The origins of the Stalinist political system offers ne
tives on Soviet political development from the October Revolution of 1917
until the outbreak of war in June 1941.

Explanations of the emergence of the Stalinist political system have hitherto concentrated upon either impersonal factors such as economic backwardness and the process of bureaucratisation or Stalin the political actor and the intricacies of elite conflict. Graeme Gill examines the relationship between institutional structures and the conventions which are created to shape the activities of individuals and considers centre/periphery relations. He divides this period into four sequential but distinct political systems and examines how the patterns of these relationships shaped the course of development to 1941. Gill convincingly argues that this development was by no means inevitable. There were at least three major points in this period at which the evolution of the political system could have been radically altered. Gill shows why conscious political decisions were made not to follow alternative paths.

This book incorporates a great deal of new material. It will become essential reading for specialists and students of Soviet history with special reference to politics under Stalin, the 1920s and the 1930s.

THE ORIGINS OF THE STALINIST POLITICAL SYSTEM

Soviet and East European Studies: 74

Editorial Board

Ronald Hill (*General editor*) Judy Batt Michael Kaser
Anthony Kemp-Welch Margot Light Alastair McAuley
James Riordan Stephen White

Soviet and East European Studies, under the auspices of Cambridge University Press and the British Association for Soviet, Slavonic and East European Studies (BASSEES), promotes the publication of works presenting substantial and original research on the economics, politics, sociology and modern history of the Soviet Union and Eastern Europe.

Soviet and East European Studies

74 GRAEME GILL
The origins of the Stalinist political system

73 SANTOSH K. MEHROTRA
India and the Soviet Union: trade and technology transfer

72 ILYA PRIZEL
Latin America through Soviet eyes
The evolution of Soviet perceptions during the Brezhnev era 1964–1982

71 ROBERT G. PATMAN
The Soviet Union in the Horn of Africa
The diplomacy of intervention and disengagement

70 IVAN T. BEREND
The Hungarian economic reforms 1953–1988

69 CHRIS WARD
Russia's cotton workers and the New Economic Policy
Shop-floor culture and state policy 1921–1929

68 LÁSZLÓ CSABA
Eastern Europe in the world economy

67 MICHAEL E. URBAN
An algebra of Soviet power
Elite circulation in the Belorussian Republic 1966–1986

66 JANE L. CURRY
Poland's journalists: professionalism and politics

65 MARTIN MYANT
The Czechoslovak economy 1948–1988
The battle for economic reform

64 XAVIER RICHET
The Hungarian model: markets and planning in a socialist economy

63 PAUL G. LEWIS
Political authority and party secretaries in Poland 1975–1986

62 BENJAMIN PINKUS
The Jews of the Soviet Union
The history of a national minority

61 FRANCESCO BENVENUTI
The Bolsheviks and the Red Army, 1918–1922

60 HIROAKI KUROMIYA
Stalin's industrial revolution
Politics and workers, 1928–1932

59 LEWIS SIEGELBAUM
Stakhanovism and the politics of productivity in the USSR 1935–1941

Series list continues on p. 451

THE ORIGINS OF THE STALINIST POLITICAL SYSTEM

GRAEME GILL

Department of Government, The University of Sydney

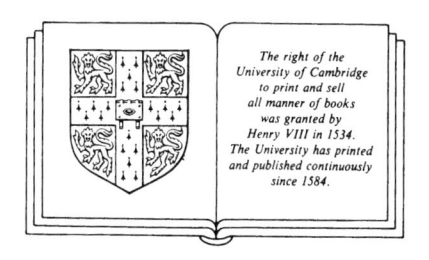

CAMBRIDGE UNIVERSITY PRESS

Cambridge
New York   Port Chester
Melbourne   Sydney

PUBLISHED BY THE PRESS SYNDICATE OF THE UNIVERSITY OF CAMBRIDGE
The Pitt Building, Trumpington Street, Cambridge, United Kingdom

CAMBRIDGE UNIVERSITY PRESS
The Edinburgh Building, Cambridge CB2 2RU, UK
40 West 20th Street, New York NY 10011-4211, USA
477 Williamstown Road, Port Melbourne, VIC 3207, Australia
Ruiz de Alarcón 13, 28014 Madrid, Spain
Dock House, The Waterfront, Cape Town 8001, South Africa

http://www.cambridge.org

© Cambridge University Press 1990

This book is in copyright. Subject to statutory exception
and to the provisions of relevant collective licensing agreements,
no reproduction of any part may take place without
the written permission of Cambridge University Press.

First published 1990
First paperback edition 2002

A catalogue record for this book is available from the British Library

Library of Congress Cataloguing in Publication data
Gill, Graeme J.
The origins of the Stalinist political system / Graeme Gill.
     p.   cm. – (Soviet and East European studies: 74)
Includes bibliographical references.
ISBN 0 521 38266 1
1. Soviet Union – Politics and government – 1917–1936. 2. Soviet Union – Politics and government – 1936–1953. 3. Stalin, Joseph, 1879–1953. I. Title.
JN6511.G53   1990
320.947–dc20   89-25153   CIP

ISBN 0 521 38266 1 hardback
ISBN 0 521 52936 0 paperback

To Heather

Contents

Preface		*Page* xi
Abbreviations		xiii
Introduction: What is Stalinism?		1

PART I COHESIVE OLIGARCHY, 1917–1922

1	The structure of sub-national politics	23
2	The structure of elite politics	51

PART II THE FRACTURED OLIGARCHY 1922–1929

3	A strong party structure?	113
4	The divided elite	135

PART III THE RE-FORMED OLIGARCHY 1930–1934

5	Regions under pressure	201
6	The Stalinist elite?	219

PART IV THE OLIGARCHY SUBDUED 1935–1941

7	The enduring structures of sub-national politics	259
8	Elite ravaged	275
	Conclusion: Why Stalinism?	307
	Notes	328
	Bibliography	427
	Index	443

Preface

This is a study of the origins of the Stalinist political system. It has its own origins in my dissatisfaction with the way in which this question has been handled by scholars in the West. For the most part, attempts to explain the emergence of the Stalinist system (as opposed to the victory of Stalin personally) have been deficient in ways that are outlined briefly in the introduction. This book attempts to fill the gap between those works which concentrate upon Stalin personally and the intricacies of the course of elite conflict, and those which place overwhelming emphasis upon contextual or metaphysical forces, like economic backwardness or bureaucratism. This book's focus is the development of those regime structures which shaped the course of systemic development in such a way that it culminated in the sort of political system which was present in 1941. Its focus is thus the structures (both institutional and value) of the Soviet system and how these changed over time. No attempt is made to provide a chronology of events during this period; individual events are discussed only insofar as they had an affect upon the structural bases of the Stalinist political system and their development. Nor is use of the word 'system' meant to imply a rationally ordered or efficiently operating network of parts, because as this study shows, the Stalinist system was not structured in this way. The word is therefore used in its vernacular rather than its technical sense.

Many people have contributed to the writing of this book, mainly by commenting upon papers which have stemmed from it or by discussing some of the issues which have arisen in it. Their contributions have been significant, and I hope that they will all recognise the thanks that is hereby given to them, albeit anonymously; to name all would be impossible, and only some invidious. However, I would like to thank personally Harry Rigby and Arch Getty for the assistance and clarification they gave in tracking down some elusive CC members. I would also like to thank the Centre for International Studies at the London School of Economics and Political Science for granting me a Visiting Fellowship in 1984–85 which enabled me to make use of the excellent library facilities in London. The University of Sydney and its Department of Government gave me leave to enable me to conduct much of the research for this book and a congenial environment within which it could be brought to fruition. Lynne Thomson struggled resolutely with an obdurate printer, and without her efforts the final draft would not have seen the light of day. But my biggest debt is owed to Heather, Fiona and Lachlan. Without their love, support and encouragement, this work would never have been finished.

Abbreviations

aktiv	the most active members of an organisation
A-R C	All-Russian Council
AUCP(b)	All-Union Communist Party (bolsheviks)
CC	Central Committee
CCC	Central Control Commission
Ch	Chairman
Cheka	Extraordinary Commission for Combating Counter-Revolution, Speculation, Sabotage and Misconduct in Office
Comintern	Communist International
Dep ch	Deputy Chairman
Desiatyi	*Desiatyi s'ezd RKP(b) mart 1921 goda. Stenograficheskii otchet* (Moscow, 1963)
Deviatyi	*Deviatyi s'ezd RKP(b) mart–aprel' 1920 goda. Protokoly* (Moscow, 1960)
ECCI	Executive Committee of the Communist International
Gensec	General Secretary
gorkom	city party committee
Gosplan	State Planning Commission
GPU	State Political Administration
guberniia	province
gubkom	province party committee
Izv ts k	*Izvestiia tsentral'nogo komiteta rossiiskoi kommunisticheskoi partii (bol'shevikov)*
Kadets	Constitutional Democratic Party
kolkhoz	collective farm
KPSS v rez	*Kommunisticheskaia partiia sovetskogo soiuza v rezoliutsiiakh i resheniiakh s'ezdov, konferentsii i plenumov Ts. K.* (Moscow, 1983)

kraikom	territory party committee
MRC	Military Revolutionary Committee
MTS	Machine Tractor Station
Narkomfin	People's Commissariat of Finance
Narkomindel	People's Commissariat of Foreign Affairs
Narkomiust	People's Commissariat of Justice
Narkomput	People's Commissariat of Transport
Narkomtorg	People's Commissariat of Trade
Narkomtrud	People's Commissariat of Labour
Narkomzem	People's Commissariat of Agriculture
NEP	New Economic Policy
NKVD	People's Commissariat of Internal Affairs
obburo	bureau of region party committee
obkom	region party committee
oblast	region
OGPU	Unified State Political Administration
okrug	area
okrugkom	area party committee
Orgotdel	Organisation-Instruction Department
Orgraspred	Organisation-Assignment Department
ORPO	Leading Party Organs Department
PCC	Party Control Commission
PPO	Primary Party Organisation
PSR	Socialist Revolutionary Party
Rabkrin	Workers' and Peasants' Inspection
raikom	district party committee
raion	district
RKI	Workers' and Peasants' Inspection
RKP	Russian Communist Party
RSFSR	Russian Socialist Federated Soviet Republic
SD	Social Democrat
skhod	traditional peasant assembly
SNK	Council of People's Commissars
sovkhoz	state farm
Sovnarkom	Council of People's Commissars
SR	Socialist Revolutionary
STO	Labour and Defence Council
TsIK	Central Executive Committee
Uchraspred	Records and Assignment Department
uezd	county
ukom	county party committee

V-C	Vice-Chairman
Vecheka	All-Russian Extraordinary Commission for Combating Counter-Revolution, Speculation, Sabotage and Misconduct in Office
Vesenkha	Supreme Council of National Economy
Vikzhel	All-Russian Executive Committee of the Union of Railway Workers
VKP(b)	All-Union Communist Party (bolsheviks)
volost	rural district, parish
vozhd'	leader, *führer*, *duce*
VTsIK	All-Russian Central Executive Committee

Introduction: What is Stalinism?

Stalinism is a much abused term. In the discourse of public politics in the West, particularly on the left of the political spectrum, it has become a form of abuse with little substantive content. In academic pursuits, too, the term has had a distinctly pejorative air. But even where it has been used in an analytical rather than a combative fashion, its use has often been characterised by a looseness of terminology and of thinking which clearly compromises its utility as a tool of both analysis and understanding. Furthermore, the difficulties with the use of the term reflect problems with the concept of Stalinism itself. The major difficulty is a lack of agreement about what should constitute Stalinism. All of those who have studied Stalinism – and there are surprisingly few studies of Stalinism as a system as opposed to Stalin as a person – have their own conceptions of what it means and these different conceptions are not always easily reconcilable. However, this is very often less a result of different positions in debate than of different foci of analysis; students often talk past one another rather than to one another. This problem of focus is well illustrated by the contemporary disputes about the role and nature of social history as applied to Stalinism.[1]

Although social history had made earlier incursions into the question of Stalinism and its origins,[2] it did not begin to make a major impact upon our conception of Stalinism until the late 1970s and early 1980s.[3] In the middle of the 1980s, a crop of new, younger historians has been making an impact upon our understanding of the Stalinist period in the USSR.[4] This 'new cohort', to use Sheila Fitzpatrick's term,[5] has been critical of the effect the totalitarian model has had upon our approach to and understanding of the Soviet system in general and Stalinism in particular. In their view, the focus upon the upper levels of the political system and the use of a cold war concept like totalitarianism obscured the reality of the system as it operated. It imposed upon that system a rationality and a consistency which did not exist. Moreover, it cast the situation in terms of an active state operating upon a passive society. In contrast to this, they argued for the adoption of the 'perspective from below'. Such a perspective highlighted the chaos and irrationalities attendant upon policy implementation, emphasised the limits of central power and portrayed the society as less a passive subject and more a partner with the state in the on-going course of Soviet development.

The social historians' 'perspective from below' raised the ire of many students of Soviet affairs. The most important criticism made of this approach is that it underestimates the importance and power of the central political authorities. By focusing upon the weakness of political controls in the countryside, the limitations of party record-keeping, or the extent of popular initiative in the collectivisation campaign, they tend at best to downplay and at worst to ignore the high degree of centralisation and the significant capacity to exercise power enjoyed by the central political authorities. Reflective of this tendency is the charge that 'the terror is ignored, obscured or minimized' in many of these works and that Stalinism is reduced to 'humdrum politics'.[6]

There is some substance to these charges in that some of the more recent works do pay scant attention to the central political authorities, to Stalin and to the Terror. However, we need to be careful in levelling this charge. It is not legitimate to argue that *all* aspects of life in the Soviet Union in the 1930s can be understood only through the prism of Stalin and the Terror. It is legitimate to demand that the study of all aspects of life in the USSR at that time, from local administration through policy implementation to social mobility, takes due account of the importance and role of Stalin and the Terror for that aspect of life. To the extent that the critics of the social historians do not accept the former position, they are being unreasonable. To the extent that individual social historians ignore the latter position, they are being unrealistic.[7]

Part of the problem is the different foci of attention of the different groups of scholars and the generalisations that have flowed from these foci. In principle, two ways of approaching Stalinism have been evident. The first can be called the descending approach. Reflected most commonly in the totalitarian model, in biographies of Stalin and in what have been called 'regime studies',[8] this approach focuses upon the structuring of national politics and the impact this has upon the society. The imagery is overwhelmingly one of an activist state dominated by a single leader who wields the political instruments of power to transform the society. The latter may be passive, as in the totalitarian model, but even when it is not so conceived, it is able to have very little influence on the internal structuring and life of the regime.

In contrast, the ascending approach utilised principally by the social historians focuses upon the mass society and, sometimes, the lower levels of the regime. At a minimum, this approach emphasises the limits of central control and the high level of improvisation on the part of local political authorities. At a maximum, it assumes that many policies are the product of initiative from below, not direction from above.[9] The political system appears much more ramshackle and much less able to impose its will on society than it does in the descending approach. Neither perspective is incorrect, but nor is either completely satisfactory.

The differences in what flows from the descending and ascending approaches simply reflect the different directions from which both approaches have come. It should not be surprising that a single phenomenon approached from different directions should appear to take on different forms. This has clearly happened to our understanding of Stalinism. But what has exacerbated this problem has been a tendency for some proponents of both approaches to reject out of hand the alternative approach, thereby claiming for their own particular position a monopoly of understanding of Stalinism. While such a position may be an understandable reaction in terms of partisan conflict, it is of little use in seeking to understand the Stalinist phenomenon and its implications. If we are to understand Stalinism, both perspectives, from above and below, must be taken into consideration.

There have been many discussions of Stalinism, but these have often involved a characterisation of Stalinism rather than an explanation of it. This is ably demonstrated by citing the words of three of the most acute observers of this period of Soviet history:

> Stalinism was not simply nationalism, bureaucratization, absence of democracy, censorship, police repression, and the rest in any precedented sense ... Instead Stalinism was excess, extraordinary extremism, in each. It was not, for example, merely coercive peasant policies, but a virtual civil war against the peasantry; not merely police repression, or even civil war-style terror, but a holocaust by terror that victimized tens of millions of people for twenty-five years; not merely a Thermidorean revival of nationalist tradition, but an

almost fascist-like chauvinism; not merely a leader cult, but deification of a despot . . . Excesses were the essence of historical Stalinism, and they are what really require explanation.[10]

Stalinism as revolution from above.[11]

Stalinism is 'Marxism of the illiterate.'[12]

None of these authors is so naive as to suggest that any of these formulations adequately summarises Stalinism either as a concept of academic discourse or a phenomenon of Soviet history. Each offers an analysis that is much more sophisticated and complete than the formulations reproduced above. However, these are useful because they demonstrate the short-hand, truncated conceptions with which many of us work when we are confronted with a phenomenon as diverse and rich as Stalinism. The problem with these formulations is not that they are wrong, but that they are all restricted and incomplete: the first relates to a mode of operation throughout much of the Stalin period without being specific about the substance of operation, the second is relevant only to the 1930s and not to the later periods of Stalinism, and the third relates only to one aspect of Stalinist life, the ideological.

The phenomenon of Stalinism is totalist. This does not mean that it embodies some totality of political control like that implied in the totalitarian model, but that Stalinism infected and shaped all spheres of life. If we are to understand Stalinism, and get away from the types of characterisations outlined above, we must see what is meant by Stalinism in each of the major spheres of Soviet life: political, economic, social and cultural. These constitute the four faces of Stalinism and will be treated in turn, but two preliminary points must be made. First, Stalinism was not a static phenomenon in any of these spheres; quite substantial changes occurred over time. Secondly, the threshold of Stalinism was not reached in all of these spheres at the same time. Only at the end of the so-called Great Terror of 1936–38[13] could one say that they all came together and that the full-blown Stalinist system was in existence; prior to that Stalinism dominated some spheres of life, but not all.

The Stalinist political system was ushered into existence through the medium of the Great Terror. Its principal features were the personal dictatorship and the associated weakness of leading political institutions, the use of terror as an instrument of governance, and the weakness of the central authorities' capacity to exercise *continuing* control over the lower levels of the political system. Each of these main points was linked, and each had significant implications for the structuring of the system as a whole.

Personal dictatorship bolstered by an extravagant leader cult is considered by most scholars to be the core of a Stalinist polity.[14] Such a perception is accurate. This does not, of course, mean that Stalin personally resolved all questions that arose. However, he did decide whatever questions he chose to decide, and whenever he intervened in an issue, that intervention was decisive. In this sense, all decision-making power ultimately was concentrated in his hands. His dominance is reflected in the way in which argument over policy issues proceeded among his leadership colleagues only until Stalin made his views known, at which point all fell in publicly behind the view that he proffered. Following 1938 he was never openly challenged on policy issues, at least as far as we know. But what is equally as important as this decision-making power was the fact that his personal position of primacy was unchallengeable. Regardless of the outcome of policy associated with his name, his position was never under threat. He was clearly superior to his colleagues and was not expendable in the same way that they were. It was only through the Terror and the resulting elimination of all potential opposition and the cowing of those who remained that he was able to consolidate this unchallenged position of primacy.

An important aspect of his personal power was the associated weakness of the leading political organs of the system. Under Stalinism, these lacked organisational integrity and coherence. This meant that Stalin could interfere at will in the operations of all political institutions, that these institutions did not have discrete spheres of responsibility and power within which they could act free from the involvement of other political actors, and that their own internal operations were not structured by a stable body of organisational norms stemming from within the institution itself. In short, all political organisations were the instruments of the vozhd', of Stalin, and were not independent from him. As this study shows, the political institutions that comprised the Soviet system never had a firmly based sense of organisational integrity or coherence, but it was the Terror which transformed them into the instruments of Stalin personally rather than of the political leadership more generally.

Being instruments of the leader does not mean that such bodies as the party, state commissariats/ministries, police, trade unions and the military did not have their own institutional interests or were active only when Stalin chose to use them. While the leading party organs atrophied,[15] along with many other bodies, much of the party and state apparatus continued in existence, even if only as a result of inertia. They continued to function, with policy suggestions still emanating from them, efforts still being made to implement central instructions and internecine bureaucratic conflicts over power and influence continuing unabated. However they were always subject to intervention from Stalin, with the result that their activities were always contingent upon the absence of objection from the leader.

One aspect of the weakness of these institutions was the importance of personalised linkages in the structuring of political life. The weakness of the formal rules designed to structure political life meant that the most important channels of political intercourse were personal. Bonds of friendship, political alliance or support became the main currency of political life. Furthermore, it was these personal relationships which were the major sinews binding the system together and the most important mechanisms for ensuring the implementation of policy. Given that the system's functioning could not be maintained through the weak institutional norms, personalised linkages were the only means through which this could be achieved. The most notable instance of this sort of phenomenon was the structure of supporters which Stalin was able to place throughout the system, but this was merely the most important instance of what was a more general phenomenon.

An important element in reducing the political organs to this instrumental state and ensuring that they remained in it was the Terror. What is crucial for the emergence of the Stalinist political system is the transformation of the Terror from an instrument of policy into an instrument of governance. Terror, defined as the use of coercion unrestrained by established rules or norms, had been used in various earlier phases of Soviet history. The most important of these was during the Civil War and at the time of agricultural collectivisation.[16] What differentiates the terror of these two periods from that of the late 1930s is that the former was generally directed at achieving specific, if large, regime goals. It was, therefore, directed at regime policy implementation. The Great Terror of 1936–38 seems to have been directed much more at consolidating the power of Stalin and his immediate supporters by destroying both potential opposition and possible institutional buffers against personal rule. At least this was its effect. Moreover, for the first time, terror was directed against functionaries of the regime itself and its principal institutional structures. In this sense, the Terror of 1936–38 was qualitatively different to that which preceded it. Similarly, the scale of the suffering rendered it qualitatively different. But what also needs to be recognised is the fundamental transformation that the Terror brought over the Soviet polity. By demolishing the barrier that previously had existed to the use of terror against political opposition within the regime, the Great Terror fundamentally altered the rules whereby politics were played out. Henceforth, the threat of terror was always present, even when it was not being used openly on the scale of 1936–38, with the result that the controller of the terror machine possessed a potent weapon which could be held over the heads of his colleagues. This constituted a firm buttress for Stalin's position.

It was thus the transformation of the Terror into an instrument of governance, reflected in the recognition by all that it could again be unleashed at the dictator's will, that fundamentally differentiated the Stalinist from the non-Stalinist political system. Always present, this potentiality pervaded all aspects of life in the USSR. Its presence was reaffirmed by those occasions in which it was openly used, most importantly the deportations from those areas incorporated into the USSR at the time of the war, the Leningrad affair of 1948 and the doctors' plot, and by the institutional prominence of the police in the Stalinist system. Indeed, the position of the police, personified by Beria's membership of the Politburo after 1939, meant that in institutional terms this was a much more important organ of the political system than were either the party or the state machines. Its prominence was always enjoyed in the shadow of the dictator, but this did nothing to ameliorate the ethos of the Terror which it exuded.

The centralisation of political power reflected in Stalin's personal dictatorship and the weakness of elite political organs was parallelled by the inability of the central authorities to exercise continuing close control over political life at sub-national levels of the Stalinist system. This does not mean that Moscow was powerless in the face of lower level intransigence or opposition. Whenever the Moscow leadership turned its attention to particular sub-national organisations, it could bring about whatever changes in membership it desired and it could ensure the implementation of central directives. However the national leadership did not have the capacity to exercise on-going close supervision of affairs in all localities. Its direct involvement in local affairs was therefore episodic rather than continuing, and the political system (including the party) was more a ramshackle structure than a highly integrated, smoothly operating entity.

The absence of continuing close supervision meant that sub-national political organs were effectively largely autonomous in their day-to-day activities. The local political machines, generally dominated by the party first secretaries, ruled their regions like medieval fiefs, ultimately answerable to Moscow but in practice able to conduct their affairs with little outside interference. Local dictators, the so-called 'little Stalins',[17] were the real powers at sub-national levels throughout the Soviet Union. The political machine under Stalinism was thus a highly segmented structure. Here lies one of the paradoxes of the Stalinist political system: a high degree of centralism was accompanied by significant practical autonomy on the part of sub-national political organs.

The second face of Stalinism is the economic. The Stalinist economic model has received considerable attention because of the rates of growth which the Soviet Union was able to achieve using this model during the 1930s. Its chief element is its directive nature. The main impetus behind economic development was not to be the interplay of market forces but the instructions and directives handed down from the central planning agencies in Moscow. While many of these directives were encapsulated in the official five year plans, too much should not be made of the extent of precise planning that was involved. Plan targets, particularly in the first half of the 1930s, rarely reflected rational economic calculations about what was feasible. They were more in the form of ambit figures reflecting the desires of the central planners, themselves under pressure from the political authorities, for increased growth at almost any cost. Better termed a command than a planned economy, its directive nature meant that it was a much more suitable instrument for the pursuit of political ends than it would have been had it relied upon market forces. The form in which it was organised also meant that, in principle if not always in practice, the low-level production units had only limited autonomy; all of the most important decisions about their operations were to be made in Moscow.

The directive nature of the economy meant that Soviet economic development was structured around the political priorities of its leaders. During the entire Stalinist period, the first priority was clearly the promotion of heavy industry, with its defence industry spin offs. Although the overwhelming emphasis upon heavy industry in the First Five Year Plan was lessened somewhat in later plan periods, popular consumption remained the poor cousin of heavy industry in terms of economic priorities. This means that economic development was unbalanced, and although it enabled rapid advances to be made in the heavy industry sector, this was at the cost of the failure to satisfy other sorts of demands elsewhere in the system.

Reliance on central direction rather than market forces plus the general emphasis upon rapid, large-scale growth meant that gross output was considered more important than quality considerations. Short-term fulfilment of plan targets expressed in quantitative terms was a higher priority than the design and production of goods to meet certain specified needs. As a result, although large quantities of goods were produced, they were often unsatisfactory for the purpose for which they were meant. The cult of bigness overshadowed considerations of utility.

This mode of operation was very wasteful of resources. Not only was much produced that was of little use, but the economic strategy was one which relied heavily upon continuing large inputs of labour and capital. This strategy was able to work only because the peasants could continually be exploited in order to produce surpluses to generate the capital required, and because of the huge labour force provided by the peasant shift to the cities. This continuing supply of labour discouraged efforts to move to a more intensive style of economic development and enabled a profligacy with resources that would have been impossible with a tighter labour market.

Reliance on continuing labour inputs was one aspect of the mobilisational nature[18] of the economic strategy. The attempt was made to mobilise all efforts into the task of economic development, something which had direct implications for social and cultural life. But the mobilisation of these forces could not rely on a market-based system of incentives because of the low priority given to the production of consumer goods. Mobilisation thus rested on a combination of material incentives, provided principally through a highly differentiated wage structure and a system of rationing of food and consumer goods, a highly developed system of symbolic and status rewards, and the use of coercion. The weighting of each of these elements differed over time, but all were present throughout the Stalinist period.

Mobilisation, and in particular its coercive aspects, was particularly evident at the time of the events which most scholars associate with the Stalinist growth model, agricultural collectivisation and forced-pace industrialisation during the First Five Year Plan. This was when the formulation 'revolution from above' was most applicable to the Stalinist economic system. Principally through a combination of enthusiastic commitment and the application of significant force, with a resulting considerable loss of life, centrally decreed economic transformation was achieved. But it is here that the limitations of the 'revolution from above' formula as a characterisation of Stalinism are most evident: the attempt at revolutionary transformation reached its peak in the early 1930s, but by the late 1940s the priority had shifted from revolutionary change to routine administration. While some echoes of the rhetoric of the earlier period may have remained and while the mobilisation of labour resources was still a primary lever of economic growth, the aim had become the running of an industrialised economy, not the transformation of an agricultural one.

Thus, while the basic ethos behind Stalinist economic development changed fundamentally from the introduction of the Stalinist economic system in 1929–30 until its mature years in the late 1940s to early 1950s, throughout this period its major structural aspects remained substantially unchanged. With its centrally directive nature, the Stalinist economic system was a clear contrast to the NEP period which preceded it.

The third face of Stalinism is the social, and here too the term 'revolution from above' is appropriate. One of the most important effects of the policies of economic transformation set in train at the end of the 1920s was the massive social mobility which they involved. Clearly there were losers in this process: those classified as kulaks, many who had owned and operated private businesses under NEP and significant numbers of technical specialists were casualties of the First Five Year Plan. Perhaps it can be said that the peasants more generally were also casualties in the sense that they were transformed from being legally free farmers into producers tied to their respective collective or state farms. At the time of the Great Terror too there were countless casualties, including those untold numbers who were killed or incarcerated in the labour camps. But at the same time, these periods witnessed unprecedented levels of upward mobility. The economic changes created large numbers of managerial and technical positions in the countryside which had to be filled principally from among those for whom such posts were a promotion. But more importantly, the industrialisation drive created an immense need for an urban labour force which could be satisfied only through the displacement of peasants from the land. Although a wrenching process for those who went into the cities, it was also a process which set their feet upon the ladder of social mobility. Furthermore, the continuing high level of demand for foremen, managerial staff and white-collar workers in the burgeoning governmental and industrial bureaucracies meant that those with ability were able to ascend swiftly to positions which their fathers did not dream of. Paradoxically, the purges contributed to this process; for everyone purged from a leading position, a replacement had to be found. The war and post-war reconstruction also provided scope for upward mobility but at a reduced level compared with the 1930s. Nevertheless, channels of mobility remained open throughout the Stalinist period.

The massive social mobility that was a central aspect of Stalinism brought about a transformation of the social structure in the USSR. This is not the place for an extended analysis of the nature of that social structure, but a couple of aspects should be mentioned. More than ever before, the contours of the social structure reflected political imperatives as perceived by the leadership. This can be seen clearly if we look at certain aspects of the structural location of four broad groups in the society. The first, and those on the lowest rung of the social ladder, were those in the labour camps scattered across the country. Although the numbers are disputed, they were clearly high. The vast majority of these people were in the camps for 'crimes' which, in other systems, would not have merited such treatment. This was particularly true of those who entered the camps during the Terror, but also applied to other people at other times who suffered as a result of what were essentially political factors. The second group were the peasants. The collectivisation of agriculture was meant to eliminate stratification in the countryside, but it was unable to do this. Peasant incomes remained dependent on the productivity of the farms on which they worked, with the result that those in poor areas were at a disadvantage compared with those in the better producing regions. Furthermore, the restrictions on private enterprise limited the capacity of many peasants to improve their standard of living; they could not produce as much as they might have done for the open market. Political constraint was also evident in the limitations on movement imposed on the peasants by the internal passport system. For many, the days of serfdom appeared to have returned.

Differentiation also appeared among the third group, the workers, as a result of the policy of highly stratified wage scales. While there was an element of payment for performance, wage inequalities also reflected vague notions of the value of different occupations for the course of socialist construction. Notions of a labour aristocracy are relevant to this sort of analysis. But differential value for different occupations was also reflected in the system of privileges. This is best seen in terms of the fourth group, the responsible office holders, or so-called nomenklatura. This group obtained their positions through appointment from above, and it was under Stalinism that the direct linkage between office and privilege that had emerged earlier became cemented into place. Each gradation of office had its own gradation of privilege. This was a means of rationing goods that were in short supply and providing an incentive for service and loyalty. The provision of these privileges for those in official positions clearly set them apart from the rest of the population; their positions and privileges were thus administratively, not market, determined. In sum, the stratification system which emerged with Stalinism was politically moulded.

Another element of the social face of Stalinism was the educational revolution. The demands of the economy stimulated the massive expansion of educational facilities and a sharp rise over a relatively short period of time in the educational level of the population. The thrust behind much of this expansion was purely instrumental; technical education was required to satisfy economic needs. While the state's massive educational effort did succeed in satisfying the need for technical cadres, it also had the important effect of increasing general educational levels.

The final face of Stalinism was the cultural [*Revolutionary culture*]. Stalinist culture became dominant in the last part of the First Five Year Plan period when it displaced the revolutionary ethos that had been evident during the cultural revolution of 1929–31. During this time culture had had a clear anti-elitist ethos; the masses were at the forefront of literature and art while all notion of hierarchy, of managers and bosses, was a distinctly subordinate strain. However from 1931 this changed. There was a new emphasis on hierarchy and on leaders, with a shift away from the 'little man' on to the 'big man', the hero, the role model.[19] Increasingly the focus was on larger than life figures who performed heroic feats in the struggle for socialism; the Stakhanovite worker was the clearest instance of this.[20] The masses became the subordinate backdrop for the stage on which the hero figure could perform his deeds.

The doctrine of socialist realism was applied, tying all cultural endeavour to the wheel of socialist construction. Cultural production was valuable as long as it contributed to the building of socialism, a demand which imposed upon the society a stultifying uniformity and conformity. Furthermore it reflected the developments fostered in other aspects of Stalinism. It confirmed economic and status stratification, reinforced the value of heavy industry over light and the urban worker over the peasant, and it embodied the sort of middle-class values which characterised many of those who had profited from the opportunities for social mobility created by the revolution from above.

Nationalism was also important in Stalinist culture, beginning during the mid-1930s and becoming highly significant during the war. The internationalist ethos of the revolution's early years was completely submerged as Russian nationalist themes moved to a prominent place in the regime's symbolic universe. The virtues of the Russian past, its great figures and cultural heritage, ceased to be objects of scorn and criticism and became major symbolic pillars of the regime's public legitimation programme. Particularly during the war, the symbolism of the past became overwhelming; the builders of the Russian state, such as Ivan the Terrible and Peter the Great; the soldiers who defended its integrity and led it to victory, such as Nevsky, Suvorov and Kutuzov; the symbols of Russian greatness, such as the Kremlin; and the pillars of Russian identity, such as the Orthodox Church were all projected as key aspects of the Soviet regime's symbolism. Indeed, the strength of this Russian revivalism was so great that it may best be described as chauvinism. Everything Russian was glorified, while all of the major advances made in virtually all spheres of endeavour from the theory of relativity to the invention of the submarine were attributed to Russians. The obverse side of this was that all things foreign were attacked and excoriated.

One of the most important aspects of Stalinism was the lavish cult of the leader which was projected throughout Soviet society during this period. Beginning in December 1929, the Stalin cult interacted with the growing cultural emphasis on heroes and on the great figures of the Russian past. It joined this symbolism with the myth of the October Revolution and Lenin to create a broad basis of legitimation both for the regime as a whole and for Stalin individually. By the mid-1930s, Stalin was the predominant cultural symbol in the USSR; he became the source of orthodoxy in all walks of life, the symbolism thereby matching the political power which he had acquired by the end of that decade.

The orthodoxy implied by the cult had dire implications for the growth and development of ideology. Under Stalinism this became highly stylised and formalised, a standardised set of concepts and formulae whose role in Soviet public life had become primarily rhetorical. Ideological language and concepts were used principally as a means of expressing policy and conducting discourse, but without themselves being major forces generating new thinking on the matters under review. Ideology became even more instrumental than it had been in previous times. Its capacity to generate a diversity of policy positions was fatally undermined by the recognition of Stalin as the infallible source of orthodoxy. Ideology thus became dead and stultified.

Stalinism was clearly a multi-faceted phenomenon, consisting of these four distinct, although linked, faces. It was also not a static phenomenon, as the change in its emphasis from revolutionary transformation to status quo orientation illustrates. Moreover, the complex nature of the phenomenon is also indicated by the fact that these four faces did not emerge at one point in time to create a single, complete 'Stalinism'. Economic and social Stalinism emerged in 1929–30, cultural Stalinism had its beginnings in 1931 but did not become dominant until closer to the middle of the decade, while political Stalinism did not emerge until the end of the 1930s. It is clear, then, that Stalinism as a general term should not be used to refer to the entire period in which Stalin was the most prominent individual in the regime. It is also clear that any attempt to explain the origins of Stalinism as a system must take account of these different faces and their different starting points. This book is more restricted in its aim. Its focus is limited to the origins of the Stalinist *political* system. The other faces of Stalinism will be taken into consideration only when they impinge upon this.

The origins of Stalinism have been an important subject of concern since the early 1930s. Most observers have seen Stalinism in a generalised way, without distinguishing between its different faces.[21] However, the nucleus of their concern has generally been what was defined above as the political face of Stalinism, the political dictatorship of one man ruling through terroristic means. Consequently the sorts of explanations successive observers have offered have been, in their focus, broadly analogous to the focus of this book.

With some simplification, explanations of the emergence of Stalinism can be divided into three types: essentialist, contextual and personalistic. None of these three types stands alone; most students seeking to explain Stalinism combine these approaches in varying combinations, but normally they give primacy to one or other type of approach. Thus, while definition of the approaches can create a neat typology, the work of individual scholars does not always fit neatly into the categories of that typology. The discussion that follows is meant to be illustrative of these approaches rather than comprehensive and aims to show the problems with the basic approaches rather than to analyse the strengths and weaknesses of the explanations offered by individual scholars.

The essentialist approach sees Stalinism as being the expression or realisation of the essence of some other historical force. The main candidates for this historical force are Marxism and, more importantly, Leninism. Leszek Kolakowski has argued that any attempt to realise the essential values of Marxism was 'likely to generate a political organization' like Stalinism.[22] This sort of position has also been evident in that array of people, particularly in the 1950s, who sought to argue that the primary moving force of Soviet policy was ideology. But of more importance has been the so-called 'continuity thesis' which seeks to draw a direct and causal link between Stalinism on the one hand and Leninism or Bolshevism (and the two are not synonymous) on the other. This line of argument has been singularly powerful in the development of Soviet studies, and has effectively structured the agenda of academic investigation for a generation.[23]

Another observer who has essentialist elements in his explanation is Trotsky. But Trotsky's starting point is quite different from those noted above in that he seeks to deny any linkage between Marxism or Bolshevism and Stalinism. Instead he sees Stalinism as the realisation of bureaucratism. Although Trotsky's thinking on Stalinism went through a number of phases[24] and also had strong elements of the contextual approach, central to it was the picture of Stalin as the representative of the social force of bureaucracy.

The essentialist approach suffers from a number of weaknesses. The definitions of what constitutes the essence of both Stalinism and its supposed progenitor are often unnecessarily restrictive, concentrating upon elements of each which fit the argument and ignoring those that do not. The view of each is thus often partial. Furthermore, the explanation usually lacks the sort of specificity which is essential to historical explanation; it builds on the commonsense point that the 'roots' of one period will be found in the period which precedes it to create an argument which extends far beyond this basic starting point. However, this is usually done without showing the mechanism whereby elements of the earlier phenomenon (the 'essence') are carried forward into the later to constitute its guiding principles. Such a mechanism can only be shown by analysing the effect of the actions of the main political actors, but once the operation of human will (and therefore of alternative possible lines of action) is allowed to enter the explanation, the force of the essentialist argument wanes. Essentialist determinism cannot coexist with any degree of independent human action, but nor can the supposed essence be transported without the action of human carriers. Once the importance of the political actors is acknowledged, essentialist characteristics become purely contextual.

The contextual approach has also been a very popular line of explanation of the Stalinist phenomenon. The predominant form this has taken has been to emphasise Russian economic backwardness. This was the source of much criticism at the time of revolution and soon after both within the party and in the Marxist movement more generally, and it has remained central to the explanations of the emergence of Stalinism by Marxist observers. Russian backwardness, accentuated by the isolation of the Russian Revolution from international revolution, remained a central motivating factor in the analysis given by Trotsky and by many of those who followed him, including Bettelheim and Deutscher.[25] Many who do not adhere to the Marxist mode of analysis also focus on the context of backwardness.[26]

Another strand of contextual explanation focuses upon culture, and in particular aspects of the culture of pre-revolutionary Russia. The most prominent exponent of this line of explanation is Robert Tucker, who draws clear parallels between various aspects of Stalinism and cultural patterns under tsarism.[27] Tucker also emphasises the way in which parallels can be drawn between the culture of the War Communism period and that of Stalinist 'revolution from above.' Culture also figures in the work of Moshe Lewin, but in this case he is more concerned with the cultural beliefs and mores of the peasant population and their role at the time of the enormous dislocation created by the revolution from above at the end of the 1920s.[28]

The contextual explanation alone, as both Tucker and Lewin recognise, cannot explain the emergence of Stalinism. Contextual factors, even those of such importance as the level of economic backwardness, cannot explain political developments without taking into account the actions of political actors. But again, once the actions of political actors are acknowledged, it is implied that these actors must have possessed various alternative possible courses of action; they could respond to the environment, to the contextual factors, in a variety of ways. Choices were available, and therefore contextual factors could not play a determining role; while they may have been able to narrow and help define options, they could not determine precisely which option would be adopted. As a result, contextual factors remain important in the explanation of Stalinism, but only in helping explain why particular courses of action were adopted rather than others.

The final approach to the explanation of Stalinism is the personalistic approach. This is most clearly reflected in the biographies of Stalin,[29] although the best of these clearly recognise the part played by contextual factors. The central argument of this approach is that the Stalinist system was created by the efforts of Stalin and his supporters who used the political power they possessed to remould both political institutions and the society as a whole. This approach has the advantage of placing the actions of political figures at the centre of the explanation and often gives due account to contextual factors. However, it is often weakened by its tendency to exaggerate the capacity of Stalin and the central leadership to bring about the changes desired. It often seems to assume that Stalin possessed the powers and abilities attributed to him by the cult because unless he did so, he would not have been able to achieve the magnitude of change associated with his name. This is because this type of explanation underestimates the role played by other forces in the development of the Soviet polity and overestimates the extent of the power exercised by the centre. Once the degree of central control is recognised as being much more limited, the role of other actors becomes commensurably more important. Stalin thereby becomes one actor – albeit the most important – among a variety of actors whose interactions resulted in the formation of Stalinism.

It is clear that, in their pure form, these three approaches are inadequate to explain the emergence of Stalinism, although elements of each can usefully be combined. The approach adopted in this book to explain the emergence of the Stalinist political system is to focus explicitly upon the internal development of the Soviet political system from the October Revolution until the outbreak of the war in 1941. The Stalinist political system was in existence only at the end of this period.

The political system will be discussed in terms of two interacting axes: politics at the sub-national levels of the system, and elite politics. The October 1917 – June 1941 period is divided into four regimes, although the boundaries between regimes are less precise and more fluid than the dates suggest: October 1917 to mid-1922, late 1922 to the end of 1929, 1930 to December 1934, and 1935 to 1941. Each regime consists of a structure of institutions and rules which, combined, produce an operating political system. Differences between regimes are produced by changes in the institutions and their functioning and in the rules (both the formally prescribed and the convention-generated) which are designed to structure political behaviour. The political system moved through these different regimes, culminating

Introduction

in the Stalinist political system at the end of the 1930s. This process was not inevitable. There were at least three, and possibly four, major points at which the course of systemic development could have been radically altered had leading political actors acted differently or adopted different decisions.

The first of these points was mid-1922 to early 1924. This was the period when it became clear that Lenin would not return to political life as he became incapacitated and eventually died. This provided an opportunity for a reappraisal of party policy and regime procedures. With NEP showing signs of bringing about a substantial revival in the economy, with opposition political parties in the country non-existent and with the massive growth of party membership by the entry into its ranks of large numbers of people who supported the official party policy of NEP, conditions did not seem unfavourable for changes of the system in a more NEPist, pluralistic direction. Of course, there would have been strong obstacles in the party to any such developments; the anti-NEP left wing of the party remained strong, the thrust of much ideology militated against seeming concessions to capitalism, and the fear of petty bourgeois infection had taken a firm hold. But what really prevented any further movement in a NEPist direction was the factional conflicts which wracked the party at this time. These transformed any consideration of party policy into a combative exercise, making reasonable argumentation and compromise impossible, and fuelled the discipline and unity ethos which helped to close off any incipient pluralism within party ranks. Factional conflict also effectively nullified the effect of Lenin's Testament; had Stalin been removed at the XIII Congress in accord with Lenin's wishes, the later course of development may have been very different. Thus as a result of conscious political decisions, reflecting the realities of elite ambitions and factional conflict, a potential alternative course of development was closed off.

The next point was 1928–29. The need for a decision to be made in the economic sphere once again created the opportunity to evaluate and review past development and future priorities. The alternatives were clearly evident to many in the party: a continuation and expansion of NEP, possibly involving greater pluralisation of political forces, or a move in the opposite direction, limiting NEP and increasing the trend away from social and political pluralism. These two alternatives were represented respectively by the Right Opposition and the group around Stalin. However, reasoned consideration of these alternatives was prevented by the same sorts of factors which had applied some five years earlier; factional conflict rigidified positions and prevented the possibility of compromise. Moreover, despite the vast influx of pro-NEP people into the party during the 1920s, the concentration of decision-making at the top and the measures against opposition taken during this decade ensured that the people who occupied positions of power and responsibility were more likely to support an authoritarian solution than one which contained the threat of greater pluralisation. Once collectivisation was begun, there was no turning back. Once again, it was political decisions (and in these Stalin played a crucial part) which set the course of development.

The third point of review was 1933–34. With the successful conclusion of the major part of the collectivisation drive and the relaxation in domestic policy, reflected in Stalin's declaration that there was 'seemingly no one left to fight', conditions seemed propitious for the continuation of the course of relaxation. Events at the XVII Congress suggest that there was a significant part of the party which favoured such a development. However, what rendered such a course of development impossible was the assassination of Kirov, an event which occurred against the background of the developing campaign against enemies inside the party. Without Kirov's death, the stimulus for the extraordinary regulations rushed in at that time and the foundation upon which the shift in the party's mood towards accepting the need for such measures would not have existed. It was Kirov's death which seems to have tilted the balance in favour of the search for enemies. Regardless of whether it was the NKVD or Stalin personally behind the Kirov assassination, it was that action which ended the prospects for further development along the line of relaxation and which pushed the system further in the direction of discipline and monocracy.

The fourth possible point for re-evaluation was at the beginning of 1937 when Stalin encountered opposition to the continuation of the Terror. Had those who opposed the Terror been able to transform what was apparently sufficient power in the CC to block the unanimity of that body into a move to replace Stalin, the Terror may not have ended in a personalised dictatorship. Of course even without Stalin the post-Terror political system would have been significantly different from that which had gone before it. But without the predominant leader figure, its contours would also have been very different from what it became.

What these re-evaluation points suggest is that at crucial stages of the Soviet system's growth, alternative lines of development were possible. At each of these points the scope for alternative development was less than at the point before. But what determined the path adopted was not any mystical inner dynamic of systemic development but conscious political decisions taken within a context of continuing flux of both institutions and values.

In order to understand why political actors throughout the system favoured a particular course of development – and therefore why the Stalinist political system emerged – we must understand the changes in institutional functioning and the shifts in party values and rules which, together, constituted the transition from one political regime to the next. It is upon these changes and shifts that this book concentrates.

Part I

Cohesive oligarchy 1917–1922

1 The structure of sub-national politics

The fall of the Provisional Government in October 1917 brought to power a small group dedicated to the transformation of Russia into a socialist form. There was common agreement within the party about the desirability of this goal and a generally shared vague conception about the forms the socialist society should take. There was, however, little agreement about the practical political forms that should characterise a society between the socialist revolution and the achievement of socialism, *The State and Revolution* notwithstanding. Indeed, the position suggested by Lenin's theoretical writings prior to October[1] and encapsulated in the general ideological perspective of most Bolsheviks implied that socialist revolution in Russia would soon be subsumed within the global socialist revolution and that national institutional forms would thus be rendered obsolete. The Bolsheviks' ideological outlook thereby discouraged all thought of constitution-building prior to the achievement of power. However, the realities of power in the days after October added to the slowly dawning recognition that international revolution may be further off than they had hoped and forced the Bolsheviks to come to grips with the problem of constructing a new set of political institutions in Russia. Not just issues of government and administration but the very survival of the revolution forced the Bolsheviks to become institution-builders, since the generation of powerful institutions was perceived to be essential to the survival of the whole enterprise.

The Bolsheviks were forced to construct a new political system out of the wreckage of the old. Their efforts in this regard were *ad hoc*, seeking to overcome problems and plug gaps through institutional innovation and tinkering rather than through the application of a well-thought-out, coherent governmental or administrative plan. The result was a bewildering array of institutional measures, decrees and reorganisations whereby the political system lurched towards a national form. This does not mean that there were no systematic efforts or consistent principles at work. Such things can be seen in various aspects of systemic construction, but it would be wrong to assume that such purposeful activity characterised all aspects of the institution-building process.

One of the most important characteristics of the development of the Soviet political system during its initial years, and indeed throughout the rest of the period of this study as well, was the weakness of its political institutions. It may seem paradoxical, given our established preconceptions about the single-party system in the Soviet Union, to speak of the institutions as weak, but this is only so if we fail to distinguish between different aspects of an institution's existence. One aspect is the capacity of an institution to carry out the basic tasks for which it was established, be those tasks administrative, political, coercive or a combination of some or all of these. Our perception of Soviet institutions as being particularly powerful has rested principally upon the belief that those institutions have been effective in successfully carrying out their tasks. The image of the party penetrating all sections of society and thereby exercising tight control over it is relevant here.

The other aspect of an institution's existence is the means whereby its internal life and functioning are structured. In this regard a strong institution would be one in which the activities of the political actors who worked within it were structured by the institution itself, its rules, conventions and principles. A weak institution would be characterised by the shaping of its internal functioning by external forces, such that its own organisational principles and rules carried very little normative authority in the structuring of its internal life. However, this is not a distinction between bodies with high and low levels of institutionalisation.

Fundamental to institutionalisation is the regularisation of behaviour, although this alone is insufficient to produce institutionalisation.[2] Such regularisation can come about on the basis of the organisational principles and rules of the institution itself, a state of affairs that can be called organisational institutionalisation. But regularisation can also occur on the basis of non-organisational factors. The most common is when a dominant leader is present in the structure but his or her position depends on factors other than the formal post the leader occupies. The leader may be the acknowledged founder of the party or regime, a position which enables him or her to exercise authority and power far beyond the powers formally attached to the particular office he or she occupies. Regularised procedures that recognise the personalised power and position of the leader may develop within the institution, but what is important about them is that they are focused upon the leader's role. This can be called patrimonial institutionalisation. Where such institutionalisation occurs, the pressures for organisational institutionalisation which inevitably stem from an organisation's functioning are checked and, in terms of the second aspect of an institution's existence noted above, the institution becomes weak. The greater the scope of power of the non-organisationally based leader,[3] the weaker will be the institution's own organisational internal regulative milieu.

An institution which does not have a high level of organisational institutionalisation lacks institutional coherence and integrity. An institution possesses integrity when its functioning is structured by itself rather than any external force; its rules are introduced, changed and enforced by the institution itself. Institutional integrity exists, therefore, when an institution is autonomous from other power centres. An institution possesses coherence when its organisational norms and internal processes are sufficiently embedded in the lore of the institution that they are able to ensure consistency and predictability in its functioning. The norms and processes must possess normative authority and thereby effectively structure the actions of the people who work within the institution. When integrity and coherence coincide, the level of organisational institutionalisation enjoyed by the institution should be high.

Central to the creation of the new political system in the USSR was the structuring of relations between regime and populace. The chief characteristic of this was the elimination of all independent channels of political activity. This was symbolised most graphically by the establishment of a one-party state following the breakdown of the abortive coalition with the Left SRs in March 1918.[4] By the middle of 1918, all non-Bolshevik parties had been suppressed,[5] and although some of them maintained shadowy existences into the early 1920s,[6] henceforth they were outside the political mainstream. Potential arenas for independent political action were also closed off, most importantly through the closure of the Constituent Assembly in January 1918[7] and the transformation of the soviets into single party organs.[8] The major channels for independent popular involvement in the political system were therefore either eliminated[9] or brought under party control. Arenas for legitimate political activity independent of the regime were abolished. This reflects the Bolsheviks' fear of their potential use by organised opposition forces. But it also reflects their concern about the nature of the popular milieu within which the new regime found itself. Bolshevik leaders were worried that the petty bourgeois nature of the vast bulk of the peasantry would infect the regime with petty bourgeois values and thereby undercut its drive towards socialism. This concern was particularly marked with regard to the party which, given the closure of the other potential avenues of political activity, attained increased importance.

The party, through its expanding membership, was the major link between regime and society. Party membership fluctuated significantly over this period, but reached a peak of some 732,521 just prior to the purge of 1921.[10] Although this figure represented a massive increase in party membership, which had almost doubled since March 1918, it still constituted a very small proportion of the populace as a whole; party membership was particularly small in the rural areas. So even though the membership growth represented a broadening of the party's, and thereby the system's, social base, that base remained narrow. Furthermore, the mass influx into the party swamped those Bolsheviks whose commitment had been demonstrated in party eyes by their service in the underground during the pre-revolutionary period. While the apparent downturn in Bolshevik fortunes in the Civil War did lead to the effluxion of some of the newer members whose reliability was under suspicion, the growth in membership up to 1921 meant that the party had within its ranks a majority whose loyalty and commitment had not been proved in the eyes of the Old Bolsheviks.[11] The concern was not just that they had not been tested by the conditions of illegal political activity, but that they were representatives of the classes against whom the revolution was ultimately directed, in particular the petty bourgeois peasantry.[12] The fears that this produced about the degeneration of the party are reflected in the almost yearly attempts to remove from party ranks those deemed deficient in some respect[13] and in the efforts made to attract the proletariat into the party in greater numbers.

The party considered itself the leading section of the proletariat and the medium through which the class would rule. Its relationship with that class, although never clearly worked out in principle, was to be organic and intimate. The urban proletariat was not just an element of the political system, but its essence. Indeed, it was the dominance of this class which guaranteed the healthy development of the new political organism, while its weakness portended the degeneration of the political structure. But there was a real problem here for the

The structure of sub-national politics

Bolsheviks given the small numbers of the proletariat in relation to the overwhelming dominance of the peasantry. How could the political dominance of the proletariat be maintained under conditions of such demographic adversity? Attempts were made to secure this institutionally by weighting political processes in favour of the proletariat. The Constitution of the RSFSR introduced in 1918 disfranchised certain categories of people and weighted electoral participation so that the vote of urban dwellers was worth more than that of those who lived in the countryside.[14] Party recruitment policy was changed at the X Congress in 1921 to reflect a vigorous pro-worker line, an orientation reaffirmed at the XI Congress twelve months later.[15] The change in emphasis in 1921 is reflected in the changing formal provisions on party entry found in successive versions of the party's Rules. Those adopted in 1919 provided for a candidacy period of no less than two months for workers and peasants, while those of 1922 established candidacy periods of six months for workers (and for Red Army men from worker and peasant backgrounds) and one year for peasants; the later Rules also made verification of applications for membership subject to a higher party level for peasants than for workers.[16] The adoption of the more pro-worker policy at the X Congress reflects leadership perceptions of the danger posed to the party by its isolation from the working class, the disintegration of the working class under War Communism and the strengthening of petty bourgeois influence as a result of these.[17]

The fear of petty bourgeois influence and the infectious effect it could have in the party, leading to the degeneration of the whole political organism, was focused principally upon the peasantry. In ideological terms the peasants constituted a backward class whose interests were, at base, fundamentally opposed to those of the proletariat. Nevertheless, prior to October 1917, Lenin had emphasised the need for an alliance between the proletariat and the poor peasantry, an alliance which the party sought to realise through the abortive policy of Committees of the Poor in mid-1918. With the failure of this policy, the party leadership looked towards an alliance between the proletariat on the one hand and the middle and poor peasants on the other.[18] This is reflected in the increased emphasis upon the recruitment of peasants into the party at the VIII Congress in March 1919,[19] a policy which continued to be implemented without restriction until the change of 1921 noted above. But the alliance with the peasants was always seen in purely tactical terms, something to be tolerated because of the power realities imposed by the balance of class forces. Peasant involvement was always viewed with considerable distrust in party ranks, and not only by such groups as the Workers' Opposition.

But if the fear of petty bourgeois influence was focused upon the peasantry, concern about its effects also permeated the party leaders' attitude to the proletariat. Party leaders recognised that, as a class, the proletariat of Russia was a differentiated entity. Sections of the class, in particular those in heavy industry, were much more class conscious and ideologically hardened than were those in other sectors of the economy. Large sections of the class were barely removed from the villages and retained close links with their rural origins, were ill-educated, badly organised and characterised by heavy concentrations of female workers. Such groups tended to be more subject to influences coming from the villages than were the more class-conscious groups, such as the metalworkers. The concern about the swamping of the class-conscious sections of the proletariat seemed to be borne out in many party members' eyes by the erosion of the party's working-class base during War Communism: the physical disintegration of the urban proletariat under the blows of food shortage and material hardship, the growth of Menshevik influence in working-class ranks and the significant spurt in strike activity and industrial action during this period impressed upon the party leaders the weakness of their social base. Despite the efforts to promote members of the working class into responsible positions, these were always tinged with caution and warnings about the lack of education and culture of this class.[20] It was this perception that the proletariat lacked the consciousness to rule directly which caused Lenin to declare in March 1919 that Soviet rule was rule for the proletariat rather than through it.[21]

Despite these negative aspects of the party leaders' evaluation of the proletariat, it is clear that members of the working class participated more widely in official political organs than they had ever done in the past. Their needs and interests were the subject of sympathetic official concern in a way which contrasted with the situation which prevailed before the Bolsheviks came to power. Through their mobilisation into the party and other official organs, the working class was a major component of the emergent political system. And in this they contrasted sharply with the bourgeoisie.

The party's attitude to the bourgeoisie was hostile. The revolution had been avowedly anti-bourgeois, and despite early attempts to reach agreement with former owners whereby they would continue to manage their enterprises under official supervision and direction, the party still sought to deny them a place in the new system. This is clearly reflected in the destruction of the bourgeois political parties and, in the economic sphere, by the wholesale nationalisation of enterprises from mid-1918.[22] But party leaders found that although they could eliminate bourgeois ownership in the economy, they could not do without the technical expertise possessed by members of the bourgeoisie. Consequently, while overall control of the economy passed into the hands of Vesenkha as the operations of this body became more regularised,[23] former owners continued to play a significant role in the running of the enterprises. Their continued involvement was accepted reluctantly and, along with the participation of the pre-revolution trained technical experts (the so-called 'bourgeois specialists'), was the subject of much acrimonious debate in the party.[24] The operation of industry under War Communism was thus conducted in large part by a group which was the object of suspicion and distrust inside the party. This economic reliance became even more marked with the introduction of NEP and the associated denationalisation of a wide range of enterprises and the imposition upon those remaining under state direction of the need to operate on strict commercial principles (khozraschet). The party was thus looking to the former owners and technical experts not only to run the private sector of the economy but also to play a part in managing the state sector on the basis of the sorts of principles which had guided the conduct of their own enterprises before the revolution. But while this group was reluctantly allowed to play a major part in the economic life of the country, it was consistently denied any legitimate role in the political sphere.

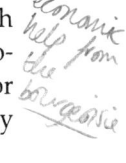

The concerns about the petty bourgeois orientation of much of the populace and the closure of avenues of independent political activity are consistent with an important principle which underlay the establishment of the political system. This principle was that the political authorities were not accountable in any direct sense to the populace for their actions. While ultimately the Bolsheviks may have considered themselves accountable before history to the proletariat as a metaphysical entity, in an immediate practical sense this was not translated into notions of the desirability of the populace passing judgement upon its rulers. With history interpreted in terms of abstract class forces, notions of responsibility and accountability in an immediate and practical sense were inappropriate. This position clearly accorded with that strand of pre-revolutionary Bolshevism which emphasised the role of intellectuals leading the proletariat and bringing class consciousness to it. The doctrine of real interests which this embodies had no room for transitory opinion and short-term political accountability. This was reflected in the structuring of the political process such that party control was not threatened through the electoral system.

The conception of the population which this implies is also evident in the absence of recognition of the need for protection of the individual by legal process. The idea of law as the instrument of the ruling class encouraged the Bolsheviks to wield legality as a sword against those in the population deemed to be opposed to the revolution. Throughout most of this period there was no formal legal code binding both subjects and authorities to its strictures; it was not until 1922 that comprehensive new codes were introduced.[25] Prior to this, in the absence of codified law, the newly established legal organs dispensed 'revolutionary justice' in an arbitrary fashion. Foremost in such activity was the Vecheka, which was established in December 1917 and permitted to operate outside legal channels; it was advocate, judge and executioner in all cases brought before it, being able to dispense justice administratively without having recourse to the courts.[26] Despite wide-ranging criticism of the Vecheka and its activities towards the end of 1918, few attempts were made to establish institutional controls over this body.[27] Some efforts were made when it was transformed into the GPU in February 1922, but little was achieved in this regard.[28]

The absence of legal and institutional constraints on the exercise of 'revolutionary justice' and the party leaders' acceptance of mass terror as a means of upholding proletarian dictatorship in the prevailing conditions[29] are reflected in the widespread use of coercive measures against those perceived to be opposed to the new regime. Such measures, which became particularly widespread with the introduction of the Red Terror in September 1918,[30] were directed not only against groups who took a stand against the Bolsheviks, but also those whose class affiliation was deemed to make their loyalty to the new regime suspect: among those who suffered under the revolutionary sword were the bourgeoisie, rich peasants, intellectuals, believers, non-Bolshevik political activists, bureaucrats, supporters of the Whites, disgruntled peasants, rebels and bandits, and even uncooperative members of the proletariat. The numbers who suffered in this way cannot be computed accurately, but what is clear is that many died, some emigrated, and some were sent to the prisons, camps and agricultural colonies based on convict labour.[31]

The widespread use of terror starkly reveals the absence among party leaders of an integrative conception of the country over which they ruled. The perceived relationship between the state and the bulk of the citizenry was an antagonistic one in which notions of guilt were defined in broad social terms. This made the attribution of guilt both unpredictable and wideranging in its effect; treasonable or criminal action by one member was sufficient to condemn a whole category of people whose only link with that individual was shared membership of that category.[32] Such an attitude may have been understandable given the harsh war-time conditions in which the new rulers of Russia were trying to create a new political structure, but one of its effects was to make the trust that the party put in such categories as the proletariat and the poor peasantry always qualified and hedged. The feeling of being under pressure and even under attack pervaded all ranks of the party.

It is difficult to overestimate the importance of the sense of isolation and threat experienced by the Bolsheviks at this time. The narrowness of the party's base, symbolised by the small and decreasing size of the proletariat and the weak penetration of the countryside, was emphasised for party leaders by such things as the minority support for the Bolsheviks in the Constituent Assembly vote, industrial activity during War Communism and the rash of popular unrest, particularly in 1920 and 1921.[33] The strength of major oppositional forces both inside and outside the country was shown by the Civil War.

In the face of such evidence, the Bolsheviks recognised the need to strengthen the basis upon which the new political system stood. In principle, two methods of this were possible. The first was by expanding the basis and seeking to draw into it a broader front of political forces; strengthening through inclusion. But it is not easy to see how such a tactic would have been viable given the party leaders' perceptions of class forces and the dangers posed by petty bourgeois infection. Moreover, all of the non-Bolshevik political forces were opposed, in varying degrees, to Bolshevik plans, and a broadening of the regime would necessarily have involved the rejection of some key Bolshevik policy positions and principles.

The second method of strengthening the system's political basis was by emphasising quality rather than quantity; instead of drawing in political forces whose loyalty and reliability were suspect, strength was more likely if all questionable elements were excluded, leaving only hardened and firm supporters to form the basis upon which the new system could rest. Such a course of action was more likely given the dangers that were perceived to surround the new system. It was also consistent with that strand of the party tradition which emphasised the importance of ideology and the need to fend off the dangerous effects of ideological heterodoxy. In the initial years of Bolshevik rule, this method of strengthening the system's basis involved the closure of avenues for independent political activity. Such a reaction was not fore-ordained by pre-1917 Bolshevik thinking nor by any supposed inner logic of Bolshevism; it was a logical response to the leaders' perceptions of the situation they faced. However, one of the problems for the Bolsheviks was that the organisational cohesion and machinery necessary to restrict membership of the system to desirable elements was severely deficient. This is clearly reflected in the structuring of sub-national politics during this period.

The most important characteristic of political life at the subnational level was the extraordinary degree of flux in organisational structures and relations. While the party may have possessed a higher degree of unity and discipline than did its opponents in October 1917, it was not a highly united or disciplined body. In the immediate aftermath of October, the party was a loose affiliation of local bodies professing allegiance to a somewhat more clearly defined centre. The boundaries of the party were fluid, with joint committees of Bolsheviks and Mensheviks remaining in existence for some time in various areas and the precise identity of the membership unclear. Within leading party bodies at all levels, differences of outlook, philosophy and temperament, not to mention education and experience, existed between many of the emigres returning to Russia and those who had spent the pre-revolutionary period in underground work inside the country. Furthermore, the links between central and local organs were weakly established, with substantial local autonomy being enjoyed by the latter throughout this period.[34] The amorphous nature of the links between centre and regions and the attempts to overcome it by the centre were to be of crucial importance for the future course of systemic development.

As an organisational entity, the party was under constant pressure throughout this period. If it was to grow into a strong, independent institution, two sorts of development were necessary. The first was the strengthening of the organisational integrity and coherence of individual party bodies. This would have involved the generation at each level of the party of an apparatus which was capable of maintaining the regularised life of the party at that level. This included carrying out the basic housekeeping functions which were essential to the party's organisational existence and implementing broader party policy in the region. In practice, these twin aims required the construction of both a 'legislative' arm – the party meeting, plenum or conference – and an executive arm – the party committee or bureau and apparatus. In addition such integrity and coherence demanded the emergence of clearly defined areas of responsibility for party organs. Such areas of responsibility had to be defined both geographically and functionally, because only in this way could jurisdictional dispute be minimised. Unless party organs at each level could ensure regularisation of their operating procedures through the development of satisfactory party machinery and spheres of jurisdiction in which they had the right to make binding decisions, they were destined to be weak organisations.

The second sort of development which was necessary if the party was to become strong and independent was the regularisation of linkages between different levels of the party. Again this involved machinery and jurisdictional parameters. What was necessary was the construction of an adequate mechanism for maintaining contact and transmitting instructions and information vertically between different levels of the party hierarchy. This had to include a mechanism for ensuring that the division of power, responsibility and accountability were not breached. These were the jurisdictional parameters which effectively ordered the rights, powers and responsibilities each level of the party possessed in relation to other levels. Unless such linkages were established, the party would not develop as a strong, national organisation, but would remain a looser association of locally based organisational structures within a single, formal but loosely articulated organisational framework. If the two sorts of development described above did not take place, the levels of organisational institutionalisation, integrity and coherence of the party would remain low. During this period there were serious deficiencies in the course of both sorts of development at the sub-national level.

From the outset of Bolshevik rule, the party came under a variety of pressures. In most areas the local party organ was anything but robust organisationally. Emerging from the underground in 1917, by October most local committees had not had time to develop their own internal procedures on a regularised basis so that they could slip easily into the role of governing. Their responses initially tended to be ad hoc in nature as they struggled to carve out for themselves a leading role in local political life. But in attempting to do so they faced significant competition from other bodies. Although for the most part such bodies as the duma and the zemstvo disappeared, party organs often faced a serious challenge to their position by the soviets which, in many areas, quickly moved to establish their positions as governing bodies.[35] Many party organs went into precipitate decline soon after the winning of power. An important reason for this was the multitude of demands made upon party personnel to staff public organs and to meet the demands for personnel at the front created by the war effort.[36] In many areas the party membership drained into the soviets either because of a naive acceptance of the 'All power to the soviets' slogan or because these institutions were seen as needing to be captured by the party. This perception at lower levels can only have been enhanced by Sverdlov's tendency to rely upon the soviet apparatus rather than the party for the conduct of administration. The result was that the party in many areas was left in a debilitated state, with insufficient personnel available to carry out basic party functions. In some instances, the party existed only as a fraction of the local soviet; many soviets thereby effectively swallowed the local party organisation.[37]

The soviets were not the only bodies against which party organs had to struggle to maintain their institutional identity. Virtually all of the *ad hoc* and permanent bodies that emerged in this period posed challenges to the party organs. Committees of the poor, military councils, food detachments, special emissaries from central party and state bodies and the local Cheka all complicated the life of party organs and, to the extent that they did not recognise the authority of those local party organs, they called into question the organisational standing of the party.[38] Measures were taken at the VIII Congress to strengthen party organs against such bodies,[39] but they could not eliminate all of the institutional confusion which resulted from the operation of numerous bodies in the same area. Particularly important in this regard was the Cheka, which had its own line of command culminating in Moscow. Although relations between this organisation and local party committees did undergo some regularisation, the wide array of powers and responsibilities which the Cheka possessed made this an institutional rival of some importance in many areas.[40]

As well as competition from other organs of the regime, local party bodies often had to cope with significant levels of popular hostility, manifested in many rural areas by continued adherence to locally based organs like the peasant skhod. Mounting hostility over Bolshevik policies, particularly War Communism, reinforced such opposition. But the problem for many local party organisations was complicated even more by the ebb and flow of the Civil War. As areas were overrun by White forces, existing party structures were crushed and known party members killed. When the Whites were driven from the area, local party organisations often had to be completely reconstructed.

The organisational structure of the party was also placed under considerable pressure by the growth of party membership during this period. Party membership grew as follows: 1917 – 24,000; 1918 – 390,000; 1919 – 350,000; 1920 – 611,978; 1921 – 732,521; 1922 – 528,354.[41] The numbers actually entering the party in any twelve-month period were greater than these figures suggest because there was also a substantial attrition rate among party members resulting from death, voluntary withdrawal and expulsion.[42] This flux in membership was exacerbated by the way in which large numbers of party workers were transferred in their party work from one region to another. Keeping track of the substantial changes in the membership of local party organisations resulting from transfers into and out of the area, new entrants to the party and departures from the party would have been a daunting task for a bureaucratic system which was fully established and operating effectively. For party committees trying to establish control in a war-ridden society, fighting to fend off the institutional challenges of other bodies, often characterised by a shortage of administrative talent and perhaps even of literate officers, with only a minimum of internal office-management procedures worked out, and an abiding fear of the danger of petty bourgeois infection, the task was well-nigh impossible. The demands of the moment tended to overwhelm the orderly development of internal party membership procedures.

The party as a whole was aware of these problems and tried to come to grips with them on a number of occasions: a general re-registration of members was announced in 1919,[43] in 1920 re-registration was to be combined with the issue of a single, standardised party card to all members,[44] and in 1921–22 a full census of party members was to be carried out.[45] This census, which was part of the purge conducted at that time, was also linked with the issue of a single party card, thereby reflecting the failure of the previous attempt to issue such a document. In addition, the party's central organs bombarded local party bodies with circulars, letters and instructions in an attempt to bring some order to the questions of registration and transfer of party members and the exclusion of class-alien elements.[46] But these sorts of measures could not, in the short term, overcome the problem at the local level. Indeed to the extent that they constituted extra administrative burdens – and even the re-registration involved a heavy administrative burden on party organisations because they had to evaluate the merits of each application to re-enter the party – they served to complicate matters for the already strained administrative machinery of the local party organs. It is perhaps not surprising that the membership records of individual party organisations could differ from the actual number of members by as much as 80 per cent.[47] Local party secretaries were often not certain who was a party member and who was not. With the party's knowledge of its own membership so uncertain, its levels of organisational coherence and integrity were very low.

Another source of pressure on local party organisations was the sort of demands made upon them from above. Many party organisations, particularly those in the countryside but also many in urban areas during the period of War Communism, found themselves in an environment of barely disguised hostility. Under such circumstances, their ability to carry out instructions from above was hindered because, at best, they could not count on popular sympathy, support or forebearance and, at worst, they had to cope with open opposition. Yet party organisations were confronted with demands which, even in more favourable conditions, would have been difficult to fulfil. The problem for lower level party organisations was that demands from above were often non-specific. Broad instructions were couched in ideological terms which may have had a degree of specificity for the ideological cognoscenti, but which for the local party secretary with little ideological training were often almost meaningless. Demands were made with little concern for their practicality or how they might be fulfilled. What was important for the centre was achievement of the aims specified rather than the means through which this was to be done. Expectations of success were high, while failure could mean a severe setback to one's career ambitions; during the Civil War it could have even more disastrous consequences. Moreover, alongside the continual pressure to perform, there was also frequently a vagueness about the criteria for successful fulfilment of central demands. Indeed, such criteria could shift as perceptions at the centre changed, and with them policy priorities. The change in official attitude to the middle peasant at the end of 1918 is a case in point; this change found many local party leaders trailing behind the centre in their move away from the committees of poor peasants.

One effect of these accumulated pressures on the party organisation was to encourage the centralisation of power at each level. But it was the form that this centralisation often took which was to be of fundamental importance for the future course of Soviet history. It should not be surprising, given the exigencies of establishing political authority in war-time Russia, the perceptions of petty bourgeois hostility and danger, the draining of party personnel into other areas of work and the weakness of democratic traditions in the operation of the party in the underground, that democratic practices atrophied in party life during this period. Along with a decline in the election of party secretaries went the weakening of the powers of plenary assemblies over their executive bodies; few plenary meetings of party bodies were held as power became concentrated in executive organs or in the local secretary personally.[48] Many secretaries were able to concentrate a large number of official positions in their own hands,[49] causing one delegate at the IX Congress to describe the situation which prevailed at the local level in many areas as a 'dictatorship'.[50]

If this centralisation of power had led to the executive bodies of the party at each level being efficient decision-making organs with the apparatus to implement those decisions and possessing close links with party levels above and below in the party hierarchy, this might have contributed to the development of the party as a powerful institution, albeit with few democratic elements in its make-up. It would have been a party openly based upon these executive bodies, and could have been efficient and powerful. However, the centralisation which occurred at each level often served to cut across party boundaries and, rather than strengthening the party as an institution, served to weaken it. What became important here were the concepts of 'localism' and 'familyness'. Throughout the period a constant source of complaint on the part of the central authorities was the localist attitude adopted by lower level party leaders.[51] In essence, this consisted of a tendency to put local interests and considerations ahead of national priorities. In practice this meant a refusal to implement central decisions because these conflicted with the perceived needs of the local area or, perhaps more commonly, the interests of the local elite. This is where 'localism' merged with 'familyness' or 'groupism'.

Familyness and groupism involved the establishment of control over a local area by a group of individuals combining together in order to consolidate and maintain that control, including the fending off of excessive outside interference. The group may have comprised the leaders of various organisations in the region, perhaps the leaders of the party organisation, soviet, trade union and cheka, and may therefore have been almost a coalition of local bureaucratic interests. Or it may have taken the form of a personality-centered power faction in local politics, with supporters grouping around a prominent local leader, shoring up his position and consolidating themselves in positions of influence in the region under his control. Kinship ties could be important in the establishment of such a structure, but they were by no means essential. At the VIII Congress Osinsky charged that such situations of individual prominence created a whole series of illegalities, including patronage, protectionism, abuse and bribery.[52] Such formations, focusing on the party leader at the sub-national level, had become common by the end of the period.

The source of the generation of such group control at the local level lay in a combination of factors. In many places, the party's survival in pre-revolutionary times had been due to the activities and commitment of one or a few party members. When power was seized, the prominence of these people in the local party organisations was often assured. But important also were the conditions of the times and the types of pressures placed on the political apparatus. Two aspects of the conditions of the times are important. The first relates to the material hardship during this period. The strains imposed on the economy by the war against Germany plus the combined effects of the revolution, Civil War and War Communism had been massive and were reflected in substantial economic disruption and hardship. Throughout most of Russia, and especially in the rural areas, luxuries were non-existent and the bare essentials of life in short supply. Food was scarce in many areas, and a large part of the country was ravaged by famine in 1920–21. Under such conditions of material deprivation, life was hard and survival a constant struggle.[53] One way of maximising one's chances of survival was to get into a position of authority in order to be able to ensure that, when goods were available, one got access to them. The result was that this leading group was frequently set off from the ordinary population and from rank-and-file party members by the standard and style of life they led. In many areas this was characterised by a sufficiency of many things which were in short supply elsewhere, a relative wealth amidst general paucity; and although in absolute terms such leaders may not have been wealthy,[54] their access to resources clearly constituted a source of privilege. The party press and party speakers frequently referred to the gap between the 'uppers' and the 'lowers', between the leaders and the workers based on privilege.[55] The emergence of a local elite was thus stimulated by the grim fight for survival in the early years of Bolshevik rule.

Also important was the magnitude of the tasks imposed upon local leaders in the immediate post-October conditions. Faced with the need to establish an effective administrative apparatus in a short period of time against a background of extremely unfavourable social and economic conditions, and with existing administrative arrangements in the party at a primitive stage of development, local leaders preferred to rely on personalised networks in an attempt to establish and exercise control in their particular regions. Far better to work directly with people, without the complicating intermediation of artificial organisational structures, and preferably with people of long acquaintance whose abilities and work habits, not to mention preferences and idiosyncrasies, were well known. Reliance upon such personalised networks clearly short-circuited potential bureaucratic hold-ups and enabled local leaders to come to grips directly with problems without having to worry too much about formal bureaucratic considerations. Local flexibility and initiative were essential if party control was to be established and maintained.

Such considerations were reinforced by the nature of the demands stemming from above. With demands that were very difficult to implement and with severe penalties for failure, local leaders sought to create a situation which would provide them with some protection against threats from on high. Formal bureaucratic procedure and working according to the regulations were not high on the central leadership's list of criteria of how the performance of local elites should be judged. There was, therefore, no benefit to be had in this regard from working through highly formalised organisational structures. The interests of the local elite were best served by the establishment of a system which would either enable them to fulfil the tasks sent down from above or would afford them some protection if they did not. In terms of task fulfilment, many saw this to lie in a network of personalised relations. For protection, too, a personalised network was useful. Control over the main formal institutions in the region meant control over the main channels of communication to Moscow and an absence of that type of institutional conflict which could draw unfavourable central attention to the region and even on occasion political intervention. Consolidation of control in the region also meant that the local leadership could direct the course of local elections and thereby ensure that no challenge was forthcoming to their position from below. As history was to show, this defence was by no means perfect, but it was probably the most for which the local elite could hope.

The establishment of control by a local personalised elite did not mean the disappearance of the party structure. The legitimacy of the local elite's position depended upon its occupation of the leading party positions in the region, so these elites did try to build up a secretarial apparatus (even if it was only an office, typewriter and one official), a party committee and bureau, and membership list. The party developed as a structure, but without a high level of standardisation across the country.[56] In most cases, party structures worked weakly. Often the bulk of the work at these levels was conducted by the local elite through the non-bureaucratic channels of personal networks. Rather than structuring the political activity of the local elite, as a strong institutional structure would have done, the local party organisation frequently acted merely as an instrument of that elite. As such, the party was unable to develop any integrity or coherence as an institution. Furthermore, the power that was exercised tended to be extra-bureaucratic, residing within the local networks which were, effectively, excrescences upon the party structure, rather than contained within the formal organs of the party; real decisions were made in the personalised cliques and brought into party bodies for ratification. While power remained personalised, party bodies could not develop significant normative authority and remained largely instrumental in nature.

The power local elites were able to exercise encouraged ambitious people who were not members of the elite to seek to seize control by ousting the incumbent leaders. So-called 'group conflict' was common at sub-national levels of the party during this period. Official spokesmen gave various typologies of the different groups which could be involved in such conflicts. At the X Congress, Krestinsky argued that squabbles for influence in the local party structure occurred among different groups of workers, uezd and guberniia organs, worker-dominated and intelligentsia-dominated parts of the gubkom, and peasant rural organs and proletarian urban ones.[57] At the XI Congress, Zinoviev argued that such clique disputes tended to be based on age, country versus city, party versus soviet, economic councils versus trade unions, and food supply committees versus economic councils.[58] Stalin provided another typology: locals versus recent arrivals (usually returning soldiers), proletarians versus intellectuals, young versus old, centre versus provinces and nationality versus nationality.[59] In such struggles, the aim was usually to capture local support and thereby oust the incumbents, although it was not uncommon for local protagonists to enlist the help of the centre either directly or indirectly.[60] The centre was often all too eager to become involved, either for factional reasons[61] or in order to try to bring about more orderly functioning within the party.

But the overthrow of one local elite did not necessarily result in any structural change to the way in which the party operated at this level. Usually it meant simply the replacement of one personalised network by another. Over time, the norms and conventions governing the mode of political action at this level structured the situation in such a way that the ability of the party organisation to generate strong organisational norms was limited. Once personalised networks became established as the main medium through which politics were played out at this level, it was difficult for incoming elites to act differently. Thus the extra-bureaucratic focus of power and the essentially instrumental nature of the party apparatus remained unshaken throughout this period.

One of the initial characteristics of the development of such personalised networks by the power-holders at sub-national levels was that many sought to act independently from Moscow. In appearance, they were akin to medieval fiefs, voicing allegiance but seeking to act independently. This state of affairs was clearly antithetical both to the party developing as a coherent institution and to effective, long-term administration and decision-making. As a result, there were powerful pressures during this period to overcome the 'fiefisation' of the political structure.[62] The main thrust of such pressures was an attempt to strengthen vertical ties at the expense of the predominantly horizontal ties of which these regional, personalised networks mainly consisted.

From the outset, the central party leadership recognised the need for the subordination of local issues to those of a national character, and therefore of the subordination of the lower level organs to the centre. This was a common theme of party leaders during this period. Zinoviev's comments at the VIII Congress were typical of this sentiment, even if they were a little more forthright than some of his colleagues may have wished at the time. While discussing organisational party work, Zinoviev declared that what was needed was a single party characterised by the strictest centralism and stern discipline, by 'internal military discipline', in which the decisions of higher party instances (and particularly the CC) should be absolutely binding on lower levels.[63] Such sentiments were frequently voiced throughout the period by prominent Bolsheviks, including Lenin,[64] although not without a good deal of criticism and opposition from below.

The views of the leaders on this question were reflected in many resolutions adopted at party congresses during this period. This was particularly evident in 1919 when a major effort was made to systematise and regularise the party structure. According to the VIII Congress resolution entitled 'On the Organisational Question':

> The party finds itself in such a position, when the strictest centralism and the most severe discipline are an absolute necessity. All decisions of a higher instance are absolutely obligatory for the lower. Each decision must first of all be implemented, and only after this is appeal to a corresponding party organ permitted. In this sense real military discipline is necessary in the party in the given period.[65]

The resolution also asserted CC control over all parts of the party regardless of nationality; CC decisions on personnel were declared binding on all; and all committees were called upon to present regular written reports on their activities to higher level bodies.[66]

The commitment to centralisation and discipline was also reflected in the first edition of the party's Rules adopted after coming to power. Adopted in December 1919, the Rules established a hierarchical order of subordination based on democratic centralism (#11 and #16) and declared that all lower level committees were to have their composition confirmed at a higher party level (#18); the CC 'organises the various institutions of the party and guides their activities, appoints the editorial boards of the central organs working under its supervision, organises and directs enterprises having general party significance, distributes the forces and funds of the party and manages the central treasury' (#24); 'The strictest party discipline is the primary duty of all party members and all party organisations. The decisions of party centres must be implemented quickly and exactly. At the same time inside the party the discussion of all contentious questions of party life is completely free until a decision is adopted' (#50); and #51 outlined a series of penalties for failure to implement the decisions of higher party bodies, including the expulsion of individuals and the dissolution of party organisations.[67] Although the Rules also declared that 'All party organisations are autonomous in solving local problems' (#12) – which seemed to involve a degree of independent initiative on the part of lower level bodies – and that the CC was to submit monthly reports on its activities to provincial and capital city party committees (#27) – which may imply a notion of accountability on the part of the CC to these lower organs—on balance, the Rules confirmed the centralist ethos of the party resolution adopted earlier at the VIII Congress.

If the resolutions of party congresses and the formal organisational charter of the party reflected the centralist emphases of the party leadership, they also mirrored the views of one of the more vocal and sustained opposition groupings, the Democratic Centralists. The Democratic Centralists were committed to the elective principle in filling party offices and to the attraction of large numbers of proletarians into responsible party work. Such principles were voiced widely throughout the upper levels of the party and were reflected in official resolutions calling for the increased role of plenary party meetings (as opposed to executive sessions), the criticism of leaders by the rank-and-file, elections based on the principles of recommendation rather than appointment, and the provision by leading bodies of regular reports to the rank-and-file party membership.[68] But as well as favouring such democratic principles, all of which constituted a potential threat from below for party leaders at all levels, the Democratic Centralists also supported a process of increasing centralisation within the party. They recognised that what was required in the dangerous conditions of the time was far greater cooperation and coordination between the centre and other levels of the party. The centre needed to give more direction to the lower levels than it had done in the past. Part of the solution to this general problem in the eyes of the Democratic Centralists involved changes in the way in which some of the central organs functioned (see below). But what was also required was a tightening of links between centre and localities. More specifically, Democratic Centralist spokesmen called for the despatch by the centre of responsible workers into the localities in greater numbers, the more frequent sending of written communications to lower party organs, and the construction of a more satisfactory personnel system; in Osinsky's words, it was necessary to establish 'tentacles into the localities'.[69]

If the congress resolutions promoting party centralisation reflected the views of both the party leadership and the Democratic Centralist opposition because of their concern to improve the efficiency of party operation, similar considerations were behind the support given to such measures by many party leaders in the provinces. Virtually from the outset of party rule, leaders in the localities were turning to the CC with pleas for assistance. With the deteriorating economic situation after October 1917 stimulating enormous popular pressure on those who sought to govern, the weakness of the party apparatus making it less able to respond effectively to those pressures, and the increased burdens imposed by the Civil War, sub-national leaders looked to greater central involvement in their affairs as a means of meeting these challenges. Appeals for both personnel and policy guidance were forthcoming from many areas of the country. There were calls for the CC to increase the flow of information and of directives to the lower level party bodies, to send responsible party workers to assist in carrying out the essential functions of the party, and even to resolve local disputes.[70] The views of many lower leaders were reflected in Mikoian's call at the VIII Conference: 'We demand more precise political directives' and in the assertion by a delegate from Yaroslavl 'that in the current situation initiative must go from the centre'.[71] Many shared the views of Nizhnii Novgorod delegate and future party leader Lazar Kaganovich, that the party was not sufficiently centralised.[72] Although such pleas from sub-national leaders were most common in the years immediately following October, complaints about the lack of leadership and the absence of CC guidance were still heard from delegates at the X Congress.[73]

However, if during this early period many sub-national leaders had welcomed greater central involvement in their regions for the benefits it brought, there were also a number of aspects of this process which they opposed. A tightening of links with the centre posed a real threat to their aspirations to consolidate personal power in their regions. This was clearly reflected in a resolution from the VIII Congress already cited in part above:

> The whole matter of the direction of party workers is in the hands of the CC of the party. Its decision is binding for all. In each guberniia, guberniia forces are distributed by the party gubkom, in the capitals by the city committees under the general guidance of the Central Committee. The Central Committee is entrusted with responsibility for the most decisive struggle against localism, or separatism in these questions.[74]

The power to allocate party personnel was thus vested specifically in the CC and, although this was to be exercised through the guberniia level party organisations, local independence in this matter was not to be permitted. But of course it was precisely such control over personnel – control over who occupied leading positions in the local area – which was the basis of the personalised power of the local barons discussed above. There was, therefore, widespread opposition at lower levels to the centralist implications of such a principle of personnel distribution. When regional leaders and Democratic Centralist spokesmen called for the injection of personnel into local party organs, they had in mind emissaries from the centre who would offer the incumbent local authorities assistance, guidance and direction. They were to work with the local leadership and, except in extraordinary circumstances, were to be subordinate to the local committees.[75] In this view, appointments should be made on the basis of local needs and should be carried out in full consultation with the local organs.

Such a position, which accorded to local elites a significant part in the making of personnel decisions in their areas, was a logical response both to the personnel needs at the lowest levels and to the need to establish an effective form of vertical coordination. However, for such a system to operate satisfactorily, what was required was an effective personnel system involving adequate personnel records at both base and apex of the party structure, regularised channels of communication between these levels, and regularised patterns and procedures of decision-making on personnel issues at the centre. If these did not exist, there was no way for the centre to evaluate local needs or to make rational decisions about how those needs could be filled. Some attempts were made during this period to move towards such a system, and these will be discussed below in relation to the establishment of a regularised personnel system. The absence of such a system meant not only that rational decisions about personnel placement on the basis of local needs could not be made,[76] but that the interests and views of local leaders were less likely to gain a prominent place in the consideration of personnel issues at the centre.

The absence of regularised procedures for 'the distribution of forces' is reflected in the early pattern of personnel appointments. Initially, many personnel were despatched into the local areas through mobilisations. This method, which was characterised by the transfer of personnel on a mass (as opposed to an individual) scale was not concerned with matching local needs with individual abilities. The principle was to overcome party weaknesses through the introduction of new party forces regardless of the suitability of those forces; the answer was quantity, not quality. It was only after the end of hostilities in the Civil War and the X Congress that personnel procedures moved away from the mobilisational method to an attempt to individualise appointments, to match needs and problems with abilities.[77] This need was sharpened by the weakness of the administrative structure and the consequent heavy reliance upon the quality of individual incumbents of leading positions and the attitudes they brought to their work.[78] The party leaders recognised the importance of individuals at the lower levels by imposing minimum periods of party membership for incumbents of leading offices in an attempt to ensure 'party mindedness' and proletarian class origins of its leading local functionaries.[79] But the decay of the party apparatus and uncertainty about the class nature, and therefore capacity and reliability, of the rank-and-file party members, meant that the principle of the free election to leading party offices involved significant dangers in the eyes of central party leaders. This is where the principle of confirmation was important.

Confirmation was meant to reconcile two other principles at the heart of the party's formal operating regime, the election of all leading positions and central responsibility for the distribution of forces. Confirmation involved the vetting of the membership of lower organs by organs at a higher level of the party[80] and may appear, superficially, to have been little more than a mechanism for higher standing party organs to keep a check upon the sort of people elected to positions of responsibility at lower levels. But the real significance of the process of confirmation was that the vetting of individuals took place before the party elections were held. Individuals were 'recommended' by higher standing party bodies to bodies at lower levels for election to certain positions and, given that usually they were the only candidates, their election was ensured. This process transformed the party election into a mere formality, a fact reflected in the complaint voiced at various times that higher bodies should ensure that they 'recommended' candidates for office and did not appoint them.[81] But the atrophy of the party structure added to doubts about the ideological soundness of many party members provided strong incentives for higher party bodies to seek to impose their will on lower level organisations. Formal support for this was sought by reference to the powers over 'the distribution of forces' noted above. As a result, 'the distribution of forces' came to mean the filling of party posts through appointment from above rather than election from below, while the filling of lower level offices reflected less the needs or demands of local party organs than the perceptions about what was appropriate held at higher levels.[82]

By 1919 vacant posts in the provinces were increasingly being filled by central appointees without any consultation with the relevant local organs. There were also cases of central appointees being sent out physically to displace an incumbent leadership.[83] Such action led to complaints about undue interference by the centre and the 'petty tutelage over local organs' which Moscow exercised.[84] By about the middle of 1921 the central organs rarely encountered problems in ensuring their nominees filled guberniia level offices while these latter were usually similarly successful at lower levels.[85] This means of gaining office – appointment from above rather than election from below – liberated party secretaries not only from the control of the rank-and-file party members in their organisations, but also from the other members of their party committees. The party secretaries at the sub-national level owed their positions to their superiors rather than to their immediate colleagues or their rank-and-file electorate, and thereby effectively became in many instances the representatives of the centre in the local organisation.[86] This was obliquely recognised by the decision in October 1920 making the party secretary, who by the end of 1919 had become (at least officially) a full-time party position down to the uezd level,[87] personally responsible for the actions of the committee.[88] The development of the principle of the distribution of forces in this way strengthened the position of the party secretaries *vis-à-vis* their local colleagues and facilitated the emergence of family groups. However, it also involved a weakening of that position in regard to the central organs and those who controlled them.

The principle of the distribution of forces involved not simply the despatch of responsible party workers from the centre into the regions, but also the cross-posting of personnel between regional organisations. This practice seems to have been stimulated by the onset of the Civil War, reaching such proportions as to cause one delegate to the VIII Conference to complain that 'party workers have been turned into nomads'.[89] Sub-national leaders complained about the disruptive effects of such practices,[90] while the so-called 'secretarial crisis', resulting from frequent changes of gubkom secretaries,[91] was in part a reflection of this. Complaints frequently were voiced also about the way in which central party organs made personnel decisions concerning party organs in the provinces without consulting the latter, but these increasingly were ignored. Leading local figures remained subject to removal and transfer by Moscow.

Such practices were inconsistent with principles of rank-and-file sovereignty and the filling of office by election, and they generated antagonism within the lower reaches of the party structure. Nevertheless, they could gain some justification on the grounds of the search for efficiency in administration through the removal of incompetent officials and those whose behaviour had, in Nogin's terms, disgraced the name of the party.[92] However, the same justifications could not as easily be made for the practice which became common in 1920 of using central power over the distribution of forces as a disciplinary measure.

In 1920 the CC's rights over personnel distribution were being used by the central leadership to discipline dissidents, to break up opposition and to resolve disputes occurring within the lower reaches of the party organisation. The first major use of these powers was in April 1920 when the CC disbanded the CC of the Communist Party of the Ukraine, a body dominated by critics of the central leadership;[93] individual oppositionists were transferred to work elsewhere in Russia. Throughout 1920 the transfer of individual dissidents and the reorganisation of local committees was used in an attempt to weaken support for the Democratic Centralist opposition in the party.[94] Such administrative measures were also turned against the Workers' Opposition in the aftermath of the X Congress.[95] The composition of local committees could be altered arbitrarily from above, sometimes with whole factions being transferred elsewhere. At the IX Congress Krestinsky justified administrative measures of this sort by claiming that factional conflict made local committees ineffective and therefore hindered the efficient operation of the party, and he admitted that such administrative action had been undertaken in the guberniia committees of Bryansk, Kazan, Saratov and Voronezh.[96] It was at about this time too that similar administrative measures began to be used against Trotsky's supporters in the party.[97] Thus from early in the system's life, central powers over the distribution of party forces were used in a disciplinary, and even partisan, way.

As well as using powers over personnel as a means of undercutting prominent local leaders, the centre also effectively reduced many such leaders by abolishing the organs of which they were members and replacing them by completely new bodies.[98] The first instance of this occurred in the armed forces. During 1918 the CC decided that, in the interests of military efficiency, elected party committees above the level of party cell in the armed forces should be abolished and that political commissars should be regarded as the party representatives. Although technically the commissar was appointed by Sovnarkom and was therefore the representative of the government in the armed forces, henceforth he was also the party spokesman and the individual charged with the implementation of party policy within the military.[99] The commissars were provided with a number of assistants, appointed rather than elected, who together constituted bodies called political departments. It was these organisations which later were extended into other areas of life, displacing party bodies as they went and achieving their greatest notoriety in connection with Trotsky's labour militarisation proposals.[100] The replacement of elected party bodies also occurred in the civilian apparatus, a number of instances of which involved leading party bodies in different areas. In late 1918 – early 1919 the party's regional committees in the Moscow, Northern and Urals regions were abolished with the CC taking over responsibility for the first two regions and a special bureau being appointed to supervise work in the Urals and Siberia. In addition, the Turkestan CC was subordinated to a special regional commission appointed by the CC. In early 1920 the Ukrainian CC was disbanded and replaced by an appointed Temporary Bureau.[101] Despite complaints about this practice,[102] the replacement of elected bodies by centrally appointed organs became a feature of party life during this period.

Sub-national politics were thus characterised by tension between forces for localism based upon the personalised political networks at levels below the centre and forces for centralisation manifested chiefly through the mechanism of personnel distribution. In the interaction between these forces, only very limited progress was made in those matters necessary for the transformation of the party into a coherent and integrated organisational entity, the development of an effective party structure and apparatus at each level and of regularised channels of communication vertically linking the different levels of the party. The undermining of the local apparatus through the excessive use of appointment powers and the consequent liberation of party secretaries from their organisations did not facilitate the development of an effective local party organisation. Indeed, to the extent that such a process created a situation in which the local secretary had no links into the local organisation, it encouraged a continuation of the sort of practice which was already emerging as the convention of political operation at sub-national levels, reliance upon the personalised network. Furthermore, despite some attempts to regularise the vertical channels within the party (see below), the principal form of centralisation remained via personnel management.

The slow development of a personnel management system meant that such appointments were also heavily reliant upon personal factors. Without satisfactory personnel records nor any reliable means of monitoring local performance, those responsible for appointments were encouraged to rely on previous associations or family ties in an attempt to secure loyalty and competence at lower levels. Personal networks stretching vertically through the party structure thus began to emerge. Pressures existed which encouraged the transformation of these relations into something more permanent, into the sorts of fractions which were forbidden at the X Congress (see ch. 2 below). But it would be wrong to assume that, by mid-1922, disciplined lines of supporters of central figures stretching throughout the apparatus had developed. Despite central powers over personnel, the local leader could remain the boss in his local area, experiencing central ire only if he drew attention to himself. Moreover, the weakness of the apparatus meant that, even though the centre could replace one local leader by another, it could not ensure that the new leader would act in the ways Moscow wanted him to act. Certainly as the period wore on, central constraints on local leaders increased, but a significant level of flux remained in the system. Thus even as the basis for a more regularised personnel system was being laid in the final stages of this period, conventions of political behaviour were becoming entrenched which interposed a strong personal element into the management of personnel matters.

2 The structure of elite politics

The politics of the elite was conducted in an institutional arena which was constructed out of the chaos of revolutionary Russia. This arena was characterised by strong personalities and weak institutional structures, a combination which, like its counterpart at sub-national levels, was not accidental. The nature of this arena is important because of its effect upon the course of politics in the initial years of the Soviet regime. The weakness of the institutions, their inability to develop a powerful sense of integrity and coherence, was also to be important for the future development of the system as a whole.

The boundaries of the elite were neither clearly defined nor impervious to influences from below. In institutional terms, the elite encompassed members of the leading organs of the party-state structure, Sovnarkom, the Politburo, CC and upper levels of the party apparatus and the control commission. Institutionally linking the elite with the sub-elite was the party congress. The developing interrelationship between these organs constituted the institutional arena within which members of the elite interacted. Institutional relations were in a state of constant flux throughout this period, partly due to the absence of any clear notions prior to the seizure of power about the institutional forms the new system should embody.[1] The unplanned growth of the new governing organs also reflected preferences within the elite for the maintenance of this fluidity and the prevention of the development of firm institutional boundaries. Such boundaries remained vague and notions of institutional competence were expansive, with the result that there was significant uncertainty about the proper role and tasks of individual organs. What initially kept this system from breaking down was the maintenance of broad consensus within the elite.[2] Within this situation of institutional flux, there was also a continuing sense of flux in the conventions which were emerging to govern political activity. As conventions were generated to structure elite politics, the regime of informal rules which grew up, like the formal institutional arena, was subject to constant change and amendment. By the time this period came to a close, the contours of elite politics were anything but fixed.

The formal institutional arena

Upon coming to power the Bolsheviks were confronted by two executive bodies spawned by the apparatus of the soviets, but neither had lasting significance as a decision-making organ. Until its abolition on 5 December 1917, the Military Revolutionary Committee (MRC) was concerned principally with food supply to the capital and the maintenance of order.[3] The All-Russian Central Executive Committee (VTsIK) was more enduring. This body was formally elected by the Congress of Soviets and, in turn, had two executive organs, a Bureau and a smaller Presidium. In addition, prior to October it had a bureaucratic apparatus of some eighteen administrative departments whose areas of competence shadowed those of the government ministries.[4] This elaborate structure with its executive/legislative head and bureaucratic body seemed to constitute the nucleus of a potential alternative governmental hierarchy. However, this potential was not realised. By the time the VTsIK elected at the II Congress was replaced by a new committee elected at the III Congress in January 1918, effective state power was centred in Sovnarkom.[5] Despite the declaration in the 1918 state constitution that the Congress of Soviets, and through it VTsIK, was the supreme organ of state,[6] VTsIK was little more than a debating forum,[7] and even this role was devalued by the exclusion of the Mensheviks and the SRs in June 1918. Its administrative bureaucracies were absorbed into the people's commissariats subordinate to Sovnarkom, and VTsIK became merely the formal head of the governmental structure.[8] Although many government measures were promulgated through VTsIK or its Presidium, especially at the beginning of the NEP period, this was a purely formal arrangement and did not reflect an increase in the real power exercised by this body. Sovnarkom was the hub of the government machine.

Sovnarkom was created at the II Congress of Soviets. Following the withdrawal of the moderates, the rump plenary session formally established Sovnarkom and accepted the list of fifteen names presented by Kamenev. Sovnarkom was initially entirely Bolshevik in composition, but after agreement with the Left SRs was reached in

November, seven members of this party took up positions as people's commissars.[9] Their tenure was short; they resigned in the wake of the Brest-Litovsk treaty, thereby restoring the one-party status of Sovnarkom. But although for most of the period Sovnarkom was an exclusively Bolshevik preserve,[10] its membership was unstable. By autumn 1918, only Lenin, Stalin and Lunacharsky remained in the same posts to which they had initially been appointed, while only two others of the original members (Trotsky and Rykov, who had both resigned and been immediately reinstated during this period) remained in Sovnarkom but in charge of different commissariats; between March 1918 and autumn of the same year, more than 66% of positions in Sovnarkom gained new incumbents. Although the rate of membership turnover declined from this point on, the overall pattern for the period remained one of substantial membership fluidity; only Lenin, Stalin and Lunacharsky retained unbroken membership throughout the entire period, with a further 52 people serving as commissars at some time.[11]

The adverse effect on Sovnarkom's institutional identity and efficiency caused by this high turnover was exacerbated by the numbers attending meetings and the type of participation exhibited by many commissars. Formally, only people's commissars had the right to attend sessions and to vote. However, the multitude of demands that were made on many commissars resulted in frequent absences from meetings and the consequent development of the use of proxies in Sovnarkom. As well as the frequent absences of many of the most prominent members of the regime, meetings of Sovnarkom were also characterised by very large attendances. Every people's commissariat was run by a people's commissar assisted and advised by a board, and in practice all members of the boards often attended Sovnarkom meetings. Accredited representatives of various central agencies (such as the Vecheka and the CC of the Trades Union Council), members of the Sovnarkom staff and the chairman of VTsIK were all frequent attenders. Members of the individual commissariats from below board level also often attended to present official reports, while others with particular expertise or interest in the issue under discussion might also be invited to attend. This combination of large attendance and comparative low status of many individual members in the regime hierarchy served to increase the power and influence within Sovnarkom which its chairman, Lenin, could wield. The only way such a large gathering could handle the crowded agendas with which it was confronted was through the exercise of strong executive control.

In recognition of this heavy workload, two executive bodies were created, the Maly Sovnarkom in December 1917 and the Defence Council, later the Labour and Defence Council (STO), in December 1918. The increased role these bodies played in handling matters which otherwise would have come before the full Sovnarkom is reflected in the declining frequency of meetings of the parent body: from daily in the immediate aftermath of October to weekly in 1921.[12] The Maly Sovnarkom became the repository of extensive power. Initially established primarily to deal with matters of financial allocation and management, by 1921 its powers had become so extensive that, with the exception of some defence and foreign affairs matters, all government business went first to the Maly Sovnarkom where in most instances a final decision was made.[13] The Maly Sovnarkom was also responsible for supervising the implementation of government decisions by the people's commissariats and government agencies.

The Defence Council, established specifically to organise the war effort, was from the outset considered virtually the equal of Sovnarkom.[14] Its powers were wide ranging and its decisions virtually unchallengeable during the war period when it was responsible for coordinating the economic effort to sustain military operations. With the end of the war, its focus of concern became purely economic. During 1920 STO was formally subordinated to Sovnarkom and given overall control and direction of the national economy; it was not only to establish a national economic plan, but it was also to ensure that this plan was implemented by the commissariats. Accordingly, a series of economic councils and boards was established down to the level of the productive enterprise and made responsible to STO, although in some instances there were problems in realising this responsibility in practice.[15] In addition, in February 1921 a new State General Planning Commission, Gosplan, was established and attached to STO, which was to appoint its membership. Thus, during this period, STO developed from the war-time coordinative centre into the overall economic supremo of the system. In doing so it effectively displaced the organ originally envisaged as the linch pin of the economy, the Supreme Council of National Economy or Vesenkha.[16]

During this period the state machine was dominated by these three interlocking bodies, with the two executive organs prominent in the major areas of governmental decision-making and Lenin, their chairman, clearly dominant in both. The full Sovnarkom was concerned mainly with the more important matters and with any questions under dispute; all other matters were the concern of the executive bodies.

Sovnarkom and its executive organs were served by the structure of government commissariats which had been built on the basis of the old tsarist ministries. As well as their purely administrative functions, these bodies constituted major sources of advice for the new Bolshevik government. Individual commissars carried the advice they received from their commissariats into policy discussions in all elite institutions, thereby ensuring that the views of these bodies had an input into policy-making. The commissariats were often also the scene of major debates on policy issues,[17] but although they may have exercised a degree of autonomy on implementation and lower level policy questions, on the major issues of the day they retained a purely advisory role.

The dominance in governmental matters exercised by Sovnarkom and its executive organs raises the question of their relationship with the party. During these early years, the dominant institutional position the party was later to attain was not yet in evidence, although trends leading in this direction were present from 1919. This is reflected in the sphere of policy-making. The initial weakness of the party's central executive and administrative machine restricted party organs largely to decisions and declarations of principle, with the task of translating those principles into workable policies being left to Sovnarkom. As a result, most decisions of importance during the initial stages of Bolshevik rule were made in Sovnarkom. The involvement of party organs in leading decisions tended to be spasmodic and unsystematic. However, with the increasing development and regularisation of the party's executive machinery following the VIII Congress in 1919, party involvement in decision-making expanded[18] and the independent profile of Sovnarkom and its agencies accordingly declined. Technical aspects of Sovnarkom's mode of operation, such as the large numbers attending meetings, the absence from those meetings of many of the more prominent Bolshevik leaders (who therefore had personal interests in shifting the centre of power to an institutional arena in which they were found), the crowded agendas and the increasingly dominant role played by its own executive organs all contributed to the erosion of Sovnarkom's authority and the weakness of its institutional coherence. The flow of authority and power to leading party organs undermined Sovnarkom's position of dominance. Lenin personally seems to have opposed this development, taking a number of steps that were designed to moderate the increasing centralisation of power in the party Politburo; he preferred a more fluid and flexible relationship between Sovnarkom and leading party organs with the writ of the former being wide and relatively untrammelled. Such an arrangement would have maximised his own power and room for manoeuvre. But the trend was clear, and the progressive decline in Lenin's involvement in government business from mid-1921 merely accelerated the already existing flow of authority and power to the party. Although Sovnarkom and its executive bodies remained of considerable importance in the political structure while Lenin was politically active, by the end of the period, its position was already substantially weakened.

Formally, the supreme body in the party was the party congress. This supremacy was recognised in the party Rules and was a reflection of the formal commitment to rank-and-file sovereignty. Such sovereignty was to be manifested through the regular election of the party leadership by the congress and the discussion and resolution by that body of the most important questions facing the party. This principle was reflected in the pre-October period in the frequent attempts by party leaders to convene party conferences and congresses in order to throw over the decisions of previous gatherings (particularly in regard to the composition of leading bodies) and to lay down new courses for party policy.[19] Not all decisions of major import were made in such gatherings and not all decisions that were made there were of great importance.[20] Nevertheless, party leaders normally were anxious to ensure that important changes which took place between congresses were ratified by the following congress if those changes were still in force. Another mechanism which was designed to express the principle of rank-and-file sovereignty was that of the verification of congress delegates' mandates. This was an attempt to ensure that only bona fide delegates participated in the congress's deliberations. While in practice it may have been used for factional ends, in principle it ensured that the correct relationship existed between rank-and-file party members, the congress and the elected party leadership. Thus when the party came to power it brought with it a principle of congress supremacy and a tradition which, though in practice not without qualification, reaffirmed that principle.

Five congresses were held at regular yearly intervals during this period.[21] Regular congresses (the VII Congress meeting in March 1918 was an 'extraordinary' congress and lasted only two days) lasted between five and eight days. They consisted of delegates elected from lower level party bodies (the number of delegates from each organisation being related to the number of party members in that organisation) plus the top party leadership found in the CC and, after 1919, its executive organs. Many of the top leaders were at the congress formally as representatives of lower level party bodies, but in many cases this was a purely fictional arrangement. The conception of the congress as a gathering of sub-national party leaders is reflected in the practice of members of the CC who were formally listed as representing that body being elected to the congress only as candidate, or non-voting delegates (for example, Lenin was in this category at the VII and VIII Congresses), while CC members listed as representing lower level party organisations were accorded the status of full, or voting, delegates. The basis of the distinction between the number of full and candidate delegates sent by each party organisation is not clear before the introduction of candidate party membership in 1919. It may represent a hold-over from pre-revolutionary times when party organisations sent more delegates than they were entitled to in an attempt to guard against the loss of delegates due to the actions of the tsar's police. Those over the organisation's entitlement would have been labelled candidates. After the introduction of candidate membership of the party, organisations were entitled to send full and candidate delegates in proportion to the number of full and candidate party members in the organisation.

The congress increased substantially in size during this period (see table 2.1).[22]

Newcomers constituted an overwhelming majority of delegates at all congresses; after the VIII Congress, a minority of delegates had joined the party prior to 1917.[23] The dominance of newcomers was partly a result of the expansion of the body as a whole and the lack of stability at the lower levels of the party which sent delegates to the congress. However, it may also reflect some manipulation by central authorities. The high turnover of delegates is consistent with central dissatisfaction with levels of opposition at successive congresses. It is likely that those who were new to the congress would be more receptive to appeals based on the authority of the leadership than were those for whom participation in such a body was not a new experience. The X Congress is interesting in this regard. This congress, which witnessed the bitter dispute about the status of the trade unions and the election of congress delegates on the basis of the platforms they supported on this issue, was characterised by: a small nucleus of delegates carried forward from the IX Congress, the smallest carryover of delegates to

Table 2.1. *Congress membership 1918–22*

	Full	Candidate	Total	Carried over to next congress (%)	Carry over as percentage of new congress
VII	47	59	106	38.1	–
VIII	286	156	442	23.3	9.0
IX	553	40	593	21.8*	17.4*
X	717	418	1135	14.7	11.4
XI	522	164	686	36.2	24.3

* Incomplete figures

the following congress in party history prior to the XVII and XVIII congresses, the largest increase in the number of delegates, the lowest proportion of full delegates who had joined the party prior to 1917 and the largest proportion who had joined after 1917 of any congress during this period. These would be consistent with attempts to build up support at the congress in the trade union dispute. In any case, the generally high levels of delegate turnover, whatever their source, clearly inhibited the development of a clear sense of institutional continuity among congress delegates.

Throughout this period the congress acted as a vigorous debating forum in which major issues of party policy were discussed and actions and policies which were proposed by the leadership came under severe criticism. Most debate took place on the floor of the congress, although issues could be referred to special sections where delegates met apart from the plenary assembly to discuss the question at hand and prepare a draft resolution for consideration by the main body.[24] The future profile of the congress as a docile and obedient creature stands in sharp contrast to the role of this institution during this period. Despite some attempts to manipulate the delegate selection process for partisan ends[25] and to structure congress proceedings for political advantage,[26] the democratic tradition in the party was sufficiently strong and the capacity of the central organs to conduct such administrative manipulation sufficiently undeveloped to ensure that no congress would consist only of people willing to accept the leaders' arguments without question. Ultimately at all congresses the leadership was able to carry the day, even if this did sometimes involve forced concessions on their part.[27] But these victories were much less the result of any stacking of the congress[28] than of a combination of the personal standing of Lenin and some of the other leading figures, of the potency of appeals for loyalty and unity in the face of the difficulties confronting the party, and of the apparent appropriateness of the policy positions they were espousing. Such successes also often reflected sustained lobbying efforts among the delegates on the part of the leadership and its supporters over the course of the congress.[29]

Debate and voting were generally free and open on the congress floor, although there were some exceptions to this. Both the military question at the VIII Congress and the Declaration of the 22 at the XI Congress were discussed behind closed doors and no stenographic report of either session was produced, while the election of the CC seems to have become much more structured with the introduction of a semi-official slate in 1921. Despite these exceptions, the openness and freedom of debate, in which the opposition took full part, ensured that the leadership and its policy were subjected to often fierce and public criticism. At the VII Congress the official policy on Brest-Litovsk came under robust criticism; at the VIII Congress the so-called Military Opposition launched an attack upon the policy of increasing centralisation and discipline in the army at the expense of the established values of democratic control, an issue so sensitive that it was discussed in closed session with its proceedings never published; at the IX Congress the leadership came under withering criticism for the development of a strongly centralist regime inside the party; at the X Congress the role of the trade unions was debated and the issue of centralism within the party was once again a point of contention. At the XI Congress open criticism of the leadership and its policies was muted, although the way in which the Declaration of the 22 was handled, in closed session with no published proceedings, suggests that a significant level of disagreement existed. Three other developments at this congress showed the limited capacity of the leadership to exercise effective control over congress delegates: a proposal to adopt the report of the Central Control Commission without debate was rejected on the floor of the congress, thereby opening the way for wide-ranging criticism of that organ; a vote to abolish the control commissions was only narrowly defeated;[30] and an official proposal to expel Shliapnikov, Medvedev and Kollantai from the party was downgraded to a formal reprimand and warning.[31] The party leadership could not take the congress for granted. It remained throughout the period an important forum for the debate and discussion of issues and was acknowledged as the supreme body in the party.

This supremacy is reflected most clearly in the policy sphere by the way in which the congress was called upon to resolve disputes within a deadlocked leadership. The VII 'extraordinary' Congress was convened specifically to resolve the question of the Brest-Litovsk peace treaty, while the X Congress was to be the forum in which the trade union question was decided. Both congresses were preceded by extensive debate in the party on the merits of the different sides of both issues. The election of delegates to the X Congress was organised on the basis of the stances taken by would-be delegates on this issue. These events constituted a clear acknowledgement of the principle of the right of the rank-and-file of the party, through the congress, to decide matters of major import. Lenin accepted this position at the time, although in a form qualified by his continued belief in the primary role to be played by the leadership, when he declared at the X Congress: 'when more or less equal groups form in the CC, the party will make a judgement and it will judge in such a way that we will unite in accordance with the party will and its instructions'.[32]

Despite the formal supremacy of the congress, real power was located in the party's executive organs. While the infrequency and growing size of party congresses contributed to this, important also was the acceptance by party opinion of the appropriateness of such a development. In the crisis conditions of the time, a premium was placed on quick decision-making. Often there was no time for prolonged discussions with all who had an interest in the particular issue under review. Decisions had to be made without delay and implemented immediately if disaster was to be avoided. This perception pervaded the party structure, and although there were some notable instances when it did not apply (the prolonged debate over the Brest-Litovsk peace is probably the best example), general recognition of the crisis conditions fostered acceptance of the need for centralised decision-making. Furthermore, the demands created by the enormous quantity of work to be completed and the speed with which decisions were required facilitated acceptance of the movement of effective decision-making power from the larger, more infrequent bodies to those with a small membership that met more frequently.

The Central Committee was an important organ throughout this period. Formally it was elected by and accountable to the congress, although the X Congress decision granting to it (in conjunction with the CCC) the power to expel its own members cut across the power of

Table 2.2. *CC membership 1918–22*

Congress	CC Full	CC Candidate	CC Total	Carried over to next CC (%)	Carryover as percentage of new CC
VII	15	8	23	56.5	–
VIII	19	8	27	77.7	48.1
IX	19	12	31	67.7	67.7
X	25	15	40	80.0	52.5
XI	27	19	46	76.0	69.6

the congress to determine its composition. The CC doubled in size between 1917 and 1922. But this increase was accompanied by a much higher level of continuity of membership than in the Congress (see table 2.2). With the exception of the CC elected at the VIII Congress in 1919, members elected from the previous committee constituted a majority in all CCs elected during this period. Perhaps a more accurate indication of the level of continuity is the continued presence of 39.1 per cent of the members of the CC elected in 1918 in that body after its election at the XI Congress in 1922. This core constituted 19.6 per cent of the 1922 CC, thereby being significantly outnumbered by more recent members.[33] Thus although there was a reasonably high level of membership continuity, the CC was a means for the introduction of new members into the party elite.

Throughout this period the CC remained the preserve of the Old Bolsheviks. Not until the XI Congress did anyone who joined the party after 1917 gain election to the CC, and then only at the candidate level; even those who joined in 1917 remained a clear minority.[34] The CC also remained an organ in which individuals who were occupied in the state machine were a much larger proportion of the membership than those in full-time party employment (see table 2.3).[35]

Two general points emerge from these figures. Firstly, the CC was not the preserve of the full-time party apparatus during this period. The high profile of the state reflects the slowness of the development of the party apparatus noted in the previous chapter and the substantial role played by state institutions in the government and administration of the country at this time. For many of these people, CC membership must have seemed less important than their state posts. The second point is more geographical than institutional. The

Table 2.3. *Bureaucratic constituencies in the CC 1918–22*

	CP Apparatus					
	Centre	Region	Total	State	Other	Uncertain
VII	8.7	4.4	13.1	47.8	39.1	–
VIII	11.1	14.8	25.9	44.4	29.6	–
IX	12.9	9.7	22.6	51.7	22.6	3.2
X	12.5	10.0	22.5	52.6	15.0	10.00
XI	10.9	23.9	34.8	47.9	17.4	–

CC constituted a forum within which both central and regional interests and views were represented. However, after an initial parity of representation in the CC elected by the VII Congress, representatives from the centre substantially outnumbered those from the regions in the committees elected by the VIII–X Congresses inclusive. At the XI Congress this pattern was dramatically reversed as regional representation surpassed that from the centre.[36] Particularly marked was the strengthening of the regional party representation at the end of this period.[37] The CC thus had a major structural division between those who were permanently located in Moscow and whose views were likely to be from an unqualified central perspective, and those whose presence in Moscow was on a part-time basis, whose power bases were in other parts of the country, and whose perspectives were therefore likely to be different from those of the full-time Muscovite. The presence of such divisions – party versus state and centre versus regions – and the consequent loyalties must have complicated the development of a clear sense of institutional identity among CC members.

The CC did not constitute an effective day-to-day policy-making body during this period. Although it decided many of the really contentious issues, dominated in all aspects of foreign policy,[38] became involved in some matters of detail[39] and set the broad directions of policy, the nitty gritty of policy questions was handled by Sovnarkom and its executive organs or, from 1919, by the Politburo. The CC's lack of activism in the policy area came in for a good deal of criticism by the Democratic Centralist opposition. As part of their argument about the weakness of links between centre and localities, the Democratic Centralists charged the CC with failing adequately to keep the lower levels informed about what it was doing or to give adequate guidance and direction. As a result, according to Osinsky, 'the activities of the party have been transferred to the CC',[40] which harboured aspirations to dictatorship over the party.[41] However, charged Osinsky, the CC had effectively ceased to exist as a collegial organ; it rarely met as a body and most decisions were taken by Lenin and Sverdlov, occasionally with the help of a few others.[42] There was some point to these criticisms, particularly in the early period. Throughout most of 1918 the CC had real problems in gaining a regular quorum. The Left Communists refused to participate in its proceedings until the summer of 1918 in protest against the signing of the Brest-Litovsk peace, while many other members of the body were frequently absent from Moscow on tasks of one kind or another; Zinoviev admitted at the VIII Congress that he took only episodic part in the work of the CC because he lived in Petrograd, although he hastened to add that this was at the instruction of the CC.[43] Of the 19 members of the CC, only ten (of whom two were candidates) were resident in the capital on a regular basis during 1919.[44] The war effort took a heavy toll on both the time and effort of individual members of the CC, and it is not surprising that, as a body, it was unable to develop a solid sense of institutional coherence and competence during this period.

The development of institutional coherence was not aided by the pattern of meetings which characterised the CC. According to the party Rules adopted in August 1917, the CC was to meet at two-monthly intervals. This was changed in the 1919 Rules to twice a month. The former schedule was clearly inadequate if the CC was to maintain effective control over the course of party affairs while the latter was impossible to attain given the chaotic conditions of the time. Table 2.4 shows the number of times the CC met during this period.[45]

If the figure for 1918 is excluded (see note 45) and account is taken of the impact of the trade union discussion – which meant that for the last third of 1920 and the first two months of 1921 the CC was meeting virtually on a weekly basis – it is clear that CC meetings were infrequent. At best, they occurred approximately monthly and rarely lasted longer than one day, a pattern which was inadequate to enable the CC to maintain close supervision over the day-to-day running of affairs of state.

The cause of institutional coherence and integrity was not assisted by the early absence of notions of collective solidarity and responsibility. This is most clearly reflected in the resolution of the VII

Table 2.4. *CC meetings 1918–22*

1918	27
March 1919–March 1920	10
March 1920–March 1921	29
March 1921–March 1922	15

Congress on the refusal of the Left Communists to enter the CC.[46] After attacking their refusal to participate as a threat to party unity, the resolution declared that those who disagreed with steps taken by the CC must register that disagreement by an appropriate declaration rather than by boycotting the body. Dissidents in the CC were thus given the right to declare openly their opposition to official positions in the party and to decisions taken by the leading body of which formally they were members, a principle which seems to run counter to the provision introduced in the 1919 Rules that discussion remained free only until a decision was taken. However, this principle seems to have been reversed with the Shliapnikov case in August 1921. The joint CC–CCC plenum which refused to expel him at that time declared that he had infringed party discipline by his speeches, declarations and criticisms of party policy outside the bounds of the CC.[47] By implication, members should confine their criticisms to sessions of that body. Such a constraint, if it had been effective, would greatly have aided the growth of a sense of institutional coherence and integrity.

These early problems of institutional coherence did not prevent the CC from playing a major role in the on-going course of elite politics. The CC remained a major arena of debate and conflict between individual members and groupings within the elite. It was in this forum that many of the chief issues of the day were fought out. Indeed, it was the failure of this body to resolve the dispute among its members which led to the issues of the Brest-Litovsk peace and the role of the trade unions being placed before the party as a whole for resolution at the congress. Given the personalities of the individuals involved, the nature of the issues confronted and the personal power plays under way, debate and discussion could be highly unpredictable. Even when the Politburo was establishing its primacy over the CC, the latter remained a forum in which opposition could be raised forcefully and publicly to the proposed actions or policies of the leaders; the difficulty Lenin had in gaining CC acceptance of his

The structure of elite politics 65

position on Brest-Litovsk[48] and that body's rejection of Lenin's calls for Shliapnikov's expulsion from the CC in August 1921[49] are two instances of this. The CC remained an unruly organ throughout this period, despite the move to regularise its composition at the X Congress; for the first time at this congress, a slate of candidates was presented for election by the delegates rather than there being an unstructured vote in the plenary meeting of the congress.[50] But the CC was dominated by political personages whose prominence within the party meant that they could not, at this stage of the system's development, be left off such a slate, and because disagreements among them were common, the course of events in the CC was bound to remain turbulent.

The body which undermined the position of the CC within the party was the Politburo. This was established formally at the VIII Congress as part of the restructuring of the leading party organs following Sverdlov's death.[51] Attempts had been made to establish such a body in 1917 and 1918, but at neither time had an effective, operating organ resulted. In the form in which it was constituted at the VIII Congress, the Politburo was to consist of five members of the CC. In an attempt to offset the fear within the CC that the smaller body would supplant its parent, all CC members were given the right to attend meetings of the Politburo without a vote. The Politburo was to take decisions on all matters that could not be delayed until the next CC meeting and was to provide a written report to the regular fortnightly meeting of its parent body. The party Rules of 1919 declared that the CC 'forms' the Politburo, a term which left the method of staffing that body somewhat uncertain.[52] Given the responsibility of the Politburo for urgent matters, the necessary regularity of meeting, the body's small size and the importance of its members, the likelihood that the Politburo would develop an organisational identity and supplant the CC and Sovnarkom as the principal political organ in the system was high. This it proceeded to do.

Throughout this period membership of the Politburo remained small and was characterised by a high level of stability (see table 2.5). Only one full member, Krestinsky, was dropped from the Politburo – a development related to his removal as a party secretary because of dissatisfaction with the way he had performed in that office. Three people joined the Politburo during this period: party secretary Molotov as a candidate member in 1921 and Tomsky and Rykov as full members in 1922. When these three joined the Politburo, their simultaneous membership of the Orgburo extended the overlap that

Table 2.5. *Politburo membership 1919–22*

	1919	1920	1921	1922
Full	Lenin	Lenin	Lenin	Lenin
	Kamenev	Kamenev	Kamenev	Kamenev
	Trotsky	Trotsky	Trotsky	Trotsky
	Stalin	Stalin	Stalin	Stalin
	Krestinsky	Krestinsky	Zinoviev	Zinoviev
				Rykov
				Tomsky
Candidate	Zinoviev	Zinoviev	Molotov	Molotov
	Bukharin	Bukharin	Bukharin	Bukharin
	Kalinin	Kalinin	Kalinin	Kalinin

already existed between these two bodies. From their establishment in 1919, the Politburo and Orgburo overlapped through the persons of Stalin and Krestinsky. With the replacement of Krestinsky by Molotov in the Politburo and the entry into the Orgburo of Politburo candidate Kalinin in 1921 and the addition of Rykov and Tomsky to the Politburo in 1922, 50 per cent of Politburo members were also members of the Orgburo.[53] This appears to represent a very significant nucleus of the full-time central party apparatus in the Politburo, but this needs to be treated with some caution. Of these five people, four also held leading positions in other institutions: Kalinin was Chairman of TsIK, Rykov was Deputy Chairman of Sovnarkom and STO, Tomsky was Chairman of the All-Russian Central Council of Trade Unions and Stalin was People's Commissar of Nationalities and, until May 1922, of Workers' and Peasants' Inspection. Only Molotov was occupied full time in the party apparatus and, as later developments showed, Stalin was the only other member of the Politburo in 1922 whose principal focus of activity lay in the party machine. The Orgburo membership of Kalinin, Rykov, and Tomsky was comparatively shortlived and their political prominence rested rather more on their non-party positions and their peripheral membership of the group of regime notables than upon their party positions.

The state machine was also prominently represented in the Politburo. In addition to the state posts held by Stalin, Rykov and Kalinin, the state was also represented by Lenin and Trotsky. Indeed, leaving out of consideration those people who combined party and state offices, the number of people who held full-time state posts consistently outnumbered the full-time party workers. What this reflects most clearly is the narrowness of the membership of the leading party body: in 1919, 1920 and 1921 62.5 per cent and in 1922 70 per cent of Politburo members were also members of the Orgburo or Sovnarkom, and were principally stationed in Moscow. All except Trotsky had joined the party before 1917.

One of the most important organisational advantages the Politburo enjoyed over the CC was the frequency of its meetings. The Politburo usually met at least once per week and, after the X Congress, twice per week (see table 2.6).[54] A weekly meeting with provision for a second meeting to handle unfinished business was probably the norm at this time.[55] There was also provision for joint meetings between the Politburo and the Orgburo, of which there were nineteen in 1919, none in 1920 and two in 1921.[56] If Lenin's notes of December 1922[57] accurately reflect the usual procedure of Politburo gatherings, meetings lasted three hours, during which time some ten to sixteen questions would have come under discussion.[58]

The rise of the Politburo to supremacy within the institutional arena was directly linked to the ability of that body to develop and strengthen a sense of its own institutional integrity and coherence. It soon emerged as an effective decision-making body, aided in this by the frequency with which it could be called together and the small size of the decision-making nucleus. Its size made it practical for contact to be maintained between Politburo members in Moscow and any who happened to be outside the capital, an important consideration for Trotsky and Stalin during the Civil War and for Zinoviev whose home base was Petrograd. The organisational efficiency of the body was also helped by the construction of an apparatus which was in part to service its needs and by the absence from it of any representatives of the leading opposition groups. This latter fact meant that although there were clear policy differences on some issues among Politburo members, the trade union dispute being the best example of this, and there were elements of personal rivalry and dislike, particularly focused on Trotsky, these divisions did not have the disruptive implications for the smooth functioning of institutional life that were experienced in the CC. The growing supremacy of this body was also facilitated by the high personal standing in which many of its members were held in the party at large; the participation of Old Bolshevik party notables clearly enhanced the profile and prestige of the Politburo.

Over the course of this period the Politburo expanded its sphere of

Table 2.6. *Politburo meetings 1919–22*

	Number of meetings	Average per month
March 1919–March 1920	72	6
March 1920–March 1921	66	5.5
March 1921–March 1922	115	9.5

competence at the expense of the CC, thereby fulfilling the public warnings to this effect issued at the time of its birth.[59] By the end of the period it was emerging as the focus of power and authority in the party. It was here that all important issues were discussed and many of the most important decisions made. This trend of development had gone so far that, at the XI Congress, one delegate was moved to complain that the Politburo had escaped CC control to such an extent that it was often impossible to discover such elementary facts as the agenda of Politburo meetings.[60]

The emergence of the Politburo as the single most important decision-making centre was greatly assisted by the systematisation of organisational matters in the party. This was achieved through the establishment of an apparatus designed to cope with that range of administrative concerns which were central to the party's internal functioning. This was also an important element in the imposition of a greater degree of organisational rigour and centralisation of control within the party structure. The organ which initially had responsibility for these organisational and administrative tasks was the CC Secretariat. Although this body was not placed on a formal and regular basis until the VIII Congress in March 1919, it was already in existence in 1917 when it played an important role in maintaining contact between the CC and the provincial organisations and in performing the necessary administrative tasks at the centre.[61] At this stage the Secretariat consisted of Yakov Sverdlov, Elena Stasova and some half dozen assistants.[62] It was therefore a very personalised organisation which depended overwhelmingly for its functioning upon the energies and capacities of Sverdlov and Stasova. The personalised nature of the Secretariat continued after the Bolsheviks came to power, although the picture presented at the VIII Congress of Sverdlov carrying all party records in his head was clearly a caricature.[63] In the immediate post-October months, Sverdlov's participation in the work of the Secretariat probably declined as a result of his appointment as Chairman of VTsIK and his propensity to use the soviet apparatus to conduct much of the business (including party business) with which he was concerned. Stasova was the practical mainstay of the organisation, but it was Sverdlov, as the most prominent Bolshevik and as one who possessed substantial administrative talent, who was its main guiding force. His influence in the organisation was probably bolstered after the government's move to Moscow in February 1918 when Stasova was replaced as his deputy by his wife Klavdia Sverdlova.

In the months following October the Secretariat laboured under enormous difficulties in attempting to carry out the tasks it was set. It was seriously under-staffed, it lacked the basic core of data on personnel and the organisational situation in most spheres of party life, and it worked under enormous pressure due to the demands for results from above, the calls for assistance from below and the carping of those who feared central encroachment on local power. One advantage that the Secretariat did enjoy was an almost indestructible link with the top through the close personal relationship between Lenin and Sverdlov. By the time of Sverdlov's death on the eve of the VIII Congress, the Secretariat still lacked a formal internal organisational structure, a fact which probably reflects Sverdlov's conviction that he could work more effectively through the soviet network than through the party. But if Sverdlov was the key to the successful implementation of the Secretariat's tasks, his death created a major problem for the party.

The challenge posed by Sverdlov's death was met by an attempt to institutionalise the Secretariat's structure and to place its operations on a more formal, regular footing. This was done in the resolution on the organisational question adopted at the VIII Congress. The resolution declared that the CC 'organises' the Secretariat, which was to consist of 'one responsible secretary, a member of the Organisational Bureau of the CC, and five technical secretaries from among experienced party workers. The Secretariat organises a series of departments. The Secretariat reports to the CC every two weeks'.[64] Moves to fill out this organisational structure were then begun, although this process of institution-building was not a smooth development. Initially five of the seven departments projected at the congress were set up: the Organisation and Instruction Department (Orgotdel) which was concerned with the institutional forms of the party apparatus and their functioning, including links between centre and provinces and the provision of guidance and assistance to local organs in the interpretation and implementation of party policy; the Records and Assignment Department (Uchraspred) which was to collect personal data and statistics on all party members to provide the basis for appointments, transfers and job postings; the Information and Statistics Department (Informotdel) which was to gather information about the organisational life of local party committees, their composition, structure, procedures and activities; the Province Inspection Department which was to supervise the activities of local party bodies through the regular despatch of officials into the regions; and the General Department which was to act as a secretarial agency or chancellery for the CC. Later in 1919, three more departments were established: the Finance Department which was created from a section of the General Department, the Rural Department, and the Department for Work Among Women.[65] In addition to these departments, a series of bureaux was established to supervise party work among the national minorities of Russia, principally work of a propaganda-educational nature.[66]

This organisational structure was hardly established before it was subjected to organisational tinkering. About the time of the IX Congress in March 1920, the Province Inspection Department was abolished and Informotdel was divided, with the Information Section being absorbed by Orgotdel and the Statistics Section by Uchraspred. In June 1920 the Department for Work Among Women was abolished. A new Conflicts sub-section was established in Uchraspred, but in September 1920 it was transferred to Orgotdel.[67] In September a new Agitation and Propaganda Department (Agitprop) was established, initially to coordinate the explanation of party policy to party members. However, its competence soon expanded as it absorbed the bureaux responsible for the national minorities and took over responsibility for the local press.[68] During 1921 both Orgotdel and the General Department experienced major internal reorganisations[69] and the Statistics section of Uchraspred was transformed into an independent Statistics Department of the Secretariat. During 1920 an attempt was made to regularise internal procedures by dividing responsibility for various aspects of the Secretariat's work among the responsible secretaries, thereby producing some division of labour among those people.

This organisational expansion was accompanied by a growth in the size of the personnel of the Secretariat. From an initial nucleus of 30 in March 1919, the Secretariat grew to 602 by February 1921, and declined to 600 in March 1922.[70] A surprising number of these workers were not party members. Official records show that in 1921 349 were full or candidate members, two were members of the youth league, and 241 were classed as non-party; by 1922 the number of non-party workers had dropped to 171.[71] Most workers in the Secretariat performed mundane tasks; they were carriers, chauffeurs, typists and clerks, and it was presumably these sorts of areas which were dominated by non-party people. This may also explain the large number of women who worked in the Secretariat; of the 602 workers in 1921, 340 were female.[72]

This expansion of the Secretariat's organisational structure and the haphazard way in which it proceeded created a variety of short-term problems, principally resulting from the absence of a clear demarcation of responsibilities between the different departments and continuing uncertainty about the relationship that should exist with the Orgburo. The resulting organisational confusion cannot have greatly improved the functioning of the Secretariat compared with its performance under Sverdlov,[73] and clearly hindered the development of a sense of organisational coherence and integrity. That the Secretariat was able to develop in this fashion, with little concerted effort from above to systematise its operations and no prominent leader willing to invest much of his personal time and effort into this organ's work until April 1922,[74] may reflect a lack of understanding of the crucial part the Secretariat could play in an organisation like the communist party; or it may reflect a reluctance on the part of the Politburo and Orgburo to relinquish any of the power they possessed. Both of these were probably true in some measure.

As early as the IX Congress in March–April 1920 complaints had been raised about the way in which Secretariat departments issued directives to their counterparts in the provinces without consulting the regular party committees.[75] The sources of such complaints and those who shared their concern would not have been reassured were they aware of the establishment in mid-1920 of a secret cipher department to maintain and strengthen the Secretariat's links with the party in the provinces.[76] Despite such worries, opponents of the centralisation of the party, and therefore those who looked upon the Secretariat with some suspicion, must have been encouraged by the leadership installed in that body after the demise of Sverdlov. At the VIII Congress N. N. Krestinsky was installed as responsible secretary, and at the following congress he was joined by L. P. Serebriakov and E. M. Preobrazhensky. Responsibility for the different departments was divided between these three secretaries,[77] but because of the illness of Krestinsky and Serebriakov, effective control resided with Preobrazhensky during 1920. All three secretaries were recognised throughout the party as individuals who were predisposed to take a conciliatory line in dealing with low level party organs, preferring to seek the cooperation of these bodies rather than indulging in actions which were likely to lead to resentment and conflict.[78] It may have been their opposition to a policy of ultra-centralism which was responsible for the continued slow development of the apparatus of the Secretariat because, despite the administrative reshuffles noted above, by the end of the period the essential tasks for effective central control had not been completed. This lack of control was clearly reflected in the outbreak of the bitter debate over the trade union issue. The Secretariat was perceived to have failed in its task of coordinating centre–periphery relations on the basis of guidance from above. As a result of this, and perhaps also reflecting their pro-Trotsky orientation, the three secretaries were replaced at the X Congress by V. M. Molotov, E. M. Yaroslavsky and V. M. Mikhailov, all of whom were proponents of greater centralisation in the party. Both Molotov and Yaroslavsky were to be closely associated with Stalin. Although none of these was a full member of the Politburo, the X Congress decided that the responsible secretary should have a consultative voice at Politburo meetings, and accordingly Molotov was made a candidate member of that body.[79]

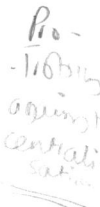

The injection of this new blood into the leadership of the Secretariat was prompted by the view that the internal functioning of that body was lacking in the coordination, coherence and efficiency that were necessary if it was to carry out its functions satisfactorily.[80] Under the guidance of the new leadership and in response to the disappearance of the sorts of personnel demands imposed by the Civil War, the internal re-ordering of the Secretariat in mid-1921 noted above was carried out. The standard of work in the organisation seems to have improved following this, although problems of coordination still occurred. Indeed, widespread dissatisfaction with the way the Secretariat was working remained, the rebuffs the party leadership received at the XI Congress being considered in some quarters as a reflection of these defects.

This dissatisfaction was instrumental in two organisational developments at this time. The first was the transformation of the auditing commission into the Central Auditing Commission at the XI Congress. Since its establishment in 1917, the former had been responsible for inspecting the central treasury and CC enterprises and reporting on these to the congress; from 1922 the new Central Auditing Commission was also responsible for inspecting 'the speed and correctness of the conduct of business in the central organs of the party and the proper functioning of the apparatus of the CC RKP'.[81] An institutional watchdog over the Secretariat was thereby established. In addition, the post of General Secretary was created, thereby establishing an institutional position of leadership in the Secretariat and putting the other secretaries much more firmly in a subordinate position than they had been before.[82] By a decision of 3 April 1922, the General Secretary was permitted to have a number of deputies and assistants to whom all but the most important work could be delegated,[83] a decision which ensured that the General Secretary himself was not swamped by petty details. Stalin was appointed General Secretary.

A key to the criticism of the Secretariat during this period lay in its inability to exert central control throughout the party. According to one discussion of the Secretariat apparatus at this time, the function of the Secretariat was to guide all the activities of the local organs of the party, to prepare cadres for those local organs, to manage the registration and distribution of party personnel and to implement all the decisions of the Orgburo, Politburo and plenum of the CC.[84] Central to the Secretariat's tasks was personnel, but it is clear that moves toward a regularised personnel system were limited in their effect during this period. Such a personnel system required adequate record-keeping and effective distribution procedures at both central and lower levels and efficient channels of communication between the various levels. In the Secretariat, these were the responsibility of Orgotdel and Uchraspred.

The principal concerns of Orgotdel were two-fold: the establishment, maintenance and servicing of links between centre and the localities, and the practical organisational questions of the daily life of the party at all levels. According to one official report from October 1921, the latter included a focus upon the structure of committees and of their working apparatuses, the method, system and maintenance of bookkeeping and information collection and storage, and a concern to bring about a standardisation in all of these.[85] This focus of concern inevitably involved personnel questions, an issue which brought Orgotdel into close and direct cooperation with Uchraspred toward the end of this period. Orgotdel was also responsible for the resolution of conflicts between party officials and between party organs, a responsibility which Orgotdel retained until the control commissions moved into this area.[86]

Throughout this period Orgotdel's capacity to carry out its functions efficiently was hampered by the immense communications difficulties in the country, the nature of the existing administrative structure, the small staff at its disposal and the amount of information and work that had to be processed. The communications problem should not be under-estimated. At this time Russia was characterised by the absence of an air communications network, a disorganised rail network that served the urban areas and left much of the hinterland isolated, and by a road system with very few all-weather surfaces and which was virtually impassable at certain times of the year. The principal form of communication was telephone and telegraph, but these too were scarcely available throughout wide expanses of the country. Faced with these sorts of problems, it is hardly surprising that complaints should frequently be heard both from the centre and the provinces about the lack of communication from the other.

Like the staff of the Secretariat as a whole, that of Orgotdel grew somewhat erratically. In the two months following the IX Congress, and therefore some 12 months following the establishment of the department, Orgotdel had only five or six people, although this was increased by the middle of the year.[87] But this was still insufficient, with the result that the quality of work by the time of the X Congress was judged to have deteriorated. The blame for this was placed squarely upon the shortage of cadres plus the illness of the department head, and it was noted that qualified staff were proving difficult to attract.[88] Staffing shortages remained pressing, reflected in the complaint from October 1921 that the Instruction section of Orgotdel needed forty people to carry out its work satisfactorily but that it had only seventeen.[89] This situation was not helped by the frequent organisational tinkering that went on in Orgotdel: the Information and Conflicts sections were added in 1920, a new statute regularising and coordinating work between subsections within the department was introduced in April 1921, later that same year a new section concerned with Transport was added to the department, and major reorganisations occurred in June 1921 and in mid-1922.[90] In practice, following the appointment of Orgburo member Zalutsky to head Orgotdel in June 1921, much business formerly handled in the Orgburo was transferred into Orgotdel.[91] Such organisational tinkering made the construction of a logical and efficient work regime within the department difficult. Indeed, at the XI Congress the internal operation of Orgotdel came under withering attack for the inefficiency and bureaucratism which characterised it.[92]

The main channels of communication between the centre and the localities were two-fold: impersonal by means of letter, report, circular or instruction, and personal through visits to the regions by central officials or emissaries and visits to the centre by local officials.[93] Both of these were conducted principally through Orgotdel.[94] Throughout the period the number of impersonal communications between centre and localities rose enormously. This suggests an improvement, over time, in the operation of the channels between centre and localities, although the sheer volume of correspondence does not prove that regular links had been established or strengthened with all party bodies.[95] Indeed, given that such an increase imposed extra administrative burdens upon Orgotdel, it is not clear that the increased communication meant a more efficient apparatus. Such communications, plus increased personal contacts, may suggest greater central knowledge of affairs in the localities, but such knowledge was of no use unless it was fed into the decision-making and administrative process at the centre. If Nogin's comments are accurate,[96] this was not happening. The picture of smooth operation which the regular reports in the party press give and which the statistics of an increasing workload may suggest, appear to conceal a situation which was much more chaotic than Orgotdel officials were willing to admit. If so, the ability of Orgotdel to establish tight links between centre and localities was limited.

The strongest bond between centre and localities was personnel appointment. For maximum strength, what was required was a regularised personnel system. A major barrier to the creation of a regularised personnel system during this period was the absence of party records. In the pre-October period, the central party organs had not tried to keep a full record of all members of the party. To the extent that such records were kept, and the underground existence of the party inside Russia militated against this, they were the responsibility of the local organs. When the identity of local members did become a matter of concern to the party centre, the procedures, machinery and methods for regularising this had to be developed. However, the large personal role played by Sverdlov in this sphere of the party's activities hindered the development of strong institutional structures. With his death the formation of such structures gathered pace, but the assembly of the necessary personnel data at the centre was much slower in realisation.

Control over the distribution of personnel was vested in the CC, although as the VIII Congress recognised, in practice in the guberniia this was to be done by the guberniia committee under the overall direction of the CC.[97] But the paucity of central records was a major problem here, so steps were taken to eliminate it. The first general registration of members took place in 1919.[98] This should have provided a means for the local organisations to get their own records in order, but the results were disappointing. This is admitted, indirectly, in a resolution of the IX Congress which called for the registration of party members on the basis of a single, uniform party card instead of the variety of cards issued by individual party organisations. In an attempt to ensure that higher standing party organs were supplied with the party talent to fill the positions that needed filling, the resolution called upon all party organs to pass to higher party organisations on a monthly or two-monthly basis lists of the 5 to 10 per cent of their members who would be of most use to those higher organisations.[99] This was clearly an attempt to overcome the paucity of personnel records in higher standing committees, including the centre, by relying upon local knowledge and regularising their access to local talent. But the lack of satisfactory progress in the course of registration is clear in the announcement of another registration to be conducted between August and October 1920.[100]

In August 1920 all guberniia committees were instructed to supply the CC with a list of responsible workers at the guberniia level, and by February 1921 all committees had complied. However, having furnished the basic list, only Riazan gubkom had bothered to inform the centre about subsequent changes, with the result that the list was not a reliable source of information upon which the centre could make personnel decisions.[101] These lists of guberniia level responsible workers were to provide the basis for Uchraspred's card index system. In September 1920 a card system had been established, but control over it was not concentrated in one section of the department. The card system provided for three types of member: the 'commanding corps' of the party who were the most active and responsible party members, those who were not currently responsible workers but were in the process of becoming so, and others. Registration of the first two categories was handled by the registration section while the last was to be found in the statistical section of Uchraspred.[102]

While the attempt to register responsible workers at the guberniia level had some initial success, the same cannot be said for the general registration which had been launched in August 1920. The IX Conference in May 1921 expressed dissatisfaction with its course[103] while a letter from responsible CC Secretary Molotov and Uchraspred head

Lisitsyn was more specific.[104] They declared that the registration of responsible workers had still not begun in the party and they blamed this on a general lack of organisation, an absence of appropriate organisations for the task, and the existence of different forms and systems of registration between and sometimes within gubkoms. In order to improve this situation they called for measures for the organisation and correct ordering of the registration-statistical apparatus in the localities, the conduct of a census within guberniias and uezds, and the introduction of some changes to the structure of guberniia committee departments. In addition, all guberniia committees were instructed to inform the centre of changes in responsible workers by 1 July. In accord with this letter, the registration departments of guberniia and oblast committees were transformed into registration-statistical sections of the local Orgotdel and were to be concerned with the registration of all types of workers and the compilation of statistics on party membership. At the same time, guberniia committees were instructed to send to the centre information about those considered suitable for transfer to other posts. This was to occur every three months and was to embrace at least 20 per cent of the total number of responsible workers.[105] Again this reflects the weakness of central records, showing that reliance had to be placed upon the judgement of the lower level leaders about those eligible for promotion and transfer. An adequate registration of guberniia level responsible workers was still not available at the time of the XI Congress, a deficiency blamed yet again on the failure of guberniia organs to keep the centre informed about changes.[106]

In an effort to overcome the *ad hoc* nature of central efforts in this sphere, on 7 July 1921 a decision was taken to conduct a census of responsible party members of the uezd level and above.[107] Unlike the previous registrations which were to be carried out by local organs and the success of which therefore depended entirely on the ability and initiative of local officials, the census was to be conducted by the newly established Statistics Department of the Secretariat. This should have given the census an organisational focus and a better chance of producing the data necessary for the central registration system which the party so badly needed. Initially the census was to be completed by 1 January 1922, but this date proved unrealistic and it did not finish until well into 1922.[108] The census was to be combined with the issue of a single, uniform party card,[109] an aim which reflects the failure of the attempt to achieve this in 1920.

As well as the difficulty of getting an accurate list of party members, there were also enormous problems in systematising and storing the data that were obtained. By the end of 1921 it had been accepted that although a standardised national system of registration was desirable, the centre could not keep an accurate register of all party members. Consequently in December 1921 a conference of secretaries of oblast committees, oblast bureaux and guberniia committees, in a resolution which was confirmed at the XI Congress some three months later,[110] set out a scheme for structuring this registration. According to this scheme, the CC would have a register of central, oblast, guberniia and uezd level workers and those on a special register. In the guberniia committee would be a register of guberniia, uezd and district level workers. A further register would be found in the uezd committee. This scheme had the advantage of taking some of the administrative weight off the shoulders of Uchraspred at the centre, but it meant the transfer of some of that weight to corresponding uchraspreds at lower levels. Most of these were in an even worse state of administrative disorder than was their central counterpart.[111]

At about the same time the Orgburo introduced a new system of responsible workers based upon their work history. This made for a much more complex system of registration,[112] but it was claimed at the time that this did not destroy the existing system. Little is known about how registration was organised, but there appears to have been a system of classification by seniority. Party workers in official positions were described as being of All-Russian, oblast, guberniia, uezd, rank-and-file and unassigned (bez ukaz) 'scale',[113] and from the context this clearly relates to a seniority ranking rather than a locational description. This sort of categorisation, presumably based on experience, performance and qualifications, was essential if a regularised personnel system was to emerge.

The compilation of data on party members and the elaboration of schemes of registration were useless unless a means could be found of keeping those registers up to date with personnel changes and of systematising and organising the data so that it could be used. Serious problems of keeping abreast of the changing personnel scene continued to plague the central organs throughout this period. There is little information on the state of internal work in Uchraspred. Reference has already been made to the way in which in late 1920 registration was split between two sections of Uchraspred, an arrangement which was organisationally clumsy and bound to lead to administrative confusion. The problem of bringing about the internal ordering of Uchraspred's administrative arrangements was complicated by the enormous workload it was called upon to shoulder: it had to process the party census as well as attend to its personnel distribution functions while suffering from an absence of clear institutional boundaries between its responsibilities and those of Orgotdel on the one hand and the Orgburo on the other, and by staffing problems.[114] The best indication of the state of internal Uchraspred work was given by Nogin at the XI Congress[115] when he reported that the files possessed by Uchraspred had gaps in them and, when there were files on individuals, those files often had insufficient information to enable decision-makers at the centre to make a realistic evaluation of the qualities an individual had in regard to a particular vacant post. Perhaps the best that can be said about the state of registration at the end of this period is that it was patchy; there may have been some files which were adequate for the tasks demanded of them, but the vast bulk of the registration system was inadequate to provide a basis for a regularised, impersonal personnel system.

The construction of a systematic personnel regime requires not just the adequate registration of party members but also a regularised system of distribution of those members. Given the slow development of the former, it should cause little surprise that the latter was also slow in emerging. Two aspects of this question are relevant: the rights over personnel disposition possessed by party committees at different levels and the forms whereby personnel distribution was carried out.

From the beginning of party rule the central organs formally had the power to distribute personnel, but in practice this power was exercised within the guberniia by the guberniia organs under CC supervision.[116] However, the compelling need for swift personnel distribution to meet emerging situations, the poor state of communications and the limitations on the ability of the central organs to make rational decisions about personnel and to meet the demands made upon them led to a situation which was in practice more anarchic than the formal rules suggest. The frequent complaints from the localities about central intrusiveness in personnel matters and from the centre about the effects of local decisions and personnel mobility reflect the way in which formal boundaries setting out the responsibilities of the different levels were being ignored. Throughout this period numerous efforts were made to demarcate more clearly the areas of responsibility for personnel transfers and postings,[117] but this was not achieved to any significant degree until the establishment of the nomenklatura system in mid-1923.

Initial efforts at personnel distribution were *ad hoc*. Much of the attention of Uchraspred in the early months after its establishment was taken up with dealing with displaced party members who turned to this party organ to find them work. They were directed into party work in various areas, but there was no pretence of trying to match the talents of these individuals with party needs. The main focus of Uchraspred's concern until about the time of the X Congress was not this sort of individual posting, but the mobilisation of large numbers of party members to fill personnel gaps elsewhere, particularly in the military. Large numbers of cadres were drafted to fill gaps regardless of their qualifications or abilities.[118] The wastefulness of this type of procedure, of simply throwing personnel at problems, was apparent to all, and as the Civil War drew to an end – with the consequent disappearance of military exigencies as a major call on personnel – the emphasis began to shift to a system characterised by a greater sense of planning. Although mobilisations occurred in 1921 and 1922, increasingly they fell below their targets in terms of the numbers expected[119] and the attention of the authorities shifted towards a more planned and systematic distribution based on data and statistics. This began after the X Congress[120] and saw the entry of Orgotdel into the personnel management field in a major way. According to Uchraspred's report on its activities for the 12 months between the X and XI Congresses, it was not adequately prepared for appointment-making on the individualised basis that was called for by the post-war circumstances. This opened the way for the involvement of Orgotdel in personnel matters, something that was clearly established by mid-1921.[121] Orgotdel used its links with lower organs to establish the needs of those organs for personnel and then passed such information on to Uchraspred, which used its power over personnel distribution to meet those needs.[122] Thus as the period wore on, the personnel system moved towards an attempt to match needs with abilities by handling questions on personnel placement on an individualised basis. The main obstacle to this was the slow development of registration procedures.

Throughout this period central personnel procedures were thus characterised by a good deal of disorganisation and confusion. Under tremendous pressure imposed by the demands for personnel, the organs of the Secretariat were slow to develop both the machinery and the procedures for instituting a regularised personnel system. By the end of the period both of these were beginning to emerge, and it is certainly true that by this time higher level organs could usually get

The structure of elite politics

their way in personnel matters concerning those party organisations below them in the party hierarchy. Nevertheless the organs of the Secretariat remained deficient in institutional coherence and integrity.

If Uchraspred and Orgotdel, as departments of the Secretariat, were responsible for most personnel matters, this was done under the general supervision of the third executive organ formalised by the VIII Congress, the Orgburo. Like the Secretariat, the Orgburo had been established in 1917 but had been overshadowed in its operations by Sverdlov.[123] After declaring that the CC 'organises' the Orgburo, the congress resolution continued:

> The Organisational Bureau consists of 5 members of the Central Committee. Each member of the Organisational Bureau manages the work of an appropriate department. The Organisational Bureau meets no less than 3 times per week. The Organisational Bureau directs all the organisational work of the party. The Organisational Bureau reports to the plenum of the CC every two weeks.[124]

Initial members of the Orgburo, all Old Bolsheviks, were Stalin, Krestinsky, A. G. Beloboradov, Serebriakov and Stasova, with Muranov as a candidate member. The membership overlapped with the Politburo (Stalin) and the Secretariat (Krestinsky). The broad relationship between these three organs was clear in principle, if difficult to realise in practice. According to Lenin in 1920, 'the Orgburo allocates forces, while the Politburo decides policy'.[125] According to an official description of the relationship between the Orgburo and the Secretariat, 'in the absence of an objection by members of the Orgburo ... the Secretariat's decision is to be regarded as a decision of the Orgburo'.[126] In theory, it was in the Orgburo that all important decisions of an administrative and personnel nature were to be made[127] and these were to be implemented by the Secretariat, which was also to provide data for Orgburo deliberations. The Politburo was to be concerned with matters of policy, with the Secretariat providing much of the data. But such sharp distinctions could not be maintained, and the Politburo frequently became involved in matters of minor importance which really fell within the sphere of the Orgburo. This was encouraged by the overlap between these bodies discussed above. Joint sessions of the Politburo and the Orgburo were also sometimes held, usually as a substitute for a CC plenum which could not be convened because of the absence of CC members from Moscow on war duty.[128] Nevertheless, although the Politburo could veto or rescind any decision of the Orgburo,[129] in practice significant scope remained for autonomous Orgburo action.

Table 2.7. *Orgburo Work Profile*

	Total meetings	Average per month	Questions handled
March 1919–March 1920	about 132	11	unknown
March 1920–Dec. 1920	81	9	2,938
March 1921–March 1922	159	13	unknown

Like the Secretariat, and in part because of the problems being experienced by that body, the Orgburo was slow to undertake its work in a systematic fashion. At the X Congress Krestinsky acknowledged the lack of planning in the Orgburo's work when he declared that it carried something of a 'shock' (udarnyi) character.[130] Nevertheless the Orgburo was busy, meeting frequently and dealing with packed agendas at each meeting. Although the figures from different sources do not match, they all suggest an organ hard at work (see table 2.7).[131]

According to Riazanov at the X Congress, at a meeting on 26 November 1920 the Orgburo made decisions on 104 cases of personnel distribution, something he referred to ironically as an 'orgy'.[132] Although the Orgburo left most cases of personnel transfer to the departments of the Secretariat and concerned itself with personnel questions relating principally to leading positions, it was nevertheless kept busy as the comment by Riazanov suggests.[133] As the state of central records improved, so the handling of personnel matters by the Orgburo moved in the same direction as in the Secretariat, towards a more systematic and regularised mode of appointment. This occurred at about the same time as the appointment powers came to be used increasingly for disciplinary or factional purposes, noted above, and meant that the Orgburo incurred significant hostility from some ranks of the party.

This hardening of the line on the use of the power of appointment was facilitated by changes in the leadership of the Orgburo. The initial membership of the Orgburo had been supplemented during the first twelve months following its formal creation by Trotsky, Kamenev, Dzerzhinsky and Rakovsky. However, the instability caused by the part-time involvement of these busy people restricted the development of the body, and by 1920 it was accepted that a greater stability of leadership was required. At that time Krestinsky, Serebriakov and

Preobrazhensky were placed at the head of the Orgburo and the Secretariat in an attempt to bring about greater coordination between both bodies.[134] Stalin remained a full member of the Orgburo, Rykov became a full member and Dzerzhinsky and Tomsky were candidates.[135] Owing to illnesses and absences due to other duties, the conciliatory Preobrazhensky took the lead in managing Orgburo affairs. However, reflecting the same sort of dissatisfaction with the Orgburo that had been directed at the Secretariat over the conduct of the trade union dispute, the membership was changed again at the X Congress. The new Orgburo, consisting of Molotov, Yaroslavsky, Mikhailov, Komarov, Stalin, Rykov and Tomsky as full members and Dzerzhinsky, Rudzutak and Kalinin as candidates was much more centralist in mood and anti-Trotsky in orientation than the one it replaced.[136] Despite further changes following the XI Congress,[137] henceforth the Orgburo was much more effective as a tool for centralisation and control than it had been prior to the X Congress. This was due to the improved technical apparatus at its control as a result of better records in the Secretariat as well as these personnel changes.

The final elite organ was the Central Control Commission (CCC). Control commissions were established at the IX Conference in September 1920,[138] but a formal charter was not fully enunciated until the X Congress six months later. This formally established commissions at the central, oblast and guberniia levels. Commissions were to be elected by the party congress at the centre and conferences at other levels to which they were to be accountable, they were to operate beside party committees using the apparatus of those committees to implement their decisions, and members of the commissions were given the right to attend all meetings of those party organisations. Members were to be of long party standing[139] and were not to have the tenure of their office cut short by transfer elsewhere. They could not simultaneously be members of party committees or hold administrative position; the control commissions were to possess a high degree of integrity and coherence and were to be independent of other party bodies.[140] These principles were enshrined in regulations for the control commissions adopted by the XI Congress.[141] But the relationship envisaged between control commissions and party committees undercut aspirations for the commissions' integrity and coherence. The commissions were to be independent of party committees[142] and yet they had to rely upon those committees for the machinery to implement their decisions. In this way their independence was compromised organisationally from the outset and inevitably they were drawn into the sorts of processes which were affecting party committees at this time.

The desired independence of the commissions was related to the tasks they were expected to carry out, while the shift in those tasks over time reflects the reality of their lack of independence.[143] Reflecting the Democratic Centralist charges of bureaucratism, the initial brief for the control commissions focused upon dealing with complaints that arose within the party. Control Commissions were originally conceived as independent arbiters in party disputes, a role which involved concern for the maintenance of high standards of party ethics and party discipline, including 'offences against the party by its members'.[144] The tasks were spelled out more fully at the X Congress:

> Control commissions are being established in order to strengthen the unity and authority of the party and their tasks include combating the bureaucratism and careerism which are creeping into the party, abuse by party members of their party and soviet positions, infringement of comradely relations in the party, dissemination of unfounded and unsubstantiated rumours and insinuations which bring disgrace to the party or to individual members and of other similar material which infringes the unity and authority of the party.[145]

While the principal concern of the control commissions remained the evil of bureaucratism, the emphasis upon the unity and authority of the party was new. It is easy to see how such a concern could be used to silence critics of party decisions or actions and thereby to contradict directly one of the principles which had been at the heart of the establishment of this institution from the outset – defending the individual party member against those in authority in the party.

It was in the direction of strengthening party unity that the control commissions developed. This is reflected clearly in the XI Congress resolution entitled 'On the Tasks and Aims of the Control Commissions'.[146] While acknowledging that under conditions of NEP the danger was growing of the corruption of the least stoic and self-controlled party members,[147] the commissions' tasks were deemed to be combating squabbles and groupism and extending the work of the verification commissions which had conducted the party purge in 1921. Furthermore the resolution declared 'that the CCC has insufficiently unified and led the work of local control commissions, and calls on the future CCC to turn more attention to this side of the matter'. This resolution shows clearly that the official aim of the control commissions had become one of discipline and that the control commission structure itself was being called on to become more centralised and unified the better to struggle with such problems. In practice, the control commissions had been moving in this direction throughout 1921–22, being used to resolve group squabbles at lower levels and to enforce discipline against oppositionist elements. It was resentment against this which led to the revolt against the control commissions on the floor of the XI Congress.

The CCC remained a small organ throughout this period. At the IX Conference a temporary membership was named consisting of three members from the centre and four from regional party organisations. From 1921, when the CCC actually came into existence (the IX Conference having set up simply a control commission), there was no statutory provision for the inclusion of regional delegates in the body. Of the initial, temporary membership, only three retained their positions after the X Congress, and of these only Sol'ts retained his seat after the XI Congress. Membership in 1922 was almost completely new,[148] a fact which may reflect the dissatisfaction with its performance in bringing the lower level commissions into line suggested by the XI Congress resolution. The new leadership of the CCC was only too willing to move in the direction called for by that resolution.

Among the temporary membership of the control commission established in 1920, three members (Dzerzhinsky, Preobrazhensky and Muranov) were also members of the CC. This was before the regulation preventing such simultaneous membership was introduced. Henceforth such dual membership did not recur. However, another form of institutional link was established between the CC and the CCC in August 1921: the joint CC–CCC plenum. Provision for such a gathering had been made in the IX Conference resolution establishing the control commissions and was reaffirmed in that part of the X Congress resolution 'On Party Unity' that was kept secret. This declared that the expulsion of CC members, CC candidates or control commission members or the reduction of CC members to candidate status could be carried out only by a two-thirds vote of a CC plenum to which all members of the Control Commission were invited.[149] The joint plenum was thus established as a high party court, and it was in this capacity that it first met in August 1921 to discuss the oppositional activities of CC member Shliapnikov. Rejecting Lenin's demand to expel Shliapnikov, the joint plenum gave him a severe reprimand.[150] The CCC's role in this case of the administration of party discipline reflected how far the perception of its functions had moved in 11 months and how, ultimately, it was impossible for the control apparatus to retain any integrity, coherence or independence from the structure of party committees.

The institutions briefly sketched above constituted the institutional arena within which the cut and thrust of politics was played out. The formal rules and official bodies helped to structure political activity, even though they had only limited success in the generation of a sense of institutional integrity and coherence; they remained throughout primarily instrumental in nature. Political activity was also structured by a range of assumptions and perceptions about what was acceptable political behaviour, about the way in which politics should be conducted. These assumptions and perceptions, combined with the actual patterns of action which emerged, created the conventions of political life which were of crucial importance in structuring the actions of individual political actors. It is to those conventions and the patterns of political behaviour which they validated that I now turn.

The conventions of political life

One of the principal characteristics of the politics of this period was the openness of debate within the party. Far from being a body of people who accepted at face value what their leaders told them, the party was a disputatious and fractious organism in which the leadership constantly had to defend itself against criticism from below. Such criticism was not alien to the ethos of the party but was rooted in its Bolshevik tradition.

The Bolshevik tradition, despite the long-held view of much Western scholarship, was not a coherent and consistent creed centred unambiguously around principles of dictatorship, elitism and centralism. Certainly these were important elements in that tradition, but they were by no means unchallenged. In broad terms, the Bolshevik tradition comprised two interacting strands, the 'democratic' and 'authoritarian'. Both strands were embodied in the official decisions and statements of party meetings, the party Rules, the writings of party actors, and the patterns of action which characterised the party and which constituted the basis for deciding what were acceptable modes of political behaviour. The bearers of this tradition were not the party elite alone, but the vast mass of party members. A particular practice or set of principles needed to be accepted by some, but not necessarily all, members of the party to become acknowledged as part of the Bolshevik tradition, with the result that different, conflicting elements could coexist within that tradition. This is what happened with the emergence of the democratic and authoritarian strands. The tension between these two strands is clear in the way the tradition handled the questions of the relationship between the party leadership and the rank-and-file and the place of opposition in the party.

The supremacy of the congress has already been noted. This was the body which was to take major decisions of policy and elect the party leadership, and was itself to be composed of delegates elected by the rank-and-file party members. This implied a principle of rank-and-file sovereignty, exercised indirectly through the congress delegates, and of leadership accountability, exercised by means of the election of party leaders. Of necessity, this implied a principle of free and open debate within the party; without such debate, notions of accountability were meaningless. This commitment to rank-and-file control can be found in some statements made by Lenin, commonly acknowledged as the most centralist of the Bolshevik leaders. In 1906, given the freer conditions created by the 1905 revolution, Lenin declared that 'the electoral principle in party organisations should be applied from top to bottom' and that it was now necessary 'to see to it that all the higher-standing bodies are elected, accountable, and subject to recall'.[151] While this is the only period in which Lenin offered broad-ranging support for the principle of rank-and-file control, it was significant because of its source and because it fed into the broader strand of Bolshevik thinking which accepted this as an important principle.

Against this clear expression of the principle of rank-and-file control through the electoral mechanism was a strong sentiment which opposed such control. This too is clearly expressed in some of Lenin's writings. Although he openly rejected rank-and-file control in 1902 because of the impossibility of open elections given the party's underground existence,[152] his opposition to such a practice was far more fundamental than simply a response to those conditions. It stemmed from his view that only correct revolutionary theory could provide an understanding of the current situation and thereby generate correct revolutionary tactics,[153] and that party leadership should therefore be held only by those who understood that theory, the professional revolutionaries. It followed that the superior understanding they possessed enabled them to decide who was best fitted to join their ranks, so that the composition of the leadership should be decided by the leadership itself rather than the rank-and-file. This view, which at its simplest constituted a claim that one's own group knew best, was widely held by different groups in the party and encouraged them to indulge in various sorts of manipulation to ensure their control and thereby negate the principle of accountability to the rank-and-file. Different groups, including both Bolsheviks and Mensheviks, sought to capture control of local organs and thereby rig representation at party congresses and conferences.[154] Congresses and conferences were sometimes convened, supposedly as a result of grass-roots pressure, but with known opponents excluded or invited in only a token capacity.[155] On other occasions party leaders, having gained control of the party's leading organs, ignored grass-roots pressure to convene a new meeting because it was politically inopportune.[156] Despite such manipulation, which completely undercut the principle of leadership accountability and rank-and-file sovereignty, congresses continued to be considered the leading organ of the party.

There was thus considerable tension within pre-October Bolshevism on the question of the relationship between leaders and the rank-and-file. The principle that major decisions should be decided by the rank-and-file through their duly elected delegates and the consequent acceptance of decisions arrived at through the voting procedure (including that of the choice of party leaders) as legitimate and binding expressions of party opinion was clearly established. But this was parallelled by acceptance of the practice of manipulating the party mechanism in order to rig the results of the voting and thereby enable the leadership to escape from effective rank-and-file control. The tension resulting from this was accompanied by a similar sort of tension over the place of opposition in the party.

A prominent strand of the Bolshevik tradition was a denial of the right of opposition to exist within party ranks. Lenin was particularly vociferous in his demands for unity and unanimity and was willing to use the party purge to remove opponents from the party's ranks if, once having brought the issue to a head, no reconciliation satisfactory to him could be achieved.[157] Unity came through struggle. But even if they did not agree with his methods, all Bolsheviks wanted unity and they worked in their own ways to bring this about: if Lenin sought to redefine the boundaries of the political grouping to exclude opposition from its ranks, the conciliators sought to achieve unity primarily through blurring boundaries and reconciling different groups. Unity and discipline were the aims of all.

Despite the strength of this anti-opposition feeling, a tradition that opposition had an accepted place in party life was spawned in the pre-October period. It was but a short step from the principles of leadership accountability and rank-and-file sovereignty to the assertion of a right for opposition to exist. The election of leaders seemed to imply a right to present separate slates of leadership candidates basing themselves upon different policy positions. The principle of free debate seemed to imply the right to form opposition groupings. Indeed, the treatment accorded to opposition groupings generally, with some exceptions, constituted effective acknowledgement that opposition had a legitimate place in party ranks. Lenin's opponents among the Bolsheviks[158] did not seek his exclusion from party political life: his right to oppose the views of what was frequently a majority was not denied, even though his action may have been deplored and the methods he used abhorred. Of course Lenin's usual tactic, once argumentation had failed, was the removal of his opponents from the ranks of the party or fraction, as he was able to do with Bogdanov and his associates in 1909. But this type of action was usually a last resort, used when other methods failed. In any case, Lenin's attempts to expel his opponents rarely met with unambiguous success; even the claimed exclusion of the Mensheviks from the party at the Prague Conference was limited in effect because many in the party refused to accept this and continued as before.[159] Lenin's inability to carry through a decisive split with his opponents because of the strength of opposition to this was a *de facto* recognition of the principle that opposition had a proper place in party life. So too was Lenin's own oppositional activity: he rejected the authority of duly elected party organs without himself seeking to leave party ranks. It was while acting in this way in 1905 that Lenin explicitly acknowledged the right of an opposition to exist, to advocate its views and to conduct ideological struggle so long as its activities did not lead to disorganisation in the party.[160] Later he also acknowledged that a party could include a variety of tendencies and factions in its structure.[161] Bolshevism was thus characterised by a tension between a strong sense of the need for unity (with a consequent disapproval of opposition activities) and a view that opposition groups had a right to pursue their activities within party ranks.

The tension between the two strands within Bolshevism sketched above is evident in the organisational formula used to describe the mode of operation of the party, democratic centralism.[162] The democratic strand was characterised by diversity (within limits), rank-and-file control over the leadership, open debate of important issues within the party and their resolution by free vote of the rank-and-file through their delegates, and an acceptance that opposition had a legitimate place in the party. The authoritarian, or centralist, strand emphasised unity, the primacy of central over local organs, the manipulation of personnel to achieve central control, the acceptance of central decisions without demur, strong leadership based on ideological rectitude, and unity through the elimination of opposition. Elements of both strands were to be found in the positions of all groups and individuals at different times. They were both intrinsic parts of the Bolshevik tradition, despite their different contours and implications for political activity. As a result of this duality, the Bolshevik tradition could not impose a single model of political action upon those who sought to exercise power in the aftermath of October 1917. The tension within the tradition ensured that it continued to justify markedly different methods of political action. The generation of conventions of political action during this initial period reflects the working out of these tensions.

The democratic strand of pre-revolutionary Bolshevism was carried into the post-October era by means of the principle of intra-party democracy. This notion, elastic in its meaning[163] and positive in its connotations, was taken up by all in the party, but interpretations of it varied between persons, groups and times. As a concept, it was directly associated in the party's mind with democratic centralism; the correct operation of centralism involved the implementation of democracy. But because interpretations of what it meant differed, the perceived implications of the formula for political action varied greatly among party members. For the Workers' Opposition, intra-party democracy was directly associated with, among other things, the promotion of workers into leading positions in the party and the elimination of the privileges possessed by those non-proletarian elements currently holding party office.[164] For the Democratic Centralists, it involved a rejection of the filling of office by appointment and the restoration of the elective principle, the implementation of some (unspecified) means whereby members of the proletariat elected to leading office were able to retain close links with the proletariat as a whole, the involvement of all party members in the decision-making process through the open discussion of issues, and the exercise of accountability on the part of leading party organs.[165] At one stage Lenin referred to democratic centralism as meaning representatives from the localities meeting and electing a representative body to do the administration and the regular election of the CC by the congress.[166] Although this view could imply a notion of accountability, it was also consistent with a view that the central leadership in the CC should have the right to make decisions unencumbered by day-to-day opposition.

But Lenin's outlook on this, as on so many other things, was dualistic. Although he recognised the advantages for efficient decision-making that flowed from having a leadership core immune from the disruptive effects of rank-and-file criticism, he also recognised the advantages such popular activism brought in terms of the health of the political organism and the generation of popular enthusiasm and commitment to the regime. He was also aware of the political consequences of opposing such action and was conscious of the fact that he was best placed of all the leaders to mobilise popular support for the positions he espoused. All of the Bolsheviks were aware of the need for a balance between an effective decision-making structure which could adequately meet the needs imposed by the dangerous times and a political structure which provided sufficient scope for rank-and-file activism. These two concerns are clearly reflected in the party's resolutions and statements of the period.

The former concern is encapsulated in the calls for unity and discipline which resounded throughout the party. In effect such calls were attempts to persuade the entire party membership to accept the decisions that were made above and to obey the instructions that were handed down. While such calls did not always specifically condemn the propensity to turn the party into a 'talking shop',[167] they emphasised the need to tighten the vertical linkages in the party and to increase the flow of power and authority to the centre. The most important instance of this was the 'On Party Unity' resolution of the X Congress discussed below.

The latter concern was reflected in a number of different types of declaration and statement. The calls to reanimate the party, to ensure that its organs met frequently and that regular reports on their activities were produced, that elections were held regularly and that the rank-and-file played a full and active part in the life of their party organisations are related to the desire to promote mass activism.[168] Resolutions seeking to encourage criticism in the party, to discourage people from simply accepting authority from above, is another reflection of this.[169] The complaints about the isolation of party leaders from the rank-and-file, and in particular the substitution of appointment for election, plus the calls for freedom of discussion clearly seek to emphasise rank-and-file activism, even at the expense of decision-making efficiency. The question was how and where the line was to be drawn between the need for the centre to make decisions and the desirability of encouraging mass activism and criticism.

An attempt to answer this question was made in the party Rules adopted in 1919. A new section in the Rules declared: 'The strictest party discipline is the primary duty of all party members and all party organisations. The decisions of party centres must be implemented quickly and exactly. At the same time inside the party the discussion of all contentious questions of party life is completely free until a decision is adopted.'[170] This seemed to offer a simple and straightforward resolution to the dilemma and thereafter was frequently repeated in party documents.[171] All major questions were to be the subject of free and open discussion throughout the party until a decision was adopted, at which point discussion was to cease and all must fall in behind the decision and support it. But in practice this solution was more apparent than real.[172] In the circumstances prevailing at the time it had two deficiencies. Firstly, it made it possible for the leadership to avoid open discussion by making a decision, claiming that the perilous times forced it to act without waiting for prolonged discussion, and calling on party members to abide by the principle by supporting the decision that had been taken. Secondly, it did not really address much of the public debate which characterised the party at that time. Much of the criticism of the leadership was less concerned with specific policy decisions than with the emergence and development of particular practices and conventions of internal party life. One of the main objects of criticism was the replacement of election by appointment and the consequent autonomy of leading levels. But far from this practice emerging as the result of the sort of policy discussion to which the above principle was meant to apply, it emerged as part of the pressures for developing a powerful political organisation in chaotic times.[173] If this practice was not the result of an open policy decision, the principle enunciated in 1919 was irrelevant.

The question of intra-party democracy, of finding a balance between the demands of speed and efficiency in central decision-making and the promotion of local activism, is intimately linked with the issue of opposition inside the party. This period witnessed the emergence of a succession of opposition groups in the party who focused upon either a single issue or a cluster of issues and attacked the leadership's handling of them. The first of the major opposition groups was the Left Communists, which emerged in early 1918 in opposition to the Brest-Litovsk treaty. Its focus soon expanded to a critique of the whole range of domestic policy and the trend of development in the country.[174] They were followed by the so-called Military Opposition in 1919 whose main concern was the policy of centralisation and discipline being imposed in the army.[175] In 1919 and 1920 the two main opposition groups were the Workers' Opposition and the Democratic Centralists. The former grew out of a concern for the perceived erosion of workers' rights, leading to a more generalised critique of the methods of operation of the party and its leadership. The latter saw their task as the restoration of democratic procedures in the working of the party and state structures.[176] A precise account of the fate of these groups will not be given here; it has been adequately recounted elsewhere. But some aspects of the history of their development and treatment in the party must be drawn out for the implications they have for the development of the internal party regime and the place in it of opposition and freedom of speech.

Prior to the X Congress there was no formal suggestion that opposition was anything but a legitimate part of party life. Although the leaders sometimes engaged in organisational manipulation in order to reduce opposition representation and effectiveness at party congresses,[177] the treatment of such groups at the congresses up until 1921 constituted a recognition of the legitimacy of their existence and activity. The VII Congress was convened specifically to resolve the issue between the leadership and the Left Communists by enabling the party rank-and-file to debate the issue and send delegates to the congress in accord with their wishes. The widespread debate within the party, while it did not support the views of the opposition, constituted a formal recognition of the right of the opposition to express their views and dissent from the leadership. At the congress Lenin declared that it was the right of a party member to disagree with and criticise the CC if he believed it to be wrong.[178] Similarly, the party-wide debate on the trade union issue preceding the X Congress and the specific provision for the election of delegates to the congress on the basis of the platform they supported on this issue seemed to confirm the legitimacy of an oppositionist stance. Moreover, at the X Congress Lenin himself affirmed that in the face of fundamental disagreements, election of congress delegates may have to be based on platforms,[179] which possibly – though not inevitably – implies a right for different groups to hold these platforms. Up until the X Congress members of the opposition usually were part of the congress presidium and took part in the special sections established by the congress to work out a resolution on the issue about which they were agitated. With the exception of the VIII Congress, where the issues raised by the Military Opposition were resolved in closed session, opposition spokesmen were allowed to address freely the congress without heckling or organisational restriction and to put alternative resolutions before the gathering; frequently opposition leaders presented what virtually amounted to an alternative political report to the keynote speech given by Lenin. Leading oppositionists were sometimes elected to the CC by the congresses at which they had taken up an oppositionist stand; the Left Communists Bukharin, Uritsky and Lomov (the first as a full member, the others as candidates) were elected at the VII congress while the Workers' Oppositionists Shliapnikov and Kutuzov were elected as full members and Kiselev as a candidate at the X Congress.

Although the successive opposition groups were defeated, this did not necessarily reflect a broad rejection of oppositional activity by the party. Each opposition group was defeated on the floor of the congress, and even though some organisational manipulation had gone into the creation of the pro-leadership majorities, they were not entirely created by central chicanery. The judicious inspection of delegates' mandates and the placing of loyal appointees in the regional and local apparatus could strengthen the anti-opposition forces at the congress, but given the limitations of the central apparatus discussed above, it is unlikely that such action could do more than reinforce the popular swell of opinion among those who made that opinion in the party. The situation the party found itself in, beset on all sides by opponents and struggling to maintain and consolidate its hold on power, meant that the leadership's arguments emphasising centralism and discipline would have appeared much more appropriate than the opposition forces' arguments for democracy and openness. Furthermore, for the local power barons discussed above, the charges and claims mounted by the opposition constituted a real threat to their positions, privileges and continued exercise of power. It is little wonder that these people should try to ensure that their local party organs chose congress delegates who would be sensitive to their needs and perceptions. So the defeat of the opposition groups did not represent a rejection of opposition in principle, but a rejection of the platform on which each group was standing.

The rejection of the oppositions' positions by many sub-national party leaders was also a consequence of the basic organisational weakness that characterised all opposition groups. None of them was a coherent, tightly organised machine; memberships were fluid around a stable leadership core (and there was a significant level of continuity between the groups); and only the Left Communists had their own press organ – and this only because a concentration of their supporters in Moscow enabled them to turn the local party organ into their mouthpiece.[180] And although the central organs hardly constituted a smoothly oiled machine, compared with the opposition groups, the organisational muscle the centre could muster was substantial. Furthermore, the opposition groups usually were confronted by a united front on the part of the ruling oligarchy. With the exception of Bukharin and the Left Communists, none of the opposition groups had within its leadership any of the Bolshevik notables. Although conflicts occurred within the oligarchy between individual leaders, these conflicts were not linked with the activity of the successive opposition groups. These groups did not, therefore, gain either a popular leader of first-rank standing within the party or someone whose political stature could enable them to carry the opposition message into leading circles. In contrast, the leadership could bring both its institutional position and the personal stature and reputation of its members into the struggle against the opposition. Particularly important in this regard was the personal primacy of Lenin, to be discussed below.

But while the acceptance of the right of an opposition to exist remained prominent in the collective consciousness of the party, a strong counter-current was also present. All of the talk about the need for centralism and discipline could be interpreted as a rejection of opposition in principle, at least in the prevailing conditions. More unambiguous in this regard were the moves taken at the X Congress. Following Lenin's strictures at the congress about the need to call a halt to discussion and to put the lid on opposition,[181] the congress adopted two resolutions. The resolution 'On the Syndicalist and Anarchist Deviation in Our Party'[182] was the first congress resolution in the post-October period to mount a sustained attack on a party opposition grouping and its views,[183] and it formally declared that the propagation of the ideas held by the Workers' Opposition was incompatible with continued membership of the party. The other resolution, 'On Party Unity',[184] was of more importance for the future development of the party. This resolution began by highlighting the dangers to the party posed by fractionalism in the contemporary circumstances and went on to urge all who would be critical of the party to be 'mindful of the party's situation, in the midst of enemy encirclement'. Although fractionalism must be destroyed, democracy and initiative must be expanded. Then came the heart of the resolution.

The congress orders the immediate dissolution, without exception, of all groups that have been formed on the basis of some platform or other and instructs all organisations to be very strict in ensuring that no fractional manifestations of any sort are tolerated. Failure to comply with this resolution of the congress will lead to unconditional and immediate expulsion from the party.

In a final section which was not made public until after the XIII Congress in 1924, the resolution placed the power to punish up to and including expulsion for fractional activity in the hands of the CC, a move which clearly violated the provisions in the party Rules which vested powers of expulsion in the member's own organisation. For members of the CC and the CCC, demotion to candidate status or expulsion from the party now required a two-thirds vote of a joint meeting of the CC and the CCC.

This resolution has often been seen as crucial in the party's development, as ineluctably setting the party on the course to the type of one-man despotism which existed much later. But this is to overstate the case. Certainly the resolution established principles of action which were deemed to be unacceptable in the party, and principles which were more wide ranging than any which had existed before; not only was organisation of a group with its own platform and discipline declared to be out of bounds, but so too was the propagation of views deemed to be a 'deviation', a 'political error' and a 'practical danger'. This was a very wide net indeed, particularly given the absence of clear definitions about what these could involve.[185] But two points need to be kept in mind. The first is that the resolution draws no distinction between factionalism and fractionalism. The Russian *fraktsionnost'* is usually taken to refer to both, but in principle fractionalism and factionalism are different. In essence, the former is a vertically structured group while the latter is horizontally structured. A fraction is a group of people with a platform and discipline of their own[186] who are scattered across different hierarchical levels of the party. There may be larger concentrations at some levels than at others, but the essence is the vertical spread. A faction is a group with a platform and a discipline of its own concentrated overwhelmingly at one level of the party hierarchy or in the one party organisation. One would, therefore, talk about a fraction with its leaders in the CC and the bulk of its membership at the oblast, guberniia and uezd levels, and a faction in the CC. While the resolution makes no distinction between these, Lenin's primary focus appears to have been the fraction. It was in the context of the struggle against such a structure, the

Workers' Opposition, that the resolution was adopted. Moreover, the view that it was the propagation rather than the mere holding of Workers' Opposition views which was incompatible with party membership suggests that it was fractionalism against which the measure was directed. Propagation involved the attempt to garner support within the party and, given the formal distribution of power and authority, this was useless unless it could be gained at both leadership and lower levels. A prohibition on fractionalism was less of a worry to Lenin because his enormous personal prestige rendered his need to gain organisational support at lower levels less pressing. Significantly, if Lenin did direct his aim at fractionalism rather than factionalism, the conception of leadership which would have remained legitimate was one in which individual leaders did not rely upon organisational manipulation. It was a conception of leadership ideally suited to someone with enormous personal prestige and no organisational power base in the party. It was thus consistent with leadership by party notables rather than party organisation men.

If the primary aim of 'On Party Unity' was to restrict fractionalism, the resolution was a defensive mechanism on the part of the oligarchy. It was an attempt to protect the oligarchy against the sorts of attacks upon it from below which it had experienced in the recent past. For the most part when confronted with such attacks from below, the oligarchy had closed ranks to fend off the challenges. Although this had not occurred in the trade union discussion, when the dispute within the oligarchy had left it open to the sort of criticism which emerged in the public discussion, the oligarchs united to put down the threat from below that seemed to be posed by the Workers' Opposition.

But the X Congress resolution was also directed against the oligarchy itself. This is most clearly reflected in the secret provisions regarding expulsion from the CC for fractional activity. In this sense, it was an attempt to impose a form of discipline on the oligarchy. But the principal purpose behind this is not clear. It is usually seen as an attempt to prevent individual oligarchs from getting together to discuss issues and combining to pursue the policy they believed most appropriate. Such an interpretation seems to have been current in the post-Lenin period, but as an explanation of its original intent this may need qualification. Lenin was the prime mover in the adoption of the measure. All of his political life he had been engaged in polemics, debating issues with colleagues and drumming up support for the position he espoused. He was not always in the majority on issues. It is unlikely that he would have fashioned an instrument that could have been mobilised against precisely this type of activity, and thereby left himself open to punishment under the discipline provisions. It is more likely that, rather than seeking to prevent politicking within the oligarchy or among the notables, he wanted to prevent this from overflowing into the party at large in an organised form. If this reasoning is correct, the X Congress resolution was designed in part to discipline the oligarchy, but not to eliminate political debate within it. It was designed to consolidate the barrier between oligarchy and rank-and-file that the trade union discussion had threatened to breach. The decision was thus an attempt to structure the relationship between oligarchy and rank-and-file rather more than an attempt to silence dissident voices in the party leadership.

The second point about this resolution is that, alone, it meant nothing. It had to be taken up and used before it could be of any practical consequence. The history of the party is littered with resolutions which were ignored almost as soon as they were adopted. The instrumental approach to rules evident in the party's history meant that this rule could have normative authority only if leading political actors sought to enforce it in intra-party life; its mere appearance in party law by itself meant nothing. Furthermore, this resolution was accompanied by a resolution which seemed to encourage something which did not sit easily with the prohibition on fractions – the free and open discussion of all important issues in the party.[187] What made the centralist and anti-oppositionist sentiments of the 'On Party Unity' resolution so important was not anything intrinsic to those sentiments, but that they were taken up and used by political actors for their own advantage. The resolution embodying these sentiments could be a weapon, but as such it was instrumental rather than generative in structuring the later course of development.

The resolution was important at the time, chiefly because of the shift in party attitude which it signified. Under the impetus of increased awareness of office-holder self interest (see below), the constant theme of the need for unity and discipline, the fears of degeneration as a result of the petty bourgeois environment,[188] and the obvious popular discontent with the Bolsheviks reflected in the peasant revolts, the Kronstadt rising and the change to NEP, the mood of the party seems to have hardened against opposition and made a call for a closing of the ranks sure to evoke a positive response within the party. This is reflected not only in the resolutions of the X Congress, but also in the change in emphasis in the tasks of the control commissions sketched above. Also significant is the increased use of administrative measures against opposition. While the purge of 1921 does not appear to have been used widely against Workers' Opposition members[189] – and the use of it for the repression of those who thought differently was openly prohibited[190] – organisational manipulation, transfers and appointments were used to break up centres of Workers' Opposition support.[191] There was little significant criticism of this within the party. But this apparent shift in mood and the resolution of the X Congress did not bring about the use of the Vecheka against party opposition during this period; party members could be arrested only after expulsion from the party. Nor did it bring an end to oppositional activity, which thrived in the next period, following Lenin's passing from the scene.

The form in which oppositional activity was conducted at this time involved an important convention of political life which was to be of significance later: political conflict must be contained within party bounds. This principle had been carried over from pre-revolutionary days and was particularly obvious on two occasions during this period. During the Brest-Litovsk affair, when the Left Communist members of the CC resigned from that body, they accompanied their resignation with the declaration 'we retain for ourselves complete freedom to agitate outside the party as well as within it for the position which we consider to be the only correct one'.[192] But despite this statement, they did not carry the debate outside the party nor did they vote against the peace in non-party fora. In contrast, in February 1922, twenty-two members of the Workers' Opposition sent the so-called 'Declaration of the 22' to the Executive Committee of the Comintern. The Declaration was an appeal to the ECCI against what they saw to be the increasingly authoritarian methods of operation of the party. This provoked a special resolution of the XI Congress[193] which, while not condemning the appeal to the Comintern, castigated the continued fractional activity of the group. However, it is clear that it was the appeal to the Comintern which provoked this action. Party disputes were to be kept within the party, because extension of those disputes outside that organisation laid the party open to attack by its enemies.

The opposition question was closely related to that of discipline. This was a term used frequently in party documents and speeches but never clearly defined. The analogy often used when discussing discipline was that of the military, but while this conveyed the appropriate sense of hierarchy, the relationship between the levels which it suggested was not that which was accepted within the party; provision for debate alone made the military analogy inappropriate. The notion of discipline which most accepted was much more consonant with the looser organisational structure of the time. It was also consistent with the principle that discussion should be free until a decision was made and with the view expressed in 1921 that what was incompatible with party membership was propagation of dissident views. Discipline was seen, purely and simply, as obedience to higher decisions; decisions of party centres were binding on all members with discussion ceasing as soon as a decision was reached and all began to implement it.[194] It was not demanded that individuals who disagreed with the official view had to reject their own views and embrace that of the centre without reservation. They had to accept that view and they had to propagate and implement it to the best of their ability, and if they did this they satisfied the demands for discipline which the party imposed.

However, this view of discipline did not apply equally to the whole party. If it had, all members of the oligarchy would at some time or another have found themselves subject to party disciplinary proceedings. In one sense, the lack of any clear agreement about the hierarchy of institutions within oligarch circles negated this rule. If, despite formal provisions, no organ was acknowledged as the ultimate authority, the decision of no body could be accepted as final. As such, no decision requiring complete obedience could be taken. This line of reasoning, although formalist in its approach, provided a basis upon which oligarch differences could be maintained even after a decision had seemingly been made. In any event, it is certain that the notion of discipline which was applied to the party at large did not impinge upon the oligarchs. There were different rules of the game at base and apex, although during this period even among those at lower levels, the use of disciplinary measures (with the exception of the purge) was sparing.

One of the characteristics of elite politics during this period was the openness of the policy-making process. Crucial questions of policy were discussed in the leading fora of the party and in the party press, with the result that any party member who regularly read the press could keep abreast of the course of policy debate at the centre. Furthermore, the different stances that members of the elite took on policy questions were clearly discernible; there was no effort to hide policy differences behind a façade of unity as individual leaders freely expressed their views on policy. But what is unique about the course of the policy debate is the elite structure within which it took place.

The structure of elite politics

The oligarchy which dominated national politics at this time was not undifferentiated in terms of the power and position possessed by its members. At its simplest, there were at least three levels in the oligarchy. At the highest level was Lenin, whose personal prestige and standing in the Bolshevik movement ensured that he was the single most important actor in the political system. At the second level of the oligarchy were those whose prominence in the movement accorded them significant personal prestige and authority. The major individuals on this level throughout this period were Trotsky, Kamenev, Zinoviev, Stalin and Bukharin, with others, such as Dzerzhinsky, Rykov, Krestinsky and Tomsky on the same broad level but distinctly lower in status than the first five named. The official positions these people occupied were for the most part products of their personal standing in the movement. Along with Lenin, these were the Bolshevik notables. The third level of the oligarchy consisted of those other members of the CC and leading figures in Sovnarkom whose profile in elite politics was low, whose individual impact on the politics was limited, and whose power and authority were essentially products of the positions they occupied. The main structures of the oligarchy were therefore highly personalised structures in which official position carried much less weight than the authority and prestige stemming from personal factors.

While the oligarchy was differentiated horizontally in this way, it was not also divided vertically into firm, enduring factional divisions. Personal dislikes and disagreements were clearly in evidence within the oligarchy throughout this period and there was increasing mistrust and resentment against the perceived parvenu, Trotsky. Some members of the oligarchy sought to use political disputes to undermine Trotsky's position in the leadership.[195] But even this anti-Trotsky sentiment had not crystallised into firm factional distinctions by the time the period drew to a close. The absence of such factions made for a freer and more wide-ranging policy process than would have existed otherwise. The resolution of policy disagreements was not achieved by lining up disciplined votes in a party forum, but by persuading leading members of the oligarchy of the merits of one's case. This was particularly important since many of the lesser members of the oligarchy seem to have taken their lead from some of the more prominent, in particular Lenin. Politics within the oligarchy was therefore personalised and free-flowing, with few hardened positions to anchor the course of policy debate. A principal reason for this fluidity was the very low profile in elite organs of the successive opposition groups. If these groups were represented at all in the oligarchy, it was by people in the third level or (with the single exception of Bukharin in 1918) at most, the second rung of the second level. No leading figure took up the banner of the opposition in elite circles, and therefore no leading figure firmly set his face against the course of systemic development. Indeed, the reverse situation applied: in the face of attacks from below by successive opposition groups, the oligarchy tended to close its ranks and maintain a high level of cohesion. The most striking instance of this was the 'On Party Unity' resolution.

The highly personalised structure of oligarchical politics facilitated the continuing low level of institutionalisation of elite political organs during this period. With politics played out and policy issues resolved in large part through the interplay of individuals, the institutional arena within which such discussion took place was essentially secondary. Because leading figures exercised power and authority more as a result of their own status than the institutional positions they occupied, there was little incentive for them to foster the growth of strong institutional structures with their own discrete spheres of competence and methods of operation. In short, leading members of the oligarchy made little attempt to work out an administrative regime which would structure the activities of the elite political organs. This is most clearly seen in the flow of decision-making in the first few years of the new political system's life.

Open and vigorous debate on policy issues took place in all of the elite political organs: Sovnarkom and its executive bodies, the CC and the Politburo. Indeed, major issues could be discussed in all of these fora, since all members of the elite were not members of all bodies. Although there was general recognition in the oligarchy that party organs were superior to state organs since they were to guide the activities of the latter, there was little sense of how this was to be brought about in practice. At the elite level, the consequent confusion was evident in the frequent appeals of decisions from one organ to another. If, for example, Lenin was defeated on some issue in Sovnarkom, he was quite willing to bring that issue up once again in the CC in an attempt to gain a reversal of the earlier decision.[19] Other members of the oligarchy followed the same course of action, reflecting a general belief that this was the right of all oligarchs. This had the effect potentially of involving all elite organs in the resolution of all issues and of ensuring wide-ranging debate within the oligarchy on all issues unrestricted by institutional boundaries. This is related to the continuing process of centralisation and the desire of individual oligarchs (most of whom had strong opinions and believed their revolutionary credentials entitled them to decisive influence in party councils) not to be excluded from the resolution of important issues on the grounds of formal institutional membership. But it also prevented the development of clear institutional boundaries and prerogatives, kept the institutional structures weakened in the face of personalised politics, and prevented the emergence of a single institutional locus of power and authority that was superior to all of the others. Only when the Politburo began to establish its predominance and authority slipped away from Sovnarkom did elite debate undergo serious restriction, and although this process was well advanced by the end of the period, it was not complete.

Although political differences and debates were freely aired at the apex of the political structure, and were therefore common knowledge among those rank-and-file members who read the party press, elite conflict was not extended to lower levels of the party in an organisational form. Party leaders did seek to generate popular support inside the party for the positions they espoused through party congresses and conferences, lower level party gatherings and the party press. The most striking instances of this were the party-wide debates in 1917–18 and 1920–21 when party leaders and their supporters conducted a form of politics that would not have been alien to politicians in countries with truly competitive elections. But such appeals for support were not buttressed by an organisational splitting of the party apparatus. Party delegations at congresses were not the disciplined troops they were to become later in the 1920s, although trends in this direction were already evident. Most party leaders did not attempt to sink their roots into the organisational structure of the party in order to press their claims, at least after the Left Communist affair, with the result that the party apparatus remained unified; it was not divided into fractions with different oligarchs at their head. The era of the political machine had not yet come. Indeed, while firm factional divisions did not emerge within the oligarchy, it is unlikely that fractional divisions with their leaders in the oligarchy would develop in the party apparatus.

One basis for the continuing unity of the oligarchy was a notion of consensus based upon shared interests. The initial Bolshevik elite was by no means cohesive, coming from a variety of social backgrounds and having a broad range of experiences in their revolutionary careers. Many of the elite, such as Lenin, Zinoviev and Kamenev, were well known to one another, having spent much of the prerevolutionary period in emigration. Others had spent much time in the emigration but had had little to do with their new colleagues; indeed, Trotsky had been a bitter opponent of many with whom he now shared power. Others, such as Stalin and Molotov, had spent most of their time in the underground or in exile inside Russia and were little known to many of their fellow oligarchs. But this diversity of background was moderated to some degree by shared commitment to the revolution and, for the most part, an extended period of party membership. Soon after coming to power, cohesive pressures began to work.

The shared commitment to the socialist future, added to success in the Civil War, generated a sense of real achievement and a consciousness that they were, in a sense, the chosen ones. They had struggled against enormous odds, and they had been successful. Braving the dangers together, struggling with the decisions that were instrumental in final success and, for the most part, overcoming the enormous pressures on them personally, engendered in the political elite, and among the notables in particular, a real *esprit de corps*. Of course this does not mean that they always agreed with their fellows. Nor does it mean that they liked their fellows. Indeed, the personal jealousies and injured pride that were to be so important later in the 1920s were already present. But while Lenin remained in charge and directed the general way forward, such personal factors tended to be subordinated. Buttressed by ideological tenets regarding the importance of correct leadership and reinforced by Bolshevik success, this group came to believe that they had not only a responsibility but almost a right to lead; they were the best qualified to lead and therefore should do so.

However, this belief in their own qualities did not lead to the closure of the elite. Large numbers of new members could still enter, as they did during this period. But it did lay the basis for the elite's claim to certain rights or prerogatives which were not available to the rank-and-file party members. Their belief in their fitness to rule justified the attempt to forestall attacks on their position from below. The attempts to discipline dissidents, the closing of the ranks against opposition in 1921, the adoption of the anti-fractional decision, and the moves to structure the election of the CC at the X Congress are all aspects of this.

But rights and prerogatives can also be seen as privileges. Although Lenin was spartan in his habits and sought to impose similar standards upon his colleagues, the combination of work demands and general socio-economic position ensured that the elite enjoyed a more privileged lifestyle than did the populace. Simple things, such as the constant supply of food and clothing, the provision of motorised transport (including chauffeur) while most of the population had to do with a ramshackle public transport system and the certainty of continuing paid employment were worth a great deal in Russia's disrupted economy. Amid general poverty and shortage, privileges such as these were of immense value. They made the difference between a life of constant struggle to survive and one into which material deprivation did not enter. The elite could justify this with the argument that they needed to be able to devote their time and efforts to the revolution and its survival rather than having to be concerned about their own personal welfare. There was some truth to this argument, but it was also very convenient. It allowed members of the elite to hold on to their privileges without abandoning their principles. Widespread criticism of this situation did not emerge principally because regional political leaders, who were the best placed to make such criticism, enjoyed similar privileges, if at a lower level. There was, then, among the elite, a common interest in ensuring the continuation of these privileges.

Another source of partial common interest emerged within the elite during this period. This was based in the permanent apparatus of the party. The development of this apparatus, focusing on the Orgburo and Secretariat but also found at lower levels of the party in the secretarial machine, spawned a set of interests and perspectives which was not always in accordance with those of either the Bolshevik elite or the party notables. Residence in the capital or major towns and possession of an official position enabled those in the command posts of the apparatus to gain a share of the privileges possessed by their political masters, so in this there were common interests. But the full-time workers in the apparatus also gained a set of priorities which were not shared by the more prominent politicians. Those in the apparatus did not depend overwhelmingly upon their political skills for survival; their future depended more upon their performance in their bureaucratic jobs. As Trotsky said, they were more concerned with administration than political principle. But this merely reflects the realities of their circumstances; their administrative performance determined their future. Moreover, it follows from this that they also had an interest in the development of that part of the apparatus in which they worked. They developed an institutional interest, one that favoured an expansion of the power and responsibilities of that institution. The early clashes between different departments of the Secretariat reflect the processes of empire-building which were proceeding.

But the interest in institutional aggrandizement was not shared by the elite as a whole because its members had diverse institutional power bases. To the extent that the oligarchs manifested such institutional interests, they were individualised because their power bases were not concentrated in one place but scattered across the country. While Zinoviev's was in Petrograd, Trotsky's was in the army and many other members of the CC had theirs in their regional seats. Thus, compared with the central administrators, the political notables had no distinctive institutional power base at hand upon which to rely and which they could collectively build up. But the full-time party workers in the Secretariat sought to build up their own departments and, because of their strategic position in both information flow to party bodies and in the implementation of party decisions, they were well placed to do this. Although the full ramifications of this were not to become clear until later in the 1920s when such interests coincided with the political interests of one of the notables, the institutional interest of the full-time party workers was already emerging.

Fractionalisation of the party apparatus was inhibited not only by the broad elite consensus, but also by the weakly developed nature of personnel procedures discussed above. While communications remained difficult and records at all levels inadequate, the physical infrastructure for the development of such procedures was weak. But as the infrastructure grew in strength, the capacity for the development of organisational machines increased, and they were clearly stronger by the end of the period than they had been at the outset. Moreover, the personalised nature of politics at the lower levels, with the development of the family groups operating more through personal ties than bureaucratic channels, were responses to pressures which also affected the elite. Incentives existed at the national level for the growth of personal ties. For those responsible for appointments and transfers, the pressures for success were enormous. But there was not the institutional infrastructure available to sustain operations on the scale demanded. One response to this problem was the same as that used at other levels, reliance upon personal contacts. The placement of personal contacts in responsible positions at lower levels of the party was a practice which provided significant potential for the development of stable fractions. But to realise this potential, long-term domination of the appointment process by a group of individuals who were aware of the possibilities and willing to exploit them and a national leader willing to play a part in this both organisationally and symbolically were required. These prerequisites were realised with the reorganisation and restaffing of the Orgburo and Secretariat in 1921 and the appointment of Stalin as General Secretary in April 1922. The consequences of these for fraction formation are discussed in chapter 4.

The absence of factional divisions at the top and of fractional divisions in the apparatus focused on the top reflects the extraordinary fluidity of politics during this period. This is also evident in the ideological realm. The ideology which the Bolsheviks brought with them provided a methodology for the analysis of social questions and a broad orientation to political issues, but very few direct guidelines for policy implementation. These were generated as the situation arose, either in the form of a prior working through of ideological positions to gain guidance for policy matters or as an *ex post facto* justification of policy positions already adopted. The centrality of the ideology to the Bolshevik outlook, in terms of its legitimation function as well as the orientation to issues which it brought, meant that all questions had to be seen and discussed in ideological terms. As the case of NEP showed, a policy did not have to be strictly in accordance with ideological tenets in order to be adopted, but the chances of adoption were much higher if such a claim could be made for it. But while the ideology, through the methodology it embodied, helped to structure the approach of the party's leaders to the problems confronting them, it offered no simple solutions. This was one of the important characteristics of the period: the ideology was not a dogma or an orthodoxy, but a living and developing intellectual universe. Furthermore, it had no recognised, living authority whose word on ideological matters was law. Not even Lenin, whose personal preeminence was unquestioned, could claim to be the ideological fount of orthodoxy and have this claim accepted. Many leaders had claims to be theoreticians, but none was accepted as *the* theoretician of the party.

In principle, the party's leadership was collective in nature. Sovereignty lay with collective organs and the party's Rules made no provision for individual positions in leading party organs. But throughout this period Lenin was the dominating force in the political system, his imprint evident at virtually all major points of the emerging structure. While Lenin's power, position and authority were linked to his chairmanship of Sovnarkom and his administrative abilities, more important was his acknowledged position as father of the party, the revolution and the Soviet state. This gave him enormous moral authority which enabled him to overcome his organisational deficiencies,.[197] As Leonard Schapiro had argued, a majority vote against Lenin was almost unthinkable in the mass ranks of the party.[198] Even oppositionists often believed in Lenin personally while opposing the policies of the leadership of which he was part; witness Workers' Opposition leader Kollontai's statement; 'Not in vain will the rank-and-file worker speak with assurance and reconciliation: "Ilyich will ponder, he will think it over, he will listen to us. And then he will decide to turn the party rudder toward the Opposition."'[199] While there may have been an element of flattery for partisan ends in this, it does express the popular view of Lenin throughout the party. Despite his disapproval, Lenin was the object of a minor personality cult among at least some sections of the masses during this period.[200] Lenin's power was personally based and essentially charismatic in nature.

The effect of the personalised authority which Lenin wielded on the early development of the Soviet system can hardly be exaggerated. If the conditions of civil war and hardship were instrumental in the centralisation of power during the early years, then the role of Lenin was fundamental to the basis upon which the central institutions grew. Lenin's part in appealing decisions from one body to another and the deleterious effects this had on the growth of institutional coherence and integrity have already been noted. But the role Lenin played was even more significant than this, and one which no one else at that time would have been able to perform. By representing a personalised form of authority, Lenin embodied a notion of authority which was completely at odds with the notion of regularised authority based upon stable institutional structures. He legitimised power and authority which was decoupled from institutional structures, thereby providing a precedent for others to make claims to authority on that basis and severely hampering the growth of authoritative institutions. If power and authority were seen in personalised terms and this became rooted in the collective consciousness of the system and its participants as the norm, the generation of normative authority by institutional structures became much more difficult. Prominent individuals, harking back to the personalised authority of the founder of the system, would always be able to challenge the organisational hierarchies on a basis acceptable in terms of political lore. It was, therefore, in the shade of Lenin's personalised authority that the early political institutions sought to grow and it was that shadow which, in significant part, hindered their growth as powerful, independent institutions.

In practice Lenin was the hub of the governmental and administrative networks. It was his personal role at the top which did much to ensure that the largely unstructured, and therefore potentially inefficient and conflictual, relationship between the bodies at the apex of the political system did not break down. He provided the lubricant as well as the driving force for governmental affairs. The extent of his influence is evident in the prominence Sovnarkom was able to retain despite the growth in the power and authority of party organs until his illness removed him from the scene. On all issues about which Lenin fought hard, he was successful. His success may have been gained by a rallying of the support of the rank-and-file (Brest-Litovsk), by partial or apparent concessions to the opposition (the organisational question at the VIII Congress), by administrative measures (after the X Congress), or by a combination of all three (the trade union debate), but it is clear that when he threw all of his efforts into the struggle, he was successful. Of course, Lenin was defeated on numerous occasions and issues, particularly in Sovnarkom,[201] but such defeats were never on major issues or were overturned by Lenin in another forum. It was this capacity to turn an issue around, albeit sometimes with difficulty, that marked Lenin as the central feature of the system. It is for this reason that the Leninist political system ceases to exist with Lenin's departure as the dominant actor in May 1922.[202]

The chief characteristic of the Leninist political system between October 1917 and May 1922 was fluidity. The system was fluid both in its institutional forms and in the conventions of political action which structured elite activity. Certainly towards the end of the period the centralist and disciplinary elements were becoming more pronounced, but they had not gathered so much momentum as to be unstoppable. Less centralist, democratic elements remained strong. The source of the fluidity in the contours of the Bolshevik system is to be found in the struggle to establish party supremacy in the absence of clear plans or agreements about how the new regime should be structured. The need for quick decision-making in the hostile environment reinforced the emphasis upon results at the expense of formal procedures; political actors at all levels were more intent on resolving immediate problems than with following any prescribed notions of procedure. The resulting weakness of institutional bodies and the diffuseness of organisational boundaries were serious obstacles to the generation of any sense of institutional integrity or cohesion or a stable pattern of institutional inter-relationships. If political bodies could be ignored or overruled at the whim of leading political figures, their importance as major structuring factors in elite political life was limited. Important here too was the personalistic basis of political life, a basis which was intrinsically at odds with the emergence of politics based on sound institutional structures. While personalistic politics was supreme, formal institutions remained instrumental, and while the oligarchy was broadly united behind a general consensus, there was little incentive to build up the institutional integrity of the organisational structures.

Nevertheless, developments in the institutional sphere during this period were significant. The most important was the growth of pressures for centralisation of decision-making. The sense of being under attack stimulated an emphasis upon control, unity and discipline as the most appropriate response. But this sort of contextual factor could only be conditioning, not determining. Of fundamental importance was the attitude of political actors, and in particular their perceptions about the appropriateness of such policies. The leading oligarchs' conviction of their own suitability to lead, buttressed by ideological tenets about the proper relationship between socialist intellectuals and the working class, was relevant here. So too was the growth of a corporate sense of identity and the perception of the oligarchy as a group with a mission to fulfil. Indeed, it was this overriding interest in the end to be achieved which was partly responsible for their failure to focus upon immediate institutional realities. When Lenin's removal threw the oligarchy off balance, this ignoring of the institutional context was to have important implications.

Part II

The fractured oligarchy 1922–1929

3 A strong party structure?

The 1920s was a period of considerable freedom and plurality within Soviet society. Following the rigours of War Communism, the policies associated with the NEP had led to a discernible easing of the political atmosphere; class war rhetoric and the politics of class struggle gave way to a policy of class conciliation as the regime sought to reach a more amicable *modus vivendi* with the populace. But despite this less overtly antagonistic relationship between regime and populace, a sense of insecurity continued to pervade large parts of the political structure. Despite the elimination of opposition parties as effective entities[1] and the smashing of the two major instances of organised opposition to emerge during this period, the Workers' Group and the Workers' Truth,[2] the control exercised by the party throughout the country was not firmly rooted.[3] Two aspects of this were significant: the isolation of the party from society at large and the internal structuring of party life.

The party's isolation is graphically shown by the weakness of its representation in rural areas. According to figures cited by Stalin at the XIII Congress, the proportion of communists in organisations at each level of the soviet hierarchy was as follows: village soviets 7 per cent, executive committees of volost soviets 48 per cent, executive committees of uezd soviets 87 per cent and executive committees of guberniia soviets 89 per cent.[4] Another speaker at the same congress declared that in three to four volosts with 50 to 60 thousand villages, there were only ten communists;[5] according to the Smolensk Archive, there was only one party member for every ten villages.[6] Another source claimed that only one out of every 25 to 30 villages had a party cell, while communists remained in the minority in soviets below the uezd level.[7] The small proportion of communists in the countryside is evident from the total numbers involved; of a total of almost 700,000 party members in 1924, some 150,000 lived outside the towns. Of

113

these 150,000, 61,000 were to be found in the central regions of the RSFSR and the Ukraine, with the remainder scattered throughout the rest of Russia; the Byelorussian and Far Eastern regions had only about 3,000 party members each.[8] Zinoviev was correct in 1923 when he declared that the party was a party of the city, based and working in the workers' quarters, which had only just begun to penetrate the countryside.[9]

This situation was little improved later in the decade. By 1927 only 23.3 per cent of party members lived in the countryside, constituting 0.52 per cent of the rural population (compared with 1.78 per cent of the urban population), while only 0.7 per cent of peasant households included a party member. In August 1928, there were 20,660 rural party cells to cover 546,747 population centres in the countryside. By 1929, only 10 per cent of delegates to village soviets were party members, with higher representation in executive positions; a third of chairmen of village soviets, 96.3 per cent of chairmen of volost and raion executive committees and 99.7 per cent of chairmen of uezd and okrug executive committees were party members.[10] As this period drew to a close, the small number of party members active in the countryside and the paucity of proletarian elements in the village organisations[11] remained a matter of major concern.

The shortage of communists to run the rural organs was accompanied by serious deficiencies in the quality of those mobilised to rural assignments. The mobilisation of cadres by the centre was a major aspect of party policy at this time,[12] but the vast majority of those who were despatched into the countryside took up their assignments without adequate administrative training. The party made some efforts to overcome this problem,[13] but the demand for trained administrators far exceeded the capacity to satisfy that demand. Furthermore, workers despatched from the centre often lacked a clear understanding of peasant interests, concerns and ways of life, while only a minority of communists had close links with the central concern of peasant life, agriculture.[14] Such a situation was exacerbated by the rapid turnover of many appointments, a practice which inhibited the acquisition of sound local knowledge by local officials. All of this was conducive to the peasant view of the party as alien and remote, unattuned to the needs of the countryside and lacking in concern for them.

Party leaders were aware of the dangers posed by isolation from the peasantry and sought to overcome this by increased recruitment from among the peasants, particularly in 1923–25. However, this posed another danger in the leaders' eyes: that of party cadres becoming too close to the peasants and of falling under the influence of petty bourgeois or kulak influence. One party member attributed this sort of development to the fact that party workers in the villages did not receive sufficient to sustain themselves and were therefore often forced to become dependent upon the kulaks simply to survive.[15] While the material difficulties of party members may have been instrumental in such a development in some instances, the dynamics of traditional village life were probably of more importance. The prominent role played in the villages by individuals who would have been labelled kulaks encouraged an outsider seeking to establish his influence in the traditional community to turn to these people to achieve his ends. If the party worker could win over local opinion leaders, his chances of successfully establishing his authority were enhanced. However, such a development could open him up to charges of joining the kulaks.[16] In the words of a CC resolution of November 1928, by which time party policy had turned decisively against the kulaks, 'in some cases' rural organs were characterised by 'a considerable proportion of well-to-do peasants, and sometimes also elements which have become intimate with the kulaks, degenerated and become completely alien to the working class'.[17] The rapid turnover of rural communists was designed, at least in part, to combat the problems of communists 'falling under the influence of the surrounding milieu'.[18]

The problem was not just the infection effect that association with kulaks could have on party members, but, as the passage cited above suggests, the way in which kulaks were able to take over and dominate low-level organisations. The cooperatives were one area in which many kulaks were able to gain positions of pre-eminence, but such a situation also developed in non-economic organisations, including the party, the soviets and the Komsomol.[19] Kulak dominance reflected in part a desire to use the new institutions to defend their interests. It was also a result of the acceptance by sections of the peasantry of the traditionally prominent role this group had played in the village and in the traditional organisations which continued to dominate peasant life;[20] at the elections for village soviets in 1925, support for supposed kulaks was stronger than it was for the communists.[21] Despite various attempts to penetrate the countryside on a wide scale,[22] official rural administration remained weak in the face of the continued strength of village-based peasant organs.

One means the party had of lifting its profile was through expansion of its membership. This occurred on a significant scale during this period: in January 1923, following a decline due to voluntary departures and the purge set in motion in 1921, membership (both full and candidate) stood at 499,100; by January 1930 it was 1,677,910.[23] This increase, in excess of threefold, was justified explicitly in terms of improving the party's position among the two main groups in the population, the proletariat and the peasantry. Throughout this period the single most important principle espoused was 'the proletarianisation of the party', the attempt to increase the proportion of workers in the party, and particularly workers from the bench. But in practice this aim was diluted by various efforts to consolidate the party's position in the countryside by drawing more peasants into its ranks.[24] The main thrusts for proletarianisation were the Lenin Enrolment launched at the XIII Conference in January 1924,[25] a second Lenin Enrolment begun a year later, a campaign beginning in 1926 and leading into the 'October Enrolment' of 1927, and a more extensive effort accompanying the upsurge in industrialisation after 1928. Emphasis upon peasant enrolment occurred in fits and starts between 1923 and 1926,[26] followed by a more concerted effort to reduce the peasant component in favour of the worker.[27] In the attempt to expand party membership, many entry requirements were substantially weakened, even to the extent of sanctioning the mass entry of candidates with a minimum of checking instead of the carefully studied acceptance of individual candidates demanded by the party Rules.[28] The mass enrolment of members of the target class overshadowed the recruitment of individual enthusiasts. But while this heightened profile among the proletariat and peasantry clearly gave the party a broader footing within these two groups, its profile among the populace as a whole remained low. The 1927 party census showed that an average of only 10.5 per cent of workers in major industry were party members while representation in the countryside was at an even lower level.[29] Furthermore, the quality of these new party members often left much to be desired and fuelled the continuing concerns about petty bourgeois infection.

These fears increased towards the end of the decade. The large-scale expansion of the proletariat resulting from increased peasant migration to the cities fuelled fears about the proletariat as a secure base of support for the party.[30] The grain procurement difficulties experienced in 1927–28 were widely interpreted in the party as reflecting continuing peasant hostility to the regime, while the Shakhty affair[31] called into question the loyalty of those technical experts upon whom much of the industrial revival of NEP had relied. The Shakhty trial of April–May 1928 was particularly important in this regard because it represented a rejection of the engineers' claims to professional autonomy. What was required of people was no longer simply their skills, labour and cooperation, but full commitment. Without this commitment, people and groups were considered to be hostile, regardless of any contributions they may have made in the past. In the struggle for socialism within a petty bourgeois environment, neutrality was no longer acceptable. This change heralded the end of the policy of class conciliation and the attempt to overcome the source of the party's isolation through industrialisation and agricultural collectivisation.

The concerns about the party's sense of isolation and the effect of the petty bourgeois environment coexisted within the party with continuing organisational tensions. The tension between localist and centralist pressures which had been evident during the earlier period continued to be a major factor structuring political activity during the 1920s. Furthermore, the playing out of this tension continued to undermine pressures for the development of a higher level of institutionalisation of the party structure based on formal, bureaucratic norms. As an organisation, the party remained unable to generate that sense of coherence and integrity that would transform it into a strong and effective organisational structure. Throughout this period the party remained organisationally very weak, which made it unprepared to deal with the increased demands made upon it during the grain collection and agricultural collectivisation campaigns at the end of the decade.[32]

One of the most important influences on party development during this period was the massive increase in party membership referred to above. The more than three-fold increase in size (at the time of the Lenin Enrolment of 1924–25 alone the party more than doubled its size) understates the flow of new members into party ranks; incomplete figures show that at least 393,000 party members were either excluded or voluntarily withdrew from the party between 1922 and May 1930.[33] Death also took an unknown number of party members. The dimensions of the renewal of party ranks was clearly immense.

The impact of this flood of recruits on the nature of the party was profound. It meant that the Old Bolsheviks, those who had joined before the revolution, and those who had joined in the dark days of the Civil War, were swamped by newcomers whose only direct experience of the party was as a governing body. Their experience of party life was not that of the struggle for power or, once attained, of its defence against military attack. For them, the creation of socialism appeared more in terms of the administration of government policy than of a life and death struggle between antagonistic social forces.[34] Indeed, for that mass of the peasantry who had flowed into the party at this time – and official figures show that by the end of 1926 almost one-third of members of village cells had been in the party less than one year and more than two-thirds for less than three years[35] – their experience of the party was as a body accepting and even encouraging the development of private enterprise. As early as the XII Congress in April 1923, prior to the mass influx of the Lenin Enrolment, a speaker complained about the small number of active Old Bolsheviks remaining in the party, a group which he declared numbered less than 2 per cent of the whole membership.[36] By the beginning of 1927 almost 60 per cent of party members had been in the party less than three years while those joining prior to February 1917 constituted less than 1 per cent of the membership.[37]

Although many may have been attracted by the vague promise of building a new society and the sense of struggle and achievement that stemmed from the victory in the Civil War, the new members usually brought with them a minimum of ideological awareness and knowledge. While such a condition cannot be measured accurately, 'political illiteracy' was characteristic of significant sections of the membership; one estimate at the XII Congress suggested that in industrial gubernii up to 50 per cent of party members were politically illiterate while the corresponding figure in agricultural gubernii was from 80 to 90 per cent.[38] Although not all observers were as pessimistic as this, there was clearly a problem of major proportions and one which was of great concern to the leadership. Recognition of this stimulated efforts by party leaders to provide greater facilities for political education, but given the extent of the need and the resources available, such a programme could have only limited impact in the short term.[39] In August 1927, it was declared that some who entered the party knew little about it and had to ask what the Politburo was.[40] Throughout this period the level of political awareness among party members remained low.

Low levels of political education were matched by low levels of general education. Between 1922 and 1927 the proportion of those with higher education increased by 0.2 per cent, those with secondary education by 1.6 per cent and those with primary education or less fell by 1.4 per cent.[41] But such positive trends were offset by the fact that over the same period the proportion of members who had completed four years of formal education declined from 82 to 71 per cent while those with only bare literacy increased.[42] Complete illiteracy within the party fell during this period from 4.6 per cent in 1922 to 2.4 per cent in 1927, although it was at much higher levels among some national groups. Semi-literacy (familiarity with the alphabet but less than four years' schooling) remained at the high level of about 25 per cent in 1927.[43] While education and literacy levels were higher among party members than among the populace as a whole, the party was still characterised by a membership with little education and virtually no training in those basic literary and administrative techniques essential to the ordered conduct of business in the sort of organisation the party was becoming.

Low levels of political education were a matter of continuing concern to the leadership. Reference has already been made to the programmes of political education which reflect this concern. Mandatory periods of party membership for office-holders was another response to this.[44] Another prominent aspect of party life during this period which reflects this concern is the party purge. Throughout the 1920s there was an almost continual process of purging, in the sense of the exclusion from party ranks of members found deficient in some respect. In the earlier period the main form which this took was the party reregistration, which involved the withdrawal of party cards and the issue of new ones. This was combined with a party census in 1921–22 and 1926–27. Two other forms of purging activity which were important during this period were the 'verification' and the 'chistka'.[45] In practice the former seems to have been part of an on-going process of monitoring the party membership in order to guard against undesirable developments or activity. Such a process involved either regular action by local control commissions in investigating alleged offences or efforts specifically directed at one particular part of the politico-administrative structure. The verification of one part of the structure was occurring virtually throughout the entire period: in 1924–25 verifications were carried out in government cells and educational institutions resulting in the expulsion of some 6,000 party members,[46] in 1925–27 in village cells involving few expulsions, and in 1928 heightened levels of 'vigilance' were demanded and a verification was carried out in local organs, among government officials and management.[47] In contrast, the chistka was a party-wide purge, in principle involving a review of the records of all party members and usually specifically directed at certain targets. Such a purge had been mounted in 1921–22 during which about 25 per cent of the membership were expelled or left voluntarily; another unrolled in 1929–30 and fell disproportionately on the rural party – it involved some 133,000 expulsions, or about 8 per cent of the membership.[48]

The formal grounds for expulsion remained broadly the same throughout the period. The CC Report to the XII Congress listed the following: squabbling, infringement of party discipline, malfeasance, criminal activity, drunkenness, religious observance, alien elements, enrichment, speculation and trade.[49] According to the resolution setting the 1929–30 purge in motion, it was directed against 'all non-communist, corrupt, alien, bureaucratised, self-seeking elements and hangers-on who take a functionary's view of their duties'.[50] In discussing the purge at the XVI Congress in June–July 1930, CCC Collegium Secretary Yaroslavsky enumerated the following grounds for expulsion: alien elements or linked with alien elements, passivity, violation of party discipline, defects in personal life and conduct, and criminal offences.[51] The purging process was thus formally related to concern about the quality of party membership and about the elimination of undesirable forms of activity. It was but a simple extension of this to the use of the purge as a weapon against oppositional activity and activists. As an unofficial reason for expulsion, oppositional activity seems to have been present from the beginning; at the XIII Congress Preobrazhensky claimed that this was the case and, in his response, Yaroslavsky seems implicitly to have acknowledged the accuracy of the charge.[52] By the end of this period opposition had become one of the formal grounds for expulsion, as reflected in the theses adopted by the XVI Conference in April 1929 which called for the expulsion of, among others, 'covert Trotskyites, Miasnikovites, Democratic Centralists and adherents of other anti-party groups'.[53] The XV Congress in December 1927 had been an important step towards this end. It approved the first large-scale expulsion of leading oppositionists and of police measures against them, and it marks the end of the regular publication of lists of expelled members and of the reasons for their expulsion. The exact number of those expelled for oppositionist activity cannot be ascertained because, as Preobrazhensky charged, false reasons were often given to cover those expelled for such activity. Nevertheless, some official figures were cited: at the XV Congress 970 people were declared to have been expelled for 'fractional activity' while at the XVI Congress such people were said to be included in the 10 per cent of party members purged for violation of party discipline.[54] As oppositionists charged, during bouts of elite conflict, the purge machinery was used against opponents in a discriminatory fashion.

One effect of the massive growth of the party membership and the continual fluidity resulting from the purging process was the maintenance of significant pressure upon the administrative regime of party organisations at all levels. This is reflected in frequent press complaints about the weak organisation and the deficiencies in the organisational work of lower level party organs.[55] Administrative procedures were *ad hoc* and unsystematic in most party organisations throughout the country; the Smolensk Archive shows how filing and communications were often conducted on any scrap bits of paper which came to hand.[56] The collection and analysis of elementary statistics was hindered by the shortage of qualified personnel at lower levels.[57] Clear, effective and streamlined office routines were not generated to cope with the flow of work with which party organs had to deal. Party bodies were often swamped with paper work,[58] committees met in plenary session infrequently, agendas were overloaded and decisions often were taken on questions that had already been decided at a higher level.[59] Communication links between the national and sub-national party bodies remained inadequate.[60] The absence of an effective administrative structure is reflected in the excessively heavy workloads which party secretaries had to bear, a consideration evident in the efforts made in the late 1920s to increase staffing levels by 20 per cent in the sub-national party apparatus and through the use of unpaid volunteers.[61]

The weak administrative regime in party organs was particularly acute in the personnel sphere where the membership fluidity imposed significant administrative burdens. Although the general registration of party workers was claimed to have been completed satisfactorily by early 1923,[62] critics suggested that the records gained thereby left much to be desired;[63] registration was often completed in a purely formal way, with some included as responsible workers when they should not have been and others incorrectly excluded. The confusion in personnel matters is reflected in the results of the attempt to establish a regularised personnel regime through the institution of nomenklatura in mid-1923. The nomenklatura system involved party committees at each level of the hierarchy having a list of positions which were within their competence to fill, plus a list of responsible workers from which appropriate personnel could be chosen to fill those positions. It was a means of standardising and dividing between party organs the responsibility for the appointment and filling of responsible positions. However, the result at lower levels was rarely the smooth streamlining of personnel procedures that was hoped for.

Problems experienced with the first nomenklatura regime established in mid-1923 led to a second being introduced in late 1925 – early 1926 in which the lower level organs were to work out their own nomenklatura listings based on central guidelines.[64] But systematic operations were slow to emerge. In August 1926 it was reported that Smolensk gubkom had worked out a nomenklatura embracing 946 workers compared with figures of 374, 364 and 393 for Stalingrad, Voronezh and Vologda gubkoms respectively.[65] Figures quoted some three months later reinforce this picture of a lack of standardisation: Stalingrad gubkom included in its nomenklatura list 147 posts, Yaroslav 190, Viatka 312, Riazan 99 and Pskov 302.[66] There were jurisdictional disputes between different organs over which had the right to fill which positions, a consequence very often of the inclusion within the nomenklatura of one organ of posts and workers whose importance or qualifications did not warrant inclusion.[67] In addition, lower level personnel work frequently was characterised by inordinately high levels of turnover of party workers, inadequate study and verification of the performance of responsible workers, inadequate planning of personnel matters and insufficient concern to coordinate needs and personnel.[68] Generally, lower level leaders were accused of paying insufficient attention to personnel work and of not strengthening the uchraspred apparatus of their committees through which the nomenklatura system was to be implemented. An integrated, efficient personnel system was clearly not in existence by the end of this period.

Although the party did not emerge from this period with an efficiently working apparatus at all levels or a tightly integrated administrative structure, efforts were made to transform it into a more regularly operating bureaucratic mechanism. The attempt to build a regularised personnel regime through the nomenklatura and the efforts to bring about some rationalisation of the party apparatus towards the end of the period are probably the best instances of this. Throughout the period a range of administrative regulations and instructions was adopted in an effort to bring a higher degree of structuring to the party's internal affairs. Two characteristics of these regulations were to be of fundamental significance for the party's development.

The first characteristic of the regulations was that they had an essentially contingent nature. Traditionally, the Bolsheviks had approached rules and laws in an essentialist way. What was important about them was not what they said but whose interests they served. Results produced were more important than formalistic interpretations. A similar attitude existed with regard to the relationship between task fulfilment and administrative regulation. While the value of the latter was recognised as a means of developing a smoothly functioning bureaucratic structure, it was at no time to stand in the way of the achievement of the political aims to which the party was committed. Although this received its most positive affirmation during the Civil War when all efforts were turned to the military conflict without regard for formal institutional boundaries, prerogatives or sensitivities, it was carried through into peace-time as one of the basic principles of the party's *modus operandi*. The continued calls from above for the achievement of specified tasks and the fulfilment of directives and the frequent complaints about lower level organs not carrying out central instructions reflects an ethos in which the emphasis was squarely upon task fulfilment, if need be at the expense of administrative considerations. The best example of this during this period was the mobilisation of all energies to implement the escalating targets of the First Five Year Plan, but this was only an extension of the practice already in operation. Formal, administrative regulations were binding only when they did not hinder the achievement of officially prescribed tasks; when those regulations got in the way of task fulfilment, they could justifiably be ignored. Of course, there was an element of ambiguity and danger here for lower level leaders; the ultimate decision about when a regulation could be ignored and when it could not lay with the central leadership and could be subject to considerations of a factional nature. An administrative regime which was considered contingent in this way was incapable of developing the sort of normative authority that was essential if the party was to emerge as a strong organisational structure.

Moreover, as these regulations emerged, it became clear that they had a significant gap in their coverage of security of tenure for political office-holders. Formal rules usually specified a period of tenure for elected positions in the party only by establishing which body elected a particular organ and the frequency with which that body was to meet. However, the process of appointment that became institutionalised through the nomenklatura could in practice undermine these tenure provisions. The growth of appointment from above as the principal pillar of personnel policy without any attendant formal security of tenure[69] created a very uncertain environment within which middle and lower level party officers had to function. This uncertainty was compounded by the national leadership's high expectations of task fulfilment; it was common for the centre to expect the achievement of results which were difficult to achieve and were made even more so by the vague way in which they were presented. In effect, this meant that lower level leaders were in a very vulnerable position: they could at any time be confronted with excessive demands from above without any institutional buffers to protect them against the wrath of their superiors should they fail to satisfy the exaggerated demands and expectations. Such uncertainty reinforced the tendency evident during the earlier period towards the development of localised power cliques.

The most prominent instances of the development of such fiefdoms involved leading oligarchs, in particular Zinoviev in Leningrad and successively Kamenev and Uglanov in Moscow. But similar developments continued to be common at the lower levels where local leaders built up their own clique or personalised political machine through which they dominated local affairs. Local bosses were often quite prominent in party life; examples from the mid-1920s include Ordzhonikidze in Tiflis, Kirov in Baku, Goloshchekin in Kazakhstan and Yaroslavsky and Lashevich in Siberia.[70] They sought to maintain their political control by judicious manipulation of personnel affairs within their particular locality and by attempting to exclude outsiders from playing any part at all.[71] Such 'feudal principalities' came under strong criticism at party gatherings and in formal party documents and decisions[72] for the way in which they violated party rules and modes of operation; for example, the leaders in Artemovsk were charged in 1928 with 'administrative' methods of leadership, suppression of debate and intra-party democracy, bureaucratism, isolation from the masses, carelessness with state funds and a groupist approach to personnel questions.[73] Criticism was also directed at the ostentatious life style led by many of these people; they were castigated for moral decay, drunkenness, sexual licence, suicide, misuse of state property for personal ends and holding banquets.[74] The names Dymovka, Artemovsk and Smolensk became synonymous in party parlance with the sort of abuses the concentration of local power could bring about.[75]

Although such local groupings were criticised for their excessive concentration of power and for disrupting the unified nature of the party, following the destruction of Zinoviev's power base in Leningrad in 1926, none of these fiefdoms was able to withstand the concerted efforts of the central authorities. When the centre sought to replace a local clique, it was always able to do so eventually. This was often accompanied by the drawing of local power holders into a more nationally oriented political structure. But this did not take place along bureaucratic lines; it rested upon personalities. Furthermore, the results of this integration process remained unstable, so that the sort of national structure that was emerging appeared to be much more firmly consolidated than it actually was.

One of the most important forces for political integration was the process of personnel appointment. Disputes within a local party organ could lead to the despatch of central functionaries whose aim was to engineer the removal of the errant comrades and their replacement by acceptable figures.[76] Or local party leaders might show too independent a disposition from Moscow, perhaps criticising party policy in unacceptable terms or siding with one of the opposition groups, thereby triggering their replacement by more reliable personnel.[77] But the most important means of this was the consolidation of the nomenklatura system through the principle of recommendation. As early as October 1923 Trotsky had declared: 'In the fiercest moment of War Communism, the system of appointment within the party did not have one-tenth of the extent that it has now. Appointment of the secretaries of provincial committees is now the rule.'[78] At the XIII Congress he complained that elections in party cells were largely a mockery because secretaries were nominated by the district committees and then members were asked: 'Is anyone opposed?' He argued that people were reluctant to oppose the central authorities, with the result that such appointments went ahead without dissent. Such a situation, he believed, was to be found 'in a slightly altered form at each successive level of our party hierarchy'.[79] In 1929 Bukharin declared 'we do not have one elected secretary of a provincial party organisation ... everything is done from above'.[80] While there may have been an element of hyperbole and rhetorical point-scoring in these charges, they clearly reflect the trend within the party toward the replacement of election by appointment. The implications of this for the growth of a more integrated political mechanism were significant. However, before looking at this, one further factor contributing to this development should be noted. This was the emphasis upon intra-party democracy.

Calls for intra-party democracy were the traditional fare of the successive opposition groups during this period, usually accompanied by a condemnation of the practice of personnel appointment. Such a criticism struck directly at the basis upon which party secretaries were increasingly coming to rest, so that it is not surprising that, as a group, they should generally oppose the opposition.[81] While the opposition was making the running on this issue, the realities of power politics within the party enabled the secretaries to ignore the implications of this call. Of course, the official leadership also made noises about the need for intra-party democracy, but this was a distinctly subordinate theme to that of the need for discipline and seems to have been treated as such by those with a personal stake in its implications. However, from about the middle of the decade this situation changed as a campaign unrolled, initially emphasising electoral abuses in the party and then moving on to embrace the principle of self-criticism.

The roots of the campaign lay in the long-time concern for intra-party democracy expressed in the formal resolutions of party meetings. A central element of the notion of intra-party democracy which prevailed at this time related to the questions of accountability and discussion. Among the measures deemed necessary in December 1923 to strengthen workers' democracy were the following: implementation of the electoral principle within the context of confirmation from above and the absence of factions; responsible figures not to be imposed upon organisations over their opposition; party organs to be accountable to those who elect them; all questions of party policy, insofar as possible, to be submitted to discussion by party cells and the masses as a whole; and discussion not to be stifled by false claims in regard to 'party discipline'.[82] These twin emphases upon election and discussion were the staple fare of the party's conception of intra-party democracy, although a prominent element remained the association of democracy with the promotion of working-class cadres into positions of responsibility; indeed, democracy and the proletarianisation of leading ranks were often seen as synonymous. An approach to democracy in terms of general principles and the promotion of workers posed little threat to the power of the secretaries whose position rested overwhelmingly on appointment. But this approach shifted in the middle of the decade with a new concern about electoral abuses.

While giving the CC's organisational report at the XIV Congress in December 1925, Molotov repeated the established wisdom that intra-party democracy was a precondition for the growth of the party, adding that there was a need to enliven or reanimate lower level party organisations.[83] Molotov returned to this issue in March 1926 when reporting on the work of the Orgburo.[84] He criticised the way in which the right of party conferences to elect leading organs could be undermined by prior decisions about the composition of those organs; such decisions were merely presented to the conference for ratification. Such preliminary decisions were often made, he declared, at higher levels, within the executive organs formally to be elected by the conference, or at lower levels where deals could be made between different party organisations to gain the leadership they wished.[85] These had the effect of circumventing the authority of the plenary assembly which formally had the power to elect the executive organs. The aim of the mounting campaign was to reanimate these assemblies;[86] they had to be given the power to choose, not simply to ratify, and although some preparatory work had to be carried out (there was to be no 'accidental' selection of party organs), this should be done in the 'senoren konvent', or conference of representatives of delegates.[87] Lists of nominations were to be devised at the senoren konvent for presentation to the conference, but such lists were not to be mandatory for the conference delegates. Thus while the lower level assemblies were to be reanimated, they were not to be allowed to act unconstrained.

This campaign was not formally directed at completely undermining local political leaders. They were still expected to exercise guidance both in the formulation of the list and in its passage through the conference; according to Molotov, where the system was operating, accidental candidates were elected only when local leaders failed to come out against them.[88] But the guiding role local leaders were now expected to exercise was to be performed in party fora which seemed to be more open than the executive organs they had previously used. The senoren konvent and the conference itself were to play a bigger role, with the result that local leaders seemed to be thrown more heavily on to the support of the rank-and-file than they previously had been. Of course, such measures could not eliminate the organisational manipulation which remained a central pillar of power for the local leaders, but by calling upon them to act more in the open, the campaign increased the level of uncertainty surrounding their positions.

Such uncertainty can only have been increased by charges at the XV Congress about local leaders' inefficiency and unsatisfactory performance,[89] by criticism of their performance in the conduct of the grain procurement campaign in early 1928,[90] and by the emergence in the same year of self-criticism as a prominent element in the evolving campaign. This had been a subsidiary element earlier,[91] but it came to the fore with a CC appeal to all party members dated 2 June 1928.[92] This appeal declared that the party had already done much to organise self-verification and self-criticism from above, but that what was needed was a 'powerful wave of creative self-criticism from below' in order to eliminate from and prevent the reappearance in the apparatus of 'bureaucratic suppression, the "mutual guarantees" of accomplices, chinovnik obsequiousness, petty tyranny, ignoring the interests of the masses and petty bourgeois tranquillity'. Without self-criticism there could be no guarantee against future Shakhty, Artemovsk or Smolensk scandals, nor could the apparatus be cleansed from kulak-capitalist elements. As well as calling for a strengthening of party work among the masses and an improvement in the quality of work and social composition of the leading organs of the party, the appeal included four measures of particular significance: the freedom of intra-party criticism without independent thought and criticism being labelled a deviation or rowdiness; the full election of party offices, including the possibility of the removal of any secretary, bureau or committee; the imposition of full penalties on wrongdoers in the party; and the need for committees to set an example for the masses and to avoid 'domestic decay'.

The theme of self-criticism was a central aspect of the campaign for the party elections occurring at the end of 1928.[93] Not only were local party organs to examine carefully their own work, but individual non-party workers also were to be called upon to evaluate the performance of the party organ in question. The electoral principle was to be implemented fully in party elections, although higher organs were to exercise 'correct and businesslike leadership' at lower levels by coming out against unsuitable candidates. But election was not to be replaced by appointment; unwanted candidates were not to be pressed on organisations; there were to be no elections by list, no prior discussion in the bureau or among the aktiv of candidates for elected organs, and no violation of voting procedures. Criticism and self-criticism were to be given full rein as party organs ensured the widespread discussion of individual candidates in order to establish the will of the party organisation. Unsatisfactory performance in regard to these points, reflected in charges about the weakness of intra-party democracy and self-criticism,[94] continued to be highlighted in the press following the elections.

The emphasis on self-criticism from the middle of 1928 injected a new element of uncertainty into the position of middle and lower level party leaders. It seemed to emphasise the way in which these people were to be subject to evaluation by the rank-and-file of the party, and even by workers who were not party members. Its impact was probably heightened by the increased attention during 1929 that the party press devoted to deficiencies in the operation of local party organs, a form of publicity which all too often portrayed party leaders as incompetent, corrupt or both.[95] This theme fed into the grounds for expulsion in the purge of 1929–30 referred to above and may have been instrumental in the high turnover rates of sub-national party leaders at this time; according to official figures, in the two years prior to June 1930, 80 per cent of kraikom and obkom secretaries and 94 per cent of okrugkom secretaries took up their current positions, while nearly half of all obkom secretaries and two-thirds of okrugkom secretaries had been in their posts for less than a year.[96] The self-criticism theme thereby complemented the campaign for intra-party democracy and for the operation of the electoral principle, and it reinforced notions of accountability to the grassroots.

As this period wore on, sub-national party leaders thus found themselves in increasingly difficult and anomalous positions. In practice, their positions rested upon appointment and their tenure depended upon satisfying those superior to them who controlled the appointment process; criticism of official policy could lead to removal or transfer.[97] The secretaries were therefore effectively independent of the local organisations they led. However, the emphasis upon intra-party democracy and self-criticism seemed to reverse this flow of power and obligation; continued tenure of their posts seemed dependent upon rank-and-file satisfaction with the way in which they were carrying out their responsibilities. The party secretaries were thus caught between the clash of two principles of party operation: the distribution of forces through the nomenklatura system based in the secretarial apparatus at all levels but culminating in the CC Orgburo and Secretariat, and the electoral principle resting upon assumptions about rank-and-file sovereignty and vesting formal control at each level in the plenary assembly, always subject of course to oversight from above. This clash of principles strengthened two sorts of developments in the party at this time.

The first was the development of 'groupism' or 'familyism', of the localised power cliques which dominated their own particular areas. The consolidation of personalised control could constitute a means of defence of the position of the local boss from threats emanating from both above and below. If the leader and his group could consolidate their control in the area by dominating all of the local political organs and by preventing possible opponents or critics from expressing their views, they could hope to make themselves relatively invulnerable to criticism from below. If their organisational control was sufficiently extensive and refined, they would be able to cut off challenges from below despite the efforts of the national leadership to encourage grassroots criticism. Potential challenges could thus be blunted at an early stage. Local control by a personalised network could also provide some hope for protection from above. If local control was sufficiently tight and the network included all of those with separate institutional channels to the centre, the local elite could hope to impose a sort of 'conspiracy of silence' on events in the area. If they could thereby limit the centre's access to the area to those channels over which they had control, the local elite could for some time convince their superiors that all was well when in fact there may have been grounds for central concern. This was a modern version of the Potemkin village. Indeed, the self-criticism campaign was one means which the centre sought to employ to overcome such localised control; encouragement of criticism from below was an attempt to circumvent the control over communications and local political life exercised by these localised cliques.

But such groups or personal networks also continued to fulfil one of those functions which was at the heart of their origin: facilitation of administration. With the formal administrative apparatus anything but a well-oiled machine, many party leaders must still have found it more effective to rely upon the informal structures emanating from the personalised network to conduct the basic tasks of administration than the more uncertain bureaucratic structure. While there were clearly costs in terms of retarding the development of the party as a coherent institutional structure, there were immediate benefits for the local party leader if he could use the informal network to improve his performance by fulfilling the tasks demanded of him. So the development of localised control through personalised networks was stimulated by the diverse pressures on local party leaders. This personalised basis of politics continued to undermine pressures for the organisational institutionalisation of the party structure. The focus of power remained outside the bureaucratic structure and in the personal networks, and the party apparatus remained instrumental in nature.

The second type of development strengthened by the clash of the principles of appointment and election was the integration of local leaderships into a nationally oriented political machine. One means of trying to protect oneself against possible attacks was to gain a high level protector. The most likely source of a high level protector for these party barons was within the secretarial hierarchy culminating in the person of the General Secretary since this structure had much of its *raison d'être* bound up with the appointment process. If lower level party leaders could find a higher level patron who could blunt or deflect attacks from above, their positions would be immeasurably strengthened. In return, lower level leaders could provide support for their patron in terms of both votes in relevant party fora and support in the implementation of their policies or the successful fulfilment of tasks accorded to them. There was, therefore, a basis for agreement resting upon mutual self interest: each side would gain a strengthening of its position through the support of the other. If these support chains were extended into the national level, leading political figures could benefit from support percolating up the structure. One important element in this process was the appointment procedure. This provided the sinews of the relationship in the sense that the act of appointment itself could constitute a means of generating a personal link upon which the patron–client relationship could rest. Even if the appointer and the appointee were not close before the appointment was made, the act of appointing could create a sense of obligation on the part of the latter toward the former. Indeed, the appointment power created an incentive for the lower placed actor to go along with the views of his patron. This has certainly been a prominent element in most Western accounts of Stalin's rise: those who had responsibility for political appointments were best placed to take advantage of patronage considerations to develop a fraction within the party spanning various levels of the hierarchy.

Prominent oppositionists were quick to point to this. As early as 1923 Trotsky declared:

> The bureaucratisation of the party apparatus has developed to unheard of proportions by means of the method of secretarial selection. There has been created a very broad stratum of party workers, entering into the apparatus of the government of the party, who completely renounce their own party opinion, at least the open expression of it, as though assuming that the secretarial hierarchy is the apparatus which creates party opinion in party decisions. Beneath this stratum ... there lies the broad mass of the party, before whom every decision stands in the form of a summons or a command.[98]

He went on to criticise the 'secretarial psychology, the principal trait of which is that the secretary is capable of deciding anything'. This attack was taken up in the Declaration of the 46[99] which distinguished between the 'secretarial hierarchy' and the 'quiet folk' who, even though they disapproved of what was happening, were afraid to speak out. Despite the hyperbole, there was some truth in this line of argument. Party secretaries did dominate their party organisations and they were generally little troubled by rank-and-file activism. But we should beware of reading into this the existence of a highly integrated political structure based on the secretarial network with its apex at the national level in the Orgburo, Secretariat and General Secretary and its roots in the cell or ukom secretaries. Such a highly integrated structure did not exist.

Those who have in the past argued for the existence of such a structure in the 1920s have tended to emphasise the importance of the appointment process in providing the cement for the structure both in terms of positive incentives for obedience and potential sanctions for disobedience. Appointment could certainly be an important factor, but it was probably a much blunter instrument for achieving obedience than it might appear. The poor state of personnel procedures and records at lower levels has already been noted. Although the situation at the centre was better than that which prevailed elsewhere, even here the situation was well below the standard required for an efficient, centralised political machine. In addition, communication problems often hindered centre–local contact, further complicating attempts to use personnel powers to enforce rigid discipline. Close, continuing supervision and contact were impossible. Furthermore, the attribution of a dominant role to the appointment process in the construction of a highly integrated political machine assumes that leaders at all levels were motivated simply by considerations of power and position, that they had few independent ideas on policy issues and any which they did possess were not held sufficiently strongly to affect their concern for their own position. Such an attitude may have been typical of some who held party office at this time, but there is no firm evidence that it was universal.[100] Indeed sub-national party leaders were at the cutting edge of the implementation of party policy and were therefore likely to have had a direct interest in policy issues. Their support for national leaders was often mediated through the policy positions adopted by those leaders. All of this is not to deny that appointment played a part in the emergence of a 'secretarial fraction' because structurally it was crucial in liberating secretaries from rank-and-file control and establishing ascending lines of responsibility. But alone it could not, at least in the form in which it existed in the 1920s, create a highly integrated political structure with a high level of unity of outlook.

The 'secretarial fraction' which emerged at this time was loosely articulated. It did not consist of a single vertical chain reaching its apex in the General Secretary, but represented an inverted fan. At each organisational level of the party (including the national level), a number of ribs of the fan spread out from the hub provided by the secretary at that level. As one approached the base, the greater was the number of ribs and the more indirect each secretary's relationship with the national level. Even if each secretary looked to the higher secretary who was responsible for his appointment, the appointment process itself could not produce a highly integrated political structure in which all lower levels unambiguously and directly followed the lead given by the General Secretary. For most of those below the regional level, this had to be mediated through intervening organisational levels. The organisational link between the General Secretary and most party secretaries was therefore indirect or segmented.

However, although the appointment power enabled the centre to remove individual secretaries at lower levels and thereby to break up existing local cliques, this power did not enable it to eliminate the conditions which produced such cliques in the first place. When a replacement leader was installed, he had to confront the same sorts of pressures as his predecessor. Moreover, he was probably moving into a political environment in which there may have been some hostility towards him from supporters of his ousted predecessor. Under these sorts of conditions, the emergence of another family group around the new leader was highly likely. The need for a local power base remained, despite the identity of the leader; personalised politics and the family group remained the norm, and with them the sort of localised concerns that did not sit easily with central demands.

Within this loosely articulated structure there were certain common interests. The secretaries were concerned to preserve their power, position and prerogatives. They tended to be more concerned with administrative and organisational affairs than with the vigorous clash of ideological principle which so concerned many of the leading party figures. Generally they opposed opposition and dissent both because of the threat oppositionist calls for intra-party democracy posed to the appointive basis upon which they stood[101] and because of the implications opposition had for efficiency and administration; opposition greatly complicated their basic tasks. These common interests provided a basis upon which a broad commonality of outlook on certain issues could emerge. This sort of perspective was espoused by General Secretary Stalin throughout much of the decade.[102] Furthermore, the change in economic policy he brought in 1928–29 would have received some, although by no means universal, support in secretarial ranks.[103] There was, then, a broad coincidence of approach between the General Secretary and the 'secretarial fraction' throughout much of the 1920s, although this was coming under considerable strain towards the end of the decade as a result of the central campaign for self-criticism and the mounting criticism of the performance of sub-national leaders.[104] This coincidence of approach and outlook was not purely a function of the use of the appointive mechanism but stemmed from the structural self interest of party secretaries at all levels. In turn, this was directly related to the continuing weakness of the party's formal organisational structures; its levels of coherence and integrity remained very low.

Throughout this period, the party's internal functioning therefore remained weakly structured. Formal lines of authority and principles of institutional organisation remained secondary in importance to a sub-national politics based upon personalised principles. The effective foci of power remained the sub-national fiefs, and even the heightening sense of urgency accompanying fears of petty bourgeois infection were insufficient to dissolve these sub-national power blocs into an integrated national machine.

4 The divided elite

The 1920s was a time of continuing elite conflict, with the strains within the ruling oligarchy bursting into the open after Lenin's death. This conflict took place within an institutional arena that was only weakly structured. The combination of continuing political conflict and weak institutions contributed substantially to the fundamental transformation of the contours of elite politics that occurred during this period. While some elements of continuity with the Leninist period remained, these were substantially overshadowed by the enormous changes which recast the face of elite politics at this time. The rules of the political game and the role and functions of many of the elite institutions had changed completely by the time this period drew to a close.

The institutional arena

One of the most important characteristics of politics during this period was the nature of policy debate. Like that during the preceding period, it was widespread, vigorous and open. Various policy positions were publicly spelled out and adopted and much debate on the merits of the different views was conducted in the open party arena. This reflects an acceptance within elite ranks of the right of individuals and groups to disagree on policy issues and to appeal within party fora for support for their stances. Such an acceptance was widespread within the elite at the opening of this period, but as the period wore on, that breadth of acceptance was substantially narrowed. Indeed, its disappearance marks the end of this period; from spring 1929, policy debate and argumentation were no longer conducted in an open, combative style.

The state machine, consisting of the multitude of government departments and associated bodies, continued to play a major part as an arena for such debate. Some leading figures used their positions in such organisations to make their views known on the issues of grand policy. Less spectacular was the on-going debate and conflict both within and between government bodies over the everyday course of administration and policy. Differences arose in all areas of concern, often generated by the vagueness of the boundaries of institutional responsibility and the propensity for departmental empire-building.[1] A prolonged and serious instance of this centres upon the related questions of finance, planning and industrial development. The introduction of NEP had thrown into a state of uncertainty the relationship between and relative responsibilities of Narkomfin, Gosplan and Vesenkha. Formally, these bodies were responsible respectively for questions of financial management, economic planning and the management of industry. Each was jealous of its own prerogatives and, in the absence of strong external pressures for the coordination of their operations, sought to press its point of view on leading economic questions to the exclusion of its rivals. This period witnessed a number of serious outbreaks of conflict between these bodies, usually over control figures for the economy.[2] This particular dispute ultimately was the issue through which Vesenkha was able by 1929 to establish its voice as the strongest in economic affairs. Its victory was due in part to the personal entrée it had into the Politburo through membership of that body by its successive presidents, Dzerzhinsky and Kuibyshev, a connection which its two rivals lacked. But at least as important was the fact that both Narkomfin and Gosplan were more conservative in their recommendations. The positions adopted by Vesenkha were more consistent with the push for industrialisation evident within the political leadership as this period drew to a close. This bureaucratic struggle illustrates the way in which the state machine constituted an arena within which alternative views on the most important issues of the day could be widely and openly canvassed and where different points of view could meet and clash.

That the governmental apparatus should act as a reservoir of ideas and expertise in the policy field should not surprise because it was here that much of the accumulated expertise available to the political leadership was concentrated. For the most part, those with abilities or training in areas relevant to the tasks of governmental administration who wished to serve the new regime were to be found in the official state structure. This meant that a prominent place in the state apparatus was held by the 'spetsy', a term with elastic boundaries but which had as its nucleus that corps of people whose training, qualifications or experience led to their occupation of leading positions in all sectors of state activity. But the need to rely upon these people was accompanied by a strong sense of mistrust of the political attitudes they were believed to have. Many of them came from groups whose commitment to the regime was deemed to be questionable: the middle class, tsarist bureaucrats, ex-members of former parties and the well educated. In 1929, even after a campaign for the dismissal of questionable people from government institutions had begun the year before, 37 per cent of personnel in Narkomfin, 27 per cent in Narkomtrud and 26 per cent in Narkomtorg had held bureaucratic office under the tsar.[3] Furthermore, Gosplan and Narkomfin were characterised by significant numbers of ex-Mensheviks and Narkomzem by ex-SRs, many in positions of prominence. The other side of this coin was the low profile of party members in the state apparatus. At the XIII Congress, one speaker declared that only 13 per cent of all commissars, deputies, department heads and collegium heads belonged to the party.[4] At the XV Congress in 1927, the proportion of party members among employees of various USSR commissariats was reported as follows: Narkomtorg 24.3 per cent, Narkomfin 18.2 per cent, Narkomput 22.0 per cent, Narkomindel 17.8 per cent, Vesenkha 20.2 per cent, Narkomzem 14.4 per cent and Narkomiust 22.4 per cent.[5] In 1929 some 25 per cent of all employees in the governmental apparatus were party members, although this figure fell to 14 per cent among those concerned with industrial administration.[6] The party tried to rectify this situation by expanding educational facilities to train Bolshevik spetsy,[7] particularly in the wake of the Shakhty affair, and by expanding party membership among the spetsy. But this was a slow process, and by the end of the period party members were still a significant minority in the state machine.[8] Throughout the period, most party leaders still viewed the state machine with an element of suspicion.

In the legislative organs of the state, the trends developed during the earlier period were maintained. The centralisation of power proceeded as the smaller executive organs displaced the plena. Although the regularisation of the governmental structure that was brought about with the new constitution of 1924[9] seemed to accord to the All-Union Congress of Soviets and its TsIK a wide range of powers, these were of little consequence. Neither body met sufficiently regularly to be able to do little more than blandly accept the reports presented to it by the smaller TsIK Presidium or by government speakers.[10] The large size of both bodies reinforced this impotence: by the second half of the 1920s, the numbers attending the congress and TsIK respectively exceeded 2,000 and 800.[11] In October 1924 TsIK was the scene of a bitter debate about the powers of the different parts of the new union (national versus republican) and in the consideration of the 1925 budget, both congress and TsIK amended the budget estimates presented to them,[12] but this sort of initiative was the exception rather than the rule. Although they could constitute an arena for the playing out of bureaucratic conflict,[13] both became largely formalistic, with their proceedings stylised and standardised.

The most important institutions in the state structure were the Presidium of TsIK and Sovnarkom. Constitutionally, both were important for the translation of decisions into legislation. Many of the day-to-day decision-making and policy implementation tasks of government were carried out here. Both could play a role as a forum for discussion of the problems of the day and for coordinating and systematising the often competing views of government departments. But both were completely subordinate to the party. The major decisions of policy (and very many of the minor ones as well) were made in party fora, not in the state. Ratification and implementation of such decisions may have taken place through state organs, but such action was purely formal. The party organs could decide whatever they chose, with the result that the effective sphere of competence of the state organs was fluid, determined by the party bodies. Certainly many decisions made in party fora relied upon advice received through the state apparatus, but in this relationship the state was distinctly subordinate. The extent of the party's role is symbolised by the practice which became common from 1929 of the issuing of decrees in the joint names of the party CC and of TsIK or its Presidium.[14] In practice, then, there was a degree of fluidity in the party–state relationship at the top, although this was in a context of clear party superiority.

Within the party sphere, formal supremacy remained vested in the congress. However, in practice, by the middle of the decade that was purely formal. One factor behind the loss of effective power was structural: the declining regularity of meeting and increasing size of assembly. A twelve-month period had separated all congresses between the VII in 1918 and the XI in 1922. This regularity now disappeared, with the intervals between congresses increasing over time (see table 4.1).

Between the final congress of this period and the first of the next (XV–XVI), a period of 30 months elapsed. National party conferences

Table 4.1 *Regularity of congresses, 1922–27*

XI–XII	March–April 1922 – April 1923	12.5 months
XII–XIII	April 1923 – May 1924	13 months
XIII–XIV	May 1924 – December 1925	18 months
XIV–XV	December 1925 – December 1927	24 months

were held during some of the intervals between congresses,[15] but these were smaller, less representative, less authoritative and lower in status than the congress.[16] They do not detract from the picture of declining institutional regularity. This trend was a clear infringement of the party's Rules which, until the amendment of 1927 changed the frequency to two years, provided for congresses to be convened annually.

The size of the congress continued to expand during this period (see table 4.2). In all congresses, first-time delegates swamped those re-elected from the previous congress. Carryover figures were, nevertheless, at a much higher level generally than those of the first period. There was some change in the profile of congress delegates over this period. From the XII Congress, delegates who worked full time in the party apparatus occupied a dominating position, as the following figures (for full delegates at the XII and XIII Congresses and for all delegates at the XIV and XV) show: XII – 55.1 per cent, XIII – 65.3 per cent, XIV – 70 per cent and XV – 54 per cent.[17] Congress delegates remained overwhelmingly male, Russian, of working-class background, poorly educated and in early middle age.[18] Over this period, the congresses came increasingly to be dominated by delegates who joined the party after power had been seized. Undergrounders constituted 59.2 per cent of delegates at the XII Congress, 48 per cent at the XIII, 44.4 per cent at the XIV and 38.5 per cent at the XV; a further 33 per cent at the XV Congress joined between 1917 and 1920.[19] Increasingly, the congress became an arena populated by poorly educated, working-class, post-1917 party members and by the full-time party officials.

The growing size of this body, the newness of its membership and the infrequency of its meetings seriously hindered its ability either to shape party policy decisively or to control adequately the party leadership based in the CC and Politburo. But in any case such tasks were rendered impossible by the way in which the body of the congress was constituted.

Table 4.2 *Congress membership, 1923–27*

Congress	Full	Candidate	Total	Carried over to next congress (%)	Carry over as (%) of new congress
XII	408	417	825	43.6	30.1
XIII	748	416	1,164	42.7	30.9
XIV	655	641	1,296	44.8	38.3
XV	898	771	1,669	38.3	34.8

Formally, delegates to national congresses were elected by delegates at regional party conferences who, in turn, were elected in the lower party organisations.[20] Manipulation of this process of selection at lower levels could result in the structuring of representation at the national congress; the congress could be stacked. During this period the central party authorities did not have the facilities to manipulate directly the delegate selection process at all levels. They lacked the relevant local information and adequate personnel records to make rational decisions about the identity of potential delegates to high gatherings. This task had to be left to the local and regional party bosses. Although the party apparatus at the disposal of such leaders was also often inadequate to structure the delegate selection process in a rational manner (as discussed in the previous chapter), the informal networks upon which their power rested were sufficient to enable this to be achieved. As a result, local and regional leaders could effectively deliver voting blocs to the higher meetings. If the central authorities could either control or win over the local and regional leaders, they could stack the national congress with their supporters. This is what happened during this period. Relying upon appointment power, organisational pressures and appeals to policy positions, that section of the leadership with its institutional base in the Orgburo and Secretariat was able to stack the congress with committed delegates, with dramatic consequences for the status and operation of the body as a whole. The higher carryover figures for this period compared with its predecessor may reflect the centre's satisfaction with the performance of congress delegates, and in particular their anti-oppositionist stance.

This process developed apace during the early part of this period. In the lead-up to the XII Congress in April 1923, the central party apparatus worked assiduously to ensure the selection of acceptable delegates. Various forms of pressure and influence were brought to bear at local and regional levels, including the attendance of members or candidate members of the CC at many of the provincial party conferences held to elect delegates. The success of such efforts is reflected in comments made by both a supporter and by opponents of this practice. Stalin declared at the congress, with an ambiguity that was not lost on delegates, that 'For the past six years the Central Committee has never once prepared a congress as it has in the present case',[21] while the Declaration of the 46, dated October 1923, complained that 'the secretarial hierarchy of the party to an ever greater extent recruits the membership of conferences and congresses, which are becoming to an ever greater extent the executive assemblies of this hierarchy'.[22] In those instances when the selection procedure was not as efficient as had been hoped, the congress Mandates Commission could make up for this deficiency. Claiming 'irregularities' in the selection of particular delegates, this body could relegate those delegates from full to candidate status, thereby depriving them of a vote, or even exclude them from the congress altogether.[23]

A change in representation practices at the time of the XIII Conference in January 1924 further undermined the possibility of opposition representation. Prior to this, if local conferences had been divided over issues, it had been the practice to send delegates proportional to the votes cast. However in late 1923 – early 1924, this principle was eroded as both sides at local levels tried to monopolise the delegates sent to the conference. The perfection of this process of delegate selection is evident in the results. In the lead-up to the XIII Conference, some 36 per cent of delegates to district party conferences in Moscow province supported the opposition, a figure which had been reduced to 18 per cent at the provincial party conference and further reduced to some 2 to 3 per cent of voting delegates at the national conference.[24] No oppositionist was a voting delegate to either the XIII or XV Congress, despite the fact that some 6,000 party members had voted for opposition candidates in the delegate selection balloting preceding the latter congress.[25] Only at the XIV Congress, where Zinoviev's control in Leningrad enabled him to hand pick the Leningrad delegation, was there a solid block of delegates who openly opposed the leadership centred around Stalin.

The capacity of the centre to structure the composition of the congress fundamentally altered the relationship between oligarchs and party rank-and-file by withdrawing from the latter the only real instrument they had for ensuring the accountability of the former. It thereby provided the means for the liberation of the leadership from rank-and-file control.

It also had another important result: it led to the transformation of the nature of party congresses and conferences and enabled the leading group to use the numbers it could generate in these fora as a weapon against successive opposition groups. Up until the time of the XIII Conference in January 1924, these party gatherings were the occasions for genuine party debate in which issues of policy were discussed and the support of the gathering was not assured by organisational means beforehand. Opposition speakers were freely accorded the right to express their opinions unhindered, and although they were always defeated on the floor of the assembly, their demise was not due primarily to the organisational manipulation of their opponents. However, from the time of the XIII Conference, this situation no longer applied.[26] Certainly party congresses and conferences remained throughout the 1920s fora within which regional leaders pressed their claims for resources[27] and thereby often criticised central priorities. They also remained the scene of scathing attacks upon the leadership and its policies by successive opposition groups. But the exchanges of which these were part had become little more than shadow-boxing.[28] The capacity of the successive groups to mount a sustained attack on the leading group was fatally flawed; not only was delegate selection manipulated in order to weaken the opposition and to strengthen the position of the leading group, but the ability of an opposition to state its case during this process of delegate selection could be hindered by the curtailment of the period of public debate preceding a congress and denial of access to printing facilities.[29] Even their participation at the congress was hindered. Prominent oppositionists were frequently present in the capacity of candidate, or non-voting, delegates, and session chairmen often discriminated against them in calling speakers to the congress podium. They were frequently excluded from participation in those bodies established to facilitate the work of the gathering, such as special commissions to investigate particular matters or to draft proposed resolutions.[30] Furthermore, in a development which clearly reflects the transformation of these gatherings, oppositionists were subjected to harassment from the floor while speaking. Such heckling occurred for the first time at the XIII Conference. By the time of the XIV Congress, the mass jeering and shouting down of speakers had become the norm, a pattern which was to be maintained until the opposition was vanquished. Only Trotsky at the XV Conference in

The divided elite

October–November 1926 could still the tongues of his tormentors, and this only because of his exceptional oratorical abilities. Nothing better shows the transformation of the congress into a weapon for pillorying the opposition than the way in which they were refused a hearing by the baying throng of delegates.

Substantial organisational coordination was behind the outbreak of heckling, as Kamenev implied at the XIV Congress,[31] at least in its initial stages. Occasional personal interventions from the floor had occurred in earlier congresses, but nothing like that of the mass scale of the mid-1920s. However, once such activity had become recognised as acceptable behaviour towards oppositionist speakers, its dependence upon conscious organisation in specific instances declined. Delegates may have come to see it as part of their role to react in this way to oppositionist speakers and may therefore have needed little prompting from political cheer leaders. It would thus have entered the culture of the institution. This was linked with a development that was of fundamental importance both to the congress as an institution and to the political system as a whole: the emergence of the principle of monolithism. The shouting down of oppositionist speakers was only one aspect of the broader task of the congress: to affirm the correct policy presented to it by the leading group. The wholesale rejection of the oppositionists and their views was the reverse side of the acceptance of the position espoused by the leading group. Furthermore, such acceptance became universal within the congress, which thereby became monolithic.[32] This development was marked, symbolically, by unanimous votes. An institutional convention which has lasted to this day was thus emerging out of the operating characteristics of the congress during the 1920s: despite possible reservations about the leadership's policy, in the public forum of the congress such reservations were not vigorously expressed and were certainly not to be manifested in the adoption of an openly oppositionist stance or vote.

An organisational lever which may have helped the emergence of monolithism in the congress was formalised during this period: the senoren konvent, or council of elders. This body was established by a CC decision two days before the XII Congress opened.[33] It met prior to the opening of the congress. Each guberniia and oblast delegation sent one representative to the senoren konvent for every ten full congress delegates, giving a total of about forty members. Officially it was summoned 'in the interest of the regulation of the organisational work of the congress and of securing the best conditions of information to the delegates'.[34] The senoren konvent probably approved the agenda and was doubtless the forum in which the party leadership consulted with and outlined for their lower level supporters the course the congress was to take.[35] This may have been the venue in which the public demonstrations against the opposition initially were organised. It is probable that this was also the arena in which soundings were taken from the lower level leaders about the identity of those it was proposed to elect formally to the CC and the Politburo.[36] The regularisation of this body was an important stage in ensuring that the congress ran smoothly.

The style and function of the congress as it developed in the 1920s was thus in stark contrast with the Leninist period. The ability of congress delegates to overturn the leadership on the floor of the congress as they had at the XI Congress had disappeared by 1923. With its disappearance came a fundamental change in the nature of the congress as an institution. A similar process of institutional transformation was evident elsewhere in the system as well.

A central place in oligarch affairs continued to be played by the CC. Between the XI and XVI Congresses, the CC met on 72 occasions,[37] twelve of which were joint sessions with the CCC. On many of the other occasions meetings were attended by some members of the CCC, something provided for by a X Congress decision according them a consultative voice at such meetings,[38] and by other specially invited representatives of different party organisations.[39] In addition, from the middle of 1924 both the CC and the Politburo engaged in the practice of meeting informally to make decisions in the absence of opposition members.[40] Despite the formal provision in the party Rules that this body should meet in plenary session once every two months, as this period wore on the formal meetings became increasingly infrequent. Although aggregate figures can be misleading (for example there were three meetings in January 1924, two of which were connected with Lenin's death), they do show the approximate frequency of CC sessions between congresses (see table 4.3).[41] By the second half of the decade, the CC was a very irregular organ, meeting only three to four times a year.

Membership changes transformed the CC fundamentally from what it had been during the Leninist period. Table 4.4 shows the figures for membership of the CC elected at successive congresses (including the XI Congress in 1922 for comparison) and the levels of carryover.[42] Between the final congresses of this and the preceding periods (XI–XV), the CC expanded in size almost three-fold. This expansion, officially justified partly in terms of Lenin's advice[43] but

Table 4.3 CC meetings, 1922–30

Congresses	Number of meetings	Average intervals between meetings	Length of plena (days)
XI-XII	19	2.75 weeks	1
XII-XIII	18	3.0 weeks	1–3
XIII-XIV	18	3.75 weeks	1–8
XIV-XV	9	11.0 weeks	2–12
XV-XVI	8	15.5 weeks	6–9

Table 4.4 CC membership, 1922–27

Congress	Full	Candidate	Total	Carried over to next CC (%)	Carryover as % of new CC
XI	27	19	46	76	–
XII	40	17	57	91.2	61.4
XIII	53	34	87	82.7	59.7
XIV	63	43	106	84.9	67.9
XV	71	50	121	84.3	74.4

actually linked to the course of factional conflict, transformed the CC into a body which was far too large for the thorough discussion of complex issues. This expansion also reflects the inflow of newer recruits to the CC, a process which was important for Stalin in building up his support. But this infusion of new blood into the CC occurred beside a substantial continuation of membership from one CC to the next. At no congress during this period was less than 82.7 per cent of all members of the CC re-elected (and this takes no account of any who may have died in the interim), although over the long run the core of long-serving members was gradually eroded; by the time of the XV Congress, 54.3 per cent of members elected at the XI Congress remained members of the CC.[44] Generally, carryover levels were higher than during the Leninist period, a development due at least in part to the changed method of selection discussed below. Full members of the CC were more likely to retain their membership than were candidates, at least until the middle of the decade.[45]

Throughout this period, the CC remained overwhelmingly the preserve of the Old Bolsheviks. This was particularly true of the full

Table 4.5 *Length of party membership of CC Members, 1922–27*

Congress	Pre-1917 Full	Pre-1917 Candidate	Pre-1917 Total	1917 Full	1917 Candidate	1917 Total	Post-1917 Full	Post-1917 Candidate	Post-1917 Total
XII	92.5	88.2	91.2	7.5	11.8	8.8	–	–	–
XIII	96.2	85.3	91.9	3.8	8.8	5.7	–	5.9	2.7
XIV	95.2	84.1	90.6	3.2	4.5	3.7	1.6	11.3	5.6
XV	98.4	82.2	92.2	–	6.6	2.6	1.6	11.0	5.3

members. Table 4.5 gives the relevant figures. All are in percentages.[46] The picture is clear. The CC remained dominated by Old Bolsheviks, with no less than 90.6 per cent of all members of that body having joined the party prior to 1917. This concentration is even more marked among full members; with the exception of Chicherin, who joined the party in 1918 but had a long career in Russian social democracy behind him, during this period the post-October generations of party recruits gained access to the CC only as candidate members.[47] The CC was thus greatly different in its membership profile from both the party as a whole and from congress delegates, both of which became dominated by post-October recruits as the period wore on. Paradoxically, during this period the CC became even more the preserve of pre-1917 recruits than it had been under Lenin; only in the final congress of the Leninist period (XI) did the proportion of members of the CC who joined the party prior to 1917 rise above the lowest level during this period (XIV). However, the path of future development was clear: of the new members elected at the XV Congress, 79.5 per cent had joined the party since the XI Congress in 1922.

This period also witnessed a strengthening of the position of the full-time party workers in the CC. The figures in table 4.6 refer to the job location of CC members in the period immediately following their election to the CC (all figures are percentages).[48] A couple of trends are interesting here. The first is the continuation, at least until 1927, of the earlier trend of a reduction in the profile of the state and an increase in that of the party. The decline in the role of the state was more retarded among full members than in the CC as a whole; full-time party workers became a majority of all members of the CC in 1923 at the XII Congress, but they did not gain a majority position among full members until 1925.[49] The emergence of the party secretaries, who were the most important group of full-time party workers, as a potentially significant force in the CC was a major stage in the evolution of this body. But another aspect of this, constituting the second major trend of development, is important here. This relates to the balance within the party workers between the central and regional functionaries. At the XI Congress the earlier trend of greater representation of central than regional party workers was reversed. Generally this process strengthened during this period, with the weight of numbers of regional workers being far greater than that of those from the centre. Such regional dominance, while it was still significant, was less marked among full members than among the committee as a

Table 4.6 *Bureaucratic constituencies in the CC, 1922–27*

Congress	CP apparatus Central	CP apparatus Regional	CP apparatus Total	State	Other	Uncertain
XI	10.9	23.9	34.8	47.9	17.4	–
XII	10.5	40.4	50.9	35.1	14.0	–
XIII	16.1	36.8	52.9	27.6	17.2	2.3
XIV	11.4	40.0	51.5	26.6	17.1	4.8
XV	14.0	35.5	49.5	28.1	15.7	6.6

whole.[50] This regional presence, and the concerns and sensitivities it embodied, was a significant element in the dynamics of the CC. Indeed, it may be that the greater infrequency of CC meetings in the latter part of this decade reflects the uncertainties felt by this group about party policy in the countryside and their resentment at the apparent attitude of party leaders towards them. Under such circumstances, central party leaders may have been reluctant to provide them with a national forum in which to air their concerns.

The emerging prominence of party secretaries in the CC reflects not just the potentially growing power of this section of the party membership, but a change in the principles of representation in this body. In the early years of the Leninist period, the CC constituted a council of party notables whose election was due mainly to the personal prominence they enjoyed in party ranks. This began to change with the X Congress, a change which was consolidated during this period. As Robert Daniels has shown,[51] the CC emerged as an arena in which various functional interests and geographical areas were represented. The CC became a body filled primarily by representatives of bureaucratic constituencies; membership became in large part a function of bureaucratic position.[52] It has remained this until the present day, and although the norms of representation[53] have changed over time, the principle of bureaucratic constituent representation was established in the 1920s and has continued to structure representation in this body. During the period under review, the party apparatus was clearly the most prominent bureaucratic constituency in the CC.

The course of development of the CC during this period militated against the generation of a strong sense of institutional coherence or identity, at least for the plenum. Meetings were generally too infrequent and numbers too large for the organ to develop the coherent, on-going institutional existence which was essential if it was to develop as a strong, independent institution. Its failure to do this is evident in the way in which it emerged as an important weapon in elite conflict. However the CC also played an important role in policy debate. Agendas seem to have been heavy[54] and the CC often established sub-committees to handle pressing business or particular problems.[55] Its importance for the formalisation of party policy is reflected in the fact that resolutions of party conferences were considered binding on the party only after they had been formally endorsed by the CC.[56] Also important was the principle enshrined in a XII Congress decision that all fundamental issues were to be decided by the plenum and that in the two to three weeks before a plenum the Politburo was to postpone all important decisions, where possible, until the meeting of its parent body.[57] In practice during this period, the competence of the CC embraced all major areas of party concern, with the result that important issues were discussed in this forum even if formal decisions were not always adopted. Most controversial issues were transferred from the Politburo to the CC, in part to secure factional advantage. In institutional terms this cast the CC in the role of arbiter between the contending sides of a split Politburo, thereby reinforcing the principle of the accountability of the latter to the former. With the exception of the congress, this did not apply to the other elite organs; there was no counterpart of that practice so common during the Leninist period of individuals appealing decisions which went against them to other elite organs, and in particular Sovnarkom.

The policy focus of the CC and its membership by leading oppositionist figures ensured that the proceedings of this body frequently were characterised by the clash of opinion ranging from the well-reasoned but perhaps impassioned argument to the most bitter and vitriolic personal attacks. Here was a major forum in which the policy positions of the various groups could be spelled out and the alternative courses of policy debated among the party leaders. Through the party press, including the publication of many leading speeches in *Pravda*, through the circulation of verbatim protocols of CC meetings to regional and district levels of the party[58] and the process of intra-party discussion, much of the course of its debates percolated throughout the party structure. But the CC also became the scene for vigorous attacks upon the opposition[59] and although the greater representation of opposition figures here than in the congress seemed to make the opposition stronger in this forum, ultimately the result was the same. From the opening of factional conflict, the leading group always had the numbers in the CC to defeat the opposition,[60] particularly with the convocation of joint CC–CCC plena discussed below.[61] The establishment of such dominance, which was linked with the expansion in size and the strengthening position of party bureaucrats in the CC, contributed greatly to the decline in the standard of CC debate. This was illustrated most clearly by the interruption and howling down of opposition speakers in the October 1927 plenum.

While majority support for the leading group was the result of a variety of factors, important was the mode of selection of members. In the first years after 1917, the CC was filled by genuine election at the party congress. Delegates voted for as many candidates as there were seats, with those receiving the highest totals taking up full membership and, prior to 1920, the runners up attaining candidate status; from 1920 these two groups were voted on separately. In 1921 at the X Congress a semi-official slate was presented to congress delegates to be voted for as a whole.[62] Henceforth, with the possible exception of the XI Congress,[63] slate-making appears to have been in evidence in the election of all CCs.[64] This development both undercut the formal sovereignty of the congress and transformed the CC into a coopted organ. The choice of membership was made from above, probably discussed in the senoren konvent, and ratified by the assembled congress delegates. In this way the ability of any opposition group to build up its power and position in this organ was undercut unless they could organise a revolt among congress delegates, which was highly unlikely given the process of delegate selection discussed above. In contrast, the leading group could ensure its supporters were in a majority through control over the process of slate-making.

The uncongenial nature of the CC for oppositional activity is clearly reflected in the practice which emerged during this period of meeting in joint session with the CCC. Provision had been made in 1921 for all members of the CCC to attend CC meetings with a consultative vote,[65] but with the growth of the CCC from seven in 1922 to sixty in 1923, provision for representation was changed. The XII Congress resolved that the right to attend and exercise a consultative vote in CC plena should be exercised only by members of the CCC Presidium[66] and reaffirmed the principle established at the time of the creation of the control commissions that a person could not simultaneously be a full member of both the CC and the CCC.[67] In addition to these provisions, a new forum was established, the joint CC–CCC plenum,

The divided elite 151

which could be attended by all members of both bodies exercising full voting rights. Twelve such plena were held during this period, with members of the CCC in the majority from 1923. The power of the CCC in the joint plenum was enhanced by the role it played in collecting and preparing material upon which discussion in the meeting rested.[68]

Until the end of 1925,[69] the joint plenum concentrated only on questions relating to issues of party discipline and unity and to the control commission structure itself. But even from the outset its brief was stated to be wider than this, embracing 'the most important general political and general party questions'.[70] This became clear from 1925 when the scope of its concerns embraced all aspects of the implementation of the CC's line, including questions of an economic nature. Indeed, many of the most important issues of the period were raised for discussion in this forum. But the most notable characteristic of the joint plenum was its concern with disciplinary matters. From the outset, these were fora within which the opposition was called upon to defend itself and at which that opposition was officially censured. Such censure could take the form of reprimands in formal resolutions[71] or could even involve expulsion from the CC or the party itself.[72] The joint plenum thus was almost a supreme court in the party where opponents were tried, found wanting and punished. This function was evident from the first joint plenum in August 1921 at which Lenin had called for disciplinary action against Shliapnikov. It is also shown by the types of decisions taken by the joint plenum compared with the CC plenum. Of all the resolutions adopted on economic matters, 79 per cent were adopted in the CC plenum, while 82 per cent of all resolutions on disciplinary matters were taken by the joint plenum.[73] These figures clearly reflect the different foci of concern of the plenum and the joint plenum.

A notion of collective responsibility on the part of the CC was voiced on a couple of occasions during this period. The refusal to allow Lominadze to move an amendment to a resolution without the assent of the CC (of which he was a candidate member) at the XVI Conference and the charge that Bukharin had published his 'Notes of an Economist' without the knowledge of the CC were both expressions of the view that CC members should tailor their actions to accord with the views of the body as a whole.[74] But despite this principle and although the CC remained an important arena of elite debate, its development as a strong and coherent institution was seriously flawed. Its use by the leading group as a weapon to attack the opposition, bolstered by the membership selection process, seriously hampered the unrolling of rational policy debate and the emergence of solidly entrenched procedural norms which could both reinforce institutional structures and bind individual actors. The relative infrequency of its meetings and the expansion in its membership, plus the practice of meeting informally without the opposition to consider questions of importance, further undermined the emergence of strong corporate norms for the CC. Furthermore, the provision for non-members to attend meetings of the CC and to enjoy voting rights hindered the emergence of any sense of institutional integrity and coherence. The pattern of operation which characterised the CC during this period was thus one which provided a very weak basis for vigorous institutional growth.

The continued erosion in the power of the CC reflected in part the increased role and functions of the Politburo and its other executive organs. Like the other leading bodies of the system, the Politburo expanded in size over this period. The Politburo elected at the CC meeting following the XI Congress consisted of seven full and three candidate members. By the end of 1929 this had grown to eight full and nine candidate members. Being elected by the CC, the Politburo could and sometimes did change in composition a number of times over a year; the Politburo elected at the CC plenum of 1 January 1926 was altered at a CC plenum of 23 July 1926 and joint CC-CCC plena on 23 October and 3 November 1926, while the Politburo elected in December 1927 was changed at CC plena in April, June and November 1929. These membership changes were directly linked with the cycle of factional conflict. This is clearly illustrated by a comparison of the Politburo elected in 1922 with that following the November 1929 plenum (see table 4.7).

Of the full members in 1922, only Stalin, Rykov and Tomsky remained full members in 1929, and of these Rykov and Tomsky were casualties of the factional conflict and were clearly on borrowed time. Two of the 1922 candidates had been promoted to full membership and retained their places while the third, Bukharin, had become a full member in 1924 but had lost that position five years later. Of the remaining four members of the 1922 Politburo, Lenin had died while the others were victims of the factional conflict. This constitutes a turnover rate of 57 per cent among full members of the Politburo. By the end of 1929, 62.5 per cent of full members or 29.4 per cent of all members had been in the Politburo when this period opened. This represents a significant membership renewal.

The divided elite   153

Table 4.7 *Politburo membership, 1922 and 1929*

	1922	1929
Full	Zinoviev, Ch Leningrad soviet	Voroshilov, War Commissar
	Kamenev, V-C Sovnarkom [a]	Kalinin, Ch TsIK
	Lenin, Ch Sovnarkom	Kuibyshev, Ch Vesenkha
	Stalin, Gensec [b]	Molotov, CC Sec.
	Trotsky, War Commissar	Rykov, Ch. Sovnarkom
	Rykov, V-C Sovnarkom	Rudzutak, V-C Sovnarkom
	Tomsky, Ch A-R C of TUs	Stalin, Gensec
		Tomsky, – [c]
Candidate	Bukharin, *Pravda* ed.	Andreev, CP Sec North Caucasus
	Kalinin, Ch TsIK	Kaganovich, CC Sec.
	Molotov, CC Sec.	Kirov, CP Sec Leningrad
		Kosior, CP Sec Ukraine
		Mikoian, Trade Commissar
		Petrovsky, Ch Ukraine TsIK
		Chubar, Ch Ukraine Sovnarkom
		Bauman, CP Sec. Moscow
		Syrtsov, Ch RSFSR TsIK

[a] Kamenev was also Chairman of the Moscow Soviet
[b] Stalin was also People's Commissar of Nationalities and of Rabkrin at the time of the XI Congress.
[c] Tomsky was in limbo, having been removed from his position as head of the trade unions in June 1929.

There is a high level of consistency in the representation of posts between these two membership profiles. The editorship of *Pravda*, chairmanship of the Leningrad Soviet and chairmanship of the All-Russian Council of Trade Unions are missing from the 1929 Politburo, absences due to the fact that their representation in 1922 owed more to their incumbents' personal standing than to the perceived importance of the offices themselves. However, Leningrad did remain represented through the candidacy of its party secretary, Kirov. The expansion in size of the Politburo meant the inclusion in that body of a range of positions not represented in 1922; of the ten new posts, five came from the state apparatus (three were from the regional state machine) and five from the party (four were from the non-central party apparatus).

Comparison of the representation of the party apparatus and the state machine is complicated by the dual occupancy of posts by many

Table 4.8 *Overlap between Politburo and Orgburo, 1922–27*

XI Congress	50%	XIV Congress	21.4%
XII Congress	54.5%	XV Congress	29.4%
XIII Congress	46%		

Politburo members. What can be said is that in 1922 50 per cent and in 1929 29.4 per cent were members of the Orgburo, while in the same years 50 per cent and 35 per cent held positions in the central state machine (these figures involve some double counting for those jointly holding party and state positions). The Politburo therefore remained a narrow elite with a predominantly central focus. Particularly important here is the overlap between Politburo and Orgburo over this period; at all times a significant proportion of Politburo members were simultaneously members of the Orgburo, as the figures in table 4.8 demonstrate. The figures (for the Politburo and Orgburo formed at the time of each congress) relate to the proportion of members of the Politburo also members of the Orgburo.

The decision of October 1923 to draft three more Politburo members (plus one CC member) into the Orgburo in order to increase Politburo supervision over it means that formally from that date until April 1924, 81.8 per cent of the Politburo were also on the Orgburo. In practice, the four new members played no part in the Orgburo's operations. But even leaving aside this exceptional period, it is clear that the Politburo overlapped considerably with the Orgburo, and that this was most pronounced in the periods of struggle against the Trotskyite and Left Oppositions. Furthermore, although the Politburo following the November 1929 plenum had only four members (23.5 per cent – Stalin, Molotov, Kaganovich and Bauman) who were simultaneously members of the Orgburo, of the other thirteen members, eight had been members of the Orgburo during the 1920s.[75] Such a leavening of central party experience ensured that as the Politburo developed during this period it remained sensitive to the concerns of the party apparatus. It was, however, from the perspective of the central party apparatus, because despite the increased regional representation in the Politburo, this remained less significant than central representation; the regional predominance in the CC was not matched in the Politburo.

An important difference between the memberships of the two Politburos lay in the nature of the individuals themselves. Of the full members in 1922, only Kamenev lacked ideological pretensions while two others (Lenin and Trotsky) were clearly in the first rank of Bolshevik theorists. The candidate Bukharin could also be added to the group of intellectuals in the Politburo, people at home in the conflict of theoretical discourse and both appreciative of and sensitive to the interplay of theoretical concepts. Furthermore, most of this group had spent their political apprenticeships in the hothouse of emigration, an environment in which the importance of theoretical disputation was bound to be inflated. In contrast, the Politburo of 1929 was filled at both full and candidate levels by individuals whose attention was focused overwhelmingly on practical matters. For these people, the conflict of ideas was less important than the imperatives of political organisation and the demands of administration. Their background was not the cafes and lodgings of the West frequented by the throng of displaced revolutionaries, but the illicit world of the Russian underground where political organisation and basic political skills were of greater importance than theoretical debate. These people, all of whom had joined the party prior to October, were not unmindful of the role of political ideas. However, such ideas were far less important for these leaders than they had been for those of a more theoretical disposition. Certainly Stalin retained his ideological pretensions, but his capacities in this regard were clearly inferior to many of those who were no longer destined to play a leading role in the Soviet political process, such as Bukharin.[76]

The later Politburo also differed from that of the Lenin period in its demographic characteristics. Although both Politburos were dominated by Russians, that of the later part of the 1920s saw a significant increase in those from peasant background (with a corresponding decrease in those coming from the working class and intelligentsia), a marked decrease in those who had higher education, and a significant reduction in the number of Jews.[77]

The personnel profile of the Politburo was directly moulded by the course of factional conflict which unrolled during this period. Throughout the 1920s the Politburo was characterised by an anti-Stalin faction, a faction which supported Stalin, and a neutralist group. While the boundaries between and the membership of these groups remained fluid, the ramifications of the dynamics of factional conflict were clear: the ultimate elimination of the anti-Stalin faction, the strengthening of the pro-Stalin group, and the continuation of the neutralist group. Of the nine people who left the Politburo during this period, three died in office (Lenin, Dzerzhinsky and Frunze) while

Ordzhonikidze was transferred to the CCC and thus rendered ineligible for Politburo membership. The other five were all opponents of Stalin at the time of their removal: Zinoviev (July 1926), Trotsky and Kamenev (October 1926), Uglanov (April 1929) and Bukharin (November 1929). Sixteen people joined the Politburo during this period of whom twelve (Voroshilov, Rudzutak, Petrovsky, Andreev, Kirov, Mikoian, Kaganovich, Chubar, Kuibyshev, Kosior, Bauman and Syrtsov) either supported Stalin or bolstered the uncommitted middle in the factional conflict.[78]

One effect of the centralising of power in the whole political process was the continual over-burdening of the Politburo. Although definitive figures are not available, those which exist suggest an organisation at full stretch, especially considering the amount of time taken up at its meetings by factional disputation. At the XII Congress it was reported that the Politburo had met on 60 occasions in the 12 months since the previous congress (an average of just over once per week) and, together with 19 meetings of the CC, had dealt with 1,322 questions.[79] In the following 12 months the Politburo met on some 86 occasions and reviewed 3,671 questions, an average of nearly 43 questions per session.[80] Between the XIII and XIV Congresses, the Politburo met on 92 occasions,[81] or an average of just over once per week. At the XV Congress Kursky reported that during the past year each Politburo member had to master 6,682 pages of material if he was to keep abreast of questions raised in that body.[82] The competence of the Politburo covered all types of questions, but the sheer scope of its concerns often meant that questions were not dealt with as fully as they should have been.[83]

No area of policy was considered outside the scope of this body,[84] although in practice many important and controversial issues were passed to the CC for discussion. But the breadth of the Politburo's concerns sometimes led to complaints about its lack of attention to particular areas of policy. One critic in 1923 suggested that a basic division of responsibility existed: the Politburo dealt principally with questions of foreign policy and finances with some attention to economic questions, while issues of party construction were left to the Orgburo and Secretariat.[85] In practice, given the power disposition and factional alignments, this suggestion was probably not far from the truth; the Politburo is likely to have exercised little more than a watching brief over the activities of the other two organs.[86] Nevertheless, real political debate did take place within the Politburo and it was recognised as the hub of decision-making. Its role was emphasised during 1928 in the wide-ranging debate between different organs on economic policy, when it seemed that the Politburo was the only body that could force agreement on these fractious organs. It even seems to have projected a weak sense of collective responsibility, and perhaps even cabinet solidarity, during this period. This was suggested by the editorial controls it sought to establish over its members[87] and the formal secrecy that surrounded its deliberations.[88]

Despite the appearance of institutional integrity and coherence in the notions of collective responsibility and cabinet solidarity, the organ remained weak in these respects. The development by the Politburo of institutional integrity and coherence was hindered by the weight of work with which that body had to deal and by the frequent attendance of non-members at its meetings. From its formal creation in 1919, members of the CC were entitled to attend Politburo meetings. At the XII Congress this principle was reaffirmed[89] and the Presidium of the CCC was granted the right to send three permanent representatives to Politburo meetings;[90] the XV Congress changed this to four full and four candidate members of the Presidium.[91] A new formal organ was also established with the creation of the joint Politburo–CCC Presidium meetings at which formal decisions were issued.[92] Specific non-members could be invited to participate in Politburo meetings from time to time,[93] while officials offering information and advice on matters under review were also frequently present.[94] The limits of attendance at the Politburo were thus elastic with a large range of non-members entitled to participate in one capacity or another. This had severe implications for institutional coherence and integrity.

One means of coming to grips with the quantity of work confronting the Politburo was the establishment of sub-committees or commissions, a practice frequently adopted during this period. Such bodies may have had a quite specific purpose, like that established in February 1929 to draft a condemnation of Bukharin's 'political errors',[95] or they may have been given a broader brief to investigate specific policy areas.[96] Such a delegation of responsibility should have improved the Politburo's efficiency, but at least one observer cast considerable doubt on this by suggesting that its effect was to duplicate and disorganise the work of the parent body.[97] The pressures of work probably also resulted in a significant level of delegation to the central party apparatus and to individual party functionaries.[98]

More important as a means of improving the Politburo's capacity to make quick policy decisions was the neutralisation of opposition in this body. Throughout this period members of the leading opposition groups were always found in the Politburo; even at the close of the period two prominent oppositionists, Tomsky and Rykov, tenuously retained their membership. Politburo politics was fractious and factionalised, with shifting coalitions of support dividing Politburo members. Four major organisational methods were used to overcome opposition in the Politburo. The first was through the monopolisation of the agenda-setting process, which the troika was able to do between 1923 and 1925.[99] The second was by meeting informally to make decisions without opposition members present.[100] Thirdly, joint Politburo–CCC Presidium sessions could be convened, thereby creating a forum in which anti-opposition sentiment was likely to be much stronger than in the Politburo alone. Alternatively, discussion could be transferred to the CC with the same effect. The final method was the stacking of the Politburo with one's supporters. From 1926 onwards, Stalin was able to promote supporters into full membership of the Politburo. He used this power initially to supplement his coalition-making to defeat opposition, but following the rout of the Right Opposition in 1929, he was able to eschew the need for coalitions and rely purely on those supporters. The key to Stalin's ability to build up his support in the Politburo lay in his power over the CC apparatus through the Orgburo and Secretariat.

The authority and power of the Orgburo and Secretariat increased during this period. Formally, the Orgburo was the more important of these two bodies, but in practical terms it was the Secretariat which emerged as the more significant organ. Both bodies carried heavy workloads, as the figures in table 4.9 show.[101] This work load was not shared equally; between the XII and XIII Congresses, the Orgburo met on 42 occasions and discussed 754 questions, but the Secretariat met 48 times and dealt with 6,972 questions.[102] The distribution of work shown in these figures supports Kursky's comment that the Orgburo concerned itself with 'the basic organisational questions' and only 'examined the most important questions concerning the personal appointment of individual comrades' while the more minor questions were handled by the Secretariat.[103] These figures also suggest a more important characteristic of the operating profile of these bodies: their inability as collective organs to monitor closely the vast range of decisions for which they were responsible. In effect, both Orgburo and Secretariat were councils of organisational notables which rested upon a hierarchy of bureaucrats in the secretarial machinery.[104] This secretarial machinery, or the apparatus of the Secretariat, was divided

Table 4.9 *Orgburo and Secretariat workloads, 1922–24*

Congresses	Meetings	Questions handled
XI–XII	106	6,834
XII–XIII	90	7,726

Table 4.10 *Orgburo and Secretariat membership, 1922–27*

	Orgburo			Secretariat		
Congress	Full	Candidate	Total	Full	Candidate	Total
XI	7	3	10	3	–	3
XII	7	2	9	4	–	4
XIII	12	4	16	4	–	4
XIV	11	5	16	5	2	7
XV	13	7	20	5	3	8

into departments (otdely) while the Secretariat itself consisted of CC secretaries who were individually responsible for the departments. The leading figure in the Secretariat was the General Secretary. Both Secretariat and Orgburo relied upon the secretarial apparatus to do the substantive work for their meetings, work which usually took the form of proposals sent into the Orgburo and Secretariat for consideration, adoption, amendment or rejection. The effect of the large number of questions which came before these bodies at each sitting (an average of 18 for the Orgburo and 145 for the Secretariat between the XII and XIII Congresses) ensured that for the most part they simply ratified the proposals emanating from the secretarial apparatus. Such a situation led to calls for the exercise by the Politburo and Orgburo of closer supervision over the party organisation,[105] to the assertion that the Orgburo and Secretariat could examine closely only some 5 per cent of questions before them, and to calls for the delegation of more responsibility by these bodies.[106] In addition, provision was made for CC members to appeal Orgburo decisions to the Politburo and Secretariat decisions to the Orgburo.[107]

One way of trying to cope with the heavy workload was to increase staff. Membership of these bodies elected by the CC following each congress, is shown in table 4.10.[108] Over this period, both organs doubled their initial sizes, but both remained comparatively small. There was little fluctuation in the size of the secretarial apparatus, as reports at successive congresses show: 1922 – 705, 1923 – 741, 1924 – 694, 1925 – 767 and 1927 – 657.[109] Surprisingly, some members of this, the administrative hub of the party, were not party members. Kursky told the XIII Congress that 25 per cent of the staff of the Secretariat were non-party people, concentrated in technical areas the party had not yet penetrated (such as accountancy) and in such less sensitive posts as typists and couriers. By the XV Congress this proportion had been reduced to 16 per cent (statisticians were cited as an example of the type of area in which the party had no resources of its own), but in the 'basic sections' non-party people accounted for no more than 4 to 6 per cent.[110] But the number of personnel alone was not enough to ensure the satisfactory handling of the volume of work passing through the secretarial apparatus, regardless of how devoted to their work these functionaries may have been.[111] One problem was the high mobility of workers in the apparatus; of the 767 people working in the apparatus at the time of the XIV Congress, 704 had changed their jobs in the preceding 18 months.[112] Such levels of mobility were not conducive to the development of a smoothly run, efficient bureaucratic machine. But what was also necessary was organisational streamlining and the rationalisation of work organisation, both of which were undertaken during this period.

A major reorganisation of the apparatus of the Secretariat occurred in 1924. The two most important departments in the Secretariat prior to the reorganisation were Uchraspred (the Records and Assignment Department) and Orgotdel (the Organisation-Instruction Department). The tasks of these departments were described in 1923 as follows: Uchraspred was responsible for

> the detailed and attentive registration of the commanding cadre of the party, the reassignment of party forces for the strengthening of the most important provincial organisations; the selection of organisers for party work, review of the leaders of oblast, guberniia and uezd party organisations and to a certain extent secretaries of cells; the replacement of workers who do not satisfy the standards set by the party congress; the selection of propagandist forces, the strengthening of the countryside and production through party workers; the strengthening of economic organs (in particular the financial apparatus) and trade unions.[113]

Orgotdel was

> to ensure the flexibility of the party apparatus, to establish CC links with local organisations in order to make possible daily study of the conditions of each organisation and the processes going on in it; to strengthen the apparatus, bring about a living link with the localities, improve the conditions of information so they embrace and reflect the work of the localities, draw nearer to the life and work of local organisations down to the lowest cells, single out the most important industrial centres and establish a direct link with them, and, on this basis, to carry on planned work directed at the strengthening and sanitation of party organisations, the liquidation of disputes, the improvement of methods of general party work and the registration and working out of those new undertakings in the realm of party work in the localities which are significant for the party.[114]

Put simply, Uchraspred was concerned with the distribution of personnel while Orgotdel was responsible for relations between the central organs of the party and those in the localities. The successful operation of both bodies was dependent upon the other; the supply of personnel was one of the major aspects of centre–local relations while the satisfactory supply of such personnel was heavily dependent upon the sort of information which Orgotdel maintained. The pressures created by this division of responsibility were instrumental in leading to the reorganisation of the Secretariat in 1924.

The principal result of the reorganisation was the creation of a new department, Orgraspred (the Organisation-Assignment Department), through the merger of Uchraspred and the Organisation Section of Orgotdel.[115] Orgraspred now became the central department of the Secretariat apparatus with very wide-ranging competence: making recommendations for appointments, promotions and transfers in the party, government, trade union, industrial and cooperative spheres; the maintenance of records on leading party workers and supervision over their assignments; supervision of questions of party structure and organisation; supervision of local party organisations directly through responsible instructors sent out periodically to these bodies and indirectly through perusal of their reports, participation in their meetings, the convocation of special meetings, the submission of advice and instruction, supervision of their personnel registration work, and oversight of their leadership selection; the systematisation of party directives and verification of their implementation; and the establishment and strengthening of links with non-party organisations.[116] In short, Orgraspred combined a concern with personnel matters, including records and appointments, with the supervision of the activities of subordinate party organs.

In addition to Orgraspred, the post-reorganisation Secretariat had the following departments: Agitation and Propaganda, Press (incorporated into Agitprop in 1928), Work among Women, Work in the Villages, Accounting, Statistics Information and the Administration of Affairs or General Department.[117] The General Department may have included the Secret Department, although the precise institutional relationship between these two bodies remains unclear. It was in the Secret Department that much of the preparatory work for the Politburo, Orgburo and Secretariat was conducted. This is important because of the special relationship that developed between it and General Secretary Stalin discussed below.[118] The broad function of these departments is clear from their titles, except perhaps for the General Department which acted as the chancellery carrying out general housekeeping functions for the central party apparatus. The broad scope of the concerns of the party organs is apparent in the organisational divisions in the Secretariat.

The main focus of Secretariat operations was undoubtedly Uchraspred/Orgraspred. It was through this organ that the life-blood of the party, the personnel to fill administrative and other positions, flowed. It was through this department that most leading appointments were made. The raw figures in table 4.11 give some idea of the scale of appointment.[119] The sharp decline following the XI Congress reflects the change in emphasis away from mass mobilisation towards more individualised appointments and an effort to relate the skills of appointees to the needs of the local organisation.[120] It also reflects the attempt to devolve responsibility for some appointments to lower levels and thereby enable the central organs to concentrate their attention on the filling of responsible posts with appropriate personnel. This involved the rationalisation of the work programme of the party apparatus.

The key to the establishment of a regularised personnel system remained what it had been during the earlier period, the creation of effective registration procedures and the construction of an efficient mode of distribution. The decision had been taken during the earlier period to restrict central registration to certain classes of worker (see ch. 2), a decision which should have lightened the administrative load on the central organs. However, some twelve months after the completion of the party census of 1921–22, the personnel records available

Table 4.11 *Scale of appointments, 1921–30*

Congress	Total appointments	Responsible workers	Av. appointments p.a.
X–XI	22,250	?	22,250
XI–XII	10,351	4,738	10,351
XII–XIII	6,082	4,569	6,082
XIII–XIV	12,277	9,419	8,184
XIV–XV	8,761	7,445	4,380
XV–XVI	11,000 approx	?	4,400 approx

in Uchraspred were still deemed to be seriously deficient.[121] A number of major attempts were made to systematise the centre's personnel records during this period. The most important were associated with the introduction and later revision of the nomenklatura system discussed below. In addition, a major new form of registration was completed in March 1924.[122] This involved some rationalisation of central records both in terms of numbers of personnel upon whom full records would be kept and the structure of central files. This means that during this period from 1922–29, there were substantial alterations to the central system of registration on a number of occasions: the establishment of the nomenklatura system in mid-1923 and its later amendment in December 1925 and, possibly, 1928 all had significant implications for the scale of registration required at the centre. In addition, minor refinements and adjustments were made from time to time.[123] The operation of an adequate registration system would have been difficult enough given this series of changes, but it was rendered even more unlikely by the high mobility levels of apparat workers and the extensive administrative pressures posed by the membership flux discussed above. In addition, the conduct of another party census in 1927 imposed extra administrative burdens on the registration apparatus. So although a greater degree of systematisation does appear to have been brought about in the registration procedure during this period, a smoothly efficient apparatus remained more a wish than a reality.

Greater success seems to have been achieved with the establishment of a regularised mode of distribution, although here too we should not assume that an impressive structure necessarily meant a highly efficient practical operation. The XII Congress in April 1923 was important for the introduction of the nomenklatura system. In one resolution, it called upon Uchraspred to 'play a very important role in the correct distribution of forces to ensure that the party exerts real leadership in all areas of the administration without exception'.[124] Another resolution declared the next task of the party to be 'the strengthening of party leadership in the sphere of the selection of leading soviet, in particular economic, and other organs, which must be achieved by means of a correct and comprehensive system of registration and selection of leading and responsible workers of soviet, economic, cooperative and trade union organisations'. The resolution went on to instruct the CC 'to take all measures for the expansion and strengthening of the records and assignment organs of the party in the centre and the localities with the aim of embracing the whole mass of communists and workers sympathetic to communism in all areas of administration and economy without exception'.[125] These demands were met by the institutionalisation of the nomenklatura in the middle of 1923.

On 12 June 1923 the Orgburo issued a resolution prescribing procedures regulating the distribution, selection and registration of responsible workers in state and economic organs. On 12 October it confirmed the lists of posts which were to comprise the party centre's personnel regime. This personnel regime comprised some 3,500 positions in the government structure that were to be filled 'through the CC' (nomenklatura number 1) and about 1,500 posts which were to be filled by the organ concerned with later notification to the CC.[126] A similar secret regime was drawn up for appointments in the party. This remained the formal charter on appointment until it was replaced by a new scheme in December 1925.[127] The new regime left the most important posts, numbering some 5,500, formally within the province of the CC. Of these, about 1,870 (category 1) were to be filled through appointment by the Politburo, Orgburo or Secretariat;[128] 1,640 (category 2) required the approval of one of the CC secretaries and was referred to the CC (or one of its executive bodies) only in cases of disagreement. A further list of 1,590 elective posts was added as a supplement to nomenklatura list 1, for which special *ad hoc* commissions would be established by the CC,[129] while a range of other assorted posts was also added as a further supplement to nomenklatura list 1. Leading appointments to positions in central bodies not on either of the CC's nomenklatura lists were the responsibility of the institutions concerned, although presumably central party organs had to be notified about such appointments. This new nomenklatura regime seems to have remained in operation for at least two years before it came under review. In early 1928 a commission was charged with working out a draft of a new nomenklatura distribution scheme for the CC.[130] There is no indication of the fate of this draft and no firm evidence that the regime adopted at the end of 1925 was replaced by a newer version at this time.

The institutionalisation of the nomenklatura system thus involved a classification of posts according to the level at which the decision about filling those posts should be made. Its introduction thereby superseded the earlier assumptions about levels of seniority of workers and set up the framework for a regularised personnel system. It did, however, take some time for the system to become fully operational; in the last quarter of 1926, 87.5 per cent of the workers who were placed by Orgraspred were not on the CC nomenklatura.[131] Nevertheless, by the end of the period the framework had been created for a regularised system of personnel distribution. Although problems still remained with registration and distribution, institutional structures had been created which would have long-term significance.

The institutionalisation of the nomenklatura in this way plus the associated expansion of Orgraspred's powers over the filling of elected positions in the party[132] brought to a head the tension in the party's rules between the principles of the election of party secretaries from below and the control over party personnel vested in the central organs. The formal means of reconciling these two conflicting principles were the processes of recommendation and confirmation. Confirmation was a process whereby the membership of party committees formally filled by election from below had to be confirmed at a higher level of the party structure. This principle was clearly enunciated in the party Rules which applied at this time.[133] But in a practical sense, such confirmation became redundant with the institutionalisation of the nomenklatura. In effect, this was the organisational vehicle for the practice of recommendation; it constituted the formal regulations governing which committees (or in practice which orgraspreds) had the right to nominate individuals to fill vacant posts. As regards elected positions in the party, the nomenklatura specified which committees had the right to recommend candidates to fill the formally elective posts. In practice, such recommendations were treated as mandatory; individuals nominated from above would duly be elected to fill the positions for which they had been nominated. In this way, the principles of central direction of personnel and rank-

and-file election of leading positions were reconciled, at least formally.

All of the most important positions in the political system were encapsulated in the nomenklatura structure, including party secretaries at all levels. Indeed, it was the party secretaries who were the key to the operation of the nomenklatura since it was through the secretarial apparatus[134] they controlled that the power of appointment which was the essence of nomenklatura was implemented. As indicated earlier, at lower levels they used this formal power to extend and consolidate the personalised political machines which had characterised local politics since 1917. Similar opportunities existed at the national level where control over the appointment process vested in the national level nomenklatura gave access to a vast range of positions throughout the system, including party secretaries at the regional and provincial levels. Potentially, control over this gave the power to move supporters into key posts throughout the party apparatus, a fact important both because of the implications this had for overall control of that apparatus and because of the prominence of party secretaries in that leading forum of elite councils, the CC. This potential was realised during this period, and became associated with acceptance of the convention that it was appropriate to use personnel powers to buttress one's own political position. While it is not clear that this was as important in determining the outcome of elite conflict as some have thought, it is clear that this was a factor in building up the power base of Stalin, the General Secretary.

The position of General Secretary was formally created in April 1922 when Stalin was named to it. Previously, following Sverdlov's death in 1919, there had been a number of CC secretaries and although a form of hierarchy had emerged among them, problems of coordination were instrumental in the decision to establish a superior position to exercise broad supervision over the secretaries and their apparatus. Initially the post was seen as being of quite low status, concerned fundamentally with questions of administration and of making the party function efficiently. The staff of the General Secretary's office seems to have been small, at least at the outset. According to Bazhanov (the timing is not clear but it was between 1922 and 1925), formally the General Secretary had three personal assistants: one doubled as secretary to the Politburo (Bazhanov), one was Stalin's personal secretary (Mekhlis) and the third (Kanner) seems to have had diverse responsibilities.[135] The bases of the power of the General Secretary were three-fold. First, he was at the crucial point of contact between the Politburo and the apparatus which did the bulk of the preparatory work for that body. As a result, the General Secretary had a significant influence on the course of information flow to the Politburo, the structuring of its agenda and the whole course of its operations.[136] Secondly, his own personal secretariat, consisting of his personal assistants and possessing significant tentacles into all areas of Soviet life, overlapped and may even have merged with the Secret Department of the CC Secretariat.[137] The extensive powers this organ could wield were thereby placed even more under the influence of the General Secretary. Thirdly, he had access to the appointment process. As the only full member of the Politburo, Orgburo and Secretariat, he was strategically placed to monitor personnel issues in all fora. For much of the time he chaired these meetings, which gave him another lever over their operations. Furthermore, he was responsible for all the activity of the Orgburo and Secretariat, including supervision of personnel questions through the secretarial apparatus. This supervision was rendered easier by the presence of supporters in these organs.[138] The position of General Secretary was clearly of crucial importance organisationally, and it was one which an ambitious man could use to further that ambition, as Stalin showed.

The final institution in the elite political arena was the CCC. The CCC and its Presidium (created in 1923) expanded significantly (see table 4.12).[139] The massive increase in CCC membership results from the mobilisation of large numbers of individuals into disciplinary work at the centre. Many of these were newcomers to the field and, because of the emphasis upon the desirability of proletarian origins, lacked a high level of political sophistication. Dissatisfaction with the quality of some of these members is suggested by high levels of turnover in the CCC. While this may reflect the presence of some oppositionist sentiment in this body, it is important to recognise that the lower proportion of carryover from 1924 on actually represents significantly higher numbers of individuals making the transition from one CCC to the next than was the case during the first two years of this period. A nucleus of competent and politically loyal officers was thus being built up in the CCC, officers whose terms of service in that body stretched to the end of this period.[140] This continuity was important for the functioning of the CCC, although each year this nucleus was outnumbered by new members, some of whom were also recent party entrants. From as early as 1924, almost a quarter of this, the main disciplinary body of the party, had not been in the party prior to 1917, and by 1927 this proportion had risen to over one-third.

Table 4.12 *CCC membership, 1920–27*[a]

	Total	Carried forward (%)	Carried forward as % of membership	Party entry (%) pre-1917	1917	post-1917
1920	7	42.8	-	100	-	-
1921	10	10.0	30.0	100	-	-
1922	7	71.4	14.3	100	-	-
1923	60	70.0	8.3	91.8	6.6	1.6
1924	151	51.6	27.8	76.2	19.2	4.6
1925	163	53.3	47.8	66.9	18.4	14.7
1927	195	43.1	44.6	63.7	22.5	13.8

[a]The CCCs elected at the X, XI and XII Congresses all had candidate as well as full members, numbering respectively three, two and ten. Slightly different figures will be found in Paul Maupin Cocks, 'Politics of party control: the historical and institutional role of party central organs in the CPSU', unpublished Ph.D thesis, Harvard University (1968), p. 169. The only noteworthy difference occurs in 1923 when his figures for pre-1917 are 96.3% and for 1917 1.7%.

This is a much higher level of representation of post-1917 recruits than in the other elite organs and seems paradoxical given the continuing emphasis throughout this period on the need to have long-time party members in this body.[141] The promotion of newer members can be explained partly in terms of the leaders' naive faith in workers from the bench as a means of ensuring the party's health. Important too were factional considerations. Nevertheless it is important to remember that pre-1917 party members remained a majority throughout, and when those who joined in 1917 are added, this majority is overwhelming. Discipline remained the preserve of the Old Bolsheviks.

Numbers also increased in the CCC Presidium, but on a lesser scale than in its parent body. Carryover figures were higher, reflecting greater stability of membership[142] and the dominating role of the Old Bolsheviks was much less eroded by newcomers to the party. Once again it was the Old Bolsheviks who sat in judgement on the successive opposition groups.

Table 4.13 CCC Presidium membership, 1923–27[a]

	Total	Carried forward (%)	Carried forward as % of membership	Party entry (%) pre-1917	1917
1923	14	78.6	-	100	
1924	21	81.0	38.1	100	
1926	30	66.6	56.6	96.7	3.3
1927	32	62.5	64.5	93.8	6.2

[a] Of the totals, respectively five, six, nine and ten were candidates. The dates of election of the presidia were 26 April 1923, 2 June 1924, 1 January 1926 and 19 December 1927.

Two important structural innovations were made to the CCC during this period. Following the lead given by Lenin before he died, the XII Congress fused the CCC with the People's Commissariat of Workers' and Peasants' Inspection (Rabkrin). The principal means whereby this was to be brought about was an interlocking of membership at the upper levels, which was meant to lead to a coordination of control activity in both party and state spheres. The other development, mentioned above, was the interlocking of the leading control bodies with the leading party organs.[143] Already mentioned have been the joint CC–CCC plena, the provision for control commission representation at CC plena, the joint Politburo–CCC Presidium sessions and the rights of the CCC Presidium to send representatives to Politburo meetings. In addition to these, the XII Congress established the right of the CCC to have three representatives at Orgburo meetings.[144] In this way the control apparatus was assured of institutional representation on the leading deliberative and administrative/personnel organs of the party despite the restrictions upon simultaneous full membership of these different sorts of bodies.

Throughout this period the CCC plenum met more frequently than the joint CC–CCC plenum; while the latter met on twelve occasions, the CCC plenum held nineteen sessions with an approximate, although variable, interval of four months between each.[145] The main focus of concern of the CCC plenum was the efficient functioning of the control apparatus and the health of the general administrative structure, and although broader issues like the state of the economy, pay levels and taxation did occupy some of its time, these were greatly overshadowed by the focus on administrative matters. Only in the plena of January and May 1925 were administrative items less numerous on the CCC's agenda than other subjects. Of course, this administrative focus included a concern with oppositional activity.

Trends begun under Lenin were continued during this period. The focus upon discipline reflected in the X Congress's call for 'strengthening the unity and authority of the party'[146] and the XI Congress's call for the commissions to combat squabbles and groupism[147] was strengthened. It is reflected in the party Rules introduced in 1925. These declared that control commissions were established 'in order to assist the party in the task of strengthening the unity and authority of the VKP(b), of ensuring in all respects the party line in the activities of soviet organs and of developing measures for the strengthening and improvement of the soviet and economic apparatus'.[148] This formulation reflects the transformation of the control commissions from supposedly independent arbiters in party disputes into an organisation with wide-ranging responsibilities in all aspects of discipline in party and state. Its role as a weapon against dissidents is clearly implied in the statement by CCC chief Kuibyshev at the XIII Congress that the commission was 'a tight ring, a united group, which has helped the CC struggle against the disorganisation of the party, for the steadfast line of bolshevism'.[149] More directly it can be seen in the regulations introduced in January 1925[150] which declared that its tasks included 'determined struggle with all kinds of groupings and tendencies towards fractions within the party ... broad, systematic study of unhealthy phenomena in the party in the field of ideology ... and purging the party of ideologically alien, harmful and demoralising elements'. Aspirations for the integrity, coherence and independence of the control apparatus had been displaced by a vision which now saw that apparatus purely in instrumental terms.

The CCC's role as a weapon against opposition is clearly evident in the part played by the joint plenum as a forum for conflict within the elite. It was in this body that much of the open conflict between the various opposition groups and the leading group took place and it was this forum which frequently passed sentence upon individual oppositionists; it was at the joint plenum of October 1926 that Trotsky was excluded from the Politburo, Zinoviev from the Comintern and Kamenev from candidate membership of the Politburo, and that of November 1927 expelled Trotsky and Zinoviev from the party, Rakovsky, Kamenev, Smilga and Evdokimov from the CC and Bakaev, Muralov and others from the CCC. The cluster of joint plena

The divided elite

at the time of the struggle against the United Opposition reflects the role this gathering played.

But the CCC was also made an important element in elite conflict through the wide-ranging powers of investigation and discipline which it possessed in its own right and through the chain of control commissions in the party and Rabkrin in the state machine. The control commissions were the principal purging instruments of the party. The CCC exercised a vigilant eye over the political health of the party and acted swiftly to excise any unhealthy elements.[151] But we should not assume that all of the CCC's actions were prompted by considerations of partisan or factional advantage. Certainly during the early part of this period there seem to have been strenuous efforts on the part of the CCC to justify its actions by reference to the moral and political shortcomings of those it acted against. There seems little reason to doubt the validity of these claims,[152] particularly given the high level of concern in leading party circles about the political health of the party during the NEP period. However, the line between moral and political shortcomings and political opposition was at best vague and indistinct, and as the period wore on, partisan political motives became much more important as central concerns of the CCC than they had been before. This is reflected in the amendment to the party Rules introduced in 1927 which made refusal to answer questions posed by the control commissions grounds for immediate expulsion from the party.[153] Independence from the political leadership and the integrity of the control commission structure was clearly a myth.

One of the main characteristics of the leading political institutions as they developed during this period was thus their inability to generate firmly based, strong institutional norms which could sustain their institutional integrity. The processes to which they were exposed, most importantly growth in size, significant levels of membership turnover, declining regularity of meeting and the impact of elite conflict, all served to undermine the development of those sorts of regularised norms that give a political body its sense of institutional existence and integrity and which could, in turn, structure the activity of individual political actors. The leading political organs were unable to develop this sort of institutional strength, with the result that the political activity of the elite was scarcely restricted by those formal organs within which it was meant to act. As a result, the institutional arena within which political conflict was played out remained weak.

Moreover, the weak institutional arena was peopled overwhelmingly by individuals who were recent arrivals in the elite political organs and, frequently, in the party itself. Most lacked any personal contact with the pre-revolutionary traditions of Bolshevism and their level of political sophistication was quite low. In conjunction with the high levels of membership turnover in the elite political organs, this meant that this group was unlikely to be strongly attached to any particular set of rules or assumptions about how political life at the apex of the system should be structured. This group therefore provided the sort of human environment which would facilitate the dramatic shift in the ground rules governing elite conflict that occurred during the 1920s.

The dynamics of elite politics

The major vehicle for the generation of norms and conventions during this period was the conflict at the top of the political hierarchy. The role of the elite in political conflict during the 1920s was very different from what it had been under Lenin. In the earlier period, individual oligarchs may have taken up an oppositionist stance on particular issues, but the elite was not continually fractured by disunity and division. With the exception of the trade union discussion of 1920–21, the Politburo did not publicly divide over a major issue. The only other occasion on which a member of the leading circle fell into open and bitter dispute with his colleagues was Bukharin on the question of the Brest-Litovsk peace, and this was not particularly longlasting. On all other occasions, leadership of the dissidents fell to second echelon leaders, usually members of the CC, who sought support from lower levels of the party while the upper echelon of the oligarchy, the Politburo members, remained broadly united against such threats from below.

During this second period of development, lower level support for opposition groups remained an important element of party life, but the focus of conflict was now the Politburo. Major opposition figures were members of the Politburo as well as the CC, many of them with long and distinguished careers in the Bolshevik movement behind them and clearly acknowledged as leading members of the new regime. The constancy of elite involvement in political conflict, of such people as Trotsky, Zinoviev, Kamenev, Bukharin, Tomsky and Rykov represents the complete fracturing of the Bolshevik political elite. They were supported by a phalanx of lesser leaders – such people as Ioffe, Lashevich, Sokol'nikov, Zalutsky, and Uglanov – and by sections of the rank-and-file membership. This three-stage structure, stretching from the top to the bottom of the political hierarchy, meant that elite politics was patterned very differently from what it had been in the Lenin period. It was no longer a case of the elite united against opposition from below (even in 1921 they were united against the challenge coming from below in the form of the Democratic Centralist and Workers' Opposition groupings), but of a divided elite seeking to build up permanent support among the lower levels. This represented a new development in the party: the on-going search for support from below by elite political actors.

The practical basis upon which this search proceeded was the personalised political machine. At its crudest, leading political figures sought to construct alliances of prominent regional and central functionaries in order to defeat their opponents at the centre. These functionaries could use their political machines to send delegates to the congress, and if a sufficiently large number of such functionaries could be recruited, a congress majority could result. In this way, the party apparatus was organisationally split by the elite conflict as lower level party leaders took sides in elite disputes. While the Left Communists had had an organisational base of sorts in Moscow and other oppositional groups during the Leninist period had sought to develop their support in various parts of the political structure, the splitting of the party apparatus did not become significant until the mid to late 1920s. The Moscow party organisation had been brought under firm central control in 1924 when Uglanov was moved in to eradicate Trotsky's influence. However, under Uglanov it became a bastion of the Right against Stalin, until it was purged in the autumn of 1928. The Leningrad party-state organisation had been solidly under Zinoviev's control from soon after the capital was shifted to Moscow in 1918. When the break came between the Zinoviev–Kamenev Left Opposition and the Stalin group, an important aspect of it was conflict between the Leningrad and Moscow party organisations, with the latter aided by the central apparatus.[154] Zinoviev's control was sufficient (if, as events were to show, not particularly firmly based) in Leningrad[155] to ensure that at the XIV Congress the Leningrad delegation supported Zinoviev against Stalin, being the only delegation to do so.

A similar process occurred in other institutional structures as their leaders picked one side or the other in the disputes and then sought to use the institution to further the interests of the side they supported. Tomsky's attempt to use the trade union structure to support the Right in the late 1920s is a good instance of this. Thus elite conflict took on an organisational form which embraced the whole structure in a way which was quite different to the structuring of conflict under Lenin. The main building blocks of this structure were the party leaders at the different levels of the political hierarchy; despite the mobilisation of them into the conflict, ordinary rank-and-file party members seem to have understood little of the disputes at the top of the political structure, at least in the middle of the decade.[156]

One of the problems for successive opposition groups was the vulnerability of these personalised machines. The powers over personnel vested in the central party apparatus enabled the centre to reward supporters and punish opponents, the latter by blocking promotion or engineering their removal from office. The collapse of Zinoviev's power base in Leningrad in early 1926 following a month's sustained pressure from the centre[157] illustrates both how unstable the personalised basis of power was in these machines and how weak they were when confronted with concerted pressure from above. No local or regional political machine could withstand the direct pressure of a hostile centre. This meant that not only was the tactic of seeking to build up an organisational power base to oppose the centre likely to fail, but so too was the reliance upon the congress for any semblance of an open hearing. The centre's personnel powers did much to ensure the increasingly monolithic nature of these assemblies,[158] even if alone they could not create a highly disciplined political machine.

The organisational basis upon which an opposition could stand was further weakened by the established convention that conflict should be restricted to the party. In some ways the opposition seemed almost implicitly to accept the reified conception of the party contained in Trotsky's 'my party right or wrong' speech (see below). This is reflected in the oppositionists' refusal to make much use of the resources available to them outside the party. At no stage did Trotsky seek to make use of his position in the armed forces to advance his political cause.[159] Zinoviev did attempt to make some use of the Comintern as a forum for verbal attacks on the leading group and for the generation of international support[160] and Tomsky used the trade union apparatus for similar purposes, but such developments were not accompanied by the intense sort of organisational efforts which might have promised greater success. No opposition group sought to appeal to the masses until the United Opposition did so in November 1927 in a last desperate effort. This sort of action clearly infringed a convention of the party dating back to the pre-revolutionary period, that party debate was conducted within party bounds.[161] Appeals outside the party were by common consent unlawful, as the reaction

The divided elite 175

to the Declaration of the Twenty-two to the Comintern in 1922 demonstrated. Restriction of conflict to the party significantly weakened the opposition because it was in this arena that the leading group's control over personnel manipulation was most marked. Furthermore, it meant that the conflict had to be fought out according to party rules, and the interpretation of these was ultimately in the hands of the recognised party leadership.

One of the rules which was important at this time was the X Congress resolution rejecting fractions in the party. From the beginning of open dispute at the apex of the party, the formal rule regarding fractionalism was brought into play with charges that the opposition had violated its principles by engaging in fractional activity. The joint CC–CCC plenum of October 1923 declared that Trotsky's letter of 8 October 1923 had 'objectively assumed the character of a fractional move, threatening to strike a blow at the unity of the party ... [and] served as a signal for a fractional grouping [the Declaration of the 46]'.[162] Such charges were pressed vigorously against Trotsky and his supporters,[163] and once they had been defeated, the same charge was directed successively against the Left, United and Right Oppositions.[164] Such charges frequently were supported by formal reaffirmations of the anti-fractional decision[165] followed by expulsion from the party. According to Yaroslavsky, in the two years between the XIV and XV congresses, 2,031 members were charged with fractional activity and 970 expelled, a statistic which provoked cries of 'too few, too few. All should be expelled' from the assembled congress delegates.[166] For the first time in post-1917 party history, during this period members of the CC were expelled from the party after first being dropped from that body.

Charges of fractional behaviour were usually denied by the opposition,[167] but in doing so they tended to criticise the way the anti-fractional decision was being interpreted and the effect this was having rather than the principle itself. A good instance of this occurred at the XII congress. Kosior claimed that conditions in the party made it very difficult for any critic of practical or organisational matters. Although the exceptional decision of the X Congress banning groups was necessary at the time, was it still essential? he asked. The only way the collective will of the party could be worked out so that the party could overcome the challenges which confronted it was to enable collective experience to develop. But this could only occur if the exceptional decision of the X Congress was not interpreted such that the collective opinion of three to six people came to be seen as a fraction.[168] Lutovinov picked up this line of argument, declaring that groups with platforms existed in the underground, but that their covert existence was a direct result of the unhealthy effect of the ban on fractions.[169] Such arguments may have made good debating points, but in an important sense they were self-defeating. They left their proponents open to the charge of wishing to allow the free formation of fractions in the party, a charge which the main opposition speakers were not able effectively to counter.[170] Indeed, some oppositionists seemed to call for precisely this: at the XIV Congress Zinoviev, while affirming the anti-fractional rule, openly called for the drawing back into party work of all former groups.[171] This view implicitly called into question the continued utility of the ban on fractions.

The ban on fractions remained a formal party rule throughout this period. However, with no independent arbiter to decide when it had been breached, in practice it constituted a major weapon in the hands of the leading group around Stalin. In structural terms, there was no difference between the oppositions' attempts to construct alliances spanning different levels of the party hierarchy and the process of moulding a political machine of the type in which Stalin was engaged. However, his capacity to have the numbers in party fora enabled Stalin and his supporters to wrap themselves in the mantle of formal party leadership and to thereby place their opponents in the position of opposing and criticising that leadership from a minority perspective. Under such circumstances it was impossible for these groups to avoid the appearance of fractionalism. Furthermore, their complaints about the actions of the leadership rang somewhat hollow in the light of their own involvement in similar sorts of overkill measures against previous opposition groups. The taunt directed against Zinoviev at the XIV Congress that: 'When there is a majority for Zinoviev, he is for iron discipline. When he has no majority ... he is against it'[172] was apt.

The continued relevance of the anti-fractional decision was buttressed by a constant emphasis upon the need for discipline. Indeed, the course of factional conflict in the elite was the main motor force for the strengthening of the disciplinary ethos within the party. The party was portrayed as a solid phalanx of committed members, albeit with some unhealthy elements, surrounded by a multitude of dangers which the party could hope to meet successfully only by maintaining the strictest Bolshevik discipline within its ranks. An instance of the type of ethos which was built up at this time comes from a resolution of the XV Conference in November 1926:

The party proceeds from the fact that 'who weakens, however so little, the iron discipline of the party of the proletariat (especially during its dictatorship) in fact helps the bourgeoisie against the proletariat' (Lenin), that intra-party democracy is essential not for weakening and breaking down proletarian discipline in the party, but for strengthening and consolidating it, that without iron discipline in the party, without a firm regime in the party which is strengthened by the sympathy and support of the proletarian millions, the dictatorship of the proletariat is impossible.[173]

This statement clearly illustrates two elements of the internal milieu within which intra-party conflict had to take place. The first is the subordination of democracy in the party to considerations of unity and discipline; democracy was useful insofar as it contributed to Bolshevik discipline. Second is the attribution to internal party opponents of an 'objective class position'. Opponents of official policy as espoused by the leading group were declared to be objectively aiding those hostile class forces which sought the overthrow of the Bolsheviks. The bourgeoisie, the Kadets, the Mensheviks, the SRs were all suggested as recipients of assistance stemming from the oppositional activity of various groups in the party. To quote Zinoviev at the XII Congress: 'Every criticism of the party line, even so-called "Left" criticism, is henceforth objectively Menshevik criticism.'[174] When cast in these terms and given the prevailing perception of a threatening environment and the dangers of infection from it, the actions of the opposition, which in many respects were within the established rules and traditions of the party, took on a malignant appearance. This was a development which the opposition was unable to combat in any effective fashion.

An important aspect of this was the erosion of both the principle and the practice of freedom of discussion inside the party. The party tradition as it was perceived during the early part of this period is well summarised by a resolution from the XIII Conference in January 1924 which defined the strengthening of workers' democracy in terms of 'the freedom of open discussion by all members of the party of the most important questions of party life, freedom of discussion by them, and also the election of leading officials and collegia from the bottom to the top. However it does not at all assume the freedom of fractional groupings.'[175] The resolution went on to warn party leaders not to consider all criticism as evidence of fractional behaviour. This theme remained prominent with the unrolling of the intra-party democracy and self-criticism campaigns in the second half of the decade discussed above. Party members were called upon to subject deficiencies in the party to businesslike and rigorous criticism, a process which was intrinsic to intra-party democracy. But such criticism was not to lead to the formation of groups or fractions.[176] Freedom of discussion and criticism were well embedded in party lore.

However, as the period wore on the position of freedom of discussion was seriously eroded, even in the heavily restricted form that linked it with avoiding the dangers of fractionalism. The phrase itself even ceased to appear in formal party resolutions. At the XII Congress Kamenev had declared that 'we must hold the development of our own intra-party discussion within definite limits' while Stalin argued that the size of the party made the discussion of issues in all party fora impossible.[177] During the debate over Trotsky's *Lessons of October* in late 1924, Safarov argued that 'the party cannot live under the Damoclean sword of endless discussions' while Kviring wrote an article entitled 'The party does not want endless discussions.'[178] These sentiments had also been evident at the XIII Conference. They were reflected in the decisions to downgrade the current discussion by moving it from the pages of *Pravda* into a separate 'Discussion Sheet',[179] and to take 'decisive measures' against 'the spreading of unverified rumours and documents forbidden for circulation and analogous techniques, which are the favourite methods of unprincipled groups, infected with petty bourgeois attitudes'.[180] The threat of decisive measures against the spreading of rumours was a clear blow against freedom of discussion in the party. The conference also decided to publish the secret clause of the X Congress 'On Party Unity' resolution which gave power over discipline for fractionalism to the CC. This change in mood on this question reinforces the view that the self-criticism campaign in the second half of the decade was more linked to attempts at central control of lower level leaders than it was a real attempt to boost discussion in principle.

The shift in the party attitude toward a narrower conception of the nature of discussion is perhaps best shown in the place this had in conceptions of intra-party democracy. In the XIV congress resolution on the CC's report, the only mention of discussion in the section dealing with intra-party democracy concerns the need to have increased involvement by the party masses in the discussion and resolution of major issues of party policy.[181] This sort of formulation was a long way removed from a principle of freedom of discussion because it failed to specify the type of involvement or the conditions under which it could take place. Formal restrictions on party-wide discussion were introduced at the XV Conference in October–November 1926. After affirming that freedom of discussion was necessary but that the party was not a debating club, the conference resolution listed three conditions, of which one had to be met, before an all-union discussion could be launched: recognition of the need for such a discussion by 'several local party organs' at the provincial or regional level, the absence of a firm majority in the CC on a vital policy issue, or recognition of the need for an open debate on the part of the CC even though a majority existed on the issue within that organ.[182] The effect of this decision was to vest in the CC the power to decide whether a free, party-wide debate was necessary since it was to this body that the 'several local party organs' had to appeal. The change in mood in the party is clearly reflected in the statements in early 1929 that the party rejected any notion of 'freedom' for the Right to defend its anti-Leninist political line and that Bukharin's article 'Notes of an Economist' created 'the danger of discussion in the party'.[183]

Thus virtually from the outset, freedom of discussion was so circumscribed as to be, in practice, little more than an unrealistic principle. It was not to contribute to the formation of fractions, but since these were seen largely in terms of any group holding contrary views to the leadership, the mere expression of opinion could be termed evidence of fractionalism. It is this which provided the impetus for the outlawing of dissent and disagreement, and with them the right to oppose. Alongside the development in the formal rules noted above, there was a similar shift in the operating conventions of the party.

This shift has already been referred to in terms of the heckling and interruption opposition speakers had to endure in leading party fora. Their participation in the life of such meetings was further constrained by under-representation due to structured delegate selection (the XV Congress was the last at which the opposition was allowed to present candidates for the election of delegates), the obvious bias of session chairmen,[184] the constriction of pre-congress debate,[185] the denial of access to printing facilities, the partial editing of some of their speeches and tracts, and their exclusion from the specialised bodies established to conduct some of the work of the congress itself. There was also significant discrimination against them in terms of access to the party press, and therefore in their capacity to reach the party rank-and-file with their message. The use of *Pravda* was particularly clear in this respect. During the public debate at the end of 1923, opposition views appeared in the press regularly until the middle of December, after which they rarely appeared and, when they did, they were always overwhelmed by articles expressing the opposite point of view.[186] By the end of the following year as the denunciation of Trotsky reached a crescendo, no voice of opposition appeared in the pages of the press. While the views of later opposition groups did gain an airing in *Pravda*, it is clear that these groups did not enjoy the sort of access to the pages of the party's leading daily which the group around Stalin enjoyed.[187] The purpose of *Pravda* was clearly stated at the XIII Conference: it was to lead a campaign against all deviations from the bases of Bolshevism.[188] The role of the press was confirmed with the establishment of *Bol'shevik* in the same year specifically to fight against deviations.[189]

The difficulties the opposition faced as a result of the constriction of the formal rights and practices of free discussion were compounded by the generation of a rigid orthodoxy in the party. This focused on the figure of Lenin and involved the generation of a myth surrounding the dead leader which transformed him into the equivalent of a secular saint and his words into formally binding instructions for future action. Lenin became a symbol and his words were turned into standardised formulae; 'Leninism' was born as an ideology during this period.

The sanctification of Lenin had begun even before he died. At the opening of the XII Congress, which Lenin was unable to attend because of his illness, Kamenev declared: 'we know only one antidote for any crisis, for any incorrect decision: this is the teaching of Vladimir Il'ich, and to this antidote the party will constantly turn in all the difficult moments, in the days of revolutionary humdrum, equally also in the days of revolutionary holidays'.[190] Zinoviev was even more lyrical:

> When we travelled to these congresses, our aim first of all was to hear this speech, since we knew in advance that in it we should find not only the considered experience of the time through which we had lived, but firm directions for the future. You remember with what thirst we always listened to this speech – a thirst like the thirst of a man who, on a sultry summer day, fell upon a clear spring to drink his fill.[191]

Again according to Kamenev: 'With his teaching we checked each time we were faced with this or that problem, this or that difficult question. Mentally each of us asked himself: and how would Vladimir Il'ich have answered this?'[192] Lenin and his teachings were clearly presented as the main inspiration and guide to the future.

This position was firmly established by the XIII Congress, the first after Lenin's death. The proceedings of the congress were studded with hortatory declarations designed to affirm continued adherence to Lenin and his ideas: 'Our banner will be Lenin, our programme will be Leninism . . . Under the banner of *Lenin*, with the teaching of *Lenin* in our hands, we will go along that path which he showed us', '*Not simply unity is necessary for us, but unity based on Leninism*', and 'the party now unites under the banner of Lenin, unites around Leninism'[193] are typical of the sentiments expressed at the congress. Furthermore, speakers referred to Lenin to support their arguments, often prefacing their comments with statements like 'according to the thought of comrade Lenin' or by directly citing some of Lenin's words.[194] This sort of treatment provided the precedent and the model for party gatherings later in the decade.

The development of the Lenin cult also took on a more symbolic – and public – aspect. At the time of his death the surviving leaders decided on a series of measures to commemorate his memory: 21 January (the day he died) was declared a day of national mourning, Petrograd was renamed Leningrad, monuments were to be erected to him in all the major cities in the country, a collected edition of all of his works was to be published and, most spectacularly of all, his embalmed body was to be placed in a mausoleum built especially for this purpose on Red Square. Ritualistic forms of veneration were introduced into political life. The first large-scale instance was the march of young pioneers to the mausoleum at the opening of the XIII Congress,[195] a ceremony in which they swore fidelity to Lenin and his cause. The symbolic figure of Lenin became the most important element in the growing cultism of the party and the developing myth of the October Revolution.[196]

The development of the cult of Lenin had important implications for intra-party life. Lenin and his thought were turned into the touchstones of orthodoxy and legitimacy in the party; the epithet 'Leninist' became the highest accolade and 'anti-Leninist' the most heinous crime. This is reflected in the form in which factional debate was conducted during the post-Lenin years. All of the protagonists sought to clothe their positions and views in Lenin's authority, continually citing Lenin's words to support their own policy preferences. The search for appropriate quotations became a major component of political needs as individual leaders sought their authority from the master's words. While for some Lenin's words (or at least a selective choice of them) did have some normative and programmatic significance, with Bukharin and his support for NEP as a case in point, for many his words were seen in a purely instrumental light. Stalin's reliance on the misquotation of a single passage from Lenin to justify his policy of socialism in one country[197] is a good example of this. In this way, Lenin's words became a weapon in the intra-elite struggle as the respective protagonists exchanged Leninist quotations in an attempt to damage their opponents and shore up their own positions.

The importance attached to Lenin's writings was reflected in the scramble by the major figures to establish themselves as the heir to those writings and the contemporary interpreter of the master's words. Both Stalin and Zinoviev produced major books which purported to present and expound Lenin's ideas,[198] while all leaders sought through publications and speeches to establish their credentials as the true followers of Lenin.[199] Attempts were also made by different leaders to project an image of themselves as long-time associates of Lenin, people whose own revolutionary careers were characterised by prolonged contact with and support for the dead leader. As early as a week after Lenin's death, Stalin effectively pre-dated his personal association with Lenin.[200] The parvenu among the leaders, Trotsky, sought to convey his familiarity with Lenin through the publication of two books, *On Lenin* (June 1924) and *Lessons of October* (October 1924), an aim which misfired.[201] Zinoviev also engaged in image manipulation. All thereby tried to obscure the differences they had had with Lenin,[202] appearing as the loyal associates whose views always coincided with those of the dead leader. What this amounted to was an attempt by the various protagonists to reinterpret Bolshevik history in a way which suited their immediate political ends.

A particularly clear instance of this was the debate surrounding the appearance of Trotsky's *Lessons of October*. The account of the revolution contained in this book was substantially accurate, but the tone of it did not fit in with the burgeoning hagiographical ethos characteristic of the treatment of Lenin at this time. Nor was the interpretation the book offered of much comfort to Trotsky's opponents. As a result, when they began to criticise the book, one strand of that criticism was to dispute the accuracy of his interpretation and, in so doing, to offer an alternative view. The history of the revolution, and indeed of Bolshevism itself, thus became a weapon in the elite conflict as individuals sought to use it to score political points against their opponents. In general, this fed into the emerging myth of the October Revolution, a myth whose constituent elements were subject to

The divided elite

change in accord with contemporary political circumstances but which throughout this period was characterised by the dominating figure of Lenin.

The emergence of party history and of the relationship with Lenin as a battleground in the elite conflict is evident in the attempts by various principals in the disputes to use the figure and words of Lenin to attack their opponents. Previous personal disputes were particularly useful in this regard. This began before Lenin had died. In December 1923 Trotsky and his associates were accused of deviations from Leninism, a charge reinforced by emphasis upon Trotsky's differences with Lenin during the Brest-Litovsk and trade union controversies.[203] These differences, plus Trotsky's bitter disputes with Lenin prior to 1917, remained central elements of the attack upon Trotsky throughout 1924 and into the period of the United Opposition. Lenin's words were quoted against Trotsky, and vice versa, as the choice was presented in stark form: 'Trotskyism or Leninism?'[204] Similarly, the differences between Lenin on the one hand and Zinoviev and Kamenev on the other were highlighted. Their 'strike-breaking' activity in 1917 over the decision to seize power and on the coalition question frequently were raised and declared to be 'not accidental'.[205] The members of the Right Opposition, and in particular Bukharin, were also subjected to this form of attack in an attempt to cast doubt on their Leninist credentials. Attempts were also made to attack Stalin on this basis, but his low profile throughout much of the party's history left much more limited scope for this than for his more prominent opponents, with the result that such attacks were not damaging to him.

The development of the cult of Lenin thus constituted a context and a currency for the playing out of elite conflict. All parties to these disputes professed adherence to Lenin and Leninism. Given the growth of the cult, none could afford not to declare such allegiance. But ultimately this worked to the detriment of the opposition groups. The leading figures in the successive opposition groups had all been involved in much more public and significant disputes with Lenin in the past than had Stalin and were therefore more vulnerable to the charge of anti-Leninism. Furthermore, the controlling position the group around Stalin was able to establish both in formal party organisations and in the press organs enabled their version of events to be projected much more easily than those of their opponents. The constant reiteration of the anti-Leninist label had its effect, destroying the principle that opposition groups had a right to a fair hearing; if they were anti-Leninist, they were opposed to the whole course of the party and therefore did not deserve to be heard. For the vast mass of the party who were new entrants to its ranks and who had little ideological training or understanding, the growth of the symbol of Lenin as the source of orthodoxy was crucial because it provided them with a criterion by which to judge the competing groups. It was the Stalin group which was best able to present itself in such a way as to meet this criterion.[206]

The rise of a Leninist orthodoxy had significant effects on the nature of ideology in the system. During the Leninist period, ideology had been a flexible body of ideas which provided both a form of intellectual legitimation for the regime and a source of broad principles of policy. But the policy direction offered by the ideology was neither clear cut nor monist; a variety of policies could be extracted from the ideological principles, with a number of policies being able to claim ideological rectitude. However, during the 1920s this situation changed.[207] The ideology became more rigidified and standardised, its intellectual content and policy-guidance function transformed into sets of formulae which could be used for *post hoc* rationalisation and justification of action. The major impetus for this development came from elite conflict.

Although the disputes of the 1920s were conducted in part in terms of loyalty to Leninism, questions of policy did constitute an important component of elite conflict. The major policy problems which emerged during this period demanded a response from the factional protagonists. They were struggling over positions of leadership and such positions naturally involved a concern with policy issues. Consequently groups and individuals could not refuse to take a stance on these issues without losing any leadership credibility they possessed. Furthermore, the tradition of political conflict within Bolshevism was one which focused upon conflict over policy issues with positions being expressed primarily in ideological terms. Failure to be involved in such conflict effectively meant an opting out of this tradition. Policy issues were thus a major focus of elite attention and a principal mode of discourse through which conflict could be articulated.

At different times the approach to ideological tenets and policy issues adopted by virtually all protagonists was instrumental in nature. None was averse to taking up a policy position with an eye to the effects this would have in the on-going elite manoeuvring at the top. Examples of this are numerous, but a couple will suffice to convey a sense of the political implications of policy conflict. Stalin first enunciated his doctrine of socialism in one country in late 1924. This came under almost immediate attack from Zinoviev and Kamenev, although this was hushed up, while Trotsky, who has been recognised as the leading apostle of world revolution, held his fire until late 1926.[208] The opposition of Zinoviev and Kamenev was not made public in an endeavour to maintain the united front of the troika against Trotsky. Trotsky's delay in responding was probably due to his belief that Zinoviev and Kamenev, rather than Stalin, constituted the main enemy and it was only when he entered an alliance with these two against Stalin that his criticisms were forthcoming.

To take another case, during 1924 Zinoviev had taken the lead in fostering a policy of concessions to the peasants, reflected in his sponsoring of the 'face to the countryside' campaign. In 1925 the leadership adopted a series of measures involving the sorts of concessions to the peasants which had been at the heart of this campaign. But these measures were greeted with scathing criticism of the leadership's 'pro-peasant line' by Zinoviev and Kamenev. The motivation behind this was an attempt to strike at Stalin, who had been moving against these two since the demise of Trotsky, rather than a major disagreement with this policy. Furthermore, the defeat of Zinoviev and Kamenev made it much easier for the leadership to adopt a more anti-kulak policy in 1926 than would otherwise have been the case. And finally, Stalin stuck to his disastrous China policy for so long in part because to change it would have meant acknowledging the accuracy of his opponents' criticisms. It is clear, then, that on some occasions the timing and content of policy positions owed much to factional considerations, and policy was seen as a political weapon.

This does not mean, however, that policy positions were adopted purely for factional reasons. There appears no reason to doubt the genuineness of Trotsky's commitment to the doctrine of world revolution (even if he found it expedient sometimes not to press the point), of Bukharin's continued support for NEP, or of Stalin's socialism in one country. However, adherence to such generalised policy positions must be seen within the context of the changing economic situation, particularly the size of the grain harvest and marketing, the extent of the restoration of pre-war industrial capacity and the consequent need for new investment in industry, and shifting inflation levels. With all of these factors fluid, flexibility among policy-makers was essential and shifts in the policy positions and priorities of groups and individuals were not to be unexpected. The erosion of the leadership consensus over NEP was a continuing development which forced all political actors constantly to review their policy commitments. Within this context, charges that Stalin merely adopted the policies of defeated opponents, expediently shifting from policy to policy as it suited his interests while secretly being committed to the sorts of economic policies adopted at the end of the decade, need to be treated with caution. Certainly the defeat of opposition groups may have facilitated a policy change, as in the case of peasant policy noted above and the introduction of full scale collectivisation following the defeat of the Right. But often there were also economic reasons which compelled a reconsideration of policy direction. Stalin's rejection of the moderate line in agriculture, a rejection evident at least as early as January 1928,[209] was one possible reaction to the grain procurement problems of 1927–28. Policy was not merely the plaything of factional considerations.

As the course of factional dispute continued, the boundaries of acceptable debate within the elite narrowed. The processes of personal vilification, of the rejection of individual policy positions and of the establishment of a conception of the 'Leninist line' all helped to narrow the range of alternative policy positions which were acceptable within the elite. This was the policy side of the emergence of a sense of orthodoxy based upon the figure of Lenin. When the policy debate disappeared behind closed doors in the spring of 1929, the ground which that debate could traverse was defined in terms of the accepted orthodoxy, Leninism. The problem was that the definition of Leninism was, in turn, dictated by the political needs and outlook of the leading group around Stalin.

The erosion of the principle of free discussion in the party and the growth of the Leninist orthodoxy ultimately was inimical to the continued right of an opposition to play a legitimate part in party life. At the outset of the period, the existence of such a right was problematic. Alongside the tradition of open discussion within the party and the history of individuals organising in order to oppose a particular leadership line was the anti-opposition ethos and the anti-fractional decision of the X Congress. This was soon reinforced by the measures against freedom of discussion taken at the XIII Conference and discussed above. But the most important blow to the rights of an opposition was the growth in the party of a sentiment denying the validity of a right to hold different opinions. This was clearly linked to the emergence of the sense of orthodoxy.

A significant step towards this was taken at the XIII Congress where, in his keynote address Zinoviev declared: 'The most sensible step, and most worthy of a bolshevik, which the opposition could take is what a bolshevik does when he happens to make some mistake or other – to come before the party or the tribune of the party congress and say: "I was mistaken, the party was correct"'[210] Zinoviev's statement amounted to a demand that those who differed from the party line should not simply submit to that line, which was the established position in the party, but should renounce their previous views. In essence, Trotsky supported this position, even though Zinoviev's comments had been directed at him. As Trotsky said:

> Comrades, none of us wishes to be nor can be right against our party. In the last analysis the party is always right, because the party is the single historical instrument that the proletariat possesses for the fulfilment of its basic tasks ... I know that it is impossible to be right against the party. It is possible to be right only with the party and through the party, because history has created no other means for the realisation of what is right. The English have an historical proverb: my country right or wrong. With much greater historical right we can say: right or wrong in particular, specific, concrete questions at particular times, but this is my party.[211]

This exchange reflected the principle that those who were out of step with the party had to come around formally to accept the official view. But acceptance of the official line did not, as before, involve merely a refusal to propagate dissident views. It also involved the renunciation of those views and adoption of the official line as one's own. This shift in the party's law is reflected in the different official positions enunciated in mid-1926 and the end of 1927. The CC–CCC joint plenum of July 1926 declared that it was the 'indisputable right' of a party member to uphold his views as long as these were not directed against decisions adopted by the party, and referred to the right in the party Rules for individuals openly and honestly to express their views in party organs.[212] The XV Congress in December 1927 openly rejected the view that an opposition could continue to hold their views but not propagate them while remaining in the party, and called for the complete ideological disarmament of those groups through the renunciation of their heterodox opinions.[213] Those who held views deemed to be anti-Leninist could not be allowed to remain in the party.[214]

The practical manifestation of this shift in the ground rules for elite conflict was the process of public recantation that successive groups of oppositionists were forced to undergo.[215] It was also reflected in various official statements, such as that of March 1926 when it was declared that the appointment of anyone who had committed an error could occur 'only when the comrade recognises his error'.[216] If during the Leninist period discipline had been defined in terms of obedience to higher decisions and the refusal to propagate dissident views, during this period it came to mean not challenging the leadership and renouncing differing opinions.

The emphasis upon the inadmissability of contrary opinion constituted a broadening of the prevailing notion of the meaning of opposition in the party. Under the terms of the anti-fractional decision of 1921, groups had both an organisational and an intellectual aspect: they not only had their own discipline, but they also had a platform of their own.[217] These elements remained significant for the notion of opposition throughout this period; for Stalin at the XV Congress, opposition was a group with its own ideology, programme, tactics and organisational principles.[218] But opposition was not tied exclusively to fractionalism and the existence of a clearly formulated programme which that implied. During this period, the forms which opposition could take were broadened. Although the concept of a 'deviation' had existed in party lore under Lenin, during this period it became much more prominent and, particularly towards the end of the period, was much more openly contrasted with the party 'line'.[219] A deviation did not necessarily have either a platform or an organisational structure. It was something that was unformed but was the beginning of an error which, unless checked, could have serious consequences.[220] Furthermore, in late-1928 the notion of a deviation was joined by a new form of opposition, the conciliatory tendency toward a deviation. This amorphous concept seemed to mean a sympathy for the positions of a deviation.[221] These sorts of formulations, which could approach real meaning only with the development of Leninism as an orthodoxy and the increased emphasis on the party line, were so vague as to be able to mean whatever the leaders wished them to mean. They therefore constituted a perfect lever for damning heterodox opinion, even when it was not organised, with the label of opposition.

This broadening of the notion of opposition was reinforced by the general atmosphere that emerged toward the end of this decade. Fears about petty bourgeois infection had been around throughout the entire period, but they became stronger as the decade approached its end. Continuing difficulties with grain supply were important in this. So too was the Shakhty affair and the subsequent warnings about saboteurs.[222] This had a number of linked ramifications. The charges laid against the Shakhty engineers brought together the fears of the effect of the petty bourgeois environment within which the system was being built and the international environment of hostility, fuelled most recently by the war scare of 1927. The Shakhty affair purported to demonstrate the existence, within significant parts of the system, of hidden enemies who, although they had worked for the building of Soviet power, ultimately aimed at undermining and toppling it. Protestations and past demonstrations of loyalty merely camouflaged the hostility of the aims they sought. What appeared to be slips and accidents could therefore be much more malign, as reflected in the economic sphere in charges of 'wrecking'.[223] Ideologically this was sustained by the Stalinist innovation that the closer socialism approached, the more bitter class struggle became.[224] Under such circumstances what was required was total loyalty and commitment; the slightest deviation was considered damning for the individual concerned and dangerous for the party as a whole.

One important effect of this heightened concentration on opposition and the demands for greater loyalty was the growth of informing in the party. If party members were aware of dissident activity by other members, they were to report this to the appropriate authorities. As early as autumn 1923 a sub-committee of the Politburo established to deal with internal party matters proposed that party members should be obliged to provide the GPU with any information they had on the membership of fractional groups.[225] According to Bakaev (a Zinoviev supporter) at the XIV Congress, informing 'is taking such forms and such a character that friend cannot tell friend his sincere thought' while in Gusev's view 'every member of the party should inform. If we suffer from anything, it is not from too much informing, but from too little'.[226] Party members who refused to assist party bodies in the conduct of an investigation by failing to report dissident activity or to identify those engaged in it were to be expelled from the party.[227] The amendment to the party Rules in 1927 providing for the expulsion of anyone who did not answer correctly the questions of the control commissions was clearly part of this emphasis upon mobilising all members into this struggle against dissidence. This new ethos was a clear reflection of the demand for total loyalty the party made upon its members, a loyalty which transcended the more intimate commitments of inter-personal relations.

Another important innovation in elite conflict during this period was the use of the security organs against party members. The first instance of the use of the GPU (from 1924 OGPU) against a leading party member appears to have been in spring 1923 when Sultan Galiev was arrested because of his nationalist views.[228] By 1924 it was charged that the police were regularly keeping a watchful eye over the opposition,[229] while by 1927 the OGPU was engaged in active counter-measures including surveillance, harassment and the arrest of opposition figures.[230] The growing police role was played in collaboration with the control commissions, a link formally acknowledged as early as 1923.[231] But the tradition of party independence from the judicial arm of the state[232] had not yet eroded sufficiently to make the party ranks subject to the sort of independent police action that was to become common in a later period; the party remained an impermeable institution. The OGPU usually could not act against a party member until he had been expelled or, at a minimum, had become an outcast in the party.[233] Even at the end of this period Politburo authorisation was necessary before a senior party member could be arrested.[234] A semblance of justification for OGPU involvement appeared with the labelling of Trotskyism a crime against the state rather than a political error in 1929;[235] this transformed political opposition into a state crime.

The increased levels of elite conflict and the effective proscription of dissidence brought heightened penalties for those who engaged in such activity. As indicated above, the centre's powers over personnel disposition were used to break up nests of opposition support. These were supplemented by the purge, with the expulsion of dissidents becoming a common feature of party life by the end of the decade. By April 1929 opposition had become one of the formal grounds for expulsion.[236] Autumn 1927 and the defeat of the United Opposition seems to have been the turning point in this, and although accurate figures on the number expelled for dissident activity are not available, it was clearly much more extensive than it had been earlier. Furthermore, it was now applied not merely to the followers of opposition leaders, but to the leaders themselves. Even Politburo members Trotsky, Zinoviev and Kamenev suffered the ultimate indignity; following their dismissal from leading party organs, they were expelled from the party.[237] Demotion both within the party and within other institutions was a frequent reaction to dissident associations and activity, while less well-known oppositionist figures could experience arrest and internal exile by the police. The posting of oppositionists abroad was another way of dealing with opposition figures: Rakovsky, Piatakov, Preobrazhensky, Kosior, Kamenev and Antonov-Ovseenko all suffered this fate, thereby joining Krestinsky who had been made ambassador to Germany in 1921. It was in late 1929 that blood was first spilled in intra-party affairs and a party member was openly arrested for a party offence when Yakov Bliumkin was accused of treasonable contact with Trotsky and was shot without trial on the authorisation of the OGPU collegium.[238] It is clear, then, that during this period the rules for handling opposition changed with penalties becoming more severe and wider ranging. But throughout the period the party retained jurisdiction over its members; police organs could not act without party sanction.

The growth of a sense of orthodoxy had implications for the nature of leadership. The collective principle continued to be affirmed throughout this period. Speeches at the XII Congress, reflecting on the fate of the party in Lenin's absence, firmly declared that only the collective experience of the party could compensate for his loss, and that: 'The party cannot be without vozhds', that leading group which alone could replace Lenin.[239] As time passed, this question was increasingly raised in a combative context in which the opposition criticised the growing consolidation of power by Stalin and the group around him, while his supporters scoffed at such charges and reaffirmed the continuing validity of the collective principle. At the conference of the Moscow provincial party organisation in early 1925, Bukharin declared: 'We can at present have only a *collective* authority. We have no man who could say: I am without sin and can interpret Lenin's teaching absolutely to a full 100 per cent. Everyone tries, but he who puts up a claim to 100 per cent attributes too large a role to his own person.'[240] At the same conference Kuibyshev echoed Bukharin's point and added: 'In the place of persons stands the collectivity. The supreme interpreter of the Leninist line can only be the central committee and the party congress.'[241] At the XIV Congress Kamenev attacked the concentration of power at the centre, including in his attack the statement: 'We are against the theory of a vozhd'; we are against making a vozhd'.'[242] He was supported by Tomsky's declaration that 'a system of individual leaders cannot exist, and will not, no will not'.[243] But it was Stalin who most strongly affirmed the collective principle: 'To lead the party otherwise than collectively is impossible. It is silly to dream of this after Il'ich, silly to talk of this.'[244] The emphasis upon collectivism was also embedded in the formal decision-making process. Formally, all decisions were still made and issued by and in the name of the party's collective organs; they did not appear as the initiative of individual party leaders but of the party's collective decision-making bodies.

However, within the context of the growth of the immodest laudation of individual party leaders,[245] a new theme emerged which tentatively promoted the possibility of a single, pre-eminent leader. Such a suggestion occurred as early as the XIV Congress, the same congress that witnessed the affirmations of collective leadership cited above. Voroshilov sought to explain Stalin's authority in leading circles in the following terms:

> Comrades, all this happens for a very simple reason. Comrade Stalin is evidently destined by nature or by fate to formulate propositions rather more successfully than any other member of the Politburo. Comrade Stalin is, I affirm, the leading member of the Politburo, without, however, ever claiming priority; he takes the most active part in the settlement of questions; his proposals are carried more often than anyone's. And these proposals are carried unanimously.[246]

At the XV Congress Andreev sought to root a leader's authority in his willingness to go along with the party and his capacity to lead the party along the correct path.[247] Such suggestions of the possibility of personal primacy within the collective advanced no further than this during this period. They were, however, taken up and dramatically extended at the opening of the following period.

The structure of the oligarchy during the first period of Bolshevik rule had been dominated by the personal primacy of Lenin. His unique position in the history of the movement enabled him to play a dominating role which none of his successors could replicate. He clearly stood apart from his colleagues in the leadership. No similar figure existed during this period, with the result that the structure of the leadership oligarchy was completely different. There were clearly two levels within the oligarchy, with the personnel at each level not remaining static. At the higher level were those more prominent leaders whose personal role in party history gave them a status that was reinforced by an important institutional position; Stalin, Zinoviev, Kamenev, Bukharin and Trotsky were among this group, although the last four departed from it during this period. Indeed, it was the troika of Zinoviev, Kamenev and Stalin which supplanted Lenin as the dominant force in daily decision-making in the immediate aftermath of Lenin's removal from the scene. At the lower level were secondary leaders who may have occupied positions of institutional importance but who lacked the personal prestige of the leaders of the highest rank.

As well as this horizontal division, the oligarchy was also split vertically by the development of those fractional groups which were

The divided elite

the essence of elite conflict and the building blocks of the type of coalition government which dominated in the Politburo during this decade. Such groups, which usually had no formal structure of their own, provided through the dynamics of their interaction the main impetus for the course of elite politics. But those dynamics were forced to take place in an arena largely unstructured by rules which were independent and considered binding by the protagonists. Certainly some principles were accepted by all; notions of cabinet responsibility in the Politburo and an opposition to the principle of fractionalism were widely accepted, although their application in particular cases was subject to the arbitrariness of factional considerations. Also accepted was the principle of collective leadership; despite factional caucusing beforehand, until the end of the decade decisions were made and announced in collective organs. However, this rule was broken with Stalin's decision to push through his policy of forced grain procurement in 1928.

Prior to January 1928 Stalin had been a model of caution, carefully preparing his ground before he acted and preferring to take a low profile in open leadership initiatives. He appeared as the epitome of collective leadership. However, in January 1928 he travelled to Siberia in an attempt to speed up the process of grain procurement. Other members of the leadership went to other parts of the country, but whereas people like Frumkin in the Southern Urals and Uglanov in the Lower Volga area were counselling local party leaders to use conciliation and to eschew undue pressure in their dealings with peasant producers, Stalin fostered the use of coercion against these people.[248] While the Politburo as a whole had accepted the need to speed up procurement, there was no consensus favouring the use of force and there was some resentment at the way in which Stalin had abandoned the consensus-building procedures which had been part of collective leadership in the immediate past. This resentment was spearheaded by the (already declining) Right, and its limits were ably demonstrated by the affair of the Frumkin letter. In mid-1928 Finance Minister Frumkin wrote a letter critical of official policy. The Politburo decided to handle this matter by circulating that letter, along with a formal reply by the Politburo, to the CC. However Stalin pre-empted this decision by writing a personal reply (in which Frumkin was effectively a stalking horse for Bukharin), an action which stimulated criticism from the Right for overriding a Politburo decision. But the weakness of their position is reflected in the fact that the Politburo's response to Stalin's action was merely to declare that his reply to

Frumkin was incomplete.[249] Thus on two important occasions in 1928, Stalin had breached the bounds of the collective and suffered no penalty.

But what is interesting about these events is that Stalin could act against the Politburo's wishes only by acting outside its bounds and presenting it with a *fait accompli*. When he sought to act within the Politburo, he was still unable to get his way on all issues. This is most clearly reflected in the rebuff he seems to have received at the 9 February 1929 Politburo session, when he sought to obtain the expulsion of those Right Opposition members from the Politburo.[250] Stalin was not yet the all-powerful leader.

However, with the defeat of the Right in April 1929, the General Secretary was less constrained by considerations of leadership collectivity. Symbolically his position was being strengthened by the build-up to the Stalin cult (which was to burst onto the scene in December 1929) and by the principle of personalised leadership of which it was an affirmation. This was symbolised by the stance taken by former oppositionist Piatakov in *Pravda* when he declared 'that one cannot be for the Party and *against* the present leadership, and that one cannot be for the Central Committee *and* against Stalin'.[251] Furthermore, he was now less reluctant to take direct action to expand and mould the elite consensus, as he did by unilaterally calling for the 'liquidation of the kulaks as a class' before the commission established to deal with 'the kulak problem' could finish its task.[252] This does not mean that Stalin could ignore his leadership colleagues; he still had to have their support and this could not always be guaranteed. However, he was no longer confronted with an entrenched and defined opposition within the Politburo, and therefore he had more room to manoeuvre.

The basis of Stalin's position was his ability to consolidate support at all levels of the political structure, but this was something at which he continually had to work. Crucial in this was his ability to influence personnel questions and, through this, to ensure that supporters filled responsible positions throughout the apparatus; Stalin and his supporters possessed the power to reward loyalty and punish those who did not give him their support. However, the mobilisation of political machines was not, by itself, an infallible method of constructing a durable power base. Obligations resulting from appointment could melt away in the absence of reinforcement, particularly given the pressures upon sub-national party leaders and the vulnerability of their positions. Stalin was able to find such means of reinforcement.

Through skilful manipulation of the symbolism of Lenin, the adoption of appealing policy positions, and the image he projected,[253] Stalin was able to generate broad support among both rank-and-file party members and responsible party officials. By the time of their defeats, the successive opposition groups appeared to have very little genuine support in the party.[254] This ability to generate support in the party fed through into the elite organs as a result of the almost continual transfusion of new blood into these bodies. Here lies the importance of the expansion of elite political organs throughout this period, with the strengthened position of party workers (and therefore people from Stalin's 'natural' bailiwick) in the CC particularly significant. Despite the consolidation of his position in this way, Stalin did not enjoy an automatic majority on all issues. Nevertheless, the prominence he achieved by the end of the decade meant that he emerged as a major challenge to the principle of collective leadership.

Of course collective leadership had always been uncertainly based in the party, as reflected in the personalistic basis of power throughout the political structure. The death of Lenin removed the primary focus of personalised power and, therefore, appeared to leave room for the growth of institutionalisation on an organisational basis. However this was not to occur, chiefly because of the changing contours of elite politics, particularly the outbreak of factional conflict within the elite.

Personal ambition and the associated outbreak of factional conflict was a prime mover both in the destruction of the fragile consensus that had emerged in the earlier period and in preventing the institutionalisation of elite organs on an organisational basis. Although Lenin's death removed the focus of the personalistic conception of power and authority, that conception did not also disappear. While none of his former colleagues could hope to occupy the same place as Lenin had, many of them assumed that the path to power led through personalised authority rather than institutional office-holding. Furthermore, through the promotion of the Lenin cult, this image of the legitimacy of personalised authority became embedded in the lore of the regime. The projection of a personalised symbol of authority, consciously fostered and promoted by Lenin's heirs, meant that would-be successors had to claim power and authority in Lenin's name, but it also had to be associated with the individual figures themselves. This was fuelled by the need to generate and maintain support in elite organs, a need which was more easily met with a personalised leadership figure than a more abstract appeal to policy positions. The projection of such a symbol pushed the leading organs of the system into a secondary position.

This statement may seem strange given that in the elite conflicts of the period decisions rejecting the positions of the successive oppositions were made in the names of the party's collective organs. This seems to suggest that it was the party which was victorious over the oppositions. The presentation of the results in this way was designed in part to reinforce the sense of party loyalty, in the process showing up the dastardly behaviour of the opposition compared with the desire for unity by the leadership. It was also in part because the symbolism of personalised leadership had not become so strong that it could dispense with the symbolism of the party, particularly in the absence of a prominent leader. But this form of presentation also subtly downgraded party institutions and elevated the notion of the importance of an individual leader. This followed from the retention in elite organs of prominent oppositionists after they had been defeated. For example, Trotsky and Kamenev both remained in the Politburo until October 1926 and Rykov until December 1930, while Bukharin, Tomsky and Rykov were all re-elected full members of the CC at the XVI Congress in July 1930. The continued inclusion of such people in the party's leading organs implies that the ability of these institutions to make the right decisions for the party did not rest upon the nature of the institutions as corporate entities, as the symbolism of the party demanded. If it did, how could they accommodate the presence in them of people who had openly opposed the official policy? Under such circumstances, correct policy had to be the result of the role played in these institutions by leaders who were aware of the most appropriate policy lines to follow. Those leaders were the victorious group surrounding Stalin. Personalised leadership was thus essential for the correct functioning of leading party organs.

The principle that this confirmed, which clearly had its roots in the earlier period and practices of Soviet history, is also reflected in the manoeuvring and decision-making that occurred outside formal party bodies during this time. The caucusing of different factions outside the formal sessions of party bodies, the attempts to line up votes by winning over any uncommitted members, and the factional organising directed at securing political advantage in the party organs, all devalued those organs as political entities. Furthermore, they reflect an attitude to party organs which was purely instrumental. Rather than organs of decision-making, they became arenas within which the opposition was to be pilloried and defeated. They were instruments for the leadership to use to consolidate its position rather than fora for the real discussion and resolution of major issues. The growth of this attitude was propelled by the ambitions at the heart of the factional conflict throughout the 1920s.

The weakness of the party's leading organs and their inability to prevent this attitude from taking hold was in part due to the involvement of all leading oligarchs in the manoeuvring outside institutional bounds, with their consequent ambivalence about promoting the growth of powerful independent institutions. It was also due to the weak position in which they had been left at the end of the Lenin period. Unable to develop a strong sense of institutional coherence or integrity under Lenin, leading party bodies remained subsidiary to the main political actors and therefore had no firm basis upon which to grow in the post-Lenin period. Lacking a powerful momentum for organisational institutionalisation, the legislative organs of the party could not develop very far in that direction.

A similar process occurred with regard to the party's administrative organs. Their tasks – effective party house-keeping and the placement of personnel to carry out the essential tasks – were directly affected by the course of elite conflict during this period. It was not difficult for those who controlled the national party machine to justify their manipulation, which ensured that people sympathetic to their point of view filled leading positions in the party. The constant attacks on the opposition and the discrediting of it was part of the process of justifying to the party as a whole their removal from the party's leading positions. By invoking the ethos of party discipline in the face of a hostile environment and by attacking the credentials of the opposition as true disciples of Lenin, the party leadership created an environment in which their removal was acceptable to the party as a whole. This was, therefore, a means of redefining leadership positions in terms of adoption of the correct policies. By the end of the period, the ethos was one which made no provision for dispute within leadership ranks. Henceforth the principal qualification for leadership was neither previous contributions to the revolution nor demonstrated personal ability and commitment; now it was support for the right line of policy.

This shift in perception about the proper qualifications for leadership was accompanied by the shift in the way in which the party's apparatus was understood. While the main task of the apparatus continued to be seen to be the efficient management of the party's domestic affairs, another principle gained general acceptance in the party: that the apparatus, and more particularly the personnel regime, could be used and manipulated for personal ends. This development was justified in terms of the need to ensure that only loyal adherents of the Leninist line filled positions of responsibility. But when the Leninist line came to be seen as located in a group of leaders or, as the cult of Stalin was to suggest, in one leader, then the personnel mechanism could legitimately be used as a weapon to cut down one's opponents.

It is not clear how far party opinion accepted this fusing of the correct Leninist line with Stalin and his immediate colleagues during this period. It was clearly far from universal. However, it may be that such acceptance was strongest at an early stage among the personnel of the central apparatus, if for no other reason than those who were opposed to Stalin (their boss) were attacking the procedures through which this group was establishing its control in the party. Their own institutional and career interests dictated such acceptance; under attack, their only real defence was provided by their high level protector, the General Secretary. Similar considerations were also at work among sub-national party functionaries, although here a series of countervailing considerations would also have been at work, making their support for the Stalin group more conditional than that of their central colleagues.[255]

Nevertheless, the nature of power and authority at all levels of the political structure was personalised. People held their positions because of the conviction at higher levels that they were the most appropriate people to occupy party office, with 'appropriate' often defined more in terms of personal loyalties than of administrative ability. This personalised nature of power and authority reinforced the personalistic principles of authority which had emerged in the time of Lenin, principles which ran directly counter to the emergence of organisational institutionalisation on the part of the formal bodies of the system. Personalised power and authority remained more strongly based than that of the formal institutions.

Thus it is clear that during the 1920s the nature of oligarchical politics was changed fundamentally. Under the impact of elite conflict, any pressures for a more pluralistic course of development were blunted. The instruments which emerged in the initial period for the consolidation of oligarch unity were redeployed and strengthened in order to eliminate opposition within elite organs. But although individual groups of opponents of Stalin were eliminated as political actors of any substance, opposition as such did not disappear. It was to recur in the 1930s, though not in the open form characteristic of this period. Herein lies a major distinction between the 1920s and the 1930s.

Part III

The re-formed oligarchy, 1930–1934

5 Regions under pressure

A sense of isolation continued to pervade the sub-national party structure as it entered the 1930s. Beside the clear evidence of popular enthusiasm for many of the policies of the 'revolution from above'[1] and the effect of substantial upward social mobility in stimulating commitment to the regime,[2] there were also immediate and unmistakable signs of popular hostility. The most marked instances of this occurred in the countryside where wide sections of the peasantry vigorously opposed agricultural collectivisation. Armed resistance was mounted in some areas while a more passive type of resistance in the form of destruction of crops, livestock and implements was widespread throughout the country. Once in the collectives, resentment continued to smoulder as the peasants found themselves pushed into new and unfamiliar work settings in which their capacity to exercise initiative independent from the authorities was much more restricted than hitherto.[3] This was perhaps best symbolised by the decision in 1932 not to grant internal passports to the peasants, a move which imposed a substantial barrier to peasant geographical mobility. The use of famine to break peasant resistance can only have deepened the opposition of those who experienced it.[4] In the towns, too, there was an undercurrent of discontent. Many displaced peasants, pushed into the urban slums and forced to submit to the unfamiliar rigours of industrial discipline resented their dramatic change in circumstances and were willing to vent their feelings through strikes and other forms of industrial action; high levels of labour mobility and absenteeism were common.[5] Difficult working conditions, the lack of defence of workers' interests by many of the organisations established in their name and the attempted regimentation of labour[6] were a continuing source of discontent among the rapidly burgeoning urban labour force.

Concern about popular hostility to the regime is reflected in the early part of this period in the approach taken to law. The initial part of this period, until the summer of 1933, witnessed the treatment of legality in a way that was consistent with the radicalism of the cultural revolution and with the struggle being waged in the countryside to bring about collectivisation. During this period penal repression was intensified[7] and the major show trials of the Industrial Party (November–December 1930), the Mensheviks (March 1931) and the Metro-Vickers engineers (April 1933) were held. In March 1933 the OGPU gained the legal right to order executions.[8] At the CC plenum in January 1933 Stalin emphasised the way in which law was a sword to be used by the state against its enemies for 'the protection of public property'.[9] This was also the period when highly restrictive measures on personal movement were introduced.

But this initial period was followed by one of relaxation, beginning about the middle of 1933 and seeming to gather pace after the XVII Congress in January–February 1934. Symbolic of this relaxation was the fate of Zinoviev and Kamenev, who had been expelled from the party at the end of 1932, and who were now brought back and allowed to confess their error. But, more importantly, there seemed to be restraints placed upon the OGPU. In June 1933 the Soviet Procuracy was established and given oversight of the OGPU, which was now prohibited from pronouncing death sentences without the procurator's sanction.[10] In July of the following year, in a move which seems designed to rein it in and downgrade its status, the OGPU was absorbed into the People's Commissariat of Internal Affairs (NKVD).[11] The middle of 1933 also witnessed a decrease in peasant deportations and the release of some of those who had been sent to labour camps in connection with collectivisation. Following the XVII Congress, and particularly following the July 1934 CC plenum, the emphasis upon law and revolutionary legality changed. Now speakers discussed revolutionary legality in terms of a body of judicial rules designed to regulate the relationship between state and citizen and even to defend the citizens against infringements by the state.[12] In discussing the role of law at this time, one student refers to this change as being a 'shift from a facilitator of social change to a protector of the status quo'.[13] The main impetus for this emphasis on legality and relaxation is not certain (Kirov has usually been associated with it – see ch. 6 below), but its effect in terms of the relationship between citizens and system was important: symbolically it removed the adversary relationship which was implicit in the view of law as a weapon, and in that sense laid the groundwork for the new state

Table 5.1. *Party membership, 1930–35*

	Full	Candidate	Total
1930	1,184,651	493,259	1,677,910
1931	1,369,406	842,819	2,212,225
1932	1,769,773	1,347,477	3,117,250
1933	2,203,951	1,351,387	3,555,338
1934	1,826,756	874,252	2,701,008
1935	1,659,104	699,610	2,358,714

constitution introduced in 1936. It was, however, somewhat at odds with the tension in party ranks at this time.

Although the policy of relaxation in the second half of this period seemed to suggest a non-antagonistic relationship between regime and populace, the sense of isolation and unease continued to pervade the party. This is despite the dramatic increase in its size during this period, particularly during the First Five Year Plan (see table 5.1).[14] Over the five-year period, the party grew by some 40.6 per cent, and if we take as our measure the highest point party membership reached at the time recruitment was halted in December 1932, it grew by 111.9 per cent over three years. Such a massive influx clearly reflects a significant broadening of the party's base, at least in numerical terms. Most of these new recruits came from the labouring classes of town and country.

Prior to the ending of all recruitment on 11 December 1932,[15] the party had sought to recruit actively among the three major social groups, the proletariat, the peasantry and the intelligentsia. In 1930 and 1931 immense efforts were turned toward the recruitment of 'workers from the bench', with the official goal being manual workers comprising half of the party. This goal could not be achieved, despite the waiving of normal entrance requirements for such candidates. Nevertheless, large numbers of these people entered the party at this time; one estimate is that more than one million production and transport workers entered the party during 1930–31.[16] Beside this concentration upon urban workers, the party also sought to draw into its ranks increased numbers of peasants. This was particularly important given the new organisational forms established in the countryside and the need to staff these with party members who retained links with their rural roots. In the 12 months from 1 January 1930,

206,163 collective farmers joined the party, constituting some 38.6 per cent of all recruits during that period.[17] At the same time, more attention began to be devoted to the intelligentsia as the party leaders recognised the important role this group would play as industrialisation proceeded. As a result, from 1930 onwards the proportion coming from the intelligentsia among new recruits rose,[18] setting in train those trends which were to lead to the professionalisation of party ranks.[19]

But although the party in the early 1930s was more proletarian in nature than it had ever been, it was still spread remarkably thinly across Soviet society. According to Kaganovich's organisational report to the XVII Congress, the number of PPO and candidate groups increased from 54,000 at the time of the XVI Congress (June–July 1930) to 139,000 on 1 October 1933,[20] but even with this increased number, many inhabited areas did not have a party organisation. The situation generally was worse in the countryside than in the cities. In the rural areas the number of primary organisations grew from 30,000 with 404,000 members in mid-1930 to 80,000 with 790,000 members on 1 October 1933.[21] The corresponding figures for the non-rural (including military) sector were 24,000 organisations with some 1,541,000 members in 1930 and 59,000 organisations with some 1,611,000 members in late 1933.[22] Despite the larger numbers of organisations in rural areas, there were clearly many fewer communists much more thinly spread than in the cities. In 1933 there were approximately 670 urban communists and 70 rural communists for every 10,000 people, a ratio that would have been exacerbated by the effects of the 1933–34 purge.[23] By mid-1932 only 20 per cent of collective farms, which were to be one of the new organisational foundations for the party in the countryside, had a party cell or organised group of communists.[24] It is clear that the party presence at the local level remained very thin throughout this period.

The thinness of this crust of party functionaries was a matter of concern to the party leadership, and the resulting sense of unease was exacerbated by the continuing doubts of many party members about the quality of the new recruits. From the early stages of this period, central organs called for the strengthening of both the work and the composition of lower level party organs,[25] a concern sharpened by the difficulties encountered in the collectivisation campaign.[26] Recruiting methods used in the push for expanded proletarian entry, including the tendency to enrol in groups rather than individually, were blamed in part for the entry into the party of individuals 'who have not justified the lofty title of member of the party'[27] and those who *Pravda* referred to as enemies with party cards in their pockets.[28] Although the problem of the quality of party members was seen as particularly acute at this time, it was not solely a function of recent recruitment practices; in 1931, 23.4 per cent of raikom secretaries had had no systematic political training.[29] The absence of satisfactory party training programmes for responsible workers continued to fuel the doubts about the quality of lower level party leaders.

In response to this perceived problem, party educational efforts were stepped up.[30] More spectacularly, a new party purge was announced in January 1933 in an attempt to ensure iron proletarian discipline and to cleanse the party from 'all unreliable, unstable, and hanger-on elements'.[31] In the formal instructions for the purge, the categories of those to be dealt with were amplified.[32] The following categories were to be purged:
1 class alien and hostile elements who enter the party by deceitful means and seek to demoralise its ranks;
2 double-dealers who deceive the party and seek to undermine its policy;
3 violators of party and state discipline who fail to carry out the decisions of party and state and who discredit those decisions by questioning their practicality;
4 degenerates who have merged with bourgeois elements and do not seek to combat kulak elements, grabbers, loafers, thieves and plunderers of public property;
5 careerists, self-seekers and bureaucratised elements who exploit their official position for their own aims and are isolated from the masses and their demands;
6 moral degenerates whose behaviour discredits the party.

These categories are elastic and vague, and although their compass could be defined broadly to include those who were not recent adherents to the party and who held official positions, the main thrust of the purge fell upon the newer members of the party. In all, some 22 per cent of the party's membership was expelled during 1933–34, with the bulk of expulsions coming from among those who had joined during the collectivisation campaign and the First Five Year Plan period. The blow fell more heavily on rural communists than on urban,[33] reflecting the difficulties encountered during the collectivisation campaign and fears that party members of peasant origin were likely to be infected by petty bourgeois sentiment. Given this focus upon relatively recent entrants, a principal effect of the purge was to erode part of the human basis which the party was seeking to build for itself among the Soviet populace, particularly in the countryside. According to one eminent historian of the party, between 1933 and 1935, the number of party organisations on collective farms fell by 50 per cent and the number of territorially based rural organisations fell by 33 per cent.[34] In terms purely of the spread of party organisations and membership, by the end of this period the party was not deeply rooted in the Soviet populace in general, and considerable doubts remained in leading ranks about the quality and commitment of many party members.

Sub-national leaders were concerned not only about the general environment within which they had to function and, often, the nature of the members within their party organisations, but also by the sustained pressure brought to bear upon them by those at the apex of the political structure. Such pressure had begun with the self-criticism campaign of 1928, but middle level party officials had sought, with considerable success, to deflect some of this pressure on to subordinates. But their success was shortlived. The campaign for self-criticism and intra-party democracy continued, albeit in somewhat muted form, throughout 1929–30[35] and the party press continued to devote significant attention to lower level party organs and their deficiencies.[36] In addition, there was a high turnover of sub-national leaders in 1929–30 as a result of the purge of those years.[37] Such high turnover levels did not disappear. In 1931, some 507,000 transfers were carried out within the party;[38] between the beginning of 1931 and mid-1932, 80 per cent of raikom secretaries in the Ukraine were changed, with a similar percentage being removed in the mid-1932 elections in Georgia. In some places, such secretaries changed from three to five times a year.[39]

The policy of agricultural collectivisation involved continuing central pressures on lower level party leaders. The ethos which had pervaded the party's internal regime during the crisis of the Civil War period recurred. Of overwhelming importance was the achievement of the goals set down from above, regardless of prevailing notions of correct behaviour or institutional relations. Party leaders at all levels were called upon to push through the central leadership's ever-increasing demands for collectivisation, regardless of obstacles. The lower level party leaders were thus caught between two unremitting forces, the opposition of dispossessed peasants from below and the excessive demands for performance by the central leaders from above. The central leadership was often critical of their performance and their achievements in the collectivisation campaign, and when that campaign ran into difficulties as a result of the excessive zeal which inspired it, the responsibility was laid right at the door of the middle and lower level officials.[40]

Criticism also was directed at the internal workings of the party at the sub-national level. This became a major theme of intra-party life in 1932–34. It is worth examining this theme at greater length because of what it tells us about the state of the institutional environment within which sub-national party leaders had to operate.

One of the principal lines of criticism of lower level party organs during this period related to the personnel question.[41] During the 1920s the party's success in generating an integrated personnel mechanism to bring order to party personnel matters had been limited. An efficiently operating mechanism which spanned all levels of the party structure had not been constructed. The inefficient personnel mechanism was unable to handle the increased pressures posed by the simultaneous purge of 1929–30, the influx into the party in the early 1930s and the cadre demands posed by the vast plans for economic development. The strains placed upon both the personnel regime and the resources of the sub-national party structure were enormous. Local record-keeping facilities had to keep track both of those whose performance and record were considered inadequate and were therefore subject to expulsion from the party and the new recruits who flocked into party ranks at this time. This task was increasingly complicated by the widescale mobilisation of cadres during the collectivisation and industrialisation campaigns, with the attendant need to keep track of membership transfers. The sub-national personnel mechanisms were unable to handle these pressures in an ordered fashion.

The demands of economic transformation and the consequent need for cadres imposed upon middle ranking party organisations responsibilities which were impossible to fulfil under the existing circumstances. A party with a more developed internal regime than that possessed by the communist party and in a society with a far higher educational level than that of Russia would have been sorely tested to meet the demands for personnel the changed economic policies generated. For the party at this time, the task was impossible.[42] The central authorities were only too ready to point to the deficiencies of lower levels on this score. Local leaders and organisations frequently were criticised for the inadequate selection, use and distribution of cadres. The posting of cadres to positions for which they lacked the requisite knowledge, experience or skills was widespread.[43] Such a development could be the result of 'familyness',[44] of consolidating clique control in a particular region. One contributory factor was certainly the absence of established training programmes and educational facilities for preparing party cadres, particularly those new entrants to the party. This was a frequent complaint of the central authorities.[45] Another contributory factor was the high level of mobility of many party cadres, a fact which militated against individuals developing a high level of expertise in particular areas of work or geographical regions. Such mobility was sometimes attributed to the poor selection of cadres in the first place.[46]

Important too was the absence of a planned approach or an ordered mechanism for handling personnel affairs at sub-national levels. Despite the restructuring of the secretarial apparatus in 1930 and again in 1934 discussed below, personnel affairs in many party organisations remained largely unplanned and lacking in system.[47] Decisions were made on what amounted to an *ad hoc* basis with little concern for consistency, matching talents with needs or with organisational rationalisation. The principal concern was to fill a gap which currently existed, and the implications this might have for the particular position or for the development of an ordered personnel apparatus were not considered. The situation is admirably expressed in the complaint that the personnel sectors of party committees were often more interested in immediate distribution than the effective organisation of the selection of workers.[48]

An important aspect of this lack of system was the state of party organisations' registration procedures. Throughout the period as a whole, but particularly in 1932–34, the poor standard of the party's registration procedures was a source of central complaint. In some cases party committees were declared to have very weak or inadequate systems of registration[49] while in others such a system was declared to be completely lacking.[50] Even when party organisations did have systems of registration, there was little uniformity throughout the party as each organisation used its own, often unique, system. Although attempts were made to bring greater order to this aspect of party life, the success achieved was limited.[51] Records remained inadequate. Often they were characterised by the presence of large numbers of 'dead souls', members who had left either the party or the area yet remained on the party organisation's register;[52] official records could be as much as 50 per cent at variance with the actual number, while in early 1934 there were declared to be 56,000 'dead souls' on the party's register.[53] Party committees often gave out duplicate party cards with little effort made to check on the particular case concerned,[54] with the result that non-members of the party could gain membership cards and people expelled by a party organisation in one area could regain entry in another.[55] Furthermore, the physical mode of record-keeping was often one which militated against the generation of an effective registration system. The Smolensk Archive[56] indicates how information was consigned to the filing cabinet on irregularly shaped, torn pieces of paper and in a way which clearly did not conform to any standardised pattern or office formula; in one place, record cards were used as a lamp shade.[57] It is no exaggeration to say that many party organs were uncertain about who was a member of the party and who was not.

An important aspect of the chaotic nature of the party's registration system was the weakness of vertical linkages between party bodies. The nomenklatura system gave responsibility for leading personnel appointments to party bodies at higher levels. But if many party organs were uncertain about membership at their own levels, they were even more unclear about the situation lower down. This is clearly reflected in the press and the common complaint that party organs did not know the state of affairs in lower standing bodies.[58] Party bodies were accused of giving a lack of attention to lower organs; they had knowledge of the situation only in general terms while being ignorant of the details which were essential to the functioning of the party at this level.[59] Even if local records were up to date, high levels of cadre mobility added to the irregularity and uncertainty of information flow upwards meant that the information possessed by party organs at higher levels was likely to be significantly behind actual developments.[60] It is clear, then, that at the sub-national level, the party's personnel mechanism was in a state of considerable disarray.

The weakness of vertical linkages in the party's personnel mechanism was symptomatic of the general state of inter-level linkages. The organisational control which higher party levels were able to exercise over lower levels was very weak indeed. Complaints about the inadequacy of the knowledge possessed by higher bodies about the situation at lower levels extended not just to personnel matters but applied to all aspects of party life. Regularised methods of ensuring the efficient transmission of information both up and down the party structure were deficient. While central instructions could be projected through the party press, and could thereby in principle be directed to all party organisations, the upward transmission of information depended overwhelmingly on lower level initiative, and this was frequently not forthcoming. The telegraph and telephone were not available to all party organisations, the paucity of sealed roads increased the isolation, and most party organs were not conveniently located to gain easy access to the rail network.

The mechanisms for ensuring that lower level organs implemented the policy formulated above were also weak. Complaints to this effect and calls for the verification of the implementation of party decisions and of the party line often appeared in the press[61] and constituted a significant theme at the XVII Congress in early 1934. Stalin's address to the congress contained an open attack upon the non-fulfilment of party directives and the non-implementation of the party line. He attacked those who carried out party decisions formally rather than practically, doing enough to avoid criticism from above and putting an unrealistic gloss on the reports they despatched to the centre. He suggested a series of antidotes to this problem, including self-criticism, popular mobilisation, increased supervision of implementation and removal of those found wanting. In his view three categories of party executives were responsible for this state of affairs: the 'incorrigible bureaucrats and red tapists', those who believed their past services to the party put them above its laws and relieved them of the responsibility for implementing party decisions, and those 'chatterboxes' who were honest but incompetent.[62] The call for concrete leadership and guidance rather than leadership by declaration and for the criticism of all shortcomings in this regard was echoed by other speakers at the congress and by the congress resolution on organisational questions.[63]

The weakness of vertical linkages in the party had serious implications for the ability of that structure to function effectively as an organisational entity. The difficulty higher levels had in ensuring the continuing compliance of lower level bodies to party decisions and in obtaining accurate, up-to-date information on what was happening at lower levels meant that the party was anything but a highly integrated mechanism of political rule. This had important ramifications for the power and position of sub-national political leaders. These will be discussed below. This was also a continuing cause for concern on the part of the national leaders, and during this period they sought to use a variety of means to overcome this organisational looseness and bring about a more effective and tightly organised party structure.

One means of seeking to achieve this was through organisational restructuring. In 1929–30 the district committees had undergone a process of consolidation and systematisation in preparation for the increased responsibilities they were to bear with the abolition of the next level up, the okrug. This was decreed on 15 July 1930.[64] However, this attempt to streamline the party apparatus by removing a superfluous level was not successful. Many district committees did not receive the extra resources required to carry out their increased responsibilities, while the links between district and regional (oblast) committees became increasingly attenuated without the intervening link of the okrug; in early 1931 it was reported that some districts saw no one from the regional centre for three to four months at a time.[65]

Another type of reorganisation occurred in the rural areas, connected with the results of agricultural collectivisation. The establishment of the new, collective forms of agriculture led to party cells based on the production principle (in the collective and state farms and the MTS) becoming more important than those organised on a territorial basis. But what became of particular importance here were the political departments established in 1933. These were extensions of the earlier (established in 1931), less successful 'support points', and were established as a means more effectively of penetrating the countryside. These were established at the joint CC–CCC plenum of January 1933. Reflecting discontent with the performance of the party organs in the grain procurement campaigns of 1931 and 1932 and with the way in which they had lacked the necessary vigilance against enemies, sometimes even coming under the influence of the enemies of collectivisation, the political departments were to exercise control over agriculture. Established in MTS and sovkhozy, but not large kolkhozy, their role was to strengthen the sovkhozy and kolkhozy, eliminate opportunist elements and the class enemy, and encourage mass political work. Appointed directly by the CC, these bodies constituted a direct link with the centre and posed a clear threat to the ordinary party apparatus and their secretaries; they possessed effective power to purge the local apparatus. Jurisdictional disputes were a constant source of conflict and, despite attempts to sort these out, they could not be resolved.[66] In November 1934 the political departments were abolished,[67] thus marking the failure of another attempt to tighten party control over the countryside and to strengthen central links with the lower extremities of the political apparatus.

Attempts were also made to restructure the secretarial apparatus in 1930 and 1934. This will be discussed more extensively in the following chapter, but for sub-national party secretaries it meant that the administrative machinery for their areas underwent two major transformations within the space of four years. In 1930, the secretarial apparatus was shifted on to a functional basis whereby, in the personnel field, one department was to be concerned solely with cadres in the party while another department was divided into eight sections covering personnel in the various branches of the national economy.[68] In 1934 this functional basis was abandoned in favour of the 'integrated production branch' principle whereby responsibility for cadres was allocated to the departments which had responsibility for those sectors of life in which the cadres were to work.[69] This change, introduced at the national level, was to be replicated throughout the party,[70] but it seems to have encountered significant resistance at the lower levels.[71] The attempt to regularise personnel matters through restructuring the appropriate sections of the sub-national secretariat clearly failed during this period. The failure of the 1930 attempt is most clearly reflected in the purge of 1933 and the reorganisation of 1934. As efforts to bring about the tighter vertical integration of the party, the attempts at secretarial restructuring were not successful.

The centre also used another form of organisational restructuring in an attempt to overcome the weakness of organisational linkages. Without doing away with such well-established party channels of central–local relations as the central press and the CC instructors and inspectors who visited lower level party organs to give advice and collect information for the centre, the central authorities established channels outside the party's formal organisational structure. Particularly important or sensitive documents continued to be sent by special NKVD couriers.[72] But what was new was the introduction of the special sectors. These too will be discussed in the following chapter, but it is important to understand the importance of these organs for politics at the middle and lower levels of the party structure. The special sectors seem to have been established at the time of the reorganisation of the Secretariat in 1934[73] and to have been established in party committees down to the regional (oblast) level.[74] They developed as a major channel of communication between Moscow and lower levels, one former functionary going so far as to declare that all communications between the centre and local committees went through the sectors.[75] Appointed from Moscow and, at least initially, possessing no immediate links with the party organisations at the levels at which they were functioning, the special sectors were meant to constitute an independent channel into those lower level party bodies.[76] They were to provide the sort of independent check which the control commissions had been supposed to provide. The effect of the establishment of such an independent channel into the localities was buttressed by the reorganisation of the control mechanism in 1934. Reflecting dissatisfaction with the performance of the CCC and RKI, these were abolished at the XVII Congress and replaced by separate Commissions for Party Control and for Soviet Control.[77] Instead of local commissions being formed, the party congress was to elect the central body, members of which were to visit the localities as representatives of the centre and to supervise the implementation of central decisions.[78] Even the rhetoric of the independence of these bodies was gone as they were presented as responsible to the centre for ensuring the fulfilment of central directives. Thus towards the end of this period the centre made a number of organisational changes designed to constrict lower level autonomy and to bind the party more tightly together. But the immediate effect of these changes was not great.

The most spectacular way in which the party leadership sought to create tighter unity within party ranks was through the purge of 1933–34.[79] The categories of people who were to be subjected to the purging process were listed earlier (see p. 205). A major thrust of the purge as defined by these categories was to weed out of the party those undesirable elements who had flocked in during the recent recruiting surge, those who had entered the party on the basis of considerations other than commitment to the party's goals and a desire to work for their achievement. Careerists and passive elements who sought possession of a party card only for the material advantages it could bring were an important target of the purge. The removal of such ballast clearly fitted in with the emphasis upon improving vertical linkages, with ensuring a higher standard of fulfilment of party decisions, and with turning the party into a more effective instrument of political rule. Furthermore, the conduct of such a purge, added to the cessation of recruitment from the end of 1932, provided a perfect opportunity for party organs at all levels to get their registration records and procedures into some order.

However, the categories of purge targets were also consistent with an attempt to get rid of those perceived to be enemies of the party or its prevailing line. The references to class alien and hostile elements, to double-dealers who sought to undermine its policy, to violators of discipline who sought to discredit decisions by claiming they were impractical and could not be realised, and to those who exploited their official positions for their own ends, all signalled an attack upon those holding offices who were unsuited to do so. They were the 'enemies with party cards in their pockets',[80] the class enemy who continued to conduct their struggle in a masked fashion within the ranks of the party.[81] This sort of language was particularly stark in the light of the general rhetoric about 'wrecking' and hidden enemies associated with the assault on the specialists in the early 1930s, the criticism of the performances of many lower level party leaders during the collectivisation campaign and the complaints about the conduct of party affairs at these lower levels. The direction of the attack against sub-national party leaders was also signalled by the centre's attempts to mobilise both rank-and-file party members and the non-party population at large into the purge to criticise the shortcomings of party leaders.[82] Thus, while one aspect of the purge clearly was directed principally at new recruits and sought to improve the party's personnel system, another was directed against those holding responsible office who were not performing in the expected fashion.

The direction of the purge against deficiencies in performance in the countryside was consistent with recent developments. The leadership was aware that during collectivisation, many low-ranking party cadres had opposed party policy.[83] The impression of low level unreliability had been reinforced by the unsatisfactory performance of many party organs in the grain procurement campaigns of 1931 and 1932. Official reaction was a purge of the party organisations in the southern grain-producing regions. Between March and November 1932, 922 district secretaries and other leading political figures were removed from their posts, an average of two people per district in the Ukraine; in the winter of 1932–33 in the Kuban, 48.7 per cent of secretaries investigated were expelled and 20.4 per cent disciplined, 47.8 per cent of rural soviet chairmen were expelled, and 48 per cent of kolkhoz chairmen were expelled and 28.6 per cent disciplined. In the Ukraine, some 23.6 per cent of those checked were expelled.[84] This focus is clearly reflected in a leading article from *Partiinoe stroitel'stvo* of December 1932:

> The party purge will expel from our ranks cheats, double-dealers, kulak degenerates and opportunists of all types, all unsteady and chance elements, all those masking themselves from the party. Spineless whimperers and sceptics, heroes of laissez-faire [samotek], conciliators to the advances of the class enemy, those who wreck the grain procurements and other economic and political campaigns will find themselves out of the party's ranks.[85]

An important theme in the attack upon the sub-national political leaders continued to be the notion of self-criticism. This theme had been extended from 1928 into 1930, but only as a subordinate strand of party life. Although it was declared to be a basic principle of party construction and was to be implemented only when it was 'directed at the defence of the general line of the party',[86] it was not being implemented satisfactorily in many areas;[87] in some cases it was being approached in a purely formal way and was sometimes undermined by 'familyness'.[88] This theme was barely evident during 1931 and 1932,[89] but it re-emerged in a more important way with the purge of 1933–34. The absence of self-criticism in the immediate past was criticised and was directly linked with the conduct of affairs 'in a family way'[90] while the purge itself was declared to be the highest expression of self-criticism.[91] Self-criticism needed to be strengthened as a weapon against the abuses at which the purge was directed.[92] Self-criticism thus re-emerged as an element of the purge and, through its appeal to rank-and-file activism against those in authority, reflects the direction of the official cutting edge of the purge against those in authority who did not measure up to expectations.

The purge did not achieve its purposes. Although some 22 per cent of party members were expelled during the purge,[93] developments in 1935 and 1936 discussed below (see ch. 7) suggest that there was little improvement in the way in which party personnel affairs were handled. Nor was the challenge to sub-national party leaders any more successful. These leaders were for the most part able to deflect the blows of the purge away from themselves and their family power bases.[94] Many dragged their feet in organising the purge or effectively refused to permit its implementation; when it was implemented it was frequently done in a half-hearted way or such that the appearance of satisfactory fulfilment masked minimal achievement of its ends.[95] The purge fell most heavily upon newer recruits to the party, and therefore primarily upon rank-and-file members, leaving middle-ranking office-holders and their immediate associates for the most part untouched.

This leads to the question of the position of these sub-national party leaders. The large-scale turnover of these leaders during 1929–30 showed that the centre had the power, if it wished to use it, to remove political figures at these levels from their offices. However, the ability to remove individuals did not equal an ability to eliminate the sorts of pressures which facilitated the development and dominance of family groups at the sub-national level. The sorts of personalistic ties which had become so common during the 1920s as the cement which bound together locally based cliques remained a prominent characteristic of sub-national political life.[96]

An interactive relationship existed between these personalised, informal political machines and the weakness of the formal apparatus of the party. The weakness of the party's internal operating regime at these levels meant that party leaders had little or no effective machinery upon which to rely in seeking to carry out the instructions which rained down on them from above. Furthermore, this period was one in which the demands were particularly heavy, initially during the collectivisation campaign and then with the concentration upon defects in party performance at this level culminating in the 1933–34 purge. Under such conditions, with much demanded of them, with criteria of success often vague and ambiguous and with no security of tenure, political leaders were bound to opt for a system which they hoped would provide some protection for them.[97] Reliance upon informal political machines, which had in any case become widely accepted as the 'normal' way of operating at this level, was thus bound to continue as the predominant operating principle at the sub-national levels of the party. Power at sub-national levels remained outside bureaucratic channels, and party organs remained the instruments of the local power cliques.

If the weakness of the party's internal regulative milieu contributed to the predominance of such a system, it also acted as a significant barrier to the generation of a workable bureaucratic system. When a family group dominated, formal bureaucratic divisions were devalued. Formal meetings were called infrequently and they rarely decided matters of importance; these were usually decided in a 'family way' and, if brought up at the meeting, merely presented for formal ratification.[98] Under such conditions, bureaucratic norms could not develop and thereby channel political behaviour into the contours provided by the formal bureaucratic structure. As a result, the institutionalisation of the party on the basis of bureaucratic norms could not proceed effectively during this period because of the place in local and regional affairs played by the family groups.

But the political position of the leaders of these family groups was exposed and vulnerable during this period. Political rules and regulations remained contingent in the way they had been during the 1920s and thus offered little protection for sub-national leaders against wrath from on high. Criteria of success remained vague and ambiguous, with the decision about whether performance matched criteria being one over which these leaders had no control. Moreover, during this period when much had been expected of them, many had been found wanting. Paradoxically, this judgement was reinforced by the form in which power was structured at this time. Personalised leadership made it more difficult for sub-national party leaders to hide behind the anonymity of the collective because their own personal prominence projected them into a position where their personal responsibility was clear to all. Furthermore, many increased their vulnerability by the dissolute lifestyle they led.[99] Reports of party committees headed by groups which engaged in an excessively high style of life including drunkenness, sexual licence and gambling portrayed such leaders in a very bad light,[100] particularly when a major focus of national political attention was on cadres and their importance for the construction of socialism. Such vulnerability was, of course, clearly brought home to these leaders by the fates of some of their predecessors in the 1929 purge.[101]

Local factions could not withstand direct, concerted pressure from above. This could lead to the displacement of the power figure and perhaps the disintegration of his faction, even if it could not lead to the elimination of the conditions making for such factional control. As a result, sub-national leaders continued to seek their defence in part through the creation of alliances of mutual support with national level figures. The most obvious of these was Stalin, because he was the foremost person in the national leadership and the one with ultimate responsibility for the personnel mechanism. However, Stalin's role in the self-criticism campaign in 1928 and in the 1929 purge showed that he was not as secure a bastion of support as they might have wished. This impression was reinforced by Stalin's direct attack upon the sub-national leaders during the collectivisation campaign,[102] the mounting of the 1933–34 purge, and Stalin's attacks at the XVII Congress on inadequate party leadership at sub-national levels. Under such circumstances the discontent with Stalin at the XVII Congress probably had as its basis a sense of disillusionment with the General Secretary on the part of many sub-national political leaders. This tension between Stalin and the sub-national leaders clearly shows the limitations of the loyalty and ties inherent in the personalised political machines.

What is clear from this summary is that the party was far from being a highly integrated structure in which localised power cliques either had no place or were fused into a nationally integrated power fraction based on the General Secretary. While the centralised appointment system left sub-national leaders vulnerable, its ability to build a broadly based political machine (as opposed to removing individual power cliques) was hampered by the physical problems of maintaining close communication between the party centre and all party organs and by the general weakness of the administrative regime inside the party. These obstacles to centralised control gave sub-national leaders more freedom of manoeuvre than the nomenklatura system seemed to suggest and later observers have believed. While sub-national leaders clearly had to watch their step because of the possibility of central intervention leading to their displacement, the centre's inability to maintain tight, continuing control over them means that the central–sub-national relationship remained very loosely articulated.

6   The Stalinist elite?

If the 'great transformation' was an important factor reinforcing personalised politics at the sub-national levels, it was also significant in shaping the politics of the elite. The searing nature of the experience of the struggle for collectivisation and industrialisation helped to shape both the institutional contours and the perceptions of political actors at the apex of the structure. New patterns of political action emerged. Conflict was no longer conducted in an open arena but was confined to the closed circles within which the elite moved, and the principles of collectivism were increasingly being subverted by personalised power. These changes were reflected in the changing institutional contours at the top of the political structure.

The institutional arena

The institutional contours of elite politics during this period remained the apex of the party-state structure, although by this time there could be no doubt about the political subordination of the state organs to those of the party. The Congress of Soviets, TsIK and its Presidium played formal and symbolic roles. This was particularly the case with the Congress of Soviets and TsIK, whose meeting schedules and sizes prevented these bodies from operating as meaningful decision-making centres. TsIK and its Presidium did provide the venue for the conduct of bureaucratic conflict between commissariats or similar state bodies, but as organs of decision-making, they were of little importance.

The predominance in the state sphere which Sovnarkom had enjoyed during the 1920s was maintained into this period. The combined legislative and executive functions constitutionally vested in this body along with the range of formal bureaucratic structures which were subordinate to it – the most important of which were the state commissariats – gave this organisation an importance and permanence which enabled it to overshadow the other leading state bodies. This dominance was also assisted by the presence of more senior party figures in Sovnarkom; in late 1930 the rightist Rykov was replaced as Chairman of Sovnarkom by the more influential Stalin-supporter Molotov. The number of leading party figures in Sovnarkom grew substantially:[1] of the top eighteen people's commissars in 1922, only five were in the Politburo and three in the CC;[2] in 1929 there were four full members and one candidate member of the Politburo';[3] by April 1931 of the fourteen leading members of Sovnarkom, there were five full members and one candidate member of the Politburo, three members of the CC and two members of the CCC.[4] The significance of Sovnarkom was also boosted by the important roles played by the commissariats in carrying the policies of industrialisation and collectivisation through to fruition.

But despite the increased role of Sovnarkom at the start of the 1930s, its primacy within the state sphere was enjoyed completely under party suzerainty. This predominance was reinforced by the revolution from above. While the strength of party oligarch representation in Sovnarkom set this body apart from the other state organs, it was also a potent means of ensuring that the oligarchy maintained tight control over this body. Indeed, the replacement of Rykov, whose rightist leanings did not fit the prevailing urgency of the Five Year Plan, by Molotov was an important mechanism for increasing such control; Molotov's personal closeness to Stalin and his membership of the leading group around the General Secretary contrasted sharply with Rykov's long institutional affiliation with Sovnarkom. Party control is reflected in the greater prominence during this period of joint Sovnarkom–CC decisions, signed by the Sovnarkom chairman and a CC Secretary (Stalin),[5] accompanied by a decline in Joint TsIK–Sovnarkom decisions. The more limited role of Sovnarkom is also shown by its meeting frequency, approximately once every ten days in 1930 and once a fortnight thereafter,[6] and by the fact that much of its work was not handled at the plenary session but at preliminary sessions of the chairman and deputy chairmen.[7] The decline in importance of STO further reflects the erosion of the position of its mother organ.

As indicated above, one of the main reasons for Sovnarkom's prominence within the state sphere was its responsibility for the implementation of the economic policies associated with the 'great transformation'. The increased pressure that this involved was concentrated most directly upon the people's commissariats. Yet these remained the object of some suspicion on the part of some party members because of their presumed domination by 'bourgeois specialists'; according to one source, in August 1930 some 11 per cent of commissariat personnel were former tsarist officials,[8] while large numbers of others were specialists whose training put them under suspicion. This was particularly the case in the specialist-baiting post-Shakhty period which lasted from mid-1928 until early 1931. But regardless of such suspicions, it was upon the advice and information emanating from these organisations that political leaders had to rely; they were the major sources of expertise available to party leaders. Like expert bodies everywhere, the commissariats and other government bodies with adjacent or overlapping concerns frequently came into conflict, in terms of both the sort of advice to be tendered and who should have primacy in offering such advice. Such bureaucratic conflict, resting upon an *esprit de corps* within the individual bureaucratic structures and a developed sense of institutional interest, was stimulated by the fluidity of much of the policy environment at this time. The turn from radicalism to a more conservative pattern of values associated with the winding down of the cultural revolution[9] created a situation in which many established bureaucratic positions were no longer appropriate, with the consequent need to sort out new policy stances. This increased the scope for bureaucratic empire-building and conflict. Bureaucratic conflict, rooted in the commissariats and government agencies and reflected in a shuffling in the importance of individual government organs, was a continuing feature of political life during this period.[10] Such disputes frequently invaded the party realm, and it is to this that we must now turn.

Formally, the supreme organ of the party remained the congress. Following the amendment to the party Rules adopted in 1927, this body was to meet every two years; this frequency was changed to every three years at the XVII Congress in 1934. However, the prescribed frequency was not met. Two congresses were convened during this period, the twice-postponed[11] XVI in June–July 1930 and the XVII in January–February 1934.[12] Both congresses were large affairs, as the figures in table 6.1 show (with the XV Congress included for comparison).

Delegates with experience of the previous congress remained a significant minority, while carryover figures were lower than during the previous period. This may reflect the uncertainty among many delegates about the course of official policy at the XV and XVI Con-

Table 6.1. *Congress membership, 1927–34*

Congress	Full	Cand-idate	Total	Carried over to next congress (%)	Carryover as % of new congress
XV	898	771	1669	38.3	34.8
XVI	1269	891	2160	33.0	29.6
XVII	1227	789	2016	3.3	36.2

gresses (the XVII Congress carryover is discussed in ch. 8). Those who worked full time in the party apparatus continued to dominate, although at the XVII Congress, for the first time since early in the Soviet regime's history,[13] a majority of full delegates did not come from the party apparatus. This may be linked with the political tensions discussed below. The figures given in the stenographic reports of both congresses for delegates with a decisive vote are given in table 6.2.[14]

It is not clear where the remaining delegates came from, but most were probably people engaged directly in production or occupants of positions very low in the hierarchy, a broad category much more strongly represented in 1934 than in 1930. Most delegates probably occupied regional positions rather than central posts, although the standing of regional delegates declined compared with those from the centre at the XVII Congress.[15] The formal class designation of most delegates was worker[16] and the vast majority had middle level education or lower;[17] a minority had also undergone courses of party education.[18] Both congresses were overwhelmingly male in their composition and Russian in their ethnic make-up;[19] the XVI Congress was also predominantly middle-aged.[20] Both remained the preserve of long-time party members, with 82.4 per cent and 80 per cent of delegates with a decisive vote at the XVI and XVII Congresses respectively having joined the party prior to the end of 1920.[21]

The size and infrequency of the congresses alone would have prevented these bodies from exercising close supervision over the leadership. But in any case the delegate selection procedures which had become institutionalised in the 1920s had created a mechanism for removing those whom the leadership wished to exclude from delegates' ranks. The existence of this mechanism, added to the principle of public monolithism in congress votes and the defeat of the most prominent oppositionists in the 1920s, meant that congresses

Table 6.2. *Bureaucratic constituencies in the congress, 1930 and 1934*

	XVI	XVII
Party work	59.2%	40.0%
Soviet-administrative organs	20.2%	10.2%
Military workers	8.9%	7.3%

during this period were not witness to the sorts of open attacks on the leadership and its policies which had been such a feature of the 1920s. Certainly some prominent oppositionists from the 1920s spoke at these congresses, but it was formally to recant and make their obeisance to the party rather than to attack Stalin and his supporters. But the absence of attacks upon the leadership at the congresses can also be seen in another light.

Important here was the precarious position the party found itself in at the time of the XVI Congress. The first onslaught of collectivisation had not brought all of the results expected of it, leading to the retreat reflected in Stalin's 'Dizzy with success' article of March 1930.[22] The outcome of events in the countryside remained uncertain, and under such circumstances a logical reaction was to close ranks within the party regardless of any misgivings about the policy which may have existed. Therefore while there was conflict at the congress (see below), this did not involve direct attacks on the leadership or upon the basic thrust of party policy.

When the XVII Congress convened in January 1934, the battle in the countryside had been won. As Stalin declared in his main address to the so-called 'Congress of victors', 'there is nothing to prove and, it seems, no one to fight'.[23] The 1933 harvest seemed to vindicate the party's general line and show the correctness of the policy of agricultural collectivisation. This may partly explain the more restrained treatment accorded to former oppositionists in 1934 compared with 1930; in the earlier year when collectivisation remained in the balance and the arguments of the Right seemed to retain some relevance for contemporary policy, former oppositionist speakers were received in a hostile fashion and subjected to frequent interjections; by the time of the XVII Congress the position of the Right was no longer relevant and these figures from the past could be treated with greater equanimity. Despite this there seems to have been a groundswell of uneasiness about Stalin in the period leading up to and at the XVII Congress and the main focus of this was the sub-national party leadership. An attitude of opposition and resentment on their part is understandable. Caught between the imperatives of their local position and of demands from above, these people would have realised how close to disaster collectivisation had been. Furthermore, they would have resented the attempt to shift the blame for early excesses on to their shoulders. The thinly veiled attacks upon the conduct of their work during 1932–33, the party purge begun in 1933 and the open attacks upon them at the XVII Congress[24] can only have increased such resentment. Awareness by Stalin and his supporters of this feeling may be reflected in the decline in the representation of regional party workers at the XVII Congress. However, such resentment is not clearly expressed in the stenographic report of the congress, unless one interprets the change of Stalin's title from General Secretary to Secretary as evidence of this.[25] But given the way the congress had been developing in the recent past, one should not expect open challenges to the leadership in this forum. The convention of public unity around the leadership at the congress had been emerging, based on the increased strength of the ethos for party unity that had been developing in the 1920s. Such an institutional constraint would have militated against an outbreak of public criticism in this forum.

But this does not mean that the congresses were not the scene of political conflict. At the XVI Congress, CCC/Rabkrin Chairman Ordzhonikidze vigorously attacked the performance of Vesenkha and in particular its waste, extravagance and propensity to set plan targets that were too conservative.[26] The attack was carried against ineffectual resistance and Ordzhonikidze clearly won the day.[27] At the XVII Congress the dispute over growth rates which had been in train for some time in the governmental apparatus erupted into party debate with a public disagreement between Sovnarkom Chairman Molotov and Vesenkha chief Ordzhonikidze. The dispute was resolved in a way that had been common earlier in Soviet history; it was directed into a special commission which supported Ordzhonikidze's proposed figure, which was itself a compromise between the high figure supported by Molotov and the lower figure which more moderate forces had supported earlier in the debate.[28] These debates were important because although they did not openly question the general line of the party, the level of the growth rate which would be sought was clearly crucial to the course of development which the party was pursuing; in principle, support for a low growth rate could constitute an attack upon the general line itself. Although the debates were couched in terms of implementation of the line, the boundary between the means of implementation and the principle of the policy itself was very fine.

But this sort of debate differed from those in the 1920s in that the policy question was not directly linked in the minds of the protagonists with the suitability of the top party leaders to continue in their positions. While Ordzhonikidze's attack at the XVI Congress seems to have been directed in part at undermining the position of Kuibyshev, it was not directed at the leadership group as a whole and may have been related in part to personal rivalries. Similarly, at the XVII Congress, the dispute concerned different trends of leadership opinion within an elite consensus about their right to rule collectively. These disputes may be better seen as part of an on-going struggle for advantage among the second echelon leadership within the elite.

The course of institutional development of the congress during this period extended those trends which had become evident during the second half of the 1920s. Its functions as a forum for self-abnegation by the opposition and of ratification of policy decisions remained. So too did the public unanimity of its decisions, even if this continued to be achieved through the non-release of voting figures for leadership positions. Although it was no longer the scene of open attacks upon the leadership, the congress remained a forum for bureaucratic conflict and for public jockeying among the second rung of the elite. It also became a major platform for the glorification of the leader. But the congress could not act as a check upon the leadership. It had no institutional integrity or coherence and was not independent of the political elite.

The main executive organ of the congress remained the CC. According to the party Rules, this was to meet in plenary session at two monthly intervals, a frequency which was changed to four months in 1934. Neither of these timetables was realised. In addition to the plenary sessions held immediately after a party congress to elect its own executive organs, CC plena were held on only seven occasions. Two of these were in joint session with the CCC.[29] Meetings remained irregular (see table 6.3, which excludes those following the party congresses). There is no pattern to these meetings, indicating that the institution lacked both system and predictability.

The size of the CC continued to mount, although more slowly than during parts of the 1920s. Table 6.4 shows the size of the CC elected at

Table 6.3. *CC meetings, 1930–34*

Month of meeting	Months from last meeting	Approximate length of plenum (in days)
Dec. 1930 (CC–CCC)	13	5
June 1931	6	5
Oct. 1931	4	4
Sept. 1932	11	5
Jan. 1933 (CC–CCC)	4	6
June–July 1934	18	3
Nov. 1934	4	4

successive congresses (including that of 1927 for comparison) and the levels of carryover.[30] The pattern of high carryover established in the 1920s was reversed at the end of this period with the new CC elected at the XVII Congress including only just over two-thirds of the members elected in 1930. Heaviest casualties occurred among candidate members.[31] This higher rate of attrition, which was to be increased substantially during the following period, may be due to the removal of some of those who shared the unease about Stalin's leadership referred to above. Nevertheless, 59.5 per cent of all members of the 1927 CC were re-elected to the CC elected at the XVII Congress, thereby constituting a solid core of experienced party executives. They are likely also to have been those who did not show any disquiet over the policies Stalin had introduced at the end of the 1920s and early 1930s.

The CC remained the preserve of the Old Bolsheviks during this period. Table 6.5 shows the extent of this dominance, with the CC elected in 1927 for comparison. As this table makes clear, although those who joined the party before the end of 1917 continued to dominate in this body, the number of those who joined after that date was rising rapidly, particularly among the candidate members.[32] The influx of newer party members was especially marked at the XVII Congress. Nevertheless this body remained dominated by long-time party members; the latest date of party entry of any member during this period was 1921.

The most important characteristic of the profile of CC membership during this period is the erosion of the position of the full-time party apparatus. This is shown in the figures in table 6.6. The period

Table 6.4. *CC membership, 1927–34*

	Full	Cand-idate	Total	Carried over to next CC (%)	Carryover as % of new CC
XV	71	50	121	84.3	74.4
XVI	71	67	138	67.4	73.9
XVII	71	68	139	17.3	66.9

Table 6.5. *Length of party membership of CC members, 1927–34*

	Pre-1917			1917			Post-1917		
	F	C	T	F	C	T	F	C	T
XV	98.4	82.2	92.2	–	6.6	2.6	1.6	11.0	5.3
XVI	98.6	62.6	81.2	1.4	22.4	11.6	–	14.9	7.2
XVII	85.9	52.9	69.8	7.0	26.5	16.5	7.0	20.6	13.7

between the XV and XVI Congresses witnessed the greatest decline in representation of the party apparatus for the whole 1917–41 period, although this was less marked among full members than the committee as a whole.[33] The decline in party representation is much greater among regional than central officials, possibly reflecting the extent of sub-national leaders' concerns in 1929–30 about the course of agricultural collectivisation and the substantial turnover of those leaders at that time. Indeed the CC elected at the XVI Congress is the only one between 1921 and 1939 in which central representatives outnumbered those from the regions.[34] The further decline in the representation of the party apparatus at the XVII Congress (although not among full members) is consistent with the sense of uneasiness with Stalin in that apparatus. The decline in party and growth in state representation is also consistent with the statisation of party organs that was occurring at this time.[35]

The source base upon which we can rest a discussion of the performance of major organs like the CC during the 1930s is much less extensive than it was for the 1920s. The official proceedings of party congresses and the party press often provide snippets of information, but these are inadequate for the construction of an organisational

Table 6.6. *Bureaucratic constituencies in the CC, 1927–34 (in %)*

	CP apparatus			State	Other	Uncertain
	Centre	Region	Total			
XV	14.0	35.5	49.5	28.1	15.7	6.6
XVI	12.3	23.9	36.2	40.5	15.9	7.2
XVII	7.2	26.6	33.8	41.0	15.1	10.1

profile along the lines of the earlier periods. Despite the inadequacies of the sources, it seems clear that the CC was much less important as an organisational entity than it had been previously. When Kaganovich declared at the XVII Congress that questions were settled quickly in the CC, he was referring to the CC apparatus controlled by Stalin rather than the plenum.[36] The relative infrequency of CC plena means that this body could not be an effective source of on-going leadership or supervision. Judging from the resolutions adopted by CC plena, this organ concerned itself principally with economic matters; of the 21 resolutions adopted, 15 were to do directly with the economy.[37] The CC had never had a monopoly of the most important decisions, but it had previously usually had a much more prominent role in crucial areas than it now seemed to occupy. Its eroded position is illustrated by the part it played in decisions about its own composition and structure. On 1 December 1930 Syrtsov was expelled from the CC by a joint Politburo–CCC Presidium meeting,[38] a move which was strictly unconstitutional because the power to remove CC members lay with a two-thirds vote of the joint CC–CCC plenum. But what seemed to emphasise the declining relevance of the CC was the fact that this decision was taken in these executive organs when a joint CC–CCC plenum was scheduled to meet only 16 days later. Furthermore, decisions about the structure of the CC apparatus were taken in the CC's executive organs and not even ratified by the plenum; the decision about the reorganisation of the apparatus was made in January 1930 and approved some five months later by the XVI Congress[39] while in October 1934 the Central Asian Bureau of the CC was liquidated,[40] again without reference to the plenum.

The decline in the decision-making role of the CC may reflect a shift in its main focus of interest into the administrative sphere. This sort of development should not be surprising given the massive economic transformation taking place and the party's desire to control it at all stages. As a result, the CC became, through its apparatus, much more an economic-administrative organ than it had been in the past. This change is reflected in the increased importance of the joint CC–Sovnarkom decisions noted above. It is also shown by the course of development of the Orgburo and Secretariat during this period (see below).

Although the importance of the CC as a decision-maker, and even a ratifier, of the most important decisions seems to have been considerably less during this period than earlier, this does not mean that the CC had no importance. Discussion in the CC ranged over a wider array of questions than those upon which formal resolutions were adopted.[41] All plenary sessions during this period lasted between three and six days, a period which was shorter than the duration of most such meetings in the second half of the 1920s but which would have been adequate to discuss major issues of policy had the body been meeting on a more regular basis. One factor which was instrumental in the longer duration of plena during the late 1920s but was absent in the early 1930s was the high profile of opposition in the CC. Leading former anti-Stalinists like Bukharin, Rykov and Tomsky (all members in 1930 and candidates in 1934) were all re-elected to the plenum, but in political terms they were lame ducks. Unlike during the 1920s, when they were in the CC by right as a result of their personal importance in the party and when their views carried real weight, now they were present by grace of the leading group. As a result, the basis upon which they could participate in elite discussions was immeasurably weaker. This means that the CC was not characterised by the same sort of basic divisions as had existed earlier and its deliberations were not as structured by strongly entrenched antagonistic positions.

This does not mean that there were not disputes within the CC. The uncertainties which pervaded the party regarding collectivisation discussed above and reflected in the activities of opposition groups during this period (see below), would doubtless have infected the CC. If reports about Stalin's inability to gain CC approval for the use of the death penalty against Riutin in 1932[42] and Nicolaevsky's suggestion that there was increased opposition to Stalin's policies at the January 1933 plenum[43] are correct, the CC was anything but a pliable instrument of the leader and his supporters. The tension between the sub-national leaders and Stalin and his supporters would also have injected into the CC an element of tension and conflict. Its relative infrequency of meeting would be consistent with attempts to avoid this. The absence of hard evidence of open conflict in the CC at this time is therefore reflective not of the absence of such disagreement, but of the changed rules governing political conflict discussed below. The debate and conflict which must have characterised CC meetings was not broadcast in the public arena but kept behind closed doors.

The restriction of elite disagreements to the CC would be consistent with the development of a true sense of corporate identity and even collective responsibility within the CC and, perhaps flowing from that, a sense of institutional integrity and coherence. However, there is no evidence that the restriction of debate in this way resulted from the generation of such institutional norms and their imposition upon elite actors. Indeed, the other characteristics of the CC's operation and the growth of its role in administration suggests that it remained an organ subject to change and without any clear sense of integrity or coherence.

Like the CC there is little hard information about the operation of the Politburo during this period. One observer has suggested that it was meeting two to three times per week at the beginning of the 1930s.[44] We have Kaganovich's assertion at the XVII Congress that the Politburo was an organ exercising effective, concrete leadership in all branches of socialist construction,[45] but there is no hard evidence against which to measure this statement. Given the constant complaints about the failure to fulfil central directives, Kaganovich's reference to effective leadership sounds more a hope than a description of reality, at least as far as the supervision of the implementation of central policy is concerned. However, caution is needed because this may reflect more the weakness of the mechanisms possessed by the centre for ensuring lower level compliance than the operation of the Politburo as an institutional entity.

The size of the Politburo remained stable over the period, settling at a level slightly lower than that elected in 1927. There was also significant membership stability. Table 6.7 lists members and their positions when elected following both congresses.[46] Of the fifteen members of the Politburo elected in 1930, only three were not re-elected in 1934; of those three, Rykov and Syrtsov lost their places as a result of their oppositional activity and Rudzutak because he moved to the Control Commission. In addition, Andreev left and returned to the body in connection with his period at the CCC. All members elected in 1930 had been in the Politburo at the close of the earlier period, with only Tomsky and Bauman being casualties from the Politburo elected at the November 1929 plenum.[47]

Table 6.7. *Politburo membership, 1930 and 1934*

1930	1934
Full	
K. E. Voroshilov, PC Defence	A. A. Andreev, PC Transport
L. M. Kaganovich, CC Sec[a]	K. E. Voroshilov, PC Defence
M. I. Kalinin, Ch TsIK	L. M. Kaganovich, CC Sec[a]
S. M. Kirov, 1st Sec L'grad	M. I. Kalinin, Ch TsIK
S. V. Kosior, Gensec CC CPU	S. M. Kirov, 1st Sec L'grad[b]
V. V. Kuibyshev, Ch Vesenkha	S. V. Kosior, Gensec CC CPU
V. M. Molotov, CC Sec[c]	V. V. Kuibyshev, Ch Soviet Control Commission
Ya. E. Rudzutak, Dep Ch SNK	V. M. Molotov, Ch SNK
A. I. Rykov, Ch SNK	G. K. Ordzhonikidze, PC H.Ind.
I. V. Stalin, Gensec	I. V. Stalin, Gensec
Candidate	
A. A. Andreev, PC RKI/Ch CCC	A. I. Mikoian, PC Food Industry
A. I. Mikoian, PC Supply	G. I. Petrovsky, Ch TsIK Ukr.
G. I. Petrovsky, Ch TsIK Ukr.	P. P. Postyshev, CC Sec, CPU
S. I. Syrtsov, Ch TsIK RSFSR	Ya. E. Rudzutak, Dep Ch SNK
V. Ya. Chubar, Ch SNK Ukr.	V. Ya. Chubar, Dep Ch SNK[d]

[a] During 1930 Kaganovich was also First Secretary of the Moscow party committee, a position he retained in 1934 along with Chairmanship of the Party Control Commission.
[b] In 1934 Kirov was also elected a Secretary of the CC, a position he never physically took up.
[c] In December 1930 Molotov also became Chairman of Sovnarkom in place of Rykov.
[d] In 1934 Chubar was also Chairman of the Sovnarkom of the Ukraine.

Turning to institutional representation in the Politburo, despite the complicating effects of joint occupancy of state and party and of central and regional posts, it is clear that the profile of the central state apparatus increased over this period. This is illustrated by the figures in table 6.8. (All figures are percentages and all assume party rather than state and central rather than regional posts in cases of joint incumbency.)[48]

In both Politburos people holding office in the state apparatus constituted more than half of the membership. However, the overall position of the central institutions strengthened at the expense of the regionally based bodies, although this was due wholly to the expan-

Table 6.8. *Bureaucratic constituencies in the Politburo, 1930 and 1934 (in %)*

	CP apparatus		State apparatus	
	Central	Regional	Central	Regional
1930	26.6	13.3	40.0	20.0
1934	13.3	20.0	60.0	6.6

sion of central state representation; indeed the level of representation of the central party apparatus was halved. But as well as this high level of state representation, there was also significant representation of the Orgburo; in 1930 three (Kaganovich, Molotov and Stalin) and in 1934 four members (Kaganovich, Kirov, Kuibyshev and Stalin) of this body were also members of the Politburo. The extent of state and Orgburo representation on the Politburo reflects the narrowing of the elite; if in 1926 three of the nine full members of the Politburo were also members of the Orgburo or Sovnarkom, by 1934 this figure had risen to eight out of ten.[49]

The increased state representation and the central rather than regional tenor of the Politburo during this period reflects the changed orientation of leading party organs towards economic management and administration noted above with regard to the CC. All members were essentially practical politicians, concerned with running the country and building socialism rather than with the intricacies of Marxist dialectics; Riazanov's quip at the XVI Conference in April 1929 'They don't need any Marxists in the Politburo'[50] had been borne out. From the membership profile, the nature of many of the decisions which emanated from central party organs and the economic orientation of the CC apparatus which served the Politburo, much of the time of the Politburo's deliberations appears to have been spent in considering economic questions.[51] Such a focus encouraged the practice of attendance at Politburo meetings by large numbers of people who were not members but had particular expertise to contribute.

It would, however, be naive to believe that the Politburo was only concerned with economic questions. It is probable that all of the most important questions of the day came before the Politburo for discussion, particularly if it was meeting a couple of times per week.[52] Furthermore, although the members of the Politburo had much to thank Stalin for in the advancement of their careers, they were not the mute instruments of the General Secretary. They were figures of some importance in the party-state structure who, if the reports about their rebuff of Stalin's demand for the death penalty in the Riutin affair are accurate,[53] collectively could stand up to Stalin and force him to back down. Politburo members were of sufficient political stature and importance to bring any issues before the Politburo if they felt this warranted, particularly in the difficult times early in this period.[54] Despite Syrtsov's apparent claim that the Politburo had been replaced by the quartet of Stalin, Molotov, Kaganovich and Ordzhonikidze,[55] major issues do seem to have been discussed in this body; the fate of successive opposition groups and questions relating to the purge of 1933–34 all appear to have come before the Politburo. Indeed, the fact that it was a joint Politburo–CCC Presidium meeting that removed Syrtsov from the CC, and presumably from the Politburo itself (an action at variance with the party Rules), shows that this body retained considerable importance.

But this does not mean that the Politburo was the unchallenged nucleus of the political system. Stalin's personal position, buttressed by his personal secretariat (see below) gave him the capacity to take decisive measures without reference to the Politburo. Perhaps the best instance of this was the directive issued on the day of Kirov's assassination right at the close of this period and discussed below. This was issued on Stalin's personal authority and was only subsequently approved by the Politburo.[56] The Politburo did not have sufficient coherence, integrity and strength to put permanent constraints upon a General Secretary who wished to flout its authority.

Problems of shortage of hard information also exist with regard to the Secretariat and the Orgburo, making the drawing of a satisfactory organisational profile difficult. In line with the rationalisation of the party apparatus that had been undertaken at the end of the 1920s, the size of both organs was reduced during this period (see table 6.9). The turnover in the Orgburo was significant: of the thirteen full and seven candidate members elected in 1927, only five retained their places, of whom one (Dogadov) was reduced from a full to a candidate member in 1930. Of the other ten members of the Orgburo elected in 1930, four had entered that body during 1928–29 at the time of the conflict with the Right Opposition, and the remaining six were new. Of the twelve members elected at the XVII Congress, eight were newly elected; of the four who retained their membership from 1930, only Stalin had been a member in 1927. Thus by the end of this period, the Orgburo's

Table 6.9. *Orgburo and Secretariat membership, 1930 and 1934*

Congress	Orgburo			Secretariat		
	Full	Candidate	Total	Full	Candidate	Total
XVI	11	4	15	5	2	7
XVII	10	2	12	4	–	4

membership had been almost entirely renewed from that which had gained office at the final congress of the preceding period. Turning to the Secretariat, of the eight members elected in 1927, only three retained their positions in 1930, of whom Stalin and Kaganovich were re-elected in 1934. While one of the four members elected in 1934 had been in the Secretariat in 1927 (Stalin), the substantial reduction in the size of that body effectively made it an organ that was qualitatively different from its predecessor of the late 1920s. All members of the Secretariat remained members of the Orgburo.

Along with the reduction in size of these two bodies went a corresponding reduction in the central apparatus, at least at the opening of the period. No figures were given at the XVII Congress, but at the XVI Congress Vladimirsky reported that there had been a 42 per cent reduction in the size of the central full-time apparatus compared with the XV Congress, resulting in a figure of 375 members.[57] The proportion of responsible to technical workers remained what it had been before, 38 per cent:62 per cent.[58]

The reduction in size of these organs may seem surprising given the scale of the economic transformation underway and the changed role envisaged for the CC apparatus in the new-style Soviet economy. This new role is evident in the structural change made in the Secretariat in 1930. The change was specifically linked to the demands created by the new economic conditions, especially the economy's need for cadres.[59] At the heart of this reorganisation was the functional principle. Questions of personnel were now to be divided between two sections of the Secretariat, the Organisation-Instruction Department and the Assignment Department. The former was to be responsible for leading all organisational party work, including the verification of the implementation of party directives, links with lower level party organs and the distribution of cadres within the party apparatus. The latter was to be concerned with the distribution of so-called administrative-economic and trade union cadres.[60] It was to be divided into eight sub-sections: Heavy Industry, Light Industry, Transport, Agriculture, Foreign Cadres, Finance-Planning-Trade, Soviet Administration, and Accounting.[61] Personnel questions in the party apparatus were therefore clearly distinguished from those within the remainder of the Soviet apparatus, while personnel questions in each major sector of the economy were to be handled by their own individual sub-sections. In order to bring about some coordination between these sub-sections and to overcome the narrow department-mindedness that was always a problem, the Chancellery was significantly strengthened through provisions which 'completely detached' individual sections of the Secretariat from their own technical apparatus and concentrated the latter in the Chancellery.[62] Such a move, involving a centralised overview of individual sections' operations, was essential if adequate supervision of the economy was to be secured. Economic supervision and the Secretariat's role in it were thus seen primarily in terms of personnel and their placement.[63]

Such changes, which were to be replicated at all levels of the party apparatus, were slow in being brought to fruition, probably in part as a result of opposition to them.[64] Nevertheless, they reflect a clear desire to increase the role of the CC and its apparatus in the administration of the economy. This is also evident in the projected agenda for the Orgburo. During the 1920s, the plan of Orgburo work was concerned principally with party affairs: reports from lower level party organisations, verification of the implementation of decisions, the processing of new party members, the press and political education, the role of the party and the trade unions in the enterprise, the role of these bodies in production and cooperation, soviet elections, the Komsomol, composition of the Red Army and the verification of workers in some branches of industry were major areas of Orgburo concern in the latter half of 1928.[65] There was no direct concern with matters of production, except in terms of the party's role in the economic sphere. In contrast, the plan of work for the Orgburo in 1931 was divided into nine sections under the following headings:[66] industry, agriculture, transport and communications, finance, supply and grain procurement, trade unions and soviets, cadres and labour (in the economy), culture and press, and intra-party work. The final category contained the following types of items: verification of the implementation of directives, party growth and educational work, cadres in specific areas, the strengthening of lower level party organs, and the state of the party in different areas of work and geographical regions. This list depicts an organisation whose major concerns have undergone a substantial reorientation. While still concerned with intra-party affairs, the main focus of its interest as reflected in the plan had become economic management. The CC apparatus had become the main centre for the direction and administration of all aspects of state-economic life, and the reorganisation of the Secretariat in 1930 was designed to facilitate the achievement of this task. Thus the shift in the CC's functions was clearly evident in the change in the organisational profile of its apparatus.

However, the reorganisation of the Secretariat conducted in 1930 was not deemed a complete success and a further reorganisation took place in 1934. The main spokesman for the change, Kaganovich, argued that organisation on the basis of function had hindered effective work and that departments should be organised on the basis of the integral production-branch principle. Instead of one department being concerned with one function across all branches of the economy, departments should be based upon those branches and be concerned with all aspects of work within them: organisational and party work, distribution and preparation of cadres, agitation-mass work, production propaganda and the verification of the implementation of party decisions by appropriate soviet-economic and party organs.[67] On this basis, the CC Secretariat was to have the following departments: Agriculture, Industry, Transport, Planning-Finance-Trade, Politico-Administrative (dealing mainly with such organisations as the soviets, Red Army and Prosecutors Departments), Leading Party Organs (ORPO), Culture and Propaganda of Leninism, Chancellery and Special Sector.[68] This reorganisation, even more than that of 1930, reflects the orientation of the CC apparatus towards direct economic administration and management and represents an attempt to increase central control over all aspects of the economy. This reorganisation was not smoothly achieved; it met entrenched opposition, particularly at lower levels.[69] Furthermore, over time its main rationale was to be undermined as ORPO expanded its competence to embrace the posting of party officials in all areas of party work rather than just within the party itself.[70]

These cases of organisational restructuring reflect the change in function of the CC and its apparatus and show us the organisational structure through which the new functions were to be carried out. However, they leave unanswered the question of how these central organs were meant to cope with the pressures created by collectivisation and the First Five Year Plan. Expenditure on maintenance and operating costs of the party apparatus escalated 2.76 times between 1930 and 1933, with most of this being spent on the lower party apparatus.[71] Although no figures on personnel are given, expenditure levels suggest that if the size of personnel in the central apparatus did increase over this period, it increased at a slower rate than that at lower levels. So the question remains: how was the central apparatus able to cope? One aspect of the answer is that it did not cope satisfactorily. This is evident in the perceived need for the reorganisation of 1934 and for another bout of restructuring in 1939, and in the continued complaints about local organs not carrying out central instructions. Another part of the answer may lie in the Secret Department/Special Sector. The extensive control which this body exercised over communication within the party and its role in personnel affairs (which seems to have amounted to at least a watching brief) added to its links with similar departments in non-party organisations,[72] suggests that this organ could have been an important instrument for the centre to maintain supervision over developments at lower levels. The current state of the sources means that there is no way of proving that this was the case. However, if the 1930 personnel figures cited above exclude members of the Secret Department/Special Sector, as they seem to have done in the 1920s,[73] this may explain the paradox of smaller staff but greater responsibilities.

These reorganisations of the CC apparatus did little to improve the central operation of the personnel system. The major element of both changes was a recasting of the organisational vehicle of the personnel system, but that system's problems were not resolved by such measures. The continuing problems with the compilation of an adequate, up-to-date register of communists at lower levels meant that regardless of how efficient central record-system processes were (and there is no evidence to show that they were efficient) the establishment and operation of an effective, centralised personnel system was impossible. The nomenklatura system remained a somewhat haphazard means of structuring the party's personnel affairs, while the Orgburo and Secretariat continued to suffer real problems in operating in an efficient, organisationally coherent fashion.

Throughout this period, until its abolition along with Rabkrin at the XVII Congress, the Central Control Commission remained an important elite body. At the XVII Congress, the CCC was replaced by the Party Control Commission (PCC) which was to be attached to the CC and, like its predecessor, to be elected by the party congress. It was to have permanent representatives at the republican, krai and oblast levels who were to be responsible to the centre rather than to the local organs which had elected them in the past.[74] The new PCC was to be headed by a CC Secretary, and Kaganovich was chosen for this post. This reorganisation, which involved the restoration of a distinction between party and state control, was justified by the need to 'strengthen supervision of the execution of party and AUCP(b) Central Committee decisions, to consolidate party discipline, and to intensify the struggle against the violation of party ethics'.[75] This reflects a dissatisfaction with the way in which the CCC had been managing intra-party affairs, the areas specified above being consistent with a charge that this body had not been an effective instrument in the centre's desire to bring lower level political leaders into line.[76] It is also consistent with a desire to bring this disciplinary arm of the party under closer CC direction, an interesting move within the context of the contemporary purge which had explicitly been taken out of the hands of the CCC as an institution. Clearly the organisation was perceived to have failed in the implementation of the disciplinary procedures which had emerged as its major focus during the 1920s. The formal imposition of CC supervision represents institutional recognition of the demise of the control commissions' aspirations for integrity and coherence.

The disciplinary focus of the control apparatus is reflected in some of its activities during this period. Between the XVI and XVII Congresses, the CCC passed judgement on 611 party members and candidates, 75 per cent of whom were expelled. Between 1931 and the first half of 1933, thirteen of the largest regional organisations handled nearly 40,000 cases of political deviation, resulting in 15,441 being expelled.[77] But disciplinary matters were not the province solely of the control commission apparatus. When the Riutin affair emerged, the CCC seems to have considered this to be outside its competence and passed it on to the Politburo for resolution.[78] Although it was a joint Politburo–CCC Presidium session which removed Syrtsov from the CC in December 1930 and a joint CC–CCC plenum which brought down a decision on the Eismont-Tolmachev-Smirnov group in January 1933,[79] the other opposition groups were not brought before such joint sessions, as they would probably have been in the 1920s. The 1933 purge was not entrusted to the CCC but to a special Central Purge Commission of which only half of the members were representatives of the CCC.[80]

Discipline was not the only concern of the CCC. The two joint

CC–CCC plena which were held during this period (December 1930 and January 1933) did not focus particularly upon disciplinary issues: of the eight resolutions which issued from them, four were concerned with economic matters, one with the soviet elections and one with the role of the political departments in the MTS and sovkhozy. The other two announced the 1933 purge and dealt with the Eismont–Tolmachev–Smirnov group. Furthermore, in the agendas for the CCC plena during this period (July 1930, December 1930, July 1931 and February 1932), the principal area of concern appears to have been internal management and the role of the control apparatus in the achievement of economic success;[81] indeed, the XVI Congress declared that it was to play a major role in accelerating economic development.[82] It seems, then, that the re-orientation of the leading party organs towards matters of economic management and administration was also reflected in the perceptions of the role that the control apparatus should play, at least early in this period. The reorganisation of the control apparatus in 1934 seems, within the context of the emphasis upon the need for verification and the search for enemies, to reflect a change in that perception and a reaffirmation of the disciplinary orientation of the control commissions.

Personnel data from the leading organs of the control apparatus provide some interesting information. This is summarised in table 6.10, with that of 1927 for comparison. The carryover figures for the CCC are interesting.[83] The carryover level from the XV to the XVI Congress was lower than for any previous CCC after 1921–22 in proportional terms, although in terms of the total number of individuals, the difference was marginal: eighty-seven from 1925 to 1927 and eighty-four from 1927 to 1930. But the drop from 1930 to 1934 was dramatic, with only 10.2 per cent, or nineteen individuals, making the transition from CCC to PCC. Part of the reason for this is the smaller size of the latter body, which was less than one-third that of its predecessor. Even so, the fact that those carried forward constituted a smaller proportion of the new body than at any time in a decade[84] suggests that the wastage rate was due at least in part to conditions specific to the period. One of these conditions would have been the need to appoint staff to two separate organs, the Party Control Commission and the Soviet Control Commission. But also relevant were the sorts of dissatisfactions which led to the elimination of the CCC itself and which were spelled out at the XVII Congress; it would have made little sense to restructure the organisation while leaving the personnel intact. Quite marked also is the drop in both pre-1917 and

Table 6.10. *CCC and CCC Presidium membership, 1927–34*

	Total	Carried over to next body %	CCC/PCC Carryover as % of current body	Party entry (%) Pre-1917	1917	Post-1917
1927	195	43.1	44.6	63.7	22.5	13.8
1930	187	10.2	44.9	62.6	17.1	20.3
1934	61		31.1	57.4	27.8	14.7

	Total	Carried over to next body %	CCC Presidium Carryover as % of current body	Party entry (%) Pre-1917	1917	Post-1917
1927	32	62.5	64.5	93.8	6.2	–
1930	31		64.5[sic]	90.3	9.7	–

post-1917 party entrants and the consequent rise in those who entered during the revolutionary year. Clearly the party leadership was dissatisfied with the performance of the control commission apparatus during the first part of the 1930s.[85]

In structural terms, the post of General Secretary remained relatively unchanged from the 1920s: the General Secretary remained at the point of overlap between the Politburo, Orgburo and Secretariat, his supervision over the organisational levers contained in the secretarial apparatus remained unimpaired, and the personal secretariat continued to function in a way which reinforced the power and position of the incumbent. But in formal terms, the office remained elastic. As far as we are aware, no formal rules existed governing the main aspects of the office: tenure, powers, mode of selection or dismissal.[86] This means that the office had no institutional integrity or coherence and was not seen as an institution independent of its incumbent. The power of the leading figure in the system remained highly personalised; the fortunes of the office rose and fell with the fortunes of the incumbent. The power and position of the office of General Secretary is thus in reality a discussion of the power and position of Stalin himself.

Stalin was clearly the most prominent political figure in the system, although he was not yet able to ignore the rest of the leadership except in exceptional circumstances such as those surrounding the Kirov assassination. His power and position rested on two main pillars, one organisational and the other symbolic. Formally, the organisational pillar was the CC apparatus, but informally and more importantly, it was Stalin's personal secretariat. This consisted of a 'considerable number' of assistants and a large administrative apparatus[87] and was intertwined with the formal apparatus. The major student of the personal secretariat[88] has suggested that this may even have been coterminous with the Secret Department/Special Sector. He has also suggested that the Secret Department/Special Sector was the party's Chancellery,[89] an organisation with increased importance following the 1930 reorganisation. However, party documents in 1934 refer to the Special Sector as well as the Chancellery,[90] which suggests that these organisations were not coterminous, although they may have overlapped. Nevertheless, even if the Secret Department/Special Sector was not simply another name for the Chancellery, its responsibility for secret communications within the party (and it is probable that most intra-party communications were secret and fell into the competence of this body)[91] and a concern for aspects of the discipline question made this a very important power centre, especially following its apparent upgrading at the time of the 1934 reorganisation.[92] As the channel for secret communications, any fusing of the Secret Department/Special Sector with Stalin's personal secretariat would have given the General Secretary an important edge over other members of the elite in terms of access to information on all important aspects of party life. To the extent that Stalin could filter the flow of information to members of the oligarchy, he could structure debate and discussion on his own terms. Of course, the other members of the oligarchy had their own sources of information and were not entirely reliant on the party's secret communication channels. Nevertheless, Stalin's position in the information flow chart of the party was an important buttress to the influence he could wield over personnel matters.

Stalin was able to strengthen his organisational position in the security apparatus at this time. The Shakhty affair had sparked off the hunt for treachery among the specialists in the economy, a process encouraged by the show trials of the Industrial Party in 1930, of former Mensheviks (many of whom had worked in the state apparatus) in March 1931 and of the Metro-Vickers engineers in 1933.[93] This expanded into a general vigilance campaign, the search for hidden enemies and the purge of 1933–34. In addition, the OGPU had played a part in the collectivisation drive, and although there had been some periods of anxiety about the outcome of this, its ultimate success added some lustre to the image of the security apparatus. The vigilance campaign threw the security apparatus right into the forefront of the regime's political focus, projecting it as the guardian of the economic and political order.[94] However, at least until the Kirov assassination, the party's impermeability and its control were maintained; party members remained immune from police actions until expelled from the party or clearly made outcasts within it, and the party's controlling role was not questioned. Indeed, the transformation of the OGPU into the NKVD in July 1934 represents an attempt further to restrict the powers of the security apparatus.[95] Its continuing subordination to the party is suggested by the fact that neither of its successive leaders during this period (Menzhinsky until July 1934 and Yagoda thereafter) attained a party status higher than CC membership and by the close oversight of OGPU action in the Riutin affair exercised by party organs. This was to change as the role, functions and status of the organisation were transformed during the following period. Important for that change was Stalin's ability to move into important positions of party control over the security apparatus people who were to be major allies in the future, in particular Ezhov, Poskrebyshev and Beria.[96] However, from July 1934 the NKVD was headed by Yagoda, who had not always agreed with Stalin in the past.[97] But if the police were not yet a major support base, the foundations were well and truly laid.

The organisational basis of Stalin's power was strengthened considerably by the continuing inability of the party's leading legislative organs – the congress, CC and Politburo – to develop a strong sense of institutional integrity and coherence. In the absence of a major commitment by leading political figures to strengthen the organisational norms and identity of these bodies, inertia and the methods of action adopted by the party leadership ensured that the weakness of these bodies that had been evident in the 1920s continued into the 1930s. In this way, they were unable to impose meaningful constraints upon the General Secretary whose own organisational weapons were now so extensive.

The symbolic pillar of Stalin's position was the Stalin cult which grew upon the edifice of Leninist orthodoxy that had been raised up in the 1920s. The theoretical underpinning for this was provided by an article by K. Popov entitled 'The Party and the Role of the Leader'.[98] Popov advanced three main grounds for recognition of the vozhd', or supreme leader. The first part of this theoretical justification was the argument that the history of the party had shown the important role that leaders had played. Such leaders were armed with Marxist-Leninist revolutionary theory, hardened by many years experience of the struggle for Leninism, hand in hand with Lenin, those who went under his leadership in the school of this struggle with 'enemies within the worker movement', with perverters of marxism and traitors to the proletariat – in the leadership of such leaders the Leninist party sees one of the most reliable guarantees of its successes and victories. Precisely among such leaders belongs comrade Stalin.[99]

The party's successes were thus related to leadership of the Leninist type.

Popov then proceeded to cite Lenin's words to show that this type of leader could play a predominant role in the party leadership. According to Popov:

In his speech about Ya. M. Sverdlov in 1919, V. I. Lenin said: 'If we have succeeded over the course of more than a year of enduring those difficulties which befell the narrow circle of selfless revolutionaries, if the leading groups could so firmly and unanimously resolve difficult questions, then this is only because a prominent place among them was taken by such an exceptionally talented organiser as Yakov Mikhailovich.' These words of Lenin in regard to Sverdlov, so vividly and distinctly show how the bolshevik collective leadership of the party combines with the exceptional role in it of talented leader organisers, the type of which there is no equal to comrade Stalin.

Moreover, in the difficult years following Lenin's death, the collective leadership of the party was able to overcome the challenges confronting it, in particular those stemming from the activity of opposition groups, 'only because of the prominent, first place among them occupied by such an exceptionally talented organiser of the struggle for the moral and organisational unity of the party as comrade Stalin'.[100]

The third aspect of Popov's justification was that the will of an individual leader could personify the will of the proletariat, a position hitherto reserved for the party. For Popov, in the struggle for Leninism, 'the will of the leading collective of the party – its CC and the will of such a leader of the party as comrade Stalin, in this struggle invariably expresses the will of hundreds of thousands and millions'. He supported this assertion with a quotation from Lenin: 'The will of hundreds and tens of thousands of people can be expressed in a single person.'[101] It was Stalin who had led the fight for Lenin's line and defended it against those who attacked it. The message of Popov's article was clear: 'Comrade Stalin is really "the first among equals", the first political leader of the party after Lenin.'[102]

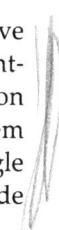

Popov's article marked an important stage in the development of party norms: it was a clear acknowledgement of the principle that individual leaders could adopt a position of pre-eminence within leading circles, that collectivism could be subordinated to individual prominence. On the basis of this supposition, the Stalin cult burgeoned.

The Stalin cult had burst onto the Soviet scene on the occasion of Stalin's fiftieth birthday. The issues of *Pravda* for the week 18–25 December 1929 dripped with lavish praise of Stalin. The epithets used and the praise heaped upon Stalin were alien even to the type of excess which had surrounded Lenin after his death.[103] One of the major themes of the cult at this time was Stalin's role as the supporter and follower of Lenin, as 'the firmest and truest pupil of Vladimir Il'ich Lenin', 'the best comrade-in-arms of Lenin', and the 'great Leninist'.[104] He was 'the true continuer of the cause of Lenin'.[105] But this sort of relationship, which clearly cast Stalin in a subordinate role to Lenin, was parallelled by two sub-themes. The first united the two figures without any notion of a superior/subordinate relationship: 'the party of Lenin–Stalin', 'the cause of Lenin–Stalin', 'the banner of Lenin–Stalin' and 'the teachings of Lenin–Stalin' were epithets typical of this sort of treatment.[106] The second sub-theme, which was little more than a faint echo at this time, portrayed Stalin as superior to Lenin. He 'further developed' Lenin's teachings, he was 'the greatest strategist of the proletarian revolution' (which by implication cast a question mark over Lenin's role), 'the best of the best', 'the hero of heroes' and 'the greatest man of all times and epochs'.[107]

Another major theme of the cult was to associate all Bolshevik successes with the name and guidance of Stalin. He was associated with all of the victories of the revolution and the Civil War,[108] a claim that was given substance by the creative rewriting of party history.[109] Achievements in the economic field, particularly the successes of agricultural collectivisation and industrial development were attributed to Stalin's guidance.[110] In the words of a letter purported to be sent to Stalin by kolkhoz youths: 'We know that You, comrade Stalin, our leader, are leading all kolkhozniks and kolkhoz children to a good and prosperous life.'[111] The image that was projected of Stalin's leadership began to take on overtones of infallibility as *Pravda* intoned: 'It is important not to forget for one minute comrade Stalin's instruction'.[112]

The third major theme of the cult at this time was the way in which Stalin's care for the people, reflected in the sort of invocation cited above, was reciprocated in their love for him. Their love for Stalin was declared to be 'boundless', they forever carried him in their hearts and they praised him and sang about him constantly.[113] The press frequently carried greetings to Stalin and the people's fervent wish that he should enjoy a long life.[114]

While the cult was projected most prominently through the press, it also resounded through formal party gatherings. At the opening of the XVI Congress, as the names of those proposed as members of the congress presidium were announced, some were met by 'applause' while, according to the published report, that of Stalin was met by 'stormy prolonged applause, the whole congress rises and greets the candidature of comrade Stalin'.[115] Although the delegates' speeches were not interlaced with invocations of Stalin's name, the greetings sent to the congress usually referred to him by name, thereby elevating him above his leadership colleagues. The XVII Congress was reported to have opened in the following way: 'The appearance in the hall of comrade Stalin is met by the stormy, prolonged applause of the whole hall. The whole congress, standing, greets its vozhd' with a fervent, prolonged ovation. Cries of "hooray". Greeting cries of "Long live comrade Stalin."'[116] His report to the congress was followed by a stormy, prolonged ovation, the singing of 'The Internationale' and invocations for his long life.[117] Many speakers at the congress referred glowingly to Stalin, including some former oppositionists in the course of their general abasement before the party.[118] As a symbol, Stalin hovered over all formal political meetings in the USSR; he was supreme in this regard by the time of the XVII Congress.

The cult was important because it projected an image of Stalin's authority which was rooted in the central pillars of Bolshevik mythology: Lenin, the October revolution, the achievement of socialism and the symbolism of the chosen people. By appropriating these symbols, the cult was immeasurably strengthening the figure of Stalin in comparison with those other figures near the apex of political life. The personalised leadership model that the cult projected accorded well with the emphasis upon the party's general line; the notion that there was one, correct, Leninist line established a need to determine what that line was. If Stalin was the embodiment of Leninism, the problem was solved: the line was whatever Stalin said it was. The special category into which Stalin was projected is reflected in the use of the term vozhd' (which has resonances of 'führer' or 'duce') for Stalin rather than the more pedestrian term for leader, rukovoditel'. Furthermore, by projecting Stalin in this way, the cult helped to shape the contours of political discourse during this period. By linking the figures of Lenin and Stalin, the cult greatly complicated any attempt to oppose Stalin by portraying this as anti-Leninist. This was a crucial pillar for Stalin, and one which may have been of great practical benefit to him. The basis of systemic legitimacy had begun to shift to Stalin, although it had not yet come to rest there.

Norms and conventions in flux

While Stalin's power and position rested on these organisational and symbolic pillars, and although throughout the period he was clearly the leading figure, his word was not law and he could not take the rest of the leadership for granted; the symbolism of collectivism still retained some force. The chink in his organisational armoury was the inability to bind appointees irrevocably to his banner. Regional political leaders, caught between the imperatives of maintaining their fiefs and of satisfying demands from above, played politics in terms of how they saw their best interests served. For the sorts of reasons outlined in the previous chapter, many sub-national party leaders appear to have become disenchanted with Stalin and to have constituted fertile soil to nourish moves to remove him. All three major opposition groups during this period, the so-called 'Left–Right Bloc' of Syrtsov and Lominadze, the Riutin group and 'the Eismont–Tolmachev–Smirnov et al. anti-party grouping'[119] included in the positions they espoused a call for Stalin's removal.[120] There have also been reports about a desire to replace Stalin by Kirov at the XVII Congress.[121] But none of these seems to have crystallised into a clear attempt to replace Stalin that had any hope of success.

Most controversial have been the reports about the strength of opposition at the XVII Congress. Some have interpreted the events and outcome of the XVII Congress as clearly indicating an attempt to downgrade Stalin. However, analysis of the congress does not inevitably lead to such a conclusion.[122] There clearly was opposition to Stalin in the elections for leading party offices; Medvedev asserts that in the election for the CC, Stalin was opposed by 270 delegates and barely gained election.[123] Such opposition was very significant given the convention of unanimity that now surrounded congress proceedings and the election of party leaders, but the numbers alone show that this opposition was unlikely to be met with success; some four-fifths of voting delegates supported Stalin's candidacy. Nor does the fact that after the congress Stalin was referred to as 'Secretary' rather than 'General Secretary' indicate a forced downgrading. On official documents, Stalin had been referred to as CC Secretary for some time[124] and this was the nomenclature used henceforth at the official level, even when there was no doubt about Stalin's dominance.[125] Furthermore, if Stalin had been downgraded, it is difficult to explain the listing of CC secretaries issued at the end of the congress; after the XVI Congress he had been listed number five, but following the XVII Congress he was listed out of alphabetical order at the top of the list.[126] It has also been suggested that at this time Stalin was considering handing over some of his administrative responsibilities in the Secretariat to someone else and wanted to avoid passing to that person the authority which went with the title General Secretary.[127] In any case the existence of a powerful and potentially successful move against Stalin at the congress is difficult to reconcile with some aspects of the proceedings of that body: the congress approved the CC Report given by Stalin in a perfunctory fashion which simply affirmed the content of his speech as the source of guidance for all party organisations and thereby effectively presented him officially as possessing the complete authority of this, the sovereign party body in the direction of party policy;[128] when the composition of the Politburo, Orgburo and Secretariat were announced, for the first time since the Lenin period they were not listed in strict alphabetical order but had Stalin at the top with the others following in order of importance; the changes to the CC apparatus which were aimed at strengthening central control over political and economic life were effectively strengthening Stalin's bailiwick; and the high levels of praise and exultation of Stalin, albeit stage-managed, do not sit easily with a concerted effort to remove him.

Nevertheless, there was an undercurrent of uneasiness about Stalin's leadership which infected both middle and upper levels of the system. While his organisational power and the symbolic legitimacy he gained through the cult were probably instrumental in preventing this uneasiness from being translated into calculated political moves, they could not eliminate it from the scene. It therefore provided a continuing backdrop to the course of Soviet politics during this period. The danger the regime confronted early in the 1930s was instrumental in muting the uneasiness with Stalin, but important too was the continuing elite consensus which characterised this period.

A major source of this consensus was the events of the 1920s, and in particular the elimination of the major opposition groups as serious political entities. One of the chief strengths of these groups had been that they were headed by prominent members of the party leadership, individuals who, until the opposition groups of which they were a part had been defeated, were certain to gain election to leading party organs because of their personal prominence in the party and its history. Their defeat and subsequent removal from the elite (Rykov's removal from the Politburo in December 1930 ended this process) left within leading circles only those who had opposed the Right Opposition and favoured in some form the course of action adopted in the economic sphere at this time. They became locked into this position by the dangers such a policy involved for the regime. Once the party's general line was deemed a success at the end of 1933, commitment to the policy was inescapable. Unlike in the 1920s, therefore, the elite was broadly united in support of the basic line of economic policy; there were no alternative economic models seriously considered and therefore no weakening of the elite's commitment to the course outlined in the Five Year Plan.

Furthermore, those at the apex of the party, while not the creatures of Stalin, owed their positions much more to Stalin than their counterparts of the 1920s had done. Nor were they revolutionaries of substance and reputation with distinguished revolutionary careers or significant theoretical pretensions. Consequently the oligarchy was intrinsically less fractious than it had been in the previous decade.

The existence of such a consensus does not mean that there were no conflicts and disputes in the leadership. However, those disputes did not question the basic thrust of economic development. Debate tended to concentrate on the issue of growth rates, on how fast collectivisation should be conducted, what level of resources should be channelled into industrial development, and what proportion of grain production should be extracted from the peasants as 'surplus'. These issues, which were also raised by the various opposition groups,[129] were vigorously debated by Stalin's lieutenants in various fora, including the party congress. Four aspects of these debates are important in differentiating them from those that went before. The first, already noted, is that these debates did not openly call into question the general line of party policy. They were about implementation, not the policy principles themselves, although clearly the line here was not always easy to draw. Secondly, the outcome of the debates did not have direct ramifications for the perceived suitability of those at the apex of the party to continue in their positions. The policy debate in the 1920s was tied to the question of who should head the party; during this period, that link was much more tenuous for all except the opposition groups. Stalin's position was not challenged by the policy debate; the last open criticism of Stalin and the CC occurred in the lead-up to the XVI Congress in June 1930, and this seems to have been permitted in order to enable the leadership to discredit that particular line of argument.[130] Thirdly, these debates neither produced nor involved organisational divisions within the party. Although many regional leaders may have favoured less speed in the countryside, the debate was not structured along central–regional lines. The debate occurred within the elite, its failure to spread openly throughout the party being partly a function of measures taken to prevent such debate from spilling into the party at large[131] and the development of norms making open dispute within the leadership unacceptable. Fourthly, although the debate was not extended organisationally into the party apparatus, it did take on an organisational form within the state. Gosplan and Vesenkha (plus its post-1932 lineal descendant, the Commissariat of Heavy Industry), plus in 1930 Rabkrin, along with various other government commissariats and agencies, threw their resources and energies into the policy debate in an attempt to ensure the outcome they desired. This had occurred in the 1920s as well, but the difference during this period is that they were the principal organisational protagonists. When party leaders addressed these questions, it was usually in their role as state spokesmen rather than party figures. This is linked with the transformation of the leading party organs into economic-administrative bodies.

The course of the debates reflects a continuing tension within the elite consensus, broadly interpreted as between moderate and radical strands.[132] Stalin's position in this moderate–radical tension is not clear. A case can be made for his support for the radical side. This would, of course, be consistent with the stance he adopted in 1928–29. It would also fit in with the interpretation that the Great Terror of 1936–38 was in part an attempt by Stalin to resolve this issue given the domination of the moderates. However, both of these points are inferential and do not relate to developments during this period. Looking at Stalin's stance at this time, his support for moderate positions seems clear in four major instances. His stepping back from the excesses of collectivisation with his 'Dizzy with success' article in March 1930,[133] his support for the Ordzhonikidze-proposed end of specialist-baiting in mid-1931,[134] the reversal of education policy along with the ending of the cultural revolution in mid-1931[135] and his endorsement of lower plan targets at the January 1933 plenum.[136] The general relaxation of 1933–34 may also be relevant here.[137] It is possible that these positions were forced on a reluctant Stalin by a moderate Politburo majority, as some have argued.[138] Or perhaps he was just inconsistent, as some claim he had been during the 1920s. But this can be framed in another way. As a politician whose political and survival skills were well developed and whose political position was not unassailable, Stalin may have adjusted his policy stances in the light of prevailing circumstances. Although he wanted economic development as quickly as possible, he recognised the dangers that would flow from a fracturing of elite unity and so at times trimmed his positions in order to accommodate the views of fellow oligarchs. In addition, he may have been willing to be guided by economic necessities when this seemed prudent, as in the change in policy towards specialists and the lower target figures for the Second Five Year Plan. So economic development was pursued, but it was tailored to serve the maintenance of elite unity. Stalin was neither an absolute dictator nor a prisoner of one or the other group in the leadership; the collective principle continued to have an impact on elite politics.

The strength of Stalin's personal position seems to be suggested by the way in which he had broken the rules of the collective leadership game by pushing through the extraordinary measures of grain collection in 1928 and the subsequent policy of collectivisation. But this appearance was deceptive. The limits to Stalin's power and authority may be reflected in the treatment of opposition during this period. Formally Syrtsov and Lominadze were excluded from the CC in December 1930, Riutin was expelled from the party in September 1930 and imprisoned in October 1932, and in January 1933 Eismont and Tolmachev were expelled from the party and Smirnov from the CC. Riutin, Tolmachev and Eismont were sent along with some former oppositionists (most importantly Zinoviev and Kamenev) into penal exile in 1933.[139] However, according to a number of sources,[140] when the Politburo discussed the Riutin case, Stalin demanded the death penalty. The Politburo rejected this demand,[141] thereby affirming the principle that party members (even when they have been expelled) should not be executed. This convention of party life remained intact, at least for the moment; the party remained impermeable. Such a rejection also constituted a reaffirmation of collective rights over the General Secretary.

This raises the question of political opposition. The tenor of the period was one that was hostile to any manifestations of opposition. A number of elements combined to create this atmosphere: the continued emphasis on the need for vigilance, the campaign of specialist-baiting and the various trials of the period,[142] the search for hidden enemies in the purge of 1933–34, and the uncertainties of the early part of the period stemming from the difficulties associated with collectivisation, were all instrumental in this. The change in the position of opposition which occurred in the 1920s, with the shift in party norms away from acceptance of the right for an opposition to exist towards a situation in which no such right existed, was extended during this period. If, towards the end of the last period, opposition figures were required to publicly recant and renounce their past views, they were now also required to show open support for the position they had hitherto opposed. At the XVI Congress Postyshev attacked the former Right Opposition for not defending party policy; they should not only acknowledge their mistakes but actively struggle against opportunism and for the general line of the party.[143] Postyshev was echoing a call made by many at the congress that the leaders of the Right Opposition had to show through deeds that their earlier declarations were not false.[144] If they failed to do this they were still struggling against the party.[145] There could be no halfway measures and no neutrality. This was expressed in Rudzutak's adage, 'Who is not with us is against us',[146] and in the abasement of Tomsky who declared that the duty of a communist was not to give any comfort to the enemy nor to call into question the authority of or faith in the party for millions of workers.[147] It was also evident in the expulsion of various party members, including Zinoviev and Kamenev, in October 1932 for having knowledge of the Riutin platform and failing to inform the authorities about it. This demand for total commitment extended to the party the principle emerging from the Shakhty affair, and reflects the dangers posed by the course of collectivisation and the concern that some sub-national leaders were not fully committed to the party line on this question.[148]

The definition of opposition remained as fluid and vague at the edges as it had ever been. Both the Syrtsov–Lominadze and Eismont–Tolmachev–Smirnov oppositions were accused of forming underground, anti-party fractional groups in order to struggle against the party line.[149] In the case of the former at least, such a charge would have been difficult to sustain.[150] The status of fractionalism as a party crime was formalised even more during this period by its inclusion in the party Rules adopted in 1934 (#58). But opposition also became much more widely interpreted than merely fractional activity; the list of categories of those to be dealt with in the purge of 1933 was effectively a catalogue of forbidden types of activity. This list was given increased formality by its incorporation, with the addition of 'passivity', in the 1934 party Rules.[151] In essence, opposition involved failure fully to support the general line as defined by the party leadership, failure to work actively and whole-heartedly for its implementation, and lack of observance of strict party discipline.[152] 'Wrecking' could be passive as well as active; failure to implement party decisions was a crime.[153] Any slackening of an individual's commitment, any failure to mobilise all efforts to work for the party line, constituted oppositional activity and support for the party's enemies. At the XVI Congress a direct line was drawn between organisational activity in the party and opposition groups and hostile classes outside the party,[154] a linkage reflecting the continued concern about the dangers of petty bourgeois infection from the countryside. At the XVII Congress, Stalin, while declaring that there was no one to fight, referred to the danger posed by survivals of capitalism in the economy and in men's minds, while Kaganovich warned that the enemy was not yet defeated and relapses toward capitalism were possible.[155] The danger from outside, a danger which was buttressed in ideological terms (see below), made any weakening of effort a party crime; in Kirov's words, 'the further we go along the road of constructing socialism, the more evident is the counter-revolutionary character of every oppositionist tendency'.[156]

In this sort of atmosphere, opposition could have no place,[157] and although some dissent on policy issues was still possible, this could not be carried into the public or party-wide arena. In line with this, groups or individuals charged with oppositional activity had no right of appeal to other organs. This broadening of the ambit of opposition imposed stern duties on party members. Not only were they to observe the strictest party discipline, but they were also urged to be watchful about the activities of their colleagues. The position established in the 1920s[158] was confirmed at the XVI Congress; after acknowledging that there had been various underground opposition groups, Yaroslavsky declared: 'it is impossible to allow even the smallest attempt to hide the existence of these organisations; if party members know of such organisations and do not report them to the party, they are responsible for these organisations, and it is necessary to apply the most decisive measures to them, right up to exclusion from the party'.[159] All had to be done to assist the party to root out and overcome any such groups, and any obstruction of the control commissions in this task rendered one subject to disciplinary measures.[160] The role in rooting out opposition played by rank-and-file party members, and even non-party members, was further emphasised by the allocation to them of a part in the conduct of the 1933–34 purge.[161]

It is important to recognise that the 1933–34 purge was directed against people whose actions and attitudes clearly rendered them opposition as far as the leadership was concerned. While the purge was in part directed at tidying up party house-keeping arrangements and bringing some order into the question of party records and registration,[162] it was also aimed at getting rid of those elements who could be classed as oppositional under the wide definition prevailing at that time. Furthermore, the definition was sufficiently all-embracing and vague as to allow personalised and fractional differences full play in the purging process, something which may have been given increased scope following the assassination of Kirov.[163] The purge of 1933–34 was an instrument that was wielded against political opposition.

An important change in the question of opposition came about at the end of 1934 with the assassination of Kirov. There is no clear, direct and unambiguous evidence that Stalin was responsible for the death of the Leningrad and CC secretary.[164] However, if those who were uneasy about Stalin saw Kirov as a possible replacement, his death would have been timely for Stalin. But regardless of the question of Stalin's complicity,[165] Kirov's death was important for a number of reasons. First, it stimulated the general ethos of vigilance, particularly since the ineptitude or complicity of the local NKVD was clear for all to see. Secondly, it provided the occasion for Stalin to act independently of the formal party organs, ramming through the extraordinary 'Law of 1 December 1934' via the TsIK Presidium[166] and only gaining subsequent party approval. Finally, the content of this extraordinary law was significant. Those accused of terrorist acts were denied any protection in the investigation of the charges. The subsequent investigation was to be conducted without delay and to be followed by immediate execution of those found guilty.[167] Furthermore, after blaming Nikolaev as a lone assassin and then linking him with a White Guard conspiracy, the official explanation for the assassination was that he acted as a follower of the Zinoviev–Kamenev opposition. On 16 December, these two plus thirteen of their associates were arrested.[168] The charges were clearly bogus, but this train of events opened a new stage in the story of opposition in the party and, more broadly, of the history of the party itself. It signified that oppositional activity followed by recantation and support for party policy was no longer adequate. Anyone who had taken up an oppositionist stance in the past could now be associated, even if indirectly, with a terrorist act of some sort and could thereby become subject to the attention of the security apparatus. Opposition was no longer what one was doing today, but extended back into the past. Moreover the anti-terrorist measures were important not only because they sped up the handling of terrorist cases, but because they effectively undermined the prohibition on the use of the death penalty against party members.[169] The party was no longer an impermeable institution. These measures thus marked a significant shift in the ground-rules according to which politics were played out.

This period also witnessed the descent to a certain standardisation in Soviet life. The diversity of NEP was eliminated as independent social and political organisation was destroyed beneath the blows of collectivisation and the First Five Year Plan. Cultural diversity almost disappeared as the cultural revolution ushered in the supremacy of proletarian values and socialist realism. Part of this was the further stultification of party ideology. The elimination of leading theoreticians like Bukharin from elite circles, the acceptance of the party's general line as constituting the true path to socialism, and the rise of a hardened orthodoxy in the form of the leader cult crowded out the possibility of vigorous ideological development and debate. So too did the political imperatives behind Stalin's quest for power, the need to ensure that no one else secured the ideological mantle he was appropriating. As a result, ideology became stolid and catechismic. Its development seemed much more directly a function of political legitimation than a development of living doctrine offering guidance to the believers. A clear case is the greater emphasis given to Stalin's thesis that the closer society approached socialism, the more fierce the resistance of the class enemy became.[170] This thesis, which has no basis in earlier ideological positions, was little more than an ideological justification for the search for hidden enemies. It was, therefore, the legitimation function of ideology which came to the fore during this period, overwhelming the policy-guidance aspects of its role in earlier times.

However, this does not mean that ideology had no policy-guidance role to play in the early 1930s. The different functions of the ideology interacted in various subtle ways, helping to establish an orthodoxy which henceforth helped to define the situation confronting policy-makers, including viable alternative policies to those being pursued. So ideology could play some part in policy choice. But it was not the same direct channel into policy formulation that it had been earlier, generally tending to be mediated through the demands of legitimation for some sort of action or situation. As such, it was largely reduced to slogans, epithets and catechisms, to be used almost mechanically when the situation demanded.

Thus, during this period, the political system remained unable to generate strong institutional structures and norms. The pressures generated by the revolution from above reinforced the weakness of institutional norms and ended any prospect of the development of pluralistic tendencies in the regime. The political scene remained fluid, even if there were no open factional conflicts and a strong sense of monolithism pervaded public political events. While formal institutional boundaries had become less important for the structuring of practical politics, the position of the individual leader remained fluid and unstable; if there were no institutional barriers which could effectively encapsulate him, nor were there firm institutional buttresses to sustain him. In this context, the course of development over the coming years was anything but determined by the state of political life at the end of 1934.

Part IV

The oligarchy subdued, 1935–1941

7 The enduring structures of sub-national politics

The sense of insecurity which had pervaded party ranks in the early part of the 1930s did not disappear in the latter half of the decade. The isolation remained, fuelled in part by continuing peasant resentment over collectivisation and a degree of popular alienation engendered by the Terror.[1] The rhetoric associated with the search for enemies and the 1936-38 Terror would have fed into and reinforced this feeling. But the extent of popular hostility should not be exaggerated. Many would have accepted the official explanation for the Terror,[2] if only because this offered at least an understandable framework for what was otherwise an incomprehensible phenomenon. The new state constitution of 1936 was also important, offering a symbolic place in the polity for the populace.[3] But of greater importance was probably the continuing expansion of opportunities for social mobility.

The processes of industrialisation and agricultural collectivisation had opened up massive opportunities for social mobility to those from the lower levels of society. The continuing expansion of industrialisation,[4] and the growth of urban areas in the Second (1933-37) and Third (1938-42) Five Year Plans ensured that the channels of mobility remained open. This was stimulated by the effect of the purges; every position left vacant by someone who was purged had to be filled by a newcomer, a development which usually involved a promotion. The scale of this was significant; according to the new First Secretary of the Western Oblast in October 1937, within the preceding three months some 1,000 people had been promoted to leading posts.[5] Thus while the purges were a tragedy for many, they were a source of advantage for others.[6] For those people moving into leading positions in Soviet society, the purges may have strengthened their commitment to the system, and thereby made the environment within which the party had to function less hostile.

Nevertheless, the party remained a small phalanx in society. In

Table 7.1. *Party membership, 1935–41*

	Full	Candidate	Total
1 Jan. 1935	1,659,104	699,610	2,358,714
1 Jan. 1941	2,490,479	1,381,986	3,872,465

crude figures, the party expanded 64.2 per cent over this period (see table 7.1).[7] This is a significant increase. However, it was not spread evenly across the period. Recruitment to the party, halted in December 1932, was not recommenced until September 1936.[8] In 1935, 1936 and 1937 the total party membership actually decreased, with the 1 January 1935 level not being regained until part way through 1939. There was a massive influx into the party in 1938, 1939 and 1940,[9] when the party increased by 1,952,463, or 101.7 per cent.[10] This means that by the end of this period in mid-1941, over half of all party members had joined the party within the past three years.

The social profile of party membership changed significantly over this period. At the XVII Congress, the new party Rules had given clear priority in recruitment to members of the working class, but nothing was achieved in the realisation of this aim because of the continuing ban on recruitment. When recruitment was renewed, 41 per cent of recruits were from the proletariat, 15.2 per cent were peasants and 43.8 per cent came from among the intelligentsia and white-collar workers. Between March 1939 and the end of the period, less than 20 per cent of recruits were workers and less than 10 per cent peasants.[11] Although definitive figures are lacking, by the end of this period workers by social class would have constituted less than half of all party members and peasants somewhere about 15 per cent.[12] Furthermore, many of these workers would have been promoted into commanding positions and would therefore no longer have been working directly in production. Their links with their class of origin would thus have become more tenuous. The recruiting balance within the party, and therefore the membership balance, shifted firmly in the direction of the intelligentsia and white-collar workers.

While the vast bulk of the population still lived in the villages, the party remained overwhelmingly an urban-based party with only a thin layer of members in the countryside. According to one speaker at the XVIII Congress in March 1939,[13] there were only 12,000 PPOs with 153,000 communists for 243,000 kolkhozy. By early 1941 there was said to have been 82,956 rural party organisations,[14] but these were dominated by people in executive positions rather than peasants tilling the soil. Indeed, membership in the countryside in 1941 was probably lower than it had been before the 1933-34 purge, as rural organisations had been particularly badly affected by that purge.[15] The weakness of the party in the countryside is well illustrated by some figures from Belyi district. In 1935 there was approximately one party member for every two collective farms, while in July 1936, of the twenty-one party cells in the district, seventeen were in the town of Belyi but only 7 per cent of the whole population lived in 'urban' areas.[16] In 1937 there was one communist for every 283.4 people in Belyi raion while the figure for the town of Belyi was one for every 47.5 residents.[17] More generally, with something over two-thirds of the population in rural areas in 1937, there were only 600,000 communists outside the towns; in the PPOs of the collective farms, there were only 350,000 communists.[18] In Belyi only four collective farms out of a total of 210 had any PPOs in 1937.[19] Indeed, until about 1939 the rural party in Belyi was in a state of decline, largely as a result of the way in which successive membership screenings fell heavily upon that sector of the party. As party organisations disappeared following the expulsion of many of their members, the party's flag in the countryside often was flown only by isolated communists.[20] It is unlikely that the situation in Belyi was unique.

There were also suspicions about the quality of many who were in the party, both among the rank-and-file and lower level officials. The purge of 1933-34 was both a reflection of such concerns and an attempt to come to grips with them. The purge, which resulted in the expulsion of some 22 per cent of party membership,[21] dragged on into 1935. It was followed almost immediately by the campaign for the Verification of Party Documents in 1935 and the Exchange of Party Cards in 1936.[22] Although both of these were presented as exercises in party accounting, a means of bringing order out of chaos in party registration matters, they also sought to eliminate undesirable elements from the party. The Verification, which resulted in the expulsion of some 9 per cent of party members,[23] involved the checking of all party members' documents and a review of their performance (although in fact only some 81 per cent of party members were processed[24]) and the expulsion of any who were found deficient. One review referred to the Verification enabling the party to rid itself of 'crooks, kulaks, white guardists, counter-revolutionary Trotskyists and Zinovievites, double dealers and other enemy elements'.[25] The

Exchange of Party Cards was also envisaged as an opportunity to get rid of undesirable elements, although in this case more 'passive' than 'hostile'.[26] The effect of these campaigns is evident in the decline in party membership over the first part of this period (although part of this decline was also due to voluntary withdrawals). However, as the quest for enemies during the Terror of 1936–38, the complaints about continuing deficiencies in party records and registration,[27] the frequent calls for the vetting of new members[28] and the need for extensive education of them[29] suggest, these campaigns did not erase the doubts held by the central leadership about the quality and reliability of the party's lower ranks.

Concern about the environment within which the party had to function and about the quality of the rank-and-file membership was combined with central worries about weaknesses in the party's vertical organisational linkages and the political views of the sub-national party leadership. The 1933–34 chistka had not shaken the power or position of sub-national leaders because they had been able to redirect the blows to lower levels and away from their power bases. But the centre maintained pressure on these leaders throughout much of this period. Initially this was done through criticism of lower level party performance, particularly in terms of the implementation of central decisions, and of the standard of record-keeping in the party.

During 1935 and 1936, the criticisms about the state of party registration procedures and records mounted, in part stimulated by the increased concern generated by the Kirov assassination. The tone of this sort of complaint was set at the outset of the period; the need to improve methods of registration of communists was associated with a call for greater care in the use and management of party documents and in particular in the delivery of party cards to the right people. It was claimed that mistakes in this left the party vulnerable to alien elements.[30] The Kirov assassination was used as clear evidence that the party had exercised insufficient vigilance against such elements[31] and the party leaders had failed to respond to earlier criticisms in this regard. The same deficiencies criticised in October 1934 were still being experienced in 1935: individual possession of more than one party card (often by non-party members), people remaining registered long after they had died or left the party, and the duplication of the same numbers on different party cards.[32] There were instances of some individuals using the party cards of dead members to gain the benefits of party membership.[33] One study from mid-1935 showed that in 39 districts of the Western Oblast, 297 members and candidates had no official party documents at all and some did not even have temporary ones; one had the wrong name listed on his card and many cards were otherwise inaccurate.[34] The main concern continued to be to ensure that enemies of the working class, alien elements, were not in possession of a party card.[35]

The problems in the process of registration and the handling of party documents meant that local party leaderships often remained unaware of the composition of their own party organisations, a complaint frequently made at this time.[36] This had important ramifications for the structure of power at this level discussed below. But it also meant that higher level party organs were often ignorant of the state of those organs they were meant to supervise and were therefore unable to provide adequate guidance and oversight;[37] according to the CC Secretariat on 8 August 1935, 'we are presently beginning only now to find out the composition of the leading party workers in the regions and districts'.[38] Such a situation was a major obstacle to the efficient operation of the nomenklatura system, a fact acknowledged at the time.[39] It therefore also weakened the main mechanism for ensuring central control and an efficiently operating party mechanism. A number of different methods were used in an attempt to rectify the appalling state of party records at most levels, the two most important being the campaigns for the Verification of Party Documents in 1935 and the Exchange of Party Cards in 1936.

The Verification was launched formally on May 13, 1935, although such a move had been foreshadowed in the months preceding this.[40] The secret CC letter of 13 May was entitled 'On disorders in the registration, distribution and safekeeping of party cards and on measures for regulating this affair'[41] and set out the conditions under which the Verification was to be conducted. It began by decrying the poor state of registration procedures and practices at all levels of the party, a fact which enabled opponents to penetrate the party and sometimes to rise to responsible positions. Consequently a verification was to be carried out within two months by comparing the details contained in the party committee's membership records with the answers received by the party secretary upon questioning each communist on that person's life, history, work, qualifications and education. Expulsion, through confiscation of the card, could follow an unsatisfactory outcome of this process. The result was thus to be an up-to-date, accurate membership record, along with the removal from party ranks of those whose performance had been unsatisfactory.

Although this exercise was presented as a membership accounting operation, it is clear that it was designed also to gain the removal from the party of those enemies who had infiltrated its ranks. This was openly stated towards the end of the campaign, which dragged on much longer than the envisaged two months: at the end of 1935 the Verification was explicitly linked with the struggle against enemies with party cards in their pockets,[42] while one of its results was declared to be 'unmasking alien persons who had made their way into the party'.[43] Even the letter launching the campaign, while focusing principally upon the book-keeping aspects of the question, had the infiltration of oppositional elements into the party as a significant theme; this was seen to be the main danger stemming from the chaotic state of registration. So although Kirov's name was not mentioned in the letter, the reference to opponents and enemies in the party had clear resonances with the developing official reaction to his assassination.[44] For many this seemed to be proof of the theme, well established in party life, of the dangers posed by internal enemies. The bringing of registration records into line with membership therefore involved some purifying of that membership.

The Verification was to be conducted under the general supervision of ORPO, the CC's Department of Leading Party Organs, but was to be carried out by the lower party secretaries. They were thus being called upon to investigate and correct their own mistakes. In this light, it is little wonder that the course and conduct of the Verification should come under central criticism. Just two months after the letter inaugurating the Verification, the centre was complaining about how it was being carried out in an unsatisfactory, formal-bureaucratic way.[45] Saratov kraikom came under direct attack by Zhdanov in August because it ignored the CC's instruction that the Verification should be conducted carefully over a two-month period and instead rushed it through, resulting in various mistakes being made.[46] Party committees were called upon to ensure that there was not just a formal, mechanical implementation of the Verification, but that an actual check was made on individual members.[47] The unsatisfactory way in which the campaign was conducted in some areas meant that some local party organs had to repeat the process; for example, in the Western Oblast the real task of the Verification was said to have been masked by enemies with party cards in their pockets so that the process had to be repeated, resulting in higher numbers of expulsions of spies, counter-revolutionary Trotskyist-Zinovievites, white guard attackers, kulaks, rogues, adventurists, embezzlers and others.[48]

The summary results of the Verification spoke about 'the successful resolution of the basic task set by the 13 May 1935 letter' and of the way in which the

> most important result ... has been that party organisations, in addition to the unmasking of alien people who had made their way into the party, in significant measure have overcome elements of this organisational dissoluteness, have brought order into the registration of party members, have made a better study of communists, and on this basis have promoted many new, able workers to leading party, soviet and economic work.[49]

However, comments during the campaign suggest that the centre was less than happy with the course of Verification. The summary results show this dissatisfaction by referring to the way in which the Verification illustrated the arbitrariness in the issuing and guarding of party documents, the chaos in registration, and the poor understanding among party organisations and members of CC directives about the need for Bolshevik vigilance and discipline. It added that only by learning from these and by improving organisational work will party organisations 'be able to extirpate completely the roots of opportunist complacency, to sharpen the Bolshevik vigilance of party members, to educate the party apparatus in the spirit of Bolshevik keenness and implacability, and to ensure that the Rules of the Party really become the unbreakable basis of its internal life'.[50] Thus while the Verification may have brought some improvement in the state of the lower level party apparatus, and led to the expulsion of some 9.1 per cent of those checked,[51] it is clear that problems still remained.

In an attempt 'to consolidate the results of the Verification', to strengthen party ranks and to overcome the current unsatisfactory state of party documents (party and candidate membership cards and registration cards), on 25 December 1935 the CC announced that there would be an Exchange of Party Documents in 1936.[52] This operation, like the Verification, was to be conducted by the local party secretaries and, it was emphasised, was not to be viewed as a 'mechanical replacement of one party card by another'; party cards did not have to be issued to party members who, although they may have passed the Verification, were 'not worthy of the high calling of party member'.[53] However, a distinction was drawn between the Verification and the Exchange:

> If during the verification of party documents the basic attention of party organisations was concentrated on disrobing those enemies of the party who had penetrated the AUCP(b) by fraudulent means, every type of rascal and rogue, then during the exchange basic

attention must be turned to freeing it from passive people, unworthy of the high calling of party member, who have by chance found themselves in the ranks of the AUCP(b).[54]

The emphasis was to be on 'passive' rather than 'hostile' elements. The instruction declared that the exchange was to be conducted between 1 February and 1 May and listed operational principles to guide its conduct.[55]

The introduction of the Exchange reflects the leadership's dissatisfaction with the results of the Verification. The stated aims of both campaigns were too similar not to reflect badly on the way in which the first had been completed: overcoming the chaos in party record-keeping and getting rid of elements who should not have been in the party. Furthermore, the initial distinction between passive and hostile elements was soon eroded as the Exchange was declared to be directed towards strengthening the party's ranks and purifying them of hostile and alien elements.[56]

The course of the Exchange seems to have been plagued by the same sorts of problems as the Verification. Like the former, it lasted for longer than the three-month period originally specified, in some areas extending into the beginning of 1937.[57] An article in June indicated some of the organisational-political mistakes that were being made during the Exchange.[58] It criticised the formal-bureaucratic approach characterised by an unnecessary formalism and concern for appearances rather than reality (an indirect admission that local party leaders were trying to protect their own power bases), the slow rate of the Exchange, the damage done to party documents, and the groundless and incorrect inclusion of communists among passive elements. Also criticised were delays in the delivery of documents to individual party members, the isolation of the Exchange from measures to improve party work, the failure to examine each communist individually and the failure of each district committee to exercise close supervision over the performance of the PPOs in this matter. Some party committees were accused of exercising inadequate vigilance, with the result that enemies of the party and people (defined as counter-revolutionary Trotskyist elements) were able to gain new party cards and continue their anti-party work.[59] In September and October CC circulars called for an end to unfair expulsions and an increase in those which were justified.[60] By the time the Exchange had drawn to a close early in 1937, most party members presumably had new party cards (since those dating from 1926 were to be invalid from the end of 1936[61]). But despite the generally positive tone of Stalin's comments at the XVIII

Congress,[62] the Exchange did not solve the party's registration problems to the satisfaction of the leadership or, if it did, that solution did not survive the upheaval of the Great Terror.

The central leadership also introduced a number of organisational measures designed to improve the personnel regime in the party. In mid-1936, some months after the beginning of the Exchange of Party Cards and therefore presumably causing some confusion and disruption at lower levels, the CC introduced a new instruction on registration which amended the previous one in force and introduced some new procedures.[63] A further set of instructions on procedures followed in November 1939[64] while principles governing the transfer of party members were spelled out in April 1938.[65] In March 1935 special cadres departments were established in some gorkoms and city raikoms in an attempt to overcome the deficiencies of personnel work in these areas[66] and in 1939 the secretarial apparatus was restructured. A major re-ordering of administrative divisions in the country in 1936 resulted in some reorganisation of the party including the multiplication of its constituent elements, a development which had clear implications for personnel matters.[67] In addition, there were frequent exhortations to higher level party organs to exercise tighter supervision over their subordinate organs.[68] But despite all of these efforts, the party continued to experience problems in the registration of party members right to the end of this period.[69] Thus throughout this period as a whole it is clear that the question of personnel registration remained an unresolved problem. This was a severe brake on the establishment of a highly centralised, disciplined machine.

The considerable defects in the functioning of the party apparatus were a major barrier to the centre's ability to exercise control over the lower levels of the party structure. One body which should have been able to facilitate this was the security apparatus. At the sub-national levels the security apparatus was not meant to be subject to effective control by the local party committee. As the Smolensk Archive shows, party organs seemed to ratify personnel appointments in the NKVD decided upon within that apparatus rather than making those decisions themselves.[70] Furthermore, the NKVD reported directly to the centre on a wide range of issues, including the performance of local party leaders.[71] But the degree of independence of this structure depended ultimately upon the personal relations that existed between party and NKVD leaders at each level. In practice, local NKVD leaders were often in close association with sub-national political leaders, and rather than acting as a central check upon them, aided and abetted them in their activities.

Major obstacles to the emergence of a centralised, disciplined machine were the position, role and activities of many sub-national political leaders. In structural terms, the position of these leaders remained as it had been in the earlier periods: caught between the imperatives of meeting and satisfying the demands emanating from above on the one hand and of maintaining their regional power bases and governing effectively on the other, many of these leaders sought sanctuary through the continuing mechanism of family group control. The continuing weakness of the local infrastructure, particularly in the field of communications such as radio, roads and telephones,[72] reinforced this reliance on informal networks for control. Throughout much of this period, the maintenance of their position was complicated by continuing hostility from the centre. Regional leaders had been able to divert the 1933–34 chistka on to lower levels and open attacks upon them at the XVII Congress had had no immediate political effects. However, between the beginnings of this period and late 1937, the centre increased the pressure on regional leaders, ultimately smashing them during the Great Terror.

An important part of this pressure was the attacks upon the way in which regional party leaders carried out their tasks of party leadership. They were accused of ignoring the principles of collective leadership by failing to convene meetings and by excluding some leaders from the decision-making process;[73] co-optation was said to be common in some party organisations,[74] thereby consolidating group control without formal accountability or election. There were accusations of misappropriation of funds for personal use[75] and of high living, abuse of position and drunkenness of some leaders.[76] These sorts of charges were made against a background of warnings about the way in which, with the victory of the general line, the tactic of the party's opponents had become one of covert opposition[77] and that extra care needed to be taken to ensure that alien elements did not gain leading positions in the party.[78] The rhetoric about 'enemies of the people' which accompanied the Great Terror fed into this line of attack; indeed, an important theme in the show trials was the penetration of the party apparatus by enemies.[79]

Both the Verification of Party Documents and the Exchange of Party Cards also constituted attacks upon the position of the regional leadership. If an effective registration system could be devised, it would be the basis of a more all-encompassing and efficient nomenklatura regime which could undermine the positions of the regional barons. These campaigns thus struck right at the heart of their power bases. However, the centre does not appear to have been adequately equipped to carry out this task with its own resources; it is likely that neither the Party Control Commission nor the Special Sector had the administrative wherewithal to undertake the accounting procedures required in these campaigns without relying heavily upon the local party secretaries themselves. The campaigns had thus to be carried out principally by those against whom the campaigns were directed.[80] It should come as little surprise that the point of the campaigns was blunted in the implementation. While the complaints about how both campaigns were being implemented could have been directed at simple bureaucratic inefficiency, it is clear that they were directed, at least in part, at the consequences of lower level leaders' efforts to subvert the main thrust of the campaigns. The CC recognised this explicitly at the end of the Verification when it talked about those people who 'approached its implementation in an opportunistic way, and in many cases directly opposed this most important measure for strengthening the ranks of the AUCP(b)'.[81] Furthermore, the fragmentary data we have on those expelled suggests (though by no means conclusively) that most expelled were rank-and-file party members,[82] a result consistent with regional leaders seeking to defend their power groupings against attack from above.

These attacks had failed because they were directed through the party apparatus and yet control over many of the crucial points of that apparatus was one of the central aspects of the power of regional leaders. A more potent weapon was the appeal to the democratic traditions of the party. There were two interwoven strands in this appeal: a revival of the campaign for self-criticism and the introduction of the Stalin Constitution with its associated emphasis upon democratic principles. This was clearly an attempt to mobilise the rank-and-file party members against their local leaders and thereby overcome the blocking mechanism which the latter had been able to deploy against attacks from above by stimulating an attack from their rear, from below. One of the keys to the success of family group control had been the ability to choke off potential complaints from below through its dominance of the communication channels. Now the rank-and-file were being given a new channel, promoted by the centre, which it was more difficult for regional leaders to block.

Self-criticism, which had burst to the fore at the end of the 1920s, remained a subordinate theme during the early and mid-1930s. In

1935 and 1936 it was still projected as an important weapon in the struggle against bureaucratism,[83] dominance by groups,[84] and alien elements and enemies.[85] The self-criticism theme became much more prominent in the press during 1937, coinciding with some of the worst excesses of the Ezhovshchina and the emphasis upon the need for vigilance, with which it was explicitly linked.[86] Similar themes to those of 1935–36 were present: lack of self-criticism was associated with the ability of class enemies to obtain new party cards,[87] a claim that was directed against sub-national party secretaries, and a direct link was drawn between the absence of self-criticism and party organisations forgetting their responsibilities under the principles of intra-party democracy.[88] Self-criticism was portrayed as the basis of party activity and 'a powerful weapon in the struggle for the general line'[89] and it was directly associated with the principle of rank-and-file control through secret ballot in the party electoral regulations of 1937 discussed below.[90] Party members were called upon to exercise Bolshevik criticism and self-criticism regardless of the person involved or the office they occupied[91] and to use it to get rid of enemies of the people in the party.[92] Self-criticism was particularly linked with the party elections of 1937 and 1938, both of which were significant for the course of the central attack upon the power and position of sub-national party leaders; thereafter it declined in prominence.

The self-criticism campaign was an important weapon against the sub-national leaders because it stimulated action against them from below,[93] but it had the weakness of lacking any institutional means of turning grievances into effective challenges to incumbent leaders.[94] The institutional means was provided by the change to the party's electoral regulations in 1937. This change was introduced amidst the surge of rhetoric on democracy associated with the adoption of the Stalin Constitution in December 1936, a rhetoric that was laced, *inter alia*, with the principle of accountability to the rank-and-file electorate.[95] In line with this sentiment and with the proclaimed intention of improving and strengthening intra-party democracy and adherence to the party Rules,[96] new electoral regulations were introduced in March 1937 to structure the forthcoming party elections.[97] The central theme of the new regulations, sponsored by CC Secretary Zhdanov, was: 'To forbid voting by list in elections to party organs. Voting must take place by individual candidatures, with all party members guaranteed unlimited right to recall of candidates and criticism of them.'[98] The regulations provided for a session in which the delegates at the electoral meeting discussed every candidate individually in order to decide whether that candidate should go forward to the actual election. The meeting was not to be presented with a pre-arranged list. Furthermore the regulations provided for election to the following offices by secret ballot:

delegates from the PPOs to district and city party conferences and delegates from district, city and okrug party conferences to oblast and krai party conferences and congresses of national communist parties;

members of the party committees and, where there were no such committees, of party organisers of the PPOs and members of the plena of raikoms, gorkoms, obkoms, kraikoms and the CCs of national communist parties;

secretaries of PPO party committees and the secretaries and members of the bureaux of raikoms, gorkoms, okrugkoms, obkoms, kraikoms and CCs of national communist parties

At all stages of the election process, including most importantly the election of party secretaries, the election was to proceed by secret ballot. This was a very important provision because it effectively denied party secretaries a means they had used previously to keep their local power base secure; with open voting, an oppositional vote was inhibited by fear of retribution. If secret ballot could be enforced, the power of the local leader was rendered more insecure.[99]

The new electoral regulations were ushered in along with exhortations for all committees to liquidate co-optation and to hold real elections for leading party organs, with a secret ballot and the presence of more candidates than there were positions to be filled.[100] They were also linked with the liquidation of a narrow, family-like approach to questions, with an end to 'the impermissible selection of workers on the rotten principle of "acquaintance", personal connections etc., an end to the toadyism, servility, flattery and mutual laudation' that was present in the apparatus.[101] However, local party leaders were warned, they were not to leave party elections unguided. They were to exercise real leadership which encouraged and promoted the exercise of Bolshevik criticism and self-criticism. Attempts at depriving party members of their rights, at suppressing self-criticism or reducing the elections to a mere formality had to be avoided.[102] The sub-national leaders were thus placed in a very difficult position: the electoral process could lead to their demise, yet they were to exercise a form of leadership which ensured that the process was not characterised by 'samotek' (or *laissez-faire*) but without limiting mass activity or freedom. For people with no experience of such elections, finding the balance between samotek and restricting the free expression of opinion would have been well nigh impossible even without the imperatives of their own political survival.

It is not surprising, then, that within two months of the regulations being introduced complaints were already appearing in the press about the way in which they were being ignored or violated. It was claimed that in some places elections were proceeding without the prior hearing and discussion of reports of party committees and organisers, leaders were refusing to exercise the appropriate guidance over the elections, cases of open rather than secret voting occurred, ineligible people participated in elections and self-criticism was suppressed.[103] Inadequate leadership of elections produced the nomination of an excessive number of candidates, much wasting of time (for example, only one report was heard in a meeting lasting sixteen hours), meetings without discussion or criticism, and even cases of Trotskyists being allowed to speak.[104] The performance of many sub-national party leaders in guiding the electoral process left Moscow dissatisfied, and while some of this may have been due to simple bureaucratic mismanagement, inexperience and confusion, there was doubtless also more than a hint of conscious opposition and sabotage. Although no final summary figures were published which allow for adequate comparison,[105] it seems that no city or regional party leaders lost their positions as a result of the election;[106] party secretaries who lost their places seem to have been confined to the district level and lower.[107] As in the chistka of 1933–34, most sub-national party leaders appear to have been able to fend off this blow from above.

The apparent victory of the sub-national leaders was short lived. From the middle of 1937 the Ezhovshchina embraced the regional party leadership. According to Getty, the formulation 'enemy of the people' was first applied to regional party secretaries in June 1937[108] and it was at about this time that the regional leadership was decimated, with virtually all obkom secretaries being removed from office.[109] It was the new incumbents of sub-national party posts who benefited from the change in electoral regulations introduced in 1938.[110] Amid charges that the 1937 elections had been characterised by an absence of correct leadership in many cases,[111] the new electoral regulations made one very significant change from those adopted a year earlier. The new regulations retained secret ballots for the election of delegates to party conferences and congresses and for members of party committees and party organisers (in PPOs where there were no committees), but introduced an open ballot for the following positions: secretaries of PPO party committees and secretaries and bureau members of raikoms, gorkoms, okrugkoms, obkoms, kraikoms and CCs of national communist parties, and for the presidia and other leading organs of party conferences and meetings. Thus the leading positions in the party, including the secretarial chain, and the bodies which ran party meetings (including electoral meetings[112]) were once again to be chosen in a forum that was open to public scrutiny and which therefore provided the local political leader with the capacity to verify who supported him and who did not. The challenge posed to sub-national leadership positions by the 1937 regulations had been removed.[113]

The decimation of the regional party leadership in the Ezhovshchina did not bring about a fundamental structural change in the centre–regional relationship. It reflected the centre's power to remove sub-national party leaders – this time on a mass scale – but this had been evident on an individual level since the early 1920s. It did not change the local conditions which gave rise to family groups. Indeed, it may even have stimulated this process. One of the factors encouraging the development of family group control was the weakness of the bureaucratic apparatus and its unsuitability for the achievement of the tasks set before the local leadership, with the concomitant need to generate a structure which would facilitate the implementation of the set tasks. To the extent that the Terror of 1936–38 severely disrupted internal party activities, both through the removal of people and the sense of uncertainty that was generated, it both weakened central institutional control and forced local leaders to rely even more heavily upon their circle of confreres.[114] With the weak institutional structure of the sub-national party organisation battered by the Terror,[115] the importance of the informal networks and structures was increased. Power remained extra-bureaucratic in its location, family groups continued to be the building blocks of sub-national power, and party organs remained overwhelmingly instrumental in nature.

Thus at the sub-national levels, the Great Terror did not facilitate the development of an effective machine based in the formal party organs, nor did it tighten up the bureaucratic links between different levels of the party.[116] Nor did the self-criticism campaign or election by secret ballot alter the structural position of sub-national leaders; self-criticism remained a minor theme during the rest of the period while secret ballot for leading positions was not restored to party elections.[117] The relationship between centre and lower levels remained loosely articulated because the bureaucratic machinery that was necessary to tie the latter more closely to the former was not yet in existence. At the end of the period, therefore, the earlier patterns of sub-national politics remained intact and the party was still not a highly centralised, integrated, efficient political machine.

8 Elite ravaged

The Great Terror had an enormous impact upon the elite, leading to the fundamental transformation of the nature of elite politics. This transformation was both structural, in terms of the formal organisational contours of the leading institutions, and personal through substantial levels of turnover in the elite. By the end of this period, the Stalinist political system as sketched in the introduction was in place.

Changing institutional parameters

The most important change in the contours of the state structure during this period was associated with the introduction of the Stalin Constitution in December 1936. This ushered in a new governmental structure in which the former All-Union Congress of Soviets was replaced by a bicameral Supreme Soviet as 'the highest organ of state power' (#30). As an executive organ, the legislature elected a Presidium which, formally, had wide powers in the issuing of decrees, the vetting of decisions and orders of Sovnarkom to ensure their legality, and the right, between sessions of the Supreme Soviet, to appoint and dismiss ministers. 'The highest executive and administrative organ' remained Sovnarkom. Formally responsible to the Supreme Soviet and its Presidium, Sovnarkom had wide powers to issue decisions and orders, and had particular responsibility in the economic sphere. This is reflected in the reorganisation of STO (The Council of Labour and Defence) into the Economic Council of Sovnarkom in 1937[1] and in the formation in 1940 of six subordinate economic councils responsible for defence industry, metallurgy and chemicals, engineering, fuels and electricity, mass consumption goods, and agriculture.[2]

Throughout this period the Supreme Soviet remained an organ which exercised purely formal functions, acting as a rubber stamp for decisions made elsewhere. Similarly, its Presidium constituted little more than a channel through which legislation could be directed, with no evidence of its playing anything more than a purely routine role. Similarly, the plenary session of Sovnarkom was a minor administrative actor during the early part of this period. On average it met no more than once a fortnight, and during 1937 it convened on only nine occasions.[3] One explanation for this is the large size of the body, with fifty members by the end of the 1930s.[4] Also important was the impact of the Great Terror, particularly in 1937. The operation of its executive bodies was another factor in the low levels of activity of the full Sovnarkom, particularly the Conference of the Chairman and Deputy Chairmen of Sovnarkom and the Economic Council.[5] Much business was handled in these fora rather than the plenary session of Sovnarkom.

The role of the state organs in decision-making during this period cannot, at this stage of our knowledge, be ascertained with any certainty. Indeed, the whole decision-making process remains unclear. However, on the basis of evidence that is certainly far from conclusive, it appears that the importance of Sovnarkom in the process of law-making underwent a significant shift during this period. During the Terror the profile of Sovnarkom declined substantially. The infrequency of Sovnarkom meetings in 1937 has already been noted. In addition, in the 1935–38 period, the party's organisational journal seems to have carried joint CC–Sovnarkom decisions or appeals on very few occasions.[6] However, Sovnarkom became more prominent following the Terror. From 1939 the party journal had a special section entitled 'In SNK–CC' and numerous issues carried joint declarations and decisions. The re-emergence of Sovnarkom seemed to be capped when Stalin assumed its chairmanship on 6 May 1941. Sovnarkom's growing importance is also reflected in the increase in the number of commissariats during this period; from twenty-one commissariats in 1938, the figure had jumped to thirty-nine in 1940 (of which twenty-four were concerned with the economy), and forty-three in June 1941.[7] This suggests a growing role for the state machine and may reflect the dire effects the purges had upon the party as an institution.

The basis of the state's position in the political system remained the expertise concentrated in the commissariats, but this expertise proved to be no defence against the Terror. Indeed, the public emphasis upon economic sabotage and wrecking as principal targets of the Terror naturally turned the cutting edge toward the governmental machine.

Virtually all sectors of state activity were affected, with individuals ranging from people's commissars[8] through to humble clerks being swept up in the Terror, and the normal operations of the state apparatus being disrupted.[9] Such disruption is clearly reflected in the difficulties encountered in compiling the Third Five Year Plan.[10] One important effect of the Terror on the state structure at this time was the resultant enormous influx of new recruits; according to Stalin, between the XVII and XVIII Congresses, the party had promoted more than half a million young party members and people close to the party into leading state and party posts,[11] and although he gave no information on the split between party and state positions, a substantial proportion of them would have entered the state apparatus. Many of these would have been the product of the educational policies set in train at the end of the 1920s, and although they may have lacked the experience of those they replaced, the level of expertise within the governmental structure was probably not greatly lowered. The state machine remained the principal source of expertise for the regime, and thereby a major source of policy ideas and recommendations. It also remained an arena of institutional conflict throughout the period. With the shift in policy at the end of 1938 to one which supported and praised office-holders instead of casting suspicion over them,[12] the scene was set for stabilisation of the bureaucratic hierarchy and the growing importance of the state organs.

The supreme organ of the party, the congress, met on only one occasion during this period, March 1939. There was also a party conference, the XVIII, in February 1941. At the XVIII Congress there were 1,570 full delegates[13] and 395 with a consultative vote, giving a total of 1,965. Workers in the party apparatus constituted 42 per cent of delegates with a decisive vote,[14] a marginal increase on the figure for the XVII Congress. Most of the delegates were from the regions rather than Moscow.[15] Although most delegates had middle level education or lower, in a sharp increase compared with the XVII Congress, more than a quarter of all delegates had completed higher education while a further 5 per cent had an incomplete higher education.[16] The delegates appear to have been younger than at the preceding two congresses,[17] a development which is connected with the disappearance of the dominance of the veteran party members among delegates; compared with the XVII Congress figure of 80 per cent of delegates with a decisive vote who had joined the party prior to 1920, at the XVIII Congress only 19.4 per cent of those delegates had joined before the end of 1920. Furthermore, 43 per cent had joined the party in the last ten years.[18] This changed profile is linked with the Terror; according to Khrushchev, of the 1,966 delegates to the XVII Congress, 1,108 were arrested 'on charges of counter-revolutionary crimes'.[19] Only 65 delegates from 1934 remained delegates in 1939, a carryover rate of only 3.3 per cent, and of those 24 were old CC members; of rank-and-file delegates in 1934, less than 2 per cent were re-elected in 1939.[20] This was the lowest carryover rate of any congress, and makes the XVIII Congress a body composed almost entirely of congress novices.

The XVIII Congress was much the most publicly united and monolithic congress in Soviet pre-war history. Although there may have been different emphases on issues given by different speakers, there were no clear conflicts of the sort which had occurred at the XVII Congress over target levels.[21] The Congress went as if scripted with no discordant notes to jar the unanimity. A central pillar around which this unanimity focused was the figure of Stalin. Much of the congress seemed little else but a forum in which to sing Stalin's praises. All speeches were laced with lavish praise of the great leader and even the laudation given to others was in large part the reflected glory of Stalin. Mikoian's entrance to the Congress is a good instance of this, being marked by stormy, prolonged, standing applause and cries of 'Long live the true comrade-in-arms of the Great Stalin! Hooray to great Stalin!'[22] The congress, at least in its public manifestations, had completed the transformation from vigorous debating shop to formal ratificatory organ. It was an instrumental body, with no institutional integrity or coherence.

The CC elected at the XVIII Congress[23] was very different from that which had been elected five years earlier. Although the size remained unchanged, the carryover figures show significant changes (see table 8.1). This was the smallest carryover rate in the party's history, marking the CC that was elected at the end of the XVIII Congress as almost a completely new organ; only sixteen full and eight candidate members were carried forward.[24] Put another way, this represents the highest attrition rate of CC members in the party's history. Some of this was doubtless due to natural causes, but many (including some who do not appear to have opposed Stalin) were clearly victims of the Terror; according to Khrushchev, ninety-eight members of the CC elected in 1934 were arrested and shot, mostly in 1937–38.[25] But as well as being composed overwhelmingly of new members, the CC elected in 1939 also marks the rise to dominance of the post-

Table 8.1. *CC membership, 1934 and 1939*

Congress	Full	Candidate	Total	Carried over to next committee (%)	Carryover as % of new committee
XVII	71	68	139	17.3	66.9
XVIII	71	68	139		17.3

Table 8.2. *Length of party membership of CC members, 1934 and 1939 (in %)*

	Pre–1917			1917			Post-1917		
	F	C	T	F	C	T	F	C	T
XVII	87.1	53.7	70.8	7.1	26.9	16.8	5.7	19.4	12.4
XVIII	29.6	6.0	18.1	9.9	3.0	6.5	60.5	91.0	75.4

revolutionary generation, in the sense of those who joined the party after the revolution (see table 8.2). These figures are a striking illustration of the way in which the political power and position of the Old Bolsheviks had been destroyed. They had been replaced by those whose allegiance to the party dated from the post-revolution period, although many of those were civil war veterans; of those who joined after 1917, 42.3 per cent were in the party by the end of 1920.[26] For many CC members, their immediate experience of the party was as a ruling body in which Stalin led the struggle for the correct line.

The occupational profile of the CC elected in 1939 shows the continuing erosion of the position of the full-time party workers (see table 8.3). Although this position did not change significantly in the CC as a whole[27] (and the large number of 'Uncertains' counsels caution), among full members, this constituency declined dramatically to constitute only just over a quarter of the full membership in 1939. Also marked was the decline in representation of regional party officials among the full members. This reflects the opposition of many of this group to Stalin and their subsequent fate in the Terror. The decline in the party's position was accompanied by some strengthening of the position of the state machine among full members, but not in the

Table 8.3. *Bureaucratic constituencies of full members of the CC, 1934 and 1939*

	CP Apparatus			State	Other	Uncertain
	Centre	Region	Total			
XVII	12.7	29.6	42.3	42.3	9.9	5.6
XVIII	8.5	18.3	26.8	46.5	19.7	7.0

committee as a whole. The main beneficiary was the 'Other' category, principally through an expanded military presence. Male Russians continued to dominate although now, consistent with the changed generation reflected in party entry dates, most were educated in the 1920s and 1930s.

The composition of the CC was altered once more during this period. Under new provisions contained in the revised party Rules adopted at the XVIII Congress, the newly established annual conference had the right to change the composition of the CC by removing individual members and replacing them by others. Such renewal could not exceed 20 per cent (#38). In line with this provision, the February 1941 conference removed four members and fifteen candidates and replaced them with six members and eighteen candidates, bringing the total membership at the close of the period to 144.[28]

The party Rules introduced in 1934 had specified a frequency of four-monthly meetings of the CC plenum, but this timetable was not met during this period. Table 8.4 shows the frequency and duration of CC plena for the period (excluding those immediately preceding and following the XVIII Congress in March 1939).[29] There is no pattern or consistency to these meetings, although the gap between January 1938 and May 1939 may be explained in part by the disappearance of many of the CC members in the Terror and the consequent problems of gaining a quorum. The CC was thus a body called into session at the whim of its leaders rather than to a timetable dictated by the party's organisational norms.

These meetings seem to have discussed many of the important economic and political issues of the day, insofar as one can judge from the decisions which issued from the plena and from the survey of topics made by one student of the period.[30] However, its deliberations seem to have been heavily oriented towards the economy; of thirteen

Table 8.4. *CC meetings, 1935–41*

Date of meeting	Months from last meeting	Approx. length of plenum (days)
Feb. 1935	2	1
June 1935	4	3
Dec. 1935	6	5
June 1936	6	4
Dec. 1936	6	?
Feb–March 1937	2	11
June 1937	3	7
Oct. 1937	4	2
Jan. 1938	3	4[b]
May. 1939	16[a]	5
March 1940	10	3
July 1940	4	3
Feb. 1941	7	1

[a] Two plena, one at the beginning and one at the end of the XVIII Congress in March 1939, occurred in this interval.
[b] These four days actually extended over a period of ten days, with each meeting day interspersed by days in which the CC did not formally convene.

published decisions, eight concerned economic matters. In the economic sphere, the attention of the CC was devoted principally to agriculture with industry receiving little attention. This is consistent with the rural concerns of many CC members, and the fact that industry was a major concern for Sovnarkom, especially after the Terror. Furthermore, given the scope and importance of the Terror, it is noteworthy that this topic was addressed formally by the CC on very few occasions; the December 1936 plenum discussed allegations against Bukharin and Rykov; the February–March 1937 plenum when Bukharin and Rykov were excluded from the party and 'enemies' within the party were discussed,[31] and the January 1938 plenum when mistakes in expulsion from the party were addressed.[32] According to Roy Medvedev, the June 1937 plenum also invested the NKVD with increased powers for the conduct of the Terror.[33]

We do not know what transpired during these plena, due to the continued operation of those rules about keeping CC deliberations secret which had emerged about the time of the revolution from above. However, it seems that the plena of December 1936, February–March 1937 and January 1938 at which the Terror was a major topic of discussion were also the scenes of significant disagreement within the CC.[34] The evidence for this regarding the December 1936 plenum is purely circumstantial. At the plenum, all speakers condemned Bukharin and Rykov and called for their expulsion from the party,[35] but Stalin, speaking last, counselled caution. Such a stance would be consistent with the presence in the assembly of significant opposition to action against these two former leaders. So too would the secrecy with which the plenum was held; no official acknowledgement of the plenum seems to have been made during Stalin's lifetime.[36] The convocation of another plenum two months later to expel these two people would also be consistent with such a view. While not conclusive, these suggest a degree of opposition from within the CC to moves against Bukharin and Rykov.

The situation is clearer for the February–March 1937 plenum. Khrushchev referred to this plenum in the following terms: 'many members actually questioned the rightness of the established course regarding mass repressions under the pretext of combating "two-facedness"', and he referred specifically to Postyshev as being prominent in expressing such doubts.[37] The thrust of this report is supported by various pieces of circumstantial evidence. This was the longest plenum of the period, lasting some eleven days. Stalin's main address to the plenum, entitled 'Deficiencies in Party Work and Methods for the Liquidation of the Trotskyists and Other Double-Dealers',[38] dwelt upon the way in which wrecking and espionage activities were widespread, how 'responsible workers' as well as rank-and-file were involved, and how many party leaders had been remiss in not uncovering such activity. The speech seems to have been received very coolly. In marked contrast to the way his other speeches were being received at this time, this one received only minimal acknowledgement; it was interrupted only once and, both on this occasion and at the end, received only 'applause' rather than the more extended and fervent reaction his words usually evoked. This should not be surprising given that this speech was, in effect, warning party leaders that they were themselves under question, a warning that would have possessed a heightened sense of threat for those regionally based CC members who had managed to survive the challenges earlier in the 1930s.[39] Furthermore, the speech was not published until 29 March, a month after its delivery, and it was not the subject of a special resolution of the meeting. Indeed, the failure of such a resolution to be issued in itself suggests the leadership's inability to carry the day in the plenum. In his concluding speech to the plenum,[40] also published after about a month's delay on 1 April, Stalin referred to an absence of 'completely clear understanding' and 'some voices' supporting particular measures. Both sorts of formulation are suggestive of less than complete unanimity over policy issues. This may be, in part, a reflection of the fact that both Bukharin and Rykov were allowed to address this plenum.

The only speech which was published immediately and upon which a formal resolution was based was that of Andrei Zhdanov.[41] His speech ushered in the changed electoral regulations (discussed in the previous chapter) which introduced secret ballot and abolished voting by list. The tone of Zhdanov's concluding remarks suggests that the debate upon his report had been characterised by heated exchanges on the substance of the changes.

If we put the circumstantial evidence sketched above with the reaction to Zhdanov's proposals, the picture of this plenum which emerges is one in which a part of the membership tried to place constraints upon the unrolling of the Terror. Their opposition appears to have been sufficiently strong to have prevented the body as a whole from coming out in open, unambiguous endorsement of the Terror.[42] It is likely that the sub-national party leaders in the CC would have supported such a restriction because it was they in particular who came under direct attack from Stalin for failing to act vigorously against enemies in the party's ranks. Clearly it was from this source that the doubts about the changed electoral regulations would also have emanated since such changes threatened their power bases. The February–March 1937 CC plenum suggests that this body was not yet the rubber stamp of a supreme leadership.

It is possible that there was also conflict at the January 1938 plenum, although there is no firm evidence to support this contention. The plenum met on four separate days, 11, 14, 18 and 20 January, a pattern unique in Soviet history. No explanation for this pattern was given. It would be consistent with a meeting in which there were significant divisions, with the intervals between sessions being used in an attempt to resolve the differences. This plenum formally removed from the Politburo the chief critic in the February–March plenum, Postyshev, but, more importantly, the only resolution which emerged from the meeting was somewhat ambiguous. The main concern of the resolution is adequately reflected in its title: 'On Errors of Party Organisations in Expelling Communists from the Party, on Formal Bureaucratic Attitudes Toward the Appeals of those Expelled from the AUCP(b), and on Measures to Eliminate These Short-comings'.[43] The main thrust of the resolution was a criticism of lower party organs and leaders for the mass, indiscriminate expulsion of party members and the slowness with which appeals were considered. Among the causes of this were the careerist desire to appear vigilant and efficient by expelling many enemies, the provocative action of masked enemies expelling honest and devoted communists, and a careless attitude to the fate of party members. The resolution then called upon party organisations and their leaders 'to unmask and *exterminate every last disguised enemy* who has penetrated our ranks' (emphasis in original) and 'in every way heighten the bolshevik vigilance of the party masses and ... unmask and uproot all voluntary and involuntary enemies of the party'. The resolution also emphasised the need for an individualised rather than a mass approach to purging and the speeding up and regularisation of re-entry procedures for those incorrectly charged. The resolution thus called for heightened vigilance against disguised enemies along with a criticism of much of the way the Terror had been conducted and a call for greater regularisation of procedures. Significantly, responsibility for the deficiencies was placed on the party and its leaders, not the NKVD. The resolution may thus have been a compromise between those who favoured a restriction of the Terror and those who wished it to continue. Whether this was the case depends in part upon whether those who had called for moderation at the February–March 1937 plenum had been removed prior to this meeting. It seems that many had disappeared from political life by this stage.[44] In any case, the number of reversals of expulsions seems to have been increased in the following months, but it is not clear that this was accompanied by any moderation in the expulsion levels.

As well as this apparent resistance to the continuation of the purges from within the CC, there may also have been some resistance to the beginning of the Terror in the first place. During the first half of 1936, the emphasis upon 'enemies' seems to have declined following the ending of the Verification of Party Documents and the comparative lack of enemies expelled. On 24 June 1936 the CC issued a document entitled 'On Errors in the Examination of Appeals from Persons Expelled from the Party during the Verification and Exchange of Documents'. Although this has not been fully published, those sections of it which have appeared attack the excesses and arbitrary treatment meted out to party members and clearly reflect a sentiment of greater moderation. However, this sense of moderation was reversed just over a month later when another document from the CC was issued on 29 July. This was entitled 'On the Terrorist Activities of the Trotskyite–Zinovievite Counter-revolutionary Bloc'. This set the scene for the forthcoming show trial by emphasising the way in which terrorists had infiltrated the party's ranks. As such, it promised anything but moderation and, in its tone, seems to conflict with what we know about the 24 June document. These two documents may reflect the tension between supporters and opponents of the mass purges.[45] Furthermore, Stalin's address to the June 1936 plenum was not published, a fact which may suggest significant opposition to the contents of that address within the elite.[46]

Throughout this period the CC seems to have addressed many of the major issues of the day, and its deliberations were not merely a passive acceptance of leadership dictates. However, as an institution, the CC had little organisational integrity or coherence. Its failure to meet according to the prescribed timetable, and indeed according to any regular pattern, is one measure of this. But more important was its inability to maintain itself intact and its limited decision-making role. The purging of most members of the CC reflects that body's weakness; it could not provide adequate defence or protection for its members against attack from without. On decision-making, although the CC had been supplanted long ago by the Politburo, it was unusual for it to be as detached from a policy development as momentous as the Great Terror. There was no published decision by a CC plenum either beginning or ending the Terror, and only the January 1938 plenum produced a published decision relating to it. Probably partly a function of the presence of opposition to the Terror in this body, this was also due to the continuing emphasis within the CC on the tasks of economic management which it had undertaken in the early 1930s.

Turning to the Politburo, it is as difficult to gain reliable information about the functioning of this body during this period as it is for the CC. One thing which is certain is its changing composition. A series of changes occurred at CC plena during this period: February 1935 A. I. Mikoian and V. Ia. Chubar were elected full members (they were previously candidates) and A. A. Zhdanov and R. I. Eikhe candidates;[47] October 1937 N. I. Ezhov was elected a candidate member;[48] January 1938 Postyshev was expelled as a candidate member and replaced by N. S. Khrushchev; February 1941 N. A. Vosnesensky, G. M. Malenkov and A. S. Shcherbakov were elected as candidate members. In addition, a new Politburo was elected following the XVIII Congress in 1939 (see table 8.5).

Table 8.5. *Politburo Membership, 1939*

Full
A. A. Andreev, CC Secretary; Ch PCC
K. E. Voroshilov, PC of Defence
A. A. Zhdanov, CC Sec; 1st Sec Leningrad
L. M. Kaganovich, Orgburo; Dep Ch SNK
M. I. Kalinin, Ch. Presidium of Supreme Soviet
A. I. Mikoian, PC of Foreign Trade
V. M. Molotov, Ch. Sovnarkom
I. V. Stalin, CC Secretary
N. S. Khrushchev, 1st Sec Ukraine

Candidate
L. P. Beria, PC NKVD
N. M. Shvernik, 1st Sec TU Council

Comparison of this body with that elected in 1934 shows a surprisingly high level of continuity compared with the CC; six of the ten full members retained their places while one of the five candidates was promoted to full membership. Clearly the common conception that the higher one was up the political ladder the more likely one was to be purged needs qualification;[49] full membership of the Politburo seems to have given a better chance of survival than any other post in the system. However, while this level of continuity is high compared with the CC, we should not under-rate the level of turnover. Of the twenty-one people who held Politburo office between 1934 and the eve of the XVIII Congress (the fifteen elected at the XVII Congress and the six added in the interim), only nine retained office in 1939, representing a carry forward rate of 42.9 per cent, and these constituted the full members of the new Politburo. This was clearly the Stalinist kernel. But it was also a long-established kernel; of the nine full members of the Politburo, only Zhdanov and Khrushchev became members later than July 1926. Conversely, of the ten people who joined the Politburo between July 1926 and the opening of the XVIII Congress, only Zhdanov and Khrushchev survived.[50] The core of Stalin's support dated from the 1920s and, like the Politburo as a whole, consisted of Old Bolsheviks; only Khrushchev, whose membership dated from 1918, joined the party after the revolution.[51]

In 1934, the occupational profile of the Politburo membership had shown a marked dominance by the state apparatus. This technocratic bias was maintained in 1939 with 55.5 per cent of full members and 54.5 per cent of all members being part of the state machine (Kaganovich held both a party and a state post). The remainder were from the party apparatus (four were members of the Orgburo – Andreev, Zhdanov, Kaganovich and Stalin; so too was Malenkov who joined in 1941) except for Shvernik who headed the trade unions. In a departure from the past, there were no representatives from the regional state apparatus. On the party side, the Moscow party organisation was not represented (Shcherbakov was party first secretary at the time of the XVIII Congress; he became a candidate member in February 1941) while Leningrad was once again represented by someone (Zhdanov) whose responsibilities were split between his regional power base and the central apparatus. The Ukrainian party retained its representation through its first secretary, but this time as a full rather than a candidate member. Another four members (Kaganovich, Mikoian, Beria and Shvernik) had previously spent some time in leading positions in the regional party apparatus. One important development during this period was the elevation to Politburo status of the head of the NKVD; in October 1937 Ezhov (who had been a CC secretary since March 1935) became a candidate member, being replaced at that level by his successor as NKVD head, Beria, in 1939. This was the first time since Dzerzhinsky had been a candidate member in 1924–26 that the security apparatus was represented at such a high level.

Looking at the changes in the composition of the Politburo it is clear that this represents the emergence of a body consisting of firm supporters of Stalin. The 1934 members who showed reservations or opposition to the course Stalin wished to pursue were removed from the body with the result that it had become by the end of the period an organ which was much more closely attuned to Stalin's wishes. Certainly the members were not undifferentiated in this regard. Leonard Schapiro[52] has divided the 1939 Politburo into two groups, the 'Old Stalinists' – Molotov, Kaganovich, Voroshilov, Kalinin, Mikoian, Andreev and Shvernik, and the 'Neo-Stalinists' – Zhdanov, Khrushchev and Beria. While the former group had supported Stalin's rise to power, they had gained prominence within the party prior to Stalin's consolidation of his leadership. The latter, in contrast, owed their advancement to Stalin. But while the former may have had an independent profile within the party, it is clear that by 1939 they were firm supporters of the CC Secretary Stalin.

Little is known of the operating procedures of the Politburo during this period. It is possible that the idiosyncratic decision-making style based upon cronies and informal groupings of Politburo members described by Khrushchev and Djilas and relating to a later period[53] was already in existence by the end of this period. Khrushchev refers to the way in which 'many decisions were taken either by one person or in a roundabout way, without collective discussions',[54] while the show trial of Zinoviev, Kamenev et al. seems to have proceeded without formal Politburo approval.[55] One scholar has argued that the Politburo was meeting only about once a month.[56] If correct, these views portray the Politburo as barely operating as an effective institution during much of this period; its level of integrity and coherence was low. It is probable that when it did meet, at least early in the period, discussion was characterised by some conflict, with those opposing Stalin's favoured course ultimately being removed from that body. There is, however, no hard evidence to support this view, although Conquest has suggested that the formal announcement of the dropping of the investigation of Bukharin and Rykov on 10 September 1936 was made as a result of opposition to the continuation of the investigation from inside the Politburo.[57] It is unlikely that opposition of this sort could have been sustained following 1938. This involves the question of Stalin's personal position, which will be discussed below.

Information on the Orgburo and Secretariat during this period is even more sketchy than for the Politburo. The Orgburo elected in March 1939 had nine full members and no candidates (compared with ten and two in 1934) of whom five had not been members in 1934.[58] Only one-third of the membership elected in 1934 retained their places on the Orgburo in 1939. The Secretariat maintained its size of four throughout this period, although only Stalin and Zhdanov retained their positions.[59] One unusual development during this period was that Ezhov retained his position as CC Secretary upon his appointment as People's Commissar of Internal Affairs in September 1936.[60] All CC secretaries remained members of the Orgburo. There appears to be no information about the size of the CC Secretariat apparatus during this period. Nor is the public record particularly enlightening about how that apparatus was operating. At the XVIII Congress Vladimirsky did refer to the efficiency of the CC apparatus in handling certain personnel matters,[61] but it is probable that Mikoian was closer to the truth when he referred to the weakness of the party's organisational work.[62]

The existence of problems in the functioning of the central apparatus during this period is suggested by its organisational restructuring. A major restructuring of the Leading Party Organs Department (ORPO) began in September 1935. A sector was created in ORPO to deal with leading cadres. Under this sector was created a series of 'groups': one for cadres in the party apparatus, one for maintaining records on their assignments, three for leading personnel in different sectors of Soviet life (industry and transport; agriculture, trade, finance and planning; and administrative, cultural and scientific organisations) and one for each of eleven territorial groups. The territorial groups, which were to work principally through 'instructors' who were totally familiar with their territories, were to be responsible for regions which overlapped existing territorial divisions. The effective concentration of all personnel work in ORPO undercut the rationale of the production branch principle established in 1934,[63] thereby overturning the new administrative arrangements before they had had a chance to become firmly established. The resulting confusion cannot have assisted the regularisation of personnel matters.

Continuing dissatisfaction led to another major restructuring at the XVIII Congress. Sponsored by Zhdanov, the new structure eliminated the industrial branch departments of the Secretariat and concentrated all personnel work in a new Cadres Administration, thereby formalising what had in practice been happening since the change to ORPO in 1935. The former integrated production branch system was criticised for artificially dividing the party's personnel work and hindering the scientific study, selection and distribution of cadres. In addition, at lower levels the industrial branch departments were accused of usurping the functions of economic and soviet organisations while their heads were becoming too involved in the direct administration of the economy.[64] Within the new administration, departments were to be established to handle the personnel needs of different sectors of political life, but these were all to be concentrated in the one organisational structure,[65] the Cadres Administration headed by Malenkov. As well as the Cadres Administration, the new structure of the CC apparatus had an Administration of Agitation and Propaganda, an Organisation-Instruction Department (for the supervision of subordinate party organisations), Agriculture Department, School Department, Special Sector and Administration of Affairs or Chancellery. The Agriculture and School Departments were maintained on the 1934 pattern rather than shifting on to the functional basis which was now the key organisational principle, reportedly because of the importance of supervision of these spheres of life.[66]

The shifting of the Secretariat apparatus away from the integrated production branch basis on to a functional basis reflects dissatisfaction with the way that apparatus had been working. It is clear from the reports that personnel matters had been excessively complicated by the organisational divisions within the Secretariat. Such divisions meant that the operation of a smoothly efficient personnel system, resting upon comprehensive records at the centre and a regularised mechanism of selection and distribution remained more hope than reality. The chaos and disruption that was produced for the party's personnel system by the Terror were far too great for a disjointed central personnel mechanism to overcome. By the end of this period, major weaknesses therefore remained in the party's central personnel system and in the organisational structure that was meant to administer it.

The functions of the Party Control Commission remained formally much as they had been outlined in the party Rules of 1934: supervision of the implementation of party decisions and calling to account those guilty of violations of party discipline and ethics; in 1939 the verification of the work of local party organs was added. But the official method of constituting the PCC was changed. In 1934 the PCC had been elected by the party congress, but in 1939 this was changed to election by the CC under whose leadership and direction it had to function.[67] The last vestige of the PCC's formal independence was eliminated as it was now unambiguously portrayed as the instrument of the leadership. But of course the myth of the independence of this organ had been punctured long before, and it continued to function as a weapon of the central leadership. Throughout this period the PCC was headed by close supporters of Stalin, including Kaganovich, Ezhov, Shkiriatov and Andreev. During the Verification of Party Documents the PCC seems vigorously to have pursued charges of corruption and bureaucratic mismanagement.[68] It seems also to have played some role, as originally envisaged, as a court of review of cases of expelled members and it reversed various decisions on expulsion taken during 1935–36.[69] However, there is no evidence to suggest that it played any meaningful restraining role during the Great Terror. Its responsibility for disciplinary matters inside the party, the great swathe cut through party membership by the Terror and the active part Ezhov had played at the apex of both PCC and NKVD suggests that this organ was a willing accomplice to the purging process and an obedient weapon in the leadership's hands.

No effort was made to define formally Stalin's position during this period. It continued to rest on the twin symbolic and organisational pillars which had sustained him earlier. The symbolic pillar remained the cult of Stalin, which reached new levels of intensity during this period.

During the second half of the 1930s the images projected through the cult underwent an important transformation. As the figure of Stalin moved to dominate the stage, that of Lenin slipped into the background. From about late 1935 the adjective 'Stalinist' began to eclipse the 'Leninist' and 'Lenin–Stalin' epithets that had been so common before. Lenin was mentioned less in the press, his words were quoted less often, and the achievements of party and regime were attributed increasingly to Stalin. Certainly the Lenin–Stalin relationship as portrayed through the cult was multi-faceted during this period, with some elements of it continuing to reflect Leninist primacy; references to Stalin as the 'pupil of Lenin'[70] and 'the true continuer of the cause of Lenin'[71] reflect this image. Others suggested a parity between the two: 'the CC of Lenin–Stalin',[72] 'the party of Lenin–Stalin',[73] 'the cause of Lenin–Stalin;'[74] 'the teachings of Lenin–Stalin',[75] and references to the two as 'great men',[76] great continuers of the cause of Marx and Engels'[77] and 'geniuses of mankind'[78] all suggest a broad equality between the two figures. There was also a suggestion of a metaphysical union between the two leaders. This is suggested in such references as 'Stalin is the Lenin of today',[79] 'Lenin is with us in wise Stalinist speeches'[80] and 'you do not look for other words, other expressions for the true characteristics of Stalin, than those with which you drew the image of Lenin'.[81] But while these sorts of images continued to resonate through the cult, during this period they came to be substantially overshadowed by an image of Stalinist primacy. One means of portraying such primacy was to attribute to Stalin qualities which could not be equalled. Thus he was 'the greatest man, the leader and teacher, our genius',[82] 'the greatest man on our planet',[83] 'The greatest thinker and leader of the socialist era of the development of mankind',[84] 'the greatest genius of mankind'[85] and 'the greatest man of our epoch'.[86] Similarly: 'There is no name on the earthly globe like the name of Stalin.'[87] Beside such a figure, Lenin paled to secondary status. In the reported words of Mikoian in 1939, 'Lenin was a very gifted man, but Stalin is a genius.'[88]

The principal strand of the Stalin cult related to Stalin's powers and abilities and the attribution of all successes to him and his guidance. This involved not simply exaggerated claims of Stalinist infallibility, but the complete rewriting of party history. The best example of this was the *Istoriia VKP(b). Kratkii kurs* published in 1938. This survey of party history showed Stalin to have been present at and to have played a decisive role in all of the most important events of the party's history. His central role in 1917 and the civil war were matters of major emphasis, as was his direct responsibility for the successes achieved since October. In speaking about agricultural collectivisation, *Pravda* declared: 'This great historical victory was achieved thanks to the genius leadership of comrade Stalin.'[89] He was the driving force behind successive Five Year Plans and the development of industry.[90] Linked to this image of Stalin as the source of all economic developments in the Soviet Union was the picture of him as the creator of a new way of life. As the 'initiator and creator of the new Constitution',[91] Stalin was 'the creator of the new life';[92] as one kolkhoz chairman said, 'thanks to our beloved comrade Stalin for the new joyful, happy, kolkhoz life'.[93] Stalin was 'the creator of happiness for the Soviet people'[94] and: 'Due to the genius of Stalin, in the epoch of Stalin, socialism has been victorious.'[95]

There were even suggestions that Stalin's powers and abilities were beyond measurement in human terms. For example, Stalin was referred to as 'the golden sun'[96] and 'the sun of a new life, enlightening the whole world'.[97] The power to create life itself was even attributed to him. Two examples are particularly striking:

> O great Stalin,
> O leader of the peoples,
> Thou who broughtest man to birth,
> Thou who fructifiest the earth,
> Thou who restorest the centuries,
> Thou who makest bloom the spring.[98]

In his paeon of praise to Stalin on the latter's sixtieth birthday, Shkiriatov declared: 'To the great leader of a great people, who gives us life, who cares for us, like a father, like a considerate parent, glory to him.'[99] The single most important theme of the cult is ably summarised in the following quotations from *Pravda* on the sixtieth birthday of the vozhd':[100] 'Comrade Stalin directs all aspects of life in our country. He is the initiator and organiser of all our victories, all the great undertakings in the construction of a new life'; 'all of our successes ... are wholly and completely linked to Stalin'; 'With the initiative, guidance and concern of comrade Stalin are linked all our successes in areas of internal and external policy.' He was the guarantor of success in the uncertain times, the constant symbol of authority, guidance and achievement. Moreover, he was garbed in the guise of the great figures of Russian history and state-building as Russian nationalism became a major symbolic prop for the system. The greatness of these past heroes only served to add gloss to Stalin's image.

The cult also projected a picture of the fervent, intense love harboured by the populace for their leader. His appearance at public meetings produced prolonged, tumultuous ovations punctuated by calls of praise. The existence of a strong emotional tie between populace and leader was suggested by such references as 'with a feeling of ardent, sincere love parents and children repeat your name'.[101] A kolkhoznik was reported as saying: 'My heart thumped joyfully when I saw that comrade Stalin was coming toward me',[102] while another reported that on leaving Stalin's presence: 'I began to run just like a youth; and joy and pride were in me, that he saw how I managed, and he was pleased.'[103] Or to quote another citizen: 'Each of us carried in his heart a fervent flame of boundless love for You – our friend, father, leader and teacher.'[104] Stalin was portrayed as the object of boundless love, devotion and adoration on the part of the populace.

The image of Stalin which the cult projected was important, particularly in the context of the uncertainty generated by the Great Terror.[105] By rewriting the historical myth of the October Revolution and replacing the symbol of Lenin by that of Stalin, the cult shifted the basis for the regime's claims to legitimacy away from both the dead founder and October itself and on to the living leader. Being cast as the creator of the system and the one whose infallible guidance was inexorably leading the country towards communism coupled the symbol of Stalin so closely with the basic ideological purposes and rationale of the regime that rejection of one became tantamount to rejection of the other. Within this context, opposition to Stalin constituted treason because it represented opposition to the move towards communism. The cult thus provided a basic rationalisation for the elimination through the Terror of those who opposed Stalin. Furthermore, by focusing upon Stalin the man rather than Stalin the party leader, the cult located systemic legitimacy in the individual person rather than the party. This removal of the party from its pedestal was a necessary pre-requisite to the permeability of the party and its demise under the blows of the NKVD. Furthermore, it firmly strengthened Stalin's political position. He became the unassailable fount of orthodoxy, with the result that by the end of the Terror, his authority was impregnable. The cult was a significant contributor to the transformation of authority within the system from the collective body where formally it resided at the opening of 1935 into the hands of the single leader where it was by 1939. Personalised leadership had become legitimate.

Of central importance here was the anti-bureaucratic thrust that the cult embodied. If the essence of bureaucratic operation and functioning is obedience to formalised laws, regulations and procedures embodied in the structured hierarchy of the bureaucracy, the cult subverted this essence. By projecting Stalin as the all-powerful leader who must be obeyed, the cult was displacing bureaucratic norms and replacing them with an authority structure that was patrimonial in nature. Lower level functionaries were expected to obey the vozhd', not the impersonal rules of the bureaucratic hierarchy. As such, the cult was a means for Stalin to by-pass the bureaucratic provisions and reach directly to the individuals who worked within the structure. It was a means of establishing a personalised tie and avoiding both the problems of communicating through an inefficient political structure and the distorting effects that structure could have on the leader's message. In this way, political support could be built up based upon that personalised tie.[106]

The anti-bureaucratic nature of Stalin's personalised leadership is also reflected in the public image of the party at this time. During 1935 and 1936, the criticism accompanying the Verification and the Exchange campaigns portrayed the party as a body which was unable to conduct its own domestic housekeeping functions in an acceptable fashion. Furthermore, in a theme which was extended in following years, it was unable to guarantee its own internal health by preventing the penetration of hostile elements. How could such an organisation be entrusted with overseeing the move into socialism? The answer was that it could carry out this function only if it followed the guidance and direction of the vozhd'. The party's special place as the repository of revolutionary values was thereby forfeited and taken over by the personalised leadership figure, Stalin. Its continued importance rested upon obedience to Stalin's will. In practical terms, this was expressed in the party's decline as an institution, its lack of integrity and coherence, and its new-found institutional permeability.

The main organisational pillar of Stalin's power remained his personal secretariat. Information on this organisation is no greater for this period than for its predecessor. However, there is no reason to assume that the close relationship between this office and the Special Sector and Chancellery of the CC Secretariat had changed. As a channel of information to Stalin (resting upon the special sectors at lower levels of the political structure) and a means of filtering the flow of that information to other members of the elite,[107] it was a very important organisation throughout this period. This role would have increased in importance as a result of the successive waves of the Verification and Exchange followed by the Great Terror. Its responsibility for secret communications in the party and the sensitive nature of all of the personnel information that was involved in the successive screenings meant that this apparatus must have had a significant part to play in the resolution of personnel matters.[108] Through Poskrebyshev, who was head of the Special Sector in Moscow and Stalin's leading personal assistant,[109] Stalin would have had direct access to whatever personnel information was available.[110] Access to this sort of information would have been very important for the direction of the Terror in that if the centre was to target particular individuals and groups, the knowledge which would have been necessary for this, if it was available at all, would have been available to the Special Sector. Furthermore the Special Sector seems to have had responsibility for the security apparatus. It thereby constituted a major weapon for influencing the course of the Terror and was a major asset for Stalin in his attempt to consolidate his position.

Stalin's power and position were also strengthened through the activities of the NKVD. It is during this period that the security apparatus reached the pinnacle of its power.[111] NKVD chief Ezhov was a candidate member of the Politburo from October 1937, a status his successor attained in March 1939. Moreover, in the second half of 1937 the campaign for heightened vigilance and the search for hidden 'enemies of the people' fed into an increased cult of the police and their leader Ezhov. Laudatory reports on the police and their activities became prominent in the national press while Ezhov himself appeared with a frequency and prominence that was surpassed only by Stalin. The cult reached its peak with the twentieth anniversary of the security apparatus in December 1937.[112] At least symbolically, the police emerged as an institution equal to if not more important than the party, as the real defender of the morality and gains of the revolution.

In practical terms, the control which the party was able to exercise over the police now slipped. Essential to the maintenance of party control was the institutional integrity of the party *vis-à-vis* the police. The best reflection of this throughout most of the regime's life was the way in which party members could not be touched by the police until they had been expelled from or discredited in the party. The party was thus able to maintain its integrity by defending its corps of members against the actions of the security apparatus. During this period, that capacity disappeared. It is not clear when the police first moved against a party member without the sanction of the party leadership. Certainly this was common at the height of the Ezhovshchina.[113] The basis for this was laid by the extraordinary measure of 1 December 1934 with its emphasis upon the immediate charging, investigation and execution of those accused of terrorism because this treated party members exactly the same as everyone else. This was reinforced by the CC resolution of the summer of 1936, extended indefinitely in June 1937, giving the NKVD extraordinary powers to destroy all enemies of the people.[114]

Khrushchev's statement that the arrest of Kosier and 'other cases of this type' was not the subject of 'an exchange of opinions or a Political Bureau decision'[115] indicates the way in which, by early 1938, Politburo members could be arrested without Politburo sanction. The February–March 1937 CC plenum which expelled Bukharin and Rykov from the party also seems to be the last at which the expulsion and arrest of CC members was dealt with. It may be that throughout much of this period, as Conquest suggests, prior to arrests the NKVD informed the party member's party organisation of what it was about to do and the organisation then expelled the member,[116] thereby formally maintaining party impermeability. But if this is the way these matters were conducted, it was farcical because the party could not prevent the arrest and it is very doubtful that the formal procedures through which expulsion was to be exercised were fulfilled. As Khrushchev declared,[117] the members of the CC arrested in 1937–38 were expelled illegally because the question of their expulsion was never discussed at a CC plenum. Thus the party's institutional integrity was breached; party membership was no longer a defence against any charge which could be fitted within the rubric of terrorism, a term with infinite flexibility, while the responsibility imposed upon the police to deal with such crimes gave them the power to override party boundaries. The superiority of their position is evident in the fact that the appointment of district, city and regional party secretaries was made subject to NKVD confirmation.[118] NKVD interest intruded into all areas of life.

The permeability of the party in general was extended to all of its constituent elements. Members of party bodies at all levels, including the CC and the Politburo, were victims of the Terror; formal office was no defence against the Ezhovshchina. Superficially this may appear to suggest that the NKVD became the supreme power in the country, with its wide-ranging powers of investigation and arrest the cudgel with which it could suppress all other political institutions. But such an impression would be misleading, because this institution too was subjected to the Terror. Individuals at all levels of the NKVD, including successive leaders Yagoda and Ezhov, were purged; indeed, the purging of a leader led to the widespread purging of his followers throughout the police structure.[119] The police was not an institution standing above the others, immune from the purging process and interfering in the political system at will.[120] While it was the key mechanism of the Terror, it was also subject to a higher authority which decided that the NKVD should itself be purged.[121] The cult of the police was not long-lasting and the wide-ranging powers of the NKVD seem to have been brought under control at the end of 1938 to early 1939;[122] in October 1938 a CC commission was created to investigate NKVD activities[123] and in February 1941 the NKVD was divided by the establishment of a new Commissariat of State Security (NKGB) alongside the NKVD.[124] The authority which was superior to the NKVD was Stalin.

New conventions in political life

In an immediate sense, Stalin's position was a function of his place in the elite, and it is to this which we must turn. Essentially this means Stalin's relationship with his fellow oligarchs. The precise nature of a personal relationship, particularly when unstructured by clearly understood formal principles, can be notoriously difficult to understand. This is particularly the case in a situation like that which applied in the Soviet Union at this time, when elite relations were even more secretive than they had been earlier. Consequently, we must rely more than we would like upon the sorts of evidence which are not themselves conclusive but rather suggestive of the particular state of affairs which may have prevailed.

Stalin's personal position changed significantly between the opening of the period and its close. At the beginning of 1935 Stalin was clearly the predominant figure in the leadership. However he did not rule over that leadership autocratically; despite the claims of the cult, his word was neither law nor holy writ within leading councils. If the traditional interpretation of Kirov's assassination is correct – namely that it was planned by Stalin as a means of introducing the

Terror and so bring the party to heel – this implies that at this time Stalin's voice alone was not sufficient to carry the day, at least on this sort of issue; he needed an excuse to bring about the change he desired. Furthermore, if the arguments presented above are correct, both the Politburo and the CC, when they met, were not mere rubber stamps of Stalin's will. If they had been, there would have been little reason for the purging of them in 1937–38. The disappearance of so many members of the elite suggests that, at the very least, there were reservations about some aspects of Stalin's policies. We know that there was direct opposition at the February–March 1937 plenum, and there is circumstantial evidence to suggest that such opposition was present both before and after that meeting. This means that although Stalin's position may not have been under threat, he was not in the position unilaterally and inevitably to carry the day in formal leadership circles.

This argument assumes Stalin's complicity in the Terror. Furthermore, it is this phenomenon which fundamentally altered Stalin's position within the elite. Both extreme positions – that Stalin bears either no responsibility or sole responsibility for the Terror – are of little help in understanding this phenomenon. Nor is it very sensible to try to attribute all of the deaths and repression *directly* to Stalin. There were forces at work within the Terror which, while left untrammelled, caused the Terror to expand and embrace increasing numbers of victims; the invidious pressures to over-fulfil quotas, the perceived need for ostentatious 'vigilance' as a means of fending off charges of being an 'enemy', the effects of personal and institutional rivalries and conflicts, and careerist motives of advancement up the ladder all appear to have been important in explaining the ever-expanding nature of the Terror. But these forces alone cannot explain the Terror. Here Stalin does bear major responsibility.

Even if we were to accept the view that Stalin had no part in the Kirov assassination, he was directly responsible for the extraordinary measures introduced in the wake of that act which left the party vulnerable to attack by the police. The reported telegram of September 1936 castigating the NKVD for being four years behind in their work in unmasking the Trotskyite–Zinovievite bloc and replacing Yagoda by Ezhov came directly from Stalin.[125] Major disciplinary instruments at this time were headed by people who had been part of Stalin's personal apparatus and therefore presumably retained close ties with him: ORPO was headed by Ezhov until 1936 and then Malenkov; in 1935 Ezhov became Chairman of the PCC; from September 1936 until December 1938 Ezhov headed the NKVD where for some of the time he was assisted by Shkiriatov and Agranov; and in May 1937 Mekhlis was made head of the Main Political Administration of the Red Army.[126] All were former members of Stalin's personal secretariat. Furthermore, although the measures of 1 December 1934 eliminated the party's impermeability to the police, it is still doubtful whether the police could have moved against members of the party oligarchy without the express permission of the leading oligarch and his supporters; if Khrushchev is correct and Stalin was routinely approving arrest lists of names of ordinary people submitted to him by Ezhov,[127] he must have exercised at least a watching brief over the elite.[128] Stalin encouraged efforts to unmask the wrecking and sabotage activities that characterised contemporary political life, both publicly through his speech at the February–March 1937 plenum and more discreetly.[129] Moreover, if Stalin was the predominant although not all-powerful oligarch early in this period, and if a portion of the leadership including Stalin opposed the Terror in some measure, the outbreak of the Terror would have to be explained by reference to the actions of a small group who could overrule the combination of Stalin and other party opponents of the Terror. This is an unlikely explanation. Finally, the fact that Stalin was left in a position of supreme and autocratic dominance, personally untouched by the Terror[130] and with his retinue of closest supporters less adversely affected by the Terror than other groups, suggests that he was able to exercise some guiding role over its course. All of these factors, which together make up the minimalist position on Stalin's responsibility, suggest that Stalin played a principal, and even activist, role in the Terror without having to have recourse to arguments about motivation.[131]

While Stalin personally was of fundamental importance for the Terror, he was supported in this by a range of associates in the upper levels of the political structure. These supporters were not mere subordinates whose whole time was taken up with pandering to the wishes of the vozhd'. They retained importance in their own right as leading political figures in the system and they had their own views on policy and desirable courses of action. Such views could differ and be the focus of conflict. There were also conflicting ambitions and struggles for power and influence between these subordinates; conflicts between Ezhov and Beria in the NKVD,[132] between Zhdanov and Ezhov over education versus purge for curing the party's ills,[133] between Malenkov and Kaganovich over personnel matters,[134] between Zhdanov and Malenkov about the role of the party in industrial management,[135] and between Molotov and Ordzhonikidze over economic growth rates[136] were among such conflicts. There has also been talk of tension between Stalin and Yagoda in the period before the latter was replaced as head of the NKVD in 1936.[137] These sorts of conflicts were bound to occur in a political structure in which one individual was pre-eminent. He could not physically take charge of all aspects of policy and place his stamp upon them. Policy generation and discussion had to occur at the second level of the elite among Stalin's lieutenants, otherwise the system would have ground to a halt. But just as such discussions did not always involve Stalin from the outset, as the leading figure in the leadership, most such discussions would sooner or later have come before his attention. Furthermore, it appears that the issue was often resolved through Stalin's intervention, particularly in the latter stages of the period; as the leading figure in the oligarchy and one whose position was becoming stronger as the period wore on, it became increasingly unlikely that a dispute between his lieutenants could be resolved in a manner of which he did not approve. By the end of the period, Stalin's fellow oligarchs generally took care not to find themselves on the opposite side of an issue to the vozhd'.

It would, however, be misleading to portray Stalin as merely the arbiter in the conflicts of his supporters, although this was one role he played. He was clearly much more than that, even at the beginning of the period. Stalin remained throughout an active politician with his own, albeit not unchanging, political views and policy preferences. Furthermore, as the predominant leader, with the support of a significant part of the party oligarchy, he was in the position to be able to push through measures he supported.[138] During the early part of the period he may have lacked sufficiently broad support within the oligarchy to get all that he wished through approved party channels; the means of introducing the measures of 1 December 1934 and of the beginning of the Terror are consistent with this.[139] Hence the making of decisions in such a way as to avoid formal party bodies may at this time have been more a reflection of Stalin's weakness in those bodies than of his political strength. However, by the end of the period the Terror had overcome any problems Stalin may have had in terms of support in elite bodies; if before the Terror Stalin remained dependent upon factional politics, after it he was independent of such considerations. His propensity to ignore formal decision-making bodies in the latter stages of the period would thus have been reflective of his strength.[140] By the end of the period, Stalin was the all-dominant political figure in the system. No major decisions could be taken that could not be overturned by Stalin. He was still not the source of all policy; subordinates continued to generate policy ideas and take up policy positions.[141] But now all was dependent upon Stalin and Stalin alone. He no longer needed the formal support of party bodies, which in any case had become automatic.

This is the important change in Stalin's position during this period: the shift from needing to rely upon the support of others to defeat opposition to a situation in which opposition did not exist. An intrinsic part of this process was the elevation of the individual leader above all other institutions in the society. Accomplished symbolically through the cult and buttressed by the course of historical revision[142] and the associated symbolic destruction of the Old Bolsheviks,[143] this was achieved in practical terms through the Terror. But it would be wrong to assume that elite relations were constructed solely on the basis of fear. For many in the elite, there would also have been a faith in and a sense of obligation to Stalin. While those in the inner circle, the Politburo, Orgburo and Secretariat, are unlikely to have been firm believers in the message of the leader cult, they may still have seen Stalin as the source of much policy which had been beneficial for the development of socialism in the USSR. Furthermore, in many respects their own careers were inextricably intertwined with that of Stalin. If they now doubted Stalin's leadership and his qualifications to exercise that leadership, it would have called into question the correctness of their previous support for him. On these grounds alone, they are likely to have acceded to the leader's wishes even had the threat been less evident.

At the lower level of the elite, among members of the CC in particular but also regional party functionaries, there may have been more widespread belief in the cult. It is impossible either to verify or disprove this, but it is likely that those who had only distant contact with the vozhd' would be more receptive to the cult's claims than those who were in close and continuing contact with him. But perhaps more important here was the enormous boost to their careers for which Stalin was believed to be responsible. The opportunities for social mobility and political promotion opened up by the Terror and administered under Stalin's name created in many of these people a sense of obligation and perhaps even faith in the leader. Where they saw their jobs, if not their lives, as being dependent on Stalin, they were much more likely to give him their support and loyalty. While there had always been something of this in the General Secretary-regional leadership relationship, the Terror made it much more evident than it had been in the past.

The elimination of party impermeability led to the destruction of all sense of integrity and coherence on the part of individual party bodies, including those at the apex of the party structure. The purging of these bodies excised opposition from them, thereby eliminating any possibility that they could play a meaningful political role in the decision-making process, and catapulted Stalin into a position of unchallenged dominance within the system as a whole. Even the security apparatus, which had been the instrument of the party's demise and which some have seen as the dominant power in the USSR at the end of the 1930s, was subordinate to the vozhd'. Certainly its profile and status as an administrative organisation was much higher at the end of the period than it had been at the outset, but it nevertheless remained one of the instruments of Soviet rule, with real power vested in the vozhd' and those immediate supporters upon whom he chose to rely. It may be that there was something of an alliance between Stalin and the NKVD as some have argued,[144] but it was an alliance in which Stalin was the superior partner. By 1941, if Stalin chose to make a decision, that decision would be adopted formally regardless of the views of the collective or the principles of system operation. The Terror had crushed all institutional constraints upon the individual leader and enormously expanded the decision-making power of that leader. What the Terror could not do was to establish an efficient administrative machine which could ensure that those decisions were implemented quickly and precisely throughout the country.

An important element of the elevation of the individual leader to a position of absolute supremacy was the attitude to opposition. During the preceding period, there had been no recognised right for opposition to exist in the USSR. This position was, if possible, strengthened during this period. The continued heavy emphasis upon the search for 'enemies of the people', the need for vigilance against saboteurs and wreckers, and the claimed presence of spies and enemy agents at all levels of the structure injected both a heightened sense of urgency and an element of paranoia into Soviet political life.[145] Dissent was opposition and this aided the enemy in his quest for the subversion of the Soviet regime. The change in imagery is suggestive: the emphasis upon deviation and ideological heterodoxy was replaced by the imagery of war. Enemies, saboteurs and spies were the new focus of concern. Not even the shadow of opposition was to be countenanced; indeed the failure to be sufficiently vigorous and successful in uncovering opposition was itself considered to be a manifestation of opposition. But even total commitment demonstrated through the vigorous and successful prosecution and persecution of oppositional elements might not be enough. According to Molotov in March 1937, enemies of the people may continually and enthusiastically support the party, even rising to positions of responsibility, but they may do this only the better to strike against the party.[146] What this represents is the effective breakdown of any discrete notion of opposition; the term was now indefinable in anything but a purely arbitrary, political and situational sense.

However, this does not mean that there were no notions of what constituted opposition. If we were to believe the catalogue of charges hurled against the victims of the Terror, acts like the formation of anti-party groups, the contemplation and planning of terrorist acts and spying for hostile powers[147] were common manifestations of oppositional activity. No one would deny that such activity should be classed as oppositional in nature. But of course in the vast majority of cases, such charges bore little resemblance to the facts. They were used as camouflage, to justify the elimination of people whose removal was actually based on other grounds. Those grounds were diverse, reflecting the different forces at work making for the expansion of the Terror noted above. What is clear is that any dissent from or opposition to Stalin and his policies either currently or in the past was likely to be interpreted as opposition. Zinoviev's admission in January 1935 that the 'political responsibility' lay with 'the former anti-party "Zinoviev" group for the [Kirov] murder'[148] established the principle that former opposition had a ripple effect throughout the party and over time and was therefore something which would be present until its potential influence was completely eradicated. Opposition could insidiously creep through party ranks unless all of its manifestations, current and previous, were extirpated. The necessary touchstone of loyalty and discipline, and therefore the reverse of opposition, was continuing ostentatious and enthusiastic commitment to the party line as enunciated by Stalin, although as Molotov's statement of March 1937 referred to above suggests, this was no certain guarantee against opposition. The linkage established by the cult between Stalin and his writings on the one hand and the country's march to communism on the other turned the failure to give total support and loyalty to Stalin into treason. Political debate which involved open rejection of Stalin's position[149] was thereby rendered unacceptable to the system; it was an instance of oppositional activity.

Following on from the two preceding periods, although on a much larger scale, the purge was a disciplinary weapon during this period, used against both enemies and mere malcontents. The continuing campaigns of searching for enemies were important in generating the atmosphere in which such measures appeared acceptable, while the effect of the collectivisation campaign and the apparent success of the use of terror in that campaign legitimised such methods. The fear of enemies in the party, stimulated by the assassination of Kirov, justified its extension into that institution. It was used both indiscriminately and with careful selection of targets and had much more of a mass character in its impact than any purge which had preceded it. The 1936–38 Terror was different from purges in earlier periods in three crucial respects. First, it was conducted against the party by a body which was neither part of the party structure nor especially set up by the party to conduct this operation, the NKVD. Here lies the importance of the party's newly established permeability; it could be purged by an outside organisation. Secondly, for the first time the penalty for party members succumbing in the purge could be death. No longer did membership of the party constitute a defence against the ultimate penalty, with the result that the party as a privileged organisation in this respect ceased to exist; it was no longer immune to the application of terroristic methods against it. Thirdly, the permeability of the party destroyed much of the barrier between it and society as a whole, with the result that purging could embrace both party members and non-party members within the one process without discrimination. Thus to the extent that the Terror was a reflection of tension within the ruling party elite,[150] it was also the mechanism for extending that tension throughout the entire apparatus and into the society as a whole.

The extension of the purge in this way reflects an important development, the politicisation of all aspects of life in the Soviet Union. The extension of the notion of opposition into the failure adequately to support and work for the party line added to the pressures to inform even on the members of one's own family for oppositional activities or views, expanded the political sphere. There was deemed to be virtually no sphere of private activity that was not directly linked with the struggle to build communism and, more immediately, to uncover enemies. In this way the boundaries of the political sphere were fundamentally redrawn as all citizens, their concerns and actions, were drawn into its ambit. Furthermore, it transformed terror from being a means of defence of the regime against foes, both real and imaginary, into a means of control of the society as a whole. The all-embracing nature of the Terror, added to the society-wide uncertainty this created, fundamentally transformed the nature of coercion in the system. It became an intrinsic part of the administrative-control system, and in so doing reshaped in a major way the course of systemic functioning.

Accompanying this redrawing of the boundaries of the political sphere was a weakening of the discreteness of institutional spheres within the political structure as a whole. The clearest instance of this is the licence given to the security apparatus to intervene in the affairs of other institutional entities. But also important was the disruption of the processes of bureaucratic decision-making and administration by the dominant individual leader. Procedures which had been developing over the life of the regime to structure the formulation and transmission of advice and the making of decisions on the basis of that advice were thrown over as Stalin chose to operate more informally through his supporters and lieutenants throughout the system. Institutional boundaries, prerogatives, sensitivities and traditions, including the established web of relationships between institutions, became of little account as Stalin's leadership style became more idiosyncratic and less regularised. He could search out and accept information and advice from wherever he chose, unconstrained by bureaucratic norms or regulations. His personal position of supremacy, supported by the uncertainty created by the Terror, meant that he shaped institutional contours and processes rather than his working style being shaped by their patterns.

Another important effect of the elevation of Stalin over the political institutions of Soviet society was the final rigidification and catechisation of ideology. With Stalin firmly entrenched as the fount of ideological orthodoxy, his words almost upon utterance entered the orthodox canon, which now developed principally through Stalinist input. But this meant that the ideology had little intellectual vigour. It became little more than a series of epithets, used mainly to legitimise the existing structure. A clear instance of this is Stalin's dictum about the intensification of class struggle and opposition the closer socialism approached, which acquired great prominence during the Terror. Like all orthodoxies, the ideology did impose some limits on the scope for policy innovation, but it was not particularly oppressive in this regard. Indeed, to the extent that the heart of the ideology formally had become Stalin's words, there was in principle a significant degree of flexibility about its role in policy formulation; when Stalin announced a new policy, it automatically obtained ideological validation. Similarly, the linkage between ideology and Stalin's words gave the ideology a certain direct, imperative quality for those at lower levels of the political structure. Obedience to Stalin's directives automatically meant acting in accord with the ideology because the two things were coterminous. But this was a purely mechanical relationship, and by linking the ideology to the leader in this way, the former was denied any independent part in the political system.

Thus by the end of this period, the essentials of the Stalinist political system sketched in the introduction were in place. The personal dominance of the leader, unencumbered by collective concerns or by high level challenge, was established. His supremacy over the institutional structures of which the regime formally consisted was consolidated, and the party had ceased to be the dominant institution in the structure. Politics had taken on a publicly monolithic and mobilisational facade, and although conflicts occurred among the second level political figures, they neither shook the position of the leader nor created major divisions in the interstices of the regime. The institutional structures remained formally in place, but they appeared much stronger than they were; they lacked institutional integrity and coherence and were completely subordinate to the vozhd'. This structure was very different from that which had existed at the opening of the period. The main agent of transformation was the Terror. But while it is important to recognise that it was principally the Terror that destroyed the institutional contours at the apex and so increased the power of the leader, the Terror left the leader's power seriously restricted in one important respect: it could not bring about any strengthening of vertical linkages in the political machine. Thus while the Stalinist political system was characterised by significant centralised, personalised power at the apex, it also had a loosely articulated structure at lower levels. Indeed, this was inevitable. At the centre, the strengthening of personalised power involved the destruction of institutional and bureaucratic structures, processes and relationships. But that personalised power could not be projected efficiently except through the operation of efficient institutional mechanisms extending vertically the length of the political structure. These had not existed at any earlier stage of the Soviet regime's life, and they were certainly not a feature of the Stalinist political system.

Conclusion: Why Stalinism?

The personalised dictatorship that was Stalinism was the product of a long process of institutional development and change and of the fundamental transformation of the notions of what was appropriate in the structuring of internal party life. Both institutional structures and values were changed to produce a political system which was significantly different from that which emerged in the immediate aftermath of October. This does not mean that the two political systems, the Leninist and the Stalinist, did not share parallels and were not linked. There were common elements between the two and some aspects of the earlier period were instrumental in setting the course of development which culminated in the personalised rule of Stalin. But the link between the two was not generative; the second did not flow automatically from the first. While it is true, as many have argued, that the roots of the Stalinist system are to be found in the Leninist, the roots of other paths of development are also present in this early period.[1] What must be explained is why, at crucial stages, these other potential paths were closed off.

For many, the answer to this question has been easy: Stalin. The standard interpretation has been that Stalin was able, through a combination of skill, luck and the incompetence of his opponents, to consolidate his own personal power and to force through the dramatic changes to the system which resulted in his own unbridled personal dictatorship. Clearly, the role of Stalin as a political actor was an important part of the course of events during this period. But we need to distinguish between the rise of the individual leader and the emergence of the whole Stalinist system. While the former is a central aspect of the latter, it is by no means the same as it. A broader explanation is required than simply an individual's ability to claw his way to the top.

An important element of the explanation, and one which has long been recognised in one form or another, is contextual (although it has often been presented less as a contextual and more as a determining factor). This is the isolation within which the new Bolshevik government found itself. But what is important here for the explanation of developments is not just the isolation and the hostile environment, but the way in which it was perceived. There is a strong case for arguing that, throughout this whole period, the leadership's conception of a hostile environment was well founded.

Domestically, Bolshevik support in the early days of the new system was restricted to a minority of the population, and although it was the strategically important working class which constituted the core of that support, this did not compensate for the narrow basis upon which the system rested. Symbolically reflected in the Constituent Assembly vote at the outset of Bolshevik rule, it was evident throughout the initial period in the armed opposition of sections of the populace in the Civil War, peasant revolts and the Kronstadt rising. Even in the cities, industrial unrest and the disintegration of the proletariat in the face of the enormous difficulties brought on by the Civil War increased the sense of isolation which faced the new rulers of Russia. This was reinforced on the international stage. The almost universal rejection of the new socialist state, evident most graphically in foreign involvement in the Civil War and in trade embargoes and boycotts, brought home to the new regime the reality of international hostility. The failure of workers' revolution in Europe emphasised the friendless status of Russia.

The sense of isolation was only marginally eased during the 1920s. Although the introduction of NEP had pacified the peasants and many of the smaller artisans and entrepreneurs who had suffered under War Communism, there was little conviction in party ranks that this new lack of restiveness in the countryside reflected popular support for the system. Distrust was still a common sentiment with regard to Russia's rulers throughout this period as much of the populace saw NEP as a welcome break from the disastrous, coercive policies of earlier years. Many saw the new policies not as a genuine change of heart on the part of the Bolsheviks, but as a temporary concession wrung from them under duress. The weakness of party representation in the countryside and the appearance of the authorities as an alien and external force reinforced this view. Similarly at the international level, the leadership in Moscow saw an outside world which had come to some sort of arrangement with Soviet Russia but which neither liked it nor saw it as a long-term relationship. The rockiness of the relationship with the United Kingdom, characterised by the so-called Zinoviev letter and the breaking off of relations in 1927, was typical of this. Similarly, the war scare of 1927 reinforced the impression of an uncertain and hostile outside world. The failure of communist revolution in China and elsewhere at this time served to emphasise the confinement of socialism to Russia.

The sense of isolation was reinforced at the time of collectivisation because, despite the surges of mass support for the new policies, these were also met by significant mass resistance. Many within the party, particularly at the middle and lower levels, knew how close to disaster collectivisation had been. They had direct experience of the level and extent of popular opposition to the new policy, and they knew that the countryside would in large measure reject the Bolsheviks and their policies if they could. The sense of isolation stemming from domestic conditions was strengthened by continuing concern about the intentions of the western powers and, more graphically, by the rise of Hitler in Germany. The nazis' accession to power confronted the Soviet Union with a foe which was recognised by the leadership as very dangerous.

The sense of hostility abated little during the rest of the decade. Although the peasantry had been brought firmly under control and the working class was now locked into the emerging structures of industrial life in the factories of the growing cities, a sense of disquiet and restiveness at the new conditions remained common among sections of the populace. Many still preferred a privatised economic existence and tolerated rather than supported the new collective forms of the economy. Internationally, the spectre of nazism continued to grow, with the Spanish Civil War and the extension of German territorial acquisitions. Backed up by the knowledge of Hitler's anti-Slav rantings, developments in Europe were seen as taking a decidedly nasty turn, particularly given the reluctance of Britain and France seriously to contemplate an anti-German alliance with the Soviet Union.

The fears of a hostile environment and of political isolation which pervaded leading ranks of the party did, therefore, have a basis in fact throughout this period. But what gave these fears a particular virulence was the way in which opposition was perceived. The basis of this perception was class analysis. Bolshevism's membership of a broader intellectual tradition which employed class analysis meant that when looking at political phenomena, Bolshevik theoreticians and politicians always searched for the fundamental social forces which gave rise to such phenomena. The problem for them was that the Russia in which they had come to power was not the sort of society where socialist revolution had been expected to occur first. In comparison with the industrialised west, Russia was not only less developed economically but, as a consequence, its working class was at a lower stage of development. It was not a hardened proletariat formed in the furnaces of the factories over a number of generations but, in large part, a class only barely removed from the villages. Levels of class consciousness, with the honourable exception of such sections as the metalworkers, were low and the capacity of the class to constitute a solid social basis for the new regime was problematic.

Concerns about the weakness of the class base were translated into constant fears about the further erosion of that base. While such developments as the evaporation of the class in 1919 and 1920 were concrete manifestations of this, far more insidious and all-pervading throughout the entire period was the fear of infection by the petty bourgeois environment. Forced to build socialism in a predominantly petty bourgeois, peasant country, as they saw it, the Bolsheviks always had to be on their guard that their efforts were not subverted by infection of their entire enterprise by petty bourgeois ideas, values and attitudes. In their eyes, this was the greatest danger; if petty bourgeois forces were able surreptitiously to enter and gain control of the political system, the achievement of socialism would be doomed. Because of the prominence that this fear had in leading Bolshevik ranks, all forms of opposition both inside and outside the party were linked with it. Such an approach only served to increase the magnitude of the danger in their own eyes; concrete opposition gave substance to the more metaphysical notions of opposition resonant in the concern with petty bourgeois attitudes.

It was this sort of approach to opposition which closed off some of the avenues of potential development. In principle, one way of overcoming the isolation which was experienced by the emerging Soviet system was inclusionist, an expansion of its boundaries in such a way as to encapsulate some of those forces currently alienated from it. This was the basic tactic adopted at the outset with regard to the Left SRs. However, what prevented this from being a viable long-term strategy was the fear of infection. It was believed that such a course of action opened the party and, more broadly, the Bolshevik political system to the danger of the free flow of petty bourgeois sentiments and values. If these were able to take a hold in the very interstices of the system, the danger of full-scale degeneration would have been greatly increased. This fear is most clearly reflected in the final suppression of the Mensheviks and the SRs at the outset of NEP; with bourgeois forces given freer rein through the economic arrangements of the NEP, these potential political channels had to be closed off. Similarly, at the time of the relaxation of 1933-34 and the associated return to political life of figures recently excluded, there was no significant support in the party for the restoration of alternative, independent channels of political activity. Single party control of the political system was essential to the maintenance of the bulwark against the dangers of petty bourgeois infection.

But the fear of infection also helped to shape developments within the party itself. Throughout the period opposition was stigmatised by its claimed association with petty bourgeois forces in the country at large. This link was explicitly made at the time of the introduction of the anti-fractional measures at the X Congress, and it was repeated in the charges made against successive opposition groups throughout the 1920s. There is no evidence that any of these groups had political links with anti-Bolshevik forces in the countryside, but in the context of fears of infection, such a link did not have to be established. Not only was opposition seen, correctly, as a potential breaching of the solid front against petty bourgeois influence by opening the party up to dissent and disunity, but the policies of some of these groups could be characterised as being pro-peasant. This seemed to validate the charge of a link with peasant forces; why else would they pursue such policies?

The validity of this mode of reasoning was confirmed for many during the collectivisation campaign. The charge that some lower level party leaders were soft-pedalling collectivisation seemed to give substance to the supposed link between extra-party enemies and opposition in the party. It reinforced the view that the surrounding petty bourgeois environment could attack the move toward socialism through its insidious influence seeping into the party structure through party members whose level of commitment was deficient. Given the continuing threat from without, the most logical answer to this problem was to eliminate the weak links from the party. Hence the fear of infection, fuelled by dissatisfaction with the performance of some sub-national party leaders, fed into the continuing search for enemies in the party, the enemies with party cards in their pockets. The uncertainty and dissatisfaction which brought this about was strengthened by the performance of these sub-national leaders in the Verification and Exchange, and was given an enormous stimulus by the assassination of Kirov. It was this sort of atmosphere which both made possible and was itself stimulated by the Terror of the latter half of the 1930s.

There was, then, the accumulation over time of a sense of the unreliability of elements within the party, of the presence within party ranks of people whose loyalty to the cause was suspect and who were, in reality, carriers of the infection of petty bourgeois values. This perception, which was an important factor in sustaining the personalised structure of power and authority (see below), was a potent stimulus to the continuing process of tightening discipline and eliminating opposition. Confronted with apparent internal enemies, centralisation, control and discipline were seen as appropriate principles of internal party life.

But the shift of the party mood away from the fluidity and comparative openness of the early years of Bolshevik rule in a more monolithic, disciplinarian direction was not due solely to the perceived dangers of infection. Another important motor force propelling party sentiment in this direction was that it was consistent with where the various sections of the party believed their interests to lie. In this regard, the party must be divided into three sections: the rank-and-file party members who held no formal party office, the sub-national party leaders and the political elite. These will be looked at in turn.

In surveying the part played by the rank-and-file, it is important to remember that for most of this period, the vast majority of party members were new to the party. Despite the way in which party purges generally fell more heavily on the more recent entrants to the party, in numerical terms the core of Old Bolsheviks was outnumbered by those whose affiliation was more recent. Moreover, those affiliations also were more suspect. Those who had joined once the party was in power were always in danger of having their loyalty questioned by suspicions of careerism. This charge, doubtless true for many, was reinforced by the way in which it appeared regularly among the categories of groups that were to be expelled during party purges. Furthermore, despite the enormous efforts put into political education and propaganda, such members were, for the most part, little schooled in the intricacies of ideology. Their knowledge of Marxism, after 1924 Marxism-Leninism, was schematic and sketchy, and yet they could see how important ideology seemed to be in party discourse. In addition, the educational level of many of these new entrants, particularly in the 1920s, was not very high.

The likely effect of this combination of factors is that many rank-

and-file members would have supported the trends toward monolithism and discipline, particularly given the form which these took. Their concerns about being tarred with the brush of careerism and their unease in ideological discourse would have encouraged them to adopt a role in which they were not personally prominent, in which they did not have to play a very active part in party affairs except in the conduct of party policy. If called upon openly to debate and discuss party policy, many such members must have felt inadequate given the ideological form that such discussion took. If this sort of reaction was common, the desire to keep their heads down and not become prominent, it would have been rational to support the drift toward dictatorship, the ending of discussion and the elimination of the opposition rather than the pressures for greater democratisation. They hoped to demonstrate their commitment through obedience. In this sense, the continuing influx of new, poorly educated recruits constituted an on-going strengthening of that sentiment in favour of authoritarian rule.[2]

Furthermore, the majority of such people entered the party at a time when the prevailing sentiment was basically anti-oppositionist, when the notion of a rightful place in party councils for dissident views was in the process of being rejected or had already been rejected. Their acceptance of this view was as natural as their adherence to any of the other rules and conventions which governed party life. This was particularly the case given that none of these people would have had any close association with the democratic strand of the Bolshevik tradition; their experience of Bolshevism and the party was that of an increasingly authoritarian structure. Moreover, the drift in the party towards monocracy involved the elimination of those who were most associated with the democratic strand and who were therefore most removed from the recent entrants. To the extent that this involved the simplification of ideology and a decline in its profile in general party life, it would have been welcomed by these ideologically untutored party members.

The support of the rank-and-file for the Stalin-focused leadership, which was itself a major force propelling the party in a monocratic direction, was also a result of the symbolism which that leadership was able to manipulate. One important element here was the leader cult of Stalin. Not only was this important for consolidating the personalised model of leadership (see below), but it was also a significant factor in embedding authority in the figure of Stalin. By linking Stalin with the supreme symbols of authority – Lenin and the revolution – and by associating this personalised leadership figure with a catechised and dogmatic ideology, the leader cult appealed to many of these new party entrants. It gave them a personalised symbol of authority to which they could direct their allegiance, thereby hopefully forestalling questions about their party commitment, and it gave them a form of ideology which they could understand.

Important too was the symbolism of building socialism. This was at its most potent during the 1930s and perhaps also at the time of War Communism. Here was the sense of excitement and enthusiasm at building a new world, the feeling of participation in a grandiose enterprise which none had done before but which was to be successfully completed in Russia. It was the association of this enterprise with the Stalin leadership that was important. Stimulated by the cult, it took little imagination to associate the march toward socialism with the Stalin leadership. It was this leadership which had pushed aside the doubters in the party like Trotsky, Zinoviev, Kamenev and Bukharin and had proceeded to the construction of socialism. To the extent that it was the achievement of socialism which provided the rationale for everything else, for the rank-and-file membership the linkage between this and the Stalin leadership was vital; it was this leadership which promised success and therefore it was this leadership which was deserving of support. In a more material sense, the opportunities for personal promotion and social mobility that flowed from the policies associated with the Stalin leadership provided an extra stimulus to the support for Stalin.

While some of these considerations doubtless played a part in the support by sub-national party leaders for the general course of development toward monocracy, important too were certain aspects of the structural position which these people occupied. The form monocracy took – a personalised power structure – was related to the structure of power at the sub-national levels.

Central to the disposition of power at the sub-national levels was the primacy of personalised power and authority over that vested in formal, party institutions. In practical terms, this meant that power was wielded by the individual political leaders and their coteries rather than by the formal institutional structures established at each level of the hierarchy. Emerging as a result of the pressures imposed by the Civil War and the policy of War Communism and of the fundamental weakness of the political mechanism which was developing at this time, the personalisation of power and authority became solidly entrenched in the lore of the party at the sub-national levels.

Despite the attempts to regularise the party structure and to improve linkages with the centre, the personalised basis of power remained largely untouched. Individual leaders favoured this type of arrangement because of the flexibility it involved, the administrative advantages of working through personalised networks compared with the ramshackle formal political machine, and the opportunities it provided for local leaders to protect themselves against attack. The removal of individual sub-national leaders could not eliminate the personalistic basis of power at these levels because it did not remove the conditions that gave rise to that type of power structure; a new incumbent, often sent from Moscow, sought to get rid of his predecessor's supporters and was therefore almost certain to replace them with his own cronies. There was, then, a very strong imperative working towards the maintenance of this type of power structure; the continuing demands and pressures on the positions of sub-national leadership encouraged the continual resort to family group means of structuring sub-national power. As a result this became institutionalised in the party's middle and lower rungs and was accepted by all as the most appropriate means of structuring political power at these levels. This had important implications for institutional development and for the growth of support for the Stalin circle, both of which are discussed below.

But if the structuring of power along personalised lines was a response to uncertainty and potential threat, it was ultimately an inadequate response. From early 1926 it was clear that the centre could, through the exercise of pressure and its control over personnel, break up individual fiefs at the sub-national levels even if it could not eliminate the conditions that led to the fiefs in the first place. Indeed, in one sense the personalisation of power may have made these leaders even more exposed. The party Rules and much of the official lore inside the party emphasised the collective principle and confirmed that decision-making was the prerogative, and indeed the duty, of the collective party organs. To the extent that the operation of party life at sub-national levels was clearly not in conformity with such notions, the leaders at these levels were placed in the position of formally breaching party norms. Consequently if the centre wished to move against them, the formal grounds for doing so existed.

The continuing uncertainty of their positions encouraged sub-national leaders to seek to establish links with prominent figures at the national level in the hope that the latter could provide them with a degree of protection. Here lies the sub-national source of the formation of fractions in the party, or in the terminology which has become current, of patron–client chains. But when these sub-national leaders looked to the centre, they did not do so in a political vacuum. They did not cast about looking for one of the political notables who might be able to provide them with what they wanted. Many of them were already linked to individuals at the top through past shared career experience, personal acquaintance or the fact that their promotion was owed to the support of a figure at higher levels. The longer the time passed, the greater the probability that such links were either with Stalin directly or with one of his supporters. This was because of Stalin's grip over the appointment process. Furthermore, when the sub-national leaders were coming under opposition criticism for their undemocratic means of operation during the 1920s, Stalin was the natural focus of their loyalty and support not only because he fought these opposition groups but because he was in charge of that section of the party machine most at fault in the opposition's eyes.

But the relationship that existed between the sub-national political leaders and the General Secretary was not one in which the former were the mere pawns or instruments of the latter. While sub-national leaders may, ultimately, have depended upon Stalin for the continued retention of their positions, Stalin needed the continued support of those leaders for the consolidation of his own position and the successful implementation of the policy lines with which he was associated. There was, therefore, a form of bargain from which both sides expected to gain. However, with the defeat of the United Opposition, this bargain seems to have come under significant strain. Stalin's support for the self-criticism campaign of 1928 reflects his move, perhaps somewhat tentative, on to the offensive against the sub-national leaders. The apparent support of some of the latter for the Right Opposition, including their agricultural policies, was part of this strain. The purge of 1929–30 and Stalin's condemnation of sub-national leaders' performance during the collectivisation campaign reflects his continuing dissatisfaction with the state of his party support base. But even in the face of such signs of central displeasure, sub-national leaders were restrained from responding by the situation in which they found themselves. The difficulties of the collectivisation campaign and the conviction that they had to close ranks if they were to survive effectively locked the sub-national leaders into a position of support for Stalin despite the reservations that many of them had about the course of policy. Such reservations came to the fore in the uneasiness at the time of the XVII Congress, a development which was greeted by a beefing up of the campaign against hidden enemies. It is at this time that the push against the sub-national leaders really gathered momentum, culminating in the elimination of them in 1937. Thus throughout much of this period the relationship between sub-national leaders and General Secretary was ambiguous, with neither completely trusting the other but also neither being able to implement measures which would remove the reasons for that distrust.

The reasons for the sub-national leaders' wariness of Stalin are easily seen. The attacks that were launched upon them from above, many of which could be associated with the General Secretary, were sufficient reason for concern on their part. But where the sub-national leaders differed from those adherents of Stalin in the central party apparatus is that the former had a personal and immediate interest in policy implementation. If central policies were decreed which they believed to be wrong-headed or counter-productive, it was these leaders who were going to have to carry them out throughout the country. Consequently their adherence to the General Secretary was always tinged with a concern for policy which was less in evidence among many of his central supporters.

The position and attitudes of the sub-national leaders facilitated the move to monocracy. The structural position of this group made it much more amenable to a personalised notion of power at the top than to one based on formal institutions and rules. They therefore provided a sound basis for patrimonialism in the party. Furthermore, the dictatorial control which they sought to exercise within their own domains provided a perfect incentive for them to support the drift towards disciplinarianism and the rejection of combative politics within the party. Despite the reservations that may have developed among them about the person of the General Secretary, they had few qualms about the general direction of development in which the system was moving. At least prior to 1937, this sort of development seemed best to serve their interests.

For the members of the elite, the drift towards monocratism and centralism seemed consonant with their interests, at least until the Terror of 1936–38 decimated their ranks. Of course many of these were the same individuals discussed above as sub-national leaders; their formal positions in the sub-national party apparatus were for many of them instrumental in their simultaneous membership of the political elite. For these people, the sorts of considerations discussed above continued to apply. Particularly important was the desire to preserve their own power positions at home, and any move towards greater accountability of the national leadership to the rank-and-file would have had direct implications for their sub-national personal bailiwicks. Moreover, these people could be confident that while the continuing centralisation of power may have strengthened their positions as central politicians, the difficulties the centre had in exerting effective control over the sub-national units would guarantee that this would not be translated into the continuing projection of intrusive central power into their lower level bailiwicks. For those sub-national leaders who were also members of the national elite, the centralisation of power may thus have strengthened their local positions because this centralisation was at the expense of notions of rank-and-file control.

But of course the sub-national leaders were not the only constituent element comprising the national elite. Important too were the full-time officials to be found in leading positions in the central apparatus of state and, in particular, party. These people, like all functionaries in national political structures, believed that their capacity to discern the national interest and to overcome the limitations imposed by a more restricted regional focus entitled them to exercise wide discretion in the pursuit of policy. Notions of accountability were clearly considered to be subordinate to the generation and implementation of correct policy. As a result, the move towards monocracy and discipline, and the associated expansion of their own power and consolidation of their position, were developments which they were likely to support.

Particularly important among these central functionaries were those who worked in the party apparatus. With the transfer of the principal arena of politics into the major party bodies, the importance of those who served in those bodies naturally increased. Those organs responsible for the secretarial work for the CC and Politburo and for implementing the decisions of these bodies increased in importance along with the higher profile of the CC and Politburo. Moreover, the importance of the apparatus was maintained after these two bodies began to wane in significance as real decision-making centres with the personalisation of power in the figure of Stalin (see below) because of the link between them and the General Secretary. As the formal head of the Secretariat, and therefore of the party's central apparatus, Stalin's personal power was linked with these executive organs. As he sought to rule and to extend his power through the organisational arms of the party, the importance of these bodies for continued party functioning remained high. Consequently, the party functionaries had their own vested interests in supporting the drift toward centralisation; it meant greater power and importance for the institutions in which they worked.

These functionaries were also in a different position in terms of their relationship with the General Secretary than were the sub-national leaders. While it would be simplistic to argue that these people had no policy views of their own, as Trotsky has argued, they seemed to place a higher priority on matters of organisational functioning and administration than upon policy discussion and debate.[3] Therefore while it is possible that, during policy discussions, their views did not completely correspond with those of Stalin, it is likely that this consideration was outweighed by the coincidence of interests in deflecting criticism against the increased bureaucratisation of the system. The contrast between the party's legislative and administrative organs is relevant here. While the former, principally the congress, CC and Politburo, were unable to develop a strong sense of organisational coherence or integrity, the full-time party apparatus did develop a real sense of institutional identity which bound together those who worked in it. Both their everyday tasks and their professional futures were bound up totally with the institutions in which they worked, and this gave them a common interest and perspective. Furthermore, unlike the sub-national leaders who could hope that distance from Moscow might provide some shield for them if they diverged significantly from Stalin's will, geographical propinquity offered no such protection for those in the central apparatus. Working under Stalin's nose and at the immediate direction of his closest supporters, any dissidence was likely to be met with dismissal or, in the late 1930s, even loss of their lives.

There was, therefore, a real coincidence of interest between Stalin and the members of the central apparatus. Because Stalin relied heavily upon this apparatus, he was intent upon protecting it from the attacks made upon it by those outside the apparatus, principally the major opposition groups. As a result Stalin was easily cast in the guise of protector, a role which therefore applied both to the institutions generally and, through his power over appointment, to their members individually. This sort of relationship welded Stalin and those in the apparatus together into a very strong partnership.

Another section of the elite also deserves attention, the notables. These were the people whose prominence rested upon their personal reputations and past service to the party and cause rather than their occupation of positions of major importance. This group, at the very apex of the political structure, do not seem to have been seriously opposed to the process of the centralisation of power that was underway throughout most of this period. Such a process seemed to involve an expansion of their own powers and roles and it ensured that those who these people believed to be best equipped to rule actually did rule. Only when individual notables lost out in the power games at the top did they come out in open criticism of this trend of development in the party; otherwise the centralisation of power remained relatively uncontroversial at this level. However, what was not greeted with such equanimity was the way in which power was coming to be structured at the party's apex.

The personal dominance Stalin was able to achieve was neither predetermined nor inevitable. It was brought about by the Terror of 1936–38 and prior to that, although Stalin may have been the most prominent individual in the party leadership, his dominance was not an inevitable development. Indeed, a substantial portion of the notables, and the elite more generally, were violently opposed to any expansion of Stalin's power. However, those who were thus opposed were eliminated during the elite conflict.

But it would be wrong to assume that those who supported Stalin during the successive bouts of elite conflict were committed from the beginning to a structure of power which had Stalin in a dominant position. Their support for Stalin stemmed from a variety of sources, including most importantly agreement with his policy positions and the personal link formed through Stalin's part in their promotion. During the 1920s these people were individuals of some note in the party independent of their positions in the Politburo. The core of Stalin's support in that body were all Old Bolsheviks and all held bureaucratic positions of some significance. They were not mere creatures of Stalin, but possessed standing in their own right. Promotion into the Politburo did not mean that these people were locked into positions of support for Stalin; as the experience of such people as Rudzutak, Kuibyshev, Petrovsky and even Voroshilov and Kalinin showed, these people retained a degree of freedom with the choice of supporting Stalin or opposing him on successive issues which arose. Support for him on a series of issues throughout the 1920s did not necessarily mean support across the board on all questions at all times. Having worked their way up the political ladder, it is unlikely that they would have envisaged the development of a system in which they were subordinate players, forever acting in the shadow of the all-powerful leader.

It is not clear that even by the mid-1930s this group was committed to the emergence of a leader-dominated system. The atmosphere of the mid- to late 1930s caused a real crystallisation of political positions; the inability of everyone except Stalin to stop the Terror forced people openly to commit themselves even more to the leader than they had in the past. Even if this Stalinist core had agreed from the outset with the Terror, and there is no evidence either to support or refute this, it does not mean that they realised that the Terror would be as extensive as it was or would lead to Stalin's personal dominance. When it became clear that that was the likely outcome, it would have been too late to do anything about it. So while the Stalinist notables may have supported their leader during the 1920s and first half of the 1930s because of patronage and policy considerations, in the latter half of the 1930s such factors would have been reinforced by concern about personal survival. Moreover, while such support for Stalin meant support for the processes of centralisation, tightened discipline and personalised leadership, they did not necessarily mean support for the sort of personalised dictatorship which emerged at the end of the 1930s.

Crucial in any explanation of the development of such a system is the person of Stalin himself. Western studies of this period of Soviet history have tended to concentrate upon Stalin, emphasising the way in which his personal characteristics and idiosyncrasies shaped the form the system took. It is instructive that most studies of the 1930s have been in the form of biographies of Stalin. It is clear that the personal characteristics, state of mind and qualities of an individual leader like Stalin can be crucial in helping to shape the development of a political system. But the individual does not act in a vacuum. His actions and his impact can be understood and evaluated only if the context of forces within which he operated is understood. Consequently, Stalin must be seen as one important factor in the developments which culminated in the personal dictatorship which is the essence of Stalinism.

One common line of argument has been that from the outset Stalin pursued supreme power, cynically adopting policy positions purely to outflank and defeat his opponents in intra-party combat. But explanations of Stalin's role do not need to rest upon unprovable assumptions about over-weening ambition. All that is necessary is to assume that, like many of the other notables, Stalin was ambitious to achieve the power that went with the top job in the Soviet political system. This does not make him, in principle, any different from many of his colleagues in the political hierarchy or from many of his counterparts in other political systems. Moreover, policy flexibility was a necessary quality for all politicians during this period. Changing economic and social conditions meant that individuals had frequently to review their policy positions in order to ensure that they remained relevant to contemporary needs and demands. Even the firmest proponents of NEP in the party shifted their positions on this during the 1920s. So all politicians showed a degree of flexibility.

But of course many would argue that Stalin was set aside from his colleagues in this respect by the timing of his policy changes. It is charged that he picked up the policy positions of his opponents once they had been defeated and then used those new positions to turn on his erstwhile allies. There is some truth in this charge. But the context needs to be borne in mind when evaluating the meaning of this. While political expediency cannot be dismissed as a component of the way Stalin acted, the effects of factional conflict were also important. What this did was to freeze policy positions. Individuals were reluctant to shift to other positions even if those they currently occupied were no longer applicable because to do so would have meant appearing to be wrong and therefore losing ground in the competition with the opposition. Consequently leading individuals changed their policy tack following the defeat of their antagonists. Furthermore, policy changes at these times should not be unexpected since the times when Stalin's major about-turns occurred (early 1926 and 1928–29) were periods when economic developments in the countryside were conducive to policy reconsiderations in Moscow. It should not be surprising that factional conflict erupted at the times when policy choices needed to be made.

It would, however, be mistaken to assume from this that Stalin was not a principal force behind the course of factional conflict during the 1920s nor that there was no opportunistic quality to his participation in this conflict. Apart from matters of timing, which were determined principally by the main protagonists including Stalin, the General Secretary was personally very important in the shaping of a number of aspects of the factional conflict which had important implications for systemic development. The emergence of a personalised notion of leadership (see below) was intimately linked with the growth of the Lenin cult which Stalin and his supporters played a major part in sponsoring. The decline in the institutional integrity of party institutions and their transformation into weapons to be used against the

Why Stalinism? 323

opposition was partly due to the ability of the Stalinist machine to stack those bodies with people who supported Stalin. The development of Stalin's personal apparatus was also central to the undermining of the top institutions evident in the way in which Stalin introduced the extraordinary measures of grain collection in 1928. Finally, the language Stalin used to attack the opposition was instrumental in hardening party opinion against opposition and making the latter unacceptable in party ranks. In all of these ways, Stalin's direct actions during the 1920s were important in structuring the development of the Soviet system.

Stalin's actions were also important for this during the 1930s. His role in forcing the pace of collectivisation and of blaming sub-national leaders for excesses were important for the course of development during this decade. So too was his introduction of the extraordinary measures on the death of Kirov (and perhaps his part in that event), which robbed the party of its permeability, and his part in the Terror of 1936–38. Indeed, Stalin was directly responsible for the decimation of the party's leading organs because, at minimum, the arrest and killing of party leaders would have been impossible without his approval. In this sense, the final shift to personal dictatorship resulted directly from his actions.

However, this does not mean that Stalin was from the outset of Bolshevik rule seeking to establish a single-person dictatorship. Certainly he worked throughout to strengthen and consolidate his own position, and the direct effect of this was to stimulate the development towards monocracy and discipline that was the major trend of systemic development during this period. Of course it is impossible to discover when Stalin adopted the establishment of such a system as one of his primary goals; in the absence of first-hand evidence, motives must always be considered uncertain. But it is possible to argue that Stalin did not adopt this as an aim until some time in 1934 at the earliest, but more likely in 1936.

His role during the 1920s was little different from those of other Bolshevik notables, except that he was much more effective at political infighting and he possessed the organisational weapons which gave him a decided advantage. All believed in their own capacities to guide the revolution victoriously to socialism and, in varying degrees, were unwilling to accept opposition or dissent from their views. But having seemingly been victorious in 1929 by defeating his open opponents in the party, Stalin found himself confronted by further opposition of undetermined dimensions, generated principally by the pressures of the collectivisation campaign. Stalin's concern at this opposition must have been strengthened by events at the XVII Congress. It may be that at this time he became convinced that he could be personally secure only by eliminating all possible opposition. If he had not reached this conclusion by then, and if he was not involved in the preparation of the Kirov assassination, his concerns would have been even further strengthened by this event. Within this context, one conclusion that could be drawn from the failure of the Verification and Exchange to achieve satisfactory results, particularly the extirpation of opposition, was that working through the party machinery was not likely to enable Stalin to eliminate those who opposed him. The failure of the party machinery to handle this question of opposition may have convinced Stalin that he could be secure personally only if opposition was once and forever eliminated. This meant a system in which his personal dominance could not be questioned, a result achieved by the Terror.

This sort of explanation cannot be proved, but it is consistent with the facts as we know them. Its advantage is that it does not rely on the attribution to Stalin of qualities of far-sightedness, ambition and level of cunning which seem to be far in excess both of what we would expect in any political leader and of what contemporary observers have to say about Stalin. Rather it sees the course of politics as driven much less by an individual's plan and much more by a combination of planning, accident and *ad hoc* response and action. This explanation is also consistent with some of the claims that have been made about Stalin's personality; his supposed paranoia, inferiority complex, propensity to hold grudges as well as his cunning can all have a part in this explanation without being the major foci of that explanation – as is the case in those studies which focus upon Stalin as a person.

An important role that Stalin did play was in stimulating the personalistic model of leadership, although it is important to recognise that this had its roots in the interstices of the political structure as a whole. At sub-national levels the structure of power was personalistic from the outset of Bolshevik rule. The weak organisational framework combined with the enormous pressures upon sub-national leaders encouraged the development of the personalistic style of rule outlined in earlier chapters. The institutionalisation of such a style of rule, initially in part a reaction to the weakness of bureaucratic procedures, in turn was a significant element undermining the growth in strength and importance of those bureaucratic procedures. The informal, personalised networks which predominated at the sub-national levels meant that formal party organs were unable to develop a strong sense of integrity and coherence; instead of being governed by their own rules and norms, these organs operated at the whim of individual political leaders. Throughout this period, political institutions were the instruments of powerful figures.

The type of power structure which existed was patrimonial. According to one student of this phenomenon, patrimonialism exists when the 'power and identity of an institution [is] defined in terms of the leader's political identity and power'.[4] With party organs dependent upon individual party leaders to breathe life into them, possessing by themselves little organisational integrity and coherence, they were instruments that could be wielded by those local leaders. Their actions and identity were determined by their leaders and the political roles those leaders sought to play. The important point is that this sort of arrangement was considered legitimate in the party at the sub-national level.

The patrimonial principle was also firmly embedded at the national level. Stemming from the historical position Lenin had occupied and sustained by the growth of the leader myth and the focus upon personalities in the discussion of issues, patrimonialism emerged as the normal, acceptable way of structuring political activity at the apex of party life. In the face of the strength of this principle, notions of collectivism were reduced to the status of formal rules which as time went on had little more than symbolic and hortatory importance.

Patrimonialism at both the national and sub-national levels combined to produce a single patrimonial structure. The entire Stalinist political system was patrimonial in nature. In an important sense, Stalin came almost to own the political structure. Through the power of appointment and his ability to remove sub-national leaders, Stalin effectively granted them a secular benefice, a share of the institution he headed. In return, they acknowledged his authority and deferred to him, but within their own backyards they were in a similar situation to Stalin: they could bestow favours on others.[5] In this sort of structure, party bodies were always subject to the personal power of political luminaries.

The dominance of patrimonialism at all levels of the party was important for the emergence of the personalised dictatorship of Stalin in two ways. The first is that it constituted a legitimation of personalised power and of personal leadership. Indeed, this was the essence of patrimonialism; as well as overriding the principles of collectivism, it justified the style of leadership which Stalin was able to attain.

Secondly, the focus upon individual leadership figures effectively retarded the development of the institutional structure of the party and the political system more widely. With the formal party structure subordinate to the patrimonial leaders and their own personal political machines, it was unable to impose any meaningful restraints upon those political leaders. The stronger the patrimonial principle became over this period, the less able were the formal institutional structures to restrict the activities of individual political leaders. Consequently the barriers to personal dictatorship, seemingly so powerful in terms of the party's formal organisational structure and ethos, were actually quite weak because of the patrimonial principle. Organisations were seen instrumentally rather than as having significant normative political authority.

Another important element in the instrumental nature of political institutions at the apex of the political structure was the course of factional conflict within the elite at this time. While disputes were inevitable given the personalities and ambitions of the political leaders and the policy matters that arose for consideration, what ensured that they had a significant systemic impact was the context within which they occurred. Prevented from developing as strong, coherent institutions with a high level of integrity by the methods of elite interaction and policy-making under Lenin, the leading organs of the system were not powerful enough to impose substantial constraints upon the course of elite conflict when it broke into the open. Furthermore, given that the rules of conflict changed over the course of the 1920s, thereby injecting a further element of uncertainty into the structuring of factional conflict, the incentive for elite actors to abide by established institutional rules, norms and conventions was reduced. Under these conditions of elite conflict within a weak institutional arena and changing rules of combat, political actors were encouraged both to see and to use the leading institutions in an instrumental fashion.

The drift toward personalised dictatorship was therefore conditioned by a wide range of factors. However, it was not inevitable. There was no inner essence of Bolshevism which propelled it to a dictatorial climax. Nor was there a carefully laid plan which culminated after many years of struggle in the emergence of the Stalinist dictatorship. The Stalinist political system was not something created by the elite in a vacuum. It was not a system imposed from the top by a dominant individual or clique upon a reluctant political system. It was a structure of rule and of values which arose from within the system itself. Certainly the person of Stalin was central at many points

Why Stalinism?

and his drive and ambition were important in the working out of the contours of the new system. So too were the interests and perceptions of the major groups of actors within the political system, and it is the pursuit of those interests which explains the decisions adopted and directions taken at those key points of re-evaluation: 1922–24, 1928–29, 1933–34 and 1937. Those interests and their satisfaction were rooted in the political structure itself. Fundamentally, therefore, the main impetus for the Stalinist political system came from within the institutional structure itself, from the subordination of those pressures for organisational institutionalisation to the demands of a patrimonial model of power.

Notes

Introduction

1 For example, see the discussion in *The Russian Review*, 45, 4 (1986), pp. 357–413; *ibid.*, 46, 4 (1987), pp. 375–431.
2 For example, see Moshe Lewin, *Russian peasants and Soviet power: a study of collectivization* (London: Allen and Unwin, 1968) and Roger Pethybridge, *The social prelude to Stalinism* (London: Macmillan, 1974).
3 In particular see Moshe Lewin, 'The social background of Stalinism', Robert C. Tucker, ed., *Stalinism. Essays in historical interpretation* (New York: W. W. Norton, 1977), pp. 111–36, Sheila Fitzpatrick, ed., *Cultural revolution in Russia 1928–1931* (Bloomington: Indiana University Press, 1978), and Sheila Fitzpatrick, *Education and social mobility in the Soviet Union, 1921–1934* (Cambridge University Press, 1979).
4 Among these are J. Arch Getty, Roberta T. Manning, Gábor Rittersporn and Lewis Siegelbaum. Strictly speaking, not all of these scholars are social historians; for example, the work of Getty and Rittersporn is more political than social history. Nevertheless all adopt the approach 'from below' of social history, and will be referred to generically as social historians.
5 Sheila Fitzpatrick, 'New perspectives on Stalinism', *The Russian Review*, 45, 4 (1986), p. 358.
6 Respectively, Stephen F. Cohen, 'Stalin's Terror as social history', *The Russian Review*, 45, 4 (1986), p. 378 and Peter Kenez, 'Stalinism as humdrum politics', *ibid.*, p. 395. Also see in the same collection Geoff Eley, 'History with the politics left out – again?' The debate has been continued in *The Russian Review*, 46, 4 (1987), pp. 375–431.
7 The work of Moshe Lewin shows how the pursuit of social history is consistent with acknowledgement of the importance of these other factors.
8 Stephen F. Cohen, 'Bolshevism and Stalinism', Tucker, *Stalinism*, p. 7.
9 The middle course is where policies are designed to appeal to or react to particular social constituencies. See the discussion in Fitzpatrick, 'New perspectives', pp. 368–72.
10 Cohen, 'Bolshevism' pp. 12–13.
11 Robert C. Tucker, 'Stalinism as revolution from above', Tucker, *Stalinism*, p. 77.

12 Isaac Deutscher, *Ironies of history. Essays on contemporary communism* (Oxford University Press, 1966), p. 185.
13 This is a somewhat unsatisfactory term for the violence of 1936–38. The term is used purely because of its general acceptance and implies no position in the argument about the extent of repression and suffering that occurred at this time.
14 This is reflected in the study by Seweryn Bialer where, in his discussion of the characteristics of 'the mature Stalinist system', he discusses six of these characteristics in one chapter while devoting one whole chapter to what he terms 'the system of personal dictatorship'. Seweryn Bialer, *Stalin's successors. Leadership, stability and change in the Soviet Union* (Cambridge University Press, 1980), chs. 1 and 2.
15 There was only one party congress between 1939 and Stalin's death and the CC met in plenary session on only six occasions between 1938 and March 1953. However, the Politburo, Orgburo and Secretariat met regularly. Bialer, *Stalin's successors*, pp. 32–3.
16 Indeed, some would argue that this was a central characteristic of the whole period of Soviet rule. The most prominent of these is Alexander Solzhenitsyn. See in particular *The Gulag Archipelago 1918–1956* (London: Collins/Fontana, 1974–78).
17 Georg Lukács, 'Reflections on the cult of Stalin', *Survey*, 47 (April 1963), p. 105.
18 This is the nucleus of the view of Stalinism as a mass mobilising developmental dictatorship under single party auspices. A. James Gregor, 'Fascism and modernization: some addenda', *World Politics*, 26, 3 (April 1974), p. 383.
19 See the studies by Katerina Clark, 'Utopian anthropology as a context for Stalinist literature', Tucker, *Stalinism*, pp. 180–98 and V. J. Dunham, *In Stalin's time: middle class values in Soviet fiction* (Cambridge University Press, 1979).
20 See Lewis H. Siegelbaum, *Stakhanovism and the politics of productivity in the USSR, 1935–1941* (Cambridge University Press, 1988).
21 A good instance of this is the recently translated study by Michal Reiman. He makes a strong case for the economic crisis of 1927–28 as the midwife of Stalinism. He sees this crisis as resulting from the isolation of the Russian economy and the reorganisation of the structure of agrarian relations which threw out of balance the relationship between industrial and agricultural production. Both of these are seen as the result of the October Revolution. The resulting crisis provided the opportunity for Stalin to force through a total re-organisation of the existing structure of the economy and of social relations, leading to the emergence of an all-embracing system of state control over society. As an explanation of the revolution from above and the economic face of Stalinism, this explanation has considerable merit, but as an explanation of full Stalinism it is less satisfactory. For Reiman, the essence of Stalinism was 'social terror', the subjugation of the population to 'exploitation and oppression of an absolutely exceptional magnitude and intensity' (Reiman, *The birth of Stalinism*.

The USSR on the eve of the 'Second Revolution' (Bloomington: Indiana University Press, 1987), p. 118). But as indicated above, this is inadequate as a description of Stalinism, even in its political face. Furthermore, it is not legitimate to argue that full Stalinism flowed automatically from the revolution from above. The introduction of the economic face of Stalinism did not determine the emergence of its political face.

22 Leszek Kolakowski, 'Marxist roots of Stalinism', Tucker, *Stalinism*, pp. 283–98. For a counter argument, see the paper in the same volume by Mihailo Markovic, 'Stalinism and Marxism', pp. 299–319. For the argument that the intellectual sources of Stalinism lie in the subordination of all considerations to the achievement of an overriding goal, a tendency associated with revolutionary maximalism within the Russian intellectual tradition, see A. Tsypko, 'Istoki stalinizma', *Nauka i zhizn'*, 11 (1988), pp. 45–55; 12 (1988), pp. 40–8; 1 (1989), pp. 46–57; and 2 (1989), pp. 53–61.

23 For a survey of those who have adopted this position, and a trenchant criticism of it, see Cohen, 'Bolshevism', pp. 3–29.

24 For example, see the discussions in Baruch Knei-Paz, *The social and political thought of Leon Trotsky* (Oxford: Clarendon Press, 1978); Robert H. McNeal, 'Trotskyist interpretations of Stalinism', Tucker, *Stalinism*, pp. 30–9; Martin Krygier, '"Bureaucracy" in Trotsky's analysis of Stalinism', Marian Sawer, ed., *Socialism and the new class: towards the analysis of structural inequality within socialist societies*, APSA Monograph No. 19 (Bedford Park, 1978), pp. 46–67; Trotsky's most famous piece where this is discussed is *The Revolution betrayed* (New York: Pathfinder Press, 1970). Also see *Stalin. An appraisal of the man and his influence* (London: MacGibbon and Kee, 1968).

25 For example, see Charles Bettelheim, *Class struggles in the USSR. First period: 1917–1923* (Brighton: Harvester Press, 1977) and *Class struggles in the USSR. Second period: 1923–1930* (Brighton: Harvester Press, 1978); and Isaac Deutscher, *Stalin. A political biography* (Harmondsworth: Penguin, 1966). Among others are Lucio Colletti, 'The question of Stalin', Robin Blackburn, ed., *Revolution and class struggle. A reader in Marxist politics* (Glasgow: Fontana/Collins, 1977) and Jean Elleinstein, *The Stalin phenomenon* (London: Lawrence and Wishart, 1976). This set of factors also provides the basis for an analysis which shares some similarities with Trotsky but is different in its mode of argument. Pavel Campeanu, *The origins of Stalinism. From leninist revolution to stalinist society* (Armonk: M. E. Sharpe, 1986) and *The genesis of the Stalinist social order* (Armonk: M. E. Sharpe, 1988) emphasise the antinomic nature of the Russian revolution, which he sees as linked to Russian backwardness. For an important argument which emphasises the legacy of Russia's historical experience of bureaucratic control over production, a control which robs the individual of personality and physical and spiritual force, see Vasilii Seliunin, 'Istoki', *Novyi Mir*, 5 (1988), pp. 162–89. According to Seliunin, this legacy is mediated through certain aspects of Lenin's policies and actions. Stalinism, seen in terms of bureaucratic control and directive planning, is thus rooted in both Leninism and Russian history more broadly.

26 For example, see Pethybridge, *Social prelude to Stalinism*.
27 Tucker, 'Stalinism as revolution from above', esp. pp. 94–108. Also see Seliunin, 'Istoki'.
28 For example, see Moshe Lewin, 'The social background of Stalinism', Tucker, *Stalinism*, pp. 111–36 and 'Grappling with Stalinism', Moshe Lewin, *The making of the Soviet system* (New York: Pantheon Books, 1985), pp. 286–314.
29 Also see Roy Medvedev, *K sudu istorii. Genezis i posledstviia Stalinizma* (New York: Alfred A. Knopf, 1974).

1 The structure of sub-national politics

1 See the study of his thought by Neil Harding, *Lenin's political thought*, vol. 1, *Theory and practice in the democratic revolution* (London: Macmillan, 1977).
2 For a more extended discussion of this question, see Graeme Gill, 'Institutionalisation and Revolution: Rules and the Soviet political system', *Soviet Studies*, 37, 2 (April 1985), pp. 212–26.
3 This is usually discussed in terms of charisma. For example, see Ann Ruth Willner, *The spellbinders. Charismatic political leadership* (New Haven: Yale University Press, 1984).
4 Formally a one-party state existed prior to the establishment of the coalition in mid-November 1917. For discussions of the coalition question, see Leonard Schapiro, *The origin of the communist autocracy. Political opposition in the Soviet state: First phase 1917–1922* (New York: Praeger, 1965), ch. 5; Robert Vincent Daniels, *The conscience of the Revolution. Communist opposition in Soviet Russia* (New York: Simon and Schuster, 1969), pp. 63–8. Contemporary views will be found in John L. H. Keep, *The debate on Soviet power. Minutes of the All-Russian Central Executive Committee of Soviets Second Convocation October 1917 – January 1918* (Oxford: Clarendon Press, 1979); and James Bunyan and H. H. Fisher, eds., *The Bolshevik Revolution 1917–1918. Documents and materials* (Stanford University Press, 1934).
5 On the Kadets, see William G. Rosenberg, *Liberals in the Russian Revolution. The Constitutional Democratic Party, 1917–1921* (Princeton University Press, 1974), Parts 3 and 4. On the Socialist Revolutionaries, see Schapiro, *Origin*, chs. 7 and 9 and Oliver Henry Radkey, *The sickle under the hammer. The Russian socialist revolutionaries in the early months of Soviet rule* (New York: Columbia University Press 1963). On the Mensheviks, see Schapiro, *Origin*, ch. 11, Leopold Haimson, ed., *The Mensheviks from the Revolution of 1917 to the Second World War* (University of Chicago Press, 1974), Parts I and II, and Israel Getzler, *Martov. A political biography of a Russian Social Democrat* (Cambridge University Press, 1967) ch. 8.
6 There was still concern about the influence such parties could wield in 1922. See the resolution of the XII Conference in August 1922. *Kommunisticheskaia partiia sovetskogo soiuza v rezoliutsiiakh i resheniiakh s'ezdov, konferentsii i plenumov Ts.K.* (Moscow, 1983), vol. 2, pp. 587–93 (hereafter *KPSS v rez*).

7 For an account of its dispersal, see John L. H. Keep, *The Russian Revolution. A study in mass mobilization* (London: Weidenfeld and Nicolson, 1976) pp. 326–33.
8 The best full-length study of the soviets remains Oskar Anweiler, *The soviets: the Russian Workers', Peasants' and Soldiers' Councils, 1905–1921* (New York: Pantheon Books, 1974). Also see Keep, *Russian Revolution*.
9 The closure of the independent press and the imposition of censorship was also important here. The debate on this will be found in Keep, *Debate*. Particularly enlightening is Bukharin's comment: 'We shall close all the papers and won't be put off by cries about freedom of the press.' Keep, *Debate*, p. 98.
10 T. H Rigby, *Communist Party membership in the USSR 1917–1967* (Princeton University Press, 1968), p. 52.
11 See *Deviatyi s'ezd RKP(b) Mart-aprel' 1920 goda. Protokoly* (Moscow, 1960), pp. 66–7; *Desiatyi s'ezd RKP(b) Mart 1921 goda. Stenograficheskii otchet* (Moscow, 1963), pp. 151–78; and *Odinnadtsatyi s'ezd RKP(b) Mart – aprel' 1922 goda. Stenograficheskii otchet* (Moscow, 1961), pp. 403–5, 442–3.
12 See the comments in Rigby, *Membership*, pp. 83–7, where he shows how between 1917 and 1921 the working-class component of the party declined and the peasant component increased. It was claimed at the VII Congress that there was virtually no check on the political affiliation of new members of local organs. *Sed'moi ekstrennyi s'ezd RKP(b) mart 1918 goda. Stenograficheskii otchet* (Moscow, 1962), p. 239. For some complaints about the quality and behaviour of party members, see *Vos'moi s'ezd RKP(b) Mart 1919 goda. Protokoly* (Moscow, 1959), pp. 166–9, 205; *Vos'maia*, pp. 157–68; *Deviatyi*, pp. 66–7. For Lenin's December 1919 call to get rid of unsatisfactory elements in the party, see *Vos'maia konferentsiia RKP(b) Dekabr' 1919 goda. Protokoly* (Moscow, 1961), pp. 23–5. At the same gathering, it was claimed that many guberniia party committees consisted only of peasants. *Vos'maia*, p. 151. For complaints about the small working class representation in the party, see *Desiatyi*, pp. 74–5, 81–2, 237, 279, 284, 290–1 and *Odinnadtsatyi*, pp. 75, 128, 196–201, 285–6, 392, 408, 445, 463, 545, 647.
13 For a discussion of these early purges, see Rigby, *Membership*, pp. 70 (1918), 76–7 (1919), 84 (1920), 96–100 (1921). The distrust of newcomers is reflected in the results of the purge of 1921. Of those expelled, the years in which they joined the party were as follows: prior to 1917 – 824; Jan–Oct 1917 – 4,360; 1918 – 13,902; 1919 – 27,499; 1920 and 1921 – 80,850. *Odinnadtsatyi*, pp. 376–377.
14 Aryeh L. Unger, *Constitutional development in the USSR. A guide to the Soviet Constitutions* (London: Methuen, 1981) provides details of the Constitution.
15 *Desiatyi*, pp. 236–41, 284, 564 and *Odinnadtsatyi*, pp. 545–59. See the discussion in Rigby, *Membership*, pp. 93–5.
16 *KPSS v rez*, vol. 2, pp. 202, 574, 575.
17 For concern about political illiteracy among new party members and for suggestions about combating it, see the IX Conference resolution (September 1920), *KPSS v rez*, vol. 2, pp. 209–12.

18 See Lenin's comments at the VIII Congress, *Vos'moi*, pp. 5, 22–3, 56–7, 346–9. Also the debate and resolution, pp. 227–72, 429–31. The new party Programme is also relevant, pp. 397–407.
19 *Vos'moi*, p. 423 where it is stated that workers and worker-peasant youths should have an open door to the party.
20 Lenin's evaluation of the capacities of the class ranged from the very optimistic in the early months after October 1917 to the pessimistic from mid-1918 to his acknowledgement of the declassing of the proletariat in 1921. For surveys, see Neil Harding, *Lenin's political thought*, vol. 2, *Theory and practice in the Socialist Revolution* (London: Macmillan, 1981) and Marcel Leibman, *Leninism under Lenin* (London: Merlin Press, 1975), part 3.
21 *Vos'moi*, p. 62. Also see his comments at the IX Congress, *Deviatyi*, p. 24.
22 There was little alternative to this given the rejection of both workers' control and agreement with the former owners. The timing of nationalisation was in part dictated by fears of a German takeover of parts of Russian industry. E. H. Carr, *The Bolshevik Revolution 1917–1923* (Harmondsworth: Penguin, 1966), vol. 2, pp. 103–5.
23 On this, see *ibid.*, pp. 181–5 and Samuel A. Oppenheim, 'The Supreme Economic Council 1917–1921', *Soviet Studies*, 25, 3 (July 1973), pp. 3–27.
24 For Lenin's defence of their use, see *Vos'moi*, pp. 18–20, 58–61 and 'Zakliuchitel'noe slovo po dokladu ob ocherednykh zadachakh sovetskoi vlasti', *Pol'noe sobranie sochinenii* (hereafter *PSS*), vol. 36, pp. 272–3. Also see his comments at the XI Congress, *Odinnadtsatyi*, pp. 29–38. For formal acceptance of their utility, see the 1919 party Programme, *Vos'moi*, pp. 404–5. This issue was associated with that of one-man management. For debate on this, see *Deviatyi*, pp. 22–5, 45–9, 51–3, 106–11, 118–24, 139, 151–2, 410–11. For the trial and shooting of some specialists in 1921, see Kendall E. Bailes, *Technology and society under Lenin and Stalin. Origins of the Soviet technical intelligentsia 1917–1941* (Princeton University Press, 1978), p. 71.
25 See the discussion of law in E. H. Carr, *Socialism in one country 1924–1926* (Harmondsworth: Penguin, 1970), vol. 1, pp. 78–101 and Eugene Huskey, *Russian lawyers and the Soviet state. The origins and development of the Soviet Bar, 1917–1939* (Princeton University Press, 1986), ch. 2. The introduction of a criminal code in May 1922 was timely, providing a legal basis for the trial of the SRs. The code was broad and vague and included provision for those who, although not having committed a crime, represented a 'social danger', and for a doctrine of analogy whereby people could be charged for something that was not provided for in the code but was analogous to something forbidden in the code.
26 On the establishment and operation of the Vecheka, see George Leggett, *The Cheka: Lenin's Political Police* (Oxford: Clarendon Press, 1981); G. H. Leggett, 'Lenin, Terror and the Political Police', *Survey*, 21, 4 (97), (1975), pp. 157–87; Alexander Solzhenitsyn, *The Gulag Archipelago 1918–1956* (London, Collins, 1974). There was considerable administrative confusion and squabbling between the different legal organs: Vecheka which answered directly to the CC, people's courts and revolutionary tribunals which were administered by the Commissariat of Justice, the commissa-

riats of Internal Affairs and of Justice, and the soviets. See E. J. Scott, 'The Cheka', *St Antony's Papers*, No. 1, Soviet affairs No. 1 (London: Chatto and Windus, 1956), pp. 15–20 and E. H. Carr, *Socialism in one country 1924–1926* (Harmondsworth: Penguin, 1969), vol. 2, ch. 24.

27 For the claim that Lenin's frequent queries about the minute details of cases concerning individuals in the hands of the Vecheka constituted an effort to control that body, see Michael Heller, 'Lenin and the Cheka: the real Lenin', *Survey*, 24, 2 (107), (1979), pp. 182–4.

28 Leggett, 'Lenin', pp. 176–81; Carr, *Bolshevik Revolution*, vol. 1, Amy W. Knight, *The KGB. Police and politics in the Soviet Union* (Boston: Unwin Hyman, 1988), ch. 1. During this period, the responsibilities of the Vecheka were not confined to dealing with instances of counter-revolution. As an organisation, it also had some responsibility for the care of orphans, for transport and fuel supply.

29 For example, see Leon Trotsky, *Terrorism and communism. A reply to Karl Kautsky* (Ann Arbor: University of Michigan Press, 1961), ch. 4. Not all party members were happy about the Vecheka. On calls to abolish it, see Leggett, *Cheka*, pp. 117–20.

30 However, terror had actually begun to be used before the formal announcement of the Red Terror. See the discussion in Leggett, *Cheka*, ch. 6.

31 For some calculations, see Solzhenitsyn, *Gulag*, p. 300 and Gregory Petrovich Maximoff, *The guillotine at work*, vol. 1, *The Leninist counter-revolution* (Sanday: Cienfuegos Press, 1979), pp. 79, 142–3, 199, 240–1. On forced labour, see David J. Dallin and Boris I. Nicolaevsky, *Forced labor in Soviet Russia* (New Haven: Yale University Press, 1947), and James Bunyan, *The origin of forced labor in the Soviet state 1917–1921. Documents and materials* (Baltimore: Johns Hopkins University Press, 1967).

32 For official statements that what was important in determining guilt was class origin, not individual identity, see Leggett, *Cheka*, pp. 114, 115.

33 For the number of risings, see *ibid.*, pp. 325, 329.

34 For one discussion of this, see Jonathan R. Adelman, 'The development of the Soviet party apparat in the Civil War: center, localities, and nationality areas', *Russian History*, 9, 1 (1982), pp. 86–110.

35 For discussions, see Anweiler, *The Soviets*, pp. 219–20 and Robert Service, *The Bolshevik Party in revolution 1917–1923. A study in organisational change* (London: Macmillan, 1979), p. 65. For reports about jurisdictional conflicts between soviets, see *Vos'maia*, p. 57.

36 On these, see Service, *Bolshevik Party*, p. 74; *Vos'moi*, p. 429; Lenin's comments in *Vos'maia*, pp. 10–11; and Merle Fainsod, *Smolensk under Soviet rule* (New York: Vintage Books, 1958), p. 39.

37 See Avanesov's comments at the VII Congress to the effect that such fractions were sending delegates to the party congress (*Sed'moi*, pp. 116–17). Also Sverdlov's comments on pp. 171–2. At the IX Congress Krestinsky confirmed that there had been little difference between party and soviet organs, but at least at the guberniia level this was no longer the case. *Deviatyi*, pp. 30–2. At the VIII Congress an attempt was made to

strengthen the local committees through the elimination of any special party organs which were operating in conflict with the local committees, by giving the local committees (under CC guidance) responsibility for the allocation of local party members to posts in all fields, and by reinforcing their directive powers over party members working in other organisations. *Vos'moi*, pp. 425, 426, 428–9. Later that same year (1919) the position of the party committees was further strengthened in relation to the soviets by a decision to finance the local committees directly by the CC instead of them having to rely totally upon the soviets for their funds *Deviatyi*, pp. 32, 504. Also see Robert H. McNeal, 'The beginning of Communist party financial exactions from the Soviet State', D. A. Loeber, ed., *Ruling communist parties and their status under law* (The Hague: Nijnhoff, 1986), p. 93 where he argues that by March 1920, 92% of party disbursements went to regional party organisations. At the VIII Congress it had also been declared that the functions of party and soviet were not to be confused and that the party was to implement its decisions through the soviets; it was 'to direct the activities of the soviets, but not replace them'. *Vos'moi*, pp. 428–9.

38 For criticisms of this, see the claim by Simbirsk delegate Vareikis that the despatch of CC emissaries outside the party framework undermined the position of the local organisations and constituted an inadmissible 'foreign intrusion into our local party affairs'. *Vos'maia*, pp. 31, 124–5. Also see *Vos'moi*, pp. 198–9, 202, 314–15.

39 See above, note 37.

40 See Leggett, *Cheka*. For an instance of conflict between Cheka and soviet, see N. Maier', 'Sluzhba v' kommissariat' iustitsii i narodnom' sud'', *Arkhiv russkoi revoliutsii*, 8 (1923) pp. 80–1.

41 Rigby, *Membership*, p. 52. The figures for 1917 and 1922 are for 1 January, the remainder are for March.

42 The exact numbers leaving the party cannot be ascertained, but isolated figures suggest that the scale was significant. According to the leading student of party membership, between March and August 1919 the party dropped from 350,000 to 150,000, and in the purge of 1921–22, nearly a quarter of the membership was expelled or withdrew voluntarily. Rigby, *Membership*, pp. 77, 97. Also see Adelman, *Development*, pp. 96–8.

43 *Izvestiia tsentral'nogo komiteta rossiiskoi kommunisticheskoi partii (bol'shevikov)*, 1 (28 May 1919) (hereafter *Izv ts k*). This was announced in the context of a concern for the health of the party resulting from its recent growth and was to be implemented in such a way that 'particular control measures' could be applied to those who joined the party after October 1917. *Vos'moi*, p. 423.

44 *Spravochnik partiinogo rabotnika* (Moscow, n.d. [1921]), vol. 1, pp. 69–77. For criticism about the excessively formalistic approach adopted toward re-registration by some party bodies, see the resolution on party construction adopted at the IX Conference, *KPSS v rez*, vol. 2, p. 299. For more general disappointment at the results of the re-registration, see the CC letter of 27 July 1921 on the purge. *KPSS v rez*, vol. 2, p. 439.

45 *Izv ts k*, 35 (1 Dec. 1921) pp. 14–15.

46 For example, see *Izv ts k*, (12 Dec. 1920), p. 20; 32 (6 August 1921), pp. 12, 17–18; 1(37) (January 1922), p. 37; and 3(39)(March 1922), p. 8.
47 For one example, see Rigby, *Membership*, p. 97, note 14.
48 See Osinsky's criticisms at the VIII and IX Congresses, *Vos'moi*, pp. 166–87 and *Deviatyi*, pp. 118–24. Also the discussion in Service, *Bolshevik Party*, pp. 100–1. One report referred to plenary assemblies as having 'a purely advisory character' with all work handled by the executive organ. *Izv ts k*, 32 (6 August 1921), p. 8. For an attempt to stimulate the plena of lower level party organisations and the rank-and-file membership and to encourage intra-party criticism, see the resolution of the IX Conference, *KPSS v rez*, vol. 2, pp. 297–8, 299–300. Centralisation also occurred in the soviets. *Vos'maia*, pp. 67–8, 75–6, 117, 122, 125. Also Keep, *Russian Revolution*, pp. 339–81, 449–63.
49 See Zinoviev's comments at the VIII Congress, *Vos'moi*, pp. 279–80.
50 *Deviatyi*, p. 62.
51 For example, see the reference to 'local "patriotism"' in the VIII Congress resolution on the organisational question. *Vos'moi*, p. 429.
52 *Vos'moi*, p.188. For a reference to 'closed groups' that were difficult for outsiders to penetrate, see *Spravochnik partiinogo rabotnika* (Moscow n.d. [1922]), vol. 2, pp. 46–7.
53 Party leaders recognised this problem. Concern was frequently expressed regarding the material standard of living of party figures in the localities. For example, see *Izv ts k*, 36 (15 December 1921), p. 5 and *Odinnadtsatyi*, pp. 551–2, 660. For some measures to alleviate this, see the resolution of the XII Conference. *KPSS v rez*, vol. 2, pp. 594–8. The effect of these material difficulties was reluctance by many cadres to take up rural posts.
54 Although clearly some were. For example, see *KPSS v rez*, vol. 2, p. 302; *Desiatyi*, pp. 59, 227–9, 250, 801–3; *Odinnadtsatyi* pp. 551–2 and Service *Bolshevik Party*, pp. 141–8.
55 For example, *Izv ts k*, 21 (4 September 1920), pp. 1–2 and 25 (11 November 1920), p. 12. For some steps taken in 1919 against abuses of office by public employees, see Leggett, *Cheka*, p. 216. Indeed, the full title of the Vecheka is instructive in this regard: All-Russian Extraordinary Commission for Combating Counter-Revolution, Speculation, Sabotage and Misconduct in Office.
56 For official concern about and measures against this, see *Izv ts k*, 24 (12 October 1921), pp. 5–8; 27 (27 January 1921), pp. 1–4; 32 (6 August 1921), pp. 8–9; 1 (37) (January 1922), pp. 40–1; and *KPSS v rez*, vol. 2, p. 264.
57 *Desiatyi*, pp. 45–6, 800–1.
58 *Odinnadtsatyi*, p. 402.
59 *Dvenadtsatyi s'ezd RKP(b) 17–25 aprelia 1923 goda. Stenograficheskii otchet* (Moscow, 1968), p. 66. For a list of nationality-based conflicts, see T. H. Rigby, 'Early provincial cliques and the rise of Stalin', *Soviet Studies*, 33, 1 (January 1981), pp. 3–28.
60 On local groups trying to use the party purge against their opponents, see *Odinnadtsatyi*, p. 371. For official prohibition of such a practice, see the CC letter of 27 July 1921 on the purge, *KPSS v rez*, vol. 2, p. 442.

61 Some conflicts at the centre were mirrored at the lower levels and resulted in central action against a dissident local leadership. For an example, see the discussion of the Brest-Litovsk issue in Service, pp. 79–83. For a discussion of local clashes which occasioned CC intervention, see *Odinnadtsatyi*, pp. 654–6. For more extended discussions of one instance, see A. I. Mikoian, *V nachale dvatsatykh* (Moscow, 1975), ch. 2 and Rigby, 'Cliques'.

62 For one call to use expulsion if necessary to eliminate the squabbles and groupings which led to the paralysis of party work, see *Odinnadtsatyi* p. 552. This phenomenon was explicitly linked with NEP.

63 *Vos'moi*, pp. 160, 287. Sol'ts also used the military analogy at the XI Congress. *Odinnadtsatyi*, p. 168.

64 For example, V. I. Lenin, 'Detskaia bolezn' "levizny" v kommunizme', *PSS*, vol. 41, pp. 5, 27.

65 *Vos'moi*, p. 426.

66 *Vos'moi*, pp. 424, 425, 426. This resolution was motivated in part by the difficulties being experienced within the Ukrainian party. Daniels, *Conscience*, pp. 98–104.

67 *Vos'maia*, pp. 193, 194, 197–8. From September 1920, the auditing commission was to monitor the implementation of central decisions by party bodies at lower levels. See the resolution of the IX Conference, *KPSS v rez*, vol. 2, pp. 298–9.

68 For example, see a resolution of the IX Conference, *KPSS v rez*, vol. 2, pp. 297–303. The other major opposition grouping during this period, the Workers' Opposition, shared the Democratic Centralists' opposition to the atrophy of party life and its replacement by politics concentrated at the executive level.

69 *Vos'moi*, p. 167. The Democratic Centralists were never able satisfactorily to reconcile this position with their championing of local initiative and autonomy in local issues for the lower level party organs. In principle, one could argue that in matters of national importance local organs must be the agents of the central authorities while in purely local affairs they should have the right of decision without interference from above. However, this distinction was more difficult to maintain in practice. See the report by Osinsky, *Vos'moi*, pp. 303–14.

70 See the discussion in Service, *Bolshevik Party*, pp. 77–8, 104, 109. For some calls for greater guidance, see *Vos'maia*, pp. 37, 39. For some details about how the central apparatus responded to such appeals, see Krestinsky's reports to the VIII Conference and the IX Congress, *Vos'maia*, pp. 27–8 and *Deviatyi*, pp. 30–1.

71 *Vos'maia*, pp. 36, 39.

72 *Vos'moi*, p. 214. For his views on the role the CC should play, see *Deviatyi*, p. 62. Also see the discussion in Service, *Bolshevik Party*, pp. 106–10.

73 *Desiatyi*, pp. 103–4.

74 *Vos'moi*, p. 426. Also see *Vos'maia*, p. 194. At the XI Congress, control over some aspects of personnel distribution was accorded to guberniia committees without the need for prior CC agreement. *Odinnadtsatyi*, p. 660.

75 This position was enunciated in an official resolution of the IX Congress. *Deviatyi*, p. 427. At the same congress, a Democratic Centralist spokesman, Maksimovsky, presented draft theses in which he called for the CC and lower committees always to act through the local committees and not to go outside them. However, earlier in his speech, he had acknowledged that in specific cases the CC should be able to ignore local opinion in matters concerning the distribution of party personnel. *Deviatyi*, pp. 318–31.
76 However, this situation had improved by the end of the period. Also note Molotov's comment at the XI Congress that there had been an attempt to supply local committees with workers in accord with their needs. *Odinnadtsatyi*, p. 56.
77 *Izv ts k*, 3 (39) (March 1922), pp. 27–8. See below.
78 At the IX Congress Kamenev referred to the allocation of party members to party work as 'the chief organisational task of the party'. This was reaffirmed in the congress resolution. *Deviatyi*, pp. 305, 424.
79 The XI Conference in December 1921 adopted a resolution which declared that secretaries of gubkoms should be of pre-October party standing and secretaries of ukoms of three years party standing, with such appointments being confirmed at higher levels. *KPSS v rez*, vol. 2, p. 474 and *Izv ts k*, 1 (37) (January 1922), p. 31. This decision was later confirmed by a meeting of secretaries of obkoms, obbureaux and gubkoms, by the CC and by the XI Congress.
80 The formal hierarchy for this was spelled out in the party Rules of 1919, #18.
81 According to the resolution on party construction adopted at the IX Conference in September 1920: 'Accepting that in principle appointment to elected posts is possible in exceptional circumstances, the CC is nevertheless advised that in the distribution of workers, appointments should in general be replaced by recommendations.' *KPSS v rez*, vol. 2, p. 300.
82 On ignoring local needs and demands, see the comments of Sapronov, Maksimovsky and Bubnov at the IX Congress, *Deviatyi*, pp. 48–52, 59.
83 For example, see Mikoian, *V nachale*.
84 For example, *Deviatyi*, p. 319 and *Desiatyi*, pp. 87–8.
85 T. H. Rigby, 'The origins of the nomenklatura system', Inge Auerbach, Andreas Hillgruber and Gottfried Schramm, eds. *Felder und Vorfelder russischer Geschichte. Studien zu Ehren von Peter Scheibert* (Frieburg: Rombach Verlag, 1985), p. 244.
86 In this regard, see the comment by Sol'ts at the X Congress that many of the complaints from the localities examined by the Central Control Commission stemmed from the sort of attitudes possessed by many local leaders, which could be summarised as follows: 'I received power and responsibility only through that organisation which entrusted this power to me, and I need not render any account to the party masses.' *Desiatyi*, p. 60. For a similar comment by Rafail, see *Desiatyi*, pp. 273–4.
87 Section 39 of the party Rules. *Vos'maia*, p. 196.
88 See *Izv ts k*, 24 (12 October 1920), pp. 5–8 for the report of a conference

held to establish a standardised structure for uezd and guberniia committees.
89 *Vos'maia*, p. 33.
90 For an example from the Ukraine, see *Deviatyi*, p. 59. At the X Congress, Shliapnikov claimed that the frequent transfer of workers from place to place had been used instead of attempting to attract more workers from below in the individual localities, with the result that local experience was not being used adequately by the party. *Desiatyi*, p. 75. At the X Conference in May 1921, calls were still being made for the transfer of workers to take place on a planned and systematic basis. *KPSS v rez*, vol. 2, p. 270. On opposition to this practice by those subject to transfer, see *Izv ts k*, 31 (20 July 1921), p. 9.
91 *Izv ts k* 33 (October 1921), p. 4. This was officially attributed to the difficulties encountered by old, experienced party workers returning to party work after the Civil War and the strains between older, more experienced party workers and newer, younger members who had joined since the revolution.
92 *Vos'moi*, pp. 168–9. Also compare the comments of Kosior and Lenin at the XI Congress. *Odinnadtsatyi*, pp. 128, 144.
93 For official admission that such practices had become common by 1920, see Krestinsky's comments at the IX Congress, *Deviatyi*, p. 43. At the same congress Lutovinov declared that 'exile had been used on the widest scale'. *Deviatyi*, p. 56. For the exchange over the charge that Shliapnikov had been sent on a diplomatic posting to Norway because of his oppositional activity, see pp. 47, 56, 80, 86. In the light of the Ukrainian action, Yakovlev's comment twelve months earlier (30 March 1919) at the IX Congress that 'the Ukraine is being turned into a place of exile. Comrades who are disagreeable to Moscow are being exiled there' is interesting. *Deviatyi*, p. 57. For Krestinsky's defence against this charge, see p. 80. Also see Robert V. Daniels, 'The secretariat and the local organizations in the Russian Communist Party, 1921–1923', *The American Slavic and East European Review*, 16, 1 (1957), p. 34 and Service, *Bolshevik Party*, pp. 127–8.
94 *ibid.*, pp. 138–9. This was despite a party conference resolution in September calling on the CC to use the method of recommendation rather than appointment and asserting that transfers should not have a punitive character. Schapiro, *Origins*, pp. 267–8.
95 The main centres of Workers' Opposition support were the metalworkers union and, in geographical terms, the Donets Basin, the Don and Kuban regions, Samara and Moscow. Daniels, *Conscience*, p. 127. For the break-up of the Samara centre, see *Odinnadtsatyi* pp. 54, 126–7, 155, 175–6, 183–4, and Daniels 'Secretariat', pp. 41–2. On the replacement of the leadership of the metalworkers union elected at the May 1921 congress by central appointees, see *Izv ts k*, 32, 6 (August 1921), pp. 3–4.
96 *Deviatyi*, pp. 43–4.
97 Service, *Bolshevik Party*, pp. 163–5, 175, 180–3.
98 The basis for such action was the section of the party Rules (#51) provid-

ing for the dissolution of any party organisation which failed to implement the decisions of a higher level body.
99 Service, *Bolshevik Party*, pp. 94–5.
100 On political departments, see Daniels, *Conscience*, p. 114 and Service, *Bolshevik Party*, pp. 136, 143. Also *Deviatyi*, pp. 142, 310–12, 318, 331–3, 413–14.
101 Service, *Bolshevik Party*, pp. 104–5, 128; Daniels, *Conscience*, pp. 98–104; Richard Pipes, *The formation of the Soviet Union*, rev. ed. (Cambridge MA: Harvard University Press, 1970, pp. 174–84.
102 For example, *Deviatyi*, p. 52; Sapronov was the speaker.

2 The structure of elite politics

1 Most Bolshevik writings prior to the seizure of power were concerned with the question of whether to seize power, with general discussions of the current situation or of the broad principles of political practice in the post-revolutionary era. No attention was paid to the institutional contours a new regime might adopt. A recent study has shown how Lenin's thoughts about the future structure of government remained fluid and unformed virtually up until the announcement of Sovnarkom. T. H. Rigby, *Lenin's government, Sovnarkom 1917–1922* (Cambridge University Press, 1978), pp. 3–6.
2 For one argument along these lines, see Robert Service, 'From polyarchy to hegemony: The party's role in the construction of the central institutions of the Soviet state, 1917–1919', *Sbornik*, 10 (1984), p. 81.
3 For a more extended discussion, see Rigby, *Sovnarkom*, pp. 14–23 and T. H. Rigby, 'The first proletarian government', *The British Journal of Political Science*, 4, 1 (1974), pp. 37–51.
4 John L. H. Keep, trans. and ed., *The debate on Soviet power. Minutes of the All-Russian Central Executive Committee of Soviets Second Convocation October 1917 – January 1918* (Oxford: Clarendon Press, 1979), p. 33.
5 A Sovnarkom decree of 30 October had vested in VTsIK the right to defer, modify or annul Sovnarkom decisions, but in the first year of Sovnarkom's existence, only 68 out of a total of 480 decrees were submitted to VTsIK for ratification. John L. H. Keep, *The Russian Revolution. A study in mass mobilization* (London: Weidenfeld and Nicolson, 1976), p. 321; James Bunyan and H. H. Fisher, eds., *The Bolshevik Revolution 1917–1918. Documents and materials* (Stanford University Press, 1934), pp. 133, 187. For complaints about the lack of accountability, see Keep, *Debate*, pp. 52–3, 60, 78–9, 80–6, 118, 120–1, 140–2, 155–8, 169, 172, 180, 181, 198, 199–201, 211, 222. At the party's VIII Congress, Osinsky proposed a series of reforms designed to restore effective power to VTsIK and to halt the flow of power into smaller executive bodies. *Vos'moi s'ezd RKP(b) Mart 1919 goda. Protokoly* (Moscow, 1959), pp. 196–8. Further discussion of this question occurred at the VIII Conference, *Vos'maia konferentsiia RKP(b) Dekabr' 1919 goda. Protokoly* (Moscow, 1961), pp. 64–5, 76–8, 123–4.
6 The Bolsheviks rejected the principle of a separation of power between executive and legislative branches. Consequently, at a formal level, there

was no difference in functions between the All-Russian Congress of Soviets, VTsIK and Sovnarkom. The formal functions of the Presidium of VTsIK remained unspecified until late 1919. *Vos'maia konferentsiia RKP(b) Dekabr' 1919 goda. Protokoly* (Moscow, 1961), pp. 59, 61–2.
7 Sverdlov was particularly skilled at directing debate from the chair. See the discussion in Charles Duval, 'Yakov M. Sverdlov and the All-Russian Central Executive Committee of Soviets (VTsIK): a study in Bolshevik consolidation of power. October 1917 – July 1918', *Soviet Studies*, 31, 1 (January 1979), pp. 3–22. For a Menshevik assertion that Sverdlov's performance as chairman was that of 'an unimpeachably "correct" parliamentarian', see Leopold H. Haimson, ed., *The Mensheviks from the Revolution of 1917 to the Second World War* (University of Chicago Press, 1974), p. 136.
8 Its decreasing importance is reflected in the diminishing frequency with which it met: four times per week in November 1917, once or twice per week in December 1917, while between July 1918 and February 1920 it appears not to have met at all. Aryeh L. Unger, *Constitutional development in the USSR. A guide to the Soviet Constitutions* (London: Methuen, 1981), p. 15. But see Rigby, *Sovnarkom*, p. 169 where it is declared that in the second half of 1918 it was meeting about once a fortnight, and that it did not meet in 1919.
9 Rigby, *Sovnarkom*, pp. 27–8. One Left SR took up a commissariat in November, the six others in December.
10 This statement applies only to the people's commissars, not to all of the other individuals who frequently attended Sovnarkom meetings and were not always members of the party.
11 Rigby, *Sovnarkom*, pp. 239–42 provides a list of all changes during the period.
12 *ibid.*, pp. 65–6. The early frequency of meetings also reflects the absence of institutionalisation of Sovnarkom and an attempt to come to grips with the multitude of problems with which the Bolsheviks were confronted.
13 All decisions of this body were final unless referred to the full Sovnarkom by the chairman of Maly Sovnarkom or were formally protested by the head of one of the Sovnarkom agencies. On the Maly Sovnarkom, see *ibid.*, pp. 34–6, 76–83.
14 *Ibid.*, ch. 8.
15 Some of these councils and boards were effectively commissions of the corresponding soviet executive committees, which had some power of veto over their decisions. There was also some rivalry with Vesenkha for control over them. *Ibid.*, pp. 93–4.
16 See a discussion of this in Samuel A. Oppenheim, 'The Supreme Economic Council 1917–1921', *Soviet Studies*, 25, 3 (July 1973), pp. 20–1.
17 See the discussions in Sheila Fitzpatrick, *The commissariat of enlightenment. Soviet organization of education and the arts under Lunacharsky* (Cambridge University Press, 1970) and Teddy J. Uldricks, *Diplomacy and ideology. The origins of Soviet foreign relations 1917–1930* (London: Sage Publications, 1979).
18 The growth of the party's role in decision-making is reflected in the

number of 'decisions' made by the party during this period: 1917 (post October) – 3, 1918 – 11, 1919 – 56, 1920 – 150, and 1921 – 291. Robert H. McNeal, ed., *Guide to the decisions of the Communist Party of the Soviet Union* (University of Toronto Press, 1972), p. xxxiv. The figure for 1921 is the highest for the 1917–67 period. For McNeal's explanation, see pp. xxxv–xxxvi. For his definition of a party 'decision', see pp. x–xviii. The growth of party dominance is also reflected in the patterns of staffing Sovnarkom over this period. See Rigby, *Sovnarkom*, ch. 10.

19 Congresses were convened at frequent intervals between the second in 1903 and the fifth in 1907, but none was convened between May 1907 and August 1917, largely for tactical reasons. However, in this period, nine party conferences were called (three without Bolshevik participation and two without Menshevik attendance), and although they were not considered to be as widely representative as party congresses, their convocation does reflect this principle of rank-and-file decision-making, albeit with an element of factional manoeuvring. For a discussion of these conferences, see Ralph Carter Elwood, *Russian Social Democracy in the underground. A study of the RSDRP in the Ukraine, 1907–1914* (Assen: Van Gorcum, 1974), pp. 117–18.

20 Indeed, many decisions of successive congresses were ignored in practice.

21 Congresses were held in March 1918 and 1919, March–April 1920 and March 1921 and 1922. Party conferences were held in December 1919, September 1920 and May and December 1921. Provision for annual conferences was not made until 1922 and their lower level of importance compared with the congress is reflected in the provision that their decisions were to come into force only when ratified by the CC. For a report of this happening, see *Izvestiia tsentral'nogo komiteta rossiiskoi kommunisticheskoi partii (bol'shevikov)* 26 (20 December 1920), p. 2 (hereafter *Izv st k*). The December 1919 conference was officially recognised as the Eighth Conference.

22 The figures for the VIII Congress come from *Vos'moi*. According to a later publication, the numbers were 301 and 102, giving a total of 403. *Kommunisticheskaia partiia sovetskogo soiuza v rezoliutsiiakh i resheniiakh s'ezdov, konferentsii i plenumov Ts.K* (Moscow, 1983), vol. 2, p. 67.

23 The percentages among full, or voting, delegates was:

Congress	Pre-1917	1917	Post-1917
VIII	77	23	–
IX	49	24	27
X	36	26	38
XI	48	26	26

24 For example, at the VIII Congress separate sections discussed the organisational, military and agriculture questions, and at the IX Congress there were sections on cooperation in the countryside and party organisation.

25 For example, on the VII Congress, see Charles Duval, 'Iakov Mikhailovich Sverdlov: founder of the Bolshevik Party machine', Ralph Carter Elwood, ed., *Reconsiderations on the Russian Revolution* (Cambridge MA: Slavica Publications, 1976), p. 227 and on the XI Congress, see Robert Service, *The Bolshevik Party in revolution 1917–1923. A study in organisational change* (London: Macmillan, 1979), pp. 181–2. Attempts at such manipulation usually involved manoeuvring at lower levels of the party structure, but there was also scope at the opening of the congress. At this time a Mandates Commission was established to verify the validity of the credentials of the delegates. Any considered deficient in this regard could be denied entry to the congress or reduced from full to candidate status. For an instance when a local organisation's choice of delegates was invalidated by the centre and an alternative imposed, see *Desiatyi s'ezd RKP(b) Mart 1921 goda. Stenograficheskii otchet* (Moscow, 1963), p. 97.

26 For example, the X Congress was the first time that members of the opposition were excluded from the Presidium of the congress, the body established to direct the congress proceedings.

27 The concessions made to the trade union leaders at the IX Congress are an instance of this. Also see the resolution of the VIII Congress on the military question, the addendum to which seems to have been added to mollify the opposition. *Vos'moi*, pp. 421–3.

28 However, the structuring of military representation at the VIII Congress was one instance when this did occur.

29 Lenin was particularly active in this regard at the X Congress. See A. I. Mikoian, *Mysli i vospominaniia o Lenine* (Moscow, 1970), p. 139.

30 When it came to a vote between a resolution to abolish local control commissions and increase CC control over the CCC on the one hand and the resolution proposed in the name of the CC (which was much more favourably disposed to the control commissions), the vote was so close that the session chairman could not tell the majority from the minority. Tellers were appointed for a second vote, and the Presidium announced the result as 223 for the CC's resolution and 89 for the dissident resolution. But the congress was attended by 520 voting delegates, so there is a clear discrepancy in the stated totals. Indeed, at the XII Congress Shkiriatov declared that the control commissions were 'saved by only a small majority (the protocols seem to show that only 89 votes were cast against but that was not so)'. *Dvenadtsatyi s'ezd RKP(b) 17–25 aprelia 1923 goda. Stenograficheskii otchet* (Moscow, 1968), p. 246. It is difficult to escape the conclusion that there was a degree of central manipulation in the resolution of this question.

31 On the expulsion question, compare the draft resolution with that adopted, *Odinnadtsatyi s'ezd RKP(b) Mart–aprel' 1922 goda. Stenograficheskii otchet* (Moscow, 1961), pp. 580, 710. For the control commission debate, see pp. 178–203.

32 *Desiatyi*, p. 122. Some of his colleagues would have been much more positive about the role of the party as a whole than this.

33 Carryover levels were higher among full than candidate members,

although the position of the latter was strengthening as the period wore on. The percentages carried forward from each CC were as follows:

Congress	Full	Candidate
VII	80.0	12.5
VIII	94.7	37.5
IX	78.9	50.0
X	84.0	73.3

34 The figures are as follows:

	Pre-1917			1917			1919		
	F	C	T	F	C	T	F	C	T
VII	93.3	75.0	87.0	6.7	25.0	13.0	–	–	–
VIII	84.2	100.0	88.9	15.8	–	11.1	–	–	–
IX	84.2	100.0	90.3	15.8	–	9.7	–	–	–
X	84.0	100.0	89.2	16.0	–	10.8	–	–	–
XI	88.8	95.0	91.5	11.2	–	6.4	–	5.0	2.1

35 For criticism of this state of affairs, see *Vos'moi*, p. 170.
36 This is shown by adding together those from the central and those from the regional party and state machines (in percentage of CC membership):

	Centre	Regions
VII	30.4	30.5
VIII	40.7	29.6
IX	45.2	29.1
X	45.0	30.0
XI	37.0	45.7

The figures do not include all CC members; the 'Other' category has been excluded. This category includes the editor of *Pravda* and (at the IX and X Congresses) the Chairman of the Executive Committee of the Comintern who were both located in Moscow, chairmen of various trade union organisations who were mostly located in the capital, people in the military who may have been serving anywhere in the country but a proportion of whom would have been in Moscow, and (at the VII Congress) two diplomatic representatives serving abroad. If anything, the above figures probably understate the level of central representation. From 1918, members of the central state apparatus were more numerous than those from the regions (in percentage of CC membership):

	Centre	Regions
VII	21.7	26.1
VIII	29.6	14.8
IX	32.3	19.4
X	32.5	20.0
XI	26.1	21.8

37 This is clearly evident in the figures for full members of the CC:

	CP Apparatus					
	Centre	Region	Total	State	Other	Uncertain
VII	13.3	6.7	20.0	46.6	33.3	–
VIII	15.8	5.3	21.1	52.6	26.3	–
IX	15.8	–	15.8	52.6	31.6	–
X	20.0	4.0	24.0	48.0	20.0	8.0
XI	11.1	18.5	29.6	51.8	18.5	–

38 On this, see E. H. Carr, *The Bolshevik Revolution 1917–1923* (Harmondsworth: Penguin, 1966), vol. 3, pp. 41ff. and Uldricks, *Diplomacy*, pp. 27, 118.
39 The CC used a series of standing and temporary commissions to study particular questions. For example, a finance commission was established after the X Congress and in 1922 a standing commission on work in the countryside was created, along with commissions on industry and the work of Vesenkha. P. A. Rodionov, *Kollektivnost'* – *vysshii printsip partiinogo rukovodstva* (Moscow, 1967), p. 85. Boris Bazhanov, *Vospominaniia byvshego sekretaria Stalina* (Paris: Tret'ia volna, 1980), pp. 32–3.
40 *Vos'moi*, p. 164.
41 *Deviatyi s'ezd RKP(b) Mart–aprel' 1920 goda. Protokoly* (Moscow, 1960), pp. 51–3. Lutovinov argued that the CC had ceased to be the guiding organ of the party and had become involved in the implementation of 'the most petty insignificant affairs', citing appointment to low level economic administrative positions as an instance of this. *Ibid.*, p. 54.
42 *Vos'moi*, p. 164.
43 *Ibid.*, p. 284.
44 Service, *Bolshevik Party*, p. 124. Also see the comments of Krestinsky at the IX Congress. *Deviatyi*, p. 38.
45 This table is a compilation, taken from a number of sources: John Lowenhardt, *The Soviet Politburo*, trans. Dymphna Clark (Edinburgh: Canongate, 1982), p. 97; Rodionov, *Kollektivnost'*, pp. 38, 62; and *Izv ts k*, 22 (18 September 1920), p. 4, 29 (7 March 1921), pp. 15–16 and 4(40) (March 1922), p. 19. Lowenhardt's figures do not match those from the other

sources. His figure for 1918 (reproduced in the table) seems high and is difficult to reconcile with complaints at the VIII Congress that the CC met rarely and with the injunction introduced into the 1919 party Rules that it should meet at least twice per month.

46 *Sed'moi ekstrennyi s'ezd RKP(b) Mart 1918 goda. Stenograficheskii otchet* (Moscow, 1962), p. 178.
47 *KPSS v rez*, vol. 2, p. 447.
48 See the minutes of the CC meeting in Ann Bone, *The Bolsheviks and the October Revolution. Minutes of the Central Committee of the Russian Social-Democratic Labour Party (bolsheviks). August 1917 – February 1918* (London: Pluto Press, 1974), Pt. 3. The issue is discussed in Leonard Schapiro, *The origin of the communist autocracy. Political opposition in the Soviet state: first phase 1917–1922* (New York: Praeger, 1965), ch. 6.
49 See Service, *Bolshevik Party*, p. 181 and Schapiro, *Origin*, pp. 326–7.
50 Evidence for this is inferential. For the argument that such a slate did not become common until later in the 1920s but was used by Lenin at the X Congress to decimate the opposition, see Robert V. Daniels, 'Evolution of leadership selection in the Central Committee 1917–1927', Walter McKenzie Pintner and Don Karl Rowney, eds., *Russian officialdom. The bureaucratization of Russian society from the seventeenth to the twentieth century* (London: Macmillan, 1980), pp. 357–60. For the suggestion that such a slate was used at the IX Congress, see Olga A. Narkiewicz, *The making of the Soviet state apparatus* (Manchester University Press, 1970), p. 15. Prior to the introduction of a slate, congress delegates voted for as many members as there were seats on the CC, with the numbers receiving the most votes being elected. By 1920 candidate members were being elected separately after the full seats had been filled. On Lenin's efforts to structure the election of the CC at the X Congress, see Robert C. Tucker, *Stalin as revolutionary 1879–1929. A study in history and personality* (London: Chatto and Windus, 1974), pp. 297–9.
51 A similar executive body was also to be created in the lower level committees above the volost level. *Vos'maia*, pp. 195–7.
52 The Rules say little about the Politburo. Most of the details given here come from the resolution on the organisational question of the VIII Congress. *Vos'moi*, pp. 424–5.
53 Bureaucratic constituency of Politburo members.

	1919		1920		1921		1922	
	F	C	F	C	F	C	F	C
Central party	2	–	2	–	1	2	3	2
Central state	2	1	2	1	2	–	2	–
Regional state	1	1	1	1	2	–	2	–
Other	–	1	–	1	–	1	–	1

The regional state category includes chairmanship of the Moscow (Kamenev) and Leningrad (Zinoviev) soviets. The other category refers to the editorship of *Pravda* (Bukharin). The two representatives of the regional state apparatus include Kamenev who became Deputy Chairman of Sovnarkom in September 1922 while retaining his chairmanship of the Moscow soviet. In 1922, Rykov, Tomsky and Kalinin have been categorised by their membership of the Orgburo rather than their non-party offices; the same applies throughout for Stalin.

54 Rodionov, *Kollektivnost'*, pp. 38, 62, 70. Lowenhardt, *The Politburo*, p. 97 gives slightly different figures:

	Number of meetings	Average per month
1919	70	6
1920	85	7
1921	110	9
1922	60	5

The Politburo's heavy workload in 1921 is evident from the following figures reproduced in the party press:

	Number of meetings	Average per month
15 March 1921 – 1 May 1921	20	14
1 May 1921 – 1 June 1921	15	15
December 1921	13	13

Source: *Izv ts k*, 31 (20 July 1921), p. 7; 32 (6 August 1921), p. 6; 1(37) (January 1922), p. 4

55 This view is supported by Lenin's proposal regarding Politburo standing orders dictated on 8 December 1922. V. I. Lenin, *Polnoe sobranie sochinenii* (Moscow, 1979–83), vol. 45, p. 327.
56 V. P. Nikolaeva, 'V. I. Lenin i Organizatsionnoe Biuro TsK RKP(b) (1919–1922gg)', *Voprosy Istorii KPSS*, 9 (1969), pp. 36–7. Also see Lowenhardt, *The Politburo*, p. 96.
57 See note 55.
58 This is calculated from figures cited in CC reports published in various issues of *Izv ts k*.
59 For example, *Vos'moi*, pp. 321–2. The basic thrust of much Democratic Centralist criticism was directed against the accretion of power by small executive bodies.
60 *Odinnadtsatyi*, pp. 86–7. Complaints were also made that the Politburo was far too concerned with matters of minute detail. *Ibid.*, pp. 84, 87, 126.
61 For a discussion of this, see Charles Duval, 'The Bolshevik Secretariat and Yakov Sverdlov: February to October 1917', *The Slavonic and East European Review*, 51, 122 (1973) and Duval, 'Sverdlov'.

62 Service, *Bolshevik*, p. 58.
63 *Vos'moi*, p. 165. Osinsky asserted, *inter alia*, that in effect the Secretariat did not exist. For some documents which refer to its activities in 1918, see *Izvestiia Ts K KPSS*, 4 (1989), pp. 141–56.
64 *Vos'moi*, pp. 424–5. An attempt to tighten the linkages between Secretariat and CC was made at the IX Congress which decided that three members of the CC should work permanently in the Secretariat. *KPSS v rez*, vol. 2, p. 264.
65 *Deviatyi*, p. 500; *Desiatyi*, pp. 48–54; Service, *Bolshevik*, pp. 125–6; Leonard Schapiro, *The Communist Party of the Soviet Union* (London: Methuen, 1970), pp. 250–1; Leonard Schapiro, 'The General Department of the CC of the CPSU', *Survey*, 21, 3(96) (Summer 1975), pp. 53–65; Janice Ali, 'Aspects of the RKP(B) Secretariat, March 1919 to April 1922', *Soviet Studies*, 26, 3 (1974), pp. 397–8.
66 For a list, see Schapiro, *Communist Party*, p. 250.
67 *Izv ts k*, 28 (5 March 1921), pp. 1, 6.
68 The expansion of Agitprop's functions was opposed by a number of departments already in existence. *Desiatyi*, p. 55; Schapiro, *Communist Party*, p. 251 and J. Ali, 'Aspects', pp. 403–4. For a call by a regional delegate for the establishment of such an organ with a view to raising the consciousness of party members and improving the quality of party instructions, see *Vos'maia*, p. 32.
69 Orgotdel was reorganised twice in 1921 and once again in mid-1922. *Izv ts k*, 33 (October 1921), pp. 1–3, 20 and 3(39) (March 1922), p. 16; J. Ali, 'Aspects', pp. 408–9, 414 and Schapiro, *Communist Party*, p. 248. In the General Department separate sub-departments were created to handle the various responsibilities which this organisation had to shoulder. In 1920, the department was divided into two, the Finance Department and Upravlenie Delami (Administration of Affairs, or Chancellery). The latter appears to have consisted of two sections, a general chancellery and the Secret Department, with the latter being concerned principally with classified, secret correspondence and material. It was here also that the secretariat for the Politburo, Secretariat and Orgburo were to be found. Niels Erik Rosenfeldt, '"The consistory of the communist church": the origins and development of Stalin's Secret Chancellery', *Russian History*, 9, 2–3 (1982), pp. 310–12 and Niels Erik Rosenfeldt, *Knowledge and power. The role of Stalin's secret chancellery in the Soviet system of government* (Copenhagen: Rosenkilde and Bagger, 1978), pp. 54–6, 204.
70 *Deviatyi*, p. 806; *Izv ts k*, 28 (5 March 1921), pp. 23–4; 3(39) (March 1922), p. 54. The figure for 1921 does not include the detachment of 140 for special appointments attached to the General Section. According to J. Ali, 'Aspects', p. 404, there were 745 workers at the end of 1920.
71 *Izv ts k*, 28 (5 March 1921), p. 24 and 3(39) (March 1922), p. 54.
72 *Izv ts k*, 28 (5 March 1921), p. 24.
73 At the VIII Conference Krestinsky argued that the performance of the central apparatus had improved, although problems still existed. These included lack of a systematic character in personnel assignment, which

still reflected demands for personnel emanating from below rather than a conscious plan from above. *Vos'maia konferentsiia RKP(b) Dekabr' 1919 goda. Protokoly* (Moscow, 1961), pp. 27–30. For his argument that links with the localities had improved by March 1920, see *Deviatyi*, pp. 30–1, 500–2.
74 For a call to place CC members in charge of Secretariat departments, see *Odinnadtsatyi*, pp. 71–2.
75 *Deviatyi*, pp. 49, 319.
76 Schapiro, *Origin*, p. 266. For a reference to the secret directive part of the General Department, see *Izv ts k*, 23 (23 September 1920), p. 3.
77 *Izv ts k*, 23 (23 September 1920), p. 1. One secretary was responsible for agitation-propaganda affairs, one for registration and distribution of party forces, and one for informational-organisational affairs.
78 Schapiro, *Origin*, p. 265. See Krestinsky's argument that certain specific personnel appointments which had come under attack had been preceded by consultation rather than being carried out arbitrarily by the central organs. *Deviatyi*, p. 80. Also see his comments at the X Congress. *Desiatyi*, p. 51. Preobrazhensky's lack of centralising zeal is reflected in his proposal that power be decentralised from the CC because of the overloading of that body and its consequent inability to carry out its tasks. *Deviatyi*, pp. 68–9.
79 Schapiro, *Origin*, p. 321.
80 See Nogin's comments at the XI Congress. *Odinnadtsatyi*, pp. 60–72. For a summary of some of his points, see J. Ali, 'Aspects', pp. 408–9. Also see the comments in Bazhanov, *Vospominaniia*, pp. 13–14, 36, 50.
81 1922 Rules, #28.
82 According to Bazhanov, this is the first time that secretaries formally were ranked, with the General Secretary followed by the second and third secretaries. He also asserts that from Sverdlov's death, party secretaries had ceased to be purely technical in their functions. Bazhanov, *Vospominaniia*, pp. 23, 30.
83 Rodionov, *Kollektivnost'*, p. 68.
84 *Izv ts k*, 23 (23 September 1920), p. 1.
85 *Izv ts k*, 33 (October 1921), pp. 3–4.
86 As late as June 1922 Orgotdel reports retained some discussion of local conflicts. See *Izv ts k*, 6(42) (June 1922), p. 8. Formally, responsibility for conflicts between organisations remained in Orgotdel while the control commissions took over responsibility for clashes between individuals and groups. *Izv ts k*, 3(39) (March 1922), p. 16.
87 *Izv ts k*, 22 (18 September 1920), p. 7.
88 *Izv ts k*, 28 (5 March 1921), p. 1. At this time Orgotdel had sixty-four staff (p. 23).
89 *Izv ts k*, 33 (October 1921), p. 2.
90 *Izv ts k*, 28 (5 March 1921), p. 1; 33 (October 1921), pp. 1–2; 36 (15 December 1921), p. 15; J. Ali, 'Aspects'. The 1921 reorganisation saw the addition of Instructors, who were to visit local party organisations with a view to improving their functioning. Schapiro, *Communist Party*, p. 248. The institution of Instructors was foreshadowed at the X Congress. *KPSS v rez*, vol. 2, pp. 332–3.

91 *Izv ts k*, 33 (October 1921), p. 3.
92 *Odinnadtsatyi*, pp. 62–4.
93 For example, see the call by the X Conference for three-monthly reports by gubkom secretaries on the work of their party organisations, and the resolution of a conference of obkom, oblast bureau and gubkom secretaries confirmed by the XI Congress. *KPSS v rez*, vol. 2, pp. 422, 515.
94 Not all centre–regional contacts went through Orgotdel. Part of the responsibility of the General Department was the handling of correspondence. Furthermore the X Congress made provision for the CC to send secret monthly letters to all gubkoms to keep them informed about international and domestic questions. *KPSS v rez*, vol. 2, p. 333.
95 On the need to improve links and for local party organs regularly to report to the centre, see *Izv ts k*, 25 (11 November 1920), p. 5; 30 (4 April 1921), pp. 1–2; 32 (6 August 1921), p. 7. For the introduction of monthly letters from secretaries of gubkoms and obkoms to keep the centre informed of their situation, see *Spravochnik partiinogo rabotnika*, 2, 1922 (Moscow, n.d.), pp. 79–80.
96 *Odinnadtsatyi*, pp. 60–72.
97 *Vos'moi*, p. 426. Control by the CC was explicitly designed to combat localism.
98 This is discussed in T. H. Rigby, *Communist Party membership in the USSR 1917–1967* (Princeton University Press, 1968), pp. 76–7.
99 *Deviatyi*, p. 425.
100 *Spravochnik partiinogo rabotnika*, 1, 1921 (Moscow, n.d.), pp. 69–77 and *Izv ts k*, 21 (4 September 1920), p. 2. This is discussed in Rigby, *Membership*, p. 84.
101 *Izv ts k*, 28 (5 March 1921), p. 13. For calls for notification of changes, see *Izv ts k*, 30 (4 April 1921), pp. 1–2; 36 (15 December 1921), p. 6.
102 *Izv ts k*, 22 (18 September 1920), p. 12.
103 *KPSS v rez*, vol. 2, p. 299.
104 *Izv ts k*, 32 (6 August 1921), pp. 17–18.
105 *Izv ts k*, 32 (6 August 1921), p. 18. An earlier instruction had called on uezd committees regularly to send 10% of their responsible workers to the guberniia committees to take up vacant positions. *Izv ts k*, 32 (6 August 1921), p. 12. The transformation of the registration departments into registration-statistical sections of Orgotdel was accompanied by the injunction that they were to be headed by senior officials, to remain in place for at least six months and to observe standardised, centrally prescribed procedures.
106 *Odinnadtsatyi*, p. 52. Although at the end of 1921 it was declared that Orgotdel (*sic*) had sufficient precise information on the composition of most leading guberniia and oblast organs to allow it systematically to supervise changes in the localities. *Izv ts k*, 36 (15 December 1921), p. 5. For one complaint about the census of guberniia level responsible workers being incomplete, see *Izv ts k*, 33 (October 1921), pp. 16–17.
107 See instructions for this in a circular dated 15 November 1921. *Izv ts k*, 35 (1 December 1921), pp. 14–15.

108 Some of the confusion is illustrated by the following. According to figures published in March 1922, there were 14,821 responsible workers in the party, of whom 3,061 were at guberniia level and higher, 9,325 at uezd level and 2,435 without responsible positions but who were capable of responsible work. *Izv ts k*, 3(39) (March 1922), p. 37. However, according to figures from November 1921, Uchraspred had 23,500 responsible workers registered. *Izv ts k*, 36 (15 December 1921), p. 6.
109 *ibid.*, p. 5.
110 *KPSS v rez*, vol. 2, p. 503.
111 For example, see the comments in *Izv ts k*, 1(37) (January 1922), pp. 51–2 and 3(39) (March 1922), p. 28.
112 There were now 14 categories of workers based on type of work rather than five. *Izv ts k*, 2(38) (February 1922), p. 12.
113 See the ranking in *Izv ts k*, 2(38) (February 1922), p. 12. Also the discussion in T. H. Rigby, 'The origins of the nomenklatura system', Inge Auerbach, Andreas Hillgruber and Gottfried Schramm, eds., *Felder und Vorfelder russischer Geschichte. Studien zu Ehren von Peter Scheibert* (Freiburg: Rombach Verlag, 1985).
114 For example, in February 1921, Uchraspred had only 26 personnel, two fewer than the much less important Women's Department, although this figure does not include the twenty-two people in the Statistics section which did not separate from Uchraspred until the July. In April 1920, Uchraspred had had only nine workers. *Izv ts k*, 28 (5 March 1921), pp. 10, 23.
115 *Odinnadtsatyi*, p. 65.
116 See Maksimovsky's comments at the IX Congress where he calls for a regularisation of the distribution of party personnel and declares that the CC should have responsibility for this task on an all-Russian scale, even to the extent of ignoring local opinion in specific cases. *Deviatyi*, pp. 326–7. In the draft theses he presented a few moments later, the CC and other committees were called upon to act through the local committees, not outside them. *Deviatyi*, p. 328. This illustrates the difficult path the Democratic Centralists were trying to tread.
117 For example, see *Izv ts k*, 26 (20 December 1920), p. 20; 1(37) (January 1922), p. 37; 5(41) (May 1922), p. 36 and 6(42) (June 1922), pp. 6, 11.
118 An indication of the numbers involved is given by the fact that in a five-month period in the middle of 1920, Uchraspred despatched 25,995 party members. *Izv ts k*, 22 (18 September 1920), p. 5.
119 For some figures on the 13 major mobilisations between the X and XI Congresses, see *Izv ts k*, 3(39) (March 1922), pp. 30–1.
120 *Izv ts k*, 26 (20 December 1920), p. 6; 28 (5 March 1921), p. 13; 33 (October 1921), p. 2 and 3(39) (March 1922), p. 28.
121 Respectively, *Izv ts k*, 3(39) (March 1922), p. 27 and 31 (20 July 1921), p. 5.
122 *Izv ts k*, 3(39) (March 1922), p. 29.
123 Charles Duval, 'The function of political sub-groups in the Russian

Revolution 1917–1918', unpublished paper, pp. 3–6. For a reference to it by Lenin in February 1918, see 'Pozitsiia Ts.K. RSDRP (bol'shevikov) v voprose o separatnom i anneksionistskom mire', *PSS*, vol. 35, p. 389.
124 *Vos'moi*, pp. 424–5.
125 *Deviatyi*, p. 86. At the same time Lenin acknowledged the practical difficulties of maintaining such a distinction.
126 *Izv ts k*, 31 (20 July 1921), p. 7. This was presented as an attempt to prevent the Orgburo from becoming bogged down in detail. To facilitate this, the Secretariat was to meet immediately before the Orgburo to handle its business.
127 According to Krestinsky, 80% of the questions dealt with by the Orgburo concerned the distribution of party workers. *Desiatyi*, p. 47. The CC report puts the figure at 'more than 85%'. *Desiatyi*, p. 805. The Orgburo had to confirm drafts of CC circulars, although the most important of these went to the Politburo for confirmation. Nikolaeva, 'Lenin', p. 38. According to one scholar, following the IX Congress, the Orgburo was able to make transfers and appointments to all party positions except those at the national level without reference to the Politburo. Schapiro, *Origin*, p. 264. This proposal, which was voiced during debate on the organisational question at the IX Congress, was certainly not included in the final congress resolution. If Schapiro is correct, this may have been adopted later in the form of an internal administrative regulation. I have been unable to find any evidence of it.
128 The first was held on 29 April 1919, with a further 21 being held up to 7 December 1922. Nikolaeva, 'Lenin', pp. 36–7.
129 Service, *Bolshevik Party*, p. 125. Also see Lenin's comments at the IX Congress to the effect that it was sufficient for one member of the CC to request that a matter handled by the Orgburo be dealt with by the Politburo for it to be done. *Deviatyi*, p. 13.
130 *Desiatyi*, pp. 56, 111. For criticism of the lack of planning, see *Desiatyi*, pp. 95–6. At the IX Congress Maksimovsky had complained that the Orgburo was functioning in a chaotic fashion. *Deviatyi*, p. 48. On the absence of a plan until spring 1920, see Schapiro, *Origin*, p. 264.
131 *Izv ts k*, 21 (4 September 1920), p. 4; 26 (20 December 1920), p. 6; 4(40) (March 1922), p. 19. For slightly different figures, see *Vos'maia*, p. 111 (April–December 1919 – 110 meetings) and *Odinnadtsatyi*, p. 661 (March 1921 – March 1922 the Orgburo and Secretariat met on 161 occasions and handled 5034 questions, but there is no breakdown between each body). According to Schapiro (*Origin*, p. 264) it was meeting an average of twice per day during part of 1920. Some meetings took place jointly with the Politburo.
132 *Desiatyi*, p. 87. For Krestinsky's response, see p. 111. According to the CC report, the Orgburo handled an average of 40 questions per session between the IX and X Congresses. *Desiatyi*, p. 805.
133 According to one scholar, by September 1920 the Orgburo had carried out transfers involving more than 25,000 party members. Schapiro, *Origins*, p. 265.

134 At the IX Congress Maksimovsky referred to 'some isolation in the work of both organs'. *Deviatyi*, p. 324.
135 This meant that the trade union chief, Cheka chief and Chairman of Vesenkha were all members of the Orgburo. This gave significant representation to the state apparatus in the Orgburo and, because of their commitments elsewhere, must have restricted its capacity to generate a sense of institutional integrity and identity.
136 The three replaced leaders were all supporters of Trotsky. As part of his onslaught on Trotsky in late 1920 – early 1921 Zinoviev had attacked the Orgburo for its 'dictatorial' actions and attitudes. Schapiro, *Origin*, pp. 270–1.
137 Following the XI Congress, the Orgburo consisted of Andreev, Dzerzhinsky, Kuibyshev, Molotov, Rykov, Stalin and Tomsky as full members and Kalinin, Rudzutak and Zelensky as candidates.
138 *KPSS v rez*, vol. 2, p. 302.
139 Ten years for the central level, five for the oblast level and post-February 1917 for the guberniia level.
140 *Desiatyi*, p. 65.
141 *Odinnadtsatyi*, pp. 563–5.
142 Party committees could not countermand the decisions of commissions; disagreements were to be referred to a joint meeting, and if no agreement could be reached, the issue would be taken to the corresponding congress or conference or to a higher control commission. *Odinnadtsatyi*, p. 565.
143 This does not mean that they played no independent part. For one instance, see the role played by the CCC in the trade union discussion. *Desiatyi*, pp. 62–3 and Schapiro, *Origin*, pp. 288–9.
144 From the CCC's initial circular to party members cited in Carr, *Bolshevik Revolution*, vol. 1, p. 203.
145 *Desiatyi*, p. 577.
146 *Odinnadtsatyi*, pp. 562–3.
147 This is linked to a description of the control commissions' tasks in mid-1921 which included the cleansing of the party from alien elements. *Izv ts k*, 32 (6 August 1921), pp. 10–11.
148 Membership changed as follows:

	1920	1921	1922
Full	Dzerzhinsky	Krivov	Varentsova
	Kuchmenko	Kuchmenko	Korostelev
	Preobrazhensky	Litvin	Chentsov
	Sol'ts	Sol'ts	Sol'ts
	Chelyshev	Chelyshev	Shkiriatov
	Shorokhov	Shvarts	
		Smidovich	
Candidate	Muranov	Batyshev	Muranov
		Dogadov	Samoilov
		Ozol	

149 *Desiatyi*, p. 573.
150 *KPSS v rez*, vol. 2, p. 447.
151 'Takticheskaia platforma k ob'edinetel'nomu s'ezdu', *PSS*, vol. 12, p. 238. For a discussion of the Bolshevik tradition, see Graeme Gill, 'Bolshevism and the party form', *The Australian Journal of Politics and History*, 34, 1 (1988), pp. 51–63.
152 'Chto delat'?', *PSS*, vol. 6, p. 140.
153 *Ibid.*, pp. 24–5.
154 For example, see Israel Getzler, *Martov. A political biography of a Russian Social Democrat* (Cambridge University Press, 1967), p. 82 and J. L. H. Keep, *The rise of Social Democracy in Russia* (Oxford: Clarendon Press, 1963), pp. 96, 109.
155 For example, the III Congress in May 1905 and the VI (Prague) Conference in January 1912.
156 For example, after Lenin gained control of the leading party organs at the V Congress in 1907.
157 The quotation from Lasalle which Lenin placed at the beginning of 'What is to be Done?' indicates his position: 'Party struggle lends a party strength and vitality; the greatest proof of a party's weakness is its diffuseness and the blurring of clear demarcations; a party becomes stronger by purging itself.' *PSS*, vol. 6, p. 1.
158 Even the Mensheviks concentrated most of their attention on outmanoeuvring Lenin inside the party rather than seeking to exclude him. Apparently Martov did favour expulsion at the time of the expropriation issue in 1908–1909, but he was opposed in this by the remainder of the Menshevik leadership. Getzler, *Martov*, pp. 120–3, 128–32.
159 For example, the Bolshevik newspaper *Pravda* established just after the conference remained outside Lenin's control throughout 1912 and fostered moves for a closer relationship with the Mensheviks by proposing to merge itself with the Menshevik newspaper *Luch*. Elwood, *Social Democracy*, pp. 211–14.
160 'Izveshchenie o III s'ezde rossiiskoi sotsial-demokraticheskoi rabochei partii', *PSS*, vol. 10, pp. 206–7.
161 'A sud'i kto?', *PSS*, vol. 16, pp. 164–5 and 'Izveshchenie o soveshchanii rasshirennoi redaktsii "Proletariia"', *PSS*, vol. 19, pp. 6–7.
162 This was introduced into the party Rules adopted in 1906, although no explanation of its meaning was given in those Rules.
163 For one definition, see the X Congress resolution on party construction which defined it in terms of the active participation of all party members in the discussion and resolution of all issues coming before the party, the election of all institutions from the bottom to the top and the accountability and responsibility of all bodies. Appointment 'as a system' was explicitly excluded. *KPSS v rez*, vol. 2, p. 327.
164 Their full programme was much more extensive than this. It included the replacement of appointment by election as the means of filling offices, widespread rank-and-file debate on all issues before decisions were made and the granting of full rein to local initiative by the workers. See

Alexandra Kollontai, *The workers' opposition* (London: London Solidarity Pamphlet 7, 1968). On privileges, see Bazhanov, *Vospominaniia*, p. 14.

165 For an outline of these views, see the speeches by Osinsky and Sapronov at the VIII Congress, *Vos'moi*, pp. 27–8, 164–7, 169–71, 187–97, 201–4, 216–18, 303–17, 319–22, and of these two plus Maksimovsky at the IX Congress, *Deviatyi*, pp. 48–53, 115–27, 139–42, 182–8, 318–30, 350–3. Bureaucratism was also one aspect of their opposition to Trotsky's militarisation proposals. At the IX Congress Osinsky declared: 'Under the flag of militarisation, you spread bureaucratism.' *Deviatyi*, p. 118.

166 *Deviatyi*, p. 85.

167 See Lenin's addresses to the X Congress. *Desiatyi*, pp. 27–9, 118–22.

168 For example, *KPSS v rez*, vol. 2, pp. 297–8.

169 For example, see #9 of the IX Conference resolution 'On the Current Tasks of Party Construction', *KPSS v rez*, vol. 2, pp. 299–300. Later in the same resolution it is declared that repression for divergent views is impermissible (p. 300). However the X Congress resolution 'On Party Unity' declared that such intra-party criticism should not take place on the basis of 'some "platform" or other'. *Desiatyi*, pp. 572–3.

170 #50.

171 For example, the X Congress resolution 'On the Question of Party Construction', *Desiatyi*, p. 563.

172 For example, see the CC appeal of 22 May 1918, *KPSS v rez*, vol. 2, p. 64.

173 This is not to say that party leaders at various levels did not take conscious decisions to structure political life in this way.

174 For a discussion of the Brest-Litovsk issue, see Daniels, *Conscience*, ch. 3 and Schapiro, *Origin*, ch. 6. The most concise outline of Left Communist theses appeared in the Moscow-based journal *Kommunist*, 20 April 1918, pp. 4–9. An abbreviated translation will be found in Bunyan and Fisher, *Bolshevik Revolution*, pp. 560–5.

175 Schapiro, *Origin*, ch. 8 and Daniels, *Conscience*, pp. 104–7.

176 Schapiro, *Origin*, chs. 14 and 15 and Daniels, *Conscience*, ch. 5.

177 For example, at the VIII Congress where the Military Opposition was defeated, only 3.2% of delegates with a full vote came from party organisations in the army (where the Military Opposition was concentrated), and yet this group constituted 9.8% of those with a consultative vote. The main spokesmen for the Military Opposition, Smirnov, Sapronov, Voroshilov and Yaroslavsky had only a consultative vote.

178 *Sed'moi*, p. 221.

179 Lenin's comment was in response to an amendment proposed by Riazanov that sought to express official disapproval of election to the congress by platform. *Desiatyi*, pp. 539–40.

180 This journal, *Kommunist*, was issued under the aegis of the Moscow Oblast Bureau. For a discussion of the nature of their regional support, see Ronald J. Kowalski, 'The Left Communism movement of 1918: a preliminary analysis of its regional strength', *Sbornik*, 12 (1986), pp. 27–63. Kowalski argues that perceptions of Left Communist strength in Moscow are exaggerated.

181 *Desiatyi*, p. 118.
182 *Ibid.*, pp. 574–6.
183 No post-October CC plenum had mounted such attacks. The VII Congress had passed a resolution 'On the Refusal of the "Left Communists" to Join the CC', but this was not a systematic attack on their views and contained no threat of party exclusion.
184 *Desiatyi*, pp. 571–3.
185 The first major application of this occurred at the XI Congress in regard to the Workers' Opposition and their appeal, as the 'Declaration of the 22', to the Executive Committee of the Comintern. The XI Congress resolution specifically declared that their making of such a declaration was not to be condemned, but that what was at issue was the perpetuation of a fractional grouping following the X Congress. This was reflected in secret meetings and both covert and overt criticism of party policy, to the joy and comfort of enemies abroad. Also, in a move which was to be extended and made more meaningful later in the decade, Shliapnikov and Medvedev were criticised for failing to raise for discussion in the CC the letters of 'the most anti-party character' which they received from their Workers' Opposition confederates. This charge is consistent with Lenin's declaration at the IX Congress: 'A good communist is at the same time a good chekist.' *Deviatyi*, p. 377. However the only two people expelled from the party formally were dismissed for organisation of a fractional group (Mitin) and for being an element alien to the proletariat (Kuznetsov). *Odinnadtsatyi*, pp. 577–80.
186 The 'On Party Unity' resolution referred to 'groups with their own platforms and with the will to close ranks to a certain extent and to create their own group discipline'. *Desiatyi*, p. 571. In practice, the distinction between a fraction and a faction was not as clear cut as the subsequent text suggests. For example, a faction in the CC may consist of a combination of regional party leaders and some from the central apparatus.
187 'On the Question of Party Construction', *Desiatyi*, p. 563.
188 The resolution 'On the Syndicalist and Anarchist Deviation in Our Party' is particularly clear in drawing a link between opposition inside and outside the party, and the way in which the former 'in practice' helped the latter. *Desiatyi*, p. 576.
189 At least no one speaking at the XI Congress charged that it had been used against them or their supporters, although Molotov did declare that, following the purge, the 'numerous currents and semi-formed factions do not exist'. *Odinnadtsatyi*, pp. 46–7. However in February 1922 Miasnikov was expelled for continued oppositional activity.
190 *KPSS v rez*, vol. 2, p. 442.
191 For example, *Odinnadtsatyi*, pp. 54, 126–7, 155, 175–6, 183–4. Workers' Opposition members were also sent on assignments far from Moscow to remove them from political life.
192 Cited in Daniels, *Conscience*, p. 76. There were rumours during 1918 and explicit charges made at the third purge trial in 1938 (in which Bukharin was a defendant) that negotiations took place between the Left Commun-

ists and the Left SRs to combine to reverse the Brest-Litovsk decision. Daniels (*Conscience*, pp. 89–90) gives credence to the story but his discussion is unconvincing. No hard evidence to support this charge has been forthcoming.
193 *Odinnadtsatyi*, pp. 577–80. See pp. 174–7 for the CCC discussion of this episode.
194 For example, see the CC appeal of 22 May 1918, *KPSS v rez*, vol. 2, p. 64.
195 In particular, Stalin and Zinoviev tried to use Trotsky's proposals for the militarisation of labour as a means of discrediting him in leading circles. This is discussed in Schapiro, *Origin*, pp. 257–61.
196 Rigby, *Sovnarkom*, p. 73.
197 The concentration of his activities in Sovnarkom may have left him somewhat out of touch with political realities in the party. It was not until his active political life had ended that he recognised that the course of development the party was following portended grave problems for the future. In particular, see his so-called 'last letters and articles', *PSS*, vol. 45, pp. 343–406. He also confessed to being unaware of central aspects of the Orgburo and the Secretariat, although this was after illness had removed him from the scene for some time. *PSS*, vol. 53, p. 300; vol. 54, p. 243. On his ability to use the Maly Sovnarkom as an instrument of control over the full Sovnarkom, see Rigby, *Sovnarkom*, pp. 34–6, 76–83.
198 Schapiro, *Origin*, p. 287.
199 Kollontai, *Workers' Opposition*, p. 48.
200 See the comments in Paul Avrich, *Kronstadt 1921* (New York: W. W. Norton, 1974), pp. 176–8. For Lenin's disapproval of such a development, see R. A. Medvedev. *K sudu istorii. Genezis i posledstviia Stalinizma* (New York: Alfred A. Knopf, 1974), pp. 306–7.
201 For example, see Fitzpatrick, *Commissariat*, p. 270. For a discussion of Lenin's role in foreign affairs, see Uldricks, *Diplomacy*, pp. 121–2. For Lenin being defeated in the CC, see Marcel Liebman, *Leninism under Lenin* (London: Merlin Press, 1975), p. 308. For Lenin's (perhaps unconscious) justification, see his statements from 28 April 1918 and 31 March 1920 respectively: 'In the history of revolutionary movements the dictatorship of single individuals has often been the expression, the vehicle, the channel, of the dictatorship of revolutionary classes ... Therefore there is decidedly no inconsistency in principle between Soviet (ie. socialist) democracy and the assumption of dictatorial power by individual persons'; and 'Soviet socialist democracy is not in the least incompatible with individual rule and dictatorship. The will of a class may sometimes be carried out by a dictator who can sometimes do more all by himself and who is frequently more essential.' *PSS*, vol. 36, p. 199; vol. 40, p. 272.
202 On 26 May 1922 Lenin suffered his first stroke, remaining in convalescence outside Moscow until 2 October. He suffered a second stroke in mid-December 1922 which rendered him unfit for regular work. He suffered a totally disabling stroke in March 1923.

3 A strong party structure?

1 In May 1924 their inability to play a major role in the political life of the country was acknowledged. *Trinadtsatyi s'ezd RKP(b). Mai 1924 goda. Stenograficheskii otchet* (Moscow, 1963), p. 793. Compare this with the assessment given at the XII Conference in August 1922 in the resolution 'On anti-Soviet parties and tendencies', *Kommunisticheskaia partiia sovetskogo soiuza v rezoliutsiiakh i resheniiakh s'ezdov, konferentsii i plenumov Ts. K.* (Moscow, 1983), vol. 2, pp. 587–93 (hereafter *KPSS v rez*). For the treatment of some of those arrested, see E. H. Carr, *Socialism in one country*, vol. 2 (Harmondsworth: Penguin, 1970), pp. 475–81.

2 The most important instances of organised political opposition took place in 1922–23 with the two underground groups, Workers' Truth and Workers' Group. Both gained adherents inside the party and both sought to use the industrial unrest of 1922 to mid–1923 to advance their causes. The former, which had actually emerged in 1921, consisted mainly of intellectuals, grew out of the Proletkult movement and was inspired by the views of Bogdanov. Its chief spokesman was the veteran party oppositionist Osinsky. The Workers' Group movement was more proletarian in composition and was headed by Miasnikov, who was expelled from the party in 1922 following the appeal of the Twenty-two to the Comintern. This group circulated its platform, anonymously, at the XII Congress of the party in April 1923. Both groups mounted a leftist critique of trends within the regime, based upon demands for a greater role by the proletariat. The significance of these groups from the perspective of the party leadership was that they sought to tap into the discontent evident among urban workers at this time and therefore potentially posed a threat to the social basis upon which the party sought to stand. The leadership reacted by mobilising the CCC against possible adherents inside the party and the GPU against those outside. Party members who joined these groups were expelled and then arrested. For contemporary discussions of these groups, see *Dvenadtsatyi s'ezd RKP(b) 17–25 aprelia 1923 goda. Stenograficheskii otchet* (Moscow, 1968), pp. 52, 120, 159 and *Trinadtsatyi*, pp. 265, 793. Also see Robert Vincent Daniels, *The conscience of the Revolution. Communist opposition in Soviet Russia* (New York: Simon and Schuster, 1969), pp. 160–1, 204–5 and E. H. Carr, *The interregnum 1923–1924* (Harmondsworth: Penguin, 1969), p. 88–92, 276–8, 300–1.

3 This does not mean the party was in imminent danger of being toppled. All who could post a direct threat to the party's continued hold on power were dealt with by the Cheka or its lineal descendants, the State Political Administration (GPU) from 1922 and Unified State Political Administration (OGPU) from 1924. Acting in a world where supervision was weak and justification on vague grounds of defence of 'the revolutionary order' or 'state security' was easy, the powers of this body expanded during this period. But even so, during the 1920s its actions directly affected a small proportion of the population, at least prior to the extraordinary measures of 1928. While the range of groups subjected to repression by the OGPU was extensive, including religious believers, certain sections of dissident

national groups, some students, former nobles, former White officers and their supporters, former members of political parties, some intellectuals, 'wreckers', those refusing to assist the security apparatus in its tasks, and some political opposition in the party, in comparison with what it was to become, its role was modest. Accurate figures are impossible to obtain, but one source suggests a total of 30,000 prisoners in OGPU camps in 1928 and a total of six camps in 1930. David J. Dallin and Boris Nicolaevsky, *Forced labor in Soviet Russia* (London: Hollis and Carter, 1948), p. 52. For a debate on the size of the camp population, see the exchange among Steven Rosefielde, Stephen Wheatcroft and Robert Conquest in various issues of *Soviet Studies*, 1981–83. Also see the discussions in Alexander Solzhenitsyn, *The Gulag Archipelago 1918–1956* (London: Collins, 1974), vol. 1, ch. 2 and D. L. Golinkov, *Krushenie antisovetskogo podpol'ia v SSSR* (Moscow, 1978), vol. 2.
4 *Trinadtsatyi*, p. 116. By 1925 these figures had declined respectively to 6.5%, 44%, 73% and 79%. *XIV s'ezd vsesoiuznoi kommunisticheskoi partii (b) 18–31 dekabria 1925g. Stenograficheskii otchet* (Moscow, 1926), p. 66. The figures for volost and above overstate the number of communists in the soviet as a whole (the figure for which the village soviet applies) because of greater efforts to ensure communist dominance of the executive committees than of the plena. Compare with the figures in Carr, *Socialism*, vol. 2, p. 333.
5 *Trinadtsatyi*, p. 471.
6 Merle Fainsod, *Smolensk under Soviet rule* (New York: Vintage Books, 1958), p. 44.
7 Carr, *Socialism*, vol. 2, p. 332.
8 ibid., pp. 332–3. Also see figures in T. H. Rigby, *Communist Party membership in the USSR 1917–1967* (Princeton University Press, 1968), pp. 133–5. At the XIV Congress, Stalin declared that the proportion of communists among the peasantry had risen from 0.26% in 1924 to 0.37% at the time of the congress. *XIV s'ezd*, p. 53.
9 *Dvenadtsatyi*, p. 39.
10 *Izvestiia tsentral'nogo komiteta rossiiskoi kommunisticheskoi partii (bol'shevikov)*, 35(255) (22 November 1928), p. 9 (hereafter *Izv ts k*) E. H. Carr, *Foundations of a planned economy 1926–1929* (Harmondsworth: Penguin, 1976), vol. 2, pp. 130, 188–9; Rigby, *Communist Party*, p. 418. Also see R. W. Davies, *The industrialisation of Soviet Russia*. vol. 1. *The socialist offensive. The collectivisation of Soviet agriculture 1929–1930* (London: Macmillan, 1980), pp. 51–2.
11 *KPSS v rez*, vol. 4, pp. 392–3.
12 Carr suggests that about half of all party members in soviet organs in 1923 were appointed by the centre and therefore presumably lacked local knowledge. Carr, *Socialism*, vol. 2, pp. 333–4. For a decision to send some 6,000 workers into the countryside in 1925, see the CC's circular to all party organisations and members dated 10 August 1925 reporting an earlier decision of the XIV Conference, *KPSS v rez*, vol. 3, pp. 403–5.
13 For example, see Stalin's proposal at the XII Congress to establish a school to train uezd party secretaries. *Dvenadtsatyi*, pp. 66–7. On rural cadres, see

M. Lewin, *Russian peasants and Soviet power. A study of collectivisation* (London: Allen and Unwin, 1968), pp. 119–27.
14 According to Carr, of party members in the countryside in 1924, only 35% were actively engaged in agricultural work and only 15% exclusively in it. Carr, *Socialism*, vol. 2, pp. 332–3. Also see Carr, *Foundations*, pp. 118–9. According to Rigby, in 1924 only 20% to 30% of members of rural cells were working peasants; many cells consisted entirely of people holding administrative or other non-manual jobs. According to a report from 1925, as little as 2% to 3% may have been wholly engaged in agriculture. Rigby, *Membership*, pp. 134, 135.
15 *Trinadtsatyi*, pp. 471–2.
16 For the term, see *KPSS v rez*, vol. 4, p. 393.
17 *KPSS v rez*, vol. 4, p. 393. Also see *Pravda*, 23 May 1929, cited in Davies, *Industrialisation*, pp. 52–3. One study gives some force to this view by showing how peasant members of the party generally tended to be wealthier in terms of ownership of the means of production than their non-party colleagues. A. Gaister and A. Levin, 'O sostave sel'skikh partorganizatsii', *Bol'shevik*, 9–10 (31 May 1929), pp. 75–90. The charge was particularly forcefully put at the time of the Smolensk scandal in 1928. Daniel R. Brower, 'The Smolensk scandal and the end of NEP', *Slavic Review*, 45, 4 (Winter 1986), pp. 689–706.
18 M. Khatsaevich, 'O sostave i rabote partiiacheiki na sele', *Bol'shevik*, 3–4 (1925), pp. 74–5. Also see the discussion in Fainsod, *Smolensk*, pp. 54–5.
19 For example, see *Trinadtsatyi*, p. 474; *KPSS v rez*, vol. 4, pp. 392–3; Carr, *Socialism*, vol. 1, p. 253; Carr, *Socialism*, vol. 2, pp. 334, 341–2; E. H. Carr and R. W. Davies, *Foundations of a planned economy 1926–1929*, (Harmondsworth: Penguin, 1974), vol. 1, pp. 159–62; Carr, *Foundations*, vol. 2, p. 190; *Dvenadtsatyi*, p. 432; and Rigby, *Membership*, pp. 170–1.
20 In 1927, 95% of agricultural land in the RSFSR remained in the traditional land commune. Carr and Davies, *Foundations*, vol. 1, p. 126. In 1926, 90% of peasants remained in the mir and the skhod continued to resolve most questions in the village. Lewin, *Russian Peasants*, pp. 26, 85–93. Beginning in that year, the Bolsheviks sought, unsuccessfully, to incorporate the skhod into the soviet network. See the discussions in Carr, *Socialism*, vol. 2, pp. 378–9 and Carr, *Foundations*, pp. 252–62.
21 See the discussion in Carr, *Socialism*, vol. 2, pp. 356–63. Carr argues that the campaign for 'the revitalisation of the soviets' was an important factor in increasing the power and influence of the kulaks, *ibid.*, ch. 22
22 Perhaps the most important was the attempt to 'revitalise the soviets' as part of the 'Face to the Countryside' campaign launched by Zinoviev in October 1924 and ending in mid-1926. This was an attempt to make the soviets more effective by increasing their links with non-party people, and achieved some limited success. For the October 1924 CC decision on improving work in the countryside, see *KPSS v rez*, vol. 3, pp. 299–304. For a discussion of the progress of this policy in the light of the 1926 elections, see the joint CC–CCC resolution 'Ob itogakh perevyborov sovetov', *KPSS v rez*, vol. 4, pp. 36–48. Also see Carr, *Socialism*, vol. 2, ch. 22 and Carr,

Foundations, vol. 2, pp. 483–92. The concern about rural administration is reflected in the attempts to strengthen the personnel of rural organs much more than in the towns. For a discussion of changing personnel levels, see Stephen Sternheimer, 'Administration for development: the emerging bureaucratic elite 1920–1930', Walter McKenzie Pinter and Don Karl Rowney, eds., *Russian officialdom. The bureaucratization of Russian society from the seventeenth to the twentieth century* (London: Macmillan, 1980), pp. 322–8, 337. Also see the discussion in Olga Narkiewicz, *The making of the Soviet state apparatus* (Manchester University Press, 1970).

23 Rigby, *Membership*, p. 52.
24 Recruitment policy was also directly shaped by the tactics of different groupings in the leadership, and in particular Stalin whose control in the apparatus enabled him to influence very substantially the actions of lower level party organs in this regard. The focus upon worker recruitment during the Lenin Enrolment was designed in part to outflank Trotsky who got little support from workers (his main support came from youth and government employees), while the mass intake of peasants in 1925–26 was directed against the Left. See *ibid.*, ch. 4.
25 *KPSS v rez*, vol. 3, pp. 157–8. As an indication of the proletarianising effect of the Lenin Enrolment, Stalin gave the following statistics on the social class of party members:

	Excluding Lenin Enrolment	Including Lenin Enrolment
Workers	45.7%	55.4%
Peasants	24.6%	23.0%
Employees	29.0%	21.6%

Source: Trinadtsatyi, p. 116.

26 For an instance of this emphasis upon the countryside, see the decision of the XIV Conference in April 1925, 'On Party Construction', KPSS v rez, vol. 3, pp. 353–68.
27 For a discussion of these trends, see Rigby, *Membership*, chs. 3, 4, 5. Representation of both groups expanded, at least in terms of current occupations of party members:

workers	18.8% (1924)	44% (1929)
individual & collective farmers	9.5% (1925)	13% (1929)

Source: Rigby, *Membership*, p. 116.

Success is also reflected in the results of the 1927 party census which shows that former workers constituted 49% of those in responsible positions in the party apparatus compared with 35% in the government and soviet bureaucracy. *Bol'shevik*, 15 (1928), p. 20. Although these figures may not be completely accurate, they are suggestive of increased peasant and particularly worker enrolment during this period, at the expense prin-

cipally of white collar workers. The result is less clear if one looks at class origin. On this basis the proportion of workers increased from 44.9% in 1923 to 61.4% in 1929, but that of peasants fell from 25.7% in 1923 to 21.7% in 1929. As the table in Rigby, *Membership*, (p. 116) shows, these trends were subject to fluctuations.
28 For a succinct discussion of changing admission criteria, see Carr, *Socialism*, vol. 2, pp. 198–201. Formal changes can be seen by comparing the party Rules of 1925 with those of 1922,.
29 Carr, *Foundations*, vol. 2, p. 114. At the XIII Congress it was stated that only 7% of workers were communists, a figure which had risen to 8% by the time of the XIV Congress. Rigby, *Membership*, pp. 151–2. Also see note 14 above. Party saturation was higher among those in responsible posts. Among enterprise directors, the proportion of party members rose from 29% in 1923 to 89% in 1928. Nicholas Lampert, *The technical intelligentsia and the Soviet state. A study of Soviet managers and technicians 1928–1935* (London: Macmillan, 1979), p. 23.
30 Hiroaki Kuromiya, *Stalin's industrial revolution. Politics and workers, 1928–1932* (Cambridge University Press, 1988), ch. 4.
31 On Shakhty, see Kendall E. Bailes, *Technology and society under Lenin and Stalin. Origins of the Soviet technical intelligentsia 1917–1941* (Princeton University Press, 1978), ch. 3; Sheila Fitzpatrick, *Education and social mobility in the Soviet Union 1921–1934* (Cambridge University Press, 1979), ch. 6; and Michal Reiman, *The Birth of Stalinism. The USSR on the eve of the 'Second Revolution'* (Bloomington: Indiana University Press, 1987), pp. 58–65.
32 The party's limitations are reflected in the way in which special plenipotentiaries were used for grain procurement programmes towards the end of the decade and mass mobilisation was used to achieve party aims in the factories. See Kuromiya, *Industrial revolution*, p. 199. On collectivisation and the mobilisation of urban workers, see Lynne Viola, *The best sons of the Fatherland. Workers in the vanguard of Soviet collectivization* (Oxford University Press, 1987), esp. ch. 3.
33 This figure is compiled from data presented in Rigby, pp. 127, 157, 178–9 and Carr, *Foundations*, vol. 2, p. 139. Also see Rigby, p. 352, where he presents figures which show that between 1920 and 1927 299,000 left the party, and *KPSS v rez*, vol. 4, p. 485 where a figure of 260,144 expelled and left voluntarily between 1922 and 1928 is cited.
34 This may need to be qualified for those who had participated in the Civil War. However it is likely that most of the Civil War militants had joined the party at that time rather than waiting until some years after the end of that conflict.
35 Cited in Rigby, *Membership*, p. 172.
36 *Dvenadtsatyi*, p. 147 where Sorin cites a figure of about 10,000 Old Bolsheviks.
37 Rigby, *Membership*, pp. 351, 352. Of some 18,000 rural cells at the beginning of 1928, 58.4% of members of cell bureaux and 56.9% of cell secretaries had been recruited in 1924 and after. *Izvestiia tsentral'nogo komiteta*

rossiiskoi kommunisticheskoi partii (bol'shevikov) 14(235), 28 April 1928, p. 20 (hereafter Izv ts k).
38 Dvenadtsatyi, p. 73.
39 For a discussion of such efforts, see Carr, Socialism, vol. 2, pp. 203–13. See p. 202 for some figures on political illiteracy.
40 Izv ts k, 32–3(205–6) (31 August 1927), p. 4. For a discussion, see pp. 1–4.
41 Rigby, Membership, p. 401.
42 ibid., p. 402.
43 ibid., pp. 403–5.
44 For example, at the XIII Congress it was decided that guberniia secretaries were to have six years' party membership instead of the former pre-October provision. Trinadtsatyi, p. 617.
45 Both terms, 'proverka' and 'chistka', were used to refer to the verification of government and higher educational cells in the XIII Congress resolution on the control commissions. Trinadtsatyi, p. 623. The absence of a clear distinction in the use of the terms is also evident in the resolution on party construction adopted by the XIV Conference in April 1925 which refers to 'general party verifications (proverki) and purges (chistki)' as 'exceptional measures' compared with the 'daily and systematic purging (ochistki) of the organisation of dissolute, unsteadfast and discredited elements'. KPSS v rez, vol. 3, p. 362.
46 Trinadtsatyi, pp. 840–1, note 113.
47 See Rigby, Membership, pp. 128, 172, 176–7 and Carr, Foundations, vol. 2, ch. 43.
48 Rigby, Membership, pp. 97, 178–9. Actually in the latter some 170,000, or 11%, were excluded, but this figure was reduced to that cited in the text by subsequent appeals and rehabilitations. For the earlier figure, see Partiinoe stroitel'stvo, 11–12(13–14) (June 1930), pp. 18, 26. This source also cites a figure of 30.3% excluded in the 1921–22 purge, which also fell heavily on the rural apparatus; 44.7% of rural communists were purged. Viola, Sons, p. 13. For the effect of the 1929–30 purge, see ibid., pp. 77, 129–31.
49 Dvenadtsatyi, pp. 793–4.
50 KPSS v rez, vol. 4, p. 489.
51 XVI s'ezd vsesoiuznoi kommunisticheskoi partii (b). Stenograficheskii otchet (Moscow, 1931), p. 340.
52 Trinadtsatyi, pp. 192–3, 223.
53 KPSS v rez, vol. 4, p. 490. See the discussion of this in regard to the 1929–30 purge in J. Arch Getty, Origins of the Great Purges. The Soviet Communist Party reconsidered 1933–1938 (Cambridge University Press, 1985), pp. 46–7.
54 Piatnadtsatyi s'ezd VKP(b). Dekabr' 1927 goda. Stenograficheskii otchet (Moscow, 1961), vol. 1, pp. 536–9 and XVI s'ezd, p. 340. According to Getty, those expelled for 'fractional activity' constituted 10% of the 10% of those expelled for violation of party discipline ie.1% of all those expelled. Getty, Origins, p. 46. An interesting figure came to light at the Moscow provincial party conference in February 1929 where Yaroslavsky reported that of those arraigned for drunkenness, 24% were expelled while such a fate befell 52% of those charged with fractional activity. Carr, Foundations, vol. 2, p. 151.

55 The XII Congress candidly acknowledged that rural party cells lacked the necessary organisational forces for the conduct of party work inside the cells themselves. *Dvenadtsatyi*, p. 721.
56 Getty, *Origins*, p. 36. This comment refers to the 1930s, but it was just as true of the earlier decade.
57 For example, see *Izv ts k*, 7(43) (July 1922), p. 21. For a complaint about the general quality of personnel, see 4(62) (April 1924), p. 19.
58 *Izv ts k*, 10–11(131–2) (27 March 1926), p. 3.
59 *Izv ts k*, 37–8(210–11) (8 October 1927), pp. 3–7. A survey of 90% of all kraikoms, national CCs, obkoms and okrugkoms for the first half of 1927 gave the following number of meetings:

	Plenum	Bureau and Presidium	Secretariat
Jan–March	169	1710	1167
April–June	94	1724	1135
Total	263	3434	2302

The plena handled an average of four to five questions per session, bureaux seven to eight and secretariats ten to twelve.
60 For a CC decision of 2 July 1926 on the state of information flow in the party and measures to improve it, see *KPSS v rez*, vol. 4, pp. 33–5.
61 *Izv ts k*, 5(226) (22 February 1928), p. 10 on workloads. For a CC decision on staffing norms in lower committees, see *Izv ts k*, 27(248) (10 September 1928), pp. 1–8. Also see *XVI s'ezd*, p. 93.
62 *Izv ts k*, 3(51) (March 1923), p. 33.
63 For example, see the exchange of views in *Pravda*, 17 July 1923, 20 July 1923, 21 July 1923, 22 July 1923, 25 July 1923, 28 July 1923, 2 Aug. 1923.
64 *Izv ts k*, 12–13(133–4) (5 April 1926), pp. vi–x; 14(135) (12 April 1926), p. 1.
65 *ibid.*, 31–2(152–3) (9 August 1926), p. 8.
66 *ibid.*, 45–6(166–7) (22 November 1926), p. 6.
67 *ibid.*, 5–6(178–9) (14 February 1927), pp. 13–14.
68 See the CC decision of 27 June 1927, *ibid.*, 29(202) (30 July 1927), pp. 6–7.
69 In any case any such formal guarantees would have been seriously weakened by the contingent nature of rules discussed earlier.
70 Carr, *Socialism*, vol. 2, pp. 243–4. For a discussion of the role of local leaders in politics in Siberia, see J. R. Hughes, 'The Irkutsk affair: Stalin, Siberian politics and the end' (sic), *Soviet Studies*, 41, 2(April 1989), pp. 228–53.
71 This could be one reason for the excessive nature of the nomenklatura lists of some party organisations noted above. For a CC instruction calling on local organs to make use of people transferred to them and to accept them as their own, see *Izv ts k*, 16–17(237–8) (25 May 1928), p. 10.
72 For example, see the statements by Komarov, Uglanov and Voroshilov at the XIV Congress, *XIV s'ezd*, pp. 221, 193, 394. The point of these was Zinoviev's control in Leningrad. Also see *KPSS v rez*, vol. 4, pp. 441–2.

73 *Izv ts k*, 8(229) (15 March 1928), pp. 4, 9–10.
74 For example, see *Izv ts k*, 9–10(57–58) (October–November 1923), pp. 20–1; 8(229) (15 March 1928), pp. 4–5, 9–11; 16(275) (14 June 1929), pp. 13–14. Corruption and illegality are reflected in the charges against many of those rural officials expelled in the 1929–30 purge. Lewin, p. 126.
75 On Dymovka, see Carr, *Socialism*, vol. 1, p. 213, on Smolensk see Fainsod, *Smolensk*, pp. 48–52, Narkiewicz, *Making*, pp. 162–73 and Brower, 'Smolensk' and on Artemovsk see *Izv ts k*, 8(229) (15 March 1928), pp. 4, 9–10. There is no discussion of this in English.
76 For example, see *Dvenadtsatyi*, pp. 796–801. For Stalin's oblique acknowledgement that this practice could stimulate squabbling in the local organs, see *Dvenadtsatyi*, pp. 65–6.
77 For example, the case of Sultan Galiev, *KPSS v rez*, vol. 3, pp. 130–2.
78 Cited by Max Schachtman, 'The struggle for the New Course', published in a single volume with his translation of Trotsky's 'The New Course', Leon Trotsky, *The New Course and the struggle for the New Course* (Ann Arbor: University of Michigan Press, 1965), p. 154. The letter to the CC from which this comes, dated 8 October 1923, has never been published in full.
79 *Trinadtsatyi*, p. 148.
80 Cited in Carr, *Foundations*, vol. 2, p. 130. The remark was purported to have been made to a joint Politburo–CCC Presidium meeting in January–February 1929.
81 The position was probably more complicated with regard to the Right because there may have been support from those in the rural areas for a continuation of the policies of NEP rather than the more militant line of the Left. See below.
82 This is from the decision of a joint Politburo–CCC Presidium meeting dated 5 December 1923. *Izv ts k*, 1(59) (January 1924), p. 7.
83 *XIV s'ezd*, p. 86. For the type of more general treatment referred to above, see the resolution on the CC's report on p. 963.
84 *Izv ts k*, 10–11(131–2) (22 March 1926), pp. 3–5.
85 The first could occur through the process of confirmation, the second could be a means of ensuring the continuation of a local clique, while the third could be the means of getting such a clique into power. For a discussion, see *Izv ts k*, 19–20(140–1) (24 May 1926), p. 1 and 40–1(161–2) (12 October 1926), p. 5.
86 For example, see the comment in the report on the state of intra-party democracy in Viatka: 'Preliminary discussion in cells of the lists for the future ukom or raikom reduces the interest of members of the conference in the elections for the raikom at the conference itself.' *Izv ts k*, 31–2(152–3) (9 August 1926), p. 6.
87 *ibid.*, 47–8(168–9) (3 December 1926), p. 6.
88 *ibid.*, 5–6(178–9) (14 February 1927), p. 16.
89 For example, see Molotov's speech, *Piatnadtsatyi*, pp. 1174–229. The Smolensk scandal was important here by highlighting the poor performance of sub-national leaders and emphasising the links they had with alien elements in the countryside. Brower, 'Smolensk'.

90 While on his grain procurement trip to Siberia in January 1928, Stalin virtually accused local leaders of sabotage and of having links with the kulaks. *Works*, vol. 11, pp. 5–6. His comments were not published at the time. However, in a letter dated 13 February and sent to all party secretaries, Stalin acknowledged that the centre had some responsibility for the current difficulties in grain procurement, but still demanded in a peremptory tone that the secretaries improve their performance and end the distortions and abuses of official policy for which they were responsible. Furthermore he declared that those 'alien' elements who had penetrated the party and sought 'to live in peace with the kulak' should be purged from the party. *Works*, vol. 11, pp. 12–22. Also see the CC resolution of April 1928, 'O khlebozagotovkakh tekushchego goda i ob organizatsii khlebozagotovitel'noi kampanii na 1928/29 god, *KPSS v rez*, vol. 4, pp. 315–23. For a complaint that some party organisations were hindering GPU efforts at grain procurement, see the document in Reiman, *Birth*, p. 157. There is some dispute over the authenticity of the documents reproduced in this book. In August 1928 Stalin wrote to lower level party officials threatening severe sanctions against their involvement in anti-semitic activity. *Ibid.*, p. 57.

91 For example, see *Izv ts k*, 14–15(187–8) (21 April 1927), p. 8 and Stalin's comments at the XV Congress, *Piatnadtsatyi*, pp. 80–1. For earlier references, see *KPSS v rez*, vol. 2, pp. 299–300 (IX Conference); and 327, 336 (X Congress).

92 *Bol'shevik*, 11 (15 June 1928), pp. 3–7. See the earlier editorial in number 10 (31 May 1928), pp. 3–7.

93 *Izv ts k*, 31(235) (21 October 1928), pp. 3–5. For the argument that the self-criticism campaign was directed specifically against industrial managers, see Kuromiya, *Industrial Revolution*, p. 76.

94 For example, *Izv ts k*, 37–8(258–9) (31 December 1928), p. 11; 2–3(261–2) (31 January 1929), p. 6; 10(269) (12 April 1929), pp. 5–6; 17–18(276–7 (29 June 1929), p. 2.

95 Such reports occurred in most issues of *Izv ts k*, during 1929. For example, see 13(272) (15 May 1929), pp. 24–5; 16(275) (14 June 1929) pp. 13–14; 20–1(279–80) (29 July 1929), pp. 10–16; 22(281) (10 August 1929), pp. 4–17.

96 *Partiinoe stroitel'stvo*, 11–12(13–14) (June 1930), p. 34. On turnover of rural soviet chairmen, see Lewin, *Russian Peasants*, p. 393.

97 According to Kosier this was happening as early as 1922. *Dvenadtsatyi*, pp. 101–3.

98 Schachtman, *New Course*, p. 154.

99 Reprinted in Carr, *Interregnum*, pp. 374–80.

100 This was despite the claims of people like Trotsky who had a personal interest in painting this type of picture.

101 In an interesting exchange at an urals party conference, one local secretary accused the Right of being out to 'get the secretaries' by blaming them for all that went wrong and questioning their mode of election. Cited in Fitzpatrick, *Russian Revolution*, p. 118.

102 According to Medvedev, during the first half of the 1920s, many of those

in the apparat regarded Stalin as 'their' man. Roy A. Medvedev, *On Stalin and Stalinism*, trans. Ellen de Kadt (Oxford University Press, 1979), p. 50.
103 On opposition to collectivisation by low level functionaries, see Fainsod, *Smolensk*, pp. 143–4, 211–20. Some regional party leaders, particularly Andreev, tried to restrain the speed of collectivisation in their regions at the November 1929 CC plenum. Davies, *Industrialisation*, p. 408. For a discussion of the nature of support for this policy, see *ibid.*, p. 399. In mid-1929, many at middle levels of the party wrote to the CC advising against the use of coercive measures against the peasants. This opposition is reflected in the fact that in December 1929 the Politburo sought to bypass the obkom/kraikom level and go straight to the okrugkom to promote speedy collectivisation. Lewin, *Russian Peasants*, pp. 310, 475.
104 This does not mean there was always a coincidence of views. For one instance of lower level uneasiness at central policies, see Carr and Davies, *Foundations*, vol. 1, p. 88. One indication of this coincidence is the figure cited by Robert Daniels: of all of those delegates listed in the protocols of the XI Congress, 16% of those in party work had engaged in oppositional activity by 1930 compared with 50% of those working in other areas. Daniels, *Conscience*, p. 170.

4 The divided elite

1 For example, see the conflicts between the Commissariat of Foreign Trade and other trading agencies over the monopoly of foreign trade in 1925–6 and between Narkomfin and Rabkrin in 1923 over their respective control functions in government departments. E. H. Carr, *The interregnum 1923–1924* (Harmondsworth: Penguin, 1969), pp. 476–81, 491–2. Also see the discussion in Stephen Blank, 'Soviet institutional development during NEP: a prelude to Stalinism', *Russian History*, 9, 2–3 (1982), pp. 325–46.
2 Some details of this can be traced in Carr, *Interregnum*, pp. 149–52 and E. H. Carr and R. W. Davies, *Foundations of a planned economy 1926–1929* (Harmondsworth: Penguin, 1974), vol. 1, chs. 12, 33, 34, 37 and pp. 777–84. For a discussion of the way in which unrealistic plan targets emerged, which reflects the part played by different government bodies and the interaction and conflict between them, see R. W. Davies and S. G. Wheatcroft, 'Further thoughts on the first Soviet Five Year Plan', *Slavic Review*, 34, 4 (December 1975), pp. 790–802. On conflict between Vesenkha and Narkompros over control of technical education in the latter half of the decade, see Sheila Fitzpatrick, *Education and social mobility in the Soviet Union 1921–1934* (Cambridge University Press, 1979), pp. 123–9.
3 E. H. Carr, *Socialism in one country 1924–1926* (Harmondsworth: Penguin, 1970), vol. 1, p. 130. For an argument that both the numbers of and fears about 'holdovers' were exaggerated, see Stephen Sternheimer, 'Administration for development: the emerging bureaucratic elite 1920–1930', Walter McKenzie Pintner and Don Karl Rowney, eds., *Russian officialdom. The bureaucratization of Russian society from the seventeenth to the twentieth century* (London: Macmillan, 1980), pp. 342–8.

4 *Trinadtsatyi s'ezd RKP(b). Mai 1924 goda. Stenograficheskii otchet* (Moscow, 1963), p. 282.
5 *Piatnadtsatyi s'ezd VKP(b). Dekabr' 1927 goda. Stenograficheskii otchet* (Moscow, 1961), vol. 1, pp. 446–7. For comparison, figures for some of the RSFSR commissariats were Narkomfin 17.0% and Narkomtrud 28.0%. Also see the discussion and figures in Sternheimer, 'Administration', pp. 337–41 and Hiroaki Kuromiya, *Stalin's industrial revolution. Politics and workers, 1928–1932* (Cambridge University Press, 1988), pp. 28–9.
6 See T. H. Rigby, *Communist Party membership in the USSR 1917–1967* (Princeton University Press, 1968), p. 420; Kuromiya, *Industrial Revolution*, p. 48; and Carr and Davies, *Foundations*, p. 132.
7 E. H. Carr, *Foundations of a planned economy 1926–1929* (Harmondsworth: Penguin, 1976), vol. 2, ch. 21; Fitzpatrick, *Education*; and Sheila Fitzpatrick, 'Stalin and the making of a new elite, 1928–1939', *Slavic Review*, 38, 3 (1979), pp. 377–402.
8 Overall figures which would enable comparison of party saturation of the state apparatus at the beginning and end of the period are not available. If the experience of Vesenkha is typical, party saturation expanded steadily: in 1923 party members constituted 5% of all officials in Vesenkha, in 1924 – 9%, in December 1925 – 14%, in April 1927 – 20% and in 1930 some 24%–25%. Rigby, *Membership*, p. 420. Party saturation was higher among 'responsible officials'. Also see Sternheimer, 'Administration', pp. 345–54.
9 Such a regularisation was also attempted in the form of bringing greater system to the structure and operation of the civil service as a whole. For one aspect of this, see Carr, *Socialism*, vol. 1, pp. 407–8.
10 The Second Congress met in January 1924, the third in May 1925, the fourth in spring 1927 and the fifth in spring 1929. TsIK met three or four times between each congress.
11 Carr, *Foundations*, p. 215.
12 Carr, *Socialism*, vol. 1, pp. 491–3 and E. H. Carr, *Socialism*, vol. 2, pp. 254-9.
13 In the conflict over target levels in 1928, TsIK was used as a means of circumventing moderate proposals emanating from Narkomzem and Gosplan. Davies and Wheatcroft, 'Further thoughts', pp. 800–1.
14 Carr, *Foundations*, p. 138. As early as 1926 a pronouncement had been issued jointly by the CC and Sovnarkom. It is also reflected, in part, in the declining frequency of meetings of Sovnarkom plena: 1923 (for five and a half months) – 24; 1924 – 55; 1925 – 62; 1926 – 53; 1927 – 50; 1928 – 43; and 1929 – 39. Ger P. van den Berg, 'The Council of Ministers of the Soviet Union', *Review of Socialist Law*, 6, 3 (1980), pp. 296, 297. Also important here was the shift of much of the workload to an executive organ, the Conference of the Chairman and Deputy Chairmen of Sovnarkom, which met frequently after its formation in 1927.
15 Conferences were held in August 1922 (XII), January 1924 (XIII), April 1925 (XIV), October-November 1926 (XV) and April 1929 (XVI).
16 A good indication of this is the fact that all decisions of the conference had to be confirmed by the CC before they became binding on the party.

Dvenadtsatyi s'ezd RKP(b) 17–25 aprelia 1923 goda. Stenograficheskii otchet (Moscow, 1968), p. 703.
17 *Dvenadtsatyi*, p. 420; *Trinadtsatyi*, p. 711; *XIV s'ezd vsesoiuznoi kommunisticheskoi partii (b) 18–31 dekabria 1925g. Stenograficheskii otchet* (Moscow, 1926), p. 810; *Piatnadtsatyi*, p. 1238. The corresponding figures for the X Congress were 24.8% and for the XVI Congress 58.2% of all delegates and 66% of full delegates. *Desiatyi s'ezd RKP(b) Mart 1921g. Stenograficheskii otchet* (Moscow, 1963), p. 762 and *XVI s'ezd vsesoiuznoi kommunisticheskoi partii (b). Stenograficheskii otchet* (Moscow, 1931), p. 599.
18 Women constituted 1% of delegates at the XII and 2.7% at the XIII Congresses. The following figures refer to the XII, XIII, XIV and XV congresses respectively. Russians comprised 60.8%, 65.2%, 61% and 62%. Official working-class background: 53%, 63.2%, 62% and 71%. Those with primary education alone constituted 49.7%, 66.8% and 66.1%; no figures were given for the XV Congress. The proportion of delegates between the ages of 30 and 39 was 52.9% (XII), 55.2% (XIII) and 62% (XV); the report at the XIV Congress gave no figures but referred to a slight increase in this age group. The older groups increased at the expense of the younger at the later congresses. The figures relate only to the voting delegates at the XII and XIII Congresses. The sources do not make this clear for the other congresses. *Dvenadtsatyi*, pp. 420–1; *Trinadtsatyi*, pp. 529–31; XIV, pp. 808–10; and *Piatnadtsatyi*, pp. 1237–40.
19 Slightly different figures emerge from analysis of the delegate lists:

	Pre-1917	1917	Post-1917
XI	49.5%	23.7%	26.6%
XII	57.5%	21.1%	21.4%
XIII	47.7%	21.4%	30.8%
XIV	45.6%	21.7%	32.7%
XV	38.6%	20.1%	41.2%

20 The formal requirements for a party conference differed, reflecting changing conceptions of that body. In the 1922 party Rules, it was to consist of representatives of party committees above the territory level, regional bureaux and political sections of the armed forces. In the 1925 Rules, the representatives were to come from local party organisations.
21 *Dvenadtsatyi*, p. 199.
22 Carr, *Interregnum*, p. 376.
23 See Kaganovich's comments at the XII Congress. *Dvenadtsatyi*, pp. 419–20. No such changes were announced at the later congresses, perhaps reflecting the increased efficiency of the selection process.
24 Carr, *Interregnum*, p. 340 and Robert Vincent Daniels, *The conscience of the Revolution Communist opposition in Soviet Russia* (New York: Simon and Schuster, 1969), p. 233.
25 Daniels, *Conscience*, p. 317.

26 For the argument that a meeting of the Moscow city party organisation on 11 December 1923 was the last occasion of full, frank and freely reported public debate which could sway party opinion, see Carr, *Interregnum*, pp. 321–2.
27 The XVI Conference was particularly important in this regard.
28 This is clearly reflected in the decision of the Politburo prior to the XIII Congress, a period when the Politburo was bitterly divided, to refrain from bitter disagreement and controversial issues at the congress. Carr, *Interregnum*, p. 25.
29 Both occurred prior to the XV Congress. Daniels, *Conscience*, p. 312 and Leonard Schapiro, *The Communist Party of the Soviet Union* (London: Methuen, 1970), p. 309.
30 For example, they were excluded from a special commission established at the XIII Congress to discuss the work of the CCC. *Trinadtsatyi*, p. 298. At the XIII Conference a proposal to add two oppositionists to the drafting commission for the resolution on the economy was rejected. Carr, *Interregnum*, p. 139.
31 Kamenev said: 'If you have instructions to interrupt me, say so openly.' *XIV s'ezd*, p. 244.
32 Somewhat surprisingly, the leadership was defeated in a vote on the congress floor on one issue at the XIII Congress. This was Molotov's proposal that guberniia conferences should meet twice per year instead of once. This was defeated by 266 votes to 259, apparently principally for technical reasons. A compromise which enabled some guberniia organisations to have only one conference per year with the approval of the CC was adopted by 322 to 246. Both votes were characterised by a large number of unexplained abstentions. Perhaps significantly, this issue was one which could directly affect the position of guberniia party leaders by increasing the occasions on which they would meet their nominal constituents. A clear instance of the imposition of monolithism on such a gathering was the refusal to allow Lominadze to move an amendment to a resolution from the floor without the prior approval of the CC. This occurred at the XVI Conference. R. W. Davies, 'The Syrtsov-Lominadze affair', *Soviet Studies*, 33 1 (January 1981), pp. 34–5.
33 *Dvenadtsatyi*, p. 768.
34 *Trinadtsatyi*, pp. 221–2.
35 It may have been this forum in which Lenin's 'Testament' was first made public just prior to the XIII Congress, although Bazhanov declares that it was an extraordinary meeting of the CC. Boris Bazhanov, *Vospominaniia byvshego sekretariia Stalina* (Paris: Tret'ia volna, 1980), p. 106.
36 Bazhanov, *Vospominaniia*, p. 128.
37 S. L. Dmitrenko, 'Ob'edinennye plenumy TsK i TsKK (1921–1933gg)', *Voprosy istorii KPSS*, 10 (1965), p. 76. Not all of these meetings were plenary in nature. Official plena are listed in *Spravochnyi tom k vos'momu izdanii 'KPSS v rezoliutsiiakh i resheniiakh s'ezdov, konferentsii i plenumov ts. k.'* (Moscow, 1984), pp. 10–11. This figure includes the closed sessions held on the eve of each congress.

38 *KPSS v rez*, vol. 2, p. 341.
39 For example, the meeting in June 1923 included representatives of national areas while the joint CC–CCC plenum of October 1926 included the Central Auditing Commission and representatives of the ECCI.
40 Zinoviev at the joint CC–CCC plenum on 19 July 1926, cited in Daniels, *Conscience*, p. 239.
41 Based on figures in Dmitrenko, 'Ob'edinennye', p. 76 and *Spravochnyi tom*, pp. 10–11. Compare with the figures in John Lowenhardt, *The Soviet Politburo* trans. Dymphna Clark (Edinburgh: Canongate, 1982), p. 97. His figures would give a slightly greater frequency, principally between the XIV and XV Congresses, where his interval is about 8.5 weeks.
42 These figures are based on the CC membership lists in *Sovetskaia Istoricheskaia Entsiklopedia* (Moscow, 1961–76), vol. 7, pp. 703–10 and Borys Levysky, 'The Soviet political elite' (Munich: unpublished, 1969), p. 17.
43 Prior to the XII Congress, Lenin had called for the enlargement of the CC by drawing into its work lower party members from among the working class and peasantry. He also favoured the practice of the CC meeting jointly with a similarly enlarged CCC as a form of 'superior party conference', a suggestion also implemented during this period. See Lenin's 'Kak nam reorganizovat' Rabkrin', 'Luchshe men'she, da luchshe' and 'Pis'mo k s'ezdu', *Polnoe sobranie sochinenii*, 5th ed. (Moscow, 1982), vol. 45, pp. 343–8, 383–406.
44 Of these 25 people, eight were re-elected at the XVIII Congress in 1939 and therefore constitute a Stalinist core. Apart from Stalin, they were Andreev, Kalinin, Molotov, Badaev, Manuilsky, Mikoian and Voroshilov.
45 Relevant carryover figures follow. Full members demoted to candidate status and candidate members promoted to full status are retained in their former category.

	F	C
XI–XII	88.8%	57.9%
XII–XIII	92.5%	88.2%
XIII–XIV	92.5%	67.6%
XIV–XV	82.5%	88.4%
XV–XVI	83.1%	86.0%

46 These figures are based on the sources listed in note 42 and the congress delegate lists at the end of each volume of congress proceedings. Some of these volumes contain statistical breakdowns of length of party membership; for the most part differences between those statistics and the figures cited here are minor. The figures cited in Levytsky have the disadvantage of not having 1917 as a category boundary, and therefore they are not strictly comparable with those cited here.
47 In terms of age profile, that generation born between 1881 and 1890 had its position slightly eroded. Among full members, the proportion slipped

from 55.5% at the XI Congress to 47% at the XV. This took place beside a significant increase in those born in the following decade; they grew from 7.5% in 1922 to 17.0% in 1927. Among the candidates, the birth dates of too many are uncertain to gain an accurate picture. See the raw figures in Levytsky, Elite, p. 10.

48 Career details are based principally on Heinrich E. Schulz, Paul K. Urban and Andrew A. Lebed, eds., Who was who in the USSR? (Metuchen: Scarecrow Press, 1972) and Levytsky, Elite. The jobs are those individuals held in the period immediately following their election to the CC because, in terms of institutional representation, it was the organisations of which they were then part which were represented. Politburo members are categorised under their other jobs. When an individual held a number of posts, the one that was politically most important has been used. The 'Other' category includes jobs in the trade unions, Comintern, Komsomol, military and *Pravda* editor. Uncertains are much higher among candidate than full members.

49 For full members only, the figures are as follows:

	CP apparatus					
	Central	Regional	Total	State	Other	Uncertain
XI	11.1	18.4	29.6	51.8	18.5	–
XII	10.0	27.5	37.5	47.0	15.0	–
XIII	16.0	24.5	40.5	37.8	20.7	–
XIV	14.3	36.5	50.8	33.3	15.9	–
XV	21.1	35.2	56.3	29.6	14.1	–

Jerry Hough provides different figures for full-time party officials among full members of the CC: X 20%, XI 26%, XII 32%, XIII 38% and XV 45%. Jerry Hough and Merle Fainsod, *How the Soviet Union is governed* (Cambridge MA: Harvard University Press, 1979), pp. 133, 145.

50 Figures for party and state combined (and excluding the Other category) in the CC as a whole are as follows (all in %):

	Centre	Region
XI	37.0	45.7
XII	26.3	59.7
XIII	32.2	48.3
XIV	30.4	47.6
XV	33.8	43.8

51 Robert V. Daniels, 'Evolution of leadership selection in the Central Committee, 1917–1927', Pintner and Rowney, *Officialdom*, pp. 355–68.
52 Although of course appointments to significant bureaucratic positions would have been made with this in mind; those who the centre did not want in the CC would not be appointed to positions entitling the incumbent to CC membership.
53 Norms of representation establish which constituencies are to be represented at what levels and by what size delegations.
54 Figures at the XIII Congress suggest an average of 15 questions per plenum between 25 April 1923 and 1 May 1924. *Trinadtsatyi*, p. 73.
55 One instance was the establishment in September 1923 of three such committees, on the scissors crisis, the wages question and on the situation inside the party. Carr, *Interregnum*, pp. 113–14, 302–3.
56 *Dvenadtsatyi*, p. 703. It was taken to an extreme in 1925 when the major resolution on the rural question was adopted not by the XIV Conference but by the CC meeting immediately after it. Carr, *Socialism*, vol. 1, p. 286. Stalin handled the issue in this way in order to avoid public criticism from his erstwhile ally Zinoviev and his supporters.
57 *Dvenadtsatyi*, pp. 701–2. According to Trotsky, the Politburo was dissuaded from introducing a spirit monopoly in 1923 by strong opposition from the CC and rank-and-file. Cited in Carr, *Interregnum*, p. 44.
58 These were circulated to obkom and raikom party secretaries in numbered copies, to be retained for a short period and then returned by special courier. Merle Fainsod, *Smolensk under Soviet rule* (New York: Vintage Books, 1958), p. 77. A decision of the joint CC–CCC plenum in April 1929 adopted measures designed to ensure the secrecy of CC decisions, something which must have imposed a restraint upon the percolation of debate throughout the party. Aleksandrov', *Kto upravliaet Rossiei? Bol'shevistskii partiino-pravitel'stvennyi apparat i Stalinizm. Istoriko-dogmaticheskii analiz* (Berlin, 1933), p. 293.
59 For example, the CC meeting of February 1927 was the scene for the recantation of two minor members of the opposition, Nikolaeva and Bakaev. Carr, *Foundations*, p. 24.
60 On the Secretariat lobbying CC members at the time of the July 1928 plenum on the question of policy toward the peasants, see Moshe Lewin, *Russian peasants and Soviet power. A study of collectivisation* (London: Allen and Unwin, 1968), p. 305.
61 The position of the leading group was further bolstered at the joint CC–CCC plenum in July 1926 by the attendance of members of the Central Auditing Commission. At the October 1926 joint plenum, representatives of the Executive Committee of the Comintern joined auditing commission members, a move designed to undercut Zinoviev's support and appearance thereof in the international movement. At the November 1928 plenum, members of the CCC and Central Auditing Commission also attended.
62 Daniels, 'Evolution', pp. 357–9.
63 *Ibid.*, p. 360. The use of the slate method is suggested by the fact that from

the XII Congress onwards, individual totals of votes were no longer announced. In addition, the composition of the newly enlarged body from this time suggests a concern with achieving a certain type of make-up.

64 The congress was presented with a list which delegates could endorse in full, or they could cross off individual names and insert others. According to Bazhanov, comparison of such entries on the list with the delegate questionnaires filled out at the beginning of each congress enabled Stalin's supporters to identify those who opposed him. Bazhanov, *Vospominaniia* pp. 128–30.
65 *KPSS v rez*, vol. 2, p. 341.
66 The CC was entitled to send representatives with a consultative vote to CCC plena.
67 *Dvenadtsatyi*, p. 701. However, a person could simultaneously be a candidate member of the CC and a member of the CCC.
68 Schapiro, *Communist Party*, p. 323. Joint plena were held in October 1923, January 1925, October 1925, July 1926, October 1926, November 1926, July–August 1927, October 1927, April 1928 and April 1929. There were two other plena, but according to Dmitrenko, 'Ob'edinennye' (p. 76) there are no details of them except that they occurred between April 1923 and May 1924. On 14 November 1927 both bodies issued a letter dealing with the public demonstrations launched by the opposition a week earlier, but no actual meeting of the joint plenum appears to have been held. See *KPSS v rez*, vol. 4, p. 253.
69 For an indication of the subjects discussed and resolutions adopted by CCC plena, see I. M. Moskalenko, *Organy partiinogo kontrolia v period stroitel'stva sotsializma (zadachi, struktura, metody deiatel'nosti kontrol'nykh komissii 1920–1934gg)* (Moscow, 1981), pp. 160–8. The decisions of joint plena are reprinted in *KPSS v rez*.
70 *Trinadtsatyi*, p. 813.
71 For example, *KPSS v rez*, vol. 3, pp. 141–2 for the attack on Trotsky and the 46 by the October 1923 joint plenum. This was also attended by representatives of ten party organisations.
72 For example, the July–August 1927 joint plenum approved of the expulsion of Trotsky and Zinoviev from the CC but later, principally as a result of Ordzhonikidze's efforts, gave the opposition leaders another chance to affirm their loyalty to the CC. They were expelled at the October joint plenum. In November 1927 they were expelled from the party and some of their supporters were expelled from the CC and the CCC in the name of the CC and the CCC.
73 Conversely, 50% of all joint plenum resolutions concerned disciplinary matters compared with only 6.5% for the CC Plenum; some 61% of all CC plenum resolutions concerned economic matters.
74 On these see Davies, 'Syrtsov-Lominadze', pp. 34–5 and *KPSS v rez*, vol. 4, pp. 437–8. Also an article by Zinoviev in September 1925 was forced to undergo 'amendments and additions' by 'members of the central committee'. Carr, *Socialism*, vol. 1, p. 324.
75 These people were Rykov (Orgburo 1921–24), Tomsky (Orgburo,

1921–24), Kalinin (Orgburo candidate 1921–24, full 1924–25), Rudzutak (Orgburo candidate 1921–23, full and Secretariat 1923–24), Kuibyshev (Secretariat and Orgburo 1922), Andreev (Orgburo 1922–28, Secretariat 1924–25), Voroshilov (Orgburo 1924–25) and Kosior (Orgburo and Secretariat 1925–28).

76 Bukharin was removed from the Politburo at the November 1929 plenum.
77 The figures upon which these generalisations are based will be found in Roy D. Laird, *The Politburo. Demographic trends, Gorbachev and the future* (Boulder: Westview Press, 1986), p. 40.
78 The remaining four were Dzerzhinsky, Frunze, Uglanov and Ordzhonikidze. The last three all opposed Stalin's opponents at the time of appointment. For the argument that Stalin was able to strengthen his position considerably in 1926 by promoting supporters to the Politburo, see Laird, *The Politburo*, p. 35.
79 *Dvenadtsatyi*, pp. 808, 809. There is no breakdown between the Politburo and the CC.
80 In his report, Zinoviev cited the figure of 86 meetings, but in the table attached to the Report of the CC, the figure cited is 88. *Trinadtsatyi*, pp. 73, 815. According to Bazhanov, the Politburo met two or three times per week and could have 150 questions on its agenda. Extraordinary meetings were held on important questions. Boris Bazhanov, *Vospominaniia*, p. 48.
81 Lowenhardt, *Politburo*, p. 97.
82 *Piatnadtsatyi*, pp. 119–20.
83 It was reported at the XV Congress that the weight of work prevented the fulfilment by the Politburo of the work schedule that had been drawn up for this body. Work schedules for the Politburo were published in the press in 1926 and 1928. They are discussed in Lowenhardt, *Politburo*, pp. 92–3 and Merle Fainsod, *How Russia is ruled* (Cambridge MA: Harvard University Press, 1964), p. 309.
84 Indeed the Frunze incident shows the scope of the Politburo's authority. This body forced War Commissar Frunze to undergo an operation which he was reluctant to undertake, a development which shows the sort of power that the Politburo had over the personal affairs of leading party members.
85 *Dvenadtsatyi*, p. 83.
86 A similar watching brief applied to the actions of the CCC. *Trinadtsatyi*, p. 268. According to Kuibyshev at the same congress, the CCC often handled questions which, ultimately, were ratified by the Politburo (*ibid*).
87 See Antipov's remark at the XIV Congress that the CC needed to exercise leadership over the speeches of individual members of the Politburo because such speeches would be seen as the speeches of the party leadership and accepted as such by the party. *XIV s'ezd*, p. 242. Also the opposition was charged with the distribution of secret material without Politburo consent. *KPSS v rez*, vol. 4, p. 49. In 1925 Zinoviev was unable to publish his article 'The philosophy of the epoch' until he had deleted parts to which the Politburo objected. *XIV s'ezd*, p. 194. (In this statement Uglanov referred to the CC, but means the Politburo.) The Frunze incident

(see note 84) also reflects a notion of collective responsibility in that it represents the assertion of the principle that the medical needs of its members is a legitimate area of its concern.
88 For example, all Politburo papers were secret and were transported from place to place by a special GPU/OGPU corps. Bazhanov, *Vospominaniia*, p. 51.
89 Despite this principle, the Politburo could take secret decisions about which the CC was unaware. An example was the date for the German revolution. *Ibid.*, p. 69.
90 *Dvenadtsatyi*, p. 702.
91 *KPSS v rez*, vol. 4, p. 314.
92 For example, see *ibid.*, p. 249 (8 September 1927) and pp. 436–47 (9 February 1929).
93 For example, party secretary Kuibyshev in late January 1924. Daniels, *Conscience*, p. 190.
94 Bazhanov, *Vospominaniia*, p. 62.
95 Daniels, *Conscience*, p. 364.
96 For example, such a body was set up early in 1925 to look into questions of hiring labour and leasing land, while another was established in December 1928 to investigate measures to relieve the tax burden on middle peasants. Respectively, Carr, *Socialism*, vol. 1, p. 274 and *KPSS v rez*, vol. 4, pp. 439–40.
97 CCC Chairman Kuibyshev at the XIII Congress. *Trinadtsatyi*, p. 268.
98 According to former Politburo secretary Bazhanov, a significant amount of work was delegated to him personally, including verification of the implementation of decisions. Bazhanov, *Vospominaniia*, pp. 55, 99–100, 109–10.
99 Bazhanov, *Vospominaniia*, p. 49.
100 Daniels, *Conscience*, p. 239 citing Zinoviev. In addition, the troika used to meet separately prior to Politburo sessions to work out their common position. Boris Bazhanov, 'Stalin closely observed', G. R. Urban, ed., *Stalinism. Its impact on Russia and the world* (London: Maurice Temple Smith, 1982), p. 9. At the time of the Right Opposition, the Stalinist group used to meet separately to define their common position.
101 *Dvenadtsatyi*, p. 809 and *Trinadtsatyi*, pp. 130, 713. One speaker at the XII Congress put the number of questions at 6312. *Dvenadtsatyi*, p. 83. An indication of the areas of concern of the Orgburo is given by the work plans designed for that body periodically since January 1925. One such plan, for February–April 1925, divided its responsibilities into eight areas: production, intra-party construction, work in the countryside, press, national policy, soviet construction, education, and military construction. *Izvestiia tsentral'nogo komiteta Rossiiskoi kommunisticheskoi partii (bol'shevikov)*, 6(81) (9 February 1925), p. 1. Later plans added to these sections a concern for the Komsomol, cooperation and trade union construction, work among women, economic construction, hearing reports from the local party organisations, state of the poor, and writers' organisation. *Izv ts k*, 35(110) (14 September 1925), p. 1; 10–11 (131–2) (22

March 1926), p. 1; 13(186) (8 April 1927), pp. 2–3; 32–3(205–6) (31 August 1927), p. 5; 16–17(237–8) (25 May 1928), pp. 1–2. According to Molotov's speech on the plan of the Orgburo's work on 28 March 1927, the centre of its attention was checking on the implementation of party directives. *Izv ts k*, 16(189) (30 April 1927), p. 1.
102 *Trinadtsatyi*, pp. 130, 713.
103 *Trinadtsatyi*, p. 130.
104 For this reason alone the attempt to curb the power of the Secretariat by electing more party luminaries to the Orgburo in October 1923 (when Trotsky and Zinoviev as full and Bukharin and Korotkov as candidates were elected to this body following the Kislovodsk incident (Daniels, *Conscience*, pp. 207–8)) was bound to fail even had these individuals been more active in their new offices. The Orgburo was even more removed from the secretarial apparatus than the Secretariat.
105 This should have been assisted by some overlap between these bodies. For example, in the organs elected by the XIV Congress, all members of the Secretariat were members of the Orgburo, while three of the latter (Stalin, Molotov and Uglanov, who were also on the Secretariat) were members of the Politburo.
106 *Dvenadtsatyi*, pp. 81–2, 83. Nogin declared that 90% of Orgotdel recommendations and 95% of Uchraspred recommendations to the Orgburo were merely ratified. *Dvenadtsatyi*, pp. 81–2.
107 *Dvenadtsatyi*, p. 702.
108 An extra full and candidate member was added to the Orgburo at the November 1924 plenum, and an extra candidate at the 1928 plenum. An additional full member had been added to the Orgburo at the November 1927 plenum. For other changes, see note 104 above.
109 *Dvenadtsatyi*, p. 79; *Trinadtsatyi*, p. 128; *XIV s'ezd*, p. 89 and *Piatnadtsatyi*, p. 123. However these figures probably exclude the staff of the Secret Department, which was somewhere between 694 and 994 people in 1921. Niels Erik Rosenfeldt, *Knowledge and power. The role of Stalin's secret chancellery in the Soviet system of government* (Copenhagen: Rosenkilde and Bagger, 1978) p. 56. At the XVI Congress, the number in the central apparatus in mid-1928 was said to be 550 following a rationalisation of the organisation. *XVI s'ezd*, p. 93.
110 *Trinadtsatyi*, p. 128 and *Piatnadtsatyi*, p. 123. The non-party proportion was said to be some 25.8% at the XIV Congress. *XIV s'ezd*, p. 90.
111 For comments on the workers, see *Trinadtsatyi*, p. 132.
112 *XIV s'ezd*, p. 89.
113 *Izv ts k*, 3(51) (March 1923), p. 28.
114 *Izv ts k* 3(51) (March 1923), p. 3. For an earlier outline, see 7(43), (July 1922), pp. 38–9.
115 The Instruction Section became the new Information Department. *Trinadtsatyi*, p. 808.
116 *Izv ts k*, 17–18(92–3) (11 May 1925), pp. 7–8.
117 There is some confusion about its exact title.
118 Schapiro, p. 315 and Schapiro, 'The General Department of the CC of the

CPSU', *Survey* 21, 3(96) (Summer 1975), pp. 53–65. Also see Niels Erik Rosenfeldt, '"The consistory of the communist church": the origins and development of Stalin's Secret Chancellery', *Russian History*, 9, 2–3 (1982), p. 312.
119 *Dvenadtsatyi*, p. 804; *Trinadtsatyi*, p. 806; Carr, *Socialism*, vol. 2, p. 222; *Piatnadtsatyi*, p. 126 and *XVI s'ezd*, p. 81. There are some discrepancies in the official figures; for example, compare the figures for the XI–XII Congress period cited in *Dvenadtsatyi* and *Trinadtsatyi*.
120 This is discussed in *Izv ts k*, 1(49) (January 1923), pp. 11–14. and *Dvenadtsatyi*, p. 801. The decision on this was made by the CC following the XI Conference in December 1921. A programme was also set up to provide for the planned rotation of leading guberniia officials into the central office and vice versa. *Izv ts k*, 3(51) (March 1923), pp. 34–41. Robert V. Daniels, 'The Secretariat and the local organizations in the Russian Communist Party, 1921–1923', *The American Slavic and East European Review*, 16 (1957), p. 36.
121 *Dvenadtsatyi*, p. 73. However, some implied that such records were available but had not been used by Uchraspred because of laxness on its part.
122 *Izv ts k*, 3(61) (March 1924), pp. 9–25, especially pp. 14–15.
123 For example, see *Spravochnik partiinogo rabotnika* 4, 1924 (Moscow, 1924), pp. 144–9; 6, vol. 1, 1927 (Moscow, 1928), pp. 527–8, 534–46, 553–4.
124 *Dvenadtsatyi*, p. 673. For the report, see pp. 62–3. Stalin announced at the congress that the staff of Uchraspred both in the centre and in the localities would gain a new deputy head specialising in personnel selection for the economic organs and the soviets. *Dvenadtsatyi*, p. 64.
125 *Dvenadtsatyi*, pp. 704–5.
126 The Orgburo resolution of 12 June 1923 has not been published. Details will be found in *Izv ts k*, 1(59) (January 1924), pp. 64–7; 4(62) (April 1924), p. 41; 1(122) (18 January 1926), p. 4. Also *Trinadtsatyi*, p. 805.
127 *Izv ts k*, 1(122) (18 January 1926), pp. 2–4.
128 Responsibility was divided between these organs in the following way: the Politburo had responsibility for 657 workers and 272 positions in 117 agencies and organisations, the Orgburo 713 workers and 513 positions in 436 agencies and organisations, and the Secretariat 542 workers and 389 positions in 287 agencies and organisations. *Izv ts k*, 9(130) (8 March 1926), p. 2.
129 Their task was to ensure that central candidates were accepted in the electoral meetings of lower organs.
130 *Izv ts k*, 6–7(227–8) (5 March 1928), p. 7.
131 *Izv ts k*, 9(182) (7 March 1927), p. 6. This situation seems to have dramatically improved in 1927. During the first and second quarters, the corresponding figures were 67.6% and 65.8%. *Izv ts k*, 19(192) (23 May 1927), p. 14; 39(212) (22 October 1927), p. 8.
132 By 1923 formal Uchraspred control over leading positions had been extended down to the uezd level. The main constraint on extension into the uezd had been the shortage of qualified personnel. Hence the establishment, on Stalin's initiative, of a school to train uezd secretaries in

Moscow. *Dvenadtsatyi*, pp. 66–7. The exercise of this power was clear in the central direction of the election of a new CC at the Georgian party conference in March 1923 and in the removal or transfer of 37 guberniia secretaries in 1922. *Izv ts k*, 3(51) (March 1923), p. 51. On the Georgian question, see Daniels, *Conscience*, p. 183.

133 The relevant section of the Rules adopted in 1922 declared: 'All lower organisations up to the uezd are confirmed by the uezd committees with the sanction of the guberniia committee, uezd committees by the guberniia committee with the sanction of the oblast committee, and in its absence by the CC, guberniia committees by the oblast committee with the sanction of the CC, and in the absence of an oblast committee, by the CC directly.' This simply repeated the provision of 1919. In the Rules adopted in 1925, this provision was omitted, but the principle remained in the individual sections of the Rules dealing with different levels of the party.

134 The size of this cannot be ascertained with a high degree of certainty. Scholars have suggested the following estimates of full-time party workers: 1922 – 15,325, 1924 – 27,250, 1925 – 25,600. Schapiro, *Communist Party*, p. 317 and Carr, *Socialism* vol. 2, p. 217.

135 Bazhanov, 'Stalin', p. 10. On Stalin's assistants, see Rosenfeldt, *Knowledge*, pp. 129–60, 165.

136 He may also have been able to control information flow in another way towards the end of this period. Special Sectors, which were part of the Secret Department, were established at all levels of the party by 1934, and may have begun to emerge in 1927–28. They were major channels of information flow and of general oversight. Rosenfeldt, 'Consistory', p. 318 n. 29.

137 According to one student of this, his personal secretariat had direct access to all policy-making areas of the political machine, had the first look at all important party documents, had its own extensive personnel records and worked closely with the security apparatus. Rosenfeldt, *Knowledge*, pp. 32–8. Some of his personal assistants were appointed to the Secret Department, including Tovstukha, Mekhlis and Poskrebyshev. Schapiro, 'General Department', pp. 53–4. According to Bazhanov, his assistants enabled him, among other things, to listen in on others' telephone calls and to discover opposition among congress delegates. Bazhanov, *Vospominaniia*, pp. 53, 56–7, 128–30.

138 The last member independent of Stalin appointed to the Secretariat was Evdokimov in January 1926. He was removed three months later. In June 1922 Kaganovich was made head of Orgotdel, three months after Stalin's appointment as General Secretary. When Orgraspred was established, he remained its head. He was to prove to be one of those closest to Stalin.

139 Calculated from lists in *Sovetskaia Istoricheskaia Entsiklopedia*, vol. 15, pp. 722–6.

140 The following table presents figures (in both percentages and actual numbers for those elected at each CCC whose service remained unbroken into the later CCCs of the period and the first CCC of the next:

	1925	1927	1930
1920	14.3% (1)	14.3% (1)	14.3% (1)
1921	10.0% (1)	10.0% (1)	10.0% (1)
1922	57.1% (4)	57.1% (4)	57.1% (4)
1923	48.3% (29)	38.3% (23)	25.0% (15)
1924	51.6% (78)	37.1% (56)	21.8% (33)
1925		53.3% (87)	21.0% (41)

The table is to be read as follows: for example, of those elected to the CCC in 1923, 48.3% were re-elected in 1925, 38.3% in 1927 and 25% in 1930.

141 For example, the XIV Congress reaffirmed the position established by the X Congress that members of the CCC had to be of at least ten years' standing. *KPSS v rez*, vol. 3, pp. 484–5. Lesser periods were demanded for control commissions at lower levels. At the XIII Congress, the period of party membership for members of guberniia control commissions was reduced from pre-February to pre-October standing. *Trinadtsatyi*, p. 619.

142 As well as the figures cited in the text, this is reflected in the long-term carryover of Presidium members. The following table gives figures (in both percentage and actual numbers) for those elected at successive presidia whose service remained unbroken into later presidia:

	1926	1927	1930
1923	71.4% (10)	50.0% (7)	42.8% (6)
1924	80.9% (17)	57.1% (12)	38.1% (8)
1926		66.6% (20)	41.9% (13)
1927			64.5% (20)

143 Actually this began in August 1921 with the joint CC–CCC meeting, but no more of these were held until 1923.
144 *Dvenadtsatyi*, p. 702.
145 On the joint plena, see Dmitrenko, 'Ob'edinennye', p. 76. For CCC plenum dates, agendas and decisions, see Moskalenko, *Organy*, pp. 160–8.
146 *KPSS v rez*, vol. 2, p. 340.
147 *Odinnadtsatyi*, p. 563.
148 *KPSS v rez*, vol. 3, p. 484.
149 *Trinadtsatyi*, p. 265. Also see comments in Bazhanov, *Vospominaniia*, p. 35.
150 *Spravochnik partiinogo rabotnika*, 5 (Moscow, 1926), pp. 500–2.
151 Although as the carryover figures suggest, the CCC was not wholly uninfected by opposition sentiment itself at times.

152 See the discussion in Carr, *Socialism*, vol. 2, pp. 234–5.
153 *Piatnadtsatyi*, p. 1470.
154 A major vehicle for this was the pages of the newspapers based in the two cities, *Leningradskaia Pravda* and *Pravda*. For a succinct discussion of a particular instance of this, relating to Sarkis' proposals on recruitment policy in late 1925, see Rigby, *Communist Party*, pp. 147–50.
155 This is despite the removal of his two supporters – Safarov from the Leningrad Komsomol and Zalutsky from the post of party secretary – during 1925. Robert V. Daniels, *Conscience* pp. 254–5.
156 Fainsod, *Smolensk*, p. 48. There seems to have been more rank-and-file awareness of and support for the Right and its positions than for any earlier opposition groups. *Ibid.*, pp. 54–5. Also see Nicolas Werth, *Etre communiste en URSS sous Staline* (Paris: Gallimard, 1981), ch. 5.
157 For details, see Carr, *Socialism*, vol. 2, pp. 168–77 and Daniels, *Conscience*, pp. 269–70. On the whiteanting of Uglanov's position in Moscow, see *ibid.*, pp. 337–41.
158 It would be a mistake to assume that this was solely due to organisational manipulation. Over the period as a whole there appears to have been very little support for the successive opposition groups. See below.
159 His historical vision and fear of being labelled a Bonapartist was also important here. However, Medvedev suggests that there was insufficient support for Trotsky in the army to make appeal to this a viable course of action. Medvedev, *Stalin*, pp. 51–6.
160 For official criticism of this type of action, see the CC–CCC decision of July 1926, 'Po delu tov. Lashevicha i dr. i o edinstve partii', *KPSS v rez*, vol. 4, p. 51.
161 For a particularly forceful reaffirmation of this principle, see the statement and decision of the CC (the decision was also given in the name of the CCC) of 11 and 14 November 1927 following the demonstrations and agitational work of the United Opposition at this time. *KPSS v rez*, vol. 4, pp. 252–5. They were charged with organising illegal anti-party meetings, the illegal publication of leaflets and circulars and the organisation of public anti-party demonstrations.
162 *KPSS v rez*, vol. 3, p. 142. The earlier action against Sultan Galiev did not, in the official resolution, mention fractionalism. He was charged, among other things, with establishing a secret organisation to oppose the measures of the central party organs and with seeking to link this organisation with elements hostile to the party both inside and outside the Soviet Union. This organisation appears not to have been within party ranks and therefore strictly did not break the anti-fractional rule. However he broke party discipline through his opposition to duly adopted decisions by central party bodies. *KPSS v rez*, vol. 3, pp. 130–2.
163 For example, see the comments by Stalin in his Report and Concluding Remarks to the XIII Conference, J. V. Stalin, *Works* (Moscow, 1953), vol. 6, pp. 7, 16, 21, 33–4. Also see the sustained attack by Bukharin in *Pravda* entitled 'Doloi fraktsionnost'' (Down with fractionalism), 28 December 1923–1 January 1924.

164 For example, see *KPSS v rez*, vol. 4, pp. 48–54 (July 1926), 105–15 (November 1926) and 429–36 (April 1929).
165 For example, *Trinadtsatyi*, pp. 771–7 which reproduces the XIII Conference resolution 'Ob itogakh diskussi i o melkoburzhuaznom uklone v partii' and Stalin's speech to that congress, pp. 231–2. See also the resolution of the joint CC–CCC plenum of July 1926, 'Po delu tov. Lashevicha i dr. i o edinstve partii', *KPSS v rez*, vol 4, pp. 48–54.
166 *Piatnadtsatyi*, p. 550. He also indicated that the CCC had been lighter than the control commissions at other levels, having arraigned 75 people of whom only 19 were excluded.
167 However, the United Opposition acknowledged that they had breached the anti-fractional rule in a public declaration in *Pravda*, 17 October 1926.
168 *Dvenadtsatyi*, pp. 103–5.
169 *Dvenadtsatyi*, pp. 115–16. Also see Trotsky's argument in *Trinadtsatyi*, pp. 150–2.
170 This was despite Trotsky's unequivocal statement that he was not in favour of allowing groupings in the party. *Trinadtsatyi*, p. 151.
171 *XIV s'ezd*, p. 467. For a more direct example, see Daniels, *Conscience*, p. 225.
172 The speaker was Mikoian. *XIV s'ezd*, p. 186.
173 *KPSS v rez*, vol. 4, p. 112. Also see *Trinadtsatyi*, pp. 602–3 and the joint CC–CCC resolution of July 1926, 'Ob itogakh perevyborov sovetov', *KPSS v rez,*, vol. 4, pp. 36–48. In the words of Alexander Barmine, 'Whatever our hesitations and our doubts, the sentiment of loyalty to the party was always the determining influence in our decisions.' Alexander Barmine, *One who survived* (New York: Putnam, 1945), pp. 216–17.
174 *Dvenadtsatyi*, pp. 52–53. For a sustained argument that the views of the United Opposition represented a social democratic deviation, see the XV Conference resolution, 'Ob oppositsionnom bloke v VKP(b)', *KPSS v rez*, vol. 4, pp. 105–16.
175 *KPSS v rez*, vol. 3, p. 147. The principle of discussion was implemented in the party-wide discussion launched in November 1923. See some details in Daniels, *Conscience*, pp. 225–30.
176 For example, see the CC–CCC decision of June–July 1927, *KPSS v rez*, vol. 4, pp. 202–9; *Piatnadtsatyi*, pp. 554, 1434; the CC appeal on self-criticism, *KPSS v rez*, vol. 4, pp. 338–42; the decision of the joint CC–CCC plenum of April 1929, *KPSS v rez*, vol. 4, pp. 429–36. See ch. 3.
177 *Dvenadtsatyi*, pp. 153, 200.
178 Cited in Carr, *Socialism*, vol. 2, p. 28.
179 Such Discussion Sheets initially were established by the IX Conference in September 1920, which directed that these be published regularly as a vehicle within which criticisms of party shortcomings could be published. *KPSS v rez*, vol. 2, pp. 299–300. For later use of the Discussion Sheet as a forum for criticism prior to a congress, see *KPSS v rez*, vol. 4, p. 249.
180 *KPSS v rez*, vol. 3, p. 159.
181 *XIV s'ezd*, p. 963. The four elements of intra-party democracy were an

increase in the activity of the broad party masses in the discussion and resolution of major issues of party policy, the election of leading party organs with promotion of new forces into them, the expansion and increased qualifications of the party aktiv, and the dissemination in party circles of the foundations of Leninist doctrine.

182 *KPSS v rez*, vol. 4, p. 113. These provisions were incorporated into the party Rules at the XV Congress. *Piatnadtsatyi*, p. 1,470.
183 *KPSS v rez*, vol. 4, pp. 434, 437–8. The latter is found in a resolution of a joint meeting of the Politburo and CCC Presidium on 9 February 1929 and ratified by a joint CC–CCC plenum on 23 April 1929.
184 For example, at the XIV Congress, Stalin's supporters were allowed free rein from the chair while oppositionists were always reminded of the time limits for speakers, even if in most instances they were permitted minor extensions on request.
185 For example, the period of pre-congress discussion prior to the XV Congress was cut from three months to one month and, some three months before the congress, the Politburo decided the opposition platform could not be printed and placed before the party rank-and-file. Daniels, *Conscience*, pp. 312–13.
186 Carr, *Interregnum*, pp. 327–28. *Pravda* staff members who sought to report both sides of the discussion impartially were dismissed at the instruction of the CCC. Daniels, *Conscience*, p. 227.
187 The position of the Right Opposition was curious in that the dispute was not broadcast into the public realm through the press for some time as both sides sought to maintain the myth of leadership unanimity. The Right was probably prompted by notions of party unity, the desire to avoid the charges of fractionalism that had been levelled at earlier opposition groups and an inflated view of their power; the Stalin group by a concern at the possible support the Right may have been able to obtain within the party. As a result, members of the Right Opposition were attacked by name only after they had been defeated. Although Stalin had attacked a deviation in January 1928 and the notion of a 'right deviation' had been emerging since mid-1928, the first open naming of members of the Right did not occur until the CC plenum of April 1929 at which Uglanov was removed as a candidate member of the Politburo. *Pravda* first published an attack on Bukharin by name on 21 August 1929. R. W. Davies, *The industrialisation of Soviet Russia*, vol. 1, *The socialist offensive. The collectivisation of Soviet agriculture, 1929–1930* (London: Macmillan, 1980), p. 132. Much of the earlier conflict had proceeded publicly through allusion and Aesopian language. In this sense, the Right Opposition was transitional between the open conflict earlier in the decade and that which occurred purely behind the scenes during the 1930s.
188 *KPSS v rez*, vol. 3, pp. 158–9.
189 *Bol'shevik*, 1 (April 1924), p. 3.
190 *Dvenadtsatyi*, p. 5.
191 *ibid.*, pp. 8–9.
192 *ibid.*, p. 523.

193 *Trinadtsatyi*, pp. 3–4, 108, 814. Emphases in original.
194 For example, *Trinadtsatyi*, pp. 45, 74, 86, 90, 92, 236, 363, 619.
195 *Trinadtsatyi*, pp. 707–9.
196 For a discussion of this, see Graeme Gill, 'Political myth and Stalin's quest for authority in the Party', T. H. Rigby, Archie Brown and Peter Reddaway, eds., *Authority, power and policy in the USSR. Essays dedicated to Leonard Schapiro* (London: Macmillan, 1980), pp. 98–117 and Medvedev, *K sudu*, pp. 300–2.
197 See the discussion in Daniels, *Conscience*, pp. 298–9. On Bukharin, see Stephen F. Cohen, *Bukharin and the Bolshevik Revolution. A political biography 1888–1938* (New York: Alfred A. Knopf, 1973), chs. 5 and 6.
198 Stalin's *Foundations of Leninism* published in April–May 1924 and Zinoviev's *Leninism. An introduction to the study of Leninism* in October 1925. The first was a down-to-earth, practical exposition which greatly simplified and catechised Lenin's thought. The latter was a much more sophisticated, theoretical treatment which was understandable only by those with a grounding in Marxist theoretical discourse. See the discussion in Gill, 'Political myth', pp. 101–2.
199 For example, Bukharin's *Politicheskoe zaveshchanie Lenina* (Moscow: 1929) and Stalin's speeches in *Works*, vol. 6, pp. 374–420; vol. 7, pp. 267–361; vol. 8, pp. 13–96, 245–310; vol. 9, pp. 1–64; vol. 10, pp. 1–96, 177–211, 275–363: vol.11, pp. 231–48; vol. 12, pp. 1–113. For a discussion of some of the speeches on Lenin's death, see Gill, 'Political myth', pp. 100–1. The appointment of Stalin's supporter Tovstukha as Secretary to the Director of the Lenin Institute when it opened in 1924 may have been significant here in providing Stalin with clear access to the storehouse of Lenin's works. Bazhanov, *Vospominaniia*, pp. 85–7.
200 In a memorial speech at the Kremlin military school on 28 January 1924 Stalin outlined his early contacts with Lenin. He claimed that in 1903 he received from Lenin a 'simple but deeply significant letter'. No evidence of the letter exists. The effect of the claim was to pre-date Stalin's association with Lenin by two years. The speech, published in *Pravda* on 12 February 1924, is reprinted in *Works*, vol. 6, pp. 54–66.
201 Gill, 'Political myth', p. 102.
202 With the partial exception of Trotsky who claimed that the differences with Lenin over the question of revolution resulted in Lenin adopting the correct, Trotskyist, position.
203 For example, see Bukharin's 'Doloi fraktsionnost'', *Pravda*, 28 December 1923–1 January 1924.
204 The title of Stalin's speech to the communist fraction of the All-Union Central Council of Trade Unions on 19 November 1924, *Pravda*, 26 November 1924, reprinted in *Works*, vol. 6, pp. 338–73. Also see the resolution of the CC plenum of 17–20 January 1925 in which Trotsky was charged with seeking to substitute Trotskyism for Leninism and linking Trotsky's current position with his previous opposition to the party. *KPSS v rez*, vol. 3, pp. 323–31.
205 To quote from Lenin's 'Testament'. 'Pis'mo k s'ezdu', *PSS* vol. 45, p. 345.

206 Important too was Stalin's systematisation of Leninism in his 'Foundations of Leninism'. This simplified Lenin's thought and made it much more easily understandable to the politically illiterate, thereby bolstering Stalin's claim to be Lenin's disciple. It is no accident that the book was dedicated to the Lenin Enrolment.

207 See the discussion in Graeme Gill, 'Ideology and system-building; the experience under Lenin and Stalin', Stephen White and Alex Pravda, eds., *Ideology and Soviet politics* (London: Macmillan, 1988). On ideological debate during the 1920s, see Cohen, *Bukharin*, ch. 6.

208 Isaac Deutscher, *The prophet unarmed, Trotsky 1921–1929* (Oxford University Press, 1959), p. 242 and Richard Day, *Leon Trotsky and the politics of economic isolation* (Cambridge University Press, 1973), pp. 3–4.

209 See the studies by Lewin and Davies. During the first half of 1928, Stalin accepted the need for an offensive against the peasants and the use of forceful means to achieve this, but he did not envisage such measures as taking place on all fronts; some peasants could be left in control of their plots. He seems to have eliminated private agriculture as an acceptable part of future agricultural arrangements, at least in his own mind, by April 1929, but he may not have come to accept collectivisation in the form it took until one or two months before the plenum of November 1929 ushered in the shift from gradualism to wholesale collectivisation in party policy. See the careful analysis in Lewin, *Russian Peasants*. For an argument that the policy crisis of 1927–28 brought to a head the conflicts with the United Opposition and the Right Opposition, see Michal Reiman, *The birth of Stalinism. The USSR on the eve of the 'Second Revolution'* (Bloomington: Indiana University Press, 1987).

210 *Trinadtsatyi*, pp. 106–7.

211 *Trinadtsatyi*, p. 158.

212 'Po delu tov. lashevicha i dr. i o edinstve partii', *KPSS v rez*, vol. 4, p. 51. Lashevich *et al.* were accused of operating conspiratorially rather than through open party channels.

213 See the resolution 'Ob oppozitsii', *Piatnadtsatyi*, p. 1469. Also see pp. 90, 225, 1391. Tomsky sought to defend the weaker position: 'We do not struggle against dreams and unexpressed convictions (commotion), but when convictions are transformed into life, begin to be expressed, begin to be propagandised, to be carried into our party, when struggle for convictions proceeds, then we have a right to keep an eye on the results of these convictions' (p. 335). For Kamenev's declaration that they could not renounce their views, see p. 281. The reported comments of Piatakov in 1928 are illuminating in this respect: 'A real Bolshevik dissolves his personality in the Party collective and so can reject any of his own approaches or decisions.' *Moscow News*, 25 (19 June 1988), p. 10.

214 *Piatnadtsatyi*, pp. 155, 413–14.

215 For example, Trotsky, Zinoviev, Kamenev, Piatakov, Sokol'nikov and Evdokimov publicly renounced their oppositional action in October 1926. *Pravda*, 17 October 1926. For the self-criticism of the Right, see *Pravda*, 26 November 1929. For discussion of the recantations of some

oppositionists, see Carr, *Foundations*, pp. 18–19, 24 and Daniels, *Conscience*, p. 369.
216 Cited in Carr, *Socialism*, vo. 2, p. 240 from the proceedings of the VII Congress of the Komsomol. Also see the editorial in *Pravda*, 'Itogi i perspektivy', 18 November 1929. In October 1926 the CC declared that real peace and unity in the party could be guaranteed only if the opposition submitted to all decisions of the party, repudiated their past activities and severed their links with critics from outside party ranks. See the CC's announcement to all party organisations of 16 October 1926, 'O vnutripartiinom polozhenii', *KPSS v rez*, vol. 4, pp. 63–6.
217 It is significant in this regard that as early as 1924 Trotskyism was classed as an ideology. Stalin, *Works*, vol. 6, p. 357.
218 *Piatnadtsatyi*, p. 82. Also see the congress resolution 'Ob oppozitsii', p. 1469. For Stalin's view that the Right did not constitute a fraction, see *Works*, vol. 11, p. 298.
219 The notion of a party line had been around formally since at least 1920 when it was acknowledged in the IX Congress resolution on the CC report. It was similarly acknowledged in the corresponding resolutions of subsequent congresses (with the exception of the X). However it was in the struggle with the Right Opposition that the differences between the line and a deviation were most clearly drawn. For example, see Stalin, *Works*, vol. 11, p. 232 and, more directly, vol. 12, pp. 3–10.
220 See Stalin's address to the XIV Congress, *XIV s'ezd*, p. 46. The term was used against Trotsky and his supporters at the XIII Conference in January 1924 when they were accused of being an expression of a petty bourgeois deviation. *KPSS v rez*, vol. 3, p. 156. Stalin declared that Trotsky's writings had led people onto the anarcho-Menshevik path. Opposition was linked with the petty bourgeoisie in the country.
221 The conciliatory tendency toward the Right consisted of those who 'are willing to proclaim a fight against the Right danger ... But they will not undertake any practical measures at all to organise the fight against the Right deviation on a firm basis, and to overcome this deviation in actual fact'. Stalin, *Works*, vol. 11, p. 244.
222 *ibid.*, vol. 11, pp. 57–67. A broad anti-religious campaign was also under way at this time.
223 For Stalin's generalisation from the Shakhty experience, see his April 1929 address to the CC. *Ibid.*, vol. 12, pp. 1–113.
224 For example, see *ibid.*, vol. 12, pp. 37–41.
225 Schapiro, *Communist Party*, pp. 278–9; Daniels, *Conscience*, pp. 211–12; and Leggett, *Cheka*, p. 357.
226 *XIV s'ezd*, pp. 566, 601. Also see pp. 570, 595–6, 612–13. Informing was also embedded in the RSFSR criminal code of 1922, Article 89. Carr, *Socialism*, vol. 2, p. 239.
227 For examples, see Carr, *Interregnum*, p. 364 and Carr, *Socialism*, vol. 2, p. 239.
228 See Carr, *Interregnum*, pp. 294–6. In summer 1923, expulsion followed by

arrest was visited upon those party members who had joined the Workers' Group and Workers' Truth oppositions.
229 Daniels, *Conscience*, p. 242 citing Max Eastman, who was very close to Trotsky, and therefore not without a personal interest in this question.
230 For example, see the affairs of Mrachkovsky *et al.* in September 1927 when an OGPU undercover agent enabled the police to locate a secret press and to implicate a number of party members in it, leading to action being taken against them. Carr, *Foundations*, pp. 37–8. Also the police disruption of opposition demonstrations in November 1927. Carr, *Foundations*, p. 45. According to Reiman, in late 1927, Stalin seems to have proposed, and the party leadership to have accepted, a suggestion by GPU head Menzhinsky that GPU surveillance cells be established in the party to seek out hostile elements. Such cells and their checking functions were opposed by many at lower levels of the party. Reiman, *Birth*, pp. 35, 46, 49, 127, 143, 145. There is some controversy over the authenticity of the documents upon which this is based.
231 *Dvenadtsatyi*, p. 243. Also see *Piatnadtsatyi*, pp. 551–2. Such cooperation seems to have begun as early as 1922. See the discussion in E. H. Carr, *The Bolshevik Revolution* (Harmondsworth: Penguin, 1966) vol. 1, pp. 196, 212, Carr, *Interregnum*, pp. 292–3 and Carr, *Socialism*, vol. 1, pp. 212–21, 452–4.
232 Such independence was also reflected in the status of the OGPU; a CC instruction of 25 May 1926 gave the local party organisations little role in the appointment of OGPU personnel in their areas. *Spravochnik partiinogo rabotnika*, 6, 1 (Moscow, 1928), p. 567.
233 Hence the process of publicly discrediting the opposition before the adoption of administrative measures against it.
234 Politburo authorisation had preceded the arrest of Sultan Galiev. He was expelled by a special conference in June 1923. *KPSS v rez*, vol. 3, pp. 130–2. In April 1925 the CC adopted a secret resolution which declared that in cases of the arrest of party members, the party had to be notified and could intervene if it believed that the accusations on which the arrest was based were groundless. Schapiro, *Communist Party*, p. 334. Some of those purged in 1929–30 were subsequently arrested or sent into administrative exile. Sheila Fitzpatrick *The Russian Revolution* (Oxford University Press, 1982), p. 157.
235 Stalin, *Works*, vol. 11, pp. 327–31, esp. p. 328.
236 *KPSS v rez*, vol. 4, p. 490.
237 In the cases of Trotsky and Zinoviev, a joint CC–CCC plenum in July–August 1927 approved the expulsion of these two from the CC, then reversed this decision in favour of a compromise whereby they were given another opportunity to affirm their loyalty. This may have been the basis for suggestions that the CCC was infected with a certain degree of oppositionist sympathy and for the smaller carryover from 1927. See note 153 above.
238 Leggett, *Cheka*, p. 81. For a discussion of Bliumkin, see Victor Serge, *Memoirs of a revolutionary 1901–1941* (Oxford University Press, 1963), pp. 255–257.

239 *Dvenadtsatyi*, pp. 103, 181.
240 Cited in Carr, *Socialism*, vol. 2, p. 136.
241 Cited in *ibid.*, p. 141.
242 *XIV s'ezd*, p. 274.
243 *ibid.*, p. 289.
244 *ibid.*, p. 508.
245 For example, as early as June 1924 towns began to be named after leaders who were still politically active. See Carr, *Socialism*, vol. 2, p. 12.
246 *XIV s'ezd*, p. 397.
247 *Piatnadtsatyi*, p. 230.
248 See Fitzpatrick, *Russian Revolution*, pp. 114–15 and Lewin, *Russian Peasants*, ch. 9.
249 *ibid.*, p. 299.
250 Cohen, *Bukharin*, p. 307.
251 *Pravda*, 23 December 1929, cited in Lewin, *Russian Peasants*, p. 451. Emphases in original.
252 *ibid.*, p. 487.
253 The type of people entering the party throughout this decade (discussed above) and Stalin's ability to direct his appeal to them was important. On his appeal to working class prejudices late in the decade, see Fitzpatrick, *Russian Revolution*, p. 132.
254 The Trotskyist opposition was able to gain majority support at some party meetings in late 1923–early 1924 (Carr, *Interregnum*, p. 331); meetings in Moscow and Leningrad in October 1926 showed respectively 171 opposition supporters out of a total of 53,208 party members and 325 out of 34,180 (*KPSS v rez*, vol. 4, p. 66); and there was said to be 5,000 to 6,000 supporters of the opposition platform in the lead-up to the XV Congress (Carr, *Foundations*, p. 44). When the United Opposition sought to generate grass roots support in the factories in September–October 1926, they were abject failures, often being met with hostility and opposition. Although according to Reiman, *Birth*, (ch. 3), the United Opposition enjoyed quite extensive support. Also see the reported reaction of some party secretaries to the Right Opposition and the low levels of oppositional activity among those in the party apparatus cited in ch. 3. For discussions of the extent of support for Stalin and for the Right, see Cohen, *Bukharin*, pp. 287–8, 326–9. According to Bazhanov, in late 1923 Stalin was able to ensure that the figures of oppositional support published in *Pravda* understated the level of that support. *Vospominaniia*, p. 80.
255 See ch. 3.

5 Regions under pressure

1 For example, see the discussion of the '25,000ers', urban workers mobilised at the end of 1929 for work in the countryside, in Lynn Viola, 'The "25,000ers": a study in a Soviet recruitment campaign during the First Five Year Plan', *Russian History*, 10, 1 (1983), pp. 22–8 and Lynne Viola, *The best*

sons of the Fatherland. Workers in the vanguard of Soviet collectivization (Oxford University Press, 1987).
2 According to one scholar, during the 1930s some one to two million peasants annually left the kolkhozy to join the industrial labour force. Sheila Fitzpatrick, *Education and social mobility in the Soviet Union 1921–1934* (Cambridge University Press, 1979), p. 178. For the numbers of communists and working-class youth mobilised into technical education at this time, see Sheila Fitzpatrick, 'Stalin and the making of a new elite, 1928–1939', *Slavic Review*, 38, 3 (September 1979), pp. 384–5 and Fitzpatrick, *Education*, ch. 11.
3 On the so-called 'wrecking activities' of anti-Soviet elements who had wormed their way into the kolkhozy, see 'Tseli i zadachi politicheskikh otdelov MTS i sovkhozov' of January 1933. *Kommunisticheskaia partiia sovetskogo soiuza v rezoliutsiiakh i resheniiakh s'ezdov, konferentsii i plenumov Ts. K.* (Moscow, 1985), vol. 6, p. 22. Also see Merle Fainsod, *Smolensk Under Soviet Rule* (New York: Vintage Books, 1958), ch. 12.
4 On famine see James Mace, 'Famine and nationalism in Soviet Ukraine', *Problems of Communism*, 33, 3 (May–June 1984), pp. 37–50 and Robert Conquest, *The harvest of sorrow. Soviet collectivisation and the terror famine* (London: Hutchinson, 1986). The motives for bringing on the famine attributed to the central authorities by these authors is a matter of some dispute.
5 Gábor Tamás Rittersporn, 'Soviet politics in the 1930s: rehabilitating society', *Studies in Comparative Communism*, 19, 2 (Summer 1986), pp. 123–4. According to Rittersporn, in 1932–35 (and 1937), the number of people leaving jobs exceeded the total number of those working in industry. On worker dissatisfaction in 1929–30, also see Fainsod, *Smolensk*, pp. 309–13, 317–18. On concerns about the 'peasantisation' of the work force in 1930–31, see Hiroaki Kuromiya, *Stalin's industrial revolution. Politics and workers, 1928–1932* (Cambridge University Press, 1988), ch. 8. Also see Donald Filtzer, *Soviet workers and Stalinist industrialisation. The formation of modern Soviet production relations* (London: Pluto Press, 1986), ch. 3.
6 In October 1930 the free movement of labour was forbidden and in December of the same year factory managers were forbidden to employ those who had left their previous jobs without permission. Prison sentences were introduced for violation of labour discipline in January 1931, initially just for railwaymen. In February compulsory labour books were introduced for all industrial and transport workers, and from March negligence was to be met with punitive measures; workers were soon held responsible for damage to materials or instruments. From July 1932 the consent of workers was no longer needed for their transfer between enterprises, and in August the death penalty was introduced for the theft of state or kolkhoz property. In November 1932 instant dismissal became the penalty for unauthorised absence from work, and in December internal passports were reintroduced. T. Szamuely, 'The elimination of opposition between the Sixteenth and Seventeenth Congresses of the CPSU', *Soviet Studies*, 17, 3 (1966),

pp. 336–7. In practice, many of these measures were ineffective. Filtzer, *Soviet workers*, ch. 6.
7 For some figures, see Gábor Tamás Rittersporn, 'Soviet officialdom and political evolution. Judiciary apparatus and penal policy in the 1930s', *Theory and Society*, 13 (1984), p. 216.
8 Robert Conquest, *The Great Terror* (Harmondsworth: Penguin, 1971), p. 727.
9 J. V. Stalin, *Problems of Leninism* (Peking, 1976), pp. 625–6. On 7 August 1932 Sovnarkom had adopted a resolution giving courts the power to impose extreme sentences, including the death penalty, for crimes against 'public property'. Rittersporn, 'Officialdom', p. 216.
10 J. Arch Getty, *Origins of the Great Purges. The Soviet Communist Party reconsidered 1933–1938* (Cambridge University Press 1985), p. 94; Boris I. Nicolaevsky, *Power and the Soviet elite. 'The letter of an Old Bolshevik' and other essays* (Ann Arbor: University of Michigan Press, 1965), p. 90; Aryeh L. Unger, *Constitutional development in the USSR. A guide to the Soviet Constitutions* (London: Methuen, 1981), p. 52; Eugene Huskey, *Russian lawyers and the Soviet state. The origins and development of the Soviet Bar, 1917–1939* (Princeton University Press, 1986), p. 185.
11 In practice, this may have had the opposite effect in that the re-organised NKVD now concentrated all civil coercive functions, principally police and security, within the one organisation.
12 For example, see *Partiinoe stroitel'stvo*, 6–7 (March 1934), p. 37 (hereafter *PS*). The elimination of the special political departments at the November 1934 CC plenum was another reflection of the return to normalcy; it implied no imminent offensive in the countryside.
13 Huskey, *Lawyers*, p. 180.
14 Figures are for 1 January. T. H. Rigby, *Communist Party membership in the USSR 1917–1967* (Princeton University Press, 1968), p. 52.
15 *KPSS v rez*, vol. 5, p. 440.
16 Rigby, *Membership*, p. 184. By April 1930, workers engaged in production were reported to constitute 48.6% of the membership. *PS* 11–12(13–14) (June 1930), p. 19.
17 Calculated from figures in Rigby, *Membership*, pp. 52, 189. A further 62,785 joined in the following three months.
18 *ibid.*, pp. 199–200.
19 For some figures on party saturation among professional groups, see *ibid.*, p. 200.
20 *XVII s'ezd vsesoiuznoi kommunisticheskoi partii (b) 26 ianvaria – 10 fevralia 1934g. Stenograficheskii otchet* (Moscow, 1934), p. 555.
21 *ibid.*, p. 557. This was associated with a decline in territorially based cells and an increase in those based on production, such as kolkhozy, sovkhozy and MTS. In any case, the increased numbers were partly a function of organisational reshuffling rather than vigorous institutional growth. In 1933 a process was set in train of breaking up large party cells into a number of smaller ones. For example, between April and June 1933, the number of kolkhoz cells in Chernigov oblast increased from 237 to 740. *PS*

12 (June 1933), p. 39. Also see the discussion in Daniel G. Thorniley, *The impact of collectivization on the Soviet rural Communist Party, 1927–1937*, unpublished Ph.D., CREES, University of Birmingham (1983).
22 The figures for numbers of organisations are obtained by subtracting the rural from the total figures given by Kaganovich. Membership figures come from comparison of those cited by Kaganovich for rural organs with the total figures cited by Rigby, (*Membership*, p. 52). The figure for 1930 is the mid-point between Rigby's figures for 1 January 1930 and 1931; for the later figure, Kaganovich's figure of October 1933 has been subtracted from Rigby's figure of 1 January 1934, so it is at best only a rough approximation.
23 Figures come from *ibid.*, p. 491. Some 78% of party members were in urban areas in 1933.
24 *ibid.*, p. 188. The situation was better in the MTS, where only 10% were without a cell. *PS* 13 (July 1932), p. 23.
25 For example, see *PS* 6(8) (March 1930), p. 7; 9(11) (May 1930), pp. 19–25.
26 Levels of voluntary withdrawal were also important here. There are no reliable figures on this. T. H. Rigby implies, although he does not state, that the proportion may have approached 11%. Rigby, *Membership*, pp. 204–5.
27 From the resolution entitled 'O chistke partii' adopted by a joint CC–CCC plenum on 28 April 1933. *KPSS v rez*, vol. 6, p. 46. For the drawing of a direct link between recruitment methods and membership quality, see *XVII s'ezd*, p. 552. On lower level party members falling under the influence of 'wrecking elements', see the CC–CCC resolution of 7–12 January 1933, 'Tseli i zadachi politicheskikh otdelov MTS i sovkhozov', *KPSS v rez*, vol. 6, pp. 22.
28 *Pravda*, 11 November 1932.
29 *PS* 11 (June 1931), p. 13.
30 For example, see the CC decision of 13 September 1930 entitled 'O zadachakh partprosveshcheniia', *KPSS v rez*, vol. 5, pp. 208–13.
31 'O chistke partii', 12 January 1933, *KPSS v rez*, vol. 6, p. 32.
32 'O chistke partii', 28 April 1933, *KPSS v rez*, vol. 6, 45–50, esp. pp. 46–7.
33 *XVII s'ezd*, p. 287 and Rigby, *Membership*, pp. 203–4. In 1934, 33% of those in rural party organisations were expelled or reduced to sympathiser status, while of those in kolkhoz party organisations the corresponding figure was 38%. *PS* 7 (April 1935), p. 33.
34 Leonard Schapiro, *The Communist Party of the Soviet Union* (London: Methuen, 1970), p. 459.
35 For example, see major articles in *PS* 9(11) (May 1930), pp. 3–7; 11–12(13–14) (June 1930), pp. 21–9.
36 See ch. 3 and note 96 below.
37 See ch. 3 above.
38 *PS*, 9 (May 1932), p. 49.
39 *PS*, 11–12 (June 1932), pp. 35, 36, 47.
40 See Stalin's 'Dizzy with success', 2 March 1930. J. V. Stalin, *Works* (Moscow, 1953), vol. 12, pp. 197–205. Also see the CC decision of 14 March 1930 'O bor'be s iskrivleniiami partliniï v kolkhoznom dvizhenii', *KPSS v*

rez, vol. 5, pp. 101–4. This decision did not appear until nearly two weeks after Stalin's article. The delay has not been explained, although it may be related to rumours that Stalin's article was written and published without Politburo approval. Conquest, *Terror*, p. 43 citing *Leningradskaia Pravda*, 2 December 1962. However, according to one study there had been pressures at the top for the publication of an article ushering in a period of relaxation. R. W. Davies, *The industrialisation of Soviet Russia*, vol. 1, *The socialist offensive. The collectivisation of Soviet agriculture 1929–1930* (London: Macmillan, 1980), pp. 267–8. Also see Stalin's comments of 3 April 1930, *Works*, vol. 12, pp. 207–34. The CC decision labelled the 'distortions' of the party line in collectivisation a leftist deviation which could only strengthen rightist elements in the party. Also see the CC letter of 24 September 1930, 'O kollektivizatsii', *KPSS v rez*, vol. 5, pp. 214–15. On lower level opposition to collectivisation, see Fainsod, *Smolensk*, pp. 143–44.

41 For the importance of the issue, see for example *PS*, 7–8(9–10) (April 1930), pp. 18–22; 7 (April 1931), pp. 14–18; 22 (November 1931), pp. 37–46; 1–2 (January 1932), p. 19; 6 (March 1932), pp. 18–20, 25–7; 22 (November 1932), pp. 24–30; 5 (March 1933), pp. 46–52.

42 The need for the large-scale mobilisation of urban inhabitants during the collectivisation campaign is but one reflection of this.

43 For example, see the reports in *PS*, 3–4 (February 1931), pp. 67–8; 17 (September 1931), p. 24.

44 *PS*, 16 (August 1934), p. 2.

45 For example, *PS*, 18 (September 1931), p. 12; 22 (November 1931), pp. 40–6; 6 (March 1932), p. 26; 14 (July 1932), p. 47; 19–20 (October 1932), pp. 28–30; 22 (November 1932), pp. 22–3; 20 (October 1933), p. 42.

46 On mobility, see *PS*, 17 (September 1931), p. 1; 6 (March 1932), pp. 25–7; 10 (May 1932), p. 28; 11–12 (June 1932), pp. 35–7; 14 (July 1932), pp. 47–8; 16 (August 1932), pp. 11, 20; 22 (November 1932), pp. 19–20; 9 (May 1933), p. 12; 11 (May 1933), pp. 43–5; 16 (August 1933), pp. 39–41. One explanation offered for the high mobility levels was the weakness of knowledge of the aktiv, with the result that personnel managers always turned to the same people to fill posts. Another was the lack of knowledge of individual party workers' skills and talents with a resultant absence of any attempts to match needs with qualities. Respectively, *PS*, 6 (March 1932), p. 27; 16 (August 1933), p. 39.

47 For these specific complaints, see *PS*, 17 (September 1931), p. 5; 16 (August 1932), p. 20. For more general complaints about the standard of the appointment machinery, see *PS*, 7–8 (April 1932), p. 12; 11–12 (June 1932), pp. 37, 40; 22 (November 1932), pp. 18–21.

48 *PS*, 7–8 (April 1932), p. 5.

49 For example, *PS*, 3–4(5–6) (February 1930), 15; 7–8(9–10) (April 1930), p. 76; 16 (August 1932), p. 21; 5 (March 1933), pp. 50–2.

50 For example, *PS*, 6 (March 1932), p. 19.

51 See the argument for a standardisation and restructuring of registration procedures in *PS*, 9 (May 1933), pp. 12–15. Also the discussion in *PS*, 16 (August 1934), pp. 19–25.

52 *PS*, 18 (September 1933), p. 4; 14 (July 1934), p. 3.
53 Respectively *PS*, 16 (August 1934), p. 24 and *XIV s'ezd*, pp. 285–6.
54 For example, *PS*, 21 (November 1934), p. 62.
55 One secretary of a party cell was in this category, having been excluded in 1929. *XVII s'ezd*, p. 289.
56 See Fainsod, *Smolensk* and Getty, *Origins*, p. 36.
57 *PS*, 4 (February 1935), p. 32.
58 For example, *PS*, 16(18) (August 1930), pp. 18–29; 11 (June 1931), p. 13; 1–2 (January 1932), p. 14; 3–4 (February 1932), p. 18; 7–8 (April 1932), p. 13; 11–12 (June 1932), p. 36; 17–18 (September 1932), p. 70; 19–20 (October 1932), p. 77; 14 (July 1934), p. 3.
59 *PS*, 1 (January 1934), pp. 1–7.
60 *PS*, 16 (August 1934), pp. 19, 23. See the CC instruction of 13 November 1933 calling on local party organisations to send the party documents of those who had died or withdrawn immediately to the obkom which was to forward them to the CC. Cited in Getty, *Origins*, p. 55.
61 For example, *PS*, 3–4(5–6) (February 1930), pp. 5–6; 7 (April 1931), p. 52; 7–8 (April 1933), p. 5; 11 (May 1933), p. 6; 1 (January 1934), pp. 1–7; 10 (May 1934), p. 1; 13 (July 1934), pp. 1–2; 16 (August 1934), pp. 1–3; 18 (September 1934), p. 3.
62 *XVII s'ezd*, pp. 33–4.
63 *XVII s'ezd*, pp. 285–7, 552, 670–1.
64 See the article in *PS*, 13–14(15–16) (July 1930), pp. 10–13. For some figures, see Davies, *Industrialisation*, p. 351.
65 *PS*, 3–4 (February 1931), p. 68.
66 See the discussion in Fainsod, *Smolensk*, pp. 280–9.
67 *KPSS v rez*, vol. 6, pp. 186–91.
68 For the introduction of this, see *XVI s'ezd vsesoiuznoi kommunisticheskoi partii (b). Stenograficheskii otchet* (Moscow, 1931), pp. 82, 94–6; *PS*, 2(4) (February 1930), pp. 1–13; *Spravochnik partiinogo rabotnika* (Moscow, 1930), 7, pp. 169–71.
69 *XVII s'ezd*, pp. 561–2, 672; *PS*, 1 (January 1934), pp. 1–7.
70 In some gubkoms and raikoms, departments were to be abolished and replaced by responsible instructors supervised by the party secretary and his assistant. *PS*, 1 (January 1934), p. 4.
71 The final structure of the 1930 reorganisation was not finally approved by the Orgburo until 7 May 1932, a delay that suggests significant opposition. *PS*, 9 (May 1932), pp. 60–1. On the 1934 restructuring, see as examples the reports in *PS*, 8 (April 1934), pp. 1–5; 9 (May 1934), pp. 1, 11–28; 11 (June 1934), pp. 10–26. Also see Kaganovich's speech in which he discusses the functions of the Leading Party Organs Departments, 'O vnutripartiinoi rabote i otdelakh rukovodiashchikh partiinykh organov', *Bol'shevik*, 12 (15 November 1934), pp. 8–19. The 1934 change also seems to have included an attempt to weaken regional leaders by including a provision that in obkoms, kraikoms and the CCs of national communist parties, secretariats should be abolished and questions requiring discussion should go directly to the bureau. This looks like an attempt to make the party secretary more

responsible to the bureau by eliminating the organisational sieve he could use to structure the agenda of bureau meetings. The secretariat referred to was clearly that body which did the secretarial work for the meeting; the same report listed the following departments that were to be formed in obkoms and kraikoms: Agriculture, Industry-transport, Soviet trade, Culture and propaganda of Leninism, Leading party organs and Special sector. *PS* 1 (January 1934), p. 4.
72 Getty, *Origins*, p. 31.
73 The main sources on the special sectors are Niels Erik Rosenfeldt, *Knowledge and power. The role of Stalin's Secret Chancellery in the Soviet system of government* (Copenhagen: Rosenkilde and Bagger, 1978), pp. 63–97; Niels Erik Rosenfeldt, '"The consistory of the communist church": The origins and development of Stalin's secret chancellery', *Russian History*, 9, 2–3 (1982), pp. 308–24; and Niels Erik Rosenfeldt, 'Stalinism as a system of communication', John W. Strong, ed., *Essays on revolutionary culture and Stalinism* (Columbus: Slavica, 1989).
74 *XVII s'ezd*, pp. 561, 672.
75 Abdurakhman Avtorkhanov, *Stalin and the Soviet Communist Party. A study in the technology of power* (New York: Praeger, 1959), p. 107.
76 According to Rosenfeldt, the special sectors had no responsibilities for administration in the local areas and therefore no reason to conceal local deficiencies or to become involved in family groups. Rosenfeldt, 'Stalinism'.
77 *XVII s'ezd*, pp. 562, 600. Dissatisfaction with the performance of these bodies is also reflected in the fact that the 1933 purge was to be conducted by a new Central Purge Commission rather than the CCC.
78 *XVII s'ezd*, pp. 562–4.
79 For one discussion, see Getty, *Origins*, ch. 2.
80 *PS*, 23–24 (December 1932), p. 6; 18 (September 1933), p. 3.
81 *PS*, 3–4 (February 1933), p. 55; 10 (May 1933), pp. 4–5.
82 *PS*, 11 (June 1933), pp. 1–11.
83 See *PS*, 18 (September 1930), pp. 42–3 and Fainsod, *Smolensk*, pp. 143–4.
84 *PS*, 1–2 (January 1933), pp. 31–2.
85 *PS*, 23–24 (December 1932), p. 3.
86 *PS*, 9(11) (May 1930), pp. 5–6.
87 *PS*, 10(12) (May 1930), pp. 32–3.
88 *PS*, 11–12(13–14) (June 1930), pp. 21–9, esp. p. 22.
89 See some articles in *PS*, 24 (December 1931), pp. 13–18; 23–4 (December 1932), p. 8.
90 *PS*, 10 (May 1933), p. 34; 11 (June 1934), pp. 1–2.
91 *PS*, 16 (August 1933), p. 10; 17 (September 1933), pp. 16–18; 11 (June 1934), p. 2.
92 *PS*, 18 (September 1934), pp. 6–7.
93 Rigby, *Membership*, pp. 203–4.
94 Although for the removal of some 200 gorkom and raikom secretaries since 1 January 1934, see *PS*, 18 (September 1934), p. 6.
95 *XVII s'ezd*, pp. 286–7. Also *PS*, 11 (June 1934), p. 2.

96 For some references to this phenomenon, see *PS*, 3–4(5–6) (February 1930), p. 88; 16(18) (August 1930), pp. 55–6; 10 (May 1933), p. 34; 11 (June 1934), p. 2; 16 (August 1934), pp. 2–3.
97 This was even though the creation of such a power base generated further pressures; they had to act in ways which would preserve and serve their local power base, action which could bring them into conflict with the central authorities. On their difficult position, see Fainsod, *Smolensk*, pp. 74–6.
98 For one complaint to this effect, see *PS*, 10 (May 1933), p. 34. For party bodies existing only on paper and others meeting infrequently, see *PS*, 10 (May 1932), p. 38; 1–2 (January 1933), p. 78.
99 On privilege and corruption at the raikom level, see Fainsod, *Smolensk*, pp. 118–21.
100 For example, *PS*, 16 (August 1934), pp. 3, 48; 22 (November 1934), pp. 14–15.
101 If needed, this may have been reinforced by the decision of the November 1934 CC plenum to place the district committee secretary and the MTS deputy director for political affairs on the CC nomenklatura. *KPSS v rez*, vol. 6, p. 190.
102 On the disillusionment of lower level leaders with the attacks at the time of collectivisation, see *PS*, 11–12(13–14) (June 1930), p. 75 and Davies, *Industrialisation*, pp. 313–23.

6 The Stalinist Elite?

1 See the discussion in Aleksandrov', *Kto upravliaet' Rossiei? Bol'shevistskii partiino-pravitel'stvennyi apparat i Stalinizm. Istoriko-dogmaticheskii analiz* (Berlin, 1933), pp. 351–6.
2 Politburo: Kamenev, Lenin, Rykov, Stalin and Trotsky; CC full: Dzerzhinsky, Sokol'nikov; CC candidate: Shmidt.
3 Full members: Rykov, Voroshilov, Rudzutak and Kuibyshev; candidate member: Mikoian.
4 Full Politburo: Molotov, Kuibyshev, Rudzutak, Voroshilov and Ordzhonikidze; candidate Politburo: Mikoian; CC: Rukhimovich, Yakovlev and Antipov; CCC: Andreev, Rozengolts and Yanson. Only Litvinov and Grinko had no leading party post.
5 Based on a survey of *Izvestiia tsentral'nogo komiteta Rossiiskoi kommunisticheskoi partii (bol'shevikov)* and *Partiinoe stroitel'stvo*. Also see Derek Watson, *The Making of Molotov's Sovnarkom. 1928–1930* (CREES Discussion Papers, SIPS No. 25, University of Birmingham, 1984), p. 2.
6 Ger P. Van den Berg, 'The Council of Ministers of the Soviet Union', *Review of Socialist Law*, 6, 3 (1980), p. 296.
7 This was called the Conference of the Chairman and Deputy Chairmen of Sovnarkom. *Ibid.*, p. 297; Watson, *Sovnarkom*, p. 12.
8 Cited in *ibid.*, p. 18. Also see the figures in Sheila Fitzpatrick, 'Ordzhonikidze's takeover of Vesenkha: a case-study in Soviet bureaucratic politics', *Soviet Studies*, 37, 2 (April 1985), pp. 156–7.

9 See Sheila Fitzpatrick, ed., *Cultural Revolution in Russia 1928–1931* (Bloomington: Indiana University Press, 1978).
10 Perhaps the most obvious victor in this conflict was the successor to Vesenkha, the Commissariat of Heavy Industry headed by Ordzhonikidze. For conflict over growth rates, see Fitzpatrick, 'Ordzhonikidze' and Eugene Zaleski, *Stalinist planning for economic growth 1933–1952* (Chapel Hill NC: University of North Carolina Press, 1980), pp. 115–29. For conflict over the attitude to the bourgeois specialists, see Kendall E. Bailes, *Technology and society under Lenin and Stalin. Origins of the Soviet technical intelligentsia 1917–1941* (Princeton University Press, 1978), pp. 126–127. For the debate over markets, see R. W. Davies, 'The socialist market: a debate in Soviet industry, 1932–33', *Slavic Review*, 42, 2 (July 1984), pp. 201–23. Also see Sheila Fitzpatrick, *The Russian Revolution* (Oxford University Press, 1982), pp. 139, 143–4.
11 The November 1929 CC plenum scheduled the congress for May 1930, but on April 6 it was announced that the congress would now open on 15 June. On 7 June it was further postponed to 26 June. R. W. Davies, *The industrialisation of Soviet Russia. 1. The socialist offensive. The collectivisation of Soviet agriculture 1929–1930* (London: Macmillan, 1980), p. 323.
12 There was also a party conference, the XVII, in January–February 1932.
13 Early congresses do not provide clear information on this point, although the VIII Congress does give a figure of 8.8% of an incomplete number of delegates (75.6%) as 'party professionals'. *Vos'moi s'ezd RKP(b) Mart 1919 goda. Protokoly* (Moscow, 1959), p. 452.
14 It is possible that the figure for soviet-administrative organs at the XVI Congress includes those listed separately under agricultural economy (10%) and transport (6%) at the XVII Congress. According to information cited by Conquest, at the XVII Congress, 1.5% of full delegates and 1.3% of all delegates were from the police. Robert Conquest, *Inside Stalin's Secret Police: NKVD politics 1936–39* (Stanford, Hoover Institution Press, 1985), p. 111 for the list of police delegates. *XVI s'ezd vsesoiuznoi kommunisticheskoi partii (b). Stenograficheskii otchet* (Moscow, 1931), p. 599 and *XVII s'ezd vsesoiuznoi kommunisticheskoi partii (b) 26 ianvaria – 10 fevralia 1934g. Stenograficheskii otchet* (Moscow, 1934), p. 303.
15 The reports only give figures for delegates with a consultative vote. At the XVI Congress, 37.8% came from central institutions and 62.2% from non-central organisations while the corresponding figures at the XVII Congress were 47% and 53%. This change may be linked with the decline in party workers noted above and the political tensions of the times.
16 At the XVI and XVII Congresses respectively 71.2% and 60%, compared with figures of 6.7% and 8.0% for peasants. *XVI s'ezd*, p. 599 and *XVII s'ezd*, p. 303.
17 Among those with a decisive vote, 4.4% (XVI) and 10.0% (XVII) had higher education. *XVI s'ezd*, p. 600 and *XVII s'ezd*, p. 303. At the XVI Congress a figure of 2.8% is also given for those with unfinished higher education; there is no corresponding figure for the XVII Congress.

18 Of those with a decisive vote, 17.9% in 1930 and 21.6% in 1934. *XVI s'ezd*, p. 600 and *XVII s'ezd*, p. 303.
19 The only figure given is one of 7.6% women in 1930. *XVI s'ezd*, p. 599. Other generalisations are based on perusal of delegates' lists.
20 The breakdown for the XVI Congress was as follows: 20–30 – 10%, 30–40 – 60.1%, 40–50 – 25% and 50+ – 5% (sic). *XVI s'ezd*, p. 599. No figures are given for the XVII Congress.
21 *XVI s'ezd*, p. 598 and *XVII s'ezd*, p. 303. Only the XVII Congress gives a later breakdown: 1921–23 – 4%, 1924–28 – 13.4% and 1929 – 2.6%.
22 *Pravda*, 2 March 1930.
23 *XVII s'ezd*, p. 28.
24 For example, see the comments of Stalin, Rudzutak and Kaganovich, *XVII s'ezd*, pp. 33–6, 285–7, 552.
25 There are reasons not to accept such arguments. See below. On moves against Stalin, see Boris I. Nicolaevsky, *Power and the Soviet elite*. 'The letter of an Old Bolshevik' and other essays (Ann Arbor: University of Michigan Press, 1965), ch. 1; Adam Ulam, *Stalin. The man and his era* (London: Allen Lane, 1974), pp. 371–5; Niels Erik Rosenfeldt, *Knowledge and power. The role of Stalin's Secret Chancellery in the Soviet system of government* (Copenhagen: Rosenkilde and Bagger, 1978), pp. 112–13; and R. A. Medvedev, *K sudu istorii. Genezis i posledstviia Stalinizma* (New York: Alfred A. Knopf, 1974), pp. 315–16. In December 1987 a previously unpublished section of Mikoian's memoirs appeared. This confirmed the rumour that a group of delegates suggested that Stalin be replaced by Kirov as General Secretary and that Kirov received the most votes of any candidate for election to the CC. *Ogonek*, 50 (1987), cited in Radio Liberty Research Bulletin 509/87 (18 December 1987) and 3/88 (23 December 1987).
26 *XVI s'ezd*, pp. 300–27 for Ordzhonikidze's report. Also the discussion in Fitzpatrick, 'Ordzhonikidze', pp. 160–2. For attempts to defend Vesenkha, see the comments of two of its deputy chairmen, Mezhlauk and Lobov on pp. 588–9, 641.
27 In December 1930 he replaced Kuibyshev as Chairman of Vesenkha.
28 *XVII s'ezd*, pp. 354, 435–6, 648–50. Also see Zaleski, *Planning*, pp. 115–29 and J. Arch Getty, *Origins of the Great Purges. The Soviet Communist Party reconsidered 1933–1938* (Cambridge University Press, 1985), pp. 15–17.
29 No official figures were given in the stenographic report of the XVII Congress. These figures are based on the list in *Spravochnyi tom k vos'momu izdaniiu 'KPSS v rezoliutsiiakh i resheniiakh s'ezdov, konferentsii i plenumov ts. k.'* (Moscow, 1984), pp. 10–11.
30 See CC membership lists in *Sovetskaia Istoricheskaia Entsiklopedia* (Moscow, 1961–76), vol. 7, pp. 703–10 and Borys Levytsky, *The Soviet political elite* (Munich: unpublished, 1969), p. 17.
31 Relevant figures are as follows. Full members demoted to candidate status and candidate members promoted to full status are retained in their former categories.

	Full (%)	Candidate (%)
XV–XVI	83.1	86.0
XVI–XVII	80.3	49.3

32 Most members of the CC were male, Russian, educated before 1917 and lacked higher education.

33 Figures for full members alone are as follows (in %):

	CP Apparatus			State	Other	Uncertain
	Centre	Region	Total			
XV	21.1	35.2	56.3	29.6	14.1	–
XVI	16.9	23.9	40.8	45.1	11.3	2.8
XVII	12.7	29.6	42.3	42.3	9.9	5.6

34 The figures are (in %):

	Centre	Region
XV	33.8	43.8
XVI	39.8	36.9
XVII	36.0	38.8

35 See the discussion of the Politburo on pp. 231–2.
36 *XVII s'ezd*, pp. 564–5. This is suggested by his reference to many problems being solved through the intervention of the CC and Stalin.
37 The other six concerned the election of soviets (12/30 joint plenum), reports from communist party organisations (10/31), the role of political departments in MTS and sovkhozy, the party purge and the anti-party group of Eismont, Tolmachev Smirnov *et al.* (1/33 joint plenum), and the role of political departments in the rural economy (11/34).
38 *Spravochnik partiinogo rabotnika* (Moscow, 1934), vyp. 8, p. 300.
39 *Spravochnik partiinogo rabotnika* (Moscow, 1930), vyp. 7, ch. 2, pp. 169–71. The congress did not formally ratify the decision, but it was spelled out by Kaganovich in the Organisational Report of the CC, and the work of this body was approved in the resolution on the CC report. *XVI s'ezd*, pp. 82, 711. The change may have been ratified at the CC meeting just prior to the congress, but even if it was, the role of the plenum remained purely ratificatory.
40 *Spravochnik partiinogo rabotnika* (Moscow, 1935), vyp. 9, p. 128.
41 This can be seen by comparing the agendas with the decisions reproduced in the volumes of *KPSS v rez*.

42 This has been confirmed in Soviet sources. See Lev Razgon, 'At long last', *Moscow News*, 26 (26 June 1988), p. 10. For earlier statements, see Nicolaevsky, *Power*, pp. 28–30, 72 and Leonard Schapiro, *The Communist Party of the Soviet Union* (London: Methuen, 1970), pp. 396–7. Also see below.
43 Nicolaevsky, *Power*, p. 74. This view is supported by an analysis of some of the speeches at the plenum.
44 T. H. Rigby, 'The Soviet political executive, 1917–1986', Archie Brown, ed., *Political leadership in the Soviet Union* (London: Macmillan, 1989).
45 *XVII s'ezd*, p. 564.
46 Some changes were made at the December 1930 joint CC–CCC plenum. Rykov was replaced as a full member by G. K. Ordzhonikidze (Chairman of Vesenkha) and Andreev was removed as a candidate in connection with his election as Chairman of the Presidium of the CCC. Syrtsov had also been removed some 16 days earlier. At the February 1932 plenum, Andreev was restored, replacing Rudzutak who moved to the CCC. Abbreviations used in the table are as follows: CC Sec. Central Committee Secretary; Ch. Chairman; 1st Sec. First Secretary of a party committee; CPU Communist Party of the Ukraine; Gensec. General Secretary; Dep/ch. Deputy Chairman; SNK Sovnarkom; PC People's Commissar; Sov. Cont.C Soviet Control Commission; PC H.Ind. People's Commissar of Heavy Industry; RSFSR Russian Soviet Federated Socialist Republic.
47 It was at this plenum that Bukharin was expelled from the Politburo.
48 This means that the representation of the state apparatus and of regional bodies is understated. If individuals are categorised by their state rather than their party posts, 53.3% came from the central state apparatus and a further 20% from the regional state machine in 1930; corresponding figures for 1934 are 60% and 6.6%. In addition, in both Politburos some members who were not currently found in regional positions had had earlier experience in regional posts.
49 In 1926 Stalin and Molotov were in the Orgburo and Rykov was a member of Sovnarkom. In 1934, among full members, only Kosior was not a member of either body: Kaganovich, Kirov, Kuibyshev and Stalin were members of the Orgburo, while Andreev, Kuibyshev, Molotov, Ordzhonikidze, Voroshilov and Kalinin were members of Sovnarkom; so too were candidates Mikoian and Rudzutak.
50 Cited in Schapiro, *Communist Party*, p. 394.
51 For example, according to one author, the Politburo discussed the sowing campaign at each meeting during February 1930. Davies, *Industrialisation*, p. 305.
52 Karl Albrecht held a high position in the party between 1928 and 1931 and attended a number of Politburo meetings. He declared that meetings were held 'twice or at most three times per week'. Cited in John Lowenhardt, *The Soviet Politburo*, trans. Dymphna Clark (Edinburgh: Canongate, 1982), p. 96. Many issues were transferred into Politburo commissions for resolution.
53 According to Nicolaevsky, a similar demand with regard to the Eismont-Tolmachev-Smirnov group was also rejected. Cited in Conquest, *Terror*,

p. 56. See the discussion of the limits of Stalin's support in the Politburo in Schapiro, *Communist Party*, p. 397.
54 There were limits to their ability to carry issues forward. If R. W. Davies is correct, pressure from the Politburo upon Ordzhonikidze encouraged him to bring the debate over the socialist market that had been appearing in the pages of the newspaper of the Commissariat of Heavy Industry (which he headed) to an end. It also constituted a clear restriction upon the ability of Politburo members to encourage open discussion of policy issues through the bureaucratic organisations they headed. Davies, *Industrialisation*, p. 220.
55 This was reported in *Biulletin' Oppozitsii* (Paris, 1931), 19 (March 1931), p. 18. The validity of this as a general statement is questionable. The claim may be more plausible in regard to economic growth rates since it was the higher rates championed by Molotov, Kaganovich and Ordzhonikidze (despite disagreements between them about the most desirable level of such rates) against which Syrtsov was reacting in 1930.
56 Schapiro, *Communist Party*, p. 401.
57 *XVI s'ezd*, p. 93.
58 ibid., p. 94.
59 See in particular Kaganovich's speech to the Orgburo published in *PS*, 2(4) (February 1930), pp. 9–13. Also the preceding article, entitled 'The party apparatus at a new stage', pp. 3–8. Also *XVI s'ezd*, pp. 82, 94–5.
60 *PS*, 2(4) (February 1930), p. 10.
61 Schapiro, *Communist Party*, p. 611.
62 *XVI s'ezd*, pp. 94–5. It also seems to have involved the consolidation of many party documents in a single archive instead of being scattered throughout different departments as before.
63 In addition, the old Agitprop department was replaced by a Department for Agitation and Mass Campaigns and a Department for Culture and Propaganda. There was also a Secret Department, which is discussed below.
64 The Orgburo did not approve the final structure until May 1932. *PS*, 9 (May 1932), pp. 60–1.
65 *Izvestiia tsentral'nogo komiteta Rossiiskoi kommunisticheskoi partii (bol'shevikov)* 16–17(237–8) (25 May 1928), pp. 1–2.
66 *PS*, 5 (March 1931), pp. 14–20. Compare this with Aleksandrov', *Kto upravliaet'* p. 318. For a discussion of the plan, see the introduction to it in the same issue of *PS*, pp. 10–14.
67 *PS*, 1 (January 1934), pp. 1–7; *XVII s'ezd*, pp. 561–2.
68 *PS*, 1 (January 1934), p. 4. Also Schapiro, *Communist Party*, p. 611. The Special Sector seems to have superseded the Secret Department. According to Nicolaevsky, (*Power*, p. 97), the Special Sector was formerly Stalin's personal secretariat. The evidence is assessed in Rosenfeldt, *Knowledge*.
69 For example, see *PS*, 8 (April 1934), pp. 1–5; 9 (May 1934), pp. 1, 11–28; 11 (June 1934), pp. 10–26.
70 Schapiro, *Communist Party*, p. 449.
71 *XVII s'ezd*, p. 38. In 1930 the party apparatus, apart from the central and

krai levels, consumed 48% of expenditure. By 1933 this had jumped to 61%. *XVII s'ezd*, p. 39.
72 The available evidence on the functions of the Secret Department/Special Sector is surveyed in Rosenfeldt, *Knowledge*, pp. 63–98. The importance of this organ with regard to the police and Stalin's position will be discussed below.
73 See ch. 4.
74 Similar provisions were to apply to the Soviet Control Commission which replaced Rabkrin. *XVII s'ezd*, pp. 673–4.
75 *XVII s'ezd*, p. 674.
76 This is echoed in Stalin's speech to the XVII Congress where he links the reorganisation specifically with the need to verify the implementation of party and CC decisions. *XVII s'ezd*, p. 35.
77 *XVII s'ezd*, p. 297.
78 Conquest, *Terror*, pp. 52–3. Some uncertainty surrounds this episode. According to the report of the Politburo commission to study materials linked with the repressions of the 1930s to 1940s and the beginning of the 1950s, Riutin had been expelled from the party in September 1930. After his manifesto became known to the leadership, he was arrested along with some others by the OGPU on 15 September 1932. On 27 September, the CCC Presidium excluded 14 members of the so-called 'Union of Marxist-Leninists' from the party. This decision was confirmed at a meeting of the CC with the CCC Presidium on 2 October, the final day of a scheduled CC plenum. This suggests that the decision to expel the 14 members taken by the CCC Presidium had to be confirmed by the CC. This would have been discussed in the Politburo before the CC meeting. Presumably the fate of Riutin, who, not being a party member was not subject to the CCC, was also discussed. On 11 October the accused, including Riutin, were sentenced to terms of imprisonment. For the commission's report, see 'O dele tak nazyvaemogo "soiuza marksistov-lenintsev",' *Izv ts k KPSS*, 6 (1989), pp. 103–15.
79 *KPSS v rez*, vol. 6, pp. 32–3. This was declared to be confirming a decision of the CCC Presidium.
80 The members were Rudzutak, Kaganovich (L. M.), Kirov, Ezhov, Yaroslavsky and Shkiriatov. Rudzutak, Yaroslavsky and Shkiriatov were from the CCC. Getty, *Origins*, p. 51.
81 Only one agenda item, the question of the verification of the implementation of the decisions of the June 1931 plenum, relates to disciplinary considerations. I. M. Moskalenko, *Organy partiinogo kontrolya v period stroitel'stva sotsializma (zadachi, struktura, metody deiatel'nosti kontrol'nykh kommissii 1920–1934gg)* (Moscow, 1981), pp. 167–8.
82 *XVI s'ezd*, p. 717.
83 The total number in the CCC Presidium includes ten candidates in 1927 and six in 1930.
84 A similar situation applied to the Soviet Control Commission. A total of seventeen individuals was carried forward from the 1930 CCC to the new SCC, constituting 9.1% of the 1930 body and 24.3% of the newly elected organ.

85 In 1933, 30% of the chairmen of local control commissions were purged for failures in fulfilling their responsibilities. Hiroaki Kuromiya, *Stalin's industrial revolution. Politics and workers. 1928–1932* (Cambridge University Press, 1988), p. 296.
86 In principle the General Secretary was formally elected by the CC, but in practice this body merely ratified the candidate for office presented to it.
87 Rosenfeldt, *Knowledge*, p. 175.
88 *ibid.*, p. 204.
89 Or 'Administration of affairs' as it was sometimes called. *Ibid.*, p. 204. He also suggested that this was headed by Stalin's private secretary (p. 177).
90 For example, *XVII s'ezd*, p. 672.
91 The range of secret communications is emphasised in Niels Erik Rosenfeldt, 'Stalinism as a system of communication', J. W. Strong, ed., *Essays on revolutionary culture and Stalinism* (Columbus: Slavica, 1989). For a list of categories dating from 1927 which would render a document secret, see Fainsod, *Smolensk*, pp. 163–4.
92 Rosenfeldt, 'Stalinism', pp. 23–8.
93 These are discussed in many places. See, for example, Conquest, *Terror*, Appendix F.
94 Its responsibility for forced labour and the role this played in economic development can only have enhanced this image.
95 Schapiro, *Communist Party*, p. 399. The attempt was not successful. The establishment of the NKVD was accompanied by an increased emphasis on revolutionary legality. When the NKVD was founded, it included a special board which could impose sentences of five years' exile, thereby negating the nominal transfer of responsibility for sentencing to the courts. In November, the board gained the power to impose exile or imprisonment on those considered to be 'socially dangerous'. John A. Armstrong, *The politics of totalitarianism. The Communist Party of the Soviet Union from 1934 to the present* (New York: Random House, 1961), p. 17.
96 According to Nicolaevsky, Poskrebyshev headed a section of Stalin's personal secretariat entitled the Special Secret Political Department of State Security. Its date of creation is said to be uncertain, but it was in existence by mid-1933. Nicolaevsky, *Power*, pp. 93–95. Poskrebyshev headed Stalin's personal secretariat, Beria (who became head of the NKVD in 1938) was made First Secretary of Georgia and Transcaucasia in 1931, and Ezhov became head of the CC cadres department in 1930 and by 1935 was CC secretary responsible for the security apparatus; in 1936 he became People's Commissar of Internal Affairs. Also a former head of the security apparatus in Azerbaizhan, Bagirov, was made First Secretary there in 1935. See Rosenfeldt, *Knowledge*.
97 Yagoda is reported to have had sympathy for the Right Opposition and to have been concerned about the speed of collectivisation. Stephen F. Cohen, *Bukharin and the Bolshevik Revolution. A political biography 1888–1938* (New York: Alfred A. Knopf), pp. 288, 448. Also Schapiro, *Communist Party*, pp. 370, 379.
98 K. Popov, 'Partiia i rol' Vozhdia', *PS*, 1 (January 1930), pp. 5–9.

99 *ibid.*, p. 6.
100 *ibid.*, pp. 6–7.
101 *ibid.*, p. 7.
102 *ibid.*, p. 9.
103 See Graeme Gill, 'Personal dominance and the collective principle: individual legitimacy in Marxist-Leninist Systems', T. H. Rigby and Ferenc Feher, eds., *Political legitimation in Communist states* (London: Macmillan, 1982), pp. 94–110; Graeme Gill, 'Political myth and Stalin's quest for authority in the party', T. H. Rigby, Archie Brown and Peter Reddaway, eds., *Authority, power and policy in the USSR. Essays dedicated to Leonard Schapiro* (London: Macmillan, 1980), pp. 98–117; Robert C. Tucker, 'The rise of Stalin's personality cult', *American Historical Review*, 84, 2 (April 1979), pp. 347–66.
104 For example, respectively, *Pravda*, 5 June 1930, 10 November 1931 and 22 April 1932.
105 *Pravda*, 7 November 1930.
106 For example, *Pravda*, 2 September 1933, 7 November 1933, 4 March 1934, 22 April 1933.
107 *Pravda*, 21 January 1933, 22 January 1934, 16 February 1933, 19 June 1934, 2 February 1934.
108 For example, *Pravda*, 10 November 1931, 23 February 1934.
109 For some discussions of this, see R. L. Garthoff, 'The Stalinist revision of history', *Problems of Communism*, 2, 3–4 (July–December 1953) and S. I. Ploss, 'Soviet Party history: the Stalinist legacy', *Problems of Communism*, 21, 4 (July–August 1973).
110 For example, *Pravda*, 22 April 1932, 16 February 1932.
111 *Pravda*, 6 January 1934.
112 *Pravda*, 1 September 1931.
113 For example, *Pravda*, 1 January 1934, 21 January 1934.
114 For example, *Pravda*, 7 November 1930, 22 April 1932.
115 *XVI s'ezd*, p. 4.
116 *XVII s'ezd*, p. 5.
117 *ibid.*, p. 36.
118 For example, Bukharin. *XVII s'ezd*, p. 125. At this congress, Kamenev effectively justified Stalin's personal leadership. He declared that in the first period of the party's rule, Lenin was the party's 'theoretical leader and foremost fighter', but in the second (1925–34) period 'the theoretical leader of all the work of the party, its practical vozhd', its commander was comrade Stalin'. *XVII s'ezd*, p. 519.
119 For discussions, see R. W. Davies, 'The Syrtsov–Lominadze affair', *Soviet Studies*, 33, 1 (January 1981), pp. 29–50; T. Szamuely, 'The elimination of opposition between the Sixteenth and Seventeenth Congresses of the CPSU', *Soviet Studies*, 17, 3 (January 1966), pp. 318–38.
120 Riutin was apparently particularly insistent about this, devoting a quarter of his long tract to a bitter condemnation of Stalin for leading the revolution into the impasse in which it found itself. Nicolaevsky, *Power*, pp. 28–9.

121 For a discussion of Kirov's policy views at the time which argues that it is difficult to discern a line propounded by Kirov that is different from the official line, see Francesco Benvenuti, *Kirov in Soviet politics 1933–34* (CREES Discussion Paper, SIPS No. 8, University of Birmingham, 1977). Roy Medvedev argues that there was an estrangement between Stalin and Kirov during 1934. Medvedev, *K sudu*, pp. 317–18. Ulam argues that the threatening international situation in 1933–34, characterised by Japanese expansion and the rise of the Nazis, helped to bolster Stalin's position. Ulam, *Stalin*, p. 369. Also see above, ch. 5.
122 Following Rosenfeldt, *Knowledge*, pp. 112–13 and Ulam, *Stalin*, pp. 371–5.
123 He suggests that only three people opposed Kirov. Medvedev, *K sudu*, pp. 315–16. On this see Ulam, *Stalin*, p. 374 n. 14, who argues that the procedures for electing the CC made Stalin's defeat in the election unlikely. He argues that the failure of 270 delegates to vote for Stalin would not have made him almost miss out on election, because such a result would have required a negative vote by some 600 delegates, or half the voting members. Nevertheless the figure cited by Medvedev, 270 delegates voting against Stalin, has now been confirmed by Mikoian. Radio Liberty Research Bulletin, 3/88 (23 December 1987). In a recent Soviet source, it was claimed that Stalin received 300 votes fewer than Kirov. Leonid Radzikhovsky, 'December 1', *Moscow News*, 48 (27 November 1988), p. 6.
124 For example, see the joint CC–Sovnarkom directives in *PS*. See Rosenfeldt, *Knowledge*, p. 113 and Ulam, *Stalin*, p. 375. This was occurring at least as early as 1931.
125 In other contexts, such as party histories, he was accorded the fuller title.
126 One other indirect argument is that if Stalin had been downgraded, it is strange that this did not emerge in Khrushchevian historiography, which would have been anxious to highlight any such attempt by the party to restrict Stalin.
127 Ulam, *Stalin*, p. 375.
128 *XVII s'ezd*, p. 659.
129 Riutin apparently went further than anyone else, advocating the abolition of the collectives and the principle of economic self-determination for the peasants. Nicolaevsky, *Power*, p. 28.
130 Davies, *Industrialisation*, p. 326.
131 Relevant here are the measures taken in April 1929 to guarantee the secrecy of Politburo and CC deliberations. Aleksandrov', *Kto upravliaet*, p. 293. It is during this period that the earlier practice of circulating the protocols of CC meetings to local party organisations ceased. Fitzpatrick, 'Stalin', p. 383.
132 See the discussions in Cohen, *Bukharin*, p. 342; Schapiro, *Communist Party*, p. 390; and Getty, ch. 1. Also see Nicolaevsky, whose views on the positions by leading figures do not accord with Getty's analysis.
133 *Pravda*, 2 March 1930. Medvedev argues, without offering any evidence, that Stalin was forced into this by the CC. Medvedev, *K sudu*, p. 191. This

article also reflects the dangers inherent in a personalised conception of leadership: if things go wrong, it is difficult to avoid personal responsibility. This is precisely what Stalin was trying to do in this article.
134 On the moderate position, see Bailes, *Technology*, ch. 5, and p. 174. For Stalin's speech, see *Works*, vol. 13, pp. 53–82.
135 Fitzpatrick, *Education*, ch. 10.
136 For his speech on the Five Year Plan, see *Works*, vol. 13, pp. 161–219. Also Getty, *Origins*, p. 15.
137 Nicolaevsky, *Power*, pp. 90–1, 95–6. Nicolaevsky argues that there was a pro-relaxation majority in the CC and Politburo following the XVII Congress and that this included Kirov. He believes that Kaganovich and Ezhov opposed it (p. 49).
138 For example, Cohen, *Bukharin*, p. 342, Fitzpatrick, *Russian Revolution*, pp. 143–4 and Medvedev, *K sudu*, p. 191.
139 Schapiro, *Communist Party*, p. 392.
140 Nicolaevsky, *Power*, pp. 28–30, 72; Schapiro, *Communist Party*, pp. 396–7; Cohen, *Bukharin*, p. 344; W. G. Krivitsky, *I was Stalin's agent* (London: Hamish Hamilton, 1940), p. 203.
141 This suggests that Szamuely is mistaken when he argues that the Riutin affair constituted the dividing line between inner-party opposition being seen as dangerous and mistaken political activity and its condemnation as a capital crime against the state. Szamuely, 'Elimination', p. 327. Stalin may also have demanded the death penalty in the Eismont *et al.* case. Schapiro, *Communist Party*, p. 392.
142 As well as the more prominent trials of the Industrial Party, the Mensheviks and the Metro-Vickers engineers, there were a number of less prominent trials embracing bacteriologists (8/30), food industry officials (9/30), historians (2/31), timber industry workers (2/32), officials of state farms (3/33) and of the Agriculture Commissariat (3/33). Szamuely, 'Elimination', p. 334.
143 *XVI s'ezd*, p. 110. For the resolution see p. 716.
144 In his concluding remarks, Stalin demanded three things from the former leaders of the Right Opposition: (a) recognise the gulf that existed between the party line and their line, which objectively leads to the victory of capitalism; (b) brand that line as anti-Leninist and dissociate themselves from it openly and honestly; (c) fall into step with us and struggle against all right deviations. *XVI s'ezd*, p. 291. The statement made by the Right at the November 1929 CC plenum condemning their past attitudes was clearly considered inadequate.
145 *XVI s'ezd*, p. 716. Interesting in this regard is the treatment of Zinoviev and Kamenev. They had been readmitted to the party during the First Five Year Plan, had been arrested and exiled in late 1932 to early 1933, were welcomed back at the XVII Congress, and were arrested at the end of 1934. This reflects a degree of uncertainty about how to deal with former oppositionists.
146 *XVII s'ezd*, p. 261. Also see the letter of 1 August 1932 from Ye. Yaroslavsky to Vera Figner which declared that there could be no neutrality in

the struggle for socialism. *Moscow News*, 45 (6 November 1988), p. 9.
147 *XVI s'ezd*, p. 148. Also see the confessions of Zinoviev, Kamenev, Lominadze, Preobrazhensky, Piatakov, Tomsky, Rykov, Radek and Bukharin at the XVII Congress. *XVII s'ezd*, pp. 124–9, 209–12, 627–9. The sentiments expressed by Tomsky may explain the re-election of Bukharin, Rykov and Tomsky to the CC and Rykov to the Politburo at the XVI Congress and the permission for Zinoviev and Kamenev to re-enter the party.
148 This concern may be reflected in the fact that in the thirty Discussion Sheets which appeared in the lead-up to the XVI Congress, for the most part secondary issues alone were raised. Davies, *Industrialisation*, p. 324.
149 *Pravda*, 2 December 1930 and *KPSS v rez*, vol. 6, p. 32. The decision on Riutin does not appear to have been published.
150 See the discussion in Davies, 'Syrtsov'.
151 Graeme Gill, *The Rules of the Communist Party of the Soviet Union* (London: Macmillan, 1988), p. 152.
152 The first duty of a party member listed in the 1934 party Rules was to 'observe the strictest party discipline' (#2). Also see the references to Tomsky, Rykov and Shmidt in the resolution of the joint CC–CCC plenum of January 1933, 'Ob antipartiinoi gruppirovke Eismonta, Tolmacheva, Smirnova A. P. i dr.', *KPSS v rez*, vol. 6, p. 33.
153 This had been incorporated in the party Rules since 1919 but was given extra impetus by the 1933–34 purge.
154 *XVI s'ezd*, pp. 36, 51–3, 131–2, 337, 712–13.
155 *XVII s'ezd*, pp. 28, 566.
156 *Pravda*, 14 October 1932.
157 The secret provision from the X Congress resolution on party unity relating to members of the CC and the CCC was included in the party Rules adopted in 1934, perhaps to reinforce the point that even opposition at this level was forbidden.
158 See ch. 4.
159 *XVI s'ezd*, p. 338.
160 *Pravda*, 2 December 1930, on Syrtsov–Lominadze.
161 *KPSS v rez*, vol. 6, p. 50.
162 This is the main thesis of Getty.
163 See the comments in T. H. Rigby, *Communist Party membership in the USSR 1917–1967* (Princeton University Press, 1968), p. 213.
164 See this question discussed in Getty, *Origins*, pp. 207–10; Nicolaevsky, *Power*, pp. 69–102; Khrushchev, 'On the cult of personality and its consequences', T. H. Rigby, ed., *The Stalin dictatorship* (Sydney University Press, 1968), pp. 97–8; Medvedev, *K sudu*, ch. 5; Conquest, *Terror*, ch. 2; and Ulam, *Stalin*, pp. 380–6.
165 A strong case could be made out for the complicity of the NKVD. If that organisation was under Stalin's control, the trail would then lead directly back to him.
166 Presidium Chairman Kalinin was not even present to sign the law, an indication of the speed with which it was enacted. See the discussion in Ulam, *Stalin*, p. 381.

167 Schapiro, *Communist Party*, p. 401. The amendment to the RSFSR criminal code of 1 December 1934 created a special procedure for crimes involving terrorism (#58.8). The preliminary investigation had to be completed within ten days; the accused received the indictment no earlier than 24 hours before the trial; neither the defendant nor his counsel was allowed in the courtroom; no appeals were permitted and the death sentence was to be carried out immediately. This was slightly modified on 11 August 1936 when public hearings were re-established along with the use of legal counsel and a three-day post-sentence appeal period. Conquest, *Terror*, p. 150. A decree of 14 September 1937 simplified court procedures, forbade appeals and petitions for clemency and made provision for secret trials, thereby reversing part of the 1936 decision. Conquest, *Police*, p. 53.
168 Getty, *Origins*, p. 209. On 17 and 21 December, they were publicly blamed for the murder. Conquest, *Terror*, pp. 88–9.
169 According to Nicolaevsky, this prohibition stemmed from Lenin's 'commandment'. *Power*, p. 29.
170 See Stalin, *Works*, vol. 12, pp. 37–41.

7 Sub-national politics

1 While recognising the difficulties in using *émigré* material as a source for popular sentiment within the Soviet Union, particularly at a distance of some 15 years, a sense of this as a source of alienation from the regime can be gained from the responses in the Harvard Interview Project. See Alex Inkeles and Raymond Bauer. *The Soviet citizen, daily life in a totalitarian society* (Cambridge MA: Harvard University Press, 1959). On responses to the harsh labour legislation introduced towards the end of the decade, see Donald Filtzer, *Soviet workers and Stalinist industrialization. The formation of modern Soviet production relations* (London: Pluto Press, 1986), ch. 9.
2 One instance is shown in the memoirs of the dissident Petro Grigorenko who believed at the time that the purges were 'historical retribution for activities against the people'. Petro G. Grigorenko, *Memoirs* (London: Harvill Press, 1982), pp. 36–7. Heightened concern about the perceived internal danger may also be a factor in helping to explain the purges. If many found it difficult to believe that former leaders of the party had committed the crimes with which they were charged in the Moscow trials, many more probably interpreted these as simply a further manifestation of the presence within of the class enemy. Indeed, if those who had spent a lifetime in the party, fought for it in the revolution and endured significant trials and tribulations during their revolutionary careers had succumbed to the class enemy, how much more likely was it that among those party members who had been in the party for a short time, the numbers thus infected would be greater? The same logic would have applied to the population at large. Thinking like this would have justified the extent of the purges to the mass of political functionaries, at least insofar as they had some idea of the range of purging activity.

3 Paradoxically, at least in Belyi, the provisions of the constitution and the debate surrounding it seem to have led to an erosion of the party's position in the countryside as the peasants looked to the new legal provisions to support action against the collective farms and to hold free elections. Roberta T. Manning, *Government in the Soviet countryside in the Stalinist thirties: the case of the Belyi Raion in 1937* (The Carl Beck Papers in Russian and European Studies, Paper no. 301, University of Pittsburgh, 1984), pp. 35–40. The law continued to be seen as an instrument to be used against enemies of the proletarian state. But generally it was implemented with little predictability. See the discussion in Gabor Tamas Rittersporn, 'Soviet officialdom and political evolution. Judiciary apparatus and penal policy in the 1930s', *Theory and Society*, 13 (1984), pp. 211–37. For the fate of the legal profession, see Eugene Huskey, *Russian lawyers and the Soviet state. The origins and development of the Soviet Bar 1917–1939* (Princeton, Princeton University Press, 1986), ch. 5.
4 For some of the symbolism of this in the form of Stakhanovism, see Lewis H. Siegelbaum, *Stakhanovism and the politics of productivity in the USSR, 1935–1941* (Cambridge University Press, 1988).
5 Of these, 188 were in leading party work, 37 in the Komsomol and about 500 in soviet assignments. See the article by Korotchenkov in *Partiinoe stroitel'stvo*, 19 (October 1937), pp. 30–5.
6 See the discussion in Sheila Fitzpatrick, 'Stalin and the making of a new elite, 1928–1939', *Slavic Review*, 38, 3 (1979), pp. 377–402.
7 Based on figures in T. H. Rigby, *Communist Party membership in the USSR 1917–1967* (Princeton University Press, 1968), p. 52.
8 'O vosobnovlenii priema novykh chlenov v VKP(b)', 29 September 1936. *Kommunisticheskaia partiia sovetskogo soiuza v rezoliutsiiakh i resheniiakh s'ezdov, konferentsii i plenumov Ts.K.* (Moscow, 1985), vol. 6, pp. 369–72. This included suitable warnings against adopting the same sort of slack entry procedures which had made the purge necessary in the first place.
9 Membership dropped in 1941. Rigby, *Membership*, p. 52.
10 Using 1 January 1938 as a base figure. It grew by almost a million in 1939 alone.
11 Rigby, *Membership*, pp. 223, 225. The XVIII Congress in 1939 gave priority in recruitment to no social group.
12 *ibid.*, pp. 226–7. In 1938 workers by social class constituted 64.3% of all members. Between 1937 and June 1941, 24% of all recruits were workers. Because the party doubled during this period, workers would have constituted less than half of all party members.
13 *XVIII s'ezd vsesoiuznoi kommunisticheskoi partii (b) 10–21 marta 1939g. Stenograficheskii otchet* (Moscow, 1939), p. 109.
14 Rigby, *Membership*, p. 235.
15 *ibid.*
16 Cited in J. Arch Getty, *Origins of the Great Purges. The Soviet Communist Party reconsidered 1933–1938* (Cambridge University Press, 1985). pp. 29 & 30.
17 Manning, *Government*, p. 8.

18 John A. Armstrong, *The politics of totalitarianism. The Communist Party of the Soviet Union from 1934 to the present* (New York: Random House, 1961), p. 100.
19 Manning, *Government*, p. 28. According to Andreev, 5% of collective farms had PPOs by 1939. *XVIII s'ezd*, p. 109.
20 See the discussion in Daniel G. Thorniley, *The impact of collectivization on the Soviet rural Communist Party, 1927–1937* unpublished Ph.D, CREES, University of Birmingham (1983).
21 Rigby, *Membership*, p. 204.
22 These are discussed in Getty, *Origins*, ch. 3.
23 ibid., p. 81.
24 ibid., p. 80.
25 *PS*, 17 (15 October 1935), p. 2.
26 *KPSS v rez*, vol. 6, p. 300. However, in April 1936 it was declared to be aimed at purifying party ranks of hostile and alien elements. *PS*, 8 (25 April 1936), p. 18.
27 This will be discussed below. Concern about records and registration was linked to worries about the quality of membership by the fear that deficiencies in the former would enable unsuitable people to penetrate the party. For continuing concern about procedures of party entry, see the decision of 16 April 1939, 'Ob itogakh priema novykh chlenov v VKP(b) za aprel' – sentiabr' 1939 goda', *KPSS v rez*, vol. 7, pp. 142–4.
28 For example, *PS*, 20 (20 October 1936), pp. 3–7; 21 (5 November 1936), pp. 39–42; 22 (20 November 1936), pp. 4–5; 1 (1 January 1938), 46–8; 7 (1 April 1938), pp. 17–22; 1 (1 January 1939), pp. 9–12; 9 (May 1939), pp. 31–5; 21 (November 1939), pp. 59–60; 13 (July 1940), pp. 3–7.
29 For example, *PS*, 20 (20 October 1936), pp. 26–30; 22 (20 November 1936), pp. 3–9; 1 (1 January 1937), pp. 32–4; 3 (1 February 1937), pp. 34–8; 14 (15 July 1937), pp. 50–2; 16 (15 August 1937), pp. 18–26. In 1936, almost 30% of party members in Belyi district were classed as functional illiterates or educationally weak and were obliged to take measures to remedy these. Manning, *Government*, p. 10. On education, also see Nicolas Werth, *Etre communiste en URSS sous Staline* (Paris, Gallimard, 1981), ch. 3.
30 *PS*, 1–2 (January 1935), pp. 37–8. A secret CC letter in December 1934 entitled 'Lessons of the events connected with the evil murder of Comrade Kirov' called on party committees to hunt down former oppositionists who remained in the party. Conquest, *Terror*, p. 85. A secret circular of 18 January 1935 called for increased vigilance and a rooting out of counter-revolutionary nests of enemies. R. A. Medvedev, *K sudu istorii. Genezis i posledstviia Stalinizma* (New York: Alfred A. Knopf, 1974), p. 330.
31 *PS*, 3 (February 1935), p. 11.
32 *PS*, 4 (February 1935), pp. 32–6; 7 (April 1935), p. 40; 13 (July 1935), p. 29.
33 *PS*, 10 (May 1935), pp. 47–8.
34 *PS*, 12 (June 1935), pp. 28–30.
35 *PS*, 19–20 (15 November 1935), p. 31. A secret CC letter of 19 May 1935 called for the special investigation of enemies of the party and the working class who had remained in the party. Conquest, *Terror*, p. 127. This concern remained into 1940. *PS*, 5–6 (March 1940), p. 47.

36 For example, see *PS*, 8 (April 1935), pp. 23–5; 19–20 (15 November 1935), p. 50; 11 (5 June 1936), p. 26.
37 For example, *PS*, 4 (February 1935), pp. 32–4; 8 (April 1935), pp. 16–19; 1 (10 January 1936), p. 22; 21 (5 November 1936), p. 61; 3 (1 February 1937), p. 28; 4 (15 February 1937), pp. 58–9; 5 (10 March 1937), p. 27; 6 (20 March 1937), p. 40; 5 (March 1939), p. 24; 10 (May 1940), p. 6; 1 (January 1941), p. 32.
38 Cited in Getty, *Origins*, p. 35.
39 For example, the Saratov kraikom was accused of moving cadres who were within the nomenklatura of the CC. *PS*, 13 (July 1935), p. 44; 15 (August 1935), p. 12. More generally, it was claimed that the nomenklatura registration of some obkoms and kraikoms included some workers who should have been in the nomenklatura of other organisations, and therefore the existing arrangements needed review in order more clearly to define which positions fell under which organisation. *PS*, 11 (5 June 1936), p. 27. For some figures on the size of the obkom nomenklatura, see Merle Fainsod, *Smolensk under Soviet rule* (New York: Vintage Books, 1958), pp. 64–6.
40 Getty, *Origins*, pp. 58–60.
41 The letter is to be found in the Smolensk Archive WKP499 pp. 308–9. The following summary is based on Getty, *Origins*, pp. 60–3.
42 *PS*, 19–20 (15 November 1935), pp. 50–1; 22–3 (15 December 1935), p. 75. In October its aim was declared to be the cleansing of party ranks from decaying elements and alien people. *PS*, 17 (15 October 1935), p. 1.
43 *KPSS v rez*, vol. 6, p. 296. On 27 June 1935 officials of the Western Oblast were censured for insufficient vigilance. Conquest, *Terror*, p. 128.
44 The argument that the Verification was planned before Kirov's death and therefore cannot be seen as a reaction to that death should be treated with some caution. If it was planned in essentials before December 1934, why was it not implemented before May 1935? If it was seen as a necessity in general terms before Kirov's death, can we assume that the aims of the campaign remained unaffected by the assassination? Indeed, even if it was planned in its essentials before December, it is still likely that its aims would have undergone some modification under the impact of the assassination.
45 *PS*, 13 (July 1935), pp. 46–8.
46 *PS*, 15 (August 1935), pp. 6–22.
47 *PS*, 17 (15 October 1935), p. 5.
48 *PS*, 19–20 (15 November 1935), pp. 49–51; 1 (10 January 1936), pp. 17–18. For a discussion of the course of the Verification including the need for some 18 or 19 party organisations to repeat the process, see Getty, *Origins*, pp. 64–85.
49 *KPSS v rez*, vol. 6, p. 296. It also referred to the way in which 'order has been established in our party house and party organisations have been cleansed from alien people as a result of the verification of party documents'. p. 299.
50 *KPSS v rez*, vol. 6, pp. 295–6, 298.
51 *PS*, 2 (January 1936), p. 12.
52 'Itogi proverki partiinykh dokumentov', *KPSS v rez*, vol. 6, pp. 295–304.

For a discussion of the Exchange, see Getty, *Origins*, pp. 87–91. The Exchange was to replace the form of card introduced in 1926 with a more comprehensive one and had initially been foreshadowed in August 1934. *PS*, 19 (October 1934), pp. 435–6.
53 *KPSS v rez*, vol. 6, p. 300.
54 *KPSS v rez*, vol. 6, p. 300.
55 These were to be supplemented by Orgburo instructions which were to be issued not later than 10 January 1936. They were actually confirmed on 14 January 1936. Getty, *Origins*, p. 238, n. 100. Also see instructions in *PS*, 5 (10 March 1936), pp. 52–7.
56 *PS*, 8 (25 April 1936), p. 18. For the same phrase, 'hostile and alien elements', see *PS*, 22 (20 November 1936), p. 3.
57 This prolongation of the campaign forced a postponement of the renewal of recruiting to the party. This had originally been going to begin on 1 June but had to be postponed until November.
58 *PS*, 11 (5 June 1936), pp. 3–8. Also 8 (25 April 1936), pp. 56–7; 22 (20 November 1936), p. 7.
59 For example, *PS*, 22 (20 November 1936), pp. 4–5 (Rostov gorkom); 24 (15 December 1936), pp. 34–5 (Kursk obkom); 6 (20 March 1937), pp. 39–42 (Dzerzhinsky raikom). According to a CC letter of 29 July 1936, some people who had been arrested had retained their party cards, illustrating a clear lack of vigilance on the part of party members against masked enemies. Conquest, *Terror*, p. 148.
60 *KPSS v rez*, vol. 6, pp. 369–75. These were dated 29 September and 21 October.
61 *PS*, 2 (January 1937), p. 64. There appears to have been no summary of the results of the campaign. Getty argues that very few were expelled during the campaign. *Origins*, pp. 89–90.
62 *XVIII s'ezd*, p. 28.
63 *PS*, 14 (20 July 1936), pp. 3–9.
64 *PS*, 22 (November 1939), pp. 49–64. Also see Vladimirsky's comments at the XVIII Congress. *XVIII s'ezd*, pp. 44–5.
65 *PS*, 10 (15 May 1938), pp. 62–4.
66 *PS*, 7 (April 1935), pp. 47–8; 8 (April 1935), pp. 16–19; 9 (May 1935), pp. 21–4.
67 Prior to the reorganisation there were seven union republics, 70 territories and regions and 2559 urban and rural districts with a party organisation in each. After the reorganisation, the figures were 11 union republics, 110 territories and regions and 3815 urban and rural districts. *XVIII s'ezd*, pp 28–9. According to Malenkov, the number of PPOs increased by 2255. *XVIII s'ezd*, p. 147.
68 For a CC instruction of this type, see *PS*, 19–20 (October 1938), p. 76. Also see the instruction of 15 October 1936 that party committees were to keep written records of their decisions and send regular reports of their meetings to superior party bodies. *PS*, 20 (20 October 1936), p. 37. This set out the timetable and content of such reports and clearly indicates earlier deficiencies in this regard.

69 For example, see the complaints in *PS*, 22 (November 1939), p. 47–8; 5–6 (March 1940), p. 48; 10 (May 1940), pp. 3–6; 18 (September 1940), pp. 52–3; 8 (April 1941), pp. 52–4. Some sense of the scale of the problem party leaders still had to cope with is suggested by the fact that in 1940 a Moscow city district committee cadres section had some 800 officials of enterprises and institutions and 425 party cadres on its nomenklatura. *PS*, 21 (November 1940), pp. 58. Also see the accompanying discussion.
70 On the lack of control exercised by the oblast party organisation over the oblast NKVD, see Fainsod, *Smolensk*, pp. 73–4, 159–60.
71 *ibid.*, p. 84.
72 For one discussion of this, see Manning, *Government*, pp. 30–2.
73 For example, *PS*, 15 (August 1935), pp. 15–16; 18 (30 October 1935), pp. 41–6; 10 (20 May 1936), p. 52; 11 (5 June 1936), p. 46; 19 (5 October 1936), p. 18; 21 (5 November 1936), p. 58; 1 (1 January 1937), p. 59; 5 (10 March 1937), pp. 24–9; 6 (20 March 1937), p. 20. For some comments about the ad hoc nature of the operation of the obkom bureau in Smolensk, see Fainsod, *Smolensk*, pp. 67–9.
74 For example, *PS*, 21 (5 November 1936), p. 58; 4 (15 February 1937), p. 9; 5 (10 March 1937), p. 24; 6 (20 March 1937), p. 20.
75 For example, *PS*, 13 (July 1935), pp. 40–2.
76 For example, *PS*, 14 (July 1935), pp. 46–7.
77 For example, *PS*, 2 (25 January 1936), p. 11.
78 For example, *PS*, 16 (August 1935), pp. 42–3; 4 (15 February 1937), p. 4; 17 (1 September 1937), p. 33.
79 Also see the CC letter of 29 July 1936 entitled 'On the terrorist activities of the Trotskyist–Zinovievite counter-revolutionary bloc'. Getty, *Origins*, p. 124.
80 This reliance upon the local secretaries was seen as one of the strengths of the Verification, but insofar as this required them, in the words of the CC resolution, 'to bring to light their own shortcomings and mistakes in party-organisational work and to adopt measures for their basic improvement', doubts must arise about the efficacy of this procedure. *KPSS v rez*, vol. 6, p. 296.
81 *KPSS v rez*, vol. 6, p. 296. Also the belated comments of Zhdanov at the XVIII Congress, *XVIII s'ezd*, pp. 519–24.
82 Getty, *Origins*, pp. 84–5, 90. This appears to have been particularly marked in the Exchange of Party Cards. Also see Fainsod, *Smolensk*, pp. 223–32.
83 For example, *PS*, 9 (May 1935), pp. 31–4.
84 For example, *PS*, 10 (May 1935), pp. 34–7; 15 (August 1935), pp. 15–17.
85 For example, *PS*, 19–20 (November 1935), pp. 49–52; 1 (10 January 1936), p. 21 (where it is linked with the Verification); 22 (20 November 1936), pp. 4–5.
86 For example, *PS*, (15 February 1937), p. 10. On the use of criticism and self-criticism in the purges in Smolensk, see Fainsod, *Smolensk*, pp. 132–7 and Werth, *Etre communiste*, pp. 196–203.
87 *PS*, 3 (1 February 1937), p. 29; 17 (1 September 1937), pp. 31–6.
88 *PS*, 4 (15 February 1937), p. 8.

89 *PS*, 5 (10 March 1937), pp. 34–9; 10 (15 May 1937), pp. 31–6.
90 *PS*, 6 (20 March 1937), pp. 14, 17, 20–1; 8 (20 April 1937), pp. 50–1; 10 (15 May 1937), p. 28. It was also prominent at the time of the 1938 party elections. On this, see *PS*, 8 (15 April 1938), pp. 6–7; 9 (1 May 1938), p. 47; 10 (15 May 1938), pp. 13, 14, 32–3, 37–8. It was much less prominent as a theme in the 1939 and 1940 elections. See *PS*, 16 (August 1939), p. 31; 3 (February 1940) p. 5; 5–6 (March 1940), p. 46.
91 *PS*, 7 (1 April 1937), pp. 39–43.
92 For example, *PS*, 16 (15 August 1938), pp. 32–5.
93 For a survey of complaints levelled against local authorities in Belyi during 1937, see Roberta T. Manning, 'Peasants and the party: rural administration in the Soviet countryside on the eve of World War II', John Strong, ed., *Essays on Revolutionary Culture and Stalinism* (Columbus: Slavica, 1989) and Fainsod, *Smolensk*, ch. 20. See the discussion relating to 1936 in Gábor T. Rittersporn, 'L'Etat en lutte contre lui-même. Tensions sociales et conflits politiques en URSS 1936–1938', *Libre*, 4 (1978), pp. 3–13 and Gábor Tamás Rittersporn, 'Soviet politics in the 1930s: rehabilitating society', *Studies in Comparative Communism*, 19, 2 (Summer 1986).
94 Some objects of complaint in Belyi were removed from office, some had criminal charges levelled against them and some were expelled from the party. Manning, 'Peasants'.
95 For example, *PS*, 8 (25 April 1936), p. 38.
96 For example, *PS*, 4 (15 February 1937), pp. 5–12; 5 (10 March 1937), pp. 24–9.
97 *PS*, 6 (20 March 1937), pp. 3–4. The February–March 1937 CC plenum which formally introduced the regulations saw significant criticisms of lower level leaders for abuse of electoral practices and for failing to act against enemies. See below and Getty, *Origins*, pp. 137–49. Similar regulations were introduced in October 1937 to structure elections to leading bodies in the legal sphere, suggesting the symbolic linkage with the democratic rhetoric associated with the new constitution. Huskey, *Lawyers*, pp. 201–2.
98 *PS*, 6 (20 March 1937), p. 3. The CC plenum was dated 27 February but the regulations were not introduced until 20 March. The instruction is reprinted in *KPSS v rez*, vol. 6, pp. 382–4.
99 This was obliquely recognised in comment at the time. For example, *PS*, 6 (20 March 1937), p. 14.
100 *ibid.*, pp. 14–16.
101 *ibid.*, p. 16. Stalin's closing speech to the CC plenum which introduced the electoral changes contained a vigorous attack on familyness, a call for the unmasking of local cliques, and an open recognition of the presence of wreckers and enemies with party cards in their pockets. *I. V. Stalin – Sochineniia* (Stanford: Hoover Institution Press, 1967), vol. 14, pp. 225–47). Also see the article by Emelian Yaroslavsky, 'Ob otvetstvennosti rukovoditelei pered massami', *Bol'shevik*, 7, 4 (April 1937), pp. 31–45.
102 *PS*, 6 (20 March 1937), p. 17.
103 For example, *PS*, 8 (20 April 1937), pp. 50–4.

104 *PS*, 10 (15 May 1937), pp. 25–8, 52–3; 11 (1 June 1937), p. 17. For a positive report of the process in the Moscow party organisation, see *PS*, 11 (1 June 1937), pp. 12–19.
105 For some partial figures, see *PS*, 10 (15 May 1937), pp. 29–30; 11 (1 June 1937), pp. 13–14.
106 Getty, *Origins*, p. 162. For a discussion of the election as a whole, with a focus on Smolensk, see pp. 153–63. More generally, see Gábor Tamás Rittersporn, *Simplifications staliniennes et complications soviétiques. Tensions sociales et conflits politiques en URSS 1933–1953* (Paris: Editions des archives contemporaines, 1988), pp. 157–69.
107 Getty, *Origins*, p. 162. Turnover levels were much higher in the PPOs. Some figures are cited in Rittersporn, *Simplifications*, p. 168.
108 Getty, *Origins*, p. 168. The charge of alien elements in leading posts resounded in the press. See, for example, *PS*, 15 (1 August 1937), pp. 40–3; 17 (1 September 1937), p. 33. According to Conquest, the purge began to fall with full effect on the countryside in May 1937. Conquest, *Terror*, ch. 8. For measures to undermine local control of the judicial process at this time, a control which was important for continuing family group dominance, see Peter H. Solomon, 'Local political power and Soviet criminal justice, 1922–41', *Soviet Studies*, 37, 3 (July 1985), pp. 318–24. On mobilisation of rank-and-file party members against office-holders through the self-criticism campaign at this time, see Rittersporn, *Simplifications*, pp. 171–92.
109 J. Arch Getty, 'Party and purge in Smolensk: 1933–1937', *Slavic Review*, 42, 1 (Spring 1983), p. 75. Four prominent sub-national leaders who were not purged were Zhdanov (Leningrad), Khrushchev (Moscow), Bagirov (Azerbaijan) and Beria (Georgia). According to Zhdanov, 60% of obkoms, 46% of gorkoms, 41% of raikoms and 35% of PPOs elected in 1938 consisted of people who were elected for the first time. *XVIII s'ezd*, p. 526. According to Medvedev, 90% of the members of oblast and city committees and republican CCs were liquidated in 1937–38. Cited in Conquest, *Terror*, p. 324. Conquest also gives the following figures: in Leningrad gorkom only two of the 65 elected in May 1937 were re-elected in 1938 (five others were transferred to other posts) while only nine of the 65 in Leningrad obkom survived in the committee elected the following year (four transferred). Between March and June 1937, 66% of obkom and 33% of local leaders were removed in the Ukraine. Conquest, *Terror*, pp. 326, 329, 348. For its effect in Smolensk, see Fainsod, pp. 233–7.
110 *PS*, 8 (15 April 1938), pp. 62–4.
111 For example, *PS*, 8 (15 April 1938), pp. 4–5.
112 The mode of election of this group had not been specified in the 1937 regulations.
113 For some reports on the course of the 1938 elections, see *PS*, 9 (1 May 1938), pp. 14–28; 10 (15 May 1938), pp. 12–14; 13 (1 July 1938), pp. 45–55. Problems still remained, as these reports demonstrate.
114 This is consistent with the charge made at the January 1938 CC plenum about leaders seeking to use the purge to protect their own positions,

seeking to portray themselves as loyal and efficient by getting rid of large numbers of presumed enemies. *KPSS v rez*, vol. 7, pp. 11–12. This resolution is an indictment of the way many sub-national leaders had acted in the Terror and reflects the fact that the replacement of these leaders did not result in a change in the way in which people who held those positions acted.

115 Recognition of the effect the purge was having in this regard may be reflected in the emphasis in the press during 1937 on the need for regularity and vitality in the party's operations.

116 The sorts of charges about bureaucratic deficiencies made earlier in this period were heard again in the post-Ezhovshchina era. For example, on the absence of knowledge about the situation at lower levels, see *PS*, 5 (March 1939), p. 24; 10 (May 1939), pp. 50–2; 1 (January 1941), p. 33; on problems in registration, *PS*, 22 (November 1939), pp. 22–8; 5–6 (March 1940), pp. 47–8; 10 (May 1940), pp. 3–6; 18 (September 1940), pp. 52–3; 8 (April 1941), pp. 52–4; on the verification of implementation of decisions, *PS*, 5 (March 1939), p. 25; 12 (June 1939), pp. 3–7. On mistakes committed under the guise of 'vigilance' by party organisations and their leaders, see the resolutions of the January 1938 CC plenum, *KPSS v rez*, vol. 7, pp. 8–17. In 1939 it was reported that in Kazakhstan there were still 120 district party organisations which lacked a telephone link to the regional centre. *XVIII s'ezd*, p. 103.

117 Indeed, the 1939 regulations made provision for a meeting of representatives of the different delegations for a preliminary discussion of the composition of the organ to be elected, thereby providing a *de facto* means for local leaders to present a list of favoured candidates to the election meeting. For the 1939 regulations, see *PS*, 16 (August 1939), pp. 45–8. The elections were not held until much later. See the reports in *PS*, 3 (February 1940), pp. 4–6; 4 (February 1940), pp. 50–3; 5–6 (March 1940), pp. 20–3, 50–2. For the 1941 elections, see the regulations in *PS*, 7 (April 1941), p. 40–5 and the reports in *PS*, 7 (April 1941), pp. 3–12; 9 (May 1941), pp. 8–13.

8 Elite ravaged

1 On the role of Gosplan, see Mark Harrison, *Soviet planning in peace and war 1928–1945* (Cambridge University Press, 1985), ch. 1.

2 *ibid.*, p. 28. Each council was responsible for the coordination of a number of commissariats and departments concerned with its particular area of responsibility.

3 According to one student, the number of plenary sessions is as follows: 1935 – 21, 1937 – 9 and 1938 – 23. Ger P. Van den Berg, 'The Council of Ministers of the Soviet Union', *Review of Socialist Law*, 6, 3 (1980), p. 296.

4 *ibid.*, p. 297.

5 The Economic Council met on average more than once per week: 1938 – 80, 1939 – 60, 1940 – 63. *ibid.*, pp. 297, 299.

6 *Partiinoe stroitel'stvo*, 2 (15 January 1937) and 21 (1 November 1938).

7 This created problems of coordination and industrial control. John A. Armstrong, *The politics of totalitarianism. The Communist Party of the Soviet Union from 1934 to the present* (New York: Random House, 1961), p. 95. Also Harrison, *Planning*, pp. 11–13.
8 For example, Finance Commissar Grinko and Gosplan chief Mezhlauk. For the effect of the purges in Gosplan, see Eugene Zaleski, *Stalinist planning for economic growth, 1933–1952* (Chapel Hill, NC: University of North Carolina Press, 1980), pp. 167–71.
9 For a discussion of this in regard to the judicial apparatus, see Gábor Tamás Rittersporn, 'Soviet officialdom and political evolution. Judiciary apparatus and penal policy in the 1930s', *Theory and Society*, 13 (1984), pp. 222–30.
10 Preparations had to be recommenced in 1938 because the work done in 1937 had been discredited by the purge of Gosplan personnel during that year. Zaleski, *Planning*, ch. 8, esp. p. 171.
11 *XVIII s'ezd vsesoiuznoi kommunisticheskoi partii (b). 10–21 marta 1939g. Stenograficheskii otchet* (Moscow, 1939), p. 30.
12 Rittersporn, 'Officialdom', p. 229.
13 The report of the Mandates Commission to the Congress referred to 1569 delegates with a decisive vote (*XVIII s'ezd*, p. 148), but the list of delegates reproduced at the back of the congress proceedings lists 1570.
14 Calculated from *XVIII s'ezd*, p. 147. At least 2.9% were from the security apparatus. Robert Conquest, *Inside Stalin's Secret Police. NKVD politics 1936–1939* (Stanford, Hoover Institution Press, 1985), p. 93.
15 Speaking of delegates with a decisive vote, the report of the Mandates Commission declared that 76 worked in the central organs and 1307 worked elsewhere. *XVIII s'ezd*, p. 148. The mathematics are obscure. On Russian representation at the congress, see Armstrong, *Totalitarianism*, p. 112.
16 For delegates with a decisive vote, the figures are: higher education 26.5% (including 12.3% having technical education), incomplete higher education 5%, middle education 22.5% and unfinished middle and lower 46%. *XVIII s'ezd*, p. 148.
17 Figures for those with a decisive vote are: 35 and less 49.5%, 36–40 – 32%, 40–50 – 15.5% and over 50 – 3%. *XVIII s'ezd*, p. 149.
18 *XVIII s'ezd*, p. 148. Among those with a consultative vote, 20.6% joined prior to the end of 1920 and 30.6% in 1930 and after. *XVIII s'ezd*, p. 150. In comparison, 70% of party members joined the party in 1929 and after, so that the relatively new arrivals were still under-represented among the delegates.
19 N. S. Khrushchev, 'On the cult of personality and its consequences', T. H. Rigby, ed., *The Stalin dictatorship* (Sydney University Press, 1968), p. 38. The total number of delegates cited by Khrushchev differs from that given in ch. 6.
20 Conquest, *The Great Terror* (Harmondsworth: Penguin, 1971), p. 632. The total carryover figure given by Conquest is 59, but this is mistaken.
21 There was not the gulf between the positions of Stalin and Zhdanov on the

results of the 1933–36 membership screenings that Getty seems to suggest. J. Arch Getty, *Origins of the Great Purges. The Soviet Communist Party reconsidered, 1933–1938* (Cambridge University Press, 1985), pp. 191–4. Both admitted that problems had occurred in the implementation of the chistka of 1933–34, but Stalin believed that the results had been, on the whole, beneficial, while Zhdanov argued that the chistka had been very positive in cleansing the party's ranks. *XVIII s'ezd*, pp. 28, 519. Both positions were ambiguous, with Zhdanov's particularly unclear.

22 *XVIII s'ezd*, p. 211.
23 Following discussion in the Senoren konvent. Roy A. Medvedev, *On Stalin and Stalinism* trans. Ellen de Kadt (Oxford University Press, 1979), p. 109.
24 Carryover levels were higher among full (22.5%) than among candidate members (11.8%). Full members in 1934 carried forward into 1939 were A. A. Andreev, A. E. Badaev, L. P. Beria, L. M. Kaganovich, M. M. Kaganovich, M. I. Kalinin, N. S. Khrushchev, M. M. Litvinov, D. Z. Manuilsky, A. I. Mikoian, V. M. Molotov, K. I. Nikolaeva, N. M. Shvernik, J. V. Stalin, K. E. Voroshilov, and A. A. Zhdanov. Candidate members carried forward were M. D. Bagirov, S. M. Budenny, N. A. Bulganin, S. A. Lozovsky, I. G. Makarov, L. Z. Mekhlis, A. N. Poskrebyshev and G. D. Veinberg. Only Makarov and Veinberg were not promoted to the status of full members.
25 Khrushchev, 'Cult of personality', p. 37. According to Medvedev, the number killed was 110. R. A. Medvedev, *K sudu istorii. Genezis i posledstviia Stalinizma* (New York: Alfred A. Knopf, 1974), p. 378. See the discussion in T. H. Rigby, 'Was Stalin a disloyal patron?' *Soviet Studies*, 38, 3 (July 1986), pp. 316–18. For details of who was repressed and when, see Mikhail Gurfinkel, 'Who was repressed', *Moscow News*, 28 (10 July 1988), p. 16.
26 Figures for those 104 members who joined the party after 1917 are as follows:

1918–20			1921–28			1929–		
F	C	T	F	C	T	F	C	T
55.8	32.8	42.3	37.2	52.5	46.2	7.0	14.7	11.5

27 Figures for all members are:

	CP Apparatus					
	Centre	Region	Total	State	Other	Uncertain
XVII	7.2	26.6	33.8	41.0	15.1	10.1
XVIII	4.4	27.0	31.4	35.8	19.7	13.1

There was also a significant decline in the number of obkom and kraikom secretaries; from 12 (16.9%) in 1934 to 3 (1.2%) in 1939 among full members. Gábor Tamás Rittersporn, 'Rethinking Stalinism', *Russian History*, 11 4 (Winter 1984), p. 345. For some different figures, see Getty, *Origins*, p. 197.
28 Armstrong, *Totalitarianism*, pp. 107–8.
29 *Spravochnyi tom k vos'momu izdaniiu 'Kommunisticheskaia partiia sovetskogo soiuza v rezoliutsiiakh i resheniiakh s'ezdov, konferentsii i plenumov ts.k.'* (Moscow, 1984), p. 11. Also see Armstrong, *Totalitarianism*, pp. 98–9.
30 *ibid*.
31 A decision on the Terror was taken at this plenum but it has never been published in full. Parts of the decision were later published in *Pravda*, 21 April 1937 and 19 January 1938 and they are reprinted in Robert H. McNeal, ed., *The Stalin Years: 1929–1953* (vol. 3 of *Resolutions and decisions of the Communist Party of the Soviet Union*, University of Toronto Press, 1974), pp. 182–4. The decision may have remained in draft form as a result of widespread opposition within the committee.
32 In addition, the results of the Verification of Party Documents were discussed in December 1935 and the question of party admissions and appeals against exclusion in June 1936. Armstrong, *Totalitarianism*, p. 98.
33 Roy Medvedev, *Nikolai Bukharin. The Last Years* (New York: W. W. Norton, 1980), p. 131.
34 According to Adam Ulam, the June 1937 plenum also witnessed one member (Kaminsky) speaking in defence of some of the accused, and being removed. Adam Ulam, *Stalin. The man and his era* (London: Allen Lane, 1974), p. 441.
35 Medvedev, *Bukharin*, pp. 131–2.
36 The plenum was confirmed in *Pravda*, 9 October 1988. The abrupt ending of the investigation into Bukharin and Rykov in September 1936 would also have been consistent with the presence of such opposition.
37 Khrushchev, 'Cult of personality', p. 42. For a discussion of the plenum, see Getty, *Origins*, pp. 137–49.
38 *I. V. Stalin – Sochineniia* (Stanford Hoover Institution Press, 1967), vol. 14, pp. 189–224.
39 This sense of challenge was confirmed by Stalin's closing speech which attacked family groups and local cliques, and called for their unmasking through a process of concerted struggle. *Ibid.*, pp. 225–47.
40 *ibid*.
41 See the discussion in Getty, *Origins*, pp. 142–3.
42 However, Roy Medvedev does suggest 'no one raised any strong objections to the extension of repressive measures within the Party' at this plenum. Medvedev, *Stalin*, p. 107. Ulam, *Stalin*, pp. 429–33 also suggests that opposition was limited.
43 *KPSS v rez*, vol. 7, pp. 8–17. For Getty's view, see *Origins*, pp. 185–9.
44 For some details, see Armstrong, *Totalitarianism*, p. 72. In contrast, Conquest says that the climax of the mass purge occurred in the first half of 1938. Conquest, *Terror*, p. 625. According to Rittersporn, 142,000 rehabili-

tations occurred in 1936–38 at the same time as some 373,963 members were expelled. Gábor Tamás Rittersporn, 'Staline en 1938: apogée du verbe et défaite politique. Eléments pour une étude du "stalinisme réel"', *Libre*, 6 (1979), p. 148.
45 These documents do not relate to the 1933 chistka, which was formally wound up at the end of 1935. For discussion, see Robert H. McNeal, 'The decisions of the CPSU and the Great Purge', *Soviet Studies* 23, 2, October 1971, pp. 180–181; Getty, pp. 110–111 and 122–125. For an extract from the June document, see KPSS v rez . . . vol. 7, p. 9. The July document is reprinted from the Smolensk Archive in McNeal, *The Stalin Years*, pp. 167–81.
46 The plenum was concerned with the new Constitution, a subject which lent itself to a discussion of the legal rights of citizens and, by implication, the question of opposition. Stalin spoke on the constitution and on the question of the rehabilitation of those wrongly expelled in 1933–36. Official communique from *Pravda*, 5 June 1936 cited in Rittersporn, 'Staline', p. 116. Disagreement at the top is also suggested by the *Pravda* editorial on 5 June 1936 which discussed the Constitution and declared that far from this removing the need for acute vigilance, it actually demanded such vigilance, compared with an article a week later entitled 'Stalinskaia konstitutsiia pobedivshego sotsializma' which failed to mention vigilance at all. *Pravda*, 12 June 1936.
47 Kirov had been assassinated in December 1934 and Kuibyshev died in January 1935.
48 Ordzhonikidze had committed suicide in February 1937.
49 See the argument in Rigby, 'Patron'.
50 Those ten and the dates of their joining the Politburo were Chubar (November 1926), Kosior (December 1927), Bauman (April 1929), Syrtsov (June 1929), Ordzhonikidze (December 1930 – previously a member from July-November 1926), Postyshev (December 1934), Zhdanov (February 1935), Eikhe (February 1935), Ezhov (October 1937) and Khrushchev (January 1938). Also see Roy D. Laird, *The Politburo. Demographic trends, Gorbachev and the future* (Boulder: Westview Press, 1986), p. 41.
51 All of those who joined the Politburo after July 1926 and were purged in the 1930s were also Old Bolsheviks, with Ezhov's date of party entry, 1917, being the latest.
52 Leonard Schapiro, *The Communist Party of the Soviet Union* (London: Methuen, 1970), p. 446.
53 Khrushchev, 'Cult of personality', pp. 80–1; Milovan Djilas, *Conversations with Stalin* (Harmondsworth: Penguin, 1963).
54 Khrushchev, 'Cult of personality', p. 80. He also refers to Politburo members not being shown the retracted confessions of many of the accused (p. 43).
55 Michal Reiman, 'Political trials of the Stalinist era', *Telos*, 54 (1982–83), p. 103.
56 Van den Berg, 'Council' p. 300. For the suggestion that it met once every

three to four weeks between March 1939 and August 1941, see Rigby, 'Political Executive'.
57 Conquest, *Terror*, p. 214. Getty, *Origins*, p. 125, suggests that it reflects the rivalry between Yagoda and Ezhov.
58 The new members were Andreev, Malenkov, Mekhlis, Mikhailov and Schcherbakov. Mekhlis had joined the Orgburo in 1938. Those who retained their positions from 1934 were Stalin, Zhdanov, Kaganovich and Shvernik.
59 New members were Andreev and Malenkov. Ezhov had also been added in February 1934, but had disappeared in 1938.
60 Conquest, *Police*, pp. 20–1. He was simultaneously Chairman of the Party Control Commission and therefore concentrated significant power in his hands.
61 *XVIII s'ezd*, pp. 45–6.
62 *ibid.*, p. 220.
63 For the change, see *PS*, 17 (15 October 1935), pp. 73–8.
64 *XVIII s'ezd*, pp. 528–9, 571–3, 670. This change did involve some withdrawal of the party from a direct role in the economy. This reflects Zhdanov's apparent position at the February–March 1937 CC plenum, a position which Stalin had refrained from endorsing at that plenum by declaring that the party was not to divorce itself from economic work. Getty, *Origins*, p. 144. However, measures were taken to rectify the party's withdrawal from the economy at the party's XVIII Conference in February 1941. The conference called on all subordinate party organisations to appoint several secretaries who were to be concerned with industrial and transport issues. Industrial sections were to be formed in republican, territory, regional and city committees. *KPSS v rez,*, vol. 7, pp. 200–1. Such sections had been established in some areas in 1940. For part of the decision establishing them, see 'O sozdanii promyshlennykh i gorkomakh partii' (29 November 1939), *KPSS v rez*, vol. 7, p. 145. Also see Armstrong, *Totalitarianism*, p. 96 and Jonathan Harris, 'The origins of the conflict between Malenkov and Zhdanov: 1939–1941', *Slavic Review*, 35, 2 (1976), pp. 287–303.
65 *PS* 13 (July 1939), pp. 3–8. The Cadres Administration included sections for the commissariats, party organisations, press and publishing, scientific institutions, Komsomol organisations and trade unions. In the obkoms, cadre sections included sectors for party organisations, soviet organisations, manufacturing, transport and communications, agriculture, agricultural procurement, trade and cooperatives, NKVD and defence organisations, procurator and judicial offices, educational and cultural bodies, health departments and Komsomol organisations.
66 *XVIII s'ezd*, p. 671.
67 *ibid*.
68 Getty, *Origins*, p. 118.
69 *KPSS v rez*, vol. 7, p. 10. The figures given in this document suggest that the PCC reversed somewhere in the vicinity of 60% of the cases brought before it.

70 For example, *Pravda*, 21 January 1935, 27 January 1936, 25 November 1936, 21 January 1937, 21 December 1939, 13 August 1940.
71 For example, *Pravda*, 5 March 1935, 5 August 1935, 7 November 1936, 7 March 1937, 10 November 1937, 21 January 1938, 9 November 1938, 5 March 1939, 7 April 1939, 21 December 1939, 7 November 1940, 3 May 1941.
72 For example, *Pravda*,1 January 1936, 11 April 1936, 24 November 1938, 6 February 1939, 5 March 1939.
73 For example, *Pravda*, 4 May 1935, 8 March 1936, 10 December 1936, 2 April 1937, 8 August 1938, 6 January 1939, 1 May 1939, 14 October 1940.
74 For example, *Pravda*, 10 November 1935, 7 July 1936, 6 September 1937, 23 May 1938, 22 February 1939, 20 October 1939, 2 July 1940, 3 May 1941.
75 For example, *Pravda*, 22 April 1935, 13 June 1936, 7 March 1937, 23 September 1938, 21 January 1939, 18 February 1940, 1 May 1941.
76 *Pravda*, 1 May 1935.
77 *Pravda*, 5 August 1935
78 *Pravda*, 6 February 1939.
79 *Pravda*, 21 January 1938.
80 *Pravda*, 22 April 1937.
81 *Pravda*, 21 December 1939.
82 *Pravda*, 8 October 1938.
83 *Pravda*, 1 January 1935.
84 *Pravda*, 17 October 1935.
85 *Pravda*, 21 December 1939.
86 *Pravda*, 1 May 1939.
87 *Pravda*, 19 December 1939.
88 Cited in R. Payne, *The rise and fall of Stalin* (London: Pan Books, 1968), p. 559.
89 *Pravda*, 12 June 1939.
90 *Pravda*, 22 February 1936.
91 *Pravda*, 13 June 1936.
92 *Pravda*, 13 June 1936.
93 *Pravda*, 1 January 1936.
94 *Pravda*, 18 July 1938.
95 *Pravda*, 21 December 1939.
96 *Pravda*, 7 November 1937.
97 Dzhambul, *Songs and poems* (Moscow, 1938) cited in Y. M. Sokolov, *Russian folklore*, trans. C. R. Smith (New York: Macmillan, 1950), p. 743.
98 *Pravda*, 28 August 1936.
99 *Pravda*, 21 December 1939.
100 *Pravda*, 21 December 1939. Stalin's speeches and writings were the means whereby he set out the path to communism and infallibly guided the society to its bright future. They were the link between the leader and his people.
101 *Pravda*, 2 September 1935.
102 *Pravda*, 7 July 1935.
103 *Pravda*, 17 May 1935.

104 *Pravda*, 25 September 1936.
105 An important aspect of this was that Stalin appeared to provide a sense of authority, stability and certainty when much was uncertain and in flux.
106 For one discussion of the cult as a means of building up personal support, see Graeme Gill, 'The Soviet leader cult: reflections on the structure of leadership in the Soviet Union', *British Journal of Political Science*, 10, 2 (April 1980), pp. 167–86.
107 See Khrushchev's comments about Stalin selecting, limiting and weighing information before passing it on to the Politburo. *Khrushchev Remembers*, ed. Strobe Talbot (London: Andre Deutsch, 1971), vol. 1, p. 156.
108 On the question of communication, see Niels Erik Rosenfeldt, 'Stalinism as a system of communication', John W. Strong, ed., *Essays on revolutionary culture and Stalinism* (Columbus: Slavica, 1989).
109 ibid.
110 Central personnel files may have expanded significantly in 1935. Niels Erik Rosenfeldt, *Knowledge and power. The role of Stalin's Secret Chancellery in the Soviet system of government* (Copenhagen: Rosenkilde and Bagger, 1978), p. 185.
111 Its responsibilities also expanded significantly in the non-security area. It became responsible for surveying and mapping, forest protection, fire brigades, main roads, motor transport, protection of property, the determination of weights and measures, registration of births, deaths, marriages and divorces, and the local militia. Jonathan R. Adelman, 'Soviet Secret Police', Jonathan R. Adelman, ed., *Terror and communist politics. The role of the Secret Police in Communist states* (Boulder: Westview Press, 1984), p. 101.
112 See the discussion in Getty, *Origins*, pp. 182–5.
113 Not all party members who were purged suffered this fate while formally remaining party members. As the CC resolution of 18 January 1938 suggests, many party members were still expelled before the NKVD sought to establish grounds for action against them. *KPSS v rez*, vol. 7, p. 11.
114 Medvedev, *K sudu*, pp. 766–7.
115 Khrushchev, 'Cult of personality', p. 49. Kosior, Postyshev and Eikhe were arrested in March–April 1938. Postyshev had been expelled from the Politburo in January 1938.
116 Conquest, *Terror*, p. 367. According to the analysis in Rittersporn, at least for lower level party leaders, arrest was preceded by criticism within and expulsion from the party. Gábor Tamás Rittersporn, *Simplifications staliniennes et complications soviétiques. Tensions sociales et conflits politiques en URSS 1933–1953* (Paris, Editions des archives contemporaines, 1988), ch. 3. He also declares that party leaders could not be arrested by police functionaries on the same level as themselves, but only by those on higher levels. p. 175.
117 Khrushchev, 'Cult of personality', p. 43. According to the party Rules, expulsion was the concern of the PPO to which a member belonged rather than the CC, although in practice the latter clearly had the effective voice.

118 Medvedev, *K sudu*, p. 765. A special section was established in the NKVD to be concerned with party members.
119 For some details, see Armstrong, *Totalitarianism*, p. 72. For the most extensive account, see Conquest, *Police*. He charts the personnel changes following the replacement of Yagoda by Ezhov (26 September 1936) and Ezhov by Beria (12 December 1938).
120 Getty argued that the involvement of Ezhov in the 1936 review of the Kirov murder represents the intrusion by the Secretariat into the affairs of the NKVD, and reflects continuing party supremacy. Getty, *Origins*, p. 122. This is better seen as part of the move to unseat NKVD boss Yagoda, which was realised on 26 September 1936.
121 This is not to deny that conflict and power struggles within the security apparatus were not also instrumental in the purging of that body.
122 Although arrests continued, at a lower level, into 1941. Medvedev, *K sudu*, pp. 471–8.
123 This consisted of Beria, Molotov, Malenkov and Vyshinsky. It brought down recommendations which formed the basis of two CC resolutions on strengthening procuratorial supervision of NKVD activities and on recruiting 'honest people' into the security organs. Roy Medvedev, 'New pages from the political biography of Stalin', Robert C. Tucker, ed., *Stalinism. Essays in historical interpretation* (New York: W. W. Norton, 1977), pp. 217–18. Also Anton Antonov-Ovseenko, *The time of Stalin*, (New York: Harper and Row, 1981), p. 124 and Conquest, *Police*, pp. 78–9.
124 This did not mean a substantial lessening of Beria's power because the new organisation was headed by his supporter, V. N. Merkulov. Armstrong, *Totalitarianism*, p. 107.
125 Khrushchev, 'Cult of personality', p. 40.
126 Rosenfeldt, *Knowledge*, p. 183. See pp. 129–60 for a list of Stalin's subordinates.
127 Khrushchev, 'Cult of personality', pp. 48–9. Also Medvedev, *K sudu*, p. 560. According to Volkogonov, Stalin was signing such lists as early as December 1933. He also reports that beginning in 1937 Beria (presumably he means Ezhov and then Beria) made annual reports to Stalin on the number of people in the prison camps and corrective colonies. 'Triumph for a tyrant, tragedy for a people', *Moscow News*, 7 (12 February 1989), p. 9. Also see the condensed version of the Preface to Volkogonov's book where he asserts that Ulrikh and Vyshinsky made regular reports to Stalin about the trials and sentences, and in 1937 monthly summaries of those sentenced for 'espionage-terrorist and subversive activities' were given to Stalin. *Literaturnaia Gazeta*, 9 December 1987. Medvedev gives Stalin a much larger role than this discussion, which is setting out a minimal position, suggests.
128 The removal of one of Stalin's oldest friends, Abel Enukidze, is relevant here. Enukidze was in charge of administration and personnel in the Kremlin. In early 1935 an alleged plot against Stalin including Kremlin guards was publicly announced. Enukidze was removed, an action

which could not have taken place without Stalin's agreement. Ulam, *Stalin*, pp. 396–8. This may have been an attempt to link the Kirov affair with danger to Stalin.
129 According to a recent Soviet source, Stalin initiated a secret instruction of 29 July 1936 on the use of any methods for furthering investigations. Yevgeny Ambartsumov, 'The poisonous mist disperses', *Moscow News*, 25 (19 June 1988), p. 10. According to the testimony of a former militia (then part of the NKVD) chief in Ivanovo in 1937, during Kaganovich's visit to the town he would telephone Stalin several times a day to report on the numbers arrested and the course of the investigation. Each call was followed by demands for increased numbers of confessions. Mikhail Shreider, 'Ivanovo 1937. From the notes of a Chekist operative', *Moscow News*, 48 (27 November 1988), p. 7. Conquest, (*Terror*, p. 604) also refers to an instruction by Stalin of April 1938 calling for 'liquidation of the consequences of wrecking', and drawing attention to 'silent politically spineless people'.
130 Indeed, because Stalin stood above the institutional structures of which the system consisted and because his personal authority did not depend upon occupation of a particular formal position, he could unleash the Terror without destroying the basis upon which he stood. The vozhd' was the only major component of the system to emerge unscathed.
131 Nevertheless, some of the arguments about Stalin's motivation may be valid. See Medvedev, *K sudu*, chs. 9 and 10.
132 Conquest, *Police*.
133 Getty, *Origins*, pp. 110–11, 118, 200.
134 Schapiro, *Communist Party*, pp. 450–1.
135 Harris, 'Origins', pp. 287–303. This conflict also turned on the structure of the CC Secretariat.
136 Getty, *Origins*, pp. 128–36.
137 Armstrong, *Totalitarianism*, p. 17. Conquest, (*Terror*, p. 217) suggests that Yagoda may have opposed extension of the purge to the Rightists and thereby have been instrumental in the dropping of the investigation into Bukharin and Rykov in September 1936. Soon after this Yagoda was replaced by Ezhov as head of the NKVD. Stalin's telegram to the Politburo of 25 September 1936 said that Yagoda had 'definitely proved himself to be incapable of unmasking the Trotskyite–Zinovievite bloc' and should be removed as People's Commissar of Internal Affairs. Khrushchev, 'Cult of personality', p. 40. He was arrested on 3 April 1937.
138 For a controversial argument that Stalin was not as powerful as this suggests, see Rittersporn, 'Staline' and *Simplifications*, ch. 4.
139 Note also the *Pravda* editorial of 27 June 1936 entitled 'Kollektivnost' v partiinom rukovodstve' which emphasised that the correct mode of leadership was collective, not individual. Although specifically directed at lower party organs, the general principle is consistent with some resistance to Stalin's primacy. However there is also evidence of Stalin being opposed to the cult. See his letter of 16 February 1938 attacking a proposed publication entitled 'Tales of Stalin's childhood' and the ten-

dency to personal adulation which it represented. Stalin, *Sochineniia*, vol. 14, p. 274. It is difficult to interpret this letter because it is clear that the cult could not have continued against concerted opposition by Stalin.
140 The sacking of Yagoda in September 1936 shows Stalin able to act without even the formality of a Politburo discussion.
141 For an example from 1941, see the memoirs of A. G. Zverev cited by Van den Berg, 'Council', p. 298. Also see Vosnesensky's initiative at the XVIII Congress for a General Plan. He set this in train although it did not receive Stalin's blessing until September 1940. Harrison, *Planning*, pp. 25–6. Also the discussion in A. Kemp–Welch, 'Stalinism and intellectual order', T. H. Rigby, Archie Brown and Peter Reddaway, eds., *Authority, power and policy in the USSR. Essays dedicated to Leonard Schapiro* (London: Macmillan, 1980), pp. 118–34.
142 The Short Course was important here. So too was the unseating of the dean of Soviet historians, M. N. Pokrovsky, whose economic determinism contradicted the emphasis upon the great figures of Russian history which fuelled the cultist image.
143 This occurred through the processes of historical revision and the elimination of such bodies as the Society of Old Bolsheviks and the Society of Former Political Exiles in 1935.
144 Amy W. Knight, *The KGB. Police and politics in the Soviet Union* (Boston: Unwin Hyman, 1988)), pp. 28, 32.
145 The show trials in Novosibirsk in November 1936 and in Moscow in January 1937 (Piatakov, Radek *et al.*) were important in this regard because they purported to prove that the high levels of industrial accidents were the result of 'wreckers' at work in the economy. So too were the trials of leading Old Bolsheviks: if the infection of oppositionist sentiments had affected people with such distinguished revolutionary careers, it was likely to be much more extensive among those who did not have good revolutionary credentials.
146 Medvedev, *K sudu*, pp. 670–1. On the vagueness of the notion 'enemy', see Rittersporn, *Simplifications*, pp. 150–4.
147 On this see the proceedings of the show trials and the CC's secret letter of 29 July 1936 found in the Smolensk Archive and reprinted in McNeal, *The Stalin years*, pp. 167–81.
148 *Pravda*, 16 January 1935.
149 This does not mean that political debate did not occur. As indicated above, it did characterise relations between Stalin's lieutenants. But it was now much more dangerous and the stakes much higher; failure to win Stalin's support could have adverse consequences for a combatant in such policy debate.
150 Party elite is here interpreted broadly to include middle-ranking party leaders. This assumes that the purges were launched by Stalin in part to remove what he believed to be opposition to him at both the middle and upper levels of the party. His recognition of the existence of middle level opposition is reflected in the report by Medvedev that, after Stalin's death, materials were found in NKVD offices which fabricated a wide

range of counter-revolutionary organisations and centres, all of which were to be headed by local party first secretaries. Medvedev, *K sudu*, pp. 574–5. The argument about the Stalin-sub-national leaders relationship is spelled out more fully in Graeme Gill, 'Stalinism and institutionalization: the nature of Stalin's regional support', John W. Strong, ed., *Essays on revolutionary culture and Stalinism* (Columbus: Slavica, 1989).

Conclusion

1 For an excellent discussion of this, see Stephen F. Cohen, 'Bolshevism and Stalinism', Robert C. Tucker, ed., *Stalinism. Essays in historical interpretation* (New York: W. W. Norton, 1977).
2 See the argument in Roger Pethybridge, *The social prelude to Stalinism* (London: Macmillan, 1974).
3 Bazhanov said that while working in the central apparatus, he was absorbed in the work of that apparatus and unaware of what was going on in the country at large. Boris Bazhanov, *Vospominaniia byvshego sekretaria Stalina* (Paris: Tret'ia volna, 1980), p. 29.
4 Kenneth Jowitt, *Revolutionary breakthroughs and national development. The case of Romania 1944–1965* (Berkeley: University of California Press, 1971), p. 69.
5 See the discussion of personal power in Guenther Roth, 'Personal rulership, patrimonialism, and empire-building in the new states', *World Politics*, 20, 2 (January 1968), pp. 194–206.

Bibliography

Documents

Bol'shevik, 1924–41.
Izvestiia tsentral'nogo komiteta rossiiskoi kommunisticheskoi partii (bol'shevikov), 1919–29. (Revived as *Izvestiia Ts K KPSS* 1989.)
Kommunisticheskaia partiia sovetskogo soiuza v rezoliutsiiakh i resheniiakh s'ezdov, konferentsii i plenumov Ts.K., Moscow, 1983–
Partiinoe stroitel'stvo, 1929–41.
Pravda, 1917–41.
Sovetskie Konstitutsii. Spravochnik, Moscow, 1963.
Spravochnik partiinogo rabotnika, 1921–35.
Sed'moi ekstrennyi s'ezd RKP(b) Mart 1918 goda. Stenograficheskii otchet, Moscow, 1962.
Vos'moi s'ezd RKP(b) Mart 1919 goda. Protokoly, Moscow, 1959.
Vos'maia konferentsiia RKP(b) Dekabr' 1919 goda. Protokoly, Moscow, 1961.
Deviatyi s'ezd RKP(b) Mart-aprel' 1920 goda. Protokoly, Moscow, 1960.
Desiatyi s'ezd RKP(b) Mart 1921 goda. Stenograficheskii otchet, Moscow, 1963.
Odinnadtsatyi s'ezd RKP(b) mart-aprel' 1922 goda. Stenograficheskii otchet, Moscow, 1961.
Dvenadtsatyi s'ezd RKP(b) 17–25 aprelia 1923 goda. Stenograficheskii otchet, Moscow, 1968.
Trinadtsatyi s'ezd RKP(b). Mai 1924 goda. Stenograficheskii otchet, Moscow, 1963.
XIV s'ezd vsesoiuznoi kommunisticheskoi partii (b) 18–31 dekabria 1925g. Stenograficheskii otchet, Moscow, 1926.
Piatnadtsatyi s'ezd VKP(b). Dekabr' 1927 goda. Stenograficheskii otchet, Moscow, 1961.
XVI s'ezd vsesoiuznoi kommunisticheskoi partii (b). Stenograficheskii otchet, Moscow, 1931.
XVII s'ezd vsesoiuznoi kommunisticheskoi partii (b) 26 ianvaria – 10 fevralia 1934g. Stenograficheskii otchet, Moscow, 1934.
XVIII s'ezd vsesoiuznoi kommunisticheskoi partii (b) 10–21 marta 1939g. Stenograficheskii otchet, Moscow, 1939.

Other works

Adelman, Jonathan R., 'The development of the Soviet party apparat in the Civil War: center, localities and nationality areas', *Russian History*, 9, 1 (1982).
'Soviet Secret Police', Jonathan R. Adelman, ed., *Terror and communist politics. The role of the Secret Police in Communist states*, Boulder: Westview Press, 1984.
Aleksandrov', Kto upravliaet Rossiei? Bol'shevistskii partiino-pravitel'stvennyi apparat i Stalinizm. Istoriko-dogmaticheskii analiz, Berlin, 1933.
Alexandrov, G. F. et al., *Joseph Stalin. A short biography*, Moscow, 1947.
Ali, Janice, 'Aspects of the RKP(B) Secretariat, March 1919 to April 1922', *Soviet Studies*, 26, 3 (1974).
Ali, Tariq, *The Stalinist legacy. Its impact on twentieth century world politics*, Harmondsworth: Penguin, 1984.
Alliluyeva, Svetlana, *Twenty letters to a friend*, Harmondsworth: Penguin, 1968.
Only one year, New York: Harper and Row, 1969.
Antonov-Ovseenko, Anton, *The time of Stalin. Portrait of a tyranny*, New York: Harper and Row, 1981.
Anweiler, Oscar, *The Soviets: the Russian Workers', Peasants' and Soldiers' Councils, 1905–1921* New York: Pantheon Books, 1974.
Armstrong, John A., *The politics of totalitarianism. The Communist Party of the Soviet Union from 1934 to the present*, New York: Random House, 1961.
Avrich, Paul, *Kronstadt 1921*, New York: W. W. Norton, 1974.
Avtorkhanov, A., *Proiskhozhdenie partokratii*, Frankfurt: Possev-Verlag, 1973, vols. 1 and 2.
Stalin and the Soviet Communist Party. A study in the technology of power, New York: Praeger, 1959.
Tekhnologiia vlasti, Frankfurt: Possev-Verlag, 1976.
Bahne, Siegried, 'Trotsky on Stalin's Russia', *Survey*, 41 (1962).
Bailes, Kendall E., *Technology and society under Lenin and Stalin. Origins of the soviet technical intelligentsia, 1917–1941*, Princeton University Press, 1978.
Barber, John, *Soviet historians in crisis 1928–1932*, London: Macmillan, 1981.
'Stalin's letter to the editors of Proletarskaya Revoliutsiya', *Soviet Studies*, 28, 1 (1976).
Barbusse, Henri, *Stalin. A new world seen through one man*, London: The Bodley Head, 1935.
Barghoorn, Frederick, 'Stalinism and the Russian cultural heritage', *Problems of Communism*, 2, 1 (1953).
Barmine, Alexander, *One who survived*, New York: Putnam, 1945.
Bazhanov, Boris, 'Stalin closely observed', G. R. Urban, ed., *Stalinism. Its Impact on Russia and the World*, London: Maurice Temple Smith, 1982.
Vospominaniia byvshego sekretaria Stalina, Paris: Tret'ia volna, 1980.
Benvenuti, Francesco, *Kirov in Soviet politics 1933–34*, CREES Discussion Paper, SIPS No. 8, University of Birmingham, 1977.
Bettelheim, Charles, *Class struggles in the USSR. First period: 1917–1923*, Brighton: Harvester, 1977.

Class struggles in the USSR. Second period: 1923–1930, Brighton: Harvester, 1978.
Bialer, Seweryn, *Stalin's successors. Leadership, stability and change in the Soviet Union,* Cambridge University Press, 1980.
Biulletin' Oppozitsii, Paris, 1931.
Blank, Stephen, 'Soviet institutional development during NEP: A prelude to Stalinism', *Russian History,* 9, 2–3 (1982).
Bone, Ann, *The Bolsheviks and the October Revolution. Minutes of the Central Committee of the Russian Social-Democratic Labour Party (bolsheviks). August 1917–February 1918,* London: Pluto Press, 1974.
Brinton, Maurice, *The Bolsheviks and workers' control 1917–1921. The state and counter-revolution,* London: Solidarity, 1970.
Browder, Robert Paul and Kerensky, Alexander F., eds., *The Russian Provisional Government 1917,* Stanford University Press, 1961.
Brower, Daniel R., 'Collectivized agriculture in Smolensk: the Party, the peasantry, and the crisis of 1932', *The Russian Review,* 36, 2 (1977).
'The Smolensk scandal and the end of NEP', *Slavic Review,* 45, 4 (Winter 1986.
'Stalinism and the "view from below"', *The Russian Review,* 46, 4 (1987).
Brunner, Georg, 'The essence of Stalinism', *Problems of Communism,* 30, 3 (1981).
Brus, Wlodzimierz, 'Stalinism and the "People's Democracies"', Robert C. Tucker, ed., *Stalinism. Essays in historical interpretation,* New York: W. W. Norton, 1977.
Buchanan, H., 'Lenin and Bukharin on the transition from capitalism to socialism: the Meshchersky controversy', *Soviet Studies,* 28, 1 (January 1976).
Bukharin, Nikolai I., *Politicheskoe zaveshchanie Lenina,* Moscow, 1929.
Bullitt, M. M., 'Towards a Marxist theory of aesthetics: the development of socialist realism in the Soviet Union', *The Russian Review,* 35, 1 (1976).
Bunyan, James, *The origin of forced labor in the Soviet state 1917–1921. Documents and materials,* Baltimore: Johns Hopkins University Press, 1967.
Bunyan, James and Fisher, H. H., eds., *The Bolshevik Revolution 1917–1918. Documents and materials,* Stanford University Press, 1934.
Campeanu, Pavel, *The genesis of the Stalinist social order,* Armonk: M. E. Sharpe, 1988.
The origins of Stalinism. From Leninist revolution to Stalinist society, Armonk: M. E. Sharpe, 1986.
Carr, E. H., *The Bolshevik Revolution 1917–1923,* Harmondsworth: Penguin, 1966, vols. 1–3.
The Interregnum 1923–1924, Harmondsworth: Penguin, 1969.
Socialism in one country 1924–1926, Harmondsworth: Penguin, 1970–72, vols. 1–3.
Foundations of a planned economy 1926–1929, Harmondsworth: Penguin, 1976, vol. 2.
'The origin and status of the Cheka', *Soviet Studies,* 10, 1 (July 1958).
The Russian Revolution from Lenin to Stalin 1917–1929, London: Macmillan, 1979.

Carr, E. H. and R. W. Davies, *Foundations of a planned economy 1926–1929*, Harmondsworth: Penguin, 1974, vol. 1.
Carrere D'Encausse, Helene, *Stalin. Order through terror*, London: Longman, 1981.
Chase, William, 'Social history and revisionism of the Stalinist era', *The Russian Review*, 46, 4 (1987).
Clark, Katerina, 'Utopian anthropology as a context for Stalinist literature', Robert C. Tucker, ed., *Stalinism. Essays in historical interpretation*, New York: W. W. Norton, 1977.
Cliff, Tony, *State capitalism in Russia*, London: Pluto Press, 1979.
Cocks, Paul Maupin, *Politics of party control: the historical and institutional role of party control organs in the CPSU*, Unpublished Ph.D., Harvard University, 1968.
Cohen, S., 'Stalin's revolution reconsidered', *Slavic Review*, 32, 2 (1973).
Cohen, Stephen F., 'Bolshevism and Stalinism', Robert C. Tucker, ed., *Stalinism. Essays in historical interpretation*, New York: W. W. Norton, 1977.
Bukharin and the Bolshevik Revolution. A political biography, 1888–1938, New York: Alfred A. Knopf, 1973.
'Stalin's Terror as social history', *The Russian Review*, 45, 4 (1986).
Colletti, Lucio, 'The question of Stalin', Robin Blackburn, ed., *Revolution and class struggle. A reader in Marxist politics*, Glasgow: Fontana/Collins, 1977.
Conquest, Robert, 'Forced labour statistics: some comments', *Soviet Studies*, 34, 3 (July 1982).
The Great Terror, Harmondsworth: Penguin, 1971.
'The Great Terror revised', *Survey*, 16, 1 (1971).
The harvest of sorrow. Soviet collectivization and the terror famine, London: Hutchinson, 1986.
Inside Stalin's Secret Police, NKVD politics 1936–1939, Stanford: Hoover Institution Press, 1985.
'Revisionizing Stalin's Russia', *The Russian Review*, 46, 4 (1987).
Dallin, David J. and Nicolaevsky, Boris I., *Forced labour in Soviet Russia*, New Haven: Yale University Press, 1947.
Daniels, Robert Vincent, *The conscience of the Revolution. Communist opposition in Soviet Russia*, New York: Simon and Schuster, 1969.
'Evolution of leadership selection in the Central Committee 1917–1927', Walter McKenzie Pintner and Don Karl Rowney, eds., *Russian officialdom. The bureaucratization of Russian society from the seventeenth to the twentieth century*, London: Macmillan, 1980.
'The Secretariat and the local organizations in the Russian Communist Party, 1921–1923', *The American Slavic and East European Review*, 16, 1 (1957).
The Stalin Revolution. Foundations of Soviet totalitarianism, Lexington DC: Heath, 1965.
'Stalin's Rise to dictatorship, 1922–29', Alexander Dallin and Alan F. Westin, eds., *Politics in the Soviet Union. 7 Cases*, New York: Harcourt, Brace and World, 1966.
Davies, R. W., *The industrialisation of Soviet Russia*, vol. 1 *The socialist offensive.*

The collectivisation of Soviet agriculture, 1929–1930, London: Macmillan, 1980.
'The socialist market: a debate in Soviet industry, 1932–33', *Slavic Review*, 42, 2 (July 1984).
'The Syrtsov–Lominadze affair', *Soviet Studies*, 33, 1, (January 1981).
Davies, R. W. and Wheatcroft, S. G., 'Further thoughts on the first Soviet Five Year Plan', *Slavic Review*, 34, 4 (December 1975).
Day, Richard, *Leon Trotsky and the politics of economic isolation*, Cambridge University Press, 1973.
De Jonge, Alex, *Stalin and the shaping of the Soviet Union*, London: Collins, 1986.
Demaitre, Edmund, 'Stalin and the era of "Rational Irrationality"', *Problems of Communism*, XVI, 6 (1967).
Deutscher, Isaac, *Ironies of history. Essays on contemporary communism*, Oxford University Press, 1966.
The prophet armed. Trotsky 1879–1921, Oxford University Press, 1954.
The prophet outcast. Trotsky 1929–1940, Oxford University Press, 1963.
The prophet unarmed. Trotsky 1921–1929 Oxford University Press, 1959.
Stalin. A political biography, Harmondsworth: Penguin, 1966.
Dewar, Margaret, *Labour policy in the USSR 1917–1928*, London: RIIA, 1956.
Djilas, Milovan, *Conversations with Stalin*, Harmondsworth: Penguin, 1963.
Dmitrenko, S. L., 'Ob'edinennye plenumy TsK i TsKK (1921–1933gg)', *Voprosy Istorii KPSS*, 10 (1965).
Dohan, M. R., 'The economic origins of Soviet autarky 1927/28–1934', *Slavic Review*, 35, 4 (1976).
Dunham, Vera J., *In Stalin's time: middle class values in Soviet fiction*, Cambridge University Press, 1979.
Duval, Charles, 'The Bolshevik Secretariat and Yakov Sverdlov: February to October 1917', *The Slavonic and East European Review*, 51, 122 (1973).
'Iakov Mikhailovich Sverdlov: founder of the Bolshevik Party machine', Ralph Carter Elwood, ed., *Reconsiderations on the Russian Revolution*, Cambridge MA: Slavica Publications, 1976.
'Yakov M. Sverdlov and the All-Russian Central Executive Committee of Soviets (VTsIK): A study in Bolshevik consolidation of power. October 1917–July 1918', *Soviet Studies*, 31, 1 (January 1979).
Eley, Geoff, 'History with the politics left out – again?', *The Russian Review*, 45, 4 (1986).
Elleinstein, Jean, *The Stalin phenomenon*, London: Lawrence and Wishart, 1976.
Elwood, Ralph Carter, *Russian Social Democracy in the underground. A study of the RSDRP in the Ukraine, 1907–1914*, Assen: Van Gorcum, 1974.
Erlich, Alexander, *The Soviet industrialization debate 1924–1928*, Cambridge MA: Harvard University Press, 1967.
'Stalinism and Marxian growth models', Robert C. Tucker, ed., *Stalinism. Essays in historical interpretation*, New York: W. W. Norton, 1977.
'Stalin's views on Soviet economic development', E. J. Simmons, ed., *Continuity and change in Russian and Soviet thought*, Cambridge MA: Harvard University Press, 1955.

Fainsod, Merle, *How Russia is ruled*, Cambridge MA: Harvard University Press, 1964.
Smolensk under Soviet rule, New York: Vintage Books, 1958.
Feher, Ferenc, Heller, Agnes and Markus, Gyorgy, *Dictatorship over needs* Oxford: Blackwell, 1983.
Filtzer, Donald, *Soviet workers and Stalinist industrialization. The formation of modern Soviet production relations, 1928–1941*, London: Pluto Press, 1986.
Fitzpatrick, Sheila, 'Afterward: revisionism revisited', *The Russian Review*, 45, 4 (1986).
The Commissariat of enlightenment. Soviet organization of education and the arts under Lunacharsky, Cambridge University Press, 1970.
'Cultural Revolution in Russia 1928–32', *Contemporary History*, 9, 1 (1974).
ed., *Cultural Revolution in Russia, 1928–1931*, Bloomington: Indiana University Press, 1978.
'Culture and politics under Stalin: a reappraisal', *Slavic Review*, 35, 2 (1976).
Education and social mobility in the Soviet Union 1921–1934, Cambridge University Press, 1979.
'The emergence of glaviskusstvo: class war on the cultural front: Moscow 1928–29', *Soviet Studies*, 23, 2 (1971).
'The foreign threat during the First Five-Year Plan', *Soviet Union*, 5, 1 (1978).
'New perspectives on Stalinism', *The Russian Review*, 45, 4 (1986).
'Ordzhonikidze's takeover of Vesenkha: a case-study in Soviet bureaucratic politics', *Soviet Studies*, 37, 2 (April 1985).
The Russian Revolution, Oxford University Press, 1982.
'The Russian Revolution and social mobility: a re-examination of the question of social support for the Soviet regime in the 1920s and 1930s', *Politics and Society*, 13, 2 (1984).
'Stalin and the making of a new elite, 1928–1939', *Slavic Review*, 38, 3 (1979).
Franklin, Bruce, ed., *The essential Stalin. Major theoretical writings 1905–52*, London: Croom Helm, 1973.
Garthoff, R. L., 'The Stalinist revision of history', *Problems of Communism*, 2, 3–4 (July–December 1953).
Geller, Mikhail and Nekrich, Aleksandr, *Utopia u vlasti. Istoriia Sovetskogo Soiuza s 1917 goda do nashikh dnei*, London: Overseas Publications Interchange, 1982.
Gerratana, Valentino, 'Althusser and Stalinism', *New Left Review*, 101–2 (January–April 1977).
'Stalin, Lenin and "Leninism"', *New Left Review*, 103 (May–June 1977).
Getty, J. Arch, *Origins of the Great Purges. The Soviet Communist Party reconsidered, 1933–1938*, Cambridge University Press, 1985.
'Party and purge in Smolensk: 1933–1937', *Slavic Review*, 42, 1 (1983). Also see the following comments by Tucker and Rosenfeldt.
'State, society and superstition', *The Russian Review*, 46, 4 (1987).
Getzler, Israel, *Martov. A political biography of a Russian Social Democrat*, Cambridge University Press, 1967.
Gill, Graeme, 'Bolshevism and the party form', *Australian Journal of Politics and History*, 34, 1 (1988).

'Ideology and system-building; the experience under Lenin and Stalin', Stephen White and Alex Pravda, eds., *Ideology and Soviet politics*, London: Macmillan, 1988.

'Institutionalisation and revolution: Rules and the Soviet political system', *Soviet Studies*, 37, 2 (April 1985).

'Personal dominance and the collective principle: individual legitimacy in Marxist-Leninist systems', T. H.Rigby and Ferenc Feher, eds., *Political legitimation in communist states*, London: Macmillan, 1982.

'Political myth and Stalin's quest for authority in the party', T. H. Rigby, Archie Brown and Peter Reddaway, eds., *Authority, power and policy in the USSR. Essays dedicated to Leonard Schapiro*, London: Macmillan, 1980.

The Rules of the Communist Party of the Soviet Union, London: Macmillan 1988.

'The single party as an agent of development: lessons from the Soviet experience', *World Politics*, 39, 4 (July 1987).

'The Soviet leader cult: reflections on the structure of leadership in the Soviet Union', *The British Journal of Political Science*, 10, 2 (April 1980).

Stalinism, London: Macmillan, 1989.

'Stalinism and institutionalization: the nature of Stalin's regional support', John W. Strong, ed., *Essays on revolutionary culture and Stalinism*, Columbus: Slavica, 1989.

Ginzburg, Evgenia, S., *Into the whirlwind*, Harmondsworth: Penguin, 1968.

Gnedin, E. A., 'V Narkomindele', *Pamiat'. Istoricheskii sbornik*, Paris: La Presse Libre, 1982.

Golinkov, D. L., *Krushenie antisovetskogo podpol'ia v SSSR*, Moscow, 1978, 2 vols.

Golubovic, Zaga 'The history of Russia under Stalin', *New Left Review*, 104 (July–August 1977).

Gouldner, Alvin W., 'Stalinism: a study of internal colonialism', *Telos*, 34 (1977–78).

Gregor, A. James, 'Fascism and modernization: some addenda', *World Politics*, 26, 3 (April 1974).

Grey, Ian, *Stalin. Man of history*, London: Abacus, 1979.

Grigorenko, Petro G., *Memoirs*, London: Harvill Press, 1982.

Gurvitch, Georges, 'L'Effondrement d'un mythe politique: Joseph Staline', *Cahiers internationaux de sociologie*, 33 (Juillet–Decembre 1962).

Haimson, Leopold, ed., *The Mensheviks from the Revolution of 1917 to the Second World War*, University of Chicago Press, 1974.

Harding, Neil, *Lenin's political thought*, London: Macmillan, 1977, 1981, 2 vols.

Harris, J., 'Historians on Stalin', *Soviet Union*, 1, 1 (1974).

'The origins of the conflict between Malenkov and Zhdanov: 1939–1941', *Slavic Review*, 35, 2 (1976).

Harrison, Mark, *Soviet planning in peace and war 1938–1945*, Cambridge University Press, 1985.

Hingley, Ronald, *Joseph Stalin: man and legend*, London: Hutchinson, 1974.

History of the Communist Party of the Soviet Union (Bolsheviks). Short course, Moscow, 1939.

Hough, Jerry F., 'The "dark forces", the totalitarian model, and Soviet history', *The Russian Review*, 46, 4 (1987).
Hough, Jerry F. and Fainsod, Merle, *How the Soviet Union is governed*, Cambridge MA: Harvard University Press, 1979.
Hughes, J. R., 'The Irkutsk affair: Stalin, Siberian politics and the end' (sic), *Soviet Studies*, 41, 2 (April 1989).
Hunter, Holland, 'The overambitious first Soviet Five Year Plan', *Slavic Review*, 32, 2 (1973).
Huskey, Eugene, *Russian lawyers and the Soviet state. The origins and development of the Soviet Bar, 1917–1939*, Princeton University Press, 1986.
Hyde, H. Montgomery, *Stalin. The history of a dictator*, London: Granada Publishing, 1971.
Inkeles, Alex and Bauer, Raymond, *The Soviet citizen, daily life in a totalitarian society*, Cambridge MA: Harvard University Press, 1959.
Jowitt, Kenneth, *Revolutionary breakthroughs and national development. The case of Romania 1944–1945*, Berkeley: University of California Press, 1971.
Keep, John L. H., trans. and ed., *The debate on Soviet power. Minutes of the All-Russian Central Executive Committee of Soviets Second Convocation October 1917–January 1918*, October: Clarendon Press, 1979.
The rise of Social Democracy in Russia, Oxford: Clarendon Press, 1963.
The Russian Revolution. A study in mass mobilization, London: Weidenfeld and Nicolson, 1976.
Kemp-Welch, A., 'Stalinism and intellectual order', T. H. Rigby, Archie Brown and Peter Reddaway, eds., *Authority, Power and Policy in the USSR. Essays dedicated to Leonard Schapiro*, London: Macmillan, 1980.
Kenez, Peter, 'Stalinism as humdrum politics', *The Russian Review*, 45, 4 (1986).
Kern, G., 'Solzhenitsyn's portrait of Stalin', *Slavic Review*, 33, 1 (1974).
Khrushchev, N. S., 'On the cult of personality and its consequences', T. H. Rigby, ed., *The Stalin dictatorship*, Sydney University Press 1968.
Khrushchev Remembers, ed. Strobe Talbot, London: Andre Deutsche, 1971, 1974, vols. 1 and 2.
Knei-Paz, Baruch, *The social and political thought of Leon Trotsky*, Oxford: Clarendon Press, 1978.
Knight, Amy W., *The KGB Police and politics in the Soviet Union*, (Boston: Unwin Hyman, 1988).
Kolakowski, Leszek, 'Marxist roots of Stalinism', Robert C. Tucker, ed., *Stalinism. Essays in historical interpretation*, New York: W. W. Norton, 1977.
Main currents of Marxism. Vol. 3. The breakdown, Oxford University Press, 1981.
Kollantai, Alexandra, *The workers' opposition*, London: London Solidarity Pamphlet 7, 1968.
Kowalski, Ronald J., 'The Left Communism Movement of 1918: a preliminary analysis of its Regional Strength', *Sbornik*, 12 (1986).
Krivitsky, W. G., *I was Stalin's agent*, London: Hamish Hamilton, 1940.
Krygier, Martin, '"Bureaucracy" in Trotsky's analysis of Stalinism', Marian Sawer, ed., *Socialism and the new class: towards the analysis of structural*

inequality within socialist societies, APSA Monograph No. 19, Bedford Park, 1978.
Kuromiya, Hiroaki, 'Stalinism and historical research', *The Russian Review*, 46, 4 (1987).
Stalin's industrial revolution. Politics and workers 1928–1932, Cambridge University Press, 1988.
Laird, Roy D., *The Politburo. Demographic trends, Gorbachev and the future*, Boulder: Westview Press, 1986.
Lampert, Nicholas, *The technical intelligentsia and the Soviet state: a study of Soviet managers and technicians 1928–1935*, London: Macmillan, 1979.
Lane, David, *Leninism: a sociological interpretation*, Cambridge University Press, 1981.
Leggett, G. H., *The Cheka: Lenin's Political Police*, Oxford: Clarendon Press, 1981.
'Lenin, Terror and the Political Police', *Survey*, 21, 4 (97) (1975).
Leites, Nathan, Bernaut, Elsa and Garthoff, Raymond L., 'Politburo images of Stalin', *World Politics*, 3, 3 (April 1951).
Lenin, V. I., *Polnoe sobranie sochinenii*, Moscow, 1979–83, 55 vols.
Levytsky, Boris, *The Soviet political elite*, Munich: unpublished, 1969.
Lewin, Moshe, *Lenin's last struggle*, New York: Pluto Press, 1968.
The making of the Soviet system. Essays in the social history of interwar Russia, New York: Pantheon Books, 1985.
Russian peasants and Soviet power. A study of collectivization, London: Allen and Unwin, 1968.
'The social background of Stalinism', Robert C. Tucker, ed., *Stalinism. Essays in historical interpretation*, New York: W. W. Norton, 1977.
'Society and the Stalinist state in the period of the Five Year Plans', *Social History*, 1 (1976).
Liebman, Marcel, *Leninism under Lenin*, London: Merlin Press, 1975.
Loeber, D. A., 'Bureaucracy in a workers' state: E. B. Pashukanis and the struggle against bureaucratism in the Soviet Union', *Soviet Union*, 6, 2 (1979).
Lowenhadt, John, *The Soviet Politburo*, trans. Dymphna Clark, Edinburgh: Canongate, 1982.
Lovell, David W., *From Marx to Lenin. An evaluation of Marx's responsibility for Soviet authoritarianism*, Cambridge University Press, 1984.
Trotsky's analysis of Soviet bureaucratization, London: Croom Helm, 1985.
Lukács, Georg, 'Reflections on the cult of Stalin', *Survey*, 47 (April 1963).
Mace, James, 'Famine and nationalism in Soviet Ukraine', *Problems of Communism*, 33, 3 (May–June 1984).
McCauley, Martin, *The Russian Revolution and the Soviet state 1917–1921. Documents*, London: Macmillan, 1975.
Stalin and Stalinism, Harlow: Longman, 1983.
Maguire, R. A., *Red virgin soil: Soviet literature in the 1920s*, Princeton University Press, 1968.
McNeal, Robert H., 'The beginning of Communist Party financial exactions from the Soviet state', D. A. Loeber, ed., *Ruling communist parties and their status under law*, The Hague: Nijnhoff, 1986.

'The decisions of the CPSU and the Great Purge', *Soviet Studies*, 23, 2 (1971)
ed., *Guide to the decisions of the Communist Party of the Soviet Union*, University of Toronto Press, 1972.
ed., *Resolutions and decisions of the Communist party of the Soviet Union*, University of Toronto Press, 1974; Vol. 4. Richard Gregor ed., *The Early Soviet Period: 1917–1929*; and Vol. 3. Robert H. McNeal, ed., *The Stalin Years: 1929–1953*.
'Trotskyist interpretations of Stalinism', Robert C. Tucker, ed., *Stalinism. Essays in historical interpretation*, New York: W. W. Norton, 1977.
Stalin's works. An annotated bibliography, Stanford University Press, 1967.
Maier', N. 'Sluzhba v' komissariat' iustitsii i narodnom' sud'', *Arkhiv russkoi revoliutsii*, 8 (1923).
Mandelstam, Nadezhda, *Hope abandoned*, Harmondsworth: Penguin, 1974.
Hope against hope, Harmondsworth: Penguin, 1971.
Manning, Roberta T., *Government in the Soviet countryside in the Stalinist thirties: the case of Belyi Raion in 1937*, The Carl Beck Papers in Russian and East European Studies, Paper No. 301, University of Pittsburgh, 1984.
'Peasants and the party: rural administration in the Soviet countryside on the eve of World War II', John W. Strong, ed., *Essays on revolutionary culture and Stalinism*, Columbus: Slavica, 1989.
'State and society in Stalinist Russia', *The Russian Review*, 46, 4 (1987).
Markovic, Mihailo, 'Stalinism and Marxism', Robert C. Tucker, ed., *Stalinism. Essays in historical interpretation*, New York: W. W. Norton, 1977.
Maximoff, Gregory Petrovich, *The guillotine at work*. Vol. 1. *The Leninist counter-revolution*, Sanday: Cienfuegos Press, 1979.
Medvedev, Roy, *All Stalin's men*, Oxford: Blackwell, 1983
K sudu istorii. Genezis i posledstviia Stalinizma, New York: Alfred A. Knopf, 1974.
'New pages from the political biography of Stalin', Robert C. Tucker, ed., *Stalinism. Essays in historical interpretation*, New York: W. W. Norton, 1977.
Nikolai Bukharin, New York: W. W. Norton, 1980.
On Stalin and Stalinism, trans. Ellen de Kadt, Oxford University Press, 1979.
Meyer, Alfred G., 'Coming to terms with the past ... and with one's older colleagues', *The Russian Review*, 45, 4 (1986).
Leninism, Cambridge MA: Harvard University Press, 1957.
'The war scare of 1927', *Soviet Union*, 5, 1 (1978).
Mikoian, A. I., *Mysli i vospominaniia o Lenine*, Moscow, 1970.
V nachale dvatsatykh, Moscow, 1975.
Miliband, Ralph, 'Stalin and after. Some comments on two books by Roy Medvedev', *The Socialist Register*, 1973.
Millar, James R. and Nove, Alec, 'A debate on collectivization. Was Stalin really necessary?', *Problems of Communism*, 25, 4 (July–August 1976).
Moscow News (Moscow, 1985–89).
Moskalenko, I. M., *Organy partiinogo kontrolia v period stroitel'stva sotsializma (zadachi, struktura, metody deiatel'nosti kontrol'nykh komissii 1920–1934gg)*, Moscow, 1981.

Narkiewicz, Olga A., *The making of the Soviet state apparatus*, Manchester University Press, 1970.
Nikolaeva, V. P., 'V. I. Lenin i Organizatsionnoe Biuro TsK RKP(b) (1919–1922gg)', *Voprosy Istorii KPSS*, 9 (1969).
Nicolaevsky, Boris I., *Power and the Soviet elite 'The letter of an Old Bolshevik' and other essays*, Ann Arbor: University of Michigan Press, 1965.
Nove, Alec, *An economic history of the USSR*, Harmondsworth: Penguin, 1972.
  'Socialism, centralised planning and the one-party state', T. H. Rigby, Archie Brown and Peter Reddaway, eds, *Authority, power and policy in the USSR. Essays dedicated to Leonard Schapiro*, London: Macmillan, 1980.
  Stalinism and After, London: Allen and Unwin, 1975.
  'Stalinism: revisionism reconsidered', *The Russian Review*, 46, 4 (1987).
  'Was Stalin really necessary?', Alec Nove, *Economic rationality and soviet politics or was Stalin really necessary?* New York: Praeger, 1964.
Oppenheim, Samuel A., 'The Supreme Economic Council 1917–1921', *Soviet Studies*, 25, 3 (July 1973).
Payne, Robert, *The rise and fall of Stalin*, London: Pan Books, 1968.
  'The personality cult', *Survey*, 63 (April 1967).
Pethybridge, Roger, *The social prelude to Stalinism*, London: Macmillan, 1974.
Pipes, Richard, *The formation of the Soviet Union*, Cambridge MA: Harvard University Press, 1970.
Ploss, S. I., 'Soviet Party history: the Stalinist legacy', *Problems of Communism*, 21, 4 (July–August 1973).
Quigley, J., 'The 1926 Soviet Family Code: retreat from free love', *Soviet Union*, VI, 2 (1979).
Radkey, Oliver Henry, *The election of the Russian Constituent Assembly of 1917*, Cambridge MA: Harvard University Press, 1950.
  The sickle under the hammer. The Russian Socialist Revolutionaries in the early months of Soviet rule, New York: Columbia University Press, 1963.
Rakovsky, Christian, *Selected writings on opposition in the USSR 1923–30*, London: Allison and Busby, 1980.
Redlich, Roman, *Stalinshchina kak dukhovnyi fenomen*, Frankfurt: Possev-Verlag, 1971.
Reichman, Henry, 'Reconsidering "Stalinism"', *Theory and Society*, 17, 1 (1988).
Reiman, Michal, *The birth of Stalinism. The USSR on the eve of the 'Second Revolution'*, Bloomington: Indiana University Press, 1987.
  'Political trials of the Stalinist era', *Telos*, 54 (1982–83).
  'The Russian Revolution and Stalinism: a political problem and its historiographic content', John W. Strong, ed., *Essays on revolutionary culture and Stalinism*, Columbus: Slavica, 1989.
Report of Court Proceedings in the Case of the anti-Soviet 'Bloc of Rights and Trotskyites', Moscow, 1938.
Report of Court Proceedings in the Case of the Anti-Soviet Trotskyite Centre, Moscow, 1937.
Report of Court Proceedings in the Case of the Trotskyite-Zinovievite Terrorist Centre, Moscow, 1936.

Rigby, T. H., *Communist Party membership in the USSR 1917–1967*, Princeton University Press, 1968.
'Early provincial cliques and the rise of Stalin', *Soviet Studies*, 33, 1 (January 1981).
'The first Proletarian Government', *The British Journal of Political Science*, 4, 1 (1974).
Lenin's government, Sovnarkom 1917–1922, Cambridge University Press, 1979.
'The origins of the Nomenklatura system', Inge Auerbach, Andreas Hillgruber and Gottfried Schramm, eds., *Felder und Vorfelder russischer Geschichte. Studien zu Ehren von Peter Scheibert*, Freiburg: Rombach Verlag, 1985.
'The Soviet political executive, 1917–1986', Archie Brown, ed., *Political leadership in the Soviet Union*, London: Macmillan, 1989.
ed., *Stalin*, Englewood Cliffs NJ: Prentice Hall, 1966.
'Stalinism and the mono-organisational society', Robert C. Tucker, ed., *Stalinism. Essays in Historical Interpretation*, New York: W. W. Norton, 1977.
'Was Stalin a disloyal patron?', *Soviet Studies*, 38, 3 (July 1986).
Rittersporn, Gábor Tamás, 'History, commemoration and hectoring rhetoric', *The Russian Review*, 46, 4 (1987).
'The 1930s in the longue durée of Soviet history', *Telos*, 53 (1982).
'L'Etat en lutte contre lui-même. Tensions sociales et conflits politiques en URSS 1936–1938', *Libre*, 4 (1978).
'Rethinking Stalinism', *Russian History*, 11, 4 (Winter 1984).
Simplifications staliniennes et complications soviétiques. Tensions sociales et conflits politiques en URSS 1933–1953, Paris: Editions des archives contemporaines, 1988.
'Société et appareil d'état soviétiques (1936–1938): contradictions et interférences', *Annales. Economies, societes, civilisations*, 34, 4 (1979).
'Soviet officialdom and political evolution. Judiciary apparatus and penal policy in the 1930s', *Theory and Society*, 13 (1984).
'Soviet politics in the 1930s: rehabilitating society', *Studies in Comparative Communism*, 19, 2 (Summer 1986).
'Staline en 1938: apogée du verbe et défaite politique. Eléments pour une étude du "stalinisme réel"', *Libre*, 6, (1979).
Rodionov, P. A., *Kollektivnost' – vysshii printsip partiinogo rukovodstva*, Moscow, 1967.
Rosefielde, Steven, 'An assessment of the sources and use of Gulag forced labour 1929–56', *Soviet Studies*, 33, 1 (January 1981).
Rosenberg, William G., *Liberals in the Russian Revolution. The Constitutional Democratic Party, 1917–1921*, Princeton University Press, 1974.
'Smolensk in the 1920s: Party–worker relations and the "vanguard" problem', *The Russian Review*, 36, 2 (1977).
Rosenfeldt, Niels Erik, '"The consistory of the communist church": The origins and development of Stalin's secret chancellery', *Russian History*, 9, 2–3 (1982).

Knowledge and Power. The role of Stalin's Secret Chancellery in the Soviet system of government, Copenhagen: Rosenkilde and Bagger, 1978.
'Stalinism as a system of communication', John W. Strong, ed., *Essays on revolutionary culture and Stalinism*, Columbus: Slavica, 1989.
Roth, Guenther, 'Personal rulership, patrimonialism, and empire-building in the new states', *World Politics*, 20, 2 (January 1968).
Sartre, Jean Paul, '"Socialism in one country"', *New Left Review*, 100 (1976-77).
Schapiro, Leonard, *The Communist Party of the Soviet Union*, London: Methuen, 1970.
'The general department of the CC of the CPSU', *Survey*, 21, 3(96) (Summer 1975).
The origin of the communist autocracy. Political opposition in the Soviet state: first phase, 1917-1922, New York; Praeger, 1965.
Schulz, Heinrich A., Urban, Paul K. and Lebed, Andrew A., eds., *Who was who in the USSR?*, Metuchen: Scarecrow Press, 1972.
Scott, E. J., 'The Cheka', *St Antony's Papers*, No. 1, Soviet Affairs No. 1, London: Chatto and Windus, 1956.
Seliunin, Vasilii, 'Istoki', *Novyi Mir*, 5 (1988).
Serge, Victor, *From Lenin to Stalin*, New York: Monad Press, 1973.
Memoirs of a revolutionary 1901-1941, Oxford University Press 1963.
Service, Robert, *The Bolshevik Party in revolution 1917-1923. A study in organisational change*, London: Macmillan, 1979.
'From polyarchy to hegemony: the Party's role in the construction of the central institutions of the Soviet state, 1917-1919', *Sbornik*, 10 (1984).
The Russian Revolution 1900-1927, London: Macmillan, 1986.
Sharlet, Robert, 'Stalinism and Soviet legal culture', Robert C. Tucker, ed., *Stalinism. Essays in historical interpretation*, New York: W. W. Norton, 1977.
Shatz, Marshall, *Stalin, the Great Purge, and Russian history: a new look at the 'new class'*, The Carl Beck Papers in Russian and East European Studies, Paper No. 305, Pittsburgh, 1984.
Shaumyan, L., 'Kul't lichnosti', *Filosofskaia entsiklopediia*, Moscow, 1964, vol. 3.
Shelley, L., 'Soviet criminology: the birth and demise 1917-1936', *Slavic Review*, 38, 4 (1979).
'The 1929 dispute on Soviet criminology', *Soviet Union*, 6, 2 (1979).
Siegelbaum, Lewis H., 'Soviet norm determination in theory and practice 1917-1941', *Soviet Studies*, 36, 1 (January 1984).
Stakhanovism and the politics of productivity in the USSR, 1935-1941, Cambridge University Press, 1988.
Skilling, H. Gordon, 'Stalinism and Czechoslovak political culture', Robert C. Tucker, ed., *Stalinism. Essays in historical interpretation*, New York: W. W. Norton, 1977.
Sokolov, Y. M., *Russian folklore*, trans. C. R. Smith, New York: Macmillan, 1950.
Solomon, Peter H., 'Local political power and Soviet criminal justice, 1922-41', *Soviet Studies*, 37, 3 (July 1985).

Solzhenitsyn, Alexander, *The Gulag Archipelago 1918–1956*, London: Collins/ Fontana, 1973–78.
Sontag, John P., 'The Soviet war scare of 1926–7', *The Russian Review*, 34, 1 (1975).
Souvarine, Boris, *Stalin: a critical survey of Bolshevism*, New York: Longmans, 1939.
Sovetskaia Istoricheskaia Entsiklopedia, Moscow, 1961–76.
Spravochnyi tom k vos'momu izdanii 'KPSS v rezoliutsiiakh i resheniiakh s'ezdov, konferentsii i plenumov ts. k.', (Moscow, 1984).
Stalin, J. V., *Problems of Leninism*, Peking, 1976.
Works, Moscow, 1953–5, vols. 1–13. *I. V. Stalin Sochineniia*, Stanford: Hoover Institution Press, 1967, vols. 14–16 (1–3).
Strong, John W., ed., *Essays on revolutionary culture and Stalinism*, Columbus: Slavica, 1989.
Szamuely, T., 'The elimination of opposition between the Sixteenth and Seventeenth Congresses of the CPSU', *Soviet Studies*, 17, 3 (1966).
Thorniley, Daniel G., *The impact of collectivization on the Soviet rural Communist Party, 1927–1937*, Unpublished Ph.D., CREES, University of Birmingham, 1983.
Tiersky, Ronald, *Ordinary Stalinism. Democratic centralism and the question of communist political development*, Boston: Allen and Unwin, 1985.
Togliatti, Palmiro, '9 Domande sullo Stalinismo', Nuovi Argomenti, No.20, June 16, 1956, reprinted in *The anti-Stalin campaign and international communism. A selection of documents*, New York: Columbia UP, 1956.
Trotsky, Leon, *The challenge of the Left Opposition (1923–25)*, New York: Pathfinder Press, 1975.
My life, New York: Pathfinder Press, 1970.
The New Course and The struggle for the new Course, Ann Arbor: University of Michigan Press, 1965.
On Lenin. Notes towards a biography, London: Harrap, 1971.
The permanent revolution and results and prospects, New York: Pathfinder Press, 1970.
The revolution betrayed, New York: Pathfinder Press, 1970.
Stalin. An appraisal of the man and his influence, London: MacGibbon and Kee, 1968.
The Stalin school of falsification, New York: Pathfinder Press, 1971.
Terrorism and communism (Ann Arbor: University of Michigan Press, 1961.
Tsypko, A., 'Istoki stalinizma', *Nauka i zhizn'*, 11 and 12 (1988), 1 and 2 (1989).
Tucker, Robert C., 'The rise of Stalin's personality cult', *American Historical Review*, 84, 2 (April 1979).
'Some questions on the scholarly agenda', Robert C. Tucker, ed., *Stalinism. Essays in historical interpretation*, New York: W. W. Norton, 1977.
The Soviet political mind. Studies in Stalinism and post-Stalin change, New York: Praeger, 1971.
Stalin as revolutionary 1879–1929. A study in history and personality, London: Chatto and Windus, 1974.
'The Stalin period as an historical problem', *The Russian Review*, 46, 4 (1987).

ed., *Stalinism. Essays in historical interpretation*, New York: W. W. Norton, 1977.
'Stalinism as revolution from above', Robert C. Tucker, ed., *Stalinism. Essays in historical interpretation*, New York: W. W. Norton, 1977.
"Svetlana Alliluyeva as witness of Stalin", *Slavic Review*, 27, 2 (1968).
Ulam, Adam B., *Stalin. The man and his era*, London: Allen Lane, 1974.
Uldricks, Teddy J., *Diplomacy and ideology. The origins of Soviet foreign relations 1917–1930*, London; Sage Publications, 1979.
Unger, Aryeh L., *Constitutional development in the USSR. A guide to the Soviet Constitutions*, London: Methuen, 1981.
Urban, G. R., *Stalinism. Its impact on Russia and the world*, London: Maurice Temple Smith, 1982.
Vaganov, F. M., *Pravyi uklon v VKP(b) i ego razgrom (1928–1930gg)*, Moscow, 1977.
Van den Berg, Ger P., 'The Council of Ministers of the Soviet Union', *Review of Socialist Law*, 6, 3 (1980).
Viola, Lynne, *The best sons of the Fatherland. Workers in the vanguard of Soviet collectivization*, Oxford University Press, 1987.
'The campaign to eliminate the Kulak as a class, winter 1929–1930: a reevaluation of the legislation', *Slavic Review*, 45, 3 (1986).
'In search of young revisionists', *The Russian Review*, 46, 4 (1987).
'The "25,000ers": a study in a Soviet recruitment campaign during the first Five Year Plan', *Russian History*, 10, 1 (1983).
Von Laue, Theodore H., 'Stalin among the moral and political imperatives, or how to judge Stalin', *Soviet Union*, 8, 1 (1981).
'Stalin in focus', *Slavic Review*, 42, 3 (1983).
'Stalin reviewed', *Soviet Union*, 11, 1 (1984).
Why Lenin? Why Stalin? A reappraisal of the Russian Revolution, 1900–1930, Philadelphia: J. B. Lippincott Co., 1964.
Watson, Derek, *The making of Molotov's Sovnarkom, 1928–1930*, CREES Discussion Papers, SIPS No.25, University of Birmingham, 1984.
Werth, Nicolas, *Etre communiste en URSS sous Staline*, Paris: Gallimard, 1981.
Wheatcroft, Stephen G., 'On assessing the size of forced concentration camp labour in the Soviet Union, 1929–56', *Soviet Studies*, 33, 2 (April 1981).
'Towards a thorough analysis of Soviet forced labour statistics', *Soviet Studies*, 35, 2 (April 1983).
Willner, Ann Ruth, *The spellbinders. Charismatic political leadership*, New Haven: Yale University Press, 1984.
Wolfe, Bertram D., *Three who made a revolution: a biographical history*, Harmondsworth: Penguin, 1964.
Zaleski, Eugene, *Stalinist planning for economic growth 1933–1952*, Chapel Hill NC: University of North Carolina Press, 1980.

Index

accountability, 87–8, 89, 90, 91, 126, 141–2, 149, 268, 270, 318
Agranov, Ia., 299
Andreev, A., 153, 156, 192, 230, 231, 286, 287, 290, 353, 371, 375, 395, 399, 417, 420
Antipov, N., 395
Antonov-Ovseenko, V., 190
apparatus, party, 32–3, 40, 43–4, 49, 51, 61, 62, 66, 67, 68, 72, 73, 74, 77, 83, 94, 103, 105–7, 121–2, 128, 129, 140, 153–4, 157, 158–62, 166–7, 173, 174, 197–8, 211–12, 216, 222, 226–8, 229, 232, 233, 234, 235, 236, 237, 240, 241, 247, 249, 265, 267, 268, 269, 271, 273, 277, 279–80, 287, 288–90, 318, 319, 372, 377, 379, 400–1, 417, 426
appointment, 45–50, 75, 82, 90, 92, 106–7, 123–4, 125, 126, 128, 129, 131–4, 140, 158, 162, 194–5, 246, 316, 319, 325, 338, 339

backwardness, 16, 309–12, 330
Badaev, A., 371, 417
Bagirov, M., 402, 414, 417
Bakaev, L., 170, 189
Batyshev, I., 353
Bauman, K., 153, 154, 156, 230, 419
Bazhanov, B., 166
Beloboradov, A., 81
Beria, L., 7, 242, 286, 287, 299, 402, 414, 417, 423
Bettelheim, C., 16
Bialer, S., 329
Bliumkin, Y., 191
Bogdanov, A., 89, 358
Bolshevik tradition, 15, 86–90, 172, 184, 313
Brest Litovsk, 53, 59, 60, 63, 64, 65, 92, 99, 109, 172, 183, 356
Budenny, S., 417
Bukharin, N., 66, 94, 95, 101, 102, 125, 151, 152, 155, 156, 157, 172, 179, 182, 183, 185, 191, 192, 193, 196, 229, 254, 281, 282, 283, 288, 296, 314, 332, 347, 356, 375, 377, 383, 399, 406, 418, 424
Bulganin, N., 417
bureaucratism, 15, 74, 84, 124, 131, 264, 266, 270, 319, 355

Central Committee, 19, 41, 42, 43, 44, 48, 49, 51, 57, 59, 60–5, 67, 68, 69, 72, 73, 75–6, 78, 79, 81, 85, 90, 91, 93, 94, 96, 97, 99, 101, 102, 104, 106, 120, 126, 128, 138, 139, 141, 143, 144–52, 154, 156, 157, 158, 159, 164, 165, 166, 169, 170, 172, 175, 178, 179, 193, 194, 195, 196, 202, 211, 220, 225–30, 232, 233, 235, 236, 237, 238, 242, 244, 246, 249, 250, 263, 264, 265, 267, 276, 278–85, 286, 290, 291, 296, 297, 298, 299, 301, 318, 319, 329, 333, 334, 335, 337, 338, 339, 342, 343, 344, 345, 346, 348, 349, 350, 351, 352, 356, 359, 362, 368, 370, 371, 372, 373, 374, 375, 376, 378, 379, 383, 386, 387, 393, 395, 396, 397, 398, 401, 402, 404, 405, 406, 413, 418, 419, 420, 422, 423
CC–CCC joint plenum, 64, 85–6, 144, 150–1, 169, 170–1, 175, 187, 211, 225, 228, 238–9, 371, 373, 374, 387, 399, 406
centralisation of power, 37–40, 43, 45–50, 55–6, 59, 60, 71–2, 93, 103, 108, 110, 124, 131–4, 137, 156, 306, 318, 319, 320, 321
centre–sub-national relations, 7–8, 32, 36, 39–50, 62–3, 69–70, 71–81, 103, 105, 117, 121, 125, 126–34, 161–6, 172–4, 176, 194–5, 198, 206–18, 237, 246, 262–74, 283–4, 294, 301–2, 306, 314–17, 318, 324–7, 337, 338, 366, 367, 393–4, 413, 414
Cheka, *see* security organs

443

444   Index

Chelyshev, M., 353
Chentsov, I., 353
chistka, *see* purge
Chubar, V., 153, 156, 231, 285, 419
Civil War, 26, 31, 35, 36, 38, 44, 45, 47,
  54, 63, 67, 72, 80, 81, 104, 108, 117,
  118, 123, 206, 244, 279, 292, 308, 314,
  339, 362
coherence, institutional, 5, 24–5, 32–3,
  40–1, 49, 51, 55, 63–5, 67, 71, 81, 83,
  86, 108–10, 117, 122–4, 130, 134,
  148–9, 151–2, 157, 170, 171, 195–8,
  225, 230, 233, 238, 240, 242, 255,
  273–4, 278, 285, 288, 294, 295–7, 302,
  305, 306, 319, 322–3, 324–7
collective leadership, 107–10, 191–2,
  193–8, 219, 225, 243–4, 246, 249, 250,
  268, 297–302, 315, 325
collectivisation, agricultural, 9–10, 11, 19,
  117, 186, 201, 202, 204, 205, 206–7,
  211, 214, 217, 219, 220, 223, 224, 227,
  229, 236–7, 241, 244, 248, 249, 250,
  251, 254, 259, 292, 304, 309, 311, 316,
  323, 324, 367, 385, 392, 402
Comintern, 59, 99, 170, 174, 175, 344,
  356, 358, 371, 372, 373
commissariats, 52, 53, 54, 55, 135–7,
  219, 220, 221, 276–7, 367, 368, 415,
  420
Commission for Soviet Control, 213, 231,
  239, 401
conference, party, 56, 88, 103, 127,
  138–9, 140, 141, 142, 149, 271, 273,
  280, 342, 368, 369
  VIII, 44, 47, 348
  IX, 76, 83, 85, 332, 382
  X, 350
  XI, 338, 378
  XII, 331
  XIII, 116, 141, 142, 177, 178, 180, 186,
    370, 386
  XIV, 373
  XV, 142–3, 176–7, 179
  XVI, 120, 151, 232, 370
  XVIII, 277, 420
congress, party, 42, 43, 51, 56–60, 73, 83,
  87, 88, 90, 93, 94, 103, 138–44, 147,
  149, 150, 173, 174, 179, 213, 221–5,
  227, 237, 242, 248, 271, 273, 277–8,
  290, 319, 329, 334, 342
  VII, 56, 57, 58, 59, 60, 61, 62, 63–4, 93,
    94, 138, 332, 334, 344, 345, 356, 374,
    396
  VIII, 27, 34, 38, 41, 42, 43, 44, 55, 57,
    58, 59, 61, 62, 63, 65, 68, 69, 71, 75,
    81, 93, 109, 333, 334, 335, 342, 343,
    344, 345, 346, 355

  IX, 37, 48, 57, 58, 59, 61, 62, 70, 71, 74,
    76, 332, 334, 342, 343, 344, 345, 348,
    351, 352, 355, 356
  X, 27, 40, 44, 45, 48, 50, 57–8, 59, 60,
    61, 62, 65, 67, 72, 74, 80, 82, 83, 84,
    85, 91, 93, 94, 95, 97, 98, 99, 104,
    109, 144, 148, 150, 163, 168, 170, 175,
    178, 186, 311, 338, 339, 342, 343, 344,
    345, 346, 349, 354, 356, 380
  XI, 27, 40, 58, 59, 61, 62, 68, 72, 74, 77,
    78, 79, 80, 83, 84, 85, 99, 138, 139,
    144, 145, 147, 148, 150, 152, 153, 154,
    159, 162, 163, 168, 170, 338, 342, 345,
    350, 356, 369, 371, 372
  XII, 118, 120, 139, 140, 143, 145, 146,
    148, 149, 150, 154, 156, 157, 158, 159,
    163, 168, 169, 175, 177, 178, 180, 191,
    343, 352, 359, 364, 369, 371, 372, 374
  XIII, 18, 96, 113, 120, 125, 137, 139,
    140, 141, 145, 146, 148, 154, 156, 158,
    159, 160, 163, 170, 181, 363, 369, 370,
    371, 372, 380
  XIV, 126, 139, 140, 141, 142, 143, 145,
    146, 147, 148, 154, 156, 159, 160, 163,
    173, 175, 176, 178, 189, 191, 192, 359,
    369, 371, 372, 380, 383
  XV, 120, 127, 137, 138, 139, 140, 141,
    144, 145, 146, 147, 148, 154, 156, 157,
    159, 160, 163, 175, 179, 187, 188, 192,
    221, 222, 227, 228, 234, 239, 369, 371,
    372, 383, 398
  XVI, 120, 138, 144, 145, 163, 196, 204,
    221, 222, 223, 224, 225, 227, 228, 234,
    238, 239, 245, 247, 249, 251, 252, 371,
    396, 398, 406
  XVII, 19, 58, 202, 204, 210, 213, 217,
    221, 222, 223, 224, 226, 227, 228, 230,
    233, 234, 237, 238, 239, 245, 246–7,
    252, 260, 268, 277, 278, 279, 280, 286,
    317, 324, 396, 398, 405, 406
  XVIII, 58, 260, 266, 277, 278, 279, 280,
    281, 285, 286, 288, 289, 329, 416, 425
Conquest, R., 288, 296
consensus, elite, 51, 103–6, 110, 185, 194,
  195, 225, 247–50
Constituent Assembly, 25, 31, 308
Constitution, 1936, 203, 259, 269, 270,
  275, 292, 408, 419
control commissions, 51, 73, 83–6, 98–9,
  119, 170, 189, 190, 213, 230, 237–40,
  252, 343, 349, 353, 382, 402
  Central Control Commission, 59, 60,
    83, 84–5, 96, 120, 144, 150–1, 156,
    157, 158, 167–71, 213, 220, 224, 230,
    233, 237–40, 338, 343, 353, 358, 365,
    370, 371, 374, 375, 379–80, 382, 387,
    394, 401, 406

Index   445

Party Control Commission, 213, 231, 237–40, 269, 286, 290, 298, 420
  see also Central Committee: CC–CCC joint plenum
conventions, 51–2, 86–110, 172–98, 246–55, 297–306
criticism – self-criticism, 43, 126–9, 130, 134, 177–8, 206, 210, 215, 217, 269–73, 316, 336
cult, leader, 5
  Lenin cult, 108, 180–4, 186, 195, 322
  Stalin cult, 13–14, 194, 198, 242–6, 254, 291–4, 301, 313, 314, 424–5

Daniels, R., 148, 357
Davies, R., 400
Declaration of the 22, 59, 99, 175, 356, 358
Declaration of the 46, 132, 141, 175
democracy, intra-party, 58, 86–7, 90–9, 109, 124, 125–9, 133, 177–80, 206, 269–73, 313
democratic centralism, 42, 89–90, 164, 382–3
Democratic Centralists, 43, 48, 62–3, 84, 90, 93, 120, 173, 337, 338, 347, 351
Deutscher, I., 16
deviation, 96, 180, 188, 189, 238, 302, 382, 383, 386, 392, 405
discipline, party, 18, 41–2, 65, 88–9, 91, 92, 94, 95–100, 109–10, 120, 126, 151, 168, 170, 176–80, 188, 197, 238–9, 252, 265, 290, 312, 313, 317, 318, 321, 323, 406
discussion, intra-party, 86, 87, 89, 90, 91, 92, 93, 94, 98, 100, 101–3, 126, 128, 135, 142, 149–50, 179–91, 248, 313, 382
Djilas, M., 288
doctors' plot, 7
Dogadov, A., 233, 353
Dzerzhinsky, F., 82, 83, 85, 101, 136, 155, 287, 353, 375, 395

education, 12, 118–19, 137, 139, 222, 249, 277, 312, 409, 416
Eikhe, R., 285, 419, 422
Eismont–Tolmachev–Smirnov group, 238, 239, 246, 250, 251, 398, 399, 405
elections, party, 43, 46, 47, 48, 49, 56, 60, 65, 87, 88, 89, 90, 91, 92, 125, 126–9, 131, 140, 150, 165–6, 268, 270–3, 274, 383, 414, 415
  1937 elections, 270–2, 283, 413
Enukidze, A., 423
Evdokimov, G., 170, 379, 385
Exchange of Party Cards, *see* purge

Ezhov, N., 242, 285, 287, 288, 290, 295, 297, 298, 299, 401, 402, 405, 419, 420, 423, 424

factional conflict, 18–19, 40–1, 48, 145, 149, 150, 152, 155–6, 158, 172, 176, 181–6, 193, 195, 197, 322, 326
factions, 60, 89, 96–9, 101, 103, 107, 126, 145, 149, 155, 196, 217, 300, 356
family groups, 37, 47, 49–50, 106, 124–6, 129–31, 133, 173–4, 208, 215–18, 268, 269, 271, 273, 315–17, 337, 394, 395, 413, 414, 418
Fitzpatrick, S., 1–2
fractions, 95–9, 103, 104, 106–7, 120, 131–4, 170, 175–6, 177, 178, 179, 188, 189, 192–3, 194–5, 217, 251, 315–17, 356, 381, 382, 383, 386
Frumkin, M., 193–4
Frunze, M., 155, 375

Galiev, Sultan, 190, 381, 387
General Secretary, 73, 107, 131, 132, 133, 134, 153, 159, 162, 166–7, 217, 220, 224, 231, 233, 240–6, 247, 250, 319, 349, 379, 402
Getty, J. Arch, 272, 328, 423
Goloshchekin, F., 124
Gosplan, 54, 136–7, 249, 416
GPU, *see* security organs
Grinko, G., 395, 416
Gusev, S., 189

ideology, 13–14, 23, 32, 107, 170, 184–5, 189, 254–5, 305–6, 312–13, 314, 386
Industrial Party, 202, 241, 405
industrialisation, 9–10, 204, 207, 219, 220, 244, 259
infection, 26–32, 35, 115, 116, 117, 134, 178, 188–9, 252, 310–12, 425
institutionalisation, 24–5, 32–3, 58, 62, 63–5, 67, 71, 86, 102, 108–10, 117, 122–4, 130, 134, 148–9, 151–2, 157, 165, 171, 195–8, 216, 230, 242, 255, 273–4, 278, 285, 288, 294, 295–7, 302, 305, 306, 319, 322–3, 324–7
integrity, institutional, 5, 24–5, 32–3, 40–1, 49, 51, 63–5, 67, 71, 81, 83, 86, 108–10, 117, 122–4, 130, 134, 148–9, 151–2, 157, 170, 171, 195–8, 225, 230, 233, 238, 240, 242, 255, 273–4, 278, 285, 288, 294, 295–7, 302, 305, 306, 319, 322–3, 324–7
international context, 16, 185, 189, 308–9
Ioffe, A., 172
isolation, 16, 31–2, 95, 113–17, 201, 203, 259, 308–12, 329

Index

Kaganovich, L., 44, 153, 154, 156, 204, 228, 230, 231, 232, 233, 234, 236, 238, 252, 286, 287, 290, 299, 379, 399, 400, 401, 405, 417, 420, 424
Kaganovich, M., 417
Kalinin, M., 66, 83, 153, 231, 286, 287, 320, 347, 353, 371, 375, 399, 406, 417
Kamenev, L., 52, 66, 82, 101, 103, 124, 143, 153, 155, 156, 170, 172, 173, 178, 180, 183, 185, 190, 191, 192, 196, 202, 250, 251, 253, 288, 314, 347, 385, 395, 403, 405, 406
Kaminsky, G., 418
Kanner, G., 166
Khrushchev, N., 278, 282, 285, 286, 287, 288, 296, 299, 414, 417, 419
Kirov, S., 19, 124, 153, 156, 202, 231, 232, 233, 240, 242, 246, 252, 253, 262, 264, 297–8, 303, 304, 312, 323, 324, 397, 399, 401, 404, 405, 409, 410, 419, 423
Kiselev, A., 94
Kolakowski, L., 15
Kollontai, A., 59, 108
Komarov, N., 83
Korostelev, A., 353
Korotkov, I., 377
Kosior, S., 153, 156, 175, 190, 231, 296, 366, 375, 399, 419, 422
Krestinsky, N., 40, 48, 65, 66, 71–2, 81, 82, 101, 190, 334, 348, 349, 352
Krivov, T., 353
Kuchmenko, N., 353
Kuibyshev, V., 136, 153, 156, 170, 191, 225, 231, 232, 320, 353, 375, 395, 399, 419
kulaks, 10, 30, 115, 128, 185, 194, 261, 264, 366
Kursky, D., 156, 158, 160
Kutuzov, I., 94
Kuznetsov, N., 356
Kviring, E., 178

Lashevich, M., 124, 172
law, 30, 202, 338, 407, 408
Left Communists, 63, 64, 92–3, 94, 95, 99, 103, 173, 355, 356–7
Left Opposition, 154, 173, 175
Left SRs, 25, 52, 310, 341, 356
Lenin, V., 18, 23, 27, 28, 42, 53, 55, 56, 57, 59, 60, 63, 64, 65, 66, 67, 69, 81, 85, 87, 88, 89, 90, 91, 93, 94, 95, 97, 99, 101, 102, 103, 104, 107–10, 135, 144, 147, 151, 152, 153, 155, 169, 170, 172, 173, 174, 177, 180–3, 186, 188, 191, 192, 195, 197, 243, 244, 245, 246, 291, 293, 313, 325, 326, 330, 332, 333, 334, 340, 346, 347, 352, 354, 356, 357, 370, 371, 384, 395, 403
Lenin enrolment, 116, 117, 118, 361, 385
Leningrad affair, 7
Leninism, 15, 180–4, 187, 188, 191, 198, 242, 243, 244, 245, 312–13, 384, 385, 405
Lewin, M., 16, 328
line, party, 188, 210, 215, 223, 224–5, 245, 248, 250, 251, 252, 254, 268, 270, 279, 303, 304, 386, 392, 405
Lisitsyn, N., 76
Litvin, Z., 353
Litvinov, M., 395, 417
Lominadze, V., 151, 246, 250, 251, 370, 406
Lomov, G., 94
Lozovsky, S., 417
Lunacharsky, A., 53
Lutovinov, L., 176, 339, 345

Makarov, I., 417
Malenkov, G., 285, 287, 298, 299, 420, 423
Manning, R., 328
Manuilsky, D., 371, 417
Marxism, 15, 312
Medvedev, R., 246, 281
Medvedev, S., 59, 356
Mekhlis, L., 166, 299, 379, 417, 420
membership, party, 18, 19, 26–7, 35–6, 116–17, 121, 203–6, 259–62, 312, 332, 335, 360, 361, 362, 408
Mensheviks, 28, 32, 52, 88, 89, 137, 177, 202, 241, 311, 341, 354, 386, 405
Menzhinsky, V., 242
Merkulov, V., 423
Metro-Vickers engineers, 202, 241, 405
Mezhlauk, V., 416
Miasnikov, G., 356, 358
Mikhailov, V., 72, 83, 420
Mikoian, A., 44, 153, 156, 231, 278, 285, 286, 287, 288, 291, 371, 395, 399, 417
Military Opposition, 59, 93, 94, 355
Military Revolutionary Committee, 52
Mitin, M., 356
Molotov, V., 65, 72, 76, 83, 104, 126–7, 153–4, 220, 224, 231, 232, 233, 286, 287, 300, 303, 353, 356, 370, 371, 377, 395, 399, 400, 417, 423
monolithism, 143, 174, 186–9, 222, 224, 225, 252, 255, 278, 312, 313, 370
Moscow, 49, 62, 63, 67, 69, 81, 95, 124, 125, 153, 173, 191, 212, 231, 272, 277, 287, 295, 308, 315, 319, 322, 339, 344, 355, 370, 388, 414
Muralov, N., 170

Muranov, M., 81, 85, 353
nationalism, 13, 190, 293
NEP, 10, 18–19, 29, 52, 84, 98, 107, 113, 117, 136, 171, 182, 185, 254, 308, 311, 322, 337, 365
Nicolaevsky, B., 229
Nikolaev, L., 253
Nikolaeva, K., 417
NKVD, see security organs
Nogin, V., 47, 75, 79
nomenklatura, 11–12, 79, 121–2, 123, 125, 129, 163, 164–6, 209, 218, 237, 263, 268–9, 364, 395, 410, 412
notables, 66, 67, 95, 97, 98, 101, 104, 105, 148, 319–21

OGPU, see security organs
Old Bolsheviks, 26, 61, 67, 81, 117, 118, 145–7, 168, 226, 279, 286, 301, 312, 320, 419, 425
oligarchy, 95, 97, 98, 100, 101–3, 106, 110, 135, 141, 192–8, 220, 241, 248, 297–300
On Party Unity, 85, 91, 95–9, 102, 175–6, 178, 186, 188, 311, 355, 356, 406
On the Syndicalist and Anarchist Deviation in Our Party, 95, 356
opposition, 7, 19, 48, 57, 59, 64, 67, 85, 88–90, 92–9, 101–2, 108, 109, 113, 120–1, 126, 133–4, 140–3, 144, 149–52, 157–8, 167–71, 172–91, 194–5, 196, 197, 222–3, 224, 225, 229, 233, 238, 246–8, 250–4, 268, 281–5, 301, 302–4, 310–12, 313, 316, 319, 321–4, 343, 367, 370, 380, 383, 386, 388, 405, 406, 425–6
Ordzhonikidze, G., 124, 156, 224, 225, 231, 233, 249, 300, 375, 395, 399, 400, 419
Orgburo, 65–6, 67, 69, 71, 73, 74, 78, 79, 81–3, 105, 107, 126, 129, 132, 140, 154, 156, 158–9, 162, 164, 167, 169, 229, 232, 233–7, 240, 247, 286, 287, 288, 301, 329, 348, 352, 353, 357, 374, 375, 376, 377, 393, 399, 400, 411, 420
Osinsky, V., 38, 43, 63, 348, 355, 358
Ozol, K., 353

patrimonialism, 25, 294, 317, 325–7
peasants, 9, 10, 11, 16, 26–8, 36, 114–16, 118, 155, 185, 201, 203–4, 259, 260, 261, 308, 309, 311, 332, 333, 360, 361, 362, 367, 371, 385, 389, 408
personal dictatorship, 5, 7, 307, 321, 323, 325–7
personal linkages, 6, 37, 47, 49–60, 106, 124–5, 129–34, 166, 173–4, 215–18, 241–2, 267–8, 271, 294, 298–302, 320–7
personal power, 24–5, 37–45, 47, 49–50, 101–3, 106, 107–10, 124–6, 127–34, 166, 173–4, 192–8, 215–18, 219, 233, 240–6, 267–74, 290–302, 306, 307, 313, 314–17, 318, 320–7, 404–5
personnel procedures, 35–6, 43, 44–50, 73–81, 82, 106, 121–2, 132, 160–6, 194, 198, 207–9, 212, 213, 217–18, 237, 261–7, 288–90, 295, 315, 337, 338, 339, 348–9, 350, 351, 378, 379, 392, 393, 409, 410, 411, 422
Petrovsky, G., 153, 156, 231, 320
Piatakov, G., 190, 194, 385, 406, 425
Pokrovsky, M., 425
policy-making, 5, 55, 60, 62–3, 67, 100–3, 135–6, 156–7, 184–7, 191, 228, 248–50, 254–5, 276, 277, 280–5, 299–301, 305–6
Politburo, 7, 51, 56, 62, 64, 65–8, 71, 72, 73, 81, 102, 103, 118, 136, 139, 144, 149, 152–8, 159, 162, 164, 167, 169, 170, 172, 189, 190, 192, 193, 194, 196, 220, 228, 230–3, 238, 240, 242, 247, 248, 250, 283, 285–8, 295, 296, 298, 301, 318, 319, 320, 329, 346, 347, 348, 352, 365, 367, 370, 372, 373, 375, 376, 377, 383, 387, 395, 399, 400, 401, 404, 405, 406, 419, 422, 425
Popov, K., 242–4
Poskrebyshev, A., 242, 295, 379, 402, 417
Postyshev, P., 231, 250, 282, 283, 285, 419, 422
Preobrazhensky, E., 71–2, 83, 85, 120, 190, 349, 353, 406
privileges, 12, 38–9, 90, 91, 104–5, 124, 217, 268
purge, 88, 100, 119–21, 170, 171, 190, 259, 304, 312, 336, 363
 1919 reregistration, 35, 76
 1920 reregistration, 35, 76, 335
 1921 census, 35, 77, 79, 119, 162
 1921 purge, 26, 35, 84, 99, 116, 132
 1926–7 census, 119, 163
 1929–30 purge, 120, 129, 206, 207, 217, 316
 1933–34 purge, 204, 205–6, 213–15, 216, 217, 224, 233, 237, 238, 239, 241, 251–2, 253, 261, 262, 268, 272, 394, 417
 Verification of Party Documents, 261, 263–5, 266, 268–9, 284, 290, 294, 295, 311, 324, 410, 412, 418
 Exchange of Party cards, 261–2, 263, 265–7, 268–9, 294, 295, 311, 324
 see also Terror, Great

Rabkrin, 66, 153, 169, 171, 213, 224, 237, 249
Radek, K., 406, 425
Rakovsky, K., 82, 170, 190
regime–populace relationship, 25–32, 34–5, 36, 98, 113–19, 201–6, 259–67, 308–12
Reiman, M., 329–30
revolution from above, 4, 9–10, 16, 201, 220, 255, 281, 329
Riazanov, D., 82, 232
Right Opposition, 18, 158, 173, 175, 183, 186, 193, 194, 223, 233, 248, 250, 316, 366, 376, 381, 383, 385, 386, 388, 402, 405
Rittersporn, G., 328
Riutin, M., 229, 233, 238, 242, 246, 250, 251, 401, 403, 404, 405
Rosengoltz, A., 395
Rudzutak, Ya., 83, 153, 156, 230, 231, 251, 320, 353, 375, 395, 399, 401
Rukhimovich, M., 395
Rules, Party, 27, 42–3, 56, 63, 92, 96, 107, 139, 144, 165, 171, 187, 189, 221, 225, 233, 251, 252, 260, 265, 270, 280, 290, 315, 339–40, 346, 354, 369, 379, 406, 422
Rykov, A., 53, 65, 83, 101, 152, 153, 158, 172, 196, 220, 229, 230, 231, 248, 281, 282, 283, 288, 296, 347, 353, 374, 395, 399, 406, 418, 424

Safarov, G., 178, 381
Samoilov, F., 353
Sapronov, T., 355
Schapiro, L., 108, 287
Secretariat, 68–81, 82, 83, 105, 106, 107, 129, 132, 140, 156, 158–66, 167, 212, 229, 233–7, 240, 247, 263, 288–90, 294, 301, 318, 329, 348, 349, 352, 357, 373, 375, 377, 379, 393–4, 423
Accounting Dept., 162
Administration of Affairs, 162, 289, 348
Agitprop, 70, 162, 289, 348, 400
Agriculture Dept., 236, 289
Assignment Dept., 234–5
Cadres Administration, 289, 420
Chancellery, 235, 236, 241, 289, 294
Culture and Propaganda of Leninism, 236
Finance Dept., 70, 348
General Dept., 70, 162, 348, 350
Industry Dept., 236
Informotdel, 70, 162, 377
Leading Party Organs Dept., 236, 264, 289, 298
Organisation-Instruction Dept., 234, 289
Orgotdel, 69–70, 73–81, 160–1, 348, 349, 350, 377, 379
Orgraspred, 161–6
Planning-Finance-Trade Dept., 236
Politico-Administrative Dept., 236
Press Dept., 162
Province Inspection Dept., 70
Rural Dept., 70
School Dept., 289
Secret Dept., 162, 167, 237, 241, 348, 377, 379, 400
Special Sector, 212–13, 236, 237, 241, 269, 289, 294, 295, 379, 394, 400
Statistics Dept., 70, 77, 162
Transport Dept., 236
Uchraspred, 70, 73, 76, 78–81, 122, 160–3, 164, 351, 377, 378
Work Among Women Dept., 70, 162, 351
Work in the Villages Dept., 162
secretaries, party, 36, 37, 47, 49, 65, 69, 70, 71–2, 76, 121, 125, 128, 129, 131–4, 141, 147, 148, 153, 159, 164, 165, 166, 205, 206, 211–12, 214, 231, 238, 246–7, 263, 264, 265, 267, 269, 270, 271, 272, 273, 286, 288, 349, 350, 363, 366, 420
security apparatus, 7, 19, 30, 34, 38, 53, 99, 189–91, 202, 212, 241–2, 253, 254, 267–8, 281, 284, 286, 287, 288, 290, 293, 295–7, 298, 299, 300, 302, 304, 305, 333, 334, 336, 353, 358–9, 366, 376, 387, 390, 401, 402, 406, 412, 420, 422, 423, 424, 425
senoren konvent, 127, 143–4, 150
Serebriakov, L., 71–2, 81, 82
Shakhty affair, 116–17, 128, 137, 188–9, 221, 241, 251
Shcherbakov, A., 285, 287
Shkiriatov, M., 290, 292, 299, 343, 353, 401
Shliapnikov, A., 59, 64, 65, 85, 94, 151, 339, 356
Shmidt, V., 395, 406
Shorokhov, D., 353
Shvarts, S., 353
Shvernik, N., 286, 287, 417, 420
Siegelbaum, L., 328
Smidovich, P., 353
Smilga, I., 170
Smirnov, V., 355
social history, 1–3, 328
social mobility, 10–11, 201, 259, 301, 314
Sokol'nikov, G., 172, 385, 395
Sol'ts, A., 85, 338, 353

sovereignty, rank-and-file, 56, 60, 87–8, 89, 129, 141–2
soviets, 25, 34, 38, 52, 69, 113, 114, 115, 137–8, 153, 170, 214, 219, 275–6, 286, 334, 335, 341, 347, 359, 360, 398
Sovnarkom, 48, 51, 52–6, 62, 65, 66, 67, 101, 102, 103, 108, 109, 138, 149, 153, 219–20, 224, 229, 231, 275–6, 281, 286, 340, 341, 347, 357, 368, 390, 399, 415
 Economic Council of Sovnarkom, 275, 276, 415
 Labour and Defence Council, 54, 66, 220, 275
 Maly Sovnarkom, 54, 341
specialists, 10, 29, 117, 136–7, 214, 221, 241–2, 250–1, 276–7
Stakhanovism, 12
Stalin, I., 2, 5, 6, 7, 14, 15, 17, 18, 19, 40, 53, 66, 67, 72, 73, 81, 83, 101, 104, 107, 113, 131, 134, 141, 145, 152, 153, 154, 155, 156, 158, 162, 166, 167, 173, 176, 178, 180, 182, 183, 184–5, 186, 188, 191, 192, 193–5, 198, 202, 210, 217, 220, 223, 224, 226, 227, 228, 229, 231, 232, 233, 234, 240–7, 248, 249, 250, 252, 253, 254, 266, 276, 277, 278, 279, 282, 283, 285, 286, 287, 288, 290, 291–302, 303, 305, 306, 307, 313, 314, 316, 317, 318, 319, 320, 321–7, 329, 347, 353, 357, 359, 361, 365, 366, 367, 371, 373, 374, 375, 377, 378, 379, 383, 384, 385, 387, 388, 392, 395, 397, 398, 399, 401, 402, 403, 404, 405, 406, 413, 416–17, 418, 420, 421, 422, 423, 424, 425
Stalinism, 1–20, 307–27, 329, 330
 cultural face, 4, 12–14
 economic face, 4, 8–10, 329
 political face, 4–8, 330
 social face 4, 10–12
 origins debate, 14–17, 307–27; contextual, 14, 16, 308–13; continuity thesis, 15–16, 307; essentialist, 14, 15–16; personalistic, 14, 17, 307, 321–4
Stasova, E., 68, 81
state, 6, 7, 61, 62, 66–7, 102, 135–8, 147–8, 153–4, 190, 227–8, 231–2, 275–7, 279–80, 286–7, 353, 399, 417
sub-national leaders, 7–8, 32, 36, 39–50, 62–3, 69–70, 71–81, 103, 105, 117, 121, 125, 126–34, 161–6, 172–4, 176, 194–5, 198, 206–18, 237, 246, 262–74, 283–4, 294, 301–2, 306, 314–17, 318, 324–7, 337, 338, 366, 367, 393–4, 413, 414

Sverdlov, Ya., 34, 63, 65, 68–9, 71, 75, 81, 166, 243, 341, 349
Sverdlova, K., 69
Syrtsov, S., 153, 156, 228, 230, 231, 233, 238, 246, 250, 251, 400, 419
Szamuely, T., 405

terror, 4, 6–7, 30–1, 304–5, 329, 334
Terror, Great, 2, 4, 5, 6–7, 10, 11, 19, 249, 259, 262, 267, 268, 272, 273, 274, 275, 276, 277, 278, 279, 280, 281, 282, 283, 284, 285, 290, 293, 295, 296, 297, 298, 299, 300, 301, 302, 303, 304, 305, 306, 312, 317, 320, 321, 323, 324, 329, 407, 414–15, 416, 418, 422, 424, 425
Tomsky, M., 65, 83, 101, 152, 153, 158, 172, 173, 174, 191, 196, 229, 230, 251, 347, 353, 374, 385, 406
Tovstukha, I., 379, 384
trade union question, 57, 58, 59, 60, 63, 64, 67, 72, 83, 93, 97, 98, 109, 172, 183
Trotsky, L., 15, 16, 48, 49, 53, 66, 67, 72, 82, 83, 101, 104, 105, 106, 125, 131, 153, 155, 156, 170, 172, 173, 174, 175, 178, 180, 182, 183, 185, 187, 190, 191, 192, 196, 314, 319, 353, 355, 357, 361, 366, 373, 374, 377, 381, 382, 384, 385, 386, 387, 395
TsIK, 52, 53, 66, 137–8, 153, 219, 220, 231, 253, 340, 341, 368
Tucker, R., 16

Uglanov, N., 124, 156, 172, 173, 193, 375, 377, 383
Ukraine, 48, 49, 114, 153, 206, 214, 231, 286, 287, 337, 339
Ulrikh, V., 423
United Opposition, 170, 174, 175, 183, 190, 316, 381, 382, 385, 388
unity, party, 18, 59, 64, 84, 88–9, 90, 91, 94, 95–9, 109–10, 151, 170, 175, 177, 195, 312
Uritsky, M., 94

Varentsova, O., 353
Vecheka, see security organs
Veinberg, G., 417
Verification of Party Documents, see purge
Vesenkha, 29, 54, 136, 137, 153, 224, 231, 249, 341, 345, 353, 368, 396
Vladimirsky, M., 234, 288
Voroshilov, K., 153, 156, 192, 231, 286, 287, 320, 355, 371, 375, 395, 399, 417
Vosnesensky, N., 285, 425

VTsIK, see TsIK
Vyshinsky, A., 423

War Communism, 16, 27, 28, 29, 31, 34, 36, 38, 113, 125, 308, 314
Workers Opposition, 28, 48, 90, 93, 94, 95, 97, 99, 108, 173, 337, 339, 356
Workers' Group, 113, 358, 387
Workers' Truth, 113, 358, 387
working class, 11–12, 26–8, 90, 116, 139, 155, 202, 203–4, 222, 243, 260, 308, 309, 310, 332, 333, 361, 362, 371, 388, 389

Yagoda, G., 242, 297, 298, 300, 402, 420, 423, 424, 425

Yakovlev, Ya., 395
Yaroslavsky, E., 72, 83, 120, 124, 175, 252, 355, 363, 401, 405

Zalutsky, P., 74, 172, 381
Zelensky, I., 353
Zhdanov, A., 264, 270, 283, 285, 286, 287, 288, 289, 299, 414, 416–17, 419, 420
Zinoviev, G., 40, 41, 63, 66, 67, 101, 103, 106, 114, 124, 125, 141, 153, 156, 170, 172, 173, 174, 176, 177, 180, 182, 183, 185, 186–7, 190, 192, 202, 250, 251, 253, 288, 302, 309, 314, 347, 353, 357, 360, 373, 374, 375, 377, 385, 387, 405, 406

Soviet and East European Studies

58 JOZEF M. VAN BRABANT
Adjustment, structural change and economic efficiency
Aspects of monetary cooperation in Eastern Europe

57 IILIANA ZLOCH-CHRISTY
EBT PROBLEMS OF ASTERN UROPE

56 SUSAN BRIDGER
Women in the Soviet countryside
Women's roles in rural development in the Soviet Union

55 ALLEN LYNCH
The Soviet study of international relations

54 DAVID GRANICK
Job rights in the Soviet Union: their consequences

53 ANITA PRAZMOWSKA
Britain, Poland and the Eastern Front, 1939

52 ELLEN JONES AND FRED GRUPP
Modernization, value change and fertility in the Soviet Union

51 CATHERINE ANDREYEV
Vlasov and the Russian liberation movement
Soviet reality and émigré theories

50 STEPHEN WHITE
The origins of détente
The Genoa Conference and Soviet-Western relations 1921–1922

49 JAMES MCADAMS
East Germany and détente
Building authority after the Wall

48 S. G. WHEATCROFT AND R. W. DAVIES (EDS.)
Materials for a balance of the Soviet national economy 1928–1930

47 SYLVANA MALLE
The economic organization of war communism, 1918–1921

46 DAVID S. MASON
Public opinion and political change in Poland, 1980–1982

45 MARK HARRISON
Soviet planning in peace and war 1938–1945

44 NIGEL SWAIN
Collective farms which work?

43 J. ARCH GETTY
Origins of the great purges
The Soviet Communist Party reconsidered, 1933–1938

42 TADEUSZ SWIETOCHOWSKI
Russian Azerbaijan 1905–1920
The shaping of national identity in a muslim community

452   Soviet and East European Studies

41 RAY TARAS
Ideology in a socialist state
Poland 1956–1983

40 SAUL ESTRIN
Self-management: economic theory and Yugoslav practice

39 S. A. SMITH
Red Petrograd
Revolution in the factories 1917–1918

38 DAVID A. DYKER
The process of investment in the Soviet Union

36 JEAN WOODALL
The socialist corporation and technocratic power
The Polish United Workers Party, industrial organisation and workforce control 1958–1980

35 WILLIAM J. CONYNGHAM
The modernization of Soviet industrial management

34 ANGELA STENT
From embargo to Ostpolitik
The political economy of West German-Soviet relations 1955–1980

32 BLAIR A. RUBLE
Soviet trade unions
Their development in the 1970s

31 R.F. LESLIE (ED.)
The history of Poland since 1863

30 JOZEF M. VAN BRABANT
Socialist economic integration
Aspects of contemporary economic problems in Eastern Europe

28 STELLA ALEXANDER
Church and state in Yugoslavia since 1945

27 SHEILA FITZPATRICK
Education and social mobility in the Soviet Union 1921–1934

23 PAUL VYSNÝ
Neo-Slavism and the Czechs 1898–1914

22 JAMES RIORDAN
Sport in Soviet society
Development of sport and physical education in Russia and the USSR

14 RUDOLF BIĆANIĆ
Economic policy in socialist Yugoslavia

The following series titles are now out of print:

1 ANDREA BOLTHO
Foreign trade criteria in socialist economies

2 SHEILA FITZPATRICK
The commissariat of enlightenment
Soviet organization of education and the arts under Lunacharsky, October 1917–1921

3 DONALD J. MALE
Russian peasant organisation before collectivisation
A study of commune and gathering 1925–1930

4 P. WILES (ED.)
The prediction of communist economic performance

5 VLADIMIR V. KUSIN
The intellectual origins of the Prague Spring
The development of reformist ideas in Czechoslovakia 1956–1967

6 GALIA GOLAN
The Czechoslovak reform movement

7 NAUN JASNY
Soviet economists of the twenties
Names to be remembered

8 ASHA L. DATAR
India's economic relations with the USSR and Eastern Europe, 1953–1969

9 T. M. PODOLSKI
Socialist banking and monetary control
The experience of Poland

10 SHMUEL GALAI
The liberation movement in Russia 1900–1905

11 GALIA GOLAN
Reform rule in Czechoslovakia
The Dubcek era 1968–1969

12 GEOFFREY A. HOSKING
The Russian constitutional experiment
Government and Duma 1907–1914

13 RICHARD B. DAY
Leon Trotsky and the politics of economic isolation

15 JAN M. CIECHANOWSKI
The Warsaw rising of 1944

16 EDWARD A. HEWITT
Foreign trade prices in the Council for Mutual Economic Assistance

17 ALICE TEICHOVA
An economic background to Munich
International business and Czechoslovakia 1918–1938

18 DANIEL F. CALHOUN
The united front: the TUC and the Russians 1923–1928

19 GALIA GOLAN
Yom Kippur and after
The Soviet Union and the Middle East crisis

454   Soviet and East European Studies

20 MAUREEN PERRIE
The agrarian policy of the Russian Socialist-Revolutionary Party
From its origins through the revolution of 1905–1907

21 GABRIEL GORODETSKY
The precarious truce: Anglo-Soviet relations 1924–1927

24 GREGORY WALKER
Soviet book publishing policy

25 FELICITY ANN O'DELL
Socialisation through children's literature
The Soviet example

26 T. H. RIGBY
Lenin's government: Sovnarkom 1917–1922

29 MARTIN CAVE
Computers and economic planning
The Soviet experience

33 MARTIN MYANT
Socialism and democracy in Czechoslovakia 1944–1948

37 ISRAEL GETZLER
Kronstadt 1917–1921
The fate of a Soviet democracy

Printed in Great Britain
by Amazon